The Prime of Life

The Autobiography of Simone de Beauvoir

Translated by Peter Green
Introduction by Toril Moi

Paragon House
New York

First Paragon edition, 1992

Published in the United States by
Paragon House Publishers
90 Fifth Avenue
New York, NY 10011

Manufactured in the United States of America
10 9 8 7 6 5 4 3 2 1

Library of Congress Cataloging-in-Publication Data
Beauvoir, Simone de, 1908–86
[Force de l'âge. English]
The prime of life : the autobiography of Simone de Beauvoir /
translated by Peter Green. — 1st Paragon House ed.
p.   cm.
Translation of: La force de l'âge.
Originally published: Cleveland : World Pub. Co., c1962.
ISBN 1-55778-522-8 : $13.95
1. Beauvoir, Simone de, 1908–86—Biography.
2. Authors, French—20th century—Biography.
3. Feminists—France—Biography.   I. Title.
PQ2603.E362Z46613   1992
848'.91409—dc20   91-36832
CIP

Introduction

IN the opening pages of *The Prime of Life*, the second volume of Simone de Beauvoir's autobiography, the reader encounters a wide-eyed, rather prim, philosophy student at the point of losing her virginity. By the end of the book, that student has become a woman much chastened by personal and political experience. Emerging from the Nazi occupation of France into the limelight of one of the most successful writing careers in postwar France, Simone de Beauvoir has finally been forced to face the weight of history: "Violence and injustice were let loose, with every kind of folly, scandal and horror," she writes, "I no longer pretended I could escape my own human condition."

In the *Prime of Life*, first published in 1960, Beauvoir represents the German occupation of France as the moment when her younger self is finally forced to face reality. In this sense, *The Prime of Life* might just as well have been called *Lost Illusions* or *Great Expectations*. Referring to her intense pursuit of individual happiness in the pre-war years as her "schizophrenia," in 1960 Beauvoir dismisses it as immature. In their early twenties, Sartre and Beauvoir turn every experience into a game; to them, nothing is serious, nothing is real. They play at being teachers, and at being a couple too, blithely indulging in the illusion of their own absolute freedom. "At every level we failed to face the weight of reality," Beauvoir writes, "we imagined ourselves to be wholly independent agents...no external hazard had ever compelled us to go against our own natural inclinations."

There were strong material reasons for their carefree attitude at this time. In the summer of 1929, when *The Prime of Life* starts, both Jean-Paul Sartre and Simone de Beauvoir have just passed the most difficult—and most prestigious—university exam in France, the *agrégation* in philosophy; he came first, she came second. The examiners, apparently, were in great doubt as to whom to rank as number one. Not surprisingly, perhaps, they eventually came down in favor of the man. Simone de Beauvoir's achievement was nevertheless considerable: at twenty-one, she was one of the youngest candidates ever, and only the eighth woman, to pass the *agrégation* in philosophy. The *agrégation* was, and remains, a severely regulated national exam, which guaranteed the successful candidate a teaching position for life in the French secondary school system. Such teachers were ranked as civil servants and could look forward to a state pension at the end of their teaching careers. Passing the *agrégation*, Simone de Beauvoir achieved economic independence and intellectual prestige at one stroke: She had every reason to be proud of herself.

By becoming a *lycée* teacher with a regular salary, Beauvoir finally escaped the stifling family life described with such unflinching integrity in *Memoirs of a Dutiful Daughter*. At a time when unemployment in Europe was reaching catastrophic levels, Sartre and Beauvoir were embarking on an existence where fourteen hours of teaching per week ensured them a modest but sufficient income for life. No wonder they felt themselves to be "radically free." The fact that it took a fascist occupation and a world war to open their eyes indicates the tenacity of that illusion.

One of the more startling effects of such philosophical idealism was Simone de Beauvoir's failure to realize that she is a woman: "Just as previously I had refused to be labelled 'a child,'" she writes, referring to herself at the age of twenty-three, "so now I did not think of myself as 'a woman.' I was *me*." The young Simone de Beauvoir, in other words, had no intellectual perception of what it meant to be a woman. Yet fifteen years later, in 1946, she sat down to write an essay about the myths of femininity. That essay became *The Second Sex*, arguably the most influential feminist text of this century. Under current social conditions, she painfully concluded in that pioneering text, "to accept oneself as a woman is to accept resignation and mutilation." The truly fascinating thing about *The Prime of Life* is that it tells us—directly and indirectly—what it took to make Simone de Beauvoir realize that an intellectual woman is more than just a free spirit.

In 1930, however, it never occurred to the young woman traveling to see her lover in Tours that she was the victim of oppression in any way. On the early morning train going back to Paris, she is constantly harassed by men "determined to indulge in a little knee-rubbing"; her main complaint is that they prevent her from catching up on her sleep. Once, reading on the banks of the Loire River, she is surprised by a masturbating exhibitionist. Fleeing in panic, she is driven to reflect on the "brutish distress" of human desire. At one point, her cousins in the south of France offer her a "Grenoble nut" after dinner. When the gift turns out to be an empty nutshell with a condom inside, Beauvoir tries her best not to look shocked. Setting out for arduous solitary walks in the mountains around Marseille, she barely escapes being raped on a couple of occasions, yet persists in refusing to let such external events impinge on her consciousness in any way. To do so, she reflects, would have meant imposing limits on her sense of freedom. Intoxicated by her own arrogant individualism, the young and carefree Simone de Beauvoir remained convinced that disasters only happen to others.

Yet, even at this time, some sense of distress penetrates her shield of complacent happiness. "I would go weeks on end in a state of euphoria," she writes, "and then for a few hours I would be ravaged by a kind of tornado that stripped me bare. To justify my condition of despair yet further, I would wallow in an abyss compounded of death, nothingness, and infinity." Taking the form of a fear of emptiness, such crises of depression induce in Beauvoir a terrible sense of desolation and abandonment. Her distress is increased by the threat of separation from Sartre; when it becomes clear that she will have to take a job in Marseille, more than five hundred miles away from Paris, her anxiety intensifies. For the young Simone de Beauvoir, her relationship with Sartre protects her from loneliness, exile, and death; her emotional dependence on her lover verges on the absolute. No wonder, then, that one of the major themes of *The Prime of Life* is her struggle against the temptation to sacrifice independence for love. This is why she represents her decision to refuse Sartre's offer of marriage and go to Marseille after all, as a major turning point in her life.

In so far as *The Prime of Life* is a narrative of lost illusions, it is interesting to note that between the lines of Beauvoir's text, one illusion she never quite abandons is the idea of a fundamental unity between herself and Sartre. In 1960 she still insists on the "identical sign on both our brows," the fact that the bond between herself and Sartre was so deep that not even the most draconian experience of separation and distance could sever it: "Even at the moment of parting we still thought as one," she claims. What Beauvoir is asking us to believe, in other words, is that the bond between herself and Sartre transcends that of, ordinary human reality. Such Romantic idealism neatly protects their relationship from the degrading effects of actual events; no matter what Sartre does, Simone de Beauvoir can always insist that their underlying emotional unity remains intact. Nothing in the material world can impinge on such spiritual harmony: "I knew," Beauvoir writes, "that no harm could ever come to me from him—unless he were to die before I died."

The difficulties of this position may not be obvious to Simone de Beauvoir at the age of twenty-one, but they become starkly apparent during the episode of the "trio," which takes place from March 1935 to March 1937. In 1935, Sartre turns thirty, and discovers that he is nothing but a provincial philosophy professor with no publications. His feeling of frustration leads to a veritable crisis of boredom and depression, culminating in hallucinations of being persecuted by lobsters. "Sartre could not resign himself to going on to the age of reason," Beauvoir wryly comments. In a desperate attempt to hold on to his youth, Sartre throws himself into a passionate, but chaste, relationship with Olga Kosakiewicz, an eighteen year old student of Beauvoir's. "I placed her so high," Sartre writes in his wartime diaries, "that for the first time in my life I felt humble and disarmed before another person, and felt that I wanted to learn." With Olga, Beauvoir notes, Sartre experiences "feelings of alarm, frenzy, and ecstasy such as he had never known with me."

Desperately trying to safeguard her fundamental union with Sartre,

Beauvoir dutifully enters into a triangular relationship. Initially, Olga loved Beauvoir more than Sartre, but when Sartre sets out to seduce Olga away from her, she can only acquiesce: "There was no question of fighting him for her," she writes, "since I could not bear any dissension between us." Perfect communion, in other words, means that when he insists, she gives way. But Beauvoir remains angry, unhappy and jealous; while Sartre passionately desires the trio, she ends up hating the very thought of it. To have to confront the existence of real emotional disunity between the two of them throws her into an agony far deeper than mere jealousy: "At times," she comments, "I asked myself whether the whole of my happiness did not rest upon a gigantic lie." Confronted with the spectacle of Sartre's passion for another woman, Beauvoir is forced to face her illusions: "When I said we are one," she writes, "I was cheating. Harmony between two individuals is never given, it must be worked for continually." Such voluntaristic reflections do little to ease the tension, however, and in the end, she falls ill. When she discovers that she is being carried out of her hotel on a stretcher, the stupefied Simone de Beauvoir suddenly realizes that this time, disaster had actually struck *her*.

In *The Prime of Life*, the outbreak of war comes across as the completion of a painful process of awakening to a new reality that had started with the experiment of the trio. The trio marks the end of Beauvoir's uncomplicated happiness with Sartre. It also marks the end of a certain kind of frankness; from now on, Beauvoir tends to conceal rather more of the sexual truth than before. After the publication in 1990 of Deirdre Bair's biography, and of Beauvoir's own letters and wartime diaries, many of Beauvoir's omissions have become public knowledge. The information now available confirms that the trio inaugurates a new era in Beauvoir's relationship with Sartre. Before 1937, neither Sartre nor Beauvoir had more than the occasional affair. After that time, however, they tended to be continuously involved in tortuous and sometimes rather shabby relationships with others. While Olga's relations with Sartre remained platonic, for instance, her involvement with Beauvoir turns out to have been less chaste. In July 1938, Beauvoir goes off walking in the Alps; according to *The Prime of Life* she is on her own, but according to her letters, she is accompanied by Jacques Laurent Bost, Olga's young lover. This trip marks the beginning of a long-lasting affair between Beauvoir and Bost, an affair kept secret from Olga—although not from Sartre—for many years. Beauvoir, in fact, did not only have sex with Olga, but also with "Lise" and Bianca. Sartre, for his part, moved on from Olga to her younger sister Wanda, with whom he carried on a relationship for the rest of his life. During the phony war, much to Beauvoir's alarm, he even proposed marriage to Wanda. In addition to this, he got involved in a seemingly endless number of more or less scandalous affairs with other women, all meticulously chronicled in his letters to Beauvoir.

Reading Beauvoir's wartime diaries, it is hard to escape the impression that for her, this is a way of life that does not always make her happy. Other lovers, male or female, can only put up a futile struggle to fill the void that opens when the absolute presence of Sartre disappears. When Sartre is with Wanda, for instance, Beauvoir's world is drained of affect: "His consciousness is such an absolute for me that this morning the world seems utterly empty," she notes in her diary in February 1940, "when I think of the substitutes: Olga, Bianca, it makes me sick."

That Beauvoir failed to tell this side of the story in *The Prime of Life* is not surprising. In 1960, almost all the people involved were still alive. To confess to lesbian relationships in pre-feminist France would have brought pain and difficulties not only to Simone de Beauvoir but to her partners as well. But perhaps the main reason she drew a veil over much of her own and Sartre's involvements with others was that she could not, in the end, bring herself truly to contemplate the nature of her unity with Sartre. In 1963, at the end of *The Force of Circumstance*, she still finds the courage to claim that her relationship with him constitutes the "one undoubted success" of her life. The paradox—and pathos—of that statement is that, in spite of everything, it is so obviously true.

Published in 1943, Simone de Beauvoir's first novel, *She Came to Stay*, is based on the devastating experience of the trio. If that experience threw her emotional life into crisis, it also enabled her finally to write with conviction. In this sense, *The Prime of Life* is a fascinating, unsentimental, and immensely honest narrative of fourteen years of courageous struggle to become a published writer. Beauvoir's honesty is not, after all, a matter of the exact amount of sexual detail included in her narrative; on the contrary, the very fact that she does not feel free to "tell all," points to the difficulty of becoming an independent woman in a patriarchal world. Precisely because it offers no ideal role model, no rosy vision of easy liberation, *The Prime of Life* forces us to examine the contradictions of our own lives.

Toril Moi

Preface

WHEN I undertook to write about myself I found that I had embarked upon a somewhat rash adventure, easier begun than left off. I had long wanted to set down the story of my first twenty years; nor did I ever forget the distress signals which my adolescent self sent out to the older woman who was afterward to absorb me, body and soul. Nothing, I feared, would survive of that girl, not so much as a pinch of ashes. I begged her successor to recall my youthful ghost, one day, from the limbo to which it had been consigned. Perhaps the only reason for writing my books was to make the fulfillment of this long-standing prayer possible. When I was fifty, it seemed to me that the time had come. I took that child and that adolescent girl, both so long given up for lost in the depths of the unrecalled past, and endowed them with my adult awareness. I gave them a new existence—in black and white, on sheets of paper.

I had no plans for taking this project any further. Adult status brought disenchantment with the future. When I had completed my *Memoirs of a Dutiful Daughter* no voice spoke to me out of my past, urging me to continue the story. I made up my mind to turn to some other task; but in the event I found myself unable to do so. Beneath the final line of that book an invisible question mark was inscribed, and I could not get my mind off it. Freedom I had—but freedom to do what? What new direction would the course of my life take as a result of all this fuss and commotion, the pitched battle that had culminated in victorious release? My first instinct was to bury myself behind my books; but they provided no solution. Indeed, their own validity was being challenged. I had chosen to be a writer, and had in fact written various works. But *why?* Why those *particular* books, *only* those and none other? Had I overshot my ambition, or fallen short of it? There could be no common ground between the boundless, infinite hopes I entertained at twenty and the actual achievement which followed. I had got at the same time both much more and much less than I wanted. Little by little I became convinced that, from my own point of view, the first volume of my *Memoirs* required a sequel. There was no point in having described how my vocation as a writer was acquired unless I then went on to show its realization.

Besides, on reflection, the task possessed an intrinsic interest for me. My life is by no means over yet, but by now it has developed a pattern which the future seems unlikely to modify very much. For various reasons, which I shall have to clarify during this autobiographical study, I have hitherto avoided asking myself just what that pattern is. I must find out now or never.

It may be objected that such an inquiry concerns no one but myself. Not so; if any individual—a Pepys or a Rousseau, an exceptional or a run-of-the-mill character—reveals himself honestly, everyone, more or less, becomes involved. It is impossible for him to shed light on his own life without at some point illuminating the lives of others. Besides, writers are constantly badgered with questions about why they write, or how they spend their time. Over and above the mere craving for gossip and personal tidbits, it does seem as though many people genuinely want to know what writing, as a profession, involves. The question can be better answered by studying an individual case than by offering generalized abstractions; this is what has encouraged me to embark on this volume. Perhaps my investigations will help to eliminate certain misunderstandings such as always arise between writers and their public, and which I have frequently experienced, to my personal annoyance. No book takes on its full meaning without the reader knowing the circumstances and background of its inception, and having some acquaintance with the personality of its author. By addressing my readers directly I hope to perform this service for them.

At the same time I must warn them that I have no intention of telling them everything. I described my childhood and adolescence without any omissions. But though I have, as I hope, managed to recount the story of my life since then without excessive embarrassment or indiscretness, I cannot treat the years of my maturity in the same detached way—nor do I enjoy a similar freedom when discussing them. I have no intention of filling these pages with spiteful gossip about myself and my friends; I lack the instincts of the scandalmonger. There are many things which I firmly intend to leave in obscurity.

On the other hand, my life has been closely linked with that of Jean-Paul Sartre. As he intends to write his own life story, I shall not attempt to perform the task for him. This book will examine neither his ideas nor his work; I propose to mention him only insofar as he played a part in my own existence.

Some critics supposed that I meant *Memoirs of a Dutiful Daughter* as an object lesson for young girls; my main desire really was to discharge a debt. The present work, at all events, has no moral purpose. I have endeavored to put down the facts concerning my life: I make no a priori assumptions, though I believe that truth in any form can be both interesting and useful. I cannot tell what purpose may be served by the truth I have attempted to outline in the following pages, nor who may benefit from it.

I only hope that my readers show a similar lack of prejudice. Lastly, though I have suppressed certain facts, I have at no point set down deliberate falsehoods. It is likely, however, that my memory has betrayed me over various small details. Such minor errors as the reader may observe should certainly not be taken as invalidating the general veracity of this narrative.

Part 1

Chapter 1

THE MOST INTOXICATING ASPECT OF MY RETURN
to Paris in September, 1929, was the freedom I now possessed. I had dreamed
of it since childhood, when I played with my sister at being a "grown-up"
girl. I have recorded elsewhere my passionate longing for it as a student.
Now, suddenly, it was mine. I was astonished to find an effortless buoyancy
in all my movements. From the moment I opened my eyes every morning
I was lost in a transport of delight. When I was about twelve I had suffered through not having a private retreat of my own at home. Leafing
through *Mon Journal* I had found a story about an English schoolgirl, and
gazed enviously at the colored illustration portraying her room. There was
a desk, and a divan, and shelves filled with books. Here, within these gaily
painted walls, she read and worked and drank tea, with no one watching
her—how envious I felt! For the first time ever I had glimpsed a more
fortunate way of life than my own. And now, at long last, I too had a
room to myself. My grandmother had stripped her drawing room of all
its armchairs, occasional tables, and knickknacks. I had bought some un-
painted furniture, and my sister had helped me to give it a coat of brown
varnish. I had a table, two chairs, a large chest which served both as a seat
and as a hold-all, shelves for my books. I papered the walls orange, and
got a divan to match. From my fifth-floor balcony I looked out over the
Lion of Belfort and the plane trees on the Rue Denfert-Rochereau. I kept
myself warm with an evil-smelling kerosene stove. Somehow its stink
seemed to protect my solitude, and I loved it. It was wonderful to be able
to shut my door and keep my daily life free of other people's inquisitiveness.
For a long time I remained indifferent to the décor of my surroundings.
Possibly because of that picture in *Mon Journal* I preferred rooms that
offered me a divan and bookshelves, but I was prepared to put up with any
sort of retreat in a pinch. To have a door that I could shut was still the
height of bliss for me.

I paid rent to my grandmother, and she treated me with the same unob-
trusive respect she showed her other lodgers. I was free to come and go as
I pleased. I could get home with the milk, read in bed all night, sleep

till midday, shut myself up for forty-eight hours at a stretch, or go out on the spur of the moment. My lunch was a bowl of borsch at Dominique's, and for supper I took a cup of hot chocolate at La Coupole. I was fond of hot chocolate, and borsch, and lengthy siestas and sleepless nights: but my chief delight was in doing as I pleased. There was practically nothing to stop me. I discovered, to my great pleasure, that "the serious business of living" on which grownups had held forth to me so interminably was not, in fact, quite so oppressive after all. Getting through my examinations, on the other hand, had been no joke. I had worked desperately hard, always with the fear of possible failure, always tired, and with various stubborn obstacles to overcome. Now I encountered no such resistance anywhere: I felt as though I were on vacation forever. A little private tutoring and a part-time teaching job at the Lycée Victor-Duruy guaranteed me enough to live on. These duties did not even prove a burden to me, since I felt that by performing them I was involved in a new sort of game: I was playing at being a grownup. Hunting for private pupils, having discussions with senior mistresses or parents, working out my budget, borrowing, paying back, adding up figures—all these activities amused me because I was doing them for the first time. I remember how tickled I was when I got my first salary check. I felt I had played a practical joke on someone.

Clothes and cosmetics had never interested me overmuch, but I nevertheless took some pleasure in dressing as *I* wanted to. I was still in mourning for my grandfather, and had no wish to shock people, so I bought myself a gray coat, with shoes and toque to match. I had two dresses made, one of the same gray, and the other in black and white. All my life I had been dressed in cotton or woolen frocks, so now I reacted by choosing silk-style materials instead—crepe de Chine and a ghastly fabric of embossed velvet called *velours frappé* which was all the rage that winter. Every morning I would make up with more dash than skill, smothering my face in powder, dabbing a patch of rouge on each cheek, and applying lipstick liberally. It struck me as ridiculous that anyone should dress up more elaborately on Sunday than during the week. Henceforth, I decided, every day was to be a holiday as far as I was concerned, and I always wore the same get-up, whatever the circumstances. It did occur to me that crepe de Chine and *velours frappé* were rather out of place in the corridors of a *lycée,* and that my evening shoes might have been less down at the heel if I hadn't tramped the Paris pavements in them from morning till night; but I couldn't have cared less. My personal appearance was one of those things that I refused to take really seriously.

I moved in, bought a new outfit, had friends in to see me, and went visiting myself; but all these were preliminary activities only. My new life really began when Sartre returned to Paris in mid-October.

Sartre had come to see me when we were in Limousin. He stayed at the Hôtel de la Boule d'Or, in Saint-Germain-les-Belles, and in order to avoid gossip we used to meet out in the country, a good way from town. In the old days I had often wandered here, bitterly hugging my loneliness;

but now I hurried blithely across the grassy parkland every morning, skipping over hurdles and plunging through dew-wet meadows. We would sit down together in the grass and talk. The first day I never supposed that, away from Paris and our friends, such an occupation would wholly suffice for us. I had suggested that we might bring some books along, and read. Sartre refused indignantly. He also swept aside all my suggestions that we might go for a walk. He was allergic to chlorophyll, he said, and all this lush green pasturage exhausted him. The only way he could put up with it was to forget it. Fair enough. Though I had received little encouragement in that direction, talking did not scare me. We picked up our discussion at the point where we had left off in Paris; and very soon I realized that even though we went on talking till Judgment Day, I would still find the time all too short. It had been early morning when we came out, and there was the luncheon bell already. I used to go home and eat with my family, while Sartre lunched on cheese or gingerbread, deposited by my cousin Madeleine in an abandoned dovecote that stood "by the house down the road"; Madeleine adored anything romantic. Hardly had the afternoon begun before it was over, and darkness falling; Sartre would then go back to his hotel and eat dinner among the commercial travelers. I had told my parents we were working together on a book, a critical study of Marxism. I hoped to butter them up by pandering to their hatred of Communism, but I cannot have been very convincing. Four days after Sartre arrived, I saw them appear at the edge of the meadow where we were sitting.

They walked toward us. Under his yellowing straw boater, my father wore a resolute but somewhat embarrassed expression. Sartre, who on this particular day happened to be wearing a decidedly aggressive red shirt, sprang to his feet, the light of battle in his eye. My father asked him, quite politely, to leave the district. People were gossiping, he said; besides, it was hoped to get my cousin married, and such apparently scandalous behavior on my part was harmful to her reputation. Sartre replied vigorously enough, but without too much violence, since he had made up his mind not to leave a minute sooner than he intended. We merely arranged somewhat more secret meeting places, in a chestnut grove a little distance away. My father did not return to the attack, and Sartre stayed on another week at the Boule d'Or. Afterward we wrote to each other daily.

By the time I met him again, in October, I had (as I describe in *Memoirs of a Dutiful Daughter*) jettisoned all past attachments, and now threw myself unreservedly into the development of this new relationship. Sartre was soon due for his military service; meanwhile he remained on vacation. He was staying with his grandparents (his mother's family, that is: their name was Schweitzer) on the Rue Saint-Jacques, and we would meet each morning in the Luxembourg Gardens, where carved stone queens gazed blindly down at us amid a dapple of gray and gold: it was late at night before we separated. We walked the streets of Paris, still talking—about ourselves and our relationship, our future life, our yet unwritten books. Today it strikes me that the most important aspect of these conversations was not so much what we said as what we took for granted, and what in fact was not so at all. We were wrong about almost everything. An accurate character sketch must needs take these errors into account, since they expressed one kind of reality—our actual situation.

As I have said elsewhere, Sartre lived for his writing. He felt he had a mission to hold forth on any subject, tackling it as best suited him in the light of circumstance. He had exhorted me to open my eyes to the manifold glories of life; I too must write, in order to snatch that vision from obliteration by time. The self-evident obviousness of our respective vocations seemed to us to guarantee their eventual fulfillment. Though we did not formulate it in such terms, we were approaching a condition of Kantian optimism, where *you should* implies *you can*. Indeed, how could one's resolution falter in doubt at the very moment of choice and affirmation? Upon such an occasion will and belief coincide. So we put our trust in the world, and in ourselves. Society as then constituted we opposed. But there was nothing sour about this enmity: it carried an implication of robust optimism. Man was to be remolded, and the process would be partly our doing. We did not envisage contributing to this change except by way of books: public affairs bored us. We counted on events turning out according to our wishes without any need for us to mix in them personally. In this respect our attitude was characteristic of that general euphoria affecting the French Left during the autumn of 1929. Peace seemed finally assured: the expansion of the German Nazi party was a mere fringe phenomenon, without any serious significance. It would not be long before colonialism folded up: Gandhi's campaign in India and the Communist agitation in French Indo-China were proof enough of that. Moreover the whole capitalist world was, at the time, being shaken by a crisis of the utmost gravity; and this encouraged the assumption that capitalism as such had had its day. We felt that we were already living in that Golden Age which for us constituted the secret truth of History, and the revelation of which remained History's final and exclusive objective.

At every level we failed to face the weight of reality, priding ourselves on what we called our "radical freedom." We clung so long and so desperately to that word "freedom" that it will be as well to make a closer examination of just what we implied by it.

There was a genuine enough field of experience for it to cover. Every activity contains its own freedom, intellectual activity in particular, because it seldom repeats itself. We had worked hard; we had been forced, unremittingly, to rediscover and revaluate; we possessed a practical, unimpeachable, intuitive awareness of the nature of freedom. The mistake we made was in failing to restrict this concept to its proper limits. We clung to the image of Kant's dove, supported rather than hindered in flight by the resistant air. We regarded any existing situation as raw material for our joint efforts, and not as a factor conditioning them: we imagined ourselves to be wholly independent agents. This spiritual pride, like our political blindness, can be explained in the first instance by the violent intensity which characterized all our plans. To be a writer, to create—this was an adventure scarcely to be embarked upon without a conviction of absolute self-mastery, absolute control over ends and means. Our boldness was inseparable from the illusions which sustained it; circumstances had favored them both. No external hazard had ever compelled us to go against our own natural inclinations. We sought knowledge, self-expression; and now we found ourselves up to our necks in just such activities. Our way of life was so exactly what we wanted that it was as though *it* had chosen *us;* we regarded this as an omen of its regular submission to our future plans. The same fate that had served our purpose also shielded us from the world's adversity.

Nor, on the other hand, did we feel any private emotional obligations. I kept on good terms with my parents, but they no longer had any real hold over me. Sartre had never known his father, and neither his mother nor his grandparents had ever represented authority in his eyes. In a sense we both lacked a real family, and we had elevated this contingency into a principle. Here we were encouraged by Cartesian rationalism, which we had picked up from Alain, and which we welcomed precisely because it happened to suit our convenience. There were no scruples, no feelings of respect or loyal affection that would stop us from making up our minds by the pure light of reason—and of our own desires. We were unaware of any cloudiness or confusion in our mental processes; we believed ourselves to consist of pure reason and pure will. This conviction was fortified by the eagerness with which we staked our all on the future; we were not tied down to any particular interest, since present and past were continually leap-frogging. We never hesitated to disagree with any point, and indeed with each other, whenever occasion demanded; it was easy for us to criticize or condemn the other's views, since every shift of opinion we regarded as a step forward. As our ignorance kept us unaware of most of the problems that might have worried us, we remained quite content with these revisions of doctrine, and indeed thought ourselves very daring.

So we went our way without let or hindrance, unembarrassed and unafraid; yet how was it that we did not at least stumble into one or two roadblocks? After all, our pockets were virtually empty. I scraped a scanty living, while Sartre was going through a small legacy he had from his paternal grandmother. The shops were laden with goods we could not buy, while all luxury resorts were closed to us. We met these prohibitions with indifference, even with active disdain. We were not ascetics, far from it; but now as before (and in this Sartre and I were alike) only those things within my reach, in particular those I could actually touch, had any true weight of reality for me. I gave myself up so completely to present desires and pleasures that I had no energy to waste on mere wishful thinking. What was the point in regretting the absence of a car, when there were so many discoveries we could make on foot, on the Bercy *quais* or along the reaches of the Saint-Martin canal? When we ate bread and *foie gras* Marie in my room, or had dinner at the Brasserie Demory (Sartre adored its heavy smell of beer and sauerkraut) we did not feel deprived of anything. In the evening we would look in at the Falstaff or the College Inn and drink our cocktails like connoisseurs—Bronxes, Sidecars, Bacardis, Alexanders, Martinis. I had a particular weakness for two specialties—mead cocktails at the Vikings' Bar, and apricot cocktails at the Bec de Gaz on the Rue Montparnasse: what more could the Ritz Bar have offered us? Occasionally we broke out and enjoyed ourselves: I remember eating chicken and cranberry sauce one evening at the Vikings' Bar while up on the dais the orchestra played a popular hit of the day called "Pagan Love Song." I am sure this celebration would not have made such an impression on me unless it had been something out of the ordinary: indeed, the very modesty of our resources served to increase my pleasure.

In any case, the pleasure to be derived from expensive possessions is not so simple or direct. They are basically a means to an end; the glamour they acquire is shed upon them by some glamorous third party. Our puritanical education and the firmness of our intellectual commitment ensured that we remained immune to dukes, millionaires, owners of Hispanos, women in mink, and all such denizens of high society. We actually stigmatized this *beau monde* as the very dregs of the earth, on the grounds that it sucked profit from a regime which we condemned. I felt a certain ironical pity for these people. When I passed by the impenetrable portals of Fouquet's or Maxim's, I pictured them, cut off from the masses, helpless prisoners of their own wealth and snobbery—surely it was they who were the real outsiders. For the most part they simply did not exist as far as I was concerned: I no more missed their refined pleasures than the Greeks of the fifth century B.C. missed cinema or radio. Obviously the cash barrier formed a block to our curiosity; but this caused us no annoyance, since we were convinced that the smart set had nothing to teach us: their mannered self-indulgence concealed a howling void.

We had no external limitations, no overriding authority, no imposed pattern of existence. We created our own links with the world, and freedom was the very essence of our existence. In our everyday lives we gave it scope by means of an activity which assumed considerable importance for us—private fantasies. Most young couples tend to enrich their normally somewhat bare past with intimate fantasies and myths. We embraced this pursuit all the more zealously since we were both active people by nature, and for the moment living a life of idleness. The comedies, parodies, or fables which we made up had a very specific object: they stopped us from taking ourselves too seriously. Seriousness as such we rejected no less vigorously than Nietzsche did, and for much the same reason: our jokes lightened the world about us by projecting it into the realm of imagination, thus enabling us to keep it at arm's length.

Of the two of us, Sartre was the most inexhaustible. He made up a whole stream of ballads, counting-out rhymes, epigrams, madrigals, thumbnail fables, and occasional poems of every description. Sometimes he would sing them to airs of his own invention. He considered neither puns nor wordplay beneath him, and enjoyed experimenting with alliteration and assonance. This was one way of coming to grips with the language—by both exploring the potential of words and discarding their everyday usage. From J. M. Synge he had borrowed the myth of Baladin, the eternal wanderer who disguises life's mediocrity with glorious lying fantasies; and James Stephens' *The Crock of Gold* had provided us with the idea of the leprechaun, a gnome who crouches under tree roots and keeps misery, boredom, and doubt at bay by cobbling tiny shoes. Both of them, the adventurer and the stay-at-home, taught the same lesson: literature above all else. But in their hands the motto lost its dogmatic weightiness; and we derived a certain backhanded pleasure from referring to our future books, so dear to our hearts, as "our tiny shoes."

We were both as healthy as horses and of a cheerful disposition. But I took any setback very badly; my face changed, I withdrew into myself and became mulish and obstinate. Sartre decided I had a double personality. Normally I was the Beaver; but occasionally this animal would be replaced by a rather irksome young lady called Mademoiselle de Beauvoir. Sartre embroidered this theme with several variations, all of which ended by making fun of me. In his own case, things very frequently got him down— especially in the morning, when his head was still foggy with sleep, or when circumstances reduced him to inactivity: he would hunch himself into a defensive ball, like a hedgehog. On such occasions he resembled a sea elephant we had once seen in the zoo at Vincennes whose misery broke our hearts. A keeper had emptied a bucketful of little fish down the beast's throat, and then jumped on its belly. The sea elephant, swamped by this internal invasion of tiny fish, raised tiny, hopeless eyes heavenward. It looked as though the whole vast bulk of his flesh were endeavoring to transmit a prayer for help through those two small apertures; but even so embryonic an attempt at communication was denied it. The mouth of the great beast gaped, and tears trickled down over its oily skin; it shook its head slowly and collapsed, defeated. When Sartre's face took on an unhappy expression, we used to pretend that the sea elephant's desolate soul had taken possession of his body. Sartre would then complete the metamorphosis by rolling his eyes up, sighing, and making silent supplication: this pantomime would restore his good spirits. Our various moods we regarded not as a kind of inevitable symptom engendered physically, but as a species of disguise that we assumed in a perverse moment and could discard at will. All through our youth, and even later, whenever we had to face a difficult or disagreeable situation we would work it out first as a private *ad hoc* drama. We turned it upside down, exaggerated it, caricatured it, and explored it in every direction; this helped us a good deal in getting it under control.

We used the same method in defining our domestic status. When we met again in Paris we found a name for our relationship before we had decided just what that relationship was to be. "It's a morganatic marriage," we said. As a couple we possessed a dual identity. In the ordinary way we were Monsieur and Madame M. Organatique, unambitious, easily satisfied, not very well off, the husband a civil servant. But sometimes I dressed up, and we would go to a cinema on the Champs Elysées, or dancing at La Coupole, and then we were an American millionaire and his wife, Mr. and Mrs. Morgan Hattick. This was not a hysterical joke designed to make us feel that, for a few hours, we were enjoying the pleasures of the idle rich; it was, rather, a parody, which confirmed us in our contempt for high socitey. Our modest celebrations were quite enough for us: there was nothing further fortune could do for us. We were asserting our actual status. But at the same time we feigned release from it. That penurious pair of *petits bourgeois* whom we called Monsieur and Madame M. Organatique had no real identity with us: by wriggling into their skins for a joke we emphasized the difference.

As I have already made clear, I also regarded my day-to-day activities—among others, my job as a teacher—in the light of a masquerade. By releasing the pressure of reality upon our lives, fantasy convinced us that life itself had no hold upon us. We belonged to no place or country, no class, profession, or generation. Our truth lay elsewhere. It was inscribed upon the face of eternity, and the future would reveal it: we were writers. Any other verdict was the merest false illusion. We believed ourselves to be following the precepts of those ancient Stoics who likewise had staked their all upon freedom. Committed body and soul to the work that depended on us, we threw off the yoke of all obligations irrelevant to this central purpose. We did not go so far as to abstain from such things altogether—we were too experience-hungry for that—but we bracketed them off as mere interludes. Circumstances permitted us a certain measure of detachment, free time, and general insouciance; it was tempting to confuse this with sovereign freedom. To explode this fallacy we would have needed to see ourselves from a distance, in perspective; and we had neither the means nor the desire to do so.

Two disciplines might have clarified our thinking, those of Marxism or psychoanalysis. We had only the most rudimentary knowledge of either. I remember a very fierce quarrel which took place at the Balzar between Sartre and Politzer, who was attempting to show Sartre up as a *petit bourgeois* at heart. Sartre did not reject the label, but maintained that it was inadequate as a complete definition of his attitude. He posed the thorny problem of the intellectual with a bourgeois background who—according to Marx himself—is capable of rising above the characteristic beliefs of his class. In what circumstances could this happen? How? Why? Politzer's shock of red hair glowed flamelike, and words poured out of him; but he failed to convince Sartre. In any case Sartre would have continued to play his part in the fight for freedom: he still believes in it to this day. But a serious analysis of the problem would have modified the ideas we held about it. Our indifference to money was a luxury we could afford only because we had enough of it to avoid real poverty and the need for hard or unpleasant work. Our open-mindedness was bound up with a cultural background and the sort of activities accessible only to people of our social class. It was our conditioning as young *petit bourgeois* intellectuals that led us to believe ourselves free of all conditioning whatsoever.

Why this particular self-indulgence rather than another? Why continual questing alertness rather than a slumberous dogmatic certainty? Psychoanalysis might have suggested some answers if we had consulted it. It was beginning to spread in France, and certain aspects of it interested us. In the sphere of psychopathology, Georges Dumas's "endocrinal monism" (our own name for his system; Dumas himself claimed to be a Cartesian dualist) seemed to us—as it did to most of our friends—quite unacceptable. We looked favorably on the notion that psychoses, neuroses, and their various symptoms had a meaning, and that this meaning must be sought in the patient's childhood. But we stopped short at this point; we rejected psychoanalysis as a tool for exploring a normal human being. We had hardly read any Freud apart from his books *The Interpretation of Dreams* and *The Psychopathology of Everyday Life*. We had absorbed the letter rather than the spirit of these works: we were put off by their dogmatic symbolism and the technique of association which vitiated them for us. Freud's pansexualism struck us as having an element of madness about it, besides offending our puritanical instincts. Above all, the importance it attached to the unconscious, and the rigidity of its mechanistic theories, meant that Freudianism, as we conceived it, was bound to eradicate human free will. No one showed us how the two might possibly be reconciled, and we were incapable of finding out for ourselves. We remained frozen in our rationalist-voluntarist position: in a clear-minded individual, we thought, freedom would win out over complexes, memories, influences, or any traumatic experience. It was a long time before we realized that our emotional detachment from, and indifference to, our respective childhoods was to be explained by what we had experienced as children.

If Marxism and psychoanalysis had so little influence on us, at a time when many young people were rallying to both, it was not only because our knowledge concerning them was so sketchy, but also because we had no wish to observe ourselves from a distance with the eyes of strangers. Our first need was to prevent any dissociation between mind and personality. Far from setting theoretical limits to our freedom, we were now practically concerned with safeguarding its existence—for it was in danger.

In this respect there was a marked difference between Sartre and me. It struck me as miraculous that I had broken free from my past, and was now self-sufficient and self-determining: I had established my autonomy once and forever, and nothing could now deprive me of it. Sartre, on the other hand, had merely moved on to a stage of his development as a man which he had long foreseen with loathing. He had more or less shed the irresponsibility of adolescence, and was entering the adult world which he so detested. His independence was threatened. First he would be obliged to do eighteen months' military service, and after that a teaching career awaited him. He had found an answer to this: a French lectureship was being advertised in Japan, and he had put in an application for October, 1931. He counted on spending two years out there, with the possibility of further foreign posts afterward. According to him the writer or storyteller should be like Synge's Baladin, and never settle anywhere for good— or with any one person. Sartre was not inclined to be monogamous by nature: he took pleasure in the company of women, finding them less comic than men. He had no intention, at twenty-three, of renouncing their tempting variety.

He explained the matter to me in his favorite terminology. "What *we* have," he said, "is an *essential* love; but it is a good idea for us also to experience *contingent* love affairs." We were two of a kind, and our relationship would endure as long as we did: but it could not make up entirely for the fleeting riches to be had from encounters with different people. How could we deliberately forego that gamut of emotions— astonishment, regret, pleasure, nostalgia—which we were as capable of sustaining as anyone else? We reflected on this problem a good deal during our walks together.

One afternoon we had been with the Nizans to a cinema on the Champs Elysées to see *Storm Over Asia*. After leaving them we walked down as far as the Carrousel Gardens, and sat down on a stone bench beneath one wing of the Louvre. There was a kind of balustrade which served as a backrest, a little way out from the wall; and in the cagelike space behind it a cat was miaowing. The poor thing was too big to get out; how had it ever gotten in? Evening was drawing on; a woman came up to the bench, a paper bag in one hand, and produced some scraps of meat. These she fed to the cat, stroking it tenderly the while. It was at this moment that Sartre said: "Let's sign a two-year lease." I could arrange to live in Paris during these two years, and we would spend them in the closest possible intimacy. Afterward, Sartre suggested, I ought to take a job abroad too. We would live apart for two or three years, and then rejoin one another somewhere—Athens, maybe—where we could, for a longer or shorter period, live more or less together. We would never become strangers to one another, and neither would appeal for the other's help in vain; nothing would prevail against this alliance of ours. But it must not be allowed to degenerate into mere duty or habit; we had at all costs to preserve it from decay of this sort. I agreed. The separation which Sartre envisaged caused me some qualms; but it lay well in the future, and I had made it a rule never to worry about anything prematurely. Despite this I did feel a flicker of fear, though I regarded it as mere weakness and made myself subdue it; I was helped by the knowledge, based on previous experience, that Sartre meant what he said. With him a proposed scheme was not mere vague talk, but a moment of actuality. If he told me one day to meet him exactly twenty-two months later on the Acropolis, at five o'clock in the afternoon, I could be sure of finding him there then, punctual to the minute. In a more general way I knew that no harm could ever come to me from him—unless he were to die before I died.

There was no question of our actually taking advantage, during our two-year "lease," of those "freedoms" which in theory we had the right to enjoy. We intended to give ourselves wholeheartedly and without reservation to this new relationship of ours. We made another pact between us: not only would we never lie to one another, but neither of us would conceal anything from the other. What is known as *la vie intérieure* aroused the greatest disgust among the students at the Ecole Normale; the gardens where sensitive, refined souls cultivated the delicate secrets they regarded as stinking swamps, the background for constant discreet trafficking in betrayal, or the consummation of filthy narcissistic pleasures.

In order to dissipate this dark miasmic atmosphere, they themelves had acquired the habit of exposing their lives, thoughts, and feelings in broad daylight. The only limit set on these public revelations was due to lack of interest: any of them who went on too much about himself would have bored the rest. But no such restrictions existed between Sartre and me; and we therefore agreed to tell one another everything. I was used to some reserve, and at first this rule of ours embarrassed me. But I soon came to realize its advantages. I no longer needed to worry about myself: all my actions were subjected to a kindly enough scrutiny, but with far greater impartiality than I could have achieved myself. The picture I thus received I regarded as objective; and this system of control protected me against all those fears, false hopes, idle scruples, fantasies, and minor brainstorms which can so easily breed in conditions of solitude. The absence of solitude did not bother me; on the contrary, I was delighted to have got away from it.

The thought that Sartre was now an open book to me, as easily read as my own mind, had a most relaxing effect on me. Later I learned better. Since he concealed nothing from me, I thought myself absolved from any necessity to think about his problems. On several occasions afterwards I perceived that this was a lazy way out. But though I reproached myself for sluggish obtuseness, I did not blame the rule that we had adopted. We were never to dispense with that rule; no other would have suited us.

This is not to suggest that in my opinion sincerity is either a universal necessity or a universal panacea: I have frequently had occasion since then to ponder its uses and abuses. I pointed out one of its dangerous qualities in one passage of my last novel, *The Mandarins*. Anne (whose prudence in this particular context I approve of) advises her daughter Nadine not to tell the young man who loves her that she has been unfaithful to him. But Nadine's actual motive is not so much to make a clean breast of things to her lover as to provoke his jealousy. Frank speaking is not only, very often, a means of communication but of action too; it isn't playing fair if, while pretending that no pressure is being brought to bear, you bludgeon someone with an indiscreet truth. Such ambiguity of language does not wholly preclude plain speaking; but it does make one or two precautions necessary. Ordinarily it will suffice to allow some little time to elapse, and then the words, will have lost their sting. After a decent interval one can, without prejudice, reveal facts and feelings that would have implied a form of intrigue, or at least some sort of interference, if blurted out on the spot.

Sartre often thrashed out this problem with me, and he also tackled it himself in *L'Age de raison (The Age of Reason)*. In the first chapter we find Mathieu and Marcelle pretending to "tell all," but in fact avoiding all serious discussion. Sometimes speech is no more than a device for saying nothing—and a neater one than silence. Even in a case where words *do* convey information, they lack the power to suppress, sidetrack, or neutralize reality; their function is to *confront* it. If two people manage to convince themselves that they possess any power over the events or people which form the subject of their mutual confidences, then they are deceiving themselves: their "honesty" is the merest pretext. There is a certain type of supposed loyalty which I have often observed, and which in fact constitutes the most flagrant hypocrisy: it is limited to the sphere of sexual relations, and its purpose, far from aiming at any intimate understanding between a man and a woman, is to supply one of them—more often the male partner—with a soothing alibi. He nurses the illusion that by confessing his infidelities he somehow redeems them; whereas actually he inflicts a double hurt upon his partner.

There is no timeless formula which guarantees all couples achieving a perfect state of understanding; it is up to the interested parties themselves to decide just what sort of agreement they want to reach. They have no a priori rights or duties. In my youth I took an opposite view; at that period I was too prone to imagine that what suited me must needs suit everybody.

Today, on the other hand, I feel irritated when outsiders praise or criticize the relationship we have built up, yet fail to take into account the peculiar characteristic which both explains and justifies it—the identical sign on both our brows. The comradeship that welded our lives together made a superfluous mockery of any other bond we might have forged for ourselves. What, for instance, was the point of living under the same roof when the whole world was our common property? Why fear to set great distances between us when we could never truly be parted? One single aim fired us, the urge to embrace all experience, and to bear witness concerning it. At times this meant that we had to follow diverse paths— though without concealing even the least of our discoveries from one another. When we were together we bent our wills so firmly to the requirements of this common task that even at the moment of parting we still thought as one. That which bound us freed us; and in this freedom we found ourselves bound as closely as possible.

I use the word "sign" here; and in *Memoirs of a Dutiful Daughter* I said that both Sartre and I were seeking some kind of "salvation." I have employed such terms because we were, in fact, a couple of mystics. Sartre had an unqualified faith in Beauty, which he treated as inseparable from Art, while I attached supreme importance to Life. Our vocations did not coincide completely. I suggested what the difference was in the notebook where I still, from time to time, jotted down my problems and worries. One day I wrote: "I want to write: I want to put down phrases on paper, to take elements from my life and turn them into words." But on another occasion I clarified this ambition more precisely: "I shall never be able to give myself to art excepting as a means of protecting my life. I shall never be a writer first and foremost, like Sartre." Despite his bursting high spirits, Sartre used to say that he attached little value to happiness; he would have gone on writing however severe his personal afflictions might have been. I knew him well enough not to query this assumption of stubbornness, though I was made of different stuff myself. I had made up my mind, in the event of some extreme misfortune overtaking me, to commit suicide. As I saw it, the resolution which Sartre displayed set him above me. I admired him for holding his destiny in his own hands, unaided; far from feeling embarrassed at the thought of his superiority, I derived comfort from it.

To achieve basic understanding with someone is a very rare privilege in any circumstances; for me it took on a literally infinite value. At the back of my memory there glowed, with unparalleled sweetness, all those long hours that Zaza and I had spent hidden in Monsieur Mabille's study, talking. I too had experienced moments of poignant pleasure when my father smiled at me, and I could tell myself that, in a sense, this peerless man was *mine*. My adolescent dreams projected these supreme moments of my childhood into the future: they were not mere insubstantial fancies, but had a real existence for me—which is why their fulfillment never struck me as miraculous. Certainly circumstances were all in my favor: I might never have found anyone with whom I could reach a state of perfect agreement. When my chance was offered me, I took it; the passion and tenacity with which I did so showed how deeply rooted the urge was in me.

Sartre was only three years older than I was—an equal, as Zaza had been—and together we set forth to explore the world. My trust in him was so complete that he supplied me with the sort of absolute unfailing security that I had once had from my parents, or from God. When I threw myself into a world of freedom, I found an unbroken sky above my head. I was free of all shackling restraint, and yet every moment of my existence possessed its own inevitability. All my most remote and deep-felt longings were now fulfilled; there was nothing left for me to wish—except that this state of triumphant bliss might continue unwaveringly forever. Its sheer intensity carried all before it; it even managed to engulf the fact of Zaza's death. I was shocked enough at the time: I wept and felt my heart would break; but it was only later that grief made its real, insidious inroads upon me. That autumn my past lay dormant; I belonged wholly to the present.

Happiness is a rarer vocation than people suppose. In my opinion Freud was quite right to link it with the satisfaction of infantile desires. Normally, unless it is crammed full to the point of imbecility, any child seethes with multitudinous appetites: what it can grasp in its hands is nothing compared to the rich harvest it can see and feel all around it. It still has to develop the sound emotional balance that will allow it to take an interest both in what it has and it has not. I have often observed that people whose early years have been ruined by a surfeit of unhappiness, humiliation, fear, or, above all, resentment are able to enjoy only abstract satisfaction when they grow up—money (if money per se does not bring happiness, said Freud, that is because no child wants money), fame, honor, power, respectability. Early victims both of others and of themselves, they turn away from a world which afterward reflects nothing for them except their own long-standing indifference. (My cousin Jacques, to whom I refer in *Memoirs of a Dutiful Daughter,* seems to me a typical example of this inaptitude for happiness, which was clearly due to the conditions of his childhood.) On the other hand, though such elements as we endow with absolute authority may weigh heavily upon us, they can also grant us unparalleled fullness of delight. I was not particularly spoiled as a small girl; but circumstances had fostered the growth in me of innumerable desires, which my studies and family life made it vital to suppress. But they only burst forth with greater violence, and to quiet them seemed a task of the utmost urgency. This proved to be a long and exacting undertaking, to which I devoted myself without stint for years. I have never met anyone, in the whole of my life, who was so well equipped for happiness as I was, or who labored so stubbornly to achieve it. No sooner had I caught a glimpse of it than I concentrated upon nothing else. If I had been promised renown and glory at the price of happiness, I should have refused. It was not merely this effervescent sensation in my heart, but also the belief that here lay the truth about my existence, indeed about the world. I longed more passionately than ever to grasp this truth; the time had come to set substantial objects, good flesh and bone, over against the images, fantasies, and mere words that had helped me to foreshadow their presence. I would not have chosen in any way to change the conditions under which I was setting about my task. Paris seemed the very center of the world to me; I was bursting with health, and had leisure at my disposal. Furthermore, I had met a traveling companion who stepped out along my own road with more self-assurance than I could muster myself. Thanks to these factors I was able to cherish the hope of turning my life into a model experience, a whole world in microcosm: they also ensured that the world and I would agree. In 1929 I believed—and said so— in peace, progress, and a glorious future. My own experience had to partake of this universal harmony; if I had been unhappy I should have felt myself an exile, and reality would have eluded me.

At the beginning of November Sartre went off to do his military service. On the advice of Raymond Aron he had studied up on meteorology. He was assigned to Saint-Cyr, where Aron was at the time a sergeant-instructor and initiated Sartre into the handling of an anemometer. I recall that I went to see Grock perform on the evening he left, and did not find the great clown funny in the least. Sartre was restricted to barracks at Saint-Cyr for a fortnight, and I could pay him only a brief visit. He received me in a kind of parlor, which was packed with other soldiers and their families. He had not resigned himself to the stupidity of military life, nor to wasting eighteen months: he was still furious. I too was repelled by any idea of constraint; as we were both antimilitarists, we felt unwilling to make any attempt to see a bright side to the present situation. This first meeting was a miserable affair: the dark-blue uniform, beret, and puttees looked to me like a convict's rig. Later Sartre had more freedom of movement: I would go off three or four times a week and meet him at Saint-Cyr in the early evening. He would be waiting for me at the station, and we would have dinner at the Soleil d'Or. The barracks were two or three miles from the town; I would walk halfway back with Sartre, and then hurry back to catch the last train, which left at nine-thirty. Once I missed it and had to walk to Versailles. Trudging alone along that black road, sometimes in the teeth of wind and rain, and watching the white distant gleam of convolvulus through the park railings, gave me an exhilarating sensation of adventure. Occasionally Sartre came into Paris for the evening: a truck would drop him and a few of his comrades at the Place de l'Etoile. He only had a couple of hours, perhaps less: we would sit in a café on the Avenue Wagram, or perhaps take a turn down the Avenue des Ternes, eating *beignets au confiture* in lieu of dinner. We called them "hunger-pluggers." He usually got off all day Sunday. In January he was assigned to Saint-Symphorien, near Tours. Together with a *chef de poste* and three assistants he lived in a villa that had been turned into a meteorological station. His chief was a civilian, and let the military personnel arrange their own lives as they pleased; they worked out a roster system that gave them an extra week off every month, over and above their official free time. So Paris remained the center of our life together.

Though we spent much time alone in each other's company, we also went out with friends. I had lost nearly all my old companions: Zaza was dead, Jacques married, and Lisa away in Saigon. Riesmann no longer interested me, and I had lost touch with Jean Pradelle. Suzanne Boigue had quarreled with me: she had tried to marry off my sister to a man in his forties—an eminently worthy match, she assured us, but poor Poupette was scared stiff by his weighty manner and bull neck. Suzanne could never forgive me for Poupette's having refused him. Shortly afterward I got a furious letter from her, saying that some anonymous caller had telephoned her and talked a lot of rubbish: she suspected me of being the practical joker in question. I denied it by return mail, but she was not convinced.

Of all the people who had mattered to me, then, I introduced Sartre to only four: my sister Poupette, Gégé, Stépha, and Fernando. Sartre always got along well with women, and he took to Fernando; but the latter went off and settled in Madrid with Stépha. André Herbaud had taken a teaching job in Coutances, and was preparing for his own examinations at the same time; so though I still kept in close touch with him, he paid only flying visits to Paris. There were really very few links with my past life surviving. On the other hand I did get to know Sartre's own circle of friends. We saw a good deal of Raymond Aron, who was just finishing his period of military service at Saint-Cyr. One day, feeling very nervous, I drove out with him alone to Trappe to find a meteorological balloon that had gone adrift. He had a little car of his own, and sometimes took us in to

Versailles from Saint-Cyr for dinner. He was a member of the Socialist Party, an organization which we despised—firstly on the grounds that it was infiltrated by the bourgeoisie, and secondly because we were temperamentally opposed to the idea of reform: society, we felt, could change only as a result of sudden cataclysmic upheaval on a global scale. But we hardly ever talked politics with Aron. Mostly he and Sartre argued bitterly about problems of philosophy. I took no part in these discussions, since my mind moved too slowly for them; nevertheless I found myself more often than not on Aron's side. Like him I had a weakness for idealism. In order to guarantee the human spirit its condition of sovereign freedom, I had come to the banal conclusion that the world must be scrapped and started again. Sartre's originality lay in the fact that while he granted the conscious mind a splendid measure of independence, he came down very heavily on the side of reality. This characteristic of his could be recognized not only in his remarkable capacity for self-revelation, but also in a certain down-to-earth quality that was impossible to minimize. He made no distinction between his own vision and the actual object he saw, which threw him into some very thorny problems—though his convictions were never shaken by mere difficulties. Should one attribute such stubborn realism to pride or to love? He would not accept the proposition that the human element in him could be duped by appearances, and he was too passionately attached to this world to write it off as mere illusion. It was his sheer vitality that fostered such optimism in him— an attitude which allowed the subjective and objective viewpoints equal validity. It is impossible to believe both in the notion of "color" and in "vibrations of the ether," so he rejected Science and followed the trail blazed by countless inheritors of Idealist criticism; but he went to unheard-of extremes in his total rejection of universals. To him general laws and concepts and all such abstractions were nothing but hot air: people, he maintained, all agreed to accept them because they effectively masked a reality which men found alarming. He, on the other hand, wanted to grapple with this living reality, and despised any analysis which limited its dissecting to corpses. He envisaged a world-wide system of intelligence centered upon the concrete—and therefore upon the individual, since only the individual entity has any real existence. The only metaphysical systems which he did not reject were those which regarded the cosmos as a synthetic totality, such as Stoicism or Spinoza's doctrines. Aron, on the other hand, enjoyed critical analysis, and set himself to tear Sartre's rash syntheses to bits. He had the knack of getting his opponent in the fork of a dilemma and then crushing him with one sharp hammer stroke. "There are two alternatives, *mon petit camarade*," he would say. "Take your choice." And a faint smile would flicker in those vivid blue eyes, which always had so intelligent and cynically disillusioned a look about them. Sartre struggled hard to avoid being cornered, but as there was more imagination than logic in his mental processes, he had his work cut out. I cannot recall one occasion on which he convinced Aron—or on which Aron succeeded in shaking Sartre's own beliefs.

Then there was Nizan—married now, and the father of a family, who was doing his military service in Paris. His in-laws had a house at Saint-Germain-en-Laye, built and furnished in the ultramodern style, where we spent an entire Sunday making a film out on the terrace. Rirette Nizan's brother was an assistant director, and owned a camera. Nizan played the part of a curé, and Sartre that of a pious young man brought up in a religious establishment. Some girls set about seducing the young man, but when they pull off his shirt they find a huge glowing scapular on his chest. Then Christ appears to him, and talks to him man to man: "Do you smoke?" Christ asks, and pulls the Sacred Heart out of his bosom and offers it to him in lieu of a lighter. In any event this bit of the scenario proved too hard to do, and we gave it up. We made do with a more benign sort of miracle: the girls, thunderstruck by their vision of the scapular, fell on their knees and worshiped God. The parts were played by Rirette, myself, and a splendid young woman at that time married to Emmanuel Berl, who shook us by smartly stepping out of her almond-green dress and parading, in broad daylight, with nothing on but black lace panties and bra. Afterward we went for a walk in the country lanes; Nizan was still wearing his soutane, and had one arm affectionately clasped round his wife's waist, a sight which made passers-by blink. The following spring he took us to Garches Fair. We knocked down stuffed dolls with the faces of well-known generals and financiers, and Nizan pointed Doriot out to us: he was shaking an old workman's hand with fine show of fraternal demonstrativeness—which elicited sharp disapproval from Sartre.

We never had discussions with Nizan: he refused to approach serious subjects directly. Instead he would tell a series of carefully selected anecdotes, and refrain from drawing any conclusion from them: he preferred to bite his nails and mutter dire prophecies and sibylline threats. As a result our differences were passed over in silence. On the other hand, like many Communist intellectuals at this period, Nizan was not so much a revolutionary as a rebel, which meant that over a whole range of topics he privately agreed with us—though in some instances this agreement rested on misconceptions which we left undisturbed. Between us we tore the bourgeoisie to shreds, tooth and nail. In the case of Sartre and myself, such hostility remained individualistic, *ergo* bourgeois: it was not so very different from that which Flaubert attributed to the "grocers" and Barrès to the "barbarians," and it was no accident that to us, as to Barrès, the engineer symbolized the "privileged enemy." He imprisoned life under his steel and concrete; he marched straight ahead, blind, unfeeling, as confident in himself as in his mathematical formulae, and implacably identifying means with ends. In the name of art, culture, and freedom we condemned him, and through him Universal Man. Despite this we did not align ourselves with the aesthetic views held by Barrès: the bourgeoisie as a class was our enemy, and we actively desired its liquidation. We sympathized in principle with the workers because they were free of any bourgeois blemish; the crude simplicity of their needs and the constant struggle they kept up against physical odds meant that they faced the human situation in its true colors. Accordingly while we shared Nizan's hopes for a revolution of the proletariat, it was only the negative aspect of such a revolution that concerned us. In the Soviet Union the great blaze of the October Revolution had long since flickered out, and, as Sartre said, by and large what was emerging there was a "technological culture." We should not, we decided, feel at all at ease in a socialist world. In every society the artist or writer remains an outsider, and one which proclaimed with such dogmatic fervor its intention of "integrating" him struck us as being about the most unfavorable environment he could have.

Sartre's most intimate friend was Pierre Pagniez, another student of his year at the Ecole Normale, who had just passed his *agrégation de lettres*. They had gone in for meteorology together, and annoyed Aron by flicking paper darts at him during his classes. Pagniez sometimes had dinner with us at the Soleil d'Or: he was fortunate enough to get a Paris assignment. Sartre met him in town every time he came up. He was of a Protestant family, and, like many Protestants, was aggressively modest by temperament. A secretive, deliberately sarcastic person, he had wide interests but few enthusiasms. He had peasant connections, and loved the country and *la vie rustique*. He used to say, laughing, that he was a *passéiste*: he believed in a bourgeois Golden Age, and in certain of the bourgeoisie's values plus the virtues of the working class. His appreciation embraced Stendhal, Proust, English fiction, classical culture, nature, travel, conversation, friendship, vintage wines, and good food. He carefully avoided ambition in any form, and did not feel obliged to write in order to justify his existence. It seemed to him quite sufficient to sample, intelligently, what this world had to offer, and to make oneself a pleasant niche in it. He used to say that there were certain special moments—for instance, when a particular landscape exactly fitted a particular mood—that gave the impression of perfect inevitability. But in general there was nothing systematic about his outlook. He would cheerfully declare that he never made up theories. Those held by Sartre amused him vastly, not because he thought them more wrongheaded than anyone else's, but because for him life and ideas always contradicted one another, and it was life that interested him.

Sartre's own interests included life and *his* ideas; those of other people bored him. He distrusted Aron's logic, Herbaud's aesthetic theories, and Nizan's Marxism. Thanks to Pagniez he learned how to garner every experience with an observant concentration unmarred by any subsequent *arrière-pensée*: Pagniez instilled into him what he called an "awareness of nuances" that acted as a corrective for his own wild enthusiasms, and this was only one of the reasons why he felt such lively appreciation for Pagniez's conversation. There were a lot of points over which he and we were in agreement. Like him, we made an a priori estimate of the artisan class, whose work we regarded as the product of untrammeled imagination, culminating in some artifact stamped with individual idiosyncrasy. About the peasants we had no opinions of our own, and were only too glad to agree with what Pagniez told us. He accepted the capitalist regime, while we condemned it; yet despite this he upbraided the ruling classes for their decadence, and attacked them in detail just as wholeheartedly as we did. For our part, we restricted our criticisms to the theoretical plane, and modeled our own way of life, with some enthusiasm, on that of the *petit bourgeois* class to which in fact we belonged: our tastes and interests were more or less identical with theirs. Sartre and Pagniez were united by their mutual passion for understanding people. They could spend hours analyzing a gesture or a tone of voice. With such common affinities to bind them together, they cherished a strong affection for one another. Pagniez went so far as to say that with his fine-chiseled nose and generous mouth Sartre was quite a handsome fellow. Sartre subjected Pagniez to humanistic views that would have made his hair stand on end coming from anyone else.

There was yet another bond between them: the admiring devotion which they both, in varying degrees, felt for Madame Lemaire. Herbaud had discussed this lady with me the previous year, in terms that aroused my interest. I was full of curiosity when I paid my first visit to her flat at the far end of the Boulevard Raspail. She was forty, which at the time I thought a great age, though exotic too. She had been born in the Argentine of French parents; after her mother's death she and her sister, who was a year older than she, had been brought up on a big, lonely *estancia* by their father. A doctor and freethinker, the latter gave them, with the aid of various governesses, a decidedly masculine education. They were taught Latin and mathematics; they acquired an abhorrence for superstition and learned the value of sound reasoning; they galloped their horses across the pampas and had absolutely no social life. When they were eighteen their father sent them to Paris. Here they were welcomed by an aunt, a colonel's wife and a very devout person, who launched them into salon life. The two girls, shattered, decided privately that *someone* must be mad—but who? The rest of the world, or themselves?

Madame Lemaire dealt with the problem by getting married, to a doctor whose means were ample enough to let him devote his life to research; her sister followed her example, but was unlucky enough to die in childbirth. Madame Lemaire no longer had anyone with whom she could share the astonishment she felt at the manners and ideas then current in society. She was particularly stupefied by the importance which people attached to one's sex life: this struck her as decidedly comic. Meanwhile she bore two children; and in 1914 Dr. Lemaire abandoned his laboratory and his rats, and went off to the front, where, under the most appalling conditions, he operated on hundreds of wounded men. After his return he took to his bed and never got up again. He lived in a draft-proof room, racked by imaginary ailments, and very seldom received visitors. During the summer he was moved either to the villa at Juan-les-Pins that Madame Lemaire had inherited from her father, or else to his own country house near Angers. Madame Lemaire devoted herself to him, and her children, and to various aging relatives or stray down-and-outs. She had given up the notion of existing for her own pleasure. When her son failed his *baccalauréat,* she engaged for the summer vacation a young tutor from the Ecole Normale, who accompanied the family into Anjou: this, of course, was Pagniez. She enjoyed shooting, and so did he; when September came they tramped across field and furrow together, and once they had started talking to each other, they never stopped. As far as Madame Lemaire was concerned, it went without saying that this friendship had to remain platonic. As Pagniez had been affected by the puritanism of his own environment, I fancy it is unlikely that the notion of overstepping certain fixed limits ever occurred to him either. But an intimacy did develop between them, which Dr. Lemaire encouraged: he trusted his wife implicity, and Pagniez rapidly won his esteem. The Lemaire boy passed his exam in October; and Sartre, on Pagniez's recommendation, now began to coach him for his *baccalauréat* in philosophy, becoming a familiar figure about the house. Pagniez spent all his spare time on the Boulevard Raspail, where he had his own room. Sartre frequently spent the night there, and even Nizan slept there on one occasion. My Valleuse cousins, who happened to live in the same block, took considerable exception to such free-and-easy hospitality, and implied that Madame Lemaire was indulging in the most lurid debauches.

She was a petite and plumpish woman, who dressed in a discreetly elegant style. Some photographs which I saw later showed that she had been a remarkably pretty girl: she had lost her striking looks, but not her attractive personality. Her face, under its halo of thick black hair, was quite round; she had a tiny mouth, an exquisite nose, and really astonishing eyes. It was not their size or color that struck one so much as their intense aliveness. From head to foot she was bursting with life: every smile and gesture and flicker of expression rippled through her entire being, without ever (to all appearances) causing her any emotional upset. Her mind, too, was ever alert; being both inquisitive and a patient listener she attracted confidence, and knew a great deal about the affairs of all those who approached her. Despite this she maintained in such relationships the starry-eyed amazement of an eighteen-year-old girl. She spoke of these people in a detached fashion, like an anthropologist, and with great felicity of phrase. Sometimes, though, she lost her temper. She affected a somewhat crotchety rationalism, which drove her to deliver furious tirades couched in most unexpected language. I found her conversation enchanting. She won my approval in another way, too; though she made light of Grundyish gossip, she remained a respectable woman. It was true that I despised marriage, and was in favor of a love affair being pushed to its logical conclusion; but I had not emancipated myself from all sexual taboos, and promiscuity in a woman still shocked me. Besides, I admired anything which made some inroad on contemporary triteness. The relationship between Madame Lemaire and Pagniez seemed to me one of unusual subtlety, and far more valuable than an ordinary liaison.

Sartre occupied a far less important place in Madame Lemaire's life than did Pagniez, but she was nevertheless extremely fond of him. His stubborn determination to be a writer and the unshakable certainty of his convictions both delighted and dumfounded her. She found him very amusing when he put himself out to entertain her—and even more so on numerous occasions when he had no intention of doing so. Two years previously he had written a novel called *Une défaite* (which Gallimard sensibly turned down) based on the love affairs of Nietzsche and of Cosima Wagner. The hero, Frédéric, with his aggressive "voluntarism," had given Madame Lemaire and Pagniez a good deal of quiet fun. They nicknamed Sartre "miserable Frédéric," and this was what Madame Lemaire called him when he tried to impose his own tastes and beliefs on her, or to dictate her actions, especially concerning the education of her son. "Listen to miserable Frédéric!" she would exclaim, laughing, to the world at large; and Sartre would join in the laughter. He accused her of treating her coterie with overindulgence, while she accused him of thoughtlessly disseminating dangerous advice. He despised traditions and morality, and exhorted people to be guided by their reason and instinct alone. This showed lack of discernment on his part. *He* might be enlightened enough to use freedom sensibly, she observed, with withering scorn, but the common run of mankind lacked his reasoning ability, and it was better to let them stick to the beaten path. They got a great deal of enjoyment out of these disputes.

Madame Lemaire did not bestow her friendship lightly, and I found favor more quickly with Pagniez. Even so, his regard was edged with a certain irony which often disconcerted me. Both of them intimidated me. They set great store on reserve, tact, and good manners; whereas I was an impetuous creature, with more passion than subtlety in my make-up. My trouble was an excess of good nature: I drove so straight for my goal that on occasion I showed myself lacking in tact. I did not have proof positive of this; but often in Madame Lemaire's presence I felt clumsy and adolescent, and was certain that she and Pagniez were passing judgment upon me. I didn't blow this up into a major worry, though: it never occurred to me that their criticism was directed at any basic element in me. Besides, only Sartre's opinions could really get under my skin; and in any case, for all their reservations, they treated me with great kindness. Just because I *was* so outspoken, this satisfied me.

Madame Lemaire, Pagniez, and Sartre set great store by observing the subtle distinctions which divided our several relationships. If I went into a restaurant with Sartre and found Madame Lemaire having dinner with Pagniez, she would cheerfully insist on our staying separate. Sometimes we went out with Pagniez but without her; sometimes we took tea in the Boulevard Raspail without Pagniez. Occasionally I would let Sartre go off alone to see his *petits camarades,* and very often he would also have a private session with Pagniez. Such habits astonished me at first; but I soon got used to them. Friendship is a delicate structure; it can adjust itself to sharing in some respects, but in others it insists upon retaining a monopoly.

Every combination we formed—whether *à deux, à trois,* or *à quatre*—had its own special features and conventions; it suited us to avoid sacrificing this diversity.

Often, however, the four of us met. We spent some delightful evenings together. Sometimes we had dinner in Madame Lemaire's kitchen, a slice of *pâté* and a couple of fried Eggs. Sometimes we ate at Chez Pierre on the Avenue d'Italie, and then, without batting an eyelid, I would wolf down a plate of hors d'oeuvres, some sort of fish done in sauce, jugged hare, and *crêpes flambées*; I can scarcely believe it looking back, but in fact my normal diet was so frugal that when I got the chance I tore through a really gigantic meal. On Christmas Eve Madame Lemaire's daughter Jacqueline, and her son, nicknamed The Tapir, had supper with us on the Boulevard Raspail. They were both roughly my own age. The table gleamed with flowers and cut glass and lacework. Pagniez had got the most famous brand of Strasbourg *foie gras* and a genuine Christmas pudding from London, not to mention some deliciously ripe African peaches. There was a lavish abundance of courses, and plenty of wine and other delicacies; our heads began to swim a little, and we were brimful of affection for one another.

When spring came we would often drive out along the banks of the Marne in Madame Lemaire's car, with Pagniez at the wheel. We would eat at the Chant des Oiseaux, or perhaps go for a spin in the forest around Saint-Germain or Fosse-Repose. This was a new experience for me; the headlights slashing their shafts of radiance through the depths of the woodland seemed a most beautiful sight. Often before returning home we would drink a cocktail or two in Montparnasse. We might all take in a new film together, or dress up and go off to listen to Jack Hylton and his boys; but most often we just talked. We would discuss various people we knew, analyzing their behavior, their motives, just where they were right and wrong, sorting out their problems for them. Madame Lemaire always advocated caution; Sartre and I would plump for bold solutions, while Pagniez normally upheld some sort of compromise. The persons concerned went their own sweet way; but we discussed them as carefully as if we had held their fates in our hands.

Some Sundays Sartre stayed in Tours, and then I would catch the first train out. He would bicycle down from the Villa Paulownia to the station (the Villa stood at the top of a small hill) and we would meet there, shortly before midday. I discovered the charms and limitations (hitherto unknown to me) of a provincial Sunday afternoon. There was a big brasserie with a female orchestra, a clutter of cafés, one or two restaurants, a seedy dance hall, an ill-kept park where lovers wandered, some pleasant family walks beside the Loire, and dozens of old, silent streets. This was quite enough to keep us amused. In those days we saw every sort of object as though it were one of those tiny handkerchiefs from which a conjuror can produce silk scarfs, streamers, flags, and yards of ribbon. A cup of coffee became a kaleidoscope in which we could spend ages watching the mutable reflections of ceiling or chandelier. We invented one past for the violinist, and quite a different one for the pianist. A great many things always happened to each of us between one meeting and the next: nothing struck us as insignificant, or was passed over by us in silence. I was acquainted with the slightest twitch of expression registered by any of Sartre's cronies; he knew, down to the last detail, everything that our friends in Paris were up to. The world at large passed endless information on to us, which we never tired of hearing.

Yet we did not have entirely the same reaction to it. I was swallowed up in transports of astonishment or delight: "Look at the Beaver," Sartre would say, "in one of her trances again!" He himself kept very cool-headed, and always tried to verbalize his visual impressions. One afternoon we were standing on the heights of Saint-Cloud, and gazing out at a wide landscape of river and woodland: I felt elated by this spectacle, and reproached Sartre for his indifference to it. He talked about the forest and the river far more eloquently than I did, yet they did not make him *feel* anything. He defended himself against this charge by asking what the real definition of feeling was. He had no taste, he said, for all those disordered physical reactions—violent palpitations of the heart, trembling, or giddiness—which paralyze verbal communication: when they were gone, nothing remained. He placed more value on what he termed "emotional abstractions." The significance of an expression or a spectacle reached him in a disembodied form; he kept himself detached enough from the event to try and catch it in words. On several occasions he explained to me that this was the only attitude a writer could possibly take. If you feel nothing, you cannot write at all; but if, on the other hand, you are so overcome by feelings of joy or horror that you cannot control them, then you are no longer able to give them adequate expression. Sometimes I admitted that Sartre was right; but on the other occasions I reflected that words have to murder reality before they can hold it captive, and that the most important aspect of reality—its here-and-now presence—always eludes them. I was led from this point to ask myself, somewhat anxiously, just what functions words could, or could not, perform. This was why I felt so personally affected by Virginia Woolf's reflections on language in general and the novel in particular. Though she emphasized the gulf that yawned between literature and life, she appeared to expect that the discovery of new techniques would allow a narrowing of the gap, and I hoped she might be right. But alas, her latest book, *Mrs. Dalloway,* suggested no answer to the problem that she raised. Sartre was of the opinion that there was an initial fallacy here, in the framing of the question itself. He too believed that any account of an event imposes a deceptive pattern upon the truth, an idea which he expounded in *La Nausée* (*Nausea*); even though the narrator resorts to verbal incoherence, and strives to grasp experience raw, in all its random scattered shapelessness, he can produce a mere imitation only, stamped with his own shortcomings. But Sartre thought it idle to deplore this discrepancy between things and words, between the world as it is and artistic creativity; on the contrary, he regarded it as the basic condition of literature, its main *raison d'être.* The writer's achievements are all gained within the limits of this apparent handicap, and instead of longing to abolish it, he ought rather to turn it to good advantage.

Perhaps; but all the same I found it hard to adapt myself to the split. I wanted to write books, yet not to give up my "trances": I was torn between two conflicting desires. It was because of this inner conflict that I clung for so long to the concept of art which I had settled for before my meeting with Sartre, and which was so very far from his own. The creative act, in his view, meant assuming responsibility for the world, giving it something it needed; whereas I felt one must turn one's back on it. It was not only "realism" I distrusted, but all pathos and tragedy, anything that smacked of the sentimental. I rated Bach much higher than Beethoven, whereas Sartre at that time much preferred the latter. I liked hermetic poems, surrealist films, abstract art, illuminated manuscripts and ancient tapestries, African masks. I had a passion for watching puppet shows: Podrecca's marionettes were too realistic for my taste, but other performances I had seen, at the Atelier and elsewhere, possessed a quality of calculated naïveté which I found enchanting. Such predilections can be partially explained by the influences I had undergone in my youth. I had rejected the notion of divinity, but not all aspects of the supernatural. Obviously I knew that a work wrought on earth can communicate only in earthly terms. But there were some that seemed to me to have broken free from their creator and absorbed something of the meaning he had tried to put into them. There they stood, foursquare and independent, dumb, inscrutable, like huge abandoned totems: in them alone I made contact with some vital, absolute element. It may seem paradoxical that I, who was so much in love with life, should have continued to demand this inhuman purity of art. But there was logic in my obstinacy: since art led me away from life, it could attain fulfillment only by denying life's claims.

Though I was less wholeheartedly committed to literature than Sartre, my thirst for knowledge rivaled his. Even so he pursued the truth far more persistently than I did. I have attempted to show, in my book *The Second Sex,* why a woman's situation still, even today, prevents her from exploring the world's basic problems. I longed to know the world, to find a way of expressing that knowledge; but I had never envisaged tearing its final secrets from it by sheer brain power. In any case I was too full of the novelty of my experiences during this year to devote much time to philosophy. I restricted myself to debating Sartre's ideas with him. The moment we met on the platform at Tours station, or in the Gare d'Austerlitz, he would grasp my hand and exclaim: "I've got a new theory." I would listen to him attentively, but with a certain wariness. Pagniez claimed that his friend's fine logical structures often rested on some hidden sophistry, and when one of Sartre's ideas annoyed me I would search for the "underlying sophistry." More than once I found it. This was how I came to shatter a certain "theory of the comic sense"—which Sartre himself, in any case, did not take overseriously. On other occasions he would stick to his guns, however: so much so, indeed, that if I pressed him hard he did not hesitate to throw common sense overboard. His aim, as I have said, was to preserve the phenomena, the realities of this world; he asserted that such phenomena coincided exactly with man's knowledge of them. If he had made adequate allowance, when evaluating his scheme of things, for the instruments by which this knowledge was acquired, his position might have been stronger. But he flatly refused to believe in science, so much so that one day I got him to defend the thesis that microbes and other animalculae invisible to the naked eye simply didn't exist at all. It was ridiculous, and he knew it; but he refused to climb down, since he also knew that when you are defending a self-evident, obvious fact—even though it is not susceptible of truth—you have to cling to it in the teeth of wind and storm, against reason itself. Since then I have learned that, in order to make discoveries, the most essential thing is not merely to observe a gleam of light here and there that other people have missed, but to drive straight for your goal, and damn everything else. I often accused Sartre of careless inaccuracy, but nevertheless I observed that his exaggerations tended to be more fruitful than my own scrupulous precision.

Sartre built his theories, fundamentally, upon certain positions which we both adhered to with some passion. Our love of freedom, our opposition to the established order of things, our individualism, and our respect for the working classes—all these brought us close to the anarchist position. But to be quite frank, our incoherence defied any sort of label. We were anticapitalist, yet not Marxists; we glorified the powers of pure mind and perfect freedom, yet we rejected the spiritual approach; though our interpretation of man and the universe was strictly materialistic, we despised science and technology. Sartre was not bothered by these inconsistencies, and refused so much as to formulate them. "When you think in terms of *problems*," he told me, "you aren't thinking at all." He himself skipped from one conviction to the next, without rhyme or reason.

What interested him above all was people. He wanted to replace the dry-as-dust analytical psychology taught at the Sorbonne with a concrete, hence synthetic, *apprehension* of individuals. He had stumbled on this notion in Jaspers, whose monograph *Psychopathology* (1913) had been translated into French in 1927: he and Nizan had read proof for the French edition. Against the causal etiology employed by science, Jaspers set up a different method of thought: this did not rest on any universal principle, but worked through independent connections between isolated sets of facts, relying on intuitive guesses which had more emotion than logic about them, and which were presented as self-evident, irrefutable truths. Jaspers defined and justified his system as a new departure in the field of phenomenology. Sartre knew nothing about this brand of philosophical thought, but the notion of "apprehension" had stuck in his mind, and now he was trying to apply it. He believed in graphology and particularly in physiognomy; he used to examine the faces of myself, my sister, and our friends and draw conclusions from them which he took perfectly seriously. I have remarked on the reasons for his distrust of psychoanalysis; but he was susceptible to any new kind of synthesis, and he eagerly devoured early popularizations of the Gestalt theory.

If the individual is a synthetic totality, one and indivisible, his actions can only be judged in a global context. On the ethical plane too we rejected the analytical position. Neither of us wanted any truck with what is known academically as "moral values." At the Ecole Normale Sartre had propounded a brisk slogan: "Science is the outer cover of a ball. Morality is the hole inside." I had an ingrained taste for the absolute, while Sartre was in revolt against universals; the result was that we both rejected not only the precepts current in our society, but any maxim whatsoever that laid claim to universal authority. Duty and virtue are concepts implying the subjection of the individual to laws outside himself. We denied such vain notions, and countered them with a living truth: wisdom. The wise man, in fact, establishes between himself and the universe a balance that is both individual and all-embracing. Wisdom is indivisible and cannot be parceled out; nor can it be attained except by patient accumulation of merit. One either has or has not got it; and the man who possesses it no longer cares about the practical details of his life: he can take disaster after disaster in his stride. Some of Stendhal's heroes, for instance, are endowed with a peculiar grace altogether denied to the common herd, and which justifies their every action. We were obviously among the elect, and this Jansenistic outlook both satisfied our intransigence and gave us authority for following the dictates of our own will, without hesitation. Liberty was the one law we possessed. We were against anyone attitudinizing, standing on his rights, or presenting himself in an overflattering light. Apropos of Meredith's *The Tragic Comedians,* we had had a long discussion on the evils of "reflexiveness." We did not by any means suppose that *amour-propre* (in the sense in which La Rochefoucauld uses the term) corrupts all human actions; merely that once it touches them total infiltration takes place. The only sentiments we allowed were those spontaneously evoked by the object in view; the only actions, those that arose from some specific situation. We measured a man's worth by what he accomplished: his deeds and his works. There were good elements in this realism of ours; our mistake was to assume that freedom of choice and action is a universal phenomenon. In this respect our morality remained bourgeois and idealist. We fondly supposed that we were representative of mankind as a whole; and thus, all unknown to ourselves, we demonstrated our identity with the very privileged class that we thought to repudiate.

These confusions of thought do not surprise me. We were lost in a world the complexities of which lay far beyond our understanding, and we possessed only the most rudimentary instruments to guide us through it. But at least we persisted in hacking out our own path. Every step we took brought fresh conflicts, and moved us on to yet further difficulties; and so during the years that followed we found ourselves swept far away from these first beginnings.

Sartre had begun writing again at Saint-Cyr. As he could not get down to a full-length work, he was trying his hand at poems. One of them was called "The Tree"; the tree's pointless proliferation symbolized "contingency," an image afterward repeated in *Nausea*. He read it over without enthusiasm, and sketched the first draft of another, of which I still remember the opening lines:

> Assuaged by the sacrifice of a violet,
> The great steel mirror leaves a purple afterglow in the eye.

Pagniez shattered his flow of inspiration by bursting out laughing. Nor was he any more indulgent with the first chapter of a novel in which Sartre intended to tell the story of Zaza's death. One morning the hero's eye glanced seaward, "stroking the sunlight the wrong way." This ruffled sunlight suffered the same reception as did the sacrificial violet, and Sartre did not press for its retention. He accepted criticism with imperturbable modesty: he always had moved on by then to something new, and from this progressive standpoint even the most recent events already seemed out of date, things of the past. Yet when an idea really laid hold of him he would pursue it through to the end: such was the case with *La Légende de la vérité* (The Legend of Truth), which he wrote while at Saint-Symphorien.

Once again he deployed his ideas through the medium of a story. It was almost impossible for him to state them directly: since he placed no faith in universals or generalizations, he denied himself the right even of formulating this repudiation in generalized terms. He had to replace proposition by demonstration. He admired those myths to which Plato, for similar reasons, had had recourse, and did not blush to imitate them. But this antiquated method imposed various irksome restrictions on his aggressive mind; and these restrictions were mirrored in the stiffness of his style. Nevertheless various new ideas did pierce through this armored carapace. In *La Légende de la vérité* Sartre's latest theories found a shop window. He was already correlating varieties in the cognitive process with structural differences between one human social group and another. "Truth," he wrote, "is a by-product of commerce," and commerce he linked with democracy: when citizens regard *themselves* as interchangeable, they must needs evaluate the world in similar terms, and science emerges as an index of their outlook. The elite of any society despise this universalized attitude: such groups hammer out so-called general ideas for their own special use, ideas which at best possess only an uncertain degree of probability. Sartre showed even greater dislike for these clique ideologies than he did for academic literary unanimism. He kept his sympathy for those thaumaturge-like characters who, shut off from the City with its logic and mathematics, wandered alone in the wilderness and only trusted the evidence of their own eyes as a guide toward knowledge. Thus it was only to the artist, the writer, or the philosopher—those whom he termed the "solitaries"—that he granted the privilege of grasping living reality. For a multitude of reasons, to which I will return later, this theory suited me very well, and I adopted it enthusiastically.

In August I took up quarters for a month in the little hotel at Saint-Radegonde, on the banks of the Loire, which was a ten-minute journey from the Villa Paulownia. So it had happened at last: I was spending a holiday away from Meyrignac. How I had once dreaded this exile! But it turned out to be nothing of the sort; on the contrary, I found myself at long last firmly anchored to the heart of my real existence. The countryside was most unattractive, but this did not matter. I found a sort of island, covered with undergrowth and easily reached without wetting one's feet, since the stream had almost dried up: I would retreat here every morning with a book. I lunched on a packet of *petits beurres* and a bar of chocolate, and then climbed the hill and met Sartre a few yards away from the meteorological station. Once every two hours he went off to take an observation, and I would see him waving a sort of miniature Eiffel Tower about in the air. We used to dine alfresco in Saint-Radegonde.

He often had the whole day off, and then he would make inroads on that legacy of his, abandoning our inn garden for more luxurious restaurants. There were La Lanterne or the Pont de Cissé on the banks of the Loire, where we ate delicious little sausages and drank good dry Vouvray. Sometimes we went to Saint-Florent-sur-Cher, and explored the roadhouses that catered to the wealthier classes in Touraine. Two or three times Sartre chartered a taxi after lunch; in this way we visited the châteaux of Amboise and Langeais, and strolled round Vouvray, under chalk escarpments pitted with ancient cave dwellings. Such plutocratic excursions always brought a lean aftermath. One September morning we got off the train at the Gare d'Austerlitz half starving: we had eaten nothing for two days except a prune tart in the station buffet at Tours. We hadn't a sou between us, and the sole of my shoe had come loose: I went stumbling through the maze in the Jardin des Plantes as though I had a blister on my heel. As soon as our favorite café, the Closerie des Lilas, opened for the day, we sat down on the *terrasse* with cups of hot chocolate and piles of *croissants* lined up in front of us. There was still the problem of paying for them, though. Sartre left me there as a kind of hostage, got into a taxi, and did not reappear for an hour. All our friends were away on holiday, and I still do not know who was responsible for coming to our rescue. We used to borrow a good deal; in order to repay these debts, Sartre dug into his legacy, while I sold my books and all the smaller jewelry I had been given as a young girl, which greatly shocked my parents.

We read omnivorously. Every Sunday I brought Sartre armfuls of books borrowed—more or less legitimately—from Adrienne Monnier's library. Being an addict of things like *Pardaillan, Fantomas,* and *Chéri-Bibi,* Sartre used to ask me insistently for "entertaining trash," as he called it. Trash I could find for him by the bucketful, but such works were never entertaining; disappointed, he authorized me to comb through the section devoted to potentially good books. Nothing very outstanding was being published in France at the time. Despite the distaste which Claudel produced in us, we admired *The Satin Slipper* (1921). We were also struck by Saint-Exupéry's *Night Flight.* Technological advances, like those of pure science, left us unmoved; we did not respond to Professor Piccard's ascents into the stratosphere. But by linking continent to continent, the development of aviation was liable to modify human relationships; and so we followed, with some interest, the exploits of men like Coste and Bellonte, or Mermoz, and were determined, one day, to view the earth from their aerial vantage point ourselves. We were keen would-be travelers, and enjoyed travel books: we tried to picture New York from Paul Morand's account of it, or India from Andrée Viollis's *L'Inde contre les Anglais*.

A foreign country can best be understood through its literature. The country which intrigued and interested us the most was the Soviet Union, and we read all the young Russian authors whose works were translated into French. Nizan specially recommended to us an extraordinary futuristic novel by Zamyatin, called *We*. In one sense this satirical work proved that individualism still survived in the U.S.S.R., since such a book could be written and printed there; but the proof remained equivocal, since the novel's tone and climax left no loophole for optimism. It seems clear Zamyatin foresaw no possible alternatives for himself save conformity or death. I have never forgotten that city of glass, so miraculously clear and crystalline hard, which he invented and set against a sky of never-changing blue. Babel's *Red Cavalry* was a collection of desolate little sketches portraying the miseries and futilities of war; while Ehrenburg's *Greed* and Pilnyak's *The Volga Falls to the Caspian Sea* showed us the hard human struggle that underlay the sovietization and hydroelectric schemes so prominent in the social structure of Communism. A country which could produce literature of this sort, and turn out such superb films as *The Battleship Potemkin* or *Storm Over Asia,* could not be accused of degenerating into a mere "technological culture." It is true, however, that other novels and films gave pride of place to cement works and tractors; our interest wavered between admiration and distrust.

Germany was at best vaguely reflected in books such as Jakob Wassermann's *The Maurizius Case* or Alfred Döblin's *Alexanderplatz, Berlin.* America, too, gave us more intriguing pictures on the screen than on the printed page. The most recent American best-seller, Sinclair Lewis's *Babbitt,* seemed to us a dull and laborious effort, and I preferred the rich, thick ferment of Dreiser's earlier novels. English writers we approached from a completely different angle. The society in which they moved was a solid, stable one, and they opened up no new horizons for us: what we appreciated in them was the quality of their art. The first novels of D. H. Lawrence had been published in France, and we recognized his talent. But we found his phallic cosmology disconcerting, while his erotic exhibitionism struck us as pedantic and childish. Despite this, his personality interested us: we read the memoirs of him written by Mabel Dodge, Brett, and Frieda Lawrence, taking sides in their various quarrels. We felt we knew them all personally. During these two years, also, translations of many English books appeared, including *Wuthering Heights,* Arnold Bennett's *The Old Wives' Tale,* Mary Webb's *Precious Bane,* Aldous Huxley's *Point Counter Point,* and Richard Hughes's *A High Wind in Jamaica.*

In the field of philosophy and political theory we found little worth the gleaning. We despised the meanderings of Keyserling, whose work was then being churned out in translation at a great rate. We paid no especial attention to Kierkegaard's *Journal of a Tempter*. Among the works of nonfiction that we found of value during this two-year period all I can find are Trotsky's *My Life*, a new translation of Hölderlin's *Empedocles*, and Jean Wahl's *Le Malheur de la conscience*, which gave us a glimpse or two of Hegel. We read every issue of the *Nouvelle Revue Française*, *Europe*, and the *Les Nouvelles littéraires*. We also got through a vast number of crime novels, which were just beginning to become fashionable. The Collection de l'Empreinte had recently been founded, and critics were devoting serious articles to Edgar Wallace, Freeman Wills Crofts, and E. Phillips Oppenheim.

There was one medium which Sartre ranked almost as high as literature: the cinema. It was while watching images flickering across a screen that he had had his revelation concerning the fundamental necessity of art, and had come to realize how lamentably "contingent" by contrast our physical background was. In most of his artistic preferences he displayed a leaning toward the classical; but this particular predilection set him among the modernists. Both our families, and indeed an enormous section of the middle-class population, still regarded the cinema as "entertainment for housemaids," and at the Ecole Normale Sartre and his friends were aware of belonging to an avant garde when they had serious discussions about their favorite films. I was less bitten by the bug than he was, but nevertheless I eagerly accompanied him to private film society screenings and little local fleapits where they dug out the most fascinating programs. We did not go there solely to enjoy ourselves; we brought the same serious approach to the occasion as young devotees show today when visiting a film library.

I have mentioned elsewhere how Sartre steered me away from "art films" and initiated me into the world of galloping cowboys and crime stories. One day he took me to Studio 28 to see William Boyd in a classic Hollywood-type feature, the story of an honest, big-hearted cop who finds out that his brother-in-law is a crook. Big moral decision. It turned out that the curtain raiser to this effort was a film called *Un Chien andalou,* by two men whose names, Bunuel and Dali, meant nothing to us. The opening sequences took our breath away, and afterward we were hard put to it to take any interest in William Boyd's problems. There were some other great films during those two years: *Storm Over Asia, The Wedding March, Mädchen in Uniform,* and *City Lights*. With somewhat uneasy curiosity we watched the debut of the talkies: *The Broadway Melody, The Green Goddess*. In *The Singing Fool* Al Jolson gave so contagiously emotional a rendering of "Sonny Boy" that when the lights went up I saw, to my astonishment, tears in Sartre's eyes. He used to cry unashamedly in the cinema, and I regretted the efforts I had made to stop myself doing the same thing. *Le Million* amused us, enchanted us, and made us laugh; it was a perfect success, but we looked on it as an exception, and did not agree with Jean Prévost when he boldly wrote: "I believe in the possibilities and artistic future of the talking film." *Hallelujah* would, all the same,

have been far less moving without the singing of its Negro cast, the beauty
of the spirituals themselves, and—during the death-hunt which forms the
film's climax—the squelch of mud and crackle of leaves at the heart of
that tragic stillness. And what would have remained of *The Blue Angel*
if Marlene Dietrich's voice had been erased from it? On this we were both
in agreement. But all the same, Sartre had been too fond of silent films
ever to admit without resentment the possibility that talkies might oust
them altogether. Doubtless they would succeed in ridding talkies of their
grosser technical shortcomings—for instance, match up voice resonance with
movements and apparent distance on the screen—but in Sartre's belief the
language of visual imagery was wholly self-sufficient. Any attempt to super-
impose another medium on it would be disastrous. The spoken word was,
according to him, incompatible with that special nonreality, at once poetic,
humorous, and heroic, which attracted him to the cinema.

As for the theater, we were discouraged by the general low standard of
drama, and seldom went to a play. In October, 1930, Baty opened the
Théâtre Montparnasse with a run of Brecht's *Threepenny Opera*. We
knew nothing about Brecht, but the way in which he presented Mack
the Knife's adventures delighted us; and pictures of Epinal suddenly jumped
into life on the stage. The work struck us as reflecting a completely anarchic
attitude; we gave warm applause to Marguerite Jamois and Lucien Nat.
Sartre knew all Kurt Weill's songs by heart, and often afterward we would
quote the catch phrase about meat first and morality afterward.

We also visited the music halls. Josephine Baker was at the Casino de
Paris, repeating the same songs and dances that had rocketed her into
celebrity several years earlier: once again she scored a triumph. At Bobino's
we heard Georgius—an old man now—and the new star Marie Dubas,
who stirred audiences to wild enthusiasm and laughter: she was exceedingly
droll when she sang numbers dating back to the 1900s (I remember one
called "Keep Your Distance, Ernest"), and we read into these parodies of
hers a satirical attack on the bourgeoisie. She also included in her repertoire
some rousing popular songs, the very crudeness of which we interpreted
as a challenge to the police-protected classes; so for us she was an anarchist,
too. Since we had made up our minds to like only those people and things
that represented our own views, we tended to push all our chosen favorites
into agreement with us by main force.

While books and entertainments meant a good deal to us, public events
touched us scarcely at all. Changes of cabinet and League of Nations
debates we found about as futile as the scuffles provoked from time to time
by the *Camelots du Roy*. Vast financial scandals did not shock us, since
for us capitalism and corruption were synonymous terms. The only difference about Oustric was that he had been unlucky, that was all. There was
nothing of real interest in the newspapers, which seemed to be concentrating
on attacks upon taxi drivers: two or three such incidents were reported
weekly. The only thing that stirred our imaginations was the affair of the
Butcher of Dusseldorf: in order really to understand something about
human beings, we thought, it was necessary to investigate cases of gross

abnormality. But by and large the world about us was a mere backdrop against which our private lives were played out.

The only moments that mattered to me were those I spent in Sartre's company; but in actuality I frequently got through the day without seeing him at all. I devoted a great deal of such time to reading, which I pursued in a haphazard fashion, according to Sartre's advice or my own whim of the moment. From time to time I would stop in at the Bibliothèque Nationale, or take out books from Adrienne Monnier's library; and I became a subscriber to the Anglo-American library run by Sylvia Beach. There I sat, hunched over my fire in winter, out on my balcony during the summer, clumsily smoking English cigarettes and catching up on my cultural education. Over and above the books I read with Sartre, I went through Whitman, Blake, Yeats, Synge, Sean O'Casey, all of Virginia Woolf, a vast quantity of Henry James, George Moore, Swinburne, Frank Swinnerton, Rebecca West, Sinclair Lewis, Theodore Dreiser, Sherwood Anderson, all the translations published in the "Feux croisés" series, and, in English, Dorothy Richardson's interminable series of novels from ten or a dozen volumes of which I learned precisely nothing. I read Alexandre Dumas, and the works of Népomucène Lemercier and Baour-Lormian. I read Gobineau's novels, all of Restif de La Bretonne, Diderot's letters to Sophie Volland, not to mention Hoffmann, Sudermann, Kellermann, Pio Baroja, and Panaït Istrati. Sartre took an interest in the psychology of mysticism, so I plunged into the writings of Catherine Emmerich and Saint Angela of Foligno. I wanted to understand Marx and Engels, and started in on *Das Kapital* at the Bibliothèque Nationale. This was not a success on my part. I made no distinction between Marxism and any other philosophy to which I had become accustomed: so much so, indeed, that the whole thing seemed immediately comprehensible to me, and in fact I grasped almost none of it. Nevertheless the theory of surplus appreciation came as a revelation to me, something with the staggering impact of Descarte's *Cogito ergo sum* or Kant's space-time critique. I wholeheartedly condemned exploitation, and felt a vast satisfaction at stripping down its functional mechanism. A new day dawned upon my world at the instant that I saw labor as the source and substance of all values. Nothing was ever to make me deny this truth: not the objections which the final sections of *Das Kapital* aroused in me, nor those which I found in other books, nor even the subtle doctrines propounded by more recent economists.

To earn my living I gave private lessons and also taught Latin at the Lycée Victor-Duruy. Previously I had taught psychology to thoughtful, well-behaved secondary-school girls in Neuilly; and this new junior class of mine took me somewhat off my guard. Learning the rudiments of Latin is a grim business for ten-year-old girls, and I thought I would soften the grimness with a few smiles. My pupils smiled back; then they came clambering up on to the dais to get a closer look at my necklace, and began pulling at the lace collar of my dress. The first time I sent them back to their places they sat more or less quiet; but in a very short while they were wriggling and whispering to each other incessantly. I tried to make my voice sound stern, and to instill a fierce gleam into my eye; but they still chattered and played up to me as much as ever. I decided to take a tough line, and gave the worst offender a black mark. She flung herself head first against the nearest wall, screaming: "My father will beat me!" The whole class took this cry up, in reproachful tones. "Her father will beat her!" they chorused. Could I, I asked myself, condemn her to paternal execution in this way? But if I let her off, how could I then punish her classmates? I found only one solution, and that was to talk so loud that my voice drowned the row they were making. The result was that those who wanted to listen could at least hear me; and I fancy my class learned about as much Latin as any other. But I more than once was summoned before an irate headmistress, and my assignment was not renewed.

In theory, after these two years' respite I had granted myself, I was supposed to take a job; but I hated the idea of leaving Paris, and looked around for some way to keep myself there. I turned to the wealthy and influential cousin who had once come to my father's aid; he gave me an introduction to Madame Poirier, one of the joint editors of L'Europe nouvelle, who was under some sort of obligation to him. Madame Poirier was married to the headmaster of a lycée; they had a rambling flat up in the school attics, full of antique furniture and Oriental rugs. To make a proper start in journalism, she told me, you had to have ideas to contribute. Did I have any ideas? No, I said, I didn't. They then advised me to stick to teaching. The husband took an interest in me. He was a tall, bald man in his sixties, with greenish eyes. Occasionally he invited me to have tea with him at the Pré Catalan, where he would promise me a lot of useful introductions and talk to me about Life, with an eager emphasis on its more libidinous aspects. At such moments he would look me straight in the eye, with a very serious expression, and his voice would become coolly clinical. He and his wife invited me to a cocktail party. It was my first sortie into the fashionable world, and I did not exactly shine. I wore a red wool dress, with a large white piqué collar—far too modest for the occasion. All the ladies on L'Europe nouvelle were dressed by couturiers: Louise Weiss, for instance, sitting there in black satin with a circle of admirers all around her. One of the guests had been told off to keep an eye on me. He cheered up a bit when he pointed out a heavily made-up old crone who, so he told me, had been the model for Mademoiselle Dax jeune fille, but thereafter conversation dragged miserably. I realized I would never be able to get on with these people, and made up my mind to go and teach in the provinces.

In the meanwhile I took what advantage of Paris I could. I had dropped nearly all the family connections—with aunts, cousins, and childhood friends —that I found boring. I quite often went for lunch with my parents. As we disliked quarrels, there were few topics of conversation open to us: they knew almost nothing about my present life. My father was annoyed at my not yet having taken a job. When friends inquired for news of me, he would tell them, in disgust, that I was having my Paris honeymoon. It is true that I enjoyed myself to the best of my ability. Sometimes I had dinner at Madame Lemaire's, with Pagniez, and they would take me to the cinema afterward. I visited La Lune Rousse with Rirette Nizan, and we finished the evening off drinking aquavit at the Vikings' Bar. I went back to the Jockey and La Jungle with my sister and Gégé; I made dates and went out with anyone—or almost anyone. Fernando had introduced me to the gatherings that used to meet in the evening at the café on the corner of the Boulevard Raspail and the Avenue Edgar Quinet, and I went there regularly. There was Robert Delaunay the artist, and his wife Sonia, who was a fabric designer; Cossio, who painted nothing but small boats; the avant-garde composer Varèse, and the Chilean poet Vincente Huidobro. Sometimes Blaise Cendrars would put in an appearance, and the moment he opened his mouth everyone uttered admiring exclamations. The evening was spent in fulminating against human stupidity, the decay of society, and currently fashionable art and literature. Someone suggested hiring the Eiffel Tower and equipping it with an electric sign that read MERDE! Someone else was for dousing the world in gasoline and setting it alight. I took no part in these vituperations, but I enjoyed the smoky atmosphere, the clink of glasses, and the buzz of conversation that grew louder and louder as silence spread over Paris. One night when the café shut, the whole gang went off to the Sphinx, and I followed them. Because of Toulouse-Lautrec and Van Gogh I pictured brothels as highly poetical establishments, and I was not disappointed. The décor, in even flashier bad taste than the interior of the Sacré-Coeur, the lighting, the half-naked girls in their flimsy harlequin tunics—all this was a great improvement on the stupid paintings and carnival booths so dear to Rimbaud's heart.

From Madrid and Budapest various artists and writers were sent on to me by Fernando and Bandi—the latter being a Hungarian journalist in love with Stépha, whom I had known at the Bibliothèque Nationale. Night after night I showed them around Paris, while they talked to me of other great unknown cities. I also went out occasionally with a young Chez Burma salesgirl, a friend of The Tapir's, whom I found a very likable character: Sartre had christened her Madame de Listomère, after one of Balzac's heroines. We went to dance halls on the Rue de Lappe, our faces smothered in powder and lipstick, and we were a great success. My favorite partner was a young butcher's assistant. One evening, over some strawberries in brandy, he urged me to go home with him. I told him I already had a boy friend. "So what?" he said. "Look, because you're fond of beef doesn't mean you can't eat a slice or two of ham occasionally, does it?" It was a great disappointment to him when I refused to countenance a change of diet.

It was seldom that I got to bed before two in the morning. This explains why I got through the day so quickly: I was asleep. On Mondays, especially, I used to be dropping from fatigue because I got back from Tours at half past five in the morning. The third-class compartments were crammed full, and as there was always some man, either beside me or opposite, determined to indulge in a little knee rubbing, I never got a wink of sleep. Despite this I had to be at the Lycée Duruy by eight-thirty. In the afternoon, during a Greek lesson, I often passed out for two or three minutes while my pupil was trying to construe some passage or other. I enjoyed my exhaustion, though; I liked overdoing things—though I hardly ever got drunk. My stomach was simply not strong enough: two or three cocktails were quite enough to upset it.

But I had no need of alcohol to achieve a state of intoxication. I passed from pleasurable surprise to carnival elation; everything enriched and delighted me. There was so much I had to learn that anything, no matter what, held a lesson for me. One Sunday The Tapir drove me out to Tours in his little car, together with Madame de Listomère. We left Sartre late in the evening, and it was midnight when we had to stop in Blois because of engine trouble. I had no idea till then how sinister all provincial towns look at night. It took us over a quarter of an hour to rouse the hotel proprietress. She put us two women in one double bed, and gave The Tapir the room adjoining. But The Tapir and I wanted to talk, so he dragged his mattress into our room and slept on the floor there. The following morning all hell broke loose. We thought the proprietress was going to call out the vice squad. I reveled in this insignificant episode and thought it a great adventure.

There was another, equally unimportant incident which gave me considerable pleasure. After the school year was over I used to spend my Sunday nights in Tours. But on August 15—at one in the morning, too— I found that the hotel where I usually stayed was fully booked. I tried two or three others, without success. I called a taxi and scoured the entire town: still no good. In the end the taxi driver offered to let me sleep in his cab, in the garage, and I accepted his offer gratefully. Then he changed his mind and said he was sure his wife would let me have their daughter's room—she was away at summer camp. I agreed, and went home with him— not out of simple-minded thoughtlessness, but because I trusted him. And sure enough, his young wife was waiting up for him in their big double bed, all smiles and make-up, gotten up as though for a party. The following morning they gave me coffee and wouldn't take a penny for their trouble. Their kindness moved me all the more because I came from a class whose members felt they had lost face if they did something for nothing. It also confirmed me in an attitude which I had adopted instinctively, and which I always hoped to stick to: when in doubt, to back my hunches and trust people or situations rather than fight shy of them.

One of my greatest pleasures was to go out in a car. Pagniez drove me to Tours three or four times, and took me over Chartres Cathedral and the Château de Chaumont. He got his discharge in February, 1931, two or three weeks before Sartre, and conceived a desire to travel across France and revisit various cousins and friends of his. Madame Lemaire lent him her car, and he suggested that I should come along with him. A car journey, a *real* car journey, the first trip of the sort I had ever made! I went straight into a kind of daze, exhilarated, too, at the thought of ten days' tête-à-tête with Pagniez: I enjoyed his conversation and his company and the prospect of sight-seeing with him.

As chance would have it, two days before my departure Herbaud turned up in Paris and told me he was staying for two weeks, without his wife: that meant he would have time to spend with me. For some time our relationship had rested on an equivocal basis. He had no intention of admitting what Sartre meant to me, and I had no intention of enlightening him on the subject. Two months previously he had found a letter in my room which made the situation quite clear: he had laughed at the time, but had shown some annoyance too—although he had never concealed the fact that he was highly interested in a girl from Coutances. He issued an ultimatum to me: if I chose to go off with Pagniez rather than take advantage of his, Herbaud's, presence, then he would never see me again. I protested that I could not possibly let Pagniez down. "Yes you can," Herbaud told me. "No I can't," I said. Upon which he broke off with me. We went to the cinema, and I kept weeping, saying over and over again, "But I *promised*." Afterward he told Sartre that this obstinacy of mine had exasperated him; he would have much preferred it if I had told him, quite bluntly, that I wanted to see something of the countryside. But in fact I was sincere in my protestations. I have always felt that to back out of a joint project, except in cases of unavoidable necessity, is an offense against any friendship, and I very much wanted to keep mine with Pagniez intact. The crux of the matter was that I now valued his intimacy more than I did Herbaud's. Pagniez stood closer both to Sartre and to me: though circumstances might limit the degree of intimacy we achieved, they also pointed to the prospect of enriching and developing it endlessly; while, on the other hand, Herbaud—and he knew this—had little further part to play in my life. He belonged to the past, and I sacrificed him to the future. I was crying when I said goodbye to him, a thing which he found irksome: I can understand this, for the decision in fact was mine, whereas my noisy grief somehow turned it into an act of fate.

It was raining through Morvan, but all I needed to cheer myself up were the whispered words *We're off—we're on our way!* Our lunch at the Hotel de la Poste in Avallon sent me into raptures. The following morning we went to see Brou Church. I was moved by the recumbent marble effigies on their tombs, and the little figures of the Virtues carved below; and no one made me admire the stained glass, which was as frightful a creation as the stonework of Saint-Maclou. When we reached Lyon, Pagniez went off to call on friends, and I descended on my eldest cousin, Sirmione, who had married a medical student. Two or three of his brothers joined us at lunch, and the same half-witted orphan was still waiting on table: her martyrdom seemed perennial. They surprised me, rather more than they had when I was a small child. Because I was traveling with a man they assumed that I must be familiar with every kind of vice, and the coarseness of their jokes took me aback. Over the dessert they offered me what they called a "Grenoble nut": this turned out to be an empty nutshell with a condom inside. They laughed so heartily over this that they spared me the need of trying not to look shocked. Afterward, though, they showed me around Lyon, which was more to the point; and my cousin Charles took me over his little factory, which turned out sockets for electric light bulbs. It was my first encounter with industry and made a violent impression on me. Though it was broad daylight outside, the workshops were gloomy as night, and the air we breathed was laden with metal dust. Numbers of women sat there in front of a moving belt, which was pierced with holes at regular intervals. On the floor beside them was a packing case; from this they took a brass cylinder and inserted it into a hole on the belt, which proceeded to whisk it away. To and fro went the arms, from case to belt and back again, with a quick, ceaseless, staccato rhythm. For how long? I asked. Eight hours at a stretch, in this heat and stench, chained to the horrible monotony of this in-and-out motion, without any respite. Eight hours, day in, day out. When my cousin saw the tears in my eyes he told me cheerfully that I must have drunk too much at lunch.

Passing across the Massif Central, I had my first sight of vast, snow-covered horizons. Pagniez was going to Tulle, and dropped me off at Uzerche. No question about it—I was revisiting the scenes of my past. I spent the night at the Hôtel Léonard, one of those places I had previously thought well-nigh unfit for human habitation, except by dregs of the earth such as peasants or commercial travelers: I was most comfortable there. Pagniez arrived to pick me up, and I recalled Proust's surprise when during his first car trip he confused *Guermantes Way* with *Swann's Way*. In a single afternoon we visited places which I had imagined on the opposite side of the world from one another: the Château de Turenne, Beaulieu Church, and Rocamadour, of which I had heard glowing descriptions all through my childhood, though no one ever took me there. I glutted myself with landscapes; and I had one great revelation—Provence. When I was small I had been most intrigued with what people told me about the Midi. How could it possibly be beautiful if there weren't any trees? I asked. There were no trees in the neighborhood of Uzès, or around the Pont du Gard, yet these places had great beauty. I loved the bareness and smell of the moorland; I loved the bleak emptiness of the Camargue as we drove down to Saintes-Maries-de-la-Mer. The real Aigues-Mortes impressed me as much as Barrès's description had done, and we lingered a long while at the foot of its ramparts, inhaling the stillness of the summer night. For the first time in my life I slept under a mosquito net; and for the first time, too, I saw rows of cypresses bent and twisted by the mistral, and learned the true color of an olive tree. When I reached Les Baux, at night, again for the first time, the wind was blowing; fires twinkled down in the plain, and a fire was crackling in the grate at the Reine Jeanne, where we were the only guests. We had dinner at a little table close to the fireplace, and drank a wine the name of which, "Le Mas de la dame," I recall to this day. For the first time ever I strolled through Avignon: we lunched on fruit and buns in a park overlooking the Rhône, under a glorious sky.

It was drizzling in Paris the next day. Herbaud had sent me a nasty little note, finally breaking off our friendship. Madame Lemaire wondered whether I had been right in refusing to yield to him, while Sartre was fulminating against the military authorities, who were releasing him later than he had reckoned. And how strange it was, after ten days of the closest intimacy, to find a sudden vast gulf (as I thought at the time) forming between Pagniez and me! The lesson of this homecoming was that even the happiest hour has its harsh moments, its occasional patches of shadow in which regret can take root and spring up.

At the age of nineteen, despite my ignorance and incompetence, I had genuinely wanted to write: I felt myself an exile, whose one remedy against solitude lay in self-expression. But now I no longer experienced this urge at all. In one way or another, every book is an appeal for help: but to whom, at this point, should I appeal—and for what help? I had all I could want. My emotions, my joys and pleasures, all constantly dragged me forward into the future with overwhelming intensity. Faced with such a press of people and events, I lacked the distance which lends perspective to one's judgments and enables one to discuss them. I could not bring myself to give up anything, and hence I was incapable of making my choice; the result was that I sank into a delectable but chaotic stew. As far as my past life was concerned, I did, it is true, feel a reaction against it: I had had more than enough of that phase. But it neither stirred me to nostalgia, which might have made me want to revive it, nor did it fire the kind of grudging resentment that drives one to a settling of old scores. I felt mere indifference, for which silence seemed the only appropriate expression.

Meanwhile, remembering my previous resolutions—not that Sartre would ever let me forget them—I decided to start work on a novel. I sat down on one of my orange-covered chairs, breathed in the fumes of the kerosene stove, and stared, with a perplexed eye, at the blank sheet of paper in front of me: I had no idea what to write *about.* Any literary work involves a portrayal of the world; I found the world's crude immediacy stupefying, and saw nothing in it; therefore I had no viewpoint of it to present. My only way out of this difficulty was by copying the imagery that other writers had employed for the task: without admitting it to myself, I was indulging in pastiche, an always regrettable habit. But why did I make things worse by choosing *Le Grand Meaulnes* and *Dusty Answer* as my models? I had loved these books. I wanted literature to get away from common humanity, and they delighted me by opening up a magic world for my benefit. Jacques and Herbaud had encouraged my taste for sublimation of this sort, since they themselves both went in for it with some enthusiasm. Sartre, on the other hand, found all faking or illusion repellent; yet this did not stop his daily myth-making activities for our joint amusement, and in his own writings fable and legend still played a considerable part. At all events, he had, without success, advised me to be honest in my work: the only kind of honesty open to me at this point would have been silence.

So I set about manufacturing a story that, I hoped, would borrow a little of Alain Fournier's and Rosamond Lehmann's magic. There was an old château with a big park, where a young girl lived with her gloomy, taciturn father. One day, out on a walk, she passed three handsome, carefree young creatures who were staying in a nearby manor house for the holidays. She reminded herself that she was eighteen years old, and a sudden urge came upon her to go where she pleased and to see something of the world. She managed to get away to Paris, where she met a girl resembling Stépha, and an older woman rather like Madame Lemaire. She was to have had all sorts of most poetic adventures, but just what they were I never found out, since I gave up at the third chapter. I became vaguely aware that the magic wasn't working in my case, though this didn't prevent me from chasing it stubbornly, and for a long time. I still kept a touch of original "Delly" about me, which was very noticeable in the first drafts of my novels.

My work lacked all real conviction. Sometimes I felt I was doing a school assignment, sometimes that I had lapsed into parody. But in any case there was no hurry. I was happy, and for the time being that was enough. Yet after a while I found it *wasn't* enough. I had hoped for something very different from myself. I no longer kept a private diary, but I still scribbled things down in a notebook from time to time: "I cannot reconcile myself to living if there is no purpose in my life," I wrote, in the spring of 1930, and a little later, in June: "I have lost my pride—and that means I have lost everything." I had sometimes lived at odds with my environment, but never with myself; during those eighteen months I learned that one's real and imagined desires may be very different—and learned, too, something of the malaise which such uncertainty can engender. Though I still enthusiastically ran after all the good things of this world, I was beginning to think that they kept me from my real vocation: I was well on the road to self-betrayal and self-destruction. I regarded this conflict—at least, there were moments when I did—as a tragedy; but looking back I fancy there was very little to worry about. In those days I could always make something out of nothing at the drop of a hat.

What, you may ask, did I reproach myself with? In the first place, there was the overeasy tenor of my life. To begin with, I had reveled in this, but very shortly it began to disgust me. The scholar in me began to revolt against such feckless truancy. My random reading was for amusement only, and led me nowhere. I did no work apart from my writing, and that I undertook without any deep conviction, because Sartre was adamant that I should. Many young people of both sexes who have the courage and ambition to battle through a tough academic course experience this kind of disappointment afterward. The struggle itself, the mastery of a subject, the daily rivalry—these bring satisfaction of a special kind, for which there is no substitute. The more passive pleasures of idleness seem dull by comparison, and time spent on other things, however dazzling, is time unjustifiably wasted.

Besides, I had not yet recovered from the blow which my first encounter with Sartre's *petits camarades* had inflicted upon me. In order to recover

my self-esteem to any extent I should have had to *do* something, and do
it well; I chose to be idle. My indolence confirmed my conviction that I
was a mediocre sort of person. I was, beyond any doubt, abdicating. Perhaps
it is hard for anyone to learn the art of peaceful coexistence with somebody
else: certainly I had never been capable of it. Either I reigned supreme or
sank into the abyss. During my subjugation by Zaza I plumbed the black
depths of humility; now the same story was repeated, except that I fell
from a greater height, and my self-confidence had been more rudely shaken.
In both cases I preserved my peace of mind: so fascinated was I by the
other person that I forgot myself, so much so indeed that no part of me
remained to register the statement: *I am nothing.* Yet this voice did raise
itself fitfully; and then I realized that I had ceased to exist on my own
account, and was now a mere parasite. When I quarreled with Herbaud
he accused me of having betrayed that concept of individualism which had
previously won me his esteem; and I had to admit he was right. What
caused me much greater pain was the fact that Sartre himself felt anxious
about me. "You used to be full of little ideas, Beaver," he said, in an
astonished voice. He also told me to watch out that I didn't become a
female introvert. There was, indeed, no danger of my turning into a mere
housewife, but he compared me to those heroines of Meredith's who after
a long battle for their independence ended up quite content to be some
man's helpmeet. I was furious with myself for disappointing him in this
way. My previous distrust of happiness had, after all, been justified. However attractive it might appear, it dragged me into every kind of compromise.
When I first met Sartre I felt I had everything, that in his company
I could not fail to fulfill myself completely. Now I reflected that to adapt
one's outlook to another person's salvation is the surest and quickest way
of losing him.

But why, when all is said and done, should I have felt such qualms of
remorse? I was certainly not a militant feminist: I had no theories concerning the rights and duties of women. Just as previously I had refused
to be labeled "a child," so now I did not think of myself as "a woman":
I was *me.* It was in this particular that I felt myself at fault. The notion
of salvation had lingered on in my mind after belief in God had vanished,
and my chief conviction was that each individual was responsible for secur-
ing his own. The difficulty nagging at me was not so much a social as a
moral, almost a religious, contradiction in terms. To accept a secondary
status in life, that of a merely ancillary being, would have been to degrade
my own humanity; and my entire past rose up in protest against such a
step. Obviously, the only reason for the problem presenting itself to me
in these terms was because I happened to be a woman. But it was qua
individual that I attempted to resolve it. The idea of feminism or the sex
war made no sense whatever to me.

My resentment would have been less acute if I had not at the same time
been forced to endure another, and more agonizing, humiliation, which
stemmed not from my external relationship but rather from a private and
intimate lack of harmony within myself. I had surrendered my virginity

with glad abandon: when heart, head, and body are all in unison, there is high delight to be had from the physical expression of that oneness. At first I had experienced nothing but pleasure, which matched my natural optimism and was balm to my pride. But very soon circumstances forced me into awareness of something which I had uneasily foreseen when I was twenty: simple physical desire. I knew nothing of such an appetite: I had never in my life suffered from hunger, or thirst, or lack of sleep. Now, suddenly, I fell a victim to it. I was separated from Sartre for days or even weeks at a time. On our Sundays in Tours we were too shy to go up to a hotel bedroom in broad daylight; and besides, I would not have love-making take on the appearance of a concerted enterprise. I was all for liberty, but dead set against deliberation. I refused to admit either that one could yield to desires against one's will, or the possibility of organizing one's pleasures in cold blood. The pleasures of love-making should be as unforeseen and as irresistible as the surge of the sea or a peach tree breaking into blossom. I could not have explained why, but the idea of any discrepancy between my physical emotions and my conscious will I found alarming in the extreme: and it was precisely this split that in fact took place. My body had its own whims, and I was powerless to control them; their violence overrode all my defenses. I found out that missing a person physically is not a mere matter of nostalgia, but an actual *pain*. From the roots of my hair to the soles of my feet a poisoned shirt was woven across my body. I hated suffering; I hated the thought that this suffering was born of my blood, that I was involved in it; I even went so far as to hate the very pulsing of the blood through my veins. Every morning in the Métro, still numb with sleep, I would stare at my fellow travelers, wondering if they too were familiar with this torture, and how it was that no book I knew had ever described its full agony. Gradually the poisoned shirt would dissolve, and I would feel the fresh morning air caressing my closed eyelids. But by nightfall my obsession would rouse itself once more, and thousands of ants would crawl across my lips: the mirror showed me bursting with health, but a hidden disease was rotting the marrow in my very bones.

A shameful disease, too. I had emancipated myself just far enough from my puritanical upbringing to be able to take unconstrained pleasure in my own body, but not so far that I could allow it to cause me any inconvenience. Starved of its sustenance, it begged and pleaded with me: I found it repulsive. I was forced to admit a truth that I had been doing my best to conceal ever since adolescence: my physical appetites were greater than I wanted them to be. In the feverish caresses and love-making that bound me to the man of my choice I could discern the movements of my heart, my freedom as an individual. But that mood of solitary, languorous excitement cried out for anyone, regardless. In the night train from Tours to Paris the touch of an anonymous hand along my leg could arouse feelings—against my conscious will—of quite shattering intensity. I said nothing about these shameful incidents. Now that I had embarked on our policy of absolute frankness, this reticence was, I felt, a kind of touchstone. If I dared not confess such things, it was because they were by definition unavowable. By driving me to such secrecy my body became a stumbling block rather than a bond of union between us, and I felt a burning resentment against it.

Though I had available a whole set of moral precedents which encouraged me to take sexual encounters lightly, I found that my personal experience gave them the lie. I was too convinced a materialist to distinguish, as Alain and his followers did, between body and mind, conceding each its due. To judge from my own case, the mind did *not* exist in isolation from the body, and my body compromised me completely. I might well have inclined toward Claudel's type of sublimation, and in particular toward that naturalistic optimism which claims to reconcile the rational and instinctive elements in man; but the truth was that for me, at any rate, this "reconciliation" simply did not work. My reason could not come to terms with my tyrannical desires. I learned with my body that humanity does *not* subsist in the calm light of the Good; men suffer the dumb, futile, cruel agonies of defenseless beasts. The face of the earth must have been hellish indeed to judge by the dark and lurid desires that, from time to time, struck me with the force of a thunderbolt.

One day I caught a glimpse of this hell on earth outside myself, in another person. I was not yet inured to such things, and it terrified me. One August afternoon I was at Sainte-Radegonde, reading, on the bank of that overgrown semi-island which I have already referred to. I heard an odd noise behind me: cracking twigs, and an animal panting that sounded like a death rattle. I turned around to find a man crouching in the bushes, a tramp, his eyes fixed on me, masturbating. I fled, panic-stricken. What brutish distress was hinted at in this solitary act of self-relief! For a long while I could not bear to recall the incident.

The notion that I partook of a condition common to all mankind gave me no consolation at all. It wounded my pride to find myself condemned to a subordinate rather than a commanding role where the private movements of my blood were concerned. It was hard for me to decide which of the many complaints I had against myself was the most important: each beyond doubt lent support to the rest. I would have found it easier to accept my unruly physical urges if I had achieved self-contentment with regard to my life as a whole; and my position as intellectual parasite would have bothered me less if I had not felt my freedom being engulfed by the flesh. But these burning pangs of desire, coupled with the pointlessness of my pursuits and my complete surrender to an alien personality, all conspired to fill me with feelings of guilt and disgrace. This emotion was too deep-rooted for me to envisage freeing myself from it by any artificial contrivance. I had no intention of faking my emotions, or feigning, whether by deed or word, a freedom I did not in fact possess. Nor did I pin my hopes upon a sudden conversion. I knew very well that a mere act of will would not suffice to restore my self-confidence, revive my wilting ambitions, or regain a genuine measure of independence.

My moral code required me to remain at the center of my life, though instinctively I preferred an existence other than my own. I realized that to restore the balance—without cheating—would mean a long, hard job.

Very soon, however, I would be forced to tackle it, and the prospect restored my equanimity. The atmosphere of happiness in which I was floundering had a somewhat precarious basis, since Sartre anticipated leaving soon for Japan. I made up my mind to go abroad too. I wrote to Fernando asking if he could find me a job in Madrid. He couldn't. But Monsieur Poirier, the headmaster, told me of an institute that would shortly be opened up in Morocco, and Bandi suggested a job at the University of Budapest. This would be exile with a vengeance, a clean break; I would have to take fresh stock of myself then, and no mistake. There was no risk of my slumbering in security forever; yet it would have been very wrong of me not to take full advantage of such opportunities, since they might well be denied me later. The future, then, offered me some sort of self-justification; but I paid a heavy price for it. I was still young enough to regard two years as a lifetime; this great gulf looming up on the horizon put the fear of death into me, and I no longer dared look directly at it. I find myself wondering, all things considered, just what the true reason for my discomposure may have been. Would I—at this stage—have protested against being caught in the toils of complacent happiness unless I was scared that someone might hook me out of it? At all events, guilt and fear, far from canceling one another out, attacked me simultaneously. I surrendered to their assault, in accordance with the dictates of a rhythmical pattern that has governed almost the entire course of my life. I would go weeks on end in a state of euphoria; and then for a few hours I would be ravaged by a kind of tornado that stripped me bare. To justify my condition of despair yet further, I would wallow in an abyss compounded of death, nothingness, and infinity. When the sky cleared again I could never be certain whether I was waking from a nightmare or relapsing into some long sky-blue fantasy, a permanent dream world.

I did not often succumb to these crises; as a normal thing I reflected but little on my own behavior, being too preoccupied with the world at large. Nevertheless, many of my experiences were colored by this malaise; and in particular I came to learn what ambiguous feelings another person can arouse in anyone who lacks confidence in himself.

There was a girl whom Sartre had been very close to, and whom he still saw on occasion: we called her Camille. His descriptions, whether of things or of people, were always painted in vivid colors, and the picture he gave me of Camille was most impressive. Herbaud knew her, and gave me to understand—in tones of amused sympathy—that she was indeed a remarkable person. Pagniez did not like her overmuch, but she had succeeded in knocking him off his perch. She was only four or five years older than I was, and in many respects, it seemed, my superior, a thought which I found most displeasing.

She existed for me only at one remove, but even so she possessed, in my eyes, all the glamour of a heroine from some novel. She was a beautiful woman, with vastly long blonde hair, blue eyes, a delicate complexion, an alluring figure, and perfect wrists and ankles. Her father owned a pharmacy in Toulouse. She was an only child; but while she was still a baby her mother had adopted a pretty little gypsy girl called Zina, who afterward became Camille's follower, accomplice, and even, as Camille was fond of saying, her slave. Though Camille worked only intermittently at the *lycée,* and was notably unenthusiastic about the various lecture courses she attended for a year or two at the university, she nevertheless was a great reader. Her father gave her a taste for Michelet, George Sand, Balzac, and Dickens, besides interesting her in the history of Toulouse, the Cathari, and Gaston Phoebus. She made up her own select pantheon, in which the principal divinities were Lucifer, Bluebeard, Pedro the Cruel, Cesare Borgia, and Louis XI; but the chief object of her cult was her own person. She marveled at the way she contrived to possess both beauty and intelligence, and at the exceptional level which each attained in her. She vowed she would achieve a destiny quite out of the ordinary. To start with, she turned to the sphere of sexual intrigue. When a child she had been patiently deflowered by a friend of the family; at the age of eighteen she began to frequent fashionable *maisons de rendez-vous.* She would say goodnight to her mother (of whom she was very fond) with great tenderness, make a pretense of going to bed, and then slip out with Zina. The latter had a rough time of it at first; her obstinate virginity intimidated her lovers, who were all gentlemen, and it was Camille who rescued her from this impasse. Sometimes they worked as a team, but Zina, a far less scintillating character than Camille, generally operated in more modest surroundings. Camille possessed an acute sense of the appropriate *mise en scène*; while awaiting a client in the room set apart for him she would stand in front of the fireplace, stark naked, her long hair combed out, reading Michelet or, at a later period, Nietzsche. Her cultured mind, her proud bearing, and the subtle technique she brought to her task knocked town clerks and lawyers flat: they wept on her pillow from sheer admiration. Some of them established a more permanent relationship with her, showered her with presents, and took her on their travels. She dressed very expensively, but chose her clothes less from the current fashion than from pictures which happened to catch her fancy: her room resembled a theatrical set for an opera. She threw parties in the cellar, which she transformed, according to circumstances, into a Renaissance palace or a medieval château. Herbaud once took part in a Roman orgy there, swathed in a toga; Camille presided over the banquet, dressed as a patrician lady of the late Empire and half reclining on a couch, with Zina sitting at her feet. The two of them thought up all sorts of games: once they concealed their own hair under a couple of wigs, dressed themselves up in rags, and went around the cathedral begging alms. At the same time Camille admired vast outbursts of passionate devotion, and affected to suffer such transports herself. She became infatuated with Conrad Veidt, and then, after seeing him play Louis XI in *Le Miracle des loups,* with Charles Dullin. Sometimes her fancy was caught by some bony, skull-like face, or a pair of long pale hands, but she never showed it. When night came she would go and gaze at the windows of this lucky man's villa, or, trembling, finger his front gate; but it was vital that he should not take any personal part in the proceedings. She regarded passionate love as a pre-eminently solitary occupation.

When she and Sartre first met, at the funeral of a mutual cousin somewhere in Périgord, she was twenty-two and he nineteen. Sartre was rigged out in a dark suit and wearing one of his stepfather's hats, which came nearly down to his eyebrows; boredom made his face expressionless, and gave him an aggressively ugly appearance. Camille was thunderstruck. "It's Mirabeau," she muttered to herself. Her own beauty had taken on a somewhat crazy quality under its black mourning crepe, and she had no trouble in arousing his interest. They stayed together for four whole days, at the end of which period they were hooked back by their worried families. Camille was being courted at the time by the son of a wealthy furnace manufacturer, and had toyed with the idea of marrying him; but she had no more intention of becoming a respectable middle-class housewife than of remaining a tart. Sartre convinced her that he alone could save her from provincial mediocrity. He encouraged her to trust her own intelligence, to read more widely, and to write: he would lend her a helping hand. She eagerly grasped this opportunity. They exchanged letters, she signing herself "Rastignac" and he "Vautrin"; she sent him her first attempts at literary essays, in the criticism of which he adroitly mingled truth and flattery. He expounded his views about life to her, and gave her a reading list which included Stendhal, Dostoevsky, and Nietzsche.

All this while he was gradually saving up enough money to make a trip to Toulouse: it took him about six months. During the next two years or so he occasionally went back there, though because of money shortage his visits were always very brief, and adhered to a more or less inflexible routine. About midnight he would stand on the pavement in front of the pharmacy and wait till the light went on in one particular window: this meant that Camille had kissed her mother good night, whereupon Zina would come down and open the front door for him. He would leave Camille's room just as dawn was breaking. Camille habitually stayed in bed till late in the afternoon; after that she was busy with her own affairs, and he would not see her again until the following evening. He was unaccustomed to sleeping during the day, and often, for motives of economy, did not even check in at a hotel, but would doze on a park bench or in the cinema. By the third or fourth night he would be dropping with fatigue, and Camille would say, contemptuously: "Oh go to sleep then; I'll read Nietzsche." When he awoke she would be reciting aloud from *Also sprach Zarathustra*—generally the passage which deals with the mastery of the body by the will. They had many other bones of contention, too, because while Camille awaited her metamorphosis into a second George Sand she made no change in her way of life. Besides, she had a positive flair for causing rows: what she wanted out of a love affair were stupendous quarrels followed by dizzy reconciliations.

During the second year of their liaison she spent two weeks in Paris and made a great impression at the Ecole Normale ball. In order to entertain her properly Sartre had borrowed money right and left, but even so his resources were very meager. She was disappointed by the poor quality of the hotel he booked for her, and the restaurants or dance halls which they visited. Besides, she disliked Paris. Sartre went to great lengths to obtain her a job in a stationer's, but she had not the least desire to sell postcards for a living, and soon went home to Toulouse. They broke off the relationship early that summer, for somewhat muddled motives.

Eighteen months later, at the beginning of 1929, he got a note from her suggesting that they might meet, and agreed to do so. The previous year she had made a second trip to Paris, together with a wealthy *entreteneur* whom she referred to as her "enlightened lover" because of his taste for the fine arts. Since Dullin had been one of her chosen heroes ever since *Le Miracle des loups,* she went to see him at the Atelier in *Les Oiseaux.* She wore her most exotic finery, had a seat in the first row, and eyed him in the most ostentatious manner conceivable; she repeated this performance several evenings in a row, and then asked for an interview. Dullin was by no means impervious to her evident admiration for him; one thing led to another, and soon he had set up both her and Zina in a ground-floor flat on the Rue Gabrielle. From time to time, however, she still spent a week or two in Toulouse with her "enlightened lover," who made up for his advancing years by the magnificence of his gifts. On these occasions she used her parents as an alibi. Dullin did not bother to investigate the situation too closely, since he himself was still living with his wife.

This situation Camille found less than satisfactory, and Paris bored her: she wanted to infuse a little high passion into her existence. So remembering the violence of her rows with Sartre, she took up with him again. He found her a different woman: more mature, and purged of her provincialisms. Dullin had developed her taste; she had come into contact with fashionable Paris, and acquired a veneer of sophistication. She took lessons at the Atelier drama school, and played bit parts, but she did not feel she wanted to be an actress. She always refused to impersonate characters with whom she could not identify herself: Agrippina was fair enough, but Junia unthinkable. In any case, the interpretative function is always a secondary art-form, and she wanted to create. She hit on an ambitious solution to her problem: she would write plays, with parts in them specially tailored for her. Meanwhile she was brooding over a novel, and had sketched out some stories, to which she gave the collective title of *Demonic Tales.*

She made no bones about citing the Prince of Darkness as her mentor, and demonstrated her loyalty to him by really spectacular pieces of misconduct. She drank a lot: one night she came on stage dead drunk, and pulled off the leading man's wig, roaring with laughter as she did so. On another occasion she hopped off on all fours, lifting her skirt waist-high as she went. Dullin wrote her reprimands, which she pinned up on the green-room notice board. She spent her nights prowling around Montparnasse with Zina, and once they brought two pimps home to the Rue Gabrielle. Next morning they went off with the girls' silver and linen, kicking them into silence when they protested.

Yet despite these diversions Camille found life very dull. She had found no one who could, in her opinion, stand up to her on equal terms. The only equals whom she acknowledged were dead: Nietzsche, Dürer (to whom, judging by one of her self-portraits, she bore a striking resemblance), and Emily Brontë, whose works she had just discovered. She would make midnight appointments with them, and talk to them; and in a manner of speaking they would answer her back. While she carried on these beyond-the-grave conversations, Sartre would sit and listen in chilly silence. On the other hand, she amused him greatly with her revelations concerning the scandalous intrigue of the theatrical world, imitating Lenormand and Steve Passeur. She would also pass on Dullin's ideas about production to him, and squash him with allusions to Spanish plays that he didn't know. She took him to the Atelier to see *Volpone,* and pointed out that when Dullin spoke the words, ". . . and next, my gold!" he turned and looked at her. But though Sartre enjoyed these meetings, he had no inclination to put their relationship on the old passionate footing again. Camille was resentful and disappointed, and the whole thing rapidly fizzled out. When the time came for Sartre to do his military service he kept up only the most intermittent acquaintance with her.

This story, of which I have done no more than sketch in the main outline, abounded in the most piquant incidents; I have since discovered that there were some discreet omissions in the telling of it, and that beyond any doubt Camille was guilty of distorting the truth on more than one occasion. This made little difference at the time: the whole thing fascinated me. The norms of credibility current in my former environment were no longer applicable, and I had not bothered to replace them. I was singularly deficient in critical common sense. My first instinct was toward belief, and on most occasions I stuck to it.

So I accepted Camille as she appeared to me through Sartre's eyes. She had meant something to him, and he could not resist the mild temptation, common among most young people, to embroider his past a little: he spoke of her to me with a warmth very much akin to admiration. He frequently set her up as an example to me when trying to goad me out of my inactivity: she spent her nights writing, she worked hard to make something of her life, and she would succeed in doing so. I reflected that she had more in common with him than I did, since, like him, she staked everything on her future work. Perhaps, despite our understanding and intimacy, Sartre had a higher regard for her than he did for me. Perhaps she was in fact a more estimable character. I should not have been so worked up about her had I not been a prey to the pangs of jealousy.

I found it perplexingly awkward to form an opinion about her. The casual way she used her body shocked me; but was it her emancipation or my puritan upbringing that should be blamed for this? My heart and body condemned her instinctively; but my rational mind argued against such a verdict. Perhaps I ought to interpret this as a mark of my own inferiority. How unpleasant it is to feel doubts concerning the sincerity of one's motives! From the moment I brought my accusation against Camille I myself became suspect, since it would give me far too much satisfaction if she were proved in the wrong. I floundered in a morass of indecision, not daring openly either to pronounce her guilty or acquit her; I would not glory in my prudery, nor yet would I discard it.

But there was at least one flaw in her attitude which sprang to the eye immediately. To sleep with a man you did not love was an experience concerning which I lacked personal insight; but I knew very well what it meant—the smile of contempt for those whom you despise. I had fought hard against the need to stoop to prostitution of this sort. Camille, like Zina and Sartre, mocked those whom she dubbed the *tiotocini*; but she was ready enough to flatter, charm, and converse with them. That she consented to such tedious self-debasement suggests a less intransigent and considerably meeker personality than would appear from the Camille legend.

I scored a point here, then, though somewhat nervously. And though she might have to endure a species of slavery that I had contrived to avoid, on the other hand—and this was far more important—she had preserved her independence, whereas I was reproaching myself with having sacrificed mine. Still, I did not let her score this advantage without comment: she had only succeeded in avoiding a condition of dependence by rejecting love, and I regarded the inability to feel love as constituting a positive infirmity. However brilliant Camille might have been, I never doubted that Sartre was worth far more than she was: according to my way of thinking she should have set him above her own comforts and pleasures, indeed above herself. The very strength that she derived from her lack of sensibility hinted at a complementary inner weakness. Yet despite all these qualifications I was hard put to it to hold my own against the picture I had formed of her. This handsome, experienced woman had already got some way in the world of art, literature, and the theater. She had embarked upon her career as a writer, too: I felt overwhelmed by her combination of luck and talent. I turned to the future for comfort, swearing that I too would write, would *do* something—all I needed was a bit of time. It occurred to me that time was on my side. But for the moment, beyond any doubt, Camille had me at a disadvantage.

I wanted to see her. She was appearing at the Atelier in the new show,

Patchouli, the work of an unknown young playwright called Salacrou. In the second act she was a dance hostess in a bar; the third brought her back as a theatrical ballet dancer. When the curtain rose for the second time I strained my eyes to spot her. There were three girls, all perched on bar stools; one was a brunette, and the other two were blondes. One of the blondes had a striking profile, with firm, proud features. I scarcely listened to the play, so busy was I retracing the Camille saga in terms of this sharply defined face, which I now substituted for those vague, blurred outlines that her name had hitherto conjured up in my mind. By the intermission this operation was more or less complete: Camille had acquired a visual personality. Once more the curtain rose, and there were the three girls again, dressed in crinolines this time—and all of them blonde. Camille was identified with some precision on the program as "1st dancer"—i.e., the one who spoke first. To my utter amazement, the sharp-profiled actress was not Camille, after all; the real Camille had been disguised by her dark wig. Now I saw her: the magnificent hair, the blue eyes, the clear complexion, and those famous wrists—but she did not entirely fit in with what I had heard about her. Her face, under its clusters of fair curls, was round, childish almost: there were childish inflections in that shrill and decidedly singsong voice. No, I could not bring myself to accept this oversized porcelain doll, especially since I had formed a totally different impression of her in advance. I muttered furiously to myself that Camille ought to have matched up to *my* version, that her head simply didn't belong to her. How on earth was I to reconcile her pride and ambition and stubborn willfulness and demoniac arrogance with the giggling, simpering, mincing airs I now beheld? Someone had made a fool of me; I didn't know who, and I felt furious with everyone impartially.

There was only one way of sorting this matter out, and that was by closer contact with Camille herself. Sartre had mentioned me to her, and her curiosity was aroused, so she invited me around. One afternoon I found myself ringing her bell on the Rue Gabrielle. When she opened the door she was wearing a long housecoat of crimson silk, under which a white tunic peeped out. She was also loaded down with heavy, exotic, antique jewelry, which clinked as she moved; her hair was coiled around her head and fell in a thick medieval plait over either shoulder. I recognized that shrill, affected voice, but her features were less obvious than they had appeared on the stage. Seen in profile they did resemble Dürer's; and though fullface they were rendered somewhat insipid by those great blue innocent-looking eyes, they lit up with extraordinary animation when Camille smiled to herself, head thrown back, nostrils quivering.

She took me into a small sitting room, pleasant enough despite its perfunctory furnishings. There were some books, and a desk, and on the walls portraits of Nietzsche and Dürer and Emily Brontë. There were also two enormous dolls, propped up in little chairs and dressed as for school: they were called Friedrich and Albrecht, and Camille referred to them as though they were real flesh-and-blood children. She kept up an easy flow of conversation: she told me about the performances of some Japanese no plays she had witnessed a few days before, and described the plot of *La Célestine,* which she was hoping to adapt and stage herself. I found her interesting. All the subjects she discussed were evoked with a wealth of gesture and mime, and she possessed a peculiarly seductive charm. Yet at the same time she irritated me. During our conversation she declared that a woman never has any difficulty catching a man in her toils: put on a little act, add a dash of coquetry and flirtation, and the thing was done. I would not admit that love could be won by such tricks; for instance, I said, even Camille would fail to get around Pagniez that way. Perhaps, she conceded, disdainfully: but that would be because he lacked passion and nobility. All the time she was talking she toyed with her bracelets, patted her curls, and kept shooting admiring little glances at herself in the mirror. I found this narcissism merely inane, and yet it contrived to annoy me. I could never have smiled at my reflection in so complacent a way. But in that case Camille was one up on me: my irony made no impression on her stupendous self-absorption, and indeed nothing but a really rousing counterblast of egocentricity could have restored the balance.

Afterward I walked for a long while through the streets of Montmartre, to the Atelier and back, suffering from a bad attack of the most unpleasant emotion that had ever laid hold on me, and which, I believe, is most often described as jealousy. Camille had not allowed any two-way relationship to be established between us: she had annexed me into *her* world, and relegated me to a very humble niche in it. I had no longer enough pride to deal with her, *mutatis mutandis,* in the same way, by pushing her to the bottom of *my* world; if I had done so I should have been forced to admit that she was a mere fraud, which both Sartre's judgment and my own acquiescence therein debarred me from doing. Another solution would have been to admit her superiority and lose myself in unqualified admiration of her; I was capable of assuming such an attitude—but not toward Camille. I felt myself to be the victim of a kind of injustice; this was all the more annoying because I was in the process of legitimizing it: I couldn't get my mind off her; whereas she had forgotten me already. I trudged up and down the steps of the Butte, obsessed by the very fact of her existence; I felt she had greater reality than I did, and rebelliously challenged the supremacy which I had myself bestowed upon her. It was this paradox that gave such a cruel twist to my jealousy; I suffered agonies from it for hours afterward.

Eventually I calmed down, but for a long time my attitude to Camille remained ambiguous: I saw her simultaneously through my eyes and hers. One day when Sartre and I went to see her together, she gave us a description of the dance she was to perform in the next show at the Atelier. She was playing the part of a gypsy and had decided to stick a patch over one eye for the occasion: she justified this notion with closely reasoned observations on gypsies, choreography, and the aesthetics of the theater, all most convincing. On the stage I found her costume, make-up, eye patch and, indeed, her dancing quite grotesque. My sister and one of her friends had come with me, and split their sides laughing. I asked Camille over one afternoon to meet Poupette and Fernando, who was passing through Paris on a short visit. She had a black velvet beret perched on her coiled-up hair, and wore a black dress smothered with large white polka dots, from which (it was low-cut) emerged a kind of tucker or chemisette, with puffed sleeves. She bore a vague but not overaccurate resemblance to a Renaissance painting, and talked at great length, con brio. After her departure I emphasized how attractive she was, and what a knack she had for creating an atmosphere all her own. Fernando said, with clumsy kindness, that *I* was the person primarily responsible for the atmosphere on this occasion. This took me by surprise, and I began to reflect that Camille might, after all, derive her disturbing powers only from me. In the end I got to know her well, and became used both to her defects and to her virtues. As I gradually got back my self-assurance I found myself free of the spell which she had at first cast over me.

In the spring of 1931 I had to make decisions about my immediate future which involved a long process of readjustment and self-discipline.

One Sunday in February Sartre received a letter advising him that someone else had been given the Japan lectureship. He was most disappointed. On the other hand, the University asked him to substitute, during the final term of the academic year, for the professor of philosophy at Le Havre, who was suffering from a nervous breakdown. He would be allowed to stay on the year after. This was a godsend, because if he had to stay in France he hoped at least to teach somewhere near Paris. He accepted the offer, and thus I was spared that major separation which I had dreaded so much. A great weight was lifted from my heart. The only snag was that, by the same token, the alibi I had contrived for my future now collapsed; I no longer had any protection against the pangs of conscience. I have found a page from a notebook on which I scribbled one evening in the Café Dupont on the Boulevard Rochechouart (no doubt after quite a bit to drink): "So there it is. Once more I shall stop thinking. A nice little pile of ideas, cheerfully self-immolated. (The bits of rope in the Hans Andersen story crackled as they burned, and the little children clapped their hands, and shouted: 'All gone! All gone!') Maybe it wasn't worth the effort of living after all. Imagine living for pleasure and comfort! . . . I wish I could recapture the art of solitude; it is so long since I have been alone!"

Such moments of remorse, as I have said, were only intermittent; in fact my fear of solitude considerably outweighed my desire for it. The time came when I had to go after a job; I was assigned one in Marseille, and felt scared stiff. I had envisaged worse exiles than this, but I had never really believed in them. Now, suddenly, it was all true. On October 2, I would find myself over five hundred miles from Paris. Faced with my state of panic, Sartre proposed to revise our plans. If we got married, he said, we would have the advantages of a double post, and in the long run such a formality would not seriously affect our way of life. This prospect took me unawares. Hitherto we had not even considered the possibility of submitting ourselves to the common customs and observances of our society, and in consequence the notion of getting married had simply not crossed our minds. It offended our principles. There were many points over which we hesitated, but our anarchism was as deep-dyed and aggressive as that of the old libertarians, and stirred us, as it had done them, to withstand any encroachment by society on our private affairs. We were against institutionalism, which seemed incompatible with freedom, and likewise opposed to the bourgeoisie, from whom such a concept stemmed. We found it normal to behave in accordance with our convictions, and took the unmarried state for granted. Only some very serious consideration could have made us bow before conventions which we found repellent.

But such a consideration had now, in fact, arisen, since the thought of going away to Marseille threw me into a state of great anxiety: in these circumstances, Sartre said, it was stupid to martyr oneself for a principle. I may say that not for one moment was I tempted to fall in with his suggestion. Marriage doubles one's domestic responsibilities, and, indeed, all one's social chores. Any modification of the relationship we maintained with the outside world would have fatally affected that existing between the two of us. The task of preserving my own independence was not particularly onerous; I would have regarded it as highly artificial to equate Sartre's absence with my own freedom—a thing I could only find, honestly, within my own head and heart. But I could see how much it cost Sartre to bid farewell to his travels, his own freedom, his youth—in order to become a provincial academic, now finally and forever grown-up. To have joined the ranks of the married men would have meant an even greater renunciation. I knew he was incapable of bearing a grudge against me; but I knew, too, how vulnerable I was to the prick of conscience, and how greatly I detested it. Mere elementary caution prevented my choosing a future that might be poisoned by remorse. I did not even have to think it over: the decision was taken without any effort on my part—no hesitations, no weighing the pros and cons.

There was only one consideration that could have carried sufficient weight to make us pass under the yoke of so-called legitimacy: the desire for children. This we did not possess. I have so often been taken up on this point, and have been asked so many questions concerning it, that an explanation is, perhaps, desirable. I had not then, and have not now, any prejudice against motherhood as such. Small babies had never interested me, but I often found slightly older children charming, and had intended to have some of my own when I was thinking of marrying my cousin Jacques. If now I turned aside from such a scheme it was, primarily, because my happiness was too complete for any new element to attract me. A child would not have strengthened the bonds that united Sartre and me; nor did I want Sartre's existence reflected and extended in some other being. He was sufficient both for himself and for me. I too was self-sufficient: I never once dreamed of rediscovering myself in the child I might bear. In any case, I felt such absence of affinity with my own parents that any sons or daughters I might have I regarded in advance as strangers; from them I expected either indifference or hostility—so great had been my own aversion to family life. So I had no dreams urging me to embrace maternity; and to look at the problem another way, maternity itself seemed incompatible with the way of life upon which I was embarking. I knew that in order to become a writer I needed a great measure of time and freedom. I had no rooted objection to playing at long odds, but this was not a game: the whole value and direction of my life lay at stake. The risk of compromising it could only have been justified had I regarded a child as no less vital a creative task than a work of art, which I did not. I have recounted elsewhere how shocked I was by Zaza's declaration— we were both fifteen at the time—that having babies was just as important as writing books: I still failed to see how any common ground could be discovered between two such objects in life. Literature, I thought, was a way of justifying the world by fashioning it anew in the pure context of imagination—and, at the same time, of preserving its own existence from oblivion. Childbearing, on the other hand, seemed no more than a purpose- less and unjustifiable increase of the world's population. It is hardly sur- prising that a Carmelite, having undertaken to pray for all mankind, also renounces the engendering of individual human beings. My vocation likewise would not admit impediments and stopped me from pursuing any plan alien to its needs. Thus the way of life I had chosen forced me to assume an attitude that would not be shaken by any of my impulses, and which I would never be tempted to discard. I never felt as though I were holding out against motherhood; it simply was not my natural lot in life, and by remaining childless I was fulfilling my proper function.

All the same, we did revise our original pact, inasmuch as we abandoned the idea of a provisional mutual "surety" between us. Our relationship had become closer and more demanding than at first; it could allow brief separations, but not vast solitary escapades. We did not swear oaths of eternal fidelity; but we did agree to postpone any possibility of separation until the distant time when we reached our thirties.

I calmed down again. Marseille, people assured me, was a fine, large city. There are only nine months in the school year, and the trains were fast: with two days off and a convenient dose of flu I could get to Paris. So I got all I could out of this last term, without a second thought. Sartre did not dislike Le Havre, and I accompanied him there on several occasions. Here I saw plenty of new sights: the port, with its ships and docks and swing bridges; high cliffs; a rough sea. In any case, Sartre spent the best part of his free time in Paris. Despite our anticolonialist convictions, we paid a visit to the Colonial Exposition, which gave Sartre a splendid opportunity to demonstrate what he termed his "aesthetic of opposition." What ugly rubbish, he snorted, and how ridiculous that papier-mâché model of the Angkor temple was! But we reveled in the hubbub and dust kicked up by the crowds.

Sartre had just finished *La Légende de la vérité,* which Nizan was trying to get accepted by Editions d'Europe. An extract was published in the periodical *Bifur,* which Ribemont-Dessaignes edited. Nizan had a finger in this pie, too: he wrote a brief Note on Contributors for each issue, and devoted a line or so to his *petit camarade*: "Young philosopher. Is at work on a volume of destructive philosophy." Bandi, who was in Paris at the time, discussed this work with me: he found it most disturbing. In the same number there appeared a French translation of Heidegger's *Was ist Metaphysik*; since we could not understand a word of it we failed to see its interest. Nizan himself had just published his first book, *Aden-Arabie.* We especially liked the aggressive opening lines: "I was twenty years old. I won't stand for anyone telling me that this is the best time in your life." The whole book pleased us, but we found it brilliant rather than profound: its sincerity seemed to us suspect. With the scatterbrained obstinacy of youth, Sartre, instead of revising his notions concerning Nizan in the light of this little work, chose to believe that his *petit camarade* had been making sacrifices for the sake of literature. He had enjoyed his life at the Ecole Normale, and did not take Nizan's furious attacks on it very seriously: nor did it occur to him that Nizan must have been in a very disturbed state indeed to embark on his Aden adventure. In *Aden-Arabie* Nizan was rebelling against that precept of Alain's which had been the hallmark of our generation: to say No. He wanted to say Yes to something, which was why on his return from Aden he joined the Communist Party. Given his liking for Nizan, Sartre clearly found it easier to minimize this aberration rather than to admit its full impact. So it came about that we sampled Nizan's virtuosity without paying too much attention to what he was actually saying.

In June, Stépha and Fernando descended on Paris, highly elated because, after a long period of agitation, upheaval, and repression, the Republic had finally been established in Spain. Stépha was heavily pregnant, and one fine July morning she entered the Tarnier Maternity Hospital in the Rue d'Assas. Fernando summoned all his friends to keep him company outside the Closerie des Lilas. Every hour or so he would rush off to the clinic and come back looking despondent. "Still nothing," he would mutter. After much reassurance and encouragement he would brighten up. Early that evening Stépha had a boy. Artists, journalists, and writers of every nationality celebrated the happy event far into the night. Stépha remained with the child in Paris while Fernando returned to Madrid. He had been forced to take a job there which he much disliked, selling radio sets, and he had very little time now for painting. Nevertheless he struggled on. His canvases, strongly influenced by Soutine, were still clumsy, but showed a decided advance on his early work.

The school year was coming to a close, and I got ready to go away on holiday with Sartre. Afterward we would go our separate ways. But now I had resigned myself to the inevitable. I reflected that solitude—in moderate doses—no doubt had its attractions as well as its more obvious virtues. I hoped that it would strengthen me against the temptation I had been dodging for two years now: that of giving up. All my life I will preserve an uneasy memory of this period, of my fear that I might betray my youthful ideals. Françoise d'Eaubonne, in her review of *The Mandarins,* observed that every writer has his King Charles's head, and that mine—as exemplified by Elisabeth, Denise, and above all by Paula—is the woman who sacrifices her independence for love. Today I ask myself how much, in fact, such a risk ever existed. If any man had proved sufficiently self-centered and commonplace to attempt my subjugation, I should have judged him, found him wanting, and left him. The only sort of person in whose favor I could ever wish to surrender my autonomy would be just the one who did his utmost to prevent any such thing. But at the time it seemed to me that the danger existed, and that by agreeing to go to Marseille I had begun to exorcise it.

Chapter 2

To TRAVEL HAD ALWAYS BEEN ONE OF MY MOST
burning desires. How nostalgically I had listened to Zaza in the old days
when she came back from Italy! Of the five senses there was one that I
valued far above the rest: sight. Despite my passion for conversation, I
was stupefied when I heard it said that the deaf are worse off than the
blind: it seemed preferable to me to have your face smashed in rather
than lose your eyesight, and if the choice had been put to me, I would
without the slightest hesitation have sacrificed my other features in order
to preserve my vision. The prospect of six weeks just strolling around
looking at things I found wonderful. Still, I was reasonable: beyond any
doubt I would one day visit Italy, Spain, and Greece, but it would have
to be later. This year, on Nizan's advice, I was contemplating a trip with
Sartre to Brittany, and could hardly believe my ears when Fernando suggested that we come to Madrid. We would live with him, he said, and the
exchange rate of the peseta was so much in our favor that our journey
would cost us practically nothing.

Neither of us had ever crossed the frontier; and when we saw the customs
inspectors at Port Bou, with their big patent-leather cocked hats, we at once
felt ourselves to be entering a new and exotic world. I shall never forget
our first evening in Figueras. We booked a room in a little *posada,* and
had dinner there; then we strolled around the town as night fell over
the plain, saying to each other: "We're in Spain!"

Sartre had converted the final crumbs of his legacy into pesetas: it was
not a very great sum. On Fernando's advice we had bought first-class
kilometricos—that is, round-trip tickets valid for two or three thousand
kilometers' travel on any route: otherwise we should only have been allowed
on the slowest trains. Even if we lived sparingly we would hardly have
enough left to make both ends meet. This I regarded as unimportant:
luxury did not exist for me, even in my imagination, and I felt far more
inclined to travel through Catalonia by country bus rather than in some
tourist-filled Pullman car. Sartre left me the task of consulting time-
tables and co-ordinating our itinerary: I organized times and distances just

as I chose, and took enthusiastic advantage of this new aspect of freedom. I thought of my childhood: what a business it was getting from Paris to Uzerche! First everyone wore themselves out packing; then the luggage had to be taken to the station and registered, and someone had to stand guard over it. My mother would get furious with the station staff, my father would insult the travelers sharing our compartment, and then the two of them would quarrel with each other. There were always long, panic-stricken delays, hours of boredom punctuated by noisy interludes. I had sworn that my own life would be very different. Our bags were far from heavy: we could pack or unpack them in a trice. And what fun it was to arrive in some unknown town and pick a hotel there! Boredom and worry were swept away for good now.

All the same, I felt a certain sense of anxiety when we reached Barcelona. The city swarmed around us, indifferent to our existence: we could not understand its language, so what means could we devise to draw it into our lives? The challenge of this problem at once put me on my mettle. We picked a place near the Cathedral, in a very third-rate *pension*. But I liked our room: during the afternoon siesta the sun gleamed fiery-bright through the red cotton curtains, and I felt it was Spain itself burning my skin. How zealously we pursued this idea of "Spain"! Like most tourists of our generation, we imagined that every place and town possessed a secret soul, some unchanging essential element that it was the traveler's business to reveal. Still, we regarded ourselves as far more up-to-date than Barrès: we knew that the key to Toledo or Venice was not to be found by searching exclusively in the museums and monuments to the past, but in the here-and-now of light and shade, the crowds and characteristic smells of the place, its special dishes. This was what we had learned from Valery Larbaud, Gide, Morand, and Drieu La Rochelle. According to Duhamel, the whole mystery of Berlin was distilled in the smell that hung about its streets and was like no other smell on earth; and Gide declared that to drink a cup of hot Spanish chocolate was to hold all Spain in one's mouth. So daily I forced myself to swallow cups of a black, saucelike liquid, heavily flavored with cinnamon; I ate sugar-almond cakes and quince tarts and buns that crumbled away between my teeth and tasted like old dust. We mingled with strollers on the Ramblas, and I dutifully breathed in the damp odor of the streets through which we wandered—sunless streets which were lent a touch of false gaiety by green-painted shutters and lines of colored washing strung across between house fronts. Convinced by the books we read that the true quality of a town is to be found only in its poorest quarters, we spent all our evenings down in the Barrio Chino, where big, graceful women sang, danced, and offered their favors from little open-air platforms. We were interested in them, but observed their audiences with rather more curiosity: by virtue of the spectacle we were all watching together, we felt ourselves assimilated in the crowd. Despite all this I was determined to work my way through the classic tourist round as well. We went up to Tibidabo, and for the first time I saw a Mediterranean city glittering beneath my feet, like a great piece of shattered quartz. I also made my first trip aboard a cable car, which whisked us up to the summit of Montserrat.

We had my sister with us on this occasion: she had just spent some time in Madrid with Fernando, and was now in Barcelona for three days. When we got back that evening there was more excitement than usual along the Ramblas, but we attached no significance to it at the time. The following afternoon all three of us went off to visit a church which was situated in one of the more thickly populated quarters. The trams were not running, and some of the main streets were almost deserted. We wondered what was up; but since our prime concern was to track down this somewhat elusive church in our street plan, we did not pay the matter any great attention. Then we came out into a street that was full of people and very noisy: men were standing along the walls in groups, arguing among themselves with vigorous gestures and loud, excited voices. Down the middle of the road came two policemen, escorting a handcuffed prisoner: we caught a glimpse of a police car in the distance. We hardly knew a word of Spanish and could not make out what anyone was saying: but their faces were decidedly grim. Being determined to reach our goal, we nevertheless went up to one of these excited groups and pro- nounced, with an interrogative inflection, the name of the church in which we were interested. People smiled at us, and one man, with the most charming and courteous manner imaginable, sketched out our route in dumb show. The moment we had thanked them, they resumed their dis- cussion. I have forgotten every detail of the church; but I know that when we got back from our walk we bought a paper and somehow man- aged to stumble through the news. The trade unions had declared a general strike against the local provincial authorities. In the street where we had inquired the way various militant union leaders had been arrested, and it was one such that we had seen being marched away by the two policemen. The crowd gathered along the sidewalk had been arguing whether they should rescue the man by force or not. The paper ended its account with the complacent old bromide about order having been restored. We felt ex- tremely mortified: we had been there, yet we had seen nothing. We con- soled ourselves by thinking of Stendhal and the Battle of Waterloo.

Before leaving Barcelona I checked through my *Guide Bleu* with frantic thoroughness: I wanted to see literally *everything*. But Sartre cate- gorically refused to stop off at Lérida just to contemplate a mountain of salt. "I don't mind Nature's beauty spots," he said, "but I draw the line at her curiosities." The only place we stopped at, for one day, was Saragossa, whence we made our way direct to Madrid. Fernando was waiting for us at the station: he installed us in his flat, which lay below the Alcalá, and then took us for a turn around the city. It seemed so hard and ruth- less a place to me that toward the end of the afternoon I shed a few tears. I suppose the truth is that, despite my affection for Fernando, I was feeling nostalgic—not so much for Barcelona as for my long private tête-à- tête with Sartre. In actual fact, thanks to Fernando, we now had a chance to escape the tourist's ambiguous status: a thing I realized that very night, when we sat in the park eating grilled *crevettes* and peach ice cream. Very soon Madrid's gaiety began to captivate me. The Republic was still astounded by its own victory, and you felt it was still celebrating every day. The deep, gloomy cafés were full of men—all most punctiliously dressed, despite the heat—who sat there building a new Spain with their impassioned rhetoric. Spain had defeated the priests and the plutocrats; Spain was to be established in a climate of freedom, would win justice for all. Fernando's friends believed that very soon the workers would take power and build a socialist state. For the moment everyone, from Democrats to Communists, felt happy; they all believed the future lay in their hands. We heard these rumors as we sat sipping our manzanillas, nibbling at black olives, and shelling large *crevettes*. Outside a certain café Valle Inclan sat enthroned a proud, bearded, one-armed figure, who would tell anyone who cared to listen just how he had lost his arm, and make a different story of it every time. In the evening we would have dinner in various cheap restaurants, which we liked because no tourist ever went near them. I remember one in a cellar, where they had goatskin bottles full of a heavy, resin-scented wine, and the waiters shouted the menu aloud. Till three o'clock in the morning the Madrid crowd continued to loaf about the streets, while we sat on the *terrasse* outside a café, breathing the fresh night air.

In theory the Republic was opposed to bullfighting, but all Republicans loved a *corrida,* and we went to one every Sunday. What I enjoyed most on my first visit was the festive atmosphere pervading the stands. I stared pop-eyed at the surging, motley crowd that stretched from top to bottom of that vast bowl-like enclosure; I sat in the burning sunlight with the rustle of fans and paper hats in my ears. But like most tyro spectators, I thought the bull followed the lure of the cape as inevitably as an automaton, and that the man's part in the proceedings was all too easy. I had not the slightest idea what it was that justified the applause or jeers of the crowd. The favorite toreadors that season were Marcia Lalanda and Ortega; the Madrileños also favored a young beginner known as El Estudiante, who distinguished himself by his great daring. I saw all three of them, and came to realize that the bull was very far from being deceived as a matter of course. The torero was caught between an unpredictable beast and the demanding attentions of the crowd: consequently he risked his life the whole time. The danger he faced was the essential stuff of his profession: with varying degrees of courage and skill he courted and calculated it, simultaneously employing a more or less sure technique for evading its consequences. Each fresh fight was a work of art, and gradually I came to discern what qualities gave it meaning and, sometimes, beauty. There was much that I still missed, but both Sartre and I had definitely become fans.

Fernando took us through the Prado, and we returned there on many occasions. We had not seen very many paintings hitherto in our lives. I had several times been through the Louvre galleries with Sartre, and had observed that, thanks to my cousin Jacques, I understood art a little better than he did. For me a picture was, basically, a plane surface covered with colors, while what Sartre reacted to was the subject matter, or the expressions on the figures' faces—so much so that he developed a liking for the work of Guido Reni. At this I attacked him sharply, and he beat a hasty retreat. I must admit that he also had the good taste to admire the Avignon "Pietà" and Grünewald's "Crucifixion." I had not converted him to abstract painting, but he had admitted that scenic interest and facial expression could not be viewed apart from the style, technique, and creative art which enabled us to "see" them. He in his turn had influenced me; my enthusiasm for "pure art" in general, with particular reference to visual art, had made me affect to ignore the *meaning* of landscape or human figure when I was confronted with them. By the time we paid our visit to the Prado we had more or less reached agreement on the subject; but we were still novices, and had to feel our way together. El Greco surpassed even what we had been led to expect of him by reading Barrès, and we put his work in first place among our enthusiasms. We were conscious of the cruelty that some of Goya's portraits revealed, and of the stark madness pervading his last canvases; but by and large, Fernando told us reprovingly, we tended to underrate him—a fair criticism. He also was of the opinion that we took excessive pleasure in the work of Hieronymus Bosch. We could, it is true, never have enough of his monstrous and tortured figures: he stirred our imaginations so strongly that we took little heed of his precise technical skill. Despite this, technical virtuosity did impress me enormously, and I would spend much time in front of the Titians. On this point Sartre took a radical stand right away: he turned aside in disgust. I told him he was exaggerating, and that the actual painting of these canvases was brilliant. "So what?" he retorted; "Titian's too *theatrical.*" In reaction against Guido Reni, he would no longer allow a painting to make any concessions to gesture or expression. His distaste for Titian was subsequently modified, but he never renounced it altogether.

We made several short trips from Madrid, to Segovia, Avila, Toledo, and the Escurial. Some places I afterward discovered which I thought more beautiful, but the beauty here had a freshness never to be recaptured.

Sartre had all my natural curiosity, but was not so gluttonous for experience. After a conscientious morning's sightseeing in Toledo, he would have been quite happy to spend the afternoon smoking his pipe in the Plaza Zocodover. I, on the other hand, at once developed a furious itch for action. I did not suppose, as I had done earlier in Limousin, that my presence was *needed;* but I had made it my aim to explore the whole world, and my time was limited, so I didn't want to waste a single instant. My task was made easier by the fact that from my viewpoint there were artists and styles and periods which quite simply didn't exist. Sartre, with vigilant loathing, was hunting down all the painters in whom he thought he could see Guido Reni's errors, and I was only only too glad to let him annihilate Murillo, Ribera, and many others. After this thinning-out process I no longer found the world more than my appetite could cope with, and determined to make a complete inventory of its contents. I had no truck with half measures, nor did I set up any order of precedence in such areas as we had not officially consigned to oblivion. I expected a total response from everything: how could I afford to miss a single item? This picture of El Greco's tucked away in the back of a sacristy might prove the key which would finally unlock his work for me, and without which—who knows?—the visual arts as a whole might remain a closed book as far as I was concerned. We intended to come back to Spain, but patience was never my strong suit. I could not bear to postpone, even for a year, the revelation which this reredos or that tympanum might bring me. The truth is that the satisfaction I got from them was in proportion to the degree of my desire, and at each fresh encounter reality took me unawares.

Sometimes this reality shook me out of myself altogether. "What's the use of traveling?" someone said to me once. "You can never get away from yourself." But I did; it was not so much that I changed my personality as lost it. Perhaps it is only those who (whether through ambition or natural energy) are constantly occupied with practical schemes who are also privileged to enjoy those moments of respite when suddenly time stands still and one's existence blends into the unmoving fullness of the universe. What peace, what recompense such an experience must bring! When we were at Avila, and I threw open the shutters of my bedroom in the morning and saw the towers of the city rising proudly against the blue sky, instantly past and future vanished, leaving nothing but a splendid immediacy—I and these ramparts were one and the same, something outside time. During my early travels such blissful entrancements occurred quite frequently.

We left Madrid at the end of September, having visited Santillana, and Pamplona, and San Sebastian, and Burgos Cathedral, and the rock paintings of bison at Altamira. I had found the harshness of the Castilian plateau attractive, but I was glad to return to the Basque hill country, with its brackenish autumnal scent. We caught the Paris train together at Hendaye, and I left it at Bayonne to pick up the Bordeaux-Marseille express.

In the whole of my life I have experienced no special moment that I can label "decisive"; but certain occasions have become so charged with significance in retrospect that they stand out from my past as clearly as if they had been truly great events. Looking back, I feel that my arrival in Marseille marked a completely new turn to my career.

I dumped my suitcase at the checkroom, and paused at the top of the main steps. Marseille, I murmured. Under a clear blue sky I saw sun-warmed tiles, patches of shadow, autumnal plane trees, and in the distance hills and the azure sea. A buzz of activity drifted up from the city to me, mingled with a whiff of scorched grass. Down in those dark, sunken streets people hurried to and fro. Marseille. I was in Marseille—alone, empty-handed, cut off from my past and everything I loved. I stood staring at this vast unknown city, where I now had to make my own way, unaided, from one day to the next. Hitherto I had been closely dependent upon other people, who had laid down rules and objectives for me; and now this wonderful piece of luck had come my way. Here no one was aware of my existence. Somewhere, under one of those roofs, I should have to teach for fourteen hours a week, but there was nothing else arranged on my behalf—not even what bed I should sleep in. It was up to me to decide my own way of spending the time. I could cultivate my own habits and pleasures. I began to walk down the steps slowly, one by one, stirred by the scene before me. These houses and trees and rocks and pavements would in due course, little by little, become familiar to me— and perhaps give me greater familiarity with myself.

On both sides of the road leading from the station there were restaurants with tables out on the sidewalk, sheltered by high glass screens. I spotted a card in a window which read "Room for Rent." It was not the kind of room that I particularly liked—it had a vast bed, and chairs, and a ward-robe—but I thought the big table would be useful for working on, and the landlady proposed reasonable *pension* terms. I went back for my case, and left it in the Restaurant de l'Amirauté. Two hours later I had called on the headmistress of my *lycée* and arranged my hours of work. Though I did not know Marseille, I already lived there. Now I set out to explore the town.

I fell in love with it at first sight. I clambered over every rock and ferreted through every back street; I breathed in the smell of tar and dead sea urchins down at the Old Port, mingled with the crowds along the Canebière, and I sat down in tree-lined avenues and public gardens and peaceful little squares where the peculiarly provincial smell of dead leaves eclipsed the sea wind's tang. I loved the clattering trams, with their grapelike clusters of passengers hanging on outside, and names like La Madrague or Mazargue or Les Chartreux or Le Roucas Blanc stuck up in front. On Thursday morning I rode to Cassis on one of the Mattéi buses: the terminus was quite close to where I lived. I trudged on foot along copper-colored cliffs all the way from Cassis to La Ciotat, and was so elated by the experience that when I caught the little green bus back that evening all I wanted to do was start off on the same trip again. The passion which caught hold of me then has persisted for over twenty years, and age alone has extinguished it: during those first twelve months it preserved me from boredom, regret, and several sorts of depression, trans-forming my exile into a holiday.

There was nothing new or surprising about this. The countryside round Marseille was at once wild and easy of access, and held promise of glinting secrets for even the least energetic walker. Such excursions formed the local inhabitants' favorite pastime. The experts joined hiking clubs, and published a regular bulletin with details of various ingenious itineraries. They also carefully maintained the brightly colored directional arrows that blazed the trail for them along their regular walks. A large number of my colleagues went off together on Sundays to climb the Marseilleveyre massif or the peaks of Sainte-Baume. I was exceptional in that I never attached myself to a group, and managed to turn a pastime into a most exacting duty. Between October 2 and July 14 I never once found myself wondering how to spend my Thursdays and Sundays. I made it a rule to be out of the house by dawn, winter and summer alike, and never to return before nightfall. I didn't bother with all the preliminaries, and never obtained the semiofficial rig of rucksack, studded shoes, rough skirt, and windbreaker. I would slip on an old dress and a pair of espadrilles, and take a few bananas and buns with me in a basket. Sometimes my friends would pass me in the hills, smiling disdainfully. On the other hand, with the aid of the *Bulletin,* the *Guide Bleu,* and a Michelin map, I used to work out my routes to the last detail. At first I limited myself to some five or six hours' walking; then I chose routes that would take nine to ten hours; in time I was doing over twenty-five miles in a day. I worked my way systematically through the entire area: I climbed every peak—Gardaban, Mont Aurélien, Mont Sainte-Victoire, and the Pilon du Roi—and clambered down every gully; I explored every valley, gorge, and defile. On I went, among those white and blinding stones, where there was no hint of path, watching out for the arrows—blue, green, red, or yellow—which led me on I knew not whither. Sometimes I lost track of them and had to hunt round in a circle, thrusting through sharp-scented bushes, scratching myself on various plants which were still new to me: resinaceous rock-roses, juniper, ilex, yellow and white asphodel. I followed all the coast guards' tracks, too; here, at the base of the cliffs, along this racked and indented coast line, the Mediterranean lacked that sweetly languorous calm which so often sickened me when I encountered it elsewhere. In morning splendor it surged fiercely again the headlands, dazzling white, and I felt that if I plunged my hand in I would have my fingers chopped off. It was splendid, too, to watch from the clifftops while with deceptive ease and sheer solid inorganic power it smashed over the breakwaters protecting the olive trees. There came a day in spring, on the Valensole plateau, when I found almond trees in blossom for the first time. I walked along red-and-ocher lanes in the flat country near Aix-en-Provence, and recognized many of Cézanne's canvases. I visited towns large and small, villages, abbeys, and châteaux. As in Spain, my curiosity gave me no respite. I looked for a revelation from each successive hilltop or valley, and always the beauty of the landscape surpassed both my memories and my expectations. With tenacious perseverance I rediscovered my mission to rescue things from oblivion. Alone I walked the mists that hung over the summit of Sainte-Victoire, and strode along the ridge of the Pilon du Roi, bracing myself against a violent wind which sent my beret spinning down into the valley below. Alone again, I got lost in a mountain ravine on the Lubéron range. Such moments, with all their warmth, tenderness, and fury, belong to me and no one else. How I loved to walk through the town while it was still dark, half asleep, and see the dawn come up behind some unknown village! I would take a midday nap with the scent of broom and pine all around me; I would clamber up the flanks of hills and go plodding across open uplands, and things foreseen and unforeseeable would befall me on my way. I never lost the pleasure of finding a dot or some lines upon a map, or three lines entered in my *Guide,* transformed into stones, trees, sky, and water.

Every time I revisit Provence I can see why I love it so much; but these reasons do not adequately explain the mad enthusiasm I felt then—an enthusiasm which I can gauge, with a certain degree of amazement, from one particular memory. Toward the end of November my sister arrived in Marseille, and I initiated her into these new pleasures of mine just as I had done with my childhood games. We saw the Roquefavour aqueduct under a bright midday sun, and ploughed through the snow round Toulon in espadrilles. My sister was unused to such activities; she suffered from agonizing blisters, yet she never complained, and managed to keep up with me. One Thursday—it was midday, and we had just reached Sainte-Baume —she developed a temperature. I told her to lie down in the hospice, have some hot toddy, and wait for the Marseille bus, which was due a few hours later. Then I finished my trek alone. That evening she took to her bed with flu, and I felt a faint twinge of remorse. Today I can scarcely imagine how I could have brought myself to leave her shivering in that gloomy refectory as I did. Generally, it is true, I showed consideration for other people, and I was very fond of my sister. Sartre often used to tell me that I was a schizophrenic, that instead of adapting my schemes to reality I pursued them in the teeth of circumstances, regarding hard facts as something merely peripheral. On Sainte-Baume, in fact, I was prepared to deny my sister's existence rather than deviate from my prepared program: she had always fallen in so loyally with all my schemes that I refused even to envisage the possibility of her disrupting them on this occasion. What Sartre called schizophrenia seemed to me an extreme and aberrant form of my particular brand of optimism. I refused, as I had done when I was twenty, to admit that life contained any wills apart from my own.

The will power that manifested itself in these fanatical walking trips of mine was something very deep-rooted. Long ago in Limousin, as I walked those deep, rutted lanes, I had promised myself that one day I would traverse France, perhaps even the whole world, so thoroughly that I left not one field or thicket unvisited. I did not really believe this; and similarly in Spain, when I claimed that I would see *everything,* I interpreted this word in a decidedly liberal sense. But here, in the limited terrain to which my job and my limited resources restricted me, the claim seemed at least a possible one. I wanted to explore Provence more fully and in a more civilized fashion than any female hiker in herringbone tweed. I had never practiced any sport, and therefore took all the more pleasure in driving my body to the very limit of its endurance, by the most ingenious possible methods. To save my energy on the highway I would thumb lifts from cars or trucks; when I was clambering over rocks in the mountains, or sliding down screes, I would work out short cuts, so that each expedition was a work of art in itself. I promised myself to cherish the proud memory of such exploits forever, and in the actual moment of accomplishment I would congratulate myself on my own achievements.

The pride which they stirred in me meant that I was forced to repeat them: how could I let myself fall from this high standard? If I had given up even one trip through indifference or to satisfy a mere whim, if I had once asked myself what the point of it all was, I would have destroyed the whole carefully contrived edifice that elevated my pleasures to the level of sacred obligations. Often during the course of my life I have resorted to such a stratagem—that is, investing my activities with the sanction of necessity—and ended by becoming its victim or dupe. This was how, at the age of eighteen, I had saved myself from boredom by plunging into frenzied action. Obviously I could not have kept up the magpie enthusiasm of the collector, as I did in Marseille, if it had been the product of a mere abstract notion; but I have already said what pleasure it gave me.

This description, incidentally, is not applicable to my case only, but will serve as a generalization for every type of obsession. An obsessed person lives in a totalitarian world, constructed on a system of rules, values, and agreements which he regards as absolute. That is why he can never admit the slightest breath of criticism, since it might show him that there was the possibility of a loophole existing in the system. This would call in question its entire *raison d'être,* and the whole edifice would collapse in ruins. No obsession can justify its continued existence except by perpetual and repeated self-affirmation.

Few real adventures befell me; yet on two or three occasions I experienced fear. Once a dog decided to follow me all the way from Aubagne to the top of the Gardaban. I shared my buns with him, but whereas I was used to going without water, he was not. On the way back I thought he was going mad, and madness in an animal was something I regarded with great alarm. When we reached the village he flung himself, howling, at the nearest brook. One afternoon I painfully struggled up a series of steep gorges that should have led me out onto a plateau. The going got steadily more difficult, but I felt incapable of getting down by the route I had clambered up, and so kept on. Finally a sheer wall of rock blocked any further advance, and I had to retrace my steps, from one basin to the next. At last I came to a fault in the rock which I dared not jump across. There was no sound except for the rustle of snakes slithering among the dry stones. No living soul would ever pass through this defile: suppose I broke a leg or twisted an ankle; what would become of me? I shouted, but got no reply: I went on calling for a quarter of an hour. The silence was appalling. In the end I plucked up my courage and got down safe and sound.

There was one danger against which my colleagues had warned me many times. My solitary rambles were against all the rules, and they were always telling me, in a prim sort of way, that I was bound to get myself raped. I treated such advice contemptuously, regarding it as a mere spinsterish obsession. I had no intention of making my life a bore with precautions of this sort; and in any case there were certain things, such as accidents, severe illnesses, or rape, which simply *could not happen* to me. I had several unpleasant incidents with truck drivers, not to mention a commercial traveler who wanted me to have a roll with him in the ditch, and left me flat in the middle of the road when I refused. But I continued to thumb lifts all the same. One afternoon I was trudging along a white, dusty road in the direction of Tarascon, under a blazing sun, when a car overtook me and pulled up. The two young men in it invited me to hop aboard, and said they would drive me into town. When we joined the main road, they turned left instead of right, saying that they were taking a little short cut they knew. I hesitated, not wanting to make a fool of myself; but when I realized that they were making for a small hill known as La Montagnette, the only deserted spot in the entire area, my doubts were at once resolved. Soon they left the road, and when they were forced to slow down at a grade crossing I opened the door and threatened to jump while the car was still moving. They pulled up and let me get out, looking somewhat sheepish. Far from teaching me a lesson, this little incident rather strengthened my presumption: with a little alertness and brisk self-assurance, I thought, one could get out of any jam. I do not regret having nursed this illusion for so long, since it supplied me with a touch of audacity which made life much easier for me.

I got much enjoyment out of the lessons I taught. They required no preparation, for my knowledge was still fresh and I spoke with easy fluency. With older pupils the question of discipline did not arise. Their minds were free of any previous instruction on the subjects I was dealing with, and I had to teach them from scratch—a proposition that stimulated me. It seemed essential to rid them of a number of preconceptions, to put them on their guard against that nonsensical shibboleth known as common sense, and to give them a real taste for discovering the truth. I derived an active pleasure from watching them struggle out of the confused state into which I had initially cast them; gradually my lessons took shape in their heads, and I could hardly have been more pleased with their progress had it been my own. Besides, I scarcely looked any older than they: at first, the mistress on duty often took me for a lycéenne. I think, too, that these girls were aware of my sympathetic attitude toward them, and probably reciprocated it. Two or three times I invited the top three members of my class home: such beginner's zeal made my colleagues sneer at me, but I far preferred talking with these big, hesitant girls than with older women whose minds were hardened by experience.

When, about the middle of the year, I embarked upon ethics things went somewhat awry. On such subjects as labor, capital, justice, and colonialism I said what I thought, and said it passionately. Most of my listeners rose in rebellion at this. Both in class and when writing their essays they belabored me with their fathers' carefully polished arguments, which I then proceeded to demolish. One of the most intelligent girls left her seat in the front row and went to the very back, where she sat, arms crossed, refusing to take notes and glaring at me with stony hatred. Meanwhile my provoking activities continued all around. I spent the periods set aside for literature in reading Proust and Gide, which at this period, in a young girls' *lycée*—and a provincial one at that—was a very daring thing to do. Worse still, through sheer thoughtlessness I put into these adolescents' hands the complete text of Lucretius' *De Rerum Natura*, and, on the subject of pain, a section of Dumas's *Traité*, which also discussed pleasure. Some parents complained, and I was sent for by the headmistress. Explanations were forthcoming and the matter went no further.

Generally speaking, the staff of the *lycée* looked somewhat askance at me. Most of them were old maids with a passion for sunshine and hiking, who reckoned on spending the remainder of their lives in Marseille. Since I was a Parisian, and eager to get back whence I had come, I was a priori an object of suspicion. My solitary walking expeditions only made things worse; besides which, I must confess, I was not exactly overpolite. Ever since I was an adolescent I have had a rooted distaste for artificial smiles or carefully contrived intonation. I would march in the staff room without saying good morning to anyone, put my things away in my pigeonhole, and sit down in a corner. I had learned a certain minimum formality: I would turn up at school wearing the approved skirt and sweater. But when spring came and I began to play tennis, I sometimes arrived without having changed, sporting a white silk pongee tennis frock, which earned me some disapproving glances. Nevertheless I was on friendly terms with two or three colleagues whose directness of manner put me at my ease. One of these became a close friend of mine.

Madame Tourmelin was thirty-five. She taught English, and looked like an Englishwoman herself: her hair was chestnut brown, her fresh and healthy complexion bore traces of acne, her lips were thin, and she wore tortoise-shell spectacles. Her plump body was austerely swathed in a brown homespun dress. Her husband was an officer, at present recovering from TB at Briançon; she went to see him during the holidays, and he paid occasional visits to Marseille. She lived in a beautiful apartment on the Prado. One afternoon she invited me to have an ice with her at the Poussin Bleu, and talked effusively to me about Katherine Mansfield. While my sister was staying with me we all three went for walks along the cliffs, and she was brimful of friendliness. She had converted her maid's room into a studio, and offered to rent it to me. It was small but fitted my ideal very well: there was a divan and bookshelves and a worktable. From the balcony I had a view out over the rooftops and the plane trees in the Prado. I was often wakened in the morning by the pleasant yet penetrating smell of a neighboring soapworks; but my walls would be flooded with sunlight, and I felt in excellent spirits.

I went out sometimes in the evening with Madame Tourmelin. We saw La Térésina and the Sakharoff sisters dance, and she introduced me to her friends. We often dined together in a little pink-walled restaurant on the Place de la Préfecture, and she would go into raptures over the young proprietress, with her pretty face and black curly hair. She loved all pretty things, whether natural or artistic; she believed in poetry and impulsiveness, though this did not prevent her being extraordinarily prudish —for instance, she found Gide repulsive, and was prone to censure vice, libertinism, or anarchic behavior. Since I had little liking for her volubly expressed enthusiasms, and did not want to discuss her prejudices, conversation tended to languish. With a sinking heart I agreed to her coming with me on a weekend trip in the neighborhood of Arles. We visited the Abbey of Montmajour, and that same evening, when we were in our big stone-flagged bedroom, I was amazed at the casual way in which she exhibited her large, well-fleshed body. All the same, I was touched by her thoughtfulness: it was to please me, she said, that she had dyed her hair, in which white threads had already begun to appear. She also bought a pink angora sweater which showed rather too much of her arms. One afternoon, when we were having tea in her drawing room, she launched into more private and confidential matters. With abrupt vehemence she confessed how much the physical act of love revolted her, how she loathed the wet sticky mess on her belly when her husband withdrew before climax. She sat lost in thought for a moment, then added that what she found romantic were the crushes she had had as a student. She believed, she added with a little smile, in going as far as kissing on the mouth, but that was all. Partly out of tact, partly because the subject did not interest me, I made no further comment on these revelations. I came to the conclusion that she was a terrible bore; and when her husband arrived in Marseille I was relieved by the thought of not seeing her for a fortnight.

But this was by no means her intention. She announced that she would come out rambling with me the following Thursday, and nothing I could say would dissuade her. She appeared complete with rucksack, studded shoes, and all the proper equipment, and tried to make me keep to the Alpinist's pace, which is very slow and steady. But we were not in the Alps, and I preferred to go at my own speed. She panted along behind me, and I derived a certain malicious satisfaction from her plight. The best things about these expeditions were the chance they gave me of solitary communion with nature and the feeling of private and individual freedom. Madame Tourmelin spoiled all my pleasure and cluttered up the landscape as well. Spurred on by hatred, I walked steadily faster and faster; from time to time I stopped for a breather in the shade, but set off once more as soon as she caught up with me. Presently we came to the edge of a ravine, where for some yards the path petered out, and we would have to clamber up a rock-face which, though steep, had plenty of easy footholds. She looked at the torrent boiling through the gorge below us, and said she would never make it. I kept on, and she decided to turn back and cut through the woods. We agreed to meet at a certain village from which a bus left for Marseille late in the afternoon. I continued my trek in a light-hearted mood, reached our rendezvous early, and sat down with a pile of newspapers in a café on the main square. The last bus left at half past five, and I had already taken my seat when (at 5:32) I spotted Madame Tourmelin, out of breath, waving frantically to the driver. She sat down beside me and didn't open her mouth till we reached Marseille; when we got out she said she was done for. She took to her bed and stayed there a week. Her doctor forbade her ever to come out on one of my expeditions again.

She bore me no grudge, however, and when her husband left we began to see each other again. He was going to come back, for good this time, late in the spring. Two days before, she asked me to dine with her at the famous Restaurant Pascal. We ate grilled perch and drank a good deal of local Cassis wine, and were very gay all the way home: we talked English to each other, and she tut-tutted at my appalling accent. I had left a school portfolio at her apartment, and went back with her to get it. As soon as we were inside she seized me in her arms. "Come on, let's drop this pretense," she gasped, and kissed me passionately. Then she burst out about how she had fallen in love with me at first sight, and it was high time to have done with all this hypocrisy, and would I—she begged me—spend the night with her? Dazed by this impetuous confession, I could only mumble, "Think of tomorrow morning—what shall we feel like then?"

"Must I kneel at your feet?" she cried, in a strangled voice.

"No, no, no!" I screamed, and fled, still obsessed with the thought of how we could possibly face one another the next day. But in the morning Madame Tourmelin managed to summon up a smile. "You didn't really believe what I told you last night, did you?" she asked. "You must have known I was joking?"

"Of course," I said. But she looked very despondent. As we walked along the Prado toward our *lycée* she murmured, "I feel as though I were walking in my own funeral procession!" Next day her husband turned up, and I left for Paris: when I got back we were hardly ever alone together, and very soon the school year drew to its close.

I have seldom felt so utterly stupefied as I did in the front hall of that apartment when Madame Tourmelin suddenly unmasked herself. Yet there had been plenty of hints which might have warned me. Under her signature in a note she sent me she had inscribed a row of *x*'s, with the comment: "I hope one day to tell you what these *x*'s mean." Obviously they stood for kisses, a symbolic representation which she must have used as a young girl. There had been the dyeing of her hair, and that pink sweater, and her coquettish behavior. But, as I have said, I was a credulous sort of person: Madame Tourmelin's virtuous declarations had convinced me of her virtuousness. Because of the moral puritanism in which my upbringing had been steeped, my judgment of people somehow never included any possible sexual motivation, and was, indeed—a point to which I shall return later—far more morally than psychologically slanted. Instead of trying to discover *what* people were doing, I simply condemned or endorsed their surface actions, and decided what they *ought* to have done.

Another friend I made, through knowing Madame Tourmelin, was a certain Marseille doctor: the relationship was unimportant in itself, but it did, somewhat indirectly, provide a stimulus to my imagination. Dr. A. looked after my sister when she had flu, and afterward I played tennis with him, once or twice a week, on the Borély Park courts. Occasionally his wife invited me to their home. He had a sister who was married to an extremely unprepossessing obstetrician, and lived in the same apartment house as he did, on the Allées. She was tubercular and permanently bed-ridden, and wore pastel-colored negligees. Her black hair was drawn back from a high white forehead, under which two small, piercing eyes looked out from a bony face. She admired Joë Bousquet and Denis Saurat, and had published a slim volume of verse. I can still remember one line: *My heart is a fragment of stale bread.* She conversed with me in a vein of lofty spirituality.

Another of Dr. A.'s sisters had been married to Dr. Bougrat, the central figure in a most resounding public scandal. A man had been found murdered in his wardrobe, and his wife had testified against him to such effect that he had been given a life sentence, though he denied his guilt throughout. Afterward he escaped from prison and reached Venezuela, where with exemplary dedication he now ran a practice devoted to the poor and destitute. Dr. A. had studied medicine with him, and described him to me as a man of outstanding intellect and character. I felt most flattered to know the family of a notorious convict. The former Madame Bougrat was a loud-mouthed, cantankerous woman with blotchy face; she had remarried, and talked openly of her son's illegitimacy. It pleased me to imagine that she had lied in court so as to ruin her first husband; I visualized Bougrat as a likable adventurer who had been made the victim of a repulsive bourgeois conspiracy, and I vaguely thought of using this story as the plot for a novel.

My parents came and spent a week with me. My father treated us to a bouillabaisse dinner at Isnard's (the best restaurant in Marseille) and I took my mother up to Sainte-Baume. My cousin Charles Sirmione passed through Marseille with his wife, and we visited an ocean liner together. The Tapir and his girl friend spent two days in town, and drove me out to see the fountain at Vaucluse. But these were negligible diversions: I preferred my solitary state. I had a vast amount of leisure time, and used it as profitably as I knew how. Sometimes I went to concerts, at one of which I heard Wanda Landowska play, or to the opera, where I sat through *Orpheus in the Underworld* or even *La Favorite.* At a small cinema I saw *L'Age d'Or,* which had lately been scandalizing Paris, and welcomed it with jubilant admiration. I found it rather hard to get books, however. There was a library, that lent texts to teachers, but it was very poorly stocked. I borrowed Jules Renard's *Journal,* and Stendhal's, together with the latter's *Correspondence* and Arbalet's critical studies of him. The most important discovery I made there was a collection of books on the history of art: these proved most instructive.

I was never bored: Marseille proved inexhaustible. I would wander along the sea-scoured, windswept jetty, watching the fishermen. They stood beside the big stone blocks of the breakwater, dabbling away in the dirty water for heaven knows what sort of catch. I would lose myself in the grim dockland wilderness, or prowl around the quarter by the Aix Gate, where sunburned hucksters chaffered endlessly over rags and old shoes.

Because of my private mythology I found the Rue Bouterie an enchanting street. I would stare at the painted women and the big garish posters stuck up above those iron bedsteads, just glimpsed through a half-open door: it was even more poetic than the mosaics at the Sphinx. Whether in the medieval quarter, with its alleys and flights of steps, or down at the fish market, or among the clamorous noises of the Old Port, there was always some new aspect of life to fill my eyes and ears.

I felt a certain self-satisfaction: here I was, well and truly pursuing the goal I had set myself at the top of that flight of steps, daily and unaided fashioning my own happiness. There were, indeed, occasional rather gloomy evenings when I came out of school, bought myself toasted cheese tidbits or some similar delicacy for supper, and trudged home as dusk fell, conscious that there was no one waiting for me in my lonely room; but even from such nostalgic moments I derived a satisfaction I had never known in all the rush and bustle of my Paris life. I had subdued my rebellious body, and was physically at peace once more: this clean break put far less strain on me than a continual seesawing between solitude and companionship. Besides, as I have said, everything hangs together; when I did get fits of impatience I bore them without resentment, because I no longer despised myself. Indeed I even felt a certain degree of complacency. That year I slightly modified the moral code which I had adopted with Sartre, and which was opposed to any kind of narcissism: I gave my life content by a process of self-observation. I was devoted to Katherine Mansfield, the *Journal* and *Letters* no less than the short stories; I had evoked her memory among the Bandol olive groves, and found her obsessive concept of the "solitary woman" romantically appealing. When I lunched on the Canebière, upstairs at the Brasserie O'Central, or had dinner at the back of Charley's Tavern— a cool, dark place, its walls covered with photographs of boxers— I told myself that I, too, personified this "solitary woman." I felt the same while I was drinking coffee under the plane trees on the Place de la Préfecture, or sitting by a window of the Café Cintra down at the Old Port. I was particularly fond of this place. On my left, where pale copper-banded casks gleamed through the shadows, I could hear soft, muffled whispering; on my right the trams went clanging past, and clamorous stallkeepers shouted their wares— clams, mussels, sea urchins—while other voices bawled departure times of boats for the Château d'If, L'Estaque, or Les Calanques. I would gaze out at the sky, at the passers-by; then I would lower my eyes to the exercise-books I was correcting or the volume I was reading. I felt wonderful.

I had too much time at my disposal not to work, so I began a new novel. I subjected myself to fiercer self-criticism than I had done during the previous year, and was dissatisfied with the phrases which I so laboriously got down on paper. I decided to get some practice in technique. I settled down in a café-brasserie near the Préfecture, where they served *tripes à la marseillaise*: the walls were bathed in a yellowish light and decorated with a festoon-and-beading motif. I made myself write out a complete description of the place, but very soon realized how absurd I was being. I returned to my novel and stuck at it assiduously till it was finished.

This book possessed somewhat firmer foundations than its predecessor. Ever since, rightly or wrongly, I had come to believe my independence, I had utilized my own life as the yardstick for all my opinions; I had examined it, in a mood of guilty remorse, and passed judgment on it. In my dealings with Sartre, as previously with Zaza, I reproached myself for failing to keep our relationship a completely honest one, and for thereby risking the loss of my own freedom. I felt that if I managed to translate this error into fictional terms I would be cleansed of it, redeemed even. For the first time I had something to say. So it was that I approached a theme that recurred in every plot line I sketched out (it still played a large part in my first published novel, *L'Invitée*), the mirage of the Other. I did not want this peculiar fascination to be confounded with a mere commonplace love affair, so I made my protagonists both women, thinking, somewhat naively, that this would preserve their relationship from all equivocal undertones of sex. I apportioned between them the two main contrasting tendencies in myself: zest for life, and the urge toward literary achievement. Though I gave an initial advantage to the former, I endowed the latter with more lasting value, and made Madame de Préliane, who represented it, a repository of every sort of charm. She was the same age as Madame Lemaire, and possessed in addition that lady's measured elegance, *savoir-vivre*, tact, reserve, capacity for silence, and pleasantly disenchanted skepticism. Though she was surrounded with numerous friends, she remained in her life a "solitary woman," dependent upon no one. I gave her Camille's artistic instinct and taste for creative work. But what sort of art? Here I hesitated. It is always hard to portray a great writer or painter, and I found it wholly impossible. On the other hand I would have found Madame de Préliane ridiculous if there had been too great a gap between her ambitions and her achievement. I chose to make her triumph in a minor medium, as the director of a puppet theater. She made and dressed the marionettes herself, besides writing the plays which they were to perform. I have already mentioned the liking I had for this type of entertainment: the puppets' nonhuman purity fitted in well with Madame de Préliane's character. I took great pains in her portrayal, but solely in order to explain the fascination she exercised. With her real nature—her interior and external relationships—I was not concerned. Once again I was making up a fairy tale.

There was more of the truth in Geneviève, to whom I gave certain characteristics of my own, greatly exaggerated. She was twenty years old, quite intelligent, and by no means a frump, but endowed with a somewhat clumsy, graceless mind, and more prone to heavy emotionalizing than to subtlety of perception. She lived, fiercely, for the moment; and lacked the psychological perspective to think or feel or will anything without reference to another person. She worshiped Madame de Préliane with passionate intensity. Her story was not so much one of disillusion as of apprenticeship; behind the idol of her own making she discovered a creature of flesh and blood. Despite her air of indifference, Madame de Préliane was in love with a man from whom fate kept her apart. She endured suffering; she was a woman, with a woman's vulnerability. But this did not make her any the less worthy of esteem and friendship, and Geneviève was not disappointed. She did, however, come to realize that no one could release her from the burden of supporting the weight of her own life and to this token of freedom she gave her consent.

Madame de Préliane felt a somewhat irritated sympathy for this young girl who bowed so humbly before her own disdainful attitude; this, however, did not supply sufficient foundation for an intrigue. I felt, moreover, that in order to evoke the rich complexity of the world it was desirable to interweave several separate stories. My own past experience suggested one that I thought tragically romantic: the death of Zaza. I set about narrating it.

I renamed Zaza Anne, and married her off to a conventional-minded bourgeois. The first chapter showed her receiving her friend Geneviève in her country home in Limousin: I tried to re-create here the atmosphere of Laubardon—the big house, Grandmama, jars of preserves. Later, in Paris, Anne met Madame de Préliane, and a great friendship developed between them. Though she loved her husband, Anne was beginning to droop in the society to which he confined her; but no sooner had she entered Madame de Préliane's circle, and been encouraged to develop her gift for music, than she at once blossomed out. Her husband forbade her to visit Madame de Préliane any more. Torn between love, duty, religious convictions and, against these, her urgent need to break out, Anne died. Geneviève and Madame de Préliane attended her funeral in Uzerche, and on the train back Geneviève, exhausted by sorrow, fell asleep, and Madame de Préliane studied her ravaged features with a kind of envy. That evening, in Paris, she spoke to her more freely than she had ever done before, and it was this conversation combined with her violent grief which brought Geneviève back to solitude and truth. The episode in the train put Geneviève at an adventage; though I refrained from flattering her character, I felt sympathetic toward her. When I was forty I hoped to be someone like Madame de Préliane: mistress of myself, slightly blasé, and incapable of bursting into tears; but it was with distinct regret that I accepted the notion of sacrificing my giddy transports and furies to this ideal detachment.

The main fault in this novel of mine was that Anne's story failed to stand up as I presented it. In order to understand Zaza's predicament you would have to begin from her childhood and the close-knit family circle to which she belonged: the devotion she felt for her mother was such that no conjugal love could ever match, let alone replace, it. A mother who has been adored and worshiped ever since childhood can keep a frightful stranglehold upon her worshiper, even though one may deplore the narrowness of her ideas and her abuse of authority; while a husband who is judged and condemned ceases to inspire any respect. Anne's husband did not, clearly, have any physical hold over her since the conflict I drew was a moral one. And how could the war between Anne's loyalty to bourgeois conventions and her admittedly casual friendship for Madame Préliane have so torn her apart that she actually died? This was quite incredible.

My mistake was in detaching this drama from the context which had given it its truth. I kept two aspects of it: on the one hand, an abstract generalization of conflict between the sclerotic bourgeoisie and the will to live; on the other, the brutal fact of Zaza's death. This was a double error. The art of fiction sanctions transposition of the truth precisely in order to avoid mere reportage, and to highlight some significant point which is not an abstraction but indissolubly rooted in actuality. (Here I am recapitulating for my own benefit ideas developed by Sartre and Blanchot: through its patent absurdity the mistake I made serves as an admirable illustration of them.)

My novel could be faulted on a number of other points. The artistic milieu in which I placed Madame de Préliane was no less artificial than she was, and the puppets with which I encumbered her trailed no end of tawdry tinsel after them. Besides, I was too inexperienced to handle more than three characters at once; when I tried to describe an animated gathering, the result was most alarming. I was interested in people's relationships with one another; I had no wish to use the convention of the *journal intime* and thus restrict myself to discussion of my own problems. Unfortunately this was something I simply could not abandon, and I quickly lapsed into the genre willy-nilly.

The most valuable thing about this apprentice work was the way I had handled the various viewpoints involved. Geneviève was observed through Anne's eyes, which lent a certain air of mystery to her otherwise simple character. Madame de Préliane and Anne were, in turn, presented as Geneviève saw them, and Geneviève was made aware that she did not understand them very well. The reader was thus invited to deduce a level of truth above and beyond her shortsightedness, and did not have this thrust crudely at him. The pity of it was that despite this carefully worked out presentation, my heroines were such inconsistent creatures.

This year I at least did not regard my work as an imposition. I would sit down beside a window in the Café Cintra, and stare through it, and breathe the atmosphere of the Old Port, and ask myself just how a forty-year-old person thought and reacted and suffered. I both envied and feared this woman in whom I was gradually becoming more and more absorbed, and felt impatient to get her various characteristics down on paper. I shall never forget that autumn afternoon when I walked round and round the Etang de Berre, working out the end of my novel. Geneviève was to be sitting in a half-dark drawing room, forehead pressed against the window, watching the first streetlamps being lit; a vast tumult was to be slowly subsiding in her heart, a prelude to true self-realization. There were some puppets lying about on the sofa. By evoking this illusory world I seemed to rise above myself and gain actual admittance, in the flesh, to the realm of pictures and statues and fictional heroes. The salt-smelling reeds and the murmur of the wind found a place in this triumphant moment. The pond was real, and so was I; but almost at once the requirements and the beauty of my newly conceived *oeuvre* transfigured both, and I found myself treading on fantasy. I had never got this feeling of elation when planning an essay or some similar piece of reportage; but it surged up whenever I gave free play to my imagination.

I went up to Paris for All Saints' Day, and returned there whenever I had a couple of days off. I spent my Christmas holiday there; besides which I wangled myself several illicit trips by pretending I had flu, or a bad liver attack. I had left my grandmother's apartment now, and used to put up in a small hotel on the Rue Gay-Lussac. Though Sartre and I wrote to each other very frequently, we still found plenty of things to discuss when we met. Above all we talked about his and my work. In October, Robertfrance, who was then in charge of Les Editions d'Europe, turned down *Le Légende de la vérité,* and Sartre shoved it away in a bottom drawer. On mature reflection he did not think much of it himself. The book contained some lively ideas, but they were frozen under a stiff, artificial, all-too-classical style. His pamphlet "on contingency," which contained the germ of *Nausea,* promised something better.

One of his letters, written in October, described his first encounter with the tree which was to occupy so important a place in that work:

> I have been to look at a tree. All you need do for such an exercise is push open the iron gate of a pleasant square off the Avenue Foch, select your victim, and find a seat. The rest is contemplation. Not far away from me, the young wife of some sea-going naval officer was holding forth to your aged grandmama on the inconveniences of her husband's profession, and your grandmama was nodding her head, as though to say, The things we have to put up with. And I sat there staring at the tree. It was extremely beautiful, and I have no hesitation about setting down here two vital pieces of information for my future biography: it was in Burgos that I first understood the meaning of a cathedral, and in Le Havre that I first understood the meaning of a tree. Unfortunately, I'm not quite sure what sort of tree it was. You'll be able to tell me. You know those toys that spin around in the wind when you wave them to and fro very fast? This tree was covered with little green stems that blew about in much the same way, and had six or seven leaves attached to their upper side just like this—rough sketch attached. I await your reply. [It was in fact a chestnut.] After about twenty minutes, having exhausted my arsenal of comparisons destined, as Mrs. Woolf would put it, to turn this tree into something other than itself, I got up and left with a good conscience . . .

Every time we met he would show me what he had written since my previous trip. In its very first draft the new pamphlet was still very much like *La Légende de la vérité,* being a lengthy, abstract dissertation on contingency. I insisted that Sartre should give Roquantin's discovery some

fictional depth, and infuse his narrative with a little of that suspense which
we enjoyed in detective novels. He agreed. I knew exactly what he was after,
and I could more nearly put myself in a reader's place than he could when
it came to judging whether he had hit the mark or not. The result was that
he invariably took my advice. I criticized him with minute and meticulous
severity, taking him to task for, among other things, overdoing his adjectives and similes. All the same I was convinced that this time he was on
the right track. He was writing the book he had been fumbling toward for
so long; and this time he would bring it off.

If my visit to Paris was a short one, I saw no one apart from Sartre and
my sister; but if I had time to spare I was always glad to look up my friends.
Nizan was teaching at Bourg, and had provoked violent attacks in the
local press by organizing a committee of unemployed persons whom he
urged to join the C.G.T.U., the Confédération Générale du Travail Universitaire; the Municipal Council, cross at having been written off by him as "a
bunch of classy illiterates," laid a complaint against him with the local
inspector of schools, who gave Nizan a straight choice between his job as
a teacher and his activities as a political agitator. But he still went on holding meetings, and actually stood in the elections: Rirette was with him
all through his campaign, wearing a pair of elbow-length red gloves—
but he collected a mere eighty votes. Pagniez, too, was a teacher, at Rheims;
he brought Madame Lemaire cases of champagne, and we killed more than
one bottle with them. Like Sartre, he spent almost all his time in Paris.
Camille was advancing confidently toward success; indeed, I fancied she
had already attained it.

During this period Dullin was putting on a series of shows designed to
promote the work of young authors, and in this program he had included
a piece by Camille called L'Ombre. This was set in medieval Toulouse, and
concerned an extremely beautiful woman—an exceptional creature in every
way—married to a pharmacist whom, of course, she did not love, and had
never loved. One day she met a marvelous grand seigneur called Gaston
Phoebus, and both of them realized, in stupefied amazement, that they were
facial doubles, who also shared identical thoughts and feelings on every
subject. The young woman fell passionately in love with this alter ego of
hers. But circumstances were all against so extraordinary an affair; and in
order to avoid worse disappointment the heroine poisoned her lover and herself died with him. Camille played the part of the pharmacist's beautiful
wife; she took me along to a rehearsal, at which Dullin confined himself to
correcting small details of production. But Camille, pacing about the stage,
seemed as wonderful to me as ever. The narcissistic theme of her play irked
me; still, in the end Dullin thought it good enough to present to the public.
Camille was playing the lead: here was her moment of triumph. On the first
night I was in Marseille and Sartre in Le Havre; but Madame Lemaire and
Pagniez went along. The décor and costumes were splendid. The two
lovers wore clothes made from the same royal-blue velvet, and on their
fair curls there sat a pair of identical berets. Camille was radiant; she
played her part with a conviction that compelled the audience's sympathy.

Despite this, when she rolled on the ground shrieking, "I wanted to close my teeth upon the lymphatic flesh of life!" the spectators burst out laughing, and the final curtain fell amid catcalls. Madame Dullin ran to and fro in the wings crying, "The Atelier is disgraced!" Antonin Artaud was the only person who clasped Camille's hands and talked of a masterpiece. Two days afterward Sartre went around to the Rue Gabrielle. The bell on the street door had been disconnected, and no one answered his knock. After three days' interval he went back to Camille's flat, and this time she admitted him. The floor of her room was littered with press cuttings. "I'll show them, the halfwits!" she snarled. For two days and nights she had crouched at Lucifer's feet, beating the furniture with her fists, and adjuring him to grant her revenge.

I had no time for the success cult—very far from it, indeed—and I admired Camille's impassioned fury as related by Sartre. All the same, her failure did not seem to me the genuine article; I found myself blaming her lack of critical sense. When I thought about her, my mind was split between astonishment and impatience.

I was so determined to see something of the countryside that I dragged Sartre off to Brittany for the Easter holidays. It was drizzling, and Mont-Saint-Michel, bare now of tourists, rose in solitary isolation between gray sky and gray sea. Somewhere in Paul Féval's *La Fée des grèves* I had read, with excitement, an account of a desperate race between the rising tide and a horse at full gallop. That beautiful word *grèves* had stuck in my mind: the pale, fluid expanse of sea flats that now lay stretched out before me seemed no less mysterious than its name. I loved Saint-Malo, with its narrow provincial streets, where the sound of the sea had once upon a time summoned corsairs to their adventures. Waves the color of milky coffee pounded against the Grand Bé, a splendid sight; but Chateaubriand's tomb struck us as so absurdly pompous in its fake simplicity that Sartre urinated on it as a mark of his contempt. Morlaix we liked, and above all Locronan, with its fine granite square and the ancient hotel, all cluttered up with bric-a-brac, where we dined on pancakes and cider. Taken all in all, however, reality for once failed to come up to my expectations. Later I did come to love Brittany, but that year transport was uncomfortable and it continued to drizzle. In order to view the moors, I forced Sartre to walk twenty-five miles around the little hill of Saint-Michel-d'Arré, which we climbed: I found the scenery somewhat limited—though twenty years later we were to drive through with a storm behind us, under an apocalyptic sky, and then we were amazed by the vast and savage splendor of the area.

It was raining at Brest, where, despite stern warnings from the proprietor of the hotel, we insisted on exploring the slum quarters. It was raining at Camaret. With enthusiasm tempered by vertigo we made the trip round the Pointe du Raz, and spent one sunny day at Douarnenez, haunted by the smell of sardines. I can still see that row of fishermen, dressed in faded pink trousers, perched along the railing above the pier, while small, gaily painted smacks got ready to put out for those deeper waters where lobsters could be caught. Finally the bad weather drove us out of Quimper and back to Paris, two days earlier than we had planned. Such a marked departure from schedule was something quite out of the ordinary: it was the rain that had defeated me.

It was during this trip that a certain rather bizarre name first came to our attention. We had just been looking at the ornamental clocks in Saint-Pol-de-Léon (nothing very interesting) and were sitting in the nearby countryside. Sartre was riffling through an issue of the *Nouvelle Revue Française,* and read out, laughing as he did so, a phrase that referred to "the three greatest novelists of the century"—Proust, Joyce, and Kafka. Kafka? So exotic a name made me smile, too. If this Kafka person had really been a great writer, we could hardly have failed to know about him . . .

We did, indeed, continue to watch out for anything new; but in literature it was a lean year. The cinema, on the other hand, had some most satisfactory items to offer us. By now we were resigned to the triumph of the talkies, reserving our indignation for the process known as "dubbing." We were all in favor of Michel Duran's vain plea that the public should boycott dubbed films. But from the practical viewpoint this made little difference to us, since the large cinemas put on the original versions. There was nothing to stop our sampling the new genre that had just appeared in America—burlesque. The last films made by Buster Keaton or Harold Lloyd, the early Eddie Cantor productions—these continued, with some charm, in the old-fashioned comic tradition. But films such as *If I Had a Million,* or *Million Dollar Legs* (which introduced us to W. C. Fields), defied reason in an even more radical fashion than the Mack Sennett comedies, and far more aggressively. The Marx Brothers brought nonsense to a fine art; no previous clowns had ever torn logic and probability to shreds in so alarming a fashion. Antonin Artaud analyzed them in the *Nouvelle Revue Française,* claiming that their weird eccentricities had all the profound significance of a delirious dream. I had enjoyed those books in which the surrealists slaughtered painting and literature; now I took much pleasure in seeing the Marx Brothers do likewise for the cinema. With furious zest they pulverized not only social conventions, organized thought, and language, but also the very *meaning* of various objects, which they occasionally supplied with a new function. When they hungrily chewed up crockery they were showing us that a dinner plate is something more than a mere utensil. Radical questioning of this sort delighted Sartre, who himself would wander through the streets of Le Havre observing (through the eyes of Antoine Roquantin) the uneasy transformations which a pair of suspenders or a tram seat were liable to undergo. Destruction and poetry, a fine double bill! Stripped of its all too human trappings, the world was rediscovering the frightful chaos which lurked beneath.

There was less virulence—and less prolixity—about the distortions and fantasies that turned up in animated cartoons, which were now becoming increasingly popular. After Mickey Mouse the screen had been invaded by that delicious character Betty Boop, whose charms struck the New York censors as so disturbing that they condemned her to death; but Fleischer offered us consolation with the exploits of Popeye the Sailor Man. Other films shown in Paris that year included Rouben Mamoulian's *Dr. Jekyll,* Fritz Lang's *M,* René Clair's *A Nous la liberté,* and Pabst's *The Threepenny Opera.*

Even then we still cared very little about what was going on in the world. The biggest news stories were the kidnaping of the Lindbergh baby, Ivar Kreuger's suicide, the arrest of Madame Hanau, and the Georges-Philippart catastrophe: we took not the slightest interest in any of them. Only the Gorguloff trial (for reasons to which I will return later) disturbed us at all. We were coming to sympathize more and more decidedly with the Communists; but though they lost 300,000 votes in the May election, Sartre had not gone to the polls, and nothing could shake us out of our apolitical attitude. Victory went to a coalition of the Left, that is, to a policy of pacifism: even the Radical-Socialists worked for disarmament and a *rapprochement* with Germany. The Right loudly denounced the growth of the Hitler movement; it seemed clear to us that they were exaggerating its importance, since in the last resort Hindenburg, not Hitler, was elected Reichpresident, and von Papen chosen as Chancellor. The future still looked peaceful.

In June, Sartre, released by the approaching *baccalauréat* exams, came and spent ten days in Marseille. Now it was my turn to give him the benefit of *my* experience; to watch him fall in love with all the spots so dear to my heart—the restaurants down at the Old Port, the cafés along the Canebière, the Château d'If, Cassis, Martigues—delighted me just as much as my own discovery of them had done. I heard that I had been appointed to a post in Rouen, we were busy making preparations for a return trip to Spain, and I was sent down to Nice to examine *baccalauréat* candidates. Everything was wonderful.

In Nice I found an enormous room with a balcony, all for ten francs a day; such windfalls meant a great deal to me, since my trips to Paris and other excursions left me absolutely penniless at the end of each month. My landlady was a heavily made-up woman in her fifties, all tricked out with satin dresses and jewelry, who spent every night at the Casino. She claimed she made an income this way, thanks to a skillful system; and I rather imagine she went in for fortunetelling as well. She would wake me at six o'clock every morning, just before she went to bed. I would hurry off to the bus station, catch a bus that took me along the coast or into the mountains, and then walk. The countryside lacked that intimacy which characterized the area round Marseille, but it was even more striking. I visited Monaco, Menton, and La Turbie in the Alpes Maritimes, while San Remo gave me a foretaste of Italy. I would come back about seven in the evening, and settle down at a café table with a sandwich and a pile of papers to correct. Afterward I would go straight to bed.

I had to stay in Nice during the orals, but I enjoyed myself nevertheless. The female candidates would turn up in the examination room wearing

large straw hats, bare-armed, their naked feet thrust into sandals. I followed
their example. The boys, too, made great display of their tanned and
muscular limbs; they looked as though they had just been taking part in an
athletic contest. No one gave any sign of treating the occasion seriously.
Obviously I was not a particularly intimidating figure: one local journalist,
seeing me sitting opposite a large and relatively mature young man, re-
versed our respective roles when he wrote up the occasion, mistaking
examiner for examinee. During the evening I would wander round the
cafés or the little dance halls on the front. With utter indifference I let
strangers sit down at my table and speak to me. I was so enchanted by the
mild night air, and the lights, and the soft lapping of water, that nothing
and no one could cause me annoyance.

The day before the prize-giving ceremony I went over to Marseille and
signed the attendance register, though I had been excused from the actual
ceremony. Madame Tourmelin begged me to stay on a day or two, but I
turned a deaf ear to her entreaties. Sartre was spending a week with his
family, and I was to join him at Narbonne; I sent my suitcase on in advance, and took to the road, carrying a basket and wearing espadrilles. I had
made longish excursions alone before, but never a real journey such as this:
it was a delightful feeling not to know each morning where you would
sleep that night. My curiosity was by no means losing its initial fervor,
very much the opposite. Now that I knew the west door of the church
in Arles I had to compare it with that at Saint-Gilles; I was aware of
architectural nuances that would previously have escaped me. The richer
the world's multiplicity, the greater the number of tasks that beckoned to
me. I stopped off by the Etang de Thau at Maguelone, and strolled around
Sète, and explored the sailors' cemetery. I saw Saint-Guilhem-le-Désert, and
Montpellier, and Minerve. I traipsed over limestone plateaus and clambered
up rock-littered gorges and defiles; I went down into the famous Grotte des
Demoiselles. I traveled by train or bus or on foot. As I trudged across
the rich dark soil of Hérault, whether along byways or on the main
road, I thought back over the past year with great satisfaction. I hadn't
read much, and my own novel was worthless; on the other hand I had
worked at my chosen profession without losing heart, and had been
enriched by a new enthusiasm. I was emerging triumphant from the
trials to which I had been subjected: separation and loneliness had not
destroyed my peace of mind. I knew that I could now rely on myself.

Madame Lemaire and Pagniez had invited us to tour southern Spain
with them by car. Meanwhile the two of us made a trip to the Balearics,
and then on into Spanish Morocco. In Tetuán I first explored the Moroccan
souks—those teeming bazaars, all light and shadow and brilliant colors,
smelling of spices and leatherwork, loud with the hammering of the copper-
smiths. I found them enchanting. We regarded the working classes as
pursuing one of the most exemplary forms of human activity, and therefore gave our unstinting approval to this picturesque scene. One thing that
disconcerted me was the way the hawkers would stand quite motionless

beside their trays for long periods. I asked Sartre what they were thinking about. "Nothing," he said. "When you have nothing to think about, you think of nothing." They had set up a void within themselves; at the very best they were daydreaming. I found this vegetablelike patience somehow a little irksome. But I enjoyed watching those quick, skilled fingers sewing slippers or knotting the threads of a carpet. At Xauen I had my first glimpse of oleanders, growing in thick profusion at the bottom of a gorge; beside the stream a group of washerwomen, in turbans and striped robes, their faces uncovered, were busy beating their laundry with wooden beetles.

We made our way back to Seville, and booked in at the Hotel Simon. When Madame Lemaire and Pagniez arrived, in the middle of the night, we fell into one another's arms in the hotel courtyard. Madame Lemaire was wearing a green silk pongee dress and a perky little hat to match: I had never seen her looking younger. Pagniez was wearing his most irresistible smile; I felt he was capable of turning everything he touched into sheer delight.

Over and above its listed attractions, which alone would have been quite enough to win our hearts, Seville next morning offered us the entertaining spectacle of a *coup d'état*. There was a great deal of hubbub outside our window, and we saw troops and cars passing by. Madame Lemaire spoke Spanish, and the chambermaid told her what was going on. The man sitting between two soldiers in that big black car was the Mayor of Seville, who had been arrested by order of General Sanjurjo. The General's men had occupied all strategic points at dawn. There was talk in the hotel office of a vast plot to overthrow the Republic. A handbill posted up near the entrance begged the public to keep calm: the troublemakers, Sanjurjo announced reassuringly, had been suitably dealt with. There were a great many soldiers out in the street, and rifles were stacked on the sidewalks; but despite this everything remained peaceful, and cafés, museums, and monuments calmly dealt with the usual flow of tourists. Next day we were told that Sanjurjo had decamped during the night: he had been relying on support from Madrid, but Madrid had not risen. A huge crowd was surging through the streets, shouting and singing and bawling. We followed it. In the Calle delle Sierpes, from under some awnings, we watched several aristocratic clubs burn. When the firemen approached—not overhurriedly—a shout of "Don't put it out!" went up. "Don't you worry," the firemen said; "we're not in any rush," and they only began to use their hoses when all the furniture had been burned. Then, suddenly, without our understanding why, panic set in, and everybody began to run, jostling and shoving. "This is too *silly*," Madame Lemaire said. She stopped, turned around, and began exhorting the crowd to keep calm. Pagniez grabbed her, and we ran with the best of them.

That afternoon we climbed up to the Giralda, and there, from the terrace, watched a triumphal procession pass below. The Mayor had been released from prison by his friends, who were now parading him through the city. Somewhere beneath us a tire burst, and the crowd, thinking that it was a shot, once more scattered frantically in all directions. All these alarms and excursions delighted us. By the next day they were all over, but a slight sense of something still lingered in the air. I went into a post office with Madame Lemaire, and people gave me very odd stares: one man spat on the ground, muttering: "None of that here!" I was stupefied. Next we went to Cook's to ask for some information we needed, and there too I heard whispering. One employee politely indicated the silk kerchief I wore, a red square dotted with little yellow anchors that somewhat resembled fleurs-de-lis. "Are you wearing those colors on purpose?" he asked. Then, seeing my astonishment, he plucked up courage and became more explicit. These were the Monarchist colors. I hurriedly discarded so seditious a piece of headgear. In the afternoon we trudged through the dusty Triana suburbs: this time there were no incidents. That evening Sartre and I visited a popular *boîte* near the Alameda, where plump Spanish women danced on the tops of barrels. Outside in the street children were selling spikenard flowers (the same that the women twined into their hair) and the scent of them filled the night air.

In my innocence I had no idea that traveling *à quatre* could be a delicate business, even though we were all friends and got on so well together. On a great many points we were in complete agreement. We unanimously detested fat Spanish businessmen and unctuous priests; in this society, which had the clear-cut simplicity of an Epinal printed fabric, our sympathies were solidly aligned with the have-nots against the haves. Yet there were great differences between Sartre and Pagniez. Pagniez was eclectic by nature, whereas Sartre was exactly the opposite. In several churches at Cadiz, for instance, there were Murillos, but he flatly refused to "waste time" looking at them. Out of politeness Madame Lemaire gave way. Pagniez took us off on a tour of the ramparts, going at a cracking pace and never once opening his mouth. Then, abruptly, he halted outside the museum, announcing that Murillo *did* interest *him*. Madame Lemaire went with him, while I stayed behind with Sartre, staring at the sea. Pagniez remained in a sour mood all day.

We spent four days in Granada, at the the Hotel Alhambra, and each of us spent the time as we liked, which avoided controversy. But the gaps between us still yawned accusingly: the only reason why Madame Lemaire and Pagniez went down into the city was to see the cathedral, while Sartre and I were at least as interested in the present as the past. We spent hours wandering through the Alhambra; but we also spent an extremely hot and dusty day out in the streets and squares where present-day Spaniards lived. Ronda struck Sartre as a dead-and-alive hole, lacking all real beauty: he found everything there tedious—the shabbily elegant houses, the courtyards and furniture and knickknacks. "They're all aristocrats' houses," he declared. "Nothing interesting about them." Pagniez grinned. "Well, they're not exactly working-class homes," he agreed.

Sartre's extremist attitudes were beginning to irk him. As long as he had regarded them as mere verbal fancies he had borne with them cheerfully enough; but when they began to influence Sartre's feelings and thoughts, and to have an effect on his actions, a gulf was opened up between the two *petits camarades*. Pagniez had no trouble in holding up Sartre's convictions to ridicule, since Sartre himself, from a practical viewpoint, gave them the lie direct: he was traveling in comfortable bourgeois style, and had no complaints on that score at all. How much truth was there in an outlook borrowed from an alien class? Pagniez was at least consistent; he adhered wholeheartedly to bourgeois liberalism, whereas Sartre had found no satisfactory vehicle for the sympathies which inclined him toward the proletariat, and his position was thus less assured. Yet even so, Pagniez disliked having his bourgeois Protestant certainties challenged by Sartre's radicalism. To Sartre he appeared just the kind of cultivated humanist that Sartre himself did not want to be, yet from which he had not, so far, managed to distinguish himself. Each saw in the other a disquieting image. Their disagreements were still amiable enough, but both instinctively felt that something more serious was involved. This, beyond any doubt, was the underlying motive behind their arguments.

What embittered them most from day to day was the fact that Pagniez only half welcomed our company. He had never before made so long a trip with Madame Lemaire, and would certainly have preferred to be on his own with her. Besides, he was the driver, and what with the heat and the bad roads, he tended to be exhausted by evening, though he still had to see to the car and find a garage. He reproached us afterward for not helping out with these chores, and I fancy that we did, in fact, use our inability to drive as a handy alibi. So he withdrew, deliberately, into a state of silent gloom, while Sartre, on the other hand, used to fly off the handle without restraint. When Pagniez's face closed up I told him he looked like an engineer. Sometimes he laughed at this monstrous insult, but not always. At Cordova, with the temperature at 108° in the shade, the two *petits camarades* came within an inch of open rupture.

Nevertheless we had some exquisite moments. We were all passionately attached to the little white Andalusian villages, the bare-trunked cork oaks and sharply tilting hills, and the way dusk came over the high sierras. Despite the magnificent view it offered (we could see the African coastline across the Straits) we all felt the peculiar desolation of Tarifa. We dined there on fish swimming in some frightful kind of oil; and a little boy of about twelve came up to our table, and said, in a way that nearly broke our hearts: "You're in luck, you can travel. I shall never get away from this place." It was true, we thought; he would grow old in this lost backwater without anything ever happening to him. Four years later something, surely, must have happened to change his life—but what?

On the return journey we let the other two go on ahead to Paris while we stopped off in Toulouse. For two days Camille showed us around; Sartre's knowledge of the place was sketchy, and I had never been there. She knew a whole cluster of anecdotes about every stick and stone, and told them extremely well. She could, on occasion, forget her myths and her own personality and take an interest in the world as it really was. This realistic vein suited her. There was an open-air restaurant on the bank of

the Garronne where she took us to dinner and entertained us vastly with
stories about the Toulouse bourgeoisie, and the *maisons de rendez-vous*
and those who frequented them, and her "enlightened lover," and her family. As we listened to her we wondered how on earth she could have wasted
her time writing *L'Ombre*. It looked as though she might be luckier with
the novel she had just begun, and which she had called *La Lierre*. This
was based on her own adolescent experiences, and both she and Zina figured
in it. She worked on it every night from midnight till six in the morning,
she told us. "Yes," said Sartre, who was regretting the all-too-slight progress
his "pamphlet" had made that year, "that's the way to work: six hours a
day, every day!" Camille no longer inspired me with feelings of jealousy
or envy, only with the urge to emulate her. I swore I would be just as
conscientious myself.

Chapter 3

A FEW DAYS BEFORE WE RETURNED TO OUR RE-
spective jobs, Sartre and I had a very significant discussion with a friend
whom I have not yet mentioned. His name was Marco; Sartre had known
him at the Cité Universitaire, where he was reading for a teachers' examination in literature. He came from Bône, and was a quite extraordinarily
handsome person: his swarthy, amber-tinted complexion, together with
that face and those burning eyes, called to mind both a Greek statue and
some of El Greco's portraits. The most remarkable thing about him was
his voice, which he trained with fanatical assiduity. He took lessons from
the very best teachers, and had no doubt that one day he would be as good
as Chaliapin. From the heights of his future fame he looked down in contempt upon his present mediocre lot, and on all those—such as Sartre,
Pagniez, and myself—who acquiesced in it. To him we were a typical
bunch of "Frenchies," and sometimes the mere sight of us was enough
to send him off in a gale of laughter. Despite this he affected to treat his
friends with the greatest consideration. He loaded us with attentions and
flattery and little kindnesses: we refused to be taken in by this gambit, but
we agreed that he did it all most gracefully. We were amused by his love
of intrigue, his indiscretions, and his scandalmongering. He assumed a
pose of unbending moral purity. He had had an affair with a girl from
Sèvres, but very soon he put the relationship on a purely platonic footing.
According to him, sexual intercourse dulled the intellect and the sensibilities: he claimed to be able to tell at first glance if one of his friends had
recently abandoned the state of chastity. He had had a flock of admirers
trailing after him at the Cité. One of them had climbed through the window of his room one night, and Marco had broken a table lamp over his
head. This incident had upset him considerably, though Sartre and Pagniez
both viewed it with some suspicion. He did not hide his indifference and
contempt where women were concerned; when he spoke enthusiastically
of his "encounters" with "gorgeous creatures," he always turned out to
be talking about some handsome boy. Still, he insisted that his only contact
with these chosen few was on the plane of lofty platonic passion, and
everyone politely pretended to believe him.

This particular afternoon we were sitting outside the Closerie des Lilas. Marco's eye swept over the customers and passers-by, and finally rested angrily upon us. "All these wretched little bourgeois creatures!" he exclaimed. "How can you possibly put up with such an existence?"

It was a fine afternoon; the autumn air smelled good, and we were, as a matter of fact, in a very contented mood.

"One day," he went on, "I shall have a *huge* car, painted white all over. I shall make a point of driving along close to the curb and splashing mud over everyone."

Sartre tried to show him how pointless fun of this sort was, at which Marco exploded into one of his bellows of laughter. "I'm sorry," he said, "but when I think of the violence of my desires, and then listen to your oh-so-reasonable arguments, I just can't help laughing!" He forced us to laugh too. Sartre said, several times, that he didn't want a Tennysonian sort of life; we expected things to happen to us, but not the kind of things that could be got for money and a lot of shouting. The contempt which we felt for the successful people of this world, and all their pomp, had by no means weakened. We wanted to be a little better off than we were, and to get posts in Paris as soon as possible. But our true ambitions were of another sort altogether, and we did not rely on fortune but ourselves to accomplish them.

It was, therefore, in a comparatively cheerful mood that we departed for the provinces once more. Sartre was quite fond of Le Havre; and I myself could not have dreamed of a better situation than Rouen—an hour's journey from Le Havre, and an hour and a half from Paris. The first thing I did on arrival was to get myself a commutation ticket. During the four years I taught there, the town center, as far as I was concerned, always remained the the station. The *lycée* was very close to it. When I went to see the headmistress she gave me a friendly welcome and passed on the address of an old lady with whom she advised me to board. I rang the bell of an elegant private house, and a dowagerlike figure escorted me to a finely furnished room, the windows of which looked out on a large and silent garden. I fled, and took a room in the Hotel La Rochefoucauld instead, from which I could hear the reassuring whistle of trains. I bought my newspapers at the station ticket office; close by on the square there was a red-painted café, La Métropole, where I had breakfast. I felt I might conceivably be living in an outlying suburb of Paris.

All the same, I was often stuck in Rouen for days on end, and Sartre and I would quite frequently spend our Thursdays there together. Accordingly I lost no time in exploring local talent. Nizan had spoken warmly to me of one of my colleagues whom he had met a couple of times. A dark-haired young Communist, he said, called Colette Audry. I contacted her. She had a pleasant face, with a pair of quick, lively eyes under close-cropped hair; in an offhandedly masculine way she affected a felt hat and a suede jacket. She too lived near the station, in a room which she had furnished and decorated most charmingly. There was rush matting on the floor and burlap on the walls, a desk strewn with papers, a divan, and books—including the works of Marx and of Rosa Luxemburg. Our first conversations were somewhat hesitant, but we soon became close friends. I introduced her to Sartre, and they got on admirably. She was not a Communist; she belonged to a Trotskyite splinter group. She knew Aimé Patri, Simone Weil, and Souvarine, and also introduced me to Michel Collinet, who taught mathematics at the boys' *lycée* and had introduced her into this group. He and I were equally self-assertive; he sang the praises of Watson and behaviorism, while I contradicted his arguments in just as aggressive a fashion. He occasionally caught a glimpse of Jacques Prévert, and had once met Gide; but he cultivated an elliptic manner, and told me nothing of this latter occasion except that Gide was a highly skilled performer with a yo-yo. This was the current craze and extraordinarily popular. People walked down the streets yo-yo in hand, and Sartre practiced from morning to night, with somber perseverance.

My other colleagues were even more rebarbative than those in Marseille, and I made no approaches to them; as for the joys of walking, I had given them up in advance. The insipid, rainy, overcivilized Normandy landscape held no inspiration for me. But the town, with its old medieval quarters and market squares, and its melancholy riverside *quais,* did possess a certain charm. I very quickly slipped into a regular routine there. Routine habits keep you company in a manner of speaking—just as some companions are often no more than acquired habits. I worked, and corrected exercises, and had lunch in the Brasserie Paul on the Rue Grand-Pont. This was a sort of long corridor, its walls covered with flyblown mirrors, its imitation-leather banquettes spilling their horsehair; down at the far end the room widened out, and men played billiards or bridge there. The waiters wore old-fashioned black dress-suits, with white aprons, and were all extremely ancient; there were few customers, because the food was not good. The silence, the casual service, and the dim yellowish light all attracted me. As a defense against the provincial wilderness it is a good thing to acquire what we called, borrowing the term from bull-ring parlance, a *querencia*: that is, a place where you feel completely sheltered from the outside world. This grubby, faded old brasserie fulfilled such a function for me. I preferred it to my room, which was a perfect commercial traveler's room, very bare and clean, which nevertheless I made good use of. I shut myself up there when I came out of school, about four or five in the afternoon, and wrote. For supper I used to cook myself a bowl of rice pudding or hot chocolate on a gas ring; then I would read for a while and go to bed. Clearly Marco would have found such an existence grotesquely inadequate; but I told myself he was wrong. One morning I was staring out of my window at the church opposite, and the faithful coming out of Mass, and the beggars attached, as it were, to the parish, when I had a sudden moment of illumination: There is, I thought, no such thing as a specially privileged situation. Every kind of situation was valid, since they all possessed a comparable degree of truth. It was a specious notion; luckily I never made the mistake of using it to justify the condition of the disinherited. When I formulated it I had only myself in mind; it struck

me as a self-evident fact that I lacked no sort of opportunity. In this respect
I suspect I was right. To be no one in particular, to thread one's way
unseen through the world, to idle—both physically and mentally—without
let or hindrance; to enjoy such a measure of leisure and solitude that one
can give one's full attention to everything; to concern oneself with the
slightest nuances either of heaven or one's own soul; to come to grips
with ennui, and defeat it—for anyone who possesses the intrepidity of youth
I cannot imagine a more profitable or desirable state.

Obviously it was Sartre's visits which did most to make my secluded
life bearable. Sometimes I would visit him at Le Havre instead, and we
both spent a good deal of time in Paris, where, thanks to Camille, we
became acquainted with Dullin, whom we found charming. He knew
how to tell a story, and it was sheer delight to listen while he recalled
his early struggles in Lyon and Paris, the glorious days of the Lapin Agile,
when he used to recite Villon, and the frightful brawls that took place
there. One morning when the charwoman swept up the broken bottles
and glasses she found a human eye rolling across the floor. But when we
questioned Dullin about his concepts of dramatic production, his face took
on a shifty expression, and he would look up at the ceiling in some embarass-
ment and avoid answering our queries. I realized why when I saw him
actually at work. He did, indeed, have certain firm principles. He condemned realism, and would not pander to his audience with cheaply
sentimental stage lighting or the other facile tricks which he criticized
in Baty's productions. But when he set about a play himself he did not
begin with any a priori theory; he preferred to adapt his *mise en scène*
to the individual art of each successive author. He did not, for instance,
treat Shakespeare as though he were Pirandello. So it was pointless to
question him *in vacuo*: the thing was to watch him working. He let us
sit in on several rehearsals of *Richard III,* and gave us the surprise of our
life. When he spoke any passage, he seemed to be re-creating it anew. His
real problem was to breathe into his actors the accent, rhythm, and intonation which he had discovered. He did not explain the text; he suggested
a mood, he wove spells around his cast. Gradually each actor, his virtues
and shortcomings skillfully utilized by Dullin, *became* the character Dullin
had created. This metamorphosis was not always accomplished painlessly.
Since Dullin was also stage manager, scene shifter, lighting director, and
a leading player himself, he often didn't know which way to turn, and on
such occasions was liable to explode. Without changing his tone he would
pick up a cue in Shakespeare with a despairing or furious string of impre-
cations. "All right," he would exclaim, "this is the *end!* Nobody's helping
me at all. We might as well forget it." He would follow this with some
very earthy profanity, and sob fit to break anyone's heart: he wouldn't go
on with the rehearsal, he wouldn't put on *Richard III* at all, he was giving
up the theater. Everyone present would freeze in attitudes of respectful
consternation, though nobody took these famous outbursts seriously, and
Dullin himself didn't really believe in them. Then, abruptly, he would
switch back into the persona of Richard. He had a singularly seductive

charm, and his face, with its mobile, flaring nostrils, its flexible mouth and mischievous eyes, could catch the expression of cruelty to perfection. Sokoloff's physique and accent produced as bizarre a Buckingham as could well have been imagined, but he brought such life and attack to the part that we were quite captivated by him. During these sessions I made the acquaintance of that lovely girl Marie-Hélène Dasté, who had inherited from her father, Jacques Copeau, both his high, smooth forehead and those large pale eyes. She was playing the part of Lady Anne, which did not suit her at all. Dullin had thought up one ingenious device, which was to hang a coarse-meshed net across the stage, dividing it in half. The lighting could then be arranged to play a scene either in front of the net, close to the audience, or else behind it, thus giving an impression of distance.

I was both intrigued and flattered to be let in on the secrets of a production; and Colette Audry gave me great pleasure by offering to take us along to see a film being shot. The film was called *Etienne,* and was adapted from a play by Jacques Deval. Colette's sister Jacqueline was working on it as a script girl. The studio was packed with people, and far too hot. Jacqueline struck me as a very chic and attractive girl; yet there were other women there even better turned out than she was, among them a slightly passé actress whose gray velvet costume I found quite stunning. Groups of supers stood about in corners, looking bored. Jacques Baumer was shooting the beginning of a scene in which he was sent for by his employer and had to say, "You wanted me, sir?"—at the same time giving a characteristic little click of his tongue. The cameraman was dissatisfied with both the lighting and the composition; Baumer repeated his little performance thirteen times, and never changed either his intonation or gesture in the slightest degree. It was a rather alarming episode, and stuck in our memories for a long time.

But we were always a little depressed when, at eight o'clock, we arrived at the Gare Saint-Lazare and boarded the train that would take us back to Rouen and Le Havre. We traveled second class, since there were no third-class compartments on the expresses. The upholstery was blue, and the compartments invariably overheated. They were adorned with photographs advertising the beauty spots of Normandy and Brittany: the Abbey of Jumièges, Caudebec Church, the Criqueboeuf marshes—all of them places I only managed to visit twenty years later. We would bury ourselves in the latest Van Dine, or some sanguinary thriller by Whitfield or Dashiell Hammett, whom the critics were acclaiming as the pioneer of "a new type of fiction." When I emerged from the station the town was already asleep. I would eat a *croissant* at the Métropole just before it shut up for the night, and go straight back to my room.

Whether in Paris, Rouen, or Le Havre, however, our main topic of conversation was the various people we knew. They occupied our minds so much that my decision not to set down details of their lives (there are obvious reasons for this reticence on my part) is bound to drain some color from the picture I am sketching of our own. But it remains true that the busy activities of these outside lives, being always somewhat unpredictable, filled our day-to-day existence and insured it against any monotony. There were problems cropping up the whole time. Gégé had married one of her former art teachers, and was now on very bad terms with her own socially superior family, who believed in piety and conformity. She and her husband had almost daily rows; she felt very bitter toward him, and yet he continued to attract her: how, we wondered, did she react to this ambivalent emotional situation? She was still on terms of great intimacy with my sister, but each of them was maturing along individual lines, so that their friendship too had its complications. Jacqueline Lemaire was going to get engaged: why to this particular suitor rather than any of the others? What were the real facts behind the row that had taken place last night between The Tapir and Madame de Listomière? When we made new acquaintances we set about turning them inside-out in every sense of the phrase, and worked like beavers to produce our own definitive portrait of them. All our various colleagues were subjected to this process. We were particularly interested in Colette Audry, and questioned her about her attitude to politics and love, her relationship with her sister, her feelings about herself. Sartre also discussed one of his pupils with me, a very intelligent boy whose studied cynicism he found amusing. Originally he had been destined for the Ecole Coloniale, but Sartre had steered him toward the study of philosophy. His name was Lionel de Roulet; his parents were divorced, and he lived in Le Havre with his mother, who was addicted to astrology and alchemy. (She both explained her son's character and predicted his future in terms of his affinity with this or that metalloid.) The boy had given Sartre a full and frank account of his difficult childhood: Sartre referred to him as "my disciple" and felt great sympathy for him.

I placed just as much emphasis upon the study of individuals as Sartre did, and shared his enthusiasm for peeling them down to the core, building them up again, and reshaping the impressions we had of them. On the other hand, I was not very good at reading their characters accurately, and my little episode with Madame Tourmelin will serve to demonstrate just how blind I was. I was always readier to judge people than to understand them. This moralistic attitude had its roots deep in the past. The innate superiority on which my family prided itself had encouraged my childish arrogance, and later, solitude had bred in me a certain aggressive pride. Circumstances still favored my leanings toward severity. Like every group of young people, this band of *petits camarades* made sharp and self-assured distinctions between what was good and bad. No sooner had I been admitted to their number than I, too, condemned all who failed to observe the laws they laid down. I showed myself more sectarian than Sartre and Pagniez; they at least tried to explain people, however fiercely they might chop them down. They exchanged amicable smiles over my lack of psychological penetration. Why did I not try to remedy this? The truth is that another childhood legacy I had was a taste for silence and mystery. Surrealism had left its mark on me because I had found an element of the supernatural in it: when confronted by other people I let myself be charmed, beguiled, and intrigued by the glittering surface appearance of things without asking myself what lay beneath. I could quite well have rid myself of such aesthetic notions had I wished; if I persevered in them, it was for very deep-seated reasons. The existence of Otherness remained a danger for me, and one which I could not bring myself to face openly. At the age of eighteen I had fought hard against sorcery that aimed to turn me into a monster, and I was still on the defensive. I had settled the anomaly of Sartre by telling myself that we formed a single entity, placed together at the world's center. Around us other people circled, pleasant, odious, or ridiculous; they had no eyes with which to observe me: I alone could see. As a result I had the most brazen indifference to public opinion. My lack of common courtesy often embarrassed Sartre, who in those days was a surprisingly polite person. We had a row one day because I wanted to sit down for a drink in Frascati's, the big luxury hotel in Le Havre. It looked straight out over the sea front, and must have had a marvelous view. But there was an enormous hole in one of my stockings, and Sartre refused emphatically. On another occasion we were in Paris, without a penny to our names, and no one available to borrow from. I suggested trying the manager of the Hôtel de Blois, where we stayed every week. Sartre protested that he found the fellow utterly nauseating. We spent over an hour arguing the point, pacing up and down the Boulevard Montparnasse. "If he disgusts you so," I said, "why should you care what goes on inside his head?" Sartre replied that the opinions one formed about the man militated against him.

It is impossible to make a really thoroughgoing job of living by a fallacy. The slightest conversation implied some sort of reciprocal contact between my questioner and myself. Since both Madame Lemaire and Pagniez stood high in Sartre's estimation as well as exercising considerable personal authority, I was very vulnerable to their comments, whether critical or ironic. I was also bothered by the spectacle of Camille's self-assurance. Colette Audry sometimes spoke of Simone Weil to me; and though I felt no great sympathy for her, this unknown woman's existence was forced upon my consciousness. She was a university teacher at Puy; it was said that she lived in a truck-drivers' hostel, and on the first of every month would put her entire salary packet out on the table and let anyone help themselves. In order to act as leader of a strike delegation and present their claims, she had herself worked alongside the railwaymen. Conduct such as this got her into trouble both with the local mayor and with her pupils' parents, and she had very nearly been run out of the university. Her intelligence, her asceticism, her total commitment, and her sheer courage— all these filled me with admiration; though I knew that, had she met me, she would have been very far from reciprocating my attitude. I could not absorb her into my universe, and this seemed to constitute a vague threat to me. Still, we lived so far apart from one another that I did not worry my head too much about this. In my day-to-day life I scarcely ever departed from the habit of cautious isolation I habitually practiced, and I refused to envisage other people as potential individuals, with consciences, like myself. I would not put myself in their shoes; and that was one reason for my addiction to irony. On more than one occasion such gratuitous stupidity involved me in difficulties and ill will and errors of judgment.

This did not stop me from picking all and sundry to pieces with Sartre till the cows came home. Indeed, they submitted to our inquiries with some docility, and my sense of independence flourished accordingly. I was a poor observer, but in any discussion when we tried to understand people's motives I managed to keep my end up. We certainly needed to work together, since we possessed no systematic method of analysis. We distrusted classical French psychology; we did not believe in behaviorism; and we had only a very limited faith in psychoanalysis. On this topic we had more than one discussion with Colette Audry. The Communists condemned psychoanalysis; Politzer, writing in *Commune,* defined it as a form of energetics, and therefore an ideal concept which could not be reconciled with Marxism. The Trotskyites and other splinter groups, however, embraced it eagerly. Colette and her friends interpreted thir feelings, behavior, and individual actions according to Freudian or Adlerian patterns.

Adler's book *The Neurotic Constitution* satisfied us more than the works of Freud because he attached somewhat less importance to sexual behavior. Nor would we agree that the idea of the "inferiority complex" could be used indiscriminately. We criticized the psychoanalysts for pulling man to pieces rather than understanding him. The quasi-mechanical application of their key concepts allowed them to make fallacious rationalizations concerning experiences which should have been analyzed individually. Such criticisms in fact had only partial validity. But we failed to distinguish between serious researchers—Freud himself, and certain of his followers and opponents—and those amateurs who applied their theories in a spirit of mere crude sectarianism. The latter we were quite justified in finding irksome. What scandalized us most was the fact that some of Colette's friends consulted psychoanalysts on how to plan their private lives. One of them was teetering between two different women, and went to ask Dr. D. (well known for having treated a large number of surrealists) which of them he should choose. "You must allow your feelings to float free by themselves, like dead leaves," the doctor replied. When Colette told us this story we were furious. We refused to accept the proposition that life was an illness, and that when a choice of actions presented itself you had to have the law laid down by a doctor instead of deciding the issue for yourself.

But in this field, as in so many others, though we might see what errors to guard against, we had no clear idea what truths to set up in their place. The concept of "apprehension," borrowed from Jaspers, we found far too vague a guide. In order to synthesize our knowledge of people without losing sight of their individual qualities we needed a systematic plan; and this we did not possess. During these years our labors were directed toward isolating and creating such a pattern, and I believe this did more for us than any amount of reading or external advice. Sartre worked out the notion of dishonesty [*mauvaise foi*] which, according to him, embraced all those phenomena which other people attributed to the unconscious mind. We set ourselves to expose this dishonesty in all its manifestations: semantic quibbling, false recollections, fugues, compensation fantasies, sublimations, and the rest. We rejoiced every time we unearthed a new loophole, another type of deception. One of my younger colleagues was a mine of dogmatic opinions and violent moods in the teachers' lounge; but when I tried to talk to her privately, I found myself plunging into mental quicksands. This contrast disconcerted me, till one day light dawned: "I've got it," I told Sartre. "Ginette Lumière is unreal, a sort of *mirage*." Thenceforth we applied this term to anyone who feigned convictions or feelings which they did not in fact possess: we had discovered, under another name, the idea of "playing a part." Sartre took a particular interest in that side of the void which corrodes human behavior, and even the seeming plenitude of what we call sensations. Once when he had a violent attack of renal colic he caused the doctor some embarrassment by asserting that he was not really suffering. Though the pain was such that it kept him pinned to his bed, he regarded it as a "porous," almost intangible entity.

Another question which preoccupied us was the relationship between our rational and physical selves. We were always trying to distinguish, both in our own lives and those of others, between the built-in physical characteristic and the freely willed act. I criticized Sartre for regarding his body as a mere bundle of striated muscles, and for having cut it out of his emotional world. If you gave way to tears or nerves or seasickness, he said, you were simply being weak. I, on the other hand, claimed that stomach and tear ducts, indeed the head itself, were all subject to irresistible forces on occasion.

In the course of this exploratory process we acquired our own individual perspectives and critical tools, and came to resent the narrowness of the area in which we were confined. We had very few friends, and hardly any relations. It was partially to offset this lack that we developed so passionate an interest in the news of the day. I often bought *Détective,* which about this time was launching an all-out attack on the police and their orthodox supporters. We were attracted by any sort of extreme, just as we were by psychoses or neuroses: here, exaggerated, distilled, and set out in striking relief were the conduct and emotions of so-called normal people. There was another reason for their moving us, too: any sort of upheaval gratified our anarchic instincts. Abnormality we found positively attractive. One of our inconsistencies was our refusal to accept the idea of the subconscious. Yet Gide, the surrealists, and, despite our resistance, Freud himself had all convinced us that in every person there lurks what André Breton called *un infracassable noyau de nuit,* an indestructible kernel of darkness, something that cannot break up social conventions or the common currency of human speech, but does, now and then, burst out in a peculiarly scandalous fashion. Every time one of these explosions took place, we believed, some truth was always revealed, and those which brought about an access of freedom we found especially impressive. We set particular store by any upheaval which exposed the defects and hypocrisy of the bourgeoisie, knocking down the façade behind which their homes and hearts took shelter. Trials no less than crimes drew our attention: the grimmer sort raised the question of individual and collective responsibility. The bulk of the verdicts reached, too, fed our indignation, for in them society shamelessly declared its class-ridden, reactionary attitudes.

Obviously we were only concerned with those affairs in which we found some social or psychological implication. The Falcou trial in Rouen produced a demonstration outside the Palais de Justice involving a crowd of some fifteen thousand: Falcou was accused of having burned his mistress alive, but enjoyed great popularity among his fellow townsfolk. After his acquittal they bore him off in triumph. I remained quite unmoved by this exhibition. On the other hand, Sartre and I spent a long time discussing another case which hardly made the headlines at all. A young chemical engineer and his wife, who had been married for three years and were very happy together, one night brought home an unknown couple that they had met in a restaurant. What orgies then took place no one knew, but next morning the engineer and his wife committed suicide. From this recollection I can deduce how unadventurously our minds still worked. We were astonished that one casual aberration could outweigh three years of love and happiness, and we were right in our surprise: we have since learned from the psychoanalysts that when a traumatic state produces really serious trouble there is invariably a history of previous circumstances predisposing the subject in the direction which he finally takes. But we should not have allowed this incident to keep us in a state of perplexity; we should have rejected the newspaper clichés, and taken the double suicide as our starting point from which to reconstruct the real relationship between the two people involved. The sex party which had preceded it was, obviously, anything but a casual accident. It never occurred to us to argue against the appearances.

All the same, if the social system happened to be involved, we were quick enough to smell out any double-dealing. The main outline of the Papin sisters' tragedy was at once intelligible to us. In Rouen as in Le Mans, and, indeed, perhaps even among the mothers of my pupils, there was to be found, beyond any doubt, the sort of woman who would deduct the price of a broken plate from her maid's wages, and wear white gloves to hunt down the least grain of forgotten dust on the furniture: in our eyes such creatures deserved the death penalty a hundred times over. How well-behaved Christine and Léa looked in the old photograph that some papers printed, with their ringlets and white collars! How had they been transformed into the haggard Furies that pictures taken after their arrest displayed for public obloquy? Respectable folk execrated them as madwomen, monsters, murderers: but it was their orphaned childhood and subsequent enslavement, the whole ghastly system that had made them what they were. The horrors of this mill-like machine could only be adequately denounced by some equally horrid, though exemplary, act of retribution. The two sisters became both the instruments and the martyrs of justice in its grimmest guise.

The papers told us that they were sexually involved with each other, and we mused on the caresses, and the hatred, that their lonely attic concealed. Yet when we read accounts of the preliminary hearing we were distinctly shaken: the elder sister was, beyond any doubt, suffering from acute paranoia, and the younger had become infected with the same disorder. We were therefore wrong in regarding their excesses as being due to the hand of rough justice, suddenly unleashed; they had, rather, struck more or less blindly, in a state of terror and confusion. We could not bring ourselves to believe this, and obstinately persisted in our admiration for them—though this did not stop our getting very cross when government psychiatrists pronounced them both of sound mind. In September, 1933, we could study, in *Détective,* the faces of those fat farmers and merchants, so sure of their own mental and moral health, whose task it was to decide the fate of these "mad sheep." They condemned the elder to death; but two days after the verdict she had to be put in a straitjacket, and was interned in an asylum for the rest of her life. We conceded the evidence. Yet though Christine's malady tarnished her crime somewhat, it also greatly increased the unworthiness of the jury. A similar verdict had sent Gorguloff to the guillotine when he was, as all the world knew, stark raving mad. He would certainly have been spared if his victim had been an ordinary person. We derived some pleasure from the discovery that our society was no more enlightened than the so-called primitive ones. If it had made any causal connection between crime and criminal, it would have concluded that both Gorguloff and the Papin sisters were not responsible for their actions. But in fact it preferred to establish a bond of "participation" between the murder and its victim. A slaughtered President of the Republic or two dismembered middle-class housewives demanded, a priori and inevitably, bloody expiation. The murderer was not so much tried as made a scapegoat. Sartre used to collect, diligently, all the examples of prerational mentality that abound in this civilized world of ours. If he repudiated the kind of rationalism practiced by engineers, this was in the name of a more justly conceived intelligibility. But by superimposing upon logic and mathematics the surviving features of a frankly magic-aligned mentality, our civilization was doing nothing but show its contempt for truth.

Most other crimes faded into insignificance when set beside the Le Mans murders. Like everybody else, we noted the exotic villainy of Hyacinthe Danse, "the sage of Boulay," who went in for some curious and orgiastic practices in his eremitical retreat before turning the place into a Chamber of Horrors by killing his mistress and her mother and leaving both bodies there—after which he went off and murdered one of his former teachers. The killing of Oscar Dufrène by an unknown sailor was a case of really classic repulsiveness. Our interests were aroused when a girl of eighteen, Violette Nozière, was convicted of poisoning her father. The trial of the Papin sisters was on at the time, and one legal correspondent managed to tie the two cases up together: he called for ruthless severity toward "all cases of youthful delinquency." From the very start of the preliminary hearing, the supposed "parricide," too, struck us as much more of a victim than a guilty person. Public opinion was somewhat shaken by her mother's attitude: she publicly told her daughter to kill herself, and brought a civil action against her concurrently with the criminal hearing. Despite this, every witness heard at the first examination, and the whole of the press as well, did everything they could to suppress the truth. Against the daughter's own accusations (corroborated by numerous witnesses) they merely set the sacred character of Fatherhood.

Reading the papers and holding regular discussions with our friends as we did, we reacted instantly when news reached us of any efforts toward a better knowledge of human nature, or any defense of human liberties. Dr. Magnus Hirschfeld had recently founded his Institute of Sexology in Berlin, and was demanding that respect for individual rights should go so far as to permit certain forms of perversion. He had successfully petitioned for the removal of "sexual anomalies" from the German criminal code. In September, shortly before the beginning of the academic year, an International Congress for Sexual Reform met at Brno and discussed such problems as birth control, voluntary sterilization, and general eugenics. We approved of this effort to free man from social conformity and emancipate him from Nature's dominion by giving him mastery over his own body. Procreation in particular was not something to be endured, but deliberately chosen. In another sphere altogether, we were strongly behind Freinet, the schoolmaster at Saint-Paul-de-Vence who had invented a wholly new method of education. Instead of instilling a code of blind obedience into his pupils, he appealed to their friendship and initiative. He took seven-year-olds and made them write compositions that were just as lively and original as paintings in this age-group can be when they are allowed to follow their natural inspiration: these he published in a little magazine called *La Gerbe*. The clergy aroused a section of the local population against him, and they threw stones at his schoolhouse windows; but he stuck it out. His success bore out our most passionately held conviction: that freedom is an inexhaustible source of discovery, and every time we give it room to develop, mankind is enriched as a result.

It did not seem to us that this emancipation would be helped by progress in technology. American economists were predicting that very soon technicians would be running the world, and the term "technocracy" had just been coined. The first telephotos were being transmitted, and television was shortly to be invented. Professor Piccard and his rivals were making numerous journeys into the stratosphere. Airmen such as Mermoz, Codos and Rossi, and Amelia Ehrhart were breaking record after record: there was a touch of high adventure in their exploits which appealed to us. But all those mechanical discoveries which so astounded the journalists left us completely cold. According to us there was only one way of preventing general madness, and that was by the overthrow of the ruling class: I was even less tolerant of its lies, stupidity, prejudices, and false virtues than I had been when I was twenty. One evening I went to a concert in Rouen, and when I saw the pampered audience all around me, preparing to digest its ration of aesthetic beauty, a feeling of misery swept over me. They were so powerful, there were so many of them: would there ever be an end of their rule? How much longer would they be allowed to believe that they embodied the very highest human values, and to go on molding their children in their own likeness? Some of my pupils sympathized with my views, and when school was over it wrung my heart to think of them going back to the same sort of miserable closed atmosphere in which I had been half choked myself at their age.

Happily the liquidation of capitalism seemed to be close at hand. The crisis which had broken in 1929 was getting steadily worse, and its more spectacular aspects struck even the dullest imagination. In Germany, England, and America literally millions of men were unemployed (the over-all figure for the countries covered by the Bureau International de Travail was about forty million), and starving bands had marched on Washington. Yet cargoes of coffee and wheat were being dumped in the sea, and in the Deep South the cotton crop was buried, while Dutchmen slaughtered their cows and fed them to the swine, and the Danes killed off a hundred thousand suckling pigs. The columns of the daily press were full of bankruptcies, scandals, and the suicides of businessmen and international financiers. The world was moving into a state of flux. Sartre often wondered whether we should not join those who were working for this revolution. I recall one conversation in particular, which took place on the *terrasse* of a big café in Rouen, the Café Victor, that looked out on the *quais*. Even in spheres where we were ideologically well-informed, to come up against some concrete fact still always had an effect on us, and would give rise to copious subsequent discussion. That was what happened on this particular afternoon. A docker, decently dressed in his blue smock, sat down at a table next to ours: the manager ejected him. The incident did not teach us anything, but it illustrated the idea of class segregation with all the naïveté of an Epinal print, and served as the point of departure for a far-reaching discussion. We got to asking ourselves whether it was enough for us to sympathize with the struggle being fought by the working classes: ought we not to join in it? More than once during these years Sartre was vaguely tempted to join the Communist Party. His ideas, aims, and temperament all militated against such a step; but though he had just as great a liking for independence as I did, his sense of responsibility was far greater. On this particular occasion we decided—our decisions were always provisional—that if you belonged to the proletariat you had to be a Communist, but that though the proletarian struggle was of concern to us, it was even so not *our* struggle; all that could be asked of us was that we should always speak out on its behalf in any argument. We had our own tasks to fulfill, and they were not compatible with joining the Party.

What we never considered was the possibility of joining a Communist splinter group. We had the very highest opinion of Trotsky, and the idea of "permanent revolution" suited our anarchist tendencies far better than that of constructing a socialist regime inside one single country. But both in the Trotskyite party and the various other dissident groups we encountered the same ideological dogmatism as we did in the Communist Party

proper; the only difference was that we had no faith in *their* effectiveness.
When Colette Audry told us that her group (which comprised five members in all) was debating the possibility of a new revolution inside Russia,
we did not conceal our skepticism. We took no more than a moderate
interest in the Stavisky Affair, over which the anti-Stalinists waxed so
fiercely partisan. All the same, we did not regard ourselves as wholly
uninvolved. We aimed to make an active personal contribution through
our discussions, our teaching, and our books: such a contribution would
be critical rather than constructive, but at this particular period in France
we felt that criticism had a most important role to fulfill.

Accordingly we continued to devote ourselves exclusively to our writing
and research. Sartre was coming to realize that in order to give the ideas
dividing his mind some coherent organization, help was essential. The first
translations of Kierkegaard appeared about this time: we had no particular
incentive to read them, and left them untouched. On the other hand,
Sartre was strongly attracted by what he had heard about German phenomenology. Raymond Aron was spending a year at the French Institute
in Berlin and studying Husserl simultaneously with preparing a historical
thesis. When he came to Paris he spoke of Husserl to Sartre. We spent
an evening together at the Bec de Gaz in the Rue Montparnasse. We
ordered the specialty of the house, apricot cocktails; Aron said, pointing
to his glass: "You see, my dear fellow, if you are a phenomenologist, you
can talk about this cocktail and make philosophy out of it!" Sartre turned
pale with emotion at this. Here was just the thing he had been longing to
achieve for years—to describe objects just as he saw and touched them,
and extract philosophy from the process. Aron convinced him that phenomenology exactly fitted in with his special preoccupations: by-passing
the antithesis of idealism and realism, affirming simultaneously both the
supremacy of reason and the reality of the visible world as it appears to
our senses. On the Boulevard Saint-Michel Sartre purchased Lévinas's book
on Husserl, and was so eager to inform himself on the subject that he
leafed through the volume as he walked along, without even having cut
the pages. His heart missed a beat when he found references to contingency:
had someone cut the ground from under his feet, then? As he read on
he reassured himself that this was not so. Contingency seemed not to play
any very important part in Husserl's system—of which, in any case, Lévinas
gave only a formal and decidedly vague outline. Sartre decided to make a
serious study of him, and took the necessary steps to succeed Aron at the
French Institute in Berlin for the coming year—this on Aron's own
instigation.

The attention which we gave to public affairs was controlled, pretty
strictly, by the tropisms I have already mentioned. Nevertheless, we were
capable of a certain eclecticism, and indeed read everything that came out,
which that year included Breton's *L'Immaculée Conception,* Michaux's *Un
Certain Plume,* Silone's *Fontamara,* Moravia's *Time of Indifference,* Von
Salomon's *La Ville,* and Marcel Aymé's *The Green Mare.* But the book
of the year for us was Céline's *Journey to the End of the Night*: we knew

whole passages of it by heart, and his type of anarchism seemed very close to ours. (*Death on the Installment Plan* opened our eyes, however: there is a certain angry contempt for the little man in it which shows a proto-Fascist attitude.) He attacked war, colonialism, the cult of mediocrity, platitudes, and society generally in a style and tone which we found enchanting. Céline had forged a new instrument: a way of writing that was as vivid as the spoken word. What a relief after the marmoreal phrases of Gide and Alain and Valéry! Sartre was strongly influenced by it; he finally abandoned the starchy verbiage he had still been using in *La Légende de la vérité.* As might be expected, we had a marked preference for private journals, collections of letters, and biographies, which enabled us to trespass on intimate territory. We read Billy's *Diderot,* and Geoffrey Scott's *Portrait of Zélide,* which introduced us to Madame de Charrière, and *Eminent Victorians,* in which Lytton Strachey cut several pompous bigwigs down to their proper size. The *N.R.F.* was running *La Condition humaine (Man's Fate)* as a serial: our reaction to it was mixed, and we admired its intentions rather more than its achievement. Taken by and large we found the technique of French novelists very crude in comparison with the major American writers. John Dos Passos' *The 42nd Parallel* had just come out in a French translation, and it taught us a good deal. Each person is conditioned by his class; no one is wholly self-determined. These are the two poles of truth between which we oscillate, and Dos Passos offered us, on the aesthetic plane, a compromise solution that struck us as quite admirable. He had worked out a bifocal perspective for the presentation of his main characters, which meant that they could be, at one and the same time, drawn as detailed individuals *and* as purely social phenomena. He did not give them all the same amount of freedom, though. In moments of need, or exhaustion, or labor, or revolt, some of the exploited had their flash of fulfillment or their instant of truth: they *lived.* But among the upper classes a radical estrangement of sympathy prevailed: a kind of collective death had frozen their every gesture and word, down to the most intimate murmurings. Five years later Sartre was to analyze the subtleties of this artistic achievement in the *N.R.F.;* but at the time we were immediately bowled over by the deliberately shocking effects that Dos Passos had contrived. Cruelly, he observed mankind both in terms of the comedy labeled "freedom" which they play out inside themselves, and also as the mere helpless projections of their situation. Sartre and I frequently attempted to observe some third person, or more often ourselves, in this stereoscopic fashion. Though we might walk through life in cheerful self-assurance, we were not guilty of self-complacency; Dos Passos had furnished us with a new critical weapon, and we took full advantage of it. For instance, we sketched out our conversation in the Café Victor as Dos Passos might have handled it: "The manager smiled in a satisfied way, and they both felt furious. Sartre drew at his pipe, and said that perhaps it was not enough merely to sympathize with the revolution. The Beaver pointed out that he had his own work to do. They ordered two large beers, and said how hard it was to sort out what you owed other people from what you owed yourself. Finally they declared that if they had been docker workers they would undoubtedly have joined the Communist Party, but in their present position all they could be expected to do was always to side with the proletariat." Two *petits bourgeois* invoking their unwritten work as an excuse for avoiding political commitment: that was the truth, and indeed we had no intention of forgetting it.

Fifty Grand and *The Sun Also Rises* introduced us to Hemingway; besides which I read a certain number of his stories in English. His individualism and his concept of human nature were both very close to ours: there was no split in any of his heroes between head, heart, or body. Whether loafing around the Mont Sainte-Geneviève or through the streets of Pamplona, talking, eating, drinking, or sleeping with women, they never held any part of themselves back. We detested the idea of eroticism—which Malraux used so plentifully in *Man's Fate*—because it implied a specialized approach that at once overinflated sex and somehow cheapened it. Hemingway's lovers were in love all the time, body and soul: actions, emotions, and words were all equally permeated with sexuality, and when they gave themselves to desire, to pleasure, it bound them together in their totality. There was another thing that pleased us. If a man brings his entire self to every situation, there can be no such thing as a "base occasion." We attached much value to the small pleasures of daily life, and Hemingway lent romantic charm to such things as a walk, a meal, or a conversation: he told us, meticulously, just what sort of wine and food his characters appreciated, just how many glasses they drank; he reported all their small talk. At the touch of his pen insignificant details suddenly took on meaning: behind the fine stories of love and death that he told us we recognized our own familiar world. For us as we then were, this measure of agreement sufficed. We were so hopelessly sidetracked by our own private notion of freedom that we failed to comprehend the fact of individualism as an attitude which relates to the world in its totality.

Hemingway's technique, with its skillful appearance of simplicity, could be accommodated to our philosophical requirements. The old kind of realism, which described things "just as they were," rested on false assumptions. Proust and Joyce had, each in his own way, opted for a form of subjectivism, which struck us as equally ill-founded. In Hemingway's work the world was still opaque and externalized, but always examined through the eyes of one particular individual: the author only gave us what could be grasped by the mind of the character he was interpreting. He managed to endow physical objects with extraordinary reality, just because he never separated them from the action in which his heroes were involved: in particular, it was by harping on the enduring quality of *things* that he suggested the passage of time. A great number of the rules which we observed in our own novels were inspired by Hemingway.

American novels, all of them, had one further advantage: they showed us something of America. We knew little about this country, and most of our information reached us through distorting lenses. We could not understand America, though jazz and Hollywood films had brought it into our lives. Like most young people at the time, we were passionately devoted to Negro spirituals, and working songs, and the blues. Our indiscriminate affections embraced "Old Man River," "St. James Infirmary," "Some of These Days," "The Man I Love," "Miss Hannah," "St. Louis Blues," "Japansy," or "Blue Skies": men's lamentations, their withered joys and shattered hopes, had found a characteristic voice—a voice which challenged the polite assumptions of conventional art, which broke harshly from the very heart of darkness and rebellion. Because they were born of huge, collective emotions, common to each and every one of us, these songs touched us individually, at that point of deep intimacy common to us all. They dwelt in our hearts, nourishing us just as certain words and cadences of our own tongue did; and through their medium America came to exist within us.

Its external existence was insured by the cinema, projected on a silver screen from the far side of the Atlantic. At first it had been a world of cowboys, riding over the vast and empty plains; but now the advent of talkies had practically driven them out of business. The scene now shifted to New York and Chicago or Los Angeles, with their gangsters and cops: during this year *Scarface, I Am a Fugitive from a Chain Gang,* and *The Big House* were all shown in Paris. We read numerous news items dealing with Al Capone and Dillinger, not to mention the sanguinary thrillers which their exploits inspired. We did not actively sympathize with these racketeers, but we did derive considerable pleasure from watching them slaughter one another and defy the forces of law and order. The press had recently made damning revelations of corruption in the American police force, exposing their collusion with bootleggers, and such excesses as grilling or the third degree. We became fed up with detective films when a wave of moral earnestness forced the scriptwriter to take the cop as his hero instead of the robber. But there were other attractions which Hollywood had to offer us, the chief of these being attractive faces. We very rarely missed films with Greta Garbo, Marlene Dietrich, Joan Crawford, Sylvia Sydney, or Kay Francis in them, even if the films themselves were mediocre or downright bad. The same year we also saw that luscious creature Mae West, in *Lady Lou* and *I'm No Angel.*

Thus America for us consisted primarily of a montage of whirling images, superimposed on a soundtrack of hoarse voices and broken rhythms: Negroes in *Hallelujah* dancing or entranced, skyscrapers towering up to heaven, prison mutinies, blast furnaces, strikes, long silk-sheathed legs, locomotives, airplanes, wild horses, and rodeos. When we managed to detach ourselves from this miscellaneous clutter, we thought of America as the country where capitalist oppression flourished in its most odious form. We loathed its racial policy, its lynchings, its twin evils of exploitation and unemployment. But there was something about life over there, something vast and unencumbered, which fascinated us at a deeper level, beyond all question of right or wrong.

We looked at the U.S.S.R. with a far less excited eye. Some Russian novels revealed aspects of the Revolution which we had not previously known about: the relationship between the towns and the countryside, for instance, between commissars whose duty it was to carry out requisitions or collectivizations and peasants who stubbornly maintained their rights as freeholders. Even in books which displayed a somewhat crude and naive technique—such as Panfërov's *Beggar's Community*, or Leonid Leonov's *The Badgers*, which did not, however, shrink from claiming affinity with Dostoevsky in its preface—we found the scope and novelty and complexity of this new adventure most exciting. The whole thing was admirably portrayed in Mikhail Sholokhov's *Seeds of Tomorrow*. We were also familiar with his other novel, *And Quiet Flows the Don*: this lengthy Cossack epic had rather put us off, and we had failed to finish it. But *Seeds of Tomorrow* struck us as a masterpiece. Like his great predecessors, Sholokhov knew how to bring a gigantic cast of characters into individual life; he got right inside their skins and motives, even when drawing a counterrevolutionary kulak. He managed to make his "positive hero," the Commissar, both human and sympathetic; but he also got us interested in the old obscurantists who were fighting to keep their corn. He let us touch the individual injustices and disappointments which are the very stuff of history. We regretted the absence of this complex approach in the Russian cinema, which had become resolutely didactic: we took care to keep away from films designed to glorify the kolkhozes. In *Road of Life*, which described the rehabilitation of a group of abandoned children, the youthful actors—in particular the one who played Mustapha, the gang leader—got into their parts so well that they saved this "pedagogic poem" from total insipidity. (There was nothing in the least insipid about the book on which the film was based, but the scriptwriter wholly omitted its tartly bitter element.) But such a film was an exception.

Thus, paradoxically, we were attracted by America, though we condemned its regime, while the U.S.S.R., the scene of a social experiment which we wholeheartedly admired, nevertheless left us quite cold. We still were not actively *for* anything. This struck us as quite reasonable, since in our opinion, as I have said, both the world and humanity were still to be created anew. I have already pointed out that there was no disenchantment in our negative attitude, far from it; our strictures on the present were made in the name of a future that must inevitably come to pass, and which our own criticisms were actively helping toward fruition. Most intellectuals took the same line as we did. Far from cutting us off from our generation, our anarchism emanated from it and set us in line with it. In our opposition to the elite we had a good number of allies, and our special crazes were shared by the bulk of our contemporaries: a passion for jazz and the cinema was a commonplace. Most of the films that we enjoyed were also generally popular, as for instance *The Private Life of Henry VIII*, which introduced us to Charles Laughton. Brecht's *Kuhle Wampe* had only a moderate success, and we were no more enthusiastic about it ourselves. It offered us that adorable actress Herta Thill as an unemployed female worker, and was so virulently *engagé* that Von Papen had it banned. We had expected great things of it, but found it ponderously conceived and executed with little artistry. In one respect we diverged from the general public: we were allergic to French films. Because of the amazing Inkichinoff, we sat through *La Tête d'un homme* without any feelings of antagonism, and were delighted by the Prévert brothers' film *L'Affaire est dans le sac*. But it was precisely that crude, flat realism, devoid of any exotic qualities, and characteristic of contemporary French films at this time, which the Prévert brothers contrived to avoid. We went to the music hall and, like everyone else, enjoyed Damia, Marie Dubas, and the petite Mireille singing *"Couchés dans le foin."* Two new stars had climbed the Parisian firmament, Gilles and Julien, a pair of antimilitary anarchists who summed up the simple hopes and clear-cut feelings of revolt which satisfied progressivist hearts in those days. Left-wing critics praised them to the skies. The first time we saw them was in a Montmartre cabaret: they were wearing evening dress and seemed very stiff and ill at ease. Dressed in black sweaters on the stage at Bobino's, they made numbers like *"Le Jeu de massacre"* and "Dollar" and a score more all the rage. We applauded them as vigorously as anyone. Generally speaking the dancer's art bored us; but in June the Ballet Jooss arrived from Vienna and put on that avant-garde, pacifist ballet, *The Green Table.* Every night they were acclaimed by packed houses, and among the spectators we had our place.

We spent our Easter vacation in London. Here was a city that was bigger than Paris, and quite new to us. We sallied forth into the streets, and walked for hours on end. Piccadilly, the City, Hampstead, Putney, Greenwich: we were determined to see everything. We would clamber up to the top deck of a big red bus, drive out to the suburbs, and make our way back on foot. We would have lunch in a Lyons or a Soho restaurant or one of the old chophouses off the Strand, and set out once more. Sometimes it rained, and we didn't know where to take shelter: the absence of cafés disconcerted us. One afternoon the only refuge we could find was in the Underground.

We amused ourselves by observing the conventions of English life. When women came down to breakfast in our hotel dining room they wore astonishing garments somewhere between a tea gown and evening dress. Men really *did* wear bowler hats and carry umbrellas in the afternoon. Soapbox orators *did* hold forth every evening at Hyde Park Corner. The shabby taxis and peeling posters and teashops and ugly window-dressing all disorientated us. We spent hours in the National Gallery, and stayed behind in the Tate to stare at Van Gogh's yellow chair and sunflowers. In the evenings we went to the cinema. We saw that beautiful creature Kay Francis in *Cynara*: "I've been faithful to thee, Cynara, in my fashion"— this quotation, screened after the credits, was to become a kind of private password between us for years afterward. I was enthralled by Maskelyne's little theater where conjurors and magicians performed the most amazing tricks, with a technical brilliance I never saw the like of anywhere else.

I had to admit that despite our private entente certain slight discrepancies of outlook existed between Sartre and myself. I went to the heart of London looking for traces of Shakespeare and Dickens; I explored the byways of Old Chiswick with a sense of rapturous discovery; I dragged Sartre around all the London parks, to Kew Gardens and even as far as Hampton Court. He lingered in lower-class districts, trying to guess at the lives and thoughts of the thousands of unemployed persons who dwelt in these joyless streets. He told me that on our next visit to England he would visit Manchester, Birmingham, all the big industrial cities. He too had his obsessions. He spent a whole day dragging me around Whitechapel in the pouring rain to find a little cinema where, according to one poster, they were showing *Outward Bound,* with Kay Francis and William Powell. The film turned out to be so good that I felt the time had been well spent. But I was the one most set on concocting schemes and bringing them about. Most of the time Sartre accommodated himself to my ideas with so good a grace that I was convinced that his enthusiasm for them matched my own. Very conveniently I persuaded myself that a foreordained harmony existed between us on every single point. "We are," I declared, "as one." This absolute certainty meant that I never went against my instinctive desires; and when, on two occasions, our desires clashed, I was completely flabbergasted.

In Canterbury we had both been struck by the beauty of the Cathedral, and spent the whole day in unclouded happiness. When we reached Oxford, Sartre was by no means averse to the streets and parks, but he found the snobbishness of the English undergraduate decidedly irksome, and refused to set foot inside any of the colleges. I went through two or three of them by myself, and reproached him for what seemed to me a mere whim. But at least he had not disturbed my own plans. I was far more put out on the afternoon of our projected visit to the British Museum, when he calmly told me he had not the slightest wish to go—though, he added, there was nothing to stop me making the trip alone. This was what I did. But it was in a very listless mood that I trailed around the bas-reliefs and statues and mummies: it had seemed so important that I should see these things, and now I began to wonder if it mattered after all. I refused to admit that my personal desires could contain any element of caprice: they were founded upon values which I regarded as absolute, and reflected imperatives that I held to be categorical. Since I was less wholly reliant upon literature than Sartre, I had a greater need to introduce necessity into my life. But this meant that I must stick to my decisions as though they were blindingly self-evident truths; otherwise my curiosity, my avidity for experience became mere personal characteristics, perhaps even personal faults. I would no longer be subject to an authoritative mandate.

I was still less able to conceive the possibility of any intellectual dissension between us. I believed in truth, and truth is one and indivisible. We thrashed out our ideas and impressions with indefatigable zeal, and were never satisfied till we had reached some agreement. Generally Sartre would propose a "theory," which I would criticize and modify; sometimes I rejected it altogether, and prevailed upon him to revise it. I accepted, with some amusement, his comparison between English cooking and Locke's empiricism, both of which, he explained to me, were founded upon the analytical principle of juxtaposition. Walking the Thames Embankment or standing before the pictures in the National Gallery, I agreed with practically everything he told me. But one evening, in a little restaurant near Euston Station, we really quarreled. We were sitting up on the first floor, eating an insipid, synthetic sort of meal, and watching the red glow on the horizon which meant a fire down near the docks. Sartre, with his usual passion for generalization, was trying to define London's place in his over-all pattern. I found the hypothesis he advanced inadequate, tendentious, and without any real value: even the principle upon which he was working irritated me. We resumed, somewhat more heatedly, the discussion that had divided us two years earlier on the heights of Saint-Cloud, and had cropped up more than once since. I maintained that reality extends beyond anything that can be said about it; that instead of reducing it to symbols capable of verbal expression, we should face it as it is—full of ambiguities, baffling, and impenetrable. Sartre replied that anyone who wished, as we did, to arrange the world in a personal pattern must do something more than observe and react; he must grasp the meaning of phenomena and pin them down in words. What made nonsense of our argument was the fact that Sartre was far from understanding London after twelve days' visit, and his résumé of it omitted countless sides of the total picture: to this extent I was justified in rejecting his theory. I reacted quite differently after reading passages in his manuscript that described Le Havre: here I did get the impression that he was revealing the true essence of the place to me. But at all events this split between us was to continue for a long time: my own prime allegiance was to life, to the here-and-now reality, while for Sartre literature came first. Still, since I wanted to write and he enjoyed living, we seldom came into open conflict.

Sartre used to read the papers, in a sketchy fashion, but assiduously. I was less conscientious about it. All the same, I went through *L'Oeuvre* and *Le Journal* daily, and read *Le Canard enchaîné* and *Marianne,* the latter recently launched by Gallimard, every week. Events taking place on the other side of the world—the Sino-Japanese War, or Gandhi's campaign in India—affected us very little. No one at this time realized what interdependence there was between every point on the globe. Our attention was concentrated on what was going on next door to us, in Germany; like everyone else on the French Left, we watched these developments quite calmly.

Hindenburg's election as Reichpresident had seemingly justified German Communist predictions that Nazism was losing its impetus. But soon such a view became quite untenable: the movement regained what the newspapers described as its "tremendous rate of expansion." In January, 1933, we saw Hitler become Chancellor, and on February 27 the Reichstag Fire opened the way for liquidating the Communist Party. Fresh elections in March served to confirm Hitler's triumph, and from May 2 onward the swastika flew over the German Embassy in Paris. A large number of German scholars and writers, particularly those of Jewish extraction, went into voluntary exile: among them was Einstein. The Institute of Sexology was closed. French opinion was profoundly disturbed by the policy which Hitler's regime adopted toward German intellectuals. In May a vast bonfire was lit on the Operaplatz in Berlin, and over twenty thousand books destroyed. A wave of anti-Semitic persecution broke loose: though there was not, as yet, any question of exterminating the Jews, the various measures passed insured their social degradation, while systematic boycotting prevented them from making a livelihood.

Today it astounds me to think how we could have stood by and watched all this so calmly. We were indignant enough, it is true: Nazism inspired even greater disgust among members of the French Left than did Mussolini's Fascist regime. But we refused to face the threat which Hitler's behavior constituted to the world: at the time no one body was more anxious to deceive itself over this than the Communist Party. With well-organized optimism the German Communists belittled the importance of those dissensions which were weakening the German proletariat, and which their own policy merely served to aggravate. Thaelmann declared that the fourteen million working-class men of Germany would never allow Fascism to be established among them permanently, and would never allow Hitler to lead them into a war. French Communists and fellow travelers took up this line with some enthusiasm. In March, 1933, Barbusse wrote, in *Le Monde,* that Hitler could not possibly restore the German economy; it was bound to collapse, and then the German proletariat would win back its heritage. In such circumstances, obviously, there was no threat to peace: the only danger was the panic that the Right was attempting to spread in France, with the aim of dragging us into war. In 1932 Romain Rolland had drawn up a manifesto, published in *Europe* and *Le Monde,* and signed by Gide among others, which called upon intellectuals to promise "resistance against war." In July, 1933, the Association of Revolutionary Writers was created, and launched the magazine *Commune,* with Barbusse, Gide, Romain Rolland, and Vallant-Couturier on the editorial board, and Aragon and Nizan as joint editors. Their first aim was to fight Fascism in France. At an international level this French anti-Fascist movement soon linked up with the big pacifist movement centered in Amsterdam. Certainly the left-wing intelligentsia did not kowtow to Hitler. They all, including Malraux, denounced the scandalous Leipzig Trials, and a mass meeting, at which Moro-Giafferi spoke, was held at the Salle Wagram in September to support the defense of Dimitroff. This did not prevent Barbusse from stepping up his antiwar appeals, and all the Left supported him. The editorial writers of *Marianne,* a Radical-Socialist weekly edited by Emmanuel Berl, preached a steady pacifist line and were never tired of announcing Hitler's imminent discomfiture. In his *Propos* Alain declared repeatedly that to believe that war might come about meant tacit consent to the idea: we were to avoid so much as dreaming of such a possibility. Everyone was convinced that we could not envisage war as a potential prospect without playing straight into the hands of the Right. But there was another reason for their pursuing this paradoxical line, to which some diehards adhered as late as September, 1938, and even after the defeat. The memory of the 1914–18 war stuck in their throats. It is dangerous and often criminal to sacrifice new and present realities for the sake of past lessons learned; but in their case the past weighed so heavily upon them that it is easy to see how they fell into the trap. In 1914 the whole of the intellectual elite, Socialists, writers, and all—no wonder Juarès was assassinated—toed a wholly chauvinistic line. Those who witnessed the debacle swore never to revive the "German barbarian" myth, and refused to pronounce this new war, if it were to break out, a justified one. From 1920 onward a large number of writers, thinkers, and academics had worked for a Franco-German *rapprochement* and continued to assert the validity of their efforts in the face of nationalist folly. To put it in a nutshell, everyone on the Left, from Radicals to Communists, were simultaneously shout-ing "Down with Fascism!" and "Disarmament!"

Our elders, then, forbade us to envisage the very possibility of a war. Sartre had too lively and horror-prone an imagination to take overmuch notice of this embargo. Certain visions, some of which left their mark on *Nausea,* haunted his mind: rioting towns, with all their steel shutters drawn, blood at the crossroads and splashed over bowls of mayonnaise in pork butchers' shops. I myself still enthusiastically pursued my old schizophrenic dream. The world existed indeed, like some parcel with endless wrappings, to unwind which would always be an adventure—but not as a field of forces quite liable to thwart my desires. This was, I fancy, due to my arbitrary way of acquiring information. Economic and social problems inter-ested me, but only from the theoretical angle: my sole concern with actual events was whether they took place a mere year or months ago, or had had time to become petrified institutions. I read Marx, and Rosa Luxem-burg, and Trotsky's *The History of the Russian Revolution,* and *Piatiletka,* Farbman's work on the Five-Year Plan, besides various studies on the economy of the NEP, the life of the American workingman, and the crisis in England. But political articles bored me to tears: I sank under their weight. To sort out what seemed to me a hopelessly muddled hodgepodge of facts would have meant predicting future events, and this I was unwilling to do. I believed in the distant future: this was determined by a dialectical process which would, in the end, justify all my expectations and moments of revolt. What I could not accept was that history was being made every day, in all its digressive complexity, and that some unforeseen event might come up over the horizon tomorrow without my knowledge or consent. Such an admission would have spelled danger for me. This concern with my own peace of mind forced me to make time stand still, until, weeks or months later, I would wake up in another period that was somehow just as static, peaceful, and undisturbed as its predecessor.

Sartre sometimes upbraided me for my insouciance, just as I became irritated when he spent too long buried in a paper. To justify my attitude I invoked the theory of the "solitary man." Sartre objected that the "solitary man" does not lack any interest in the course of events: though his thought may not depend on external supporting opinion, this does not imply that he opts for ignorance. Sartre's counterattack shook me, but I persevered in my attitude. I wanted people to despise the futile contingencies of daily life, as I thought Rimbaud and Lautréamont and Van Gogh had done. The position I had adopted suited me somewhat ill; there was nothing in me of the visionary, or the solitary, or indeed of the lyric poet. I was really indulging in escapism, putting myself into blinkers so as to safeguard my peace of mind. For a long while I stuck obstinately to this "rejection of humanity," which was also the inspiration for my aesthetic views. I liked those landscapes in which there was no apparent sign of man's presence, or else the sort of camouflage—local color, picturesque background—which concealed such presence from me. In Rouen my favorite spot was the Rue Eau-de-Robec: its shapeless, rickety houses, lapped by filthy water, looked very much as though they might be destined for some wholly alien species of inhabitant. I was attracted by those people, such as madmen, prostitutes, or tramps, who had in one way or another denied their own humanity.

Sartre's position in relation to his contemporaries was by no means clear either. He jeered at all humanistic shibboleths: it was impossible, he thought, to cherish an entity called "Man," or indeed to hate it either. Yet both of us, wherever we happened to be, whether it was on the great Paris boulevards or in a fairground, or at the ringside in Madrid or Valencia, derived great pleasure from being in a jostling crowd. Why was this? Why, in London, did we feel such affection for the grimy shop fronts in the Strand, for the docks and boats and warehouses and factory chimneys? Such objects were not works of art; they lacked all baroque or poetic charm. These unlovely houses and streets neither rose above the condition of mankind nor sought to escape it: they were its concrete embodiment. If we were so passionately attached to this incarnation of *la condition humaine,* the reason, surely, was that we were far from indifferent to mankind itself? We discussed this at length but came to no conclusion. In fact, like Antoine Roquantin in *Nausea,* Sartre detested certain specific social groups, but never inveighed against the human race as a whole: his severity was directed solely at those who professed to fawn upon it. Several years back a lady who owned a dozen or so cats reproachfully asked Jean Genet whether it was true that he disliked animals. Genet said: "I don't like people who like animals." That was precisely Sartre's attitude to humanity.

When Nizan politely asked me one day what I was doing with myself, I replied that I had begun a novel. In a slightly bantering tone he asked whether it was a story I had made up, and this vexed me greatly. I spent two years working on this new book, and it did have very lofty pretensions: single-handed I was going to settle society's hash. There was a German refugee who had been introduced to me by Colette Audry, and who came two or three times a week to teach me his language; he eyed the sheets piling up on my desk with some alarm. "Normally," he told me, "people begin with short stories. When you have learned something about technique it's time enough to tackle a novel." I smiled at this. There was no question of my scribbling little anecdotes; I wanted my book to be a totality.

It was the arbitrary nature of my project that explained its ambitious aims. I had been washed clean of all my fears and remorse in Marseille; I had become disinterested in myself. Other people I viewed externally, and felt unconcerned about their existence; I did not even feel the urge to discuss them. By and large everything was either too dull or too insignificant for me to be tempted to put it into words. Words broke down when confronted with the plenitude of my happiness; and the trifling incidents of my daily life merited nothing but oblivion. As in my adolescence, I was proposing to put the whole world into a book, though I had nothing concrete to say about it.

All the same, my hatred of bourgeois society was genuine enough, and it was this which deflected me from fantasy. I had during the past year been making a close study of Stendhal, and it was he I now took as my model. I decided to borrow his bold romantic technique in order to tell a story which, in broad outline, was my own—an individualistic revolt against this stagnating society of ours. I would draw a general picture of the postwar scene, denounce the Establishment and its misdeeds, and set against it two heroes, a brother and sister, who would be united in a close bond of sympathy and embody the moral I wanted to present. This couple were not based upon any real or imagined personal experience; I made use of them to describe the years of apprenticeship from a double viewpoint, both masculine and feminine.

So I plunged into a long narrative, the protagonists of which were up-to-date versions of Julien Sorel and Lamiel. I called them Pierre and Madeleine Labrousse. They spent a miserable childhood in an apartment modeled upon that of my maternal grandparents; their adolescent years were passed somewhere near Uzerche. They had a somewhat mixed relationship, veering between friendship, envy, hatred, and contempt, with the children of two big local families, the Beaumonts and Estignacs—which were themselves interlinked by adultery. I endowed Marguerite de Beaumont with the formal charms that had so appealed to me in Marguerite de Théricourt. I drew heavily upon my own childhood memories for this first chapter. Sartre approved of it, and Pagniez, to whom I voluntarily submitted it, for the first time paid me a compliment on my work: he said that the narrative possessed the same charm as certain English novels.

But almost at once the tone began to change: I found myself sliding into cynicism and satire. I had had the Bougrat affair on my mind for some time, and now it provided me with inspiration. Pierre, condemned by his father to a humdrum existence, was to seduce and marry Marguerite de Beaumont—simply to get the money with which to pursue his studies and cover his living expenses. He was to be coldly set on exploiting the great family to which he now belonged, and which I intended to portray as viciously as I knew how. Yet I thought then, and still do, that anyone who claims to be using nasty people for his own ends is really compromising with their standards. Pierre was to perceive this, and break off the relationship. He was then going to live by his wits, and during this period he would enter on a touching platonic love affair with a woman who, I planned, should contain elements both of Madame Lemaire and Madame de Rénal. A chain of grim misunderstandings was to lead him to the guillotine, and his *amie* to poison herself. Then there was his sister, a ruthless and sophisticated adventuress, who opposed the marriage, and so on. I did not get very far with this first draft; it struck me as much too melodramatic. Anyway, I was an optimist by nature, so settled for a somewhat more cheerful denouement.

In the final version I kept the childhood chapter only. Afterward Pierre had a violent quarrel with his father, who wanted Madeleine to marry an elderly scion of the Estignac family. Pierre then went off to Paris, where at first he was supported by a rich and aged aunt. Abandoning her, he got a job singing in a cabaret, based on Dullin's description of the Lapin Agile. Like Dullin, he wanted to be an actor-manager, and give the theater a new shot of life. He was no longer an ordinary careerist, but a man who nursed the highest of all ambitions, to be a creative artist. I could, therefore, saddle him with all the perplexed problems that I had to face at the time myself.

I set his break with his family in 1920. In order to reproduce the correct period atmosphere, I went to the Rouen Public Library and read through back numbers of *L'Illustration* and *L'Humanité*. A comparison between the two left me gasping. The two accounts of the period were contemporary, and set in the same country; yet they had not one thing in common. I wasted no more time over them, but simply garnered one or two useful facts from their pages. The chapter in which Pierre reached Paris opened with a fine bravura flourish. He strolled through the galleries of the Louvre, and was greatly moved by El Greco's "St. Louis"; then, quite accidentally, he found himself watching the ceremony in the Place de l'Hôtel de Ville during which Poincaré decorated Paris with the Croix de guerre. Depressed by this masquerade, he began to ask himself a whole series of questions, such as: How can the portrait of an abominable person still be great art? What *is* artistic truth, and at what point does it become a betrayal of one's principles? Shortly afterward he made friends with some young Communists, and though he agreed with most of their ideas, he rejected their determinist view of the world. Against their humanism he upheld his devotion to the nonhuman poetry of things, of objects; and above all, he regarded individualistic values as more important than collective interests. Such discussions were not entirely gratuitous, since I had correlated them with a sentimental intrigue that every day forced him to admit the importance both of his own feelings and of a beloved face.

The face in question was Zaza's, whom once again I rechristened Anne, and whose appearance I was still trying to evoke in memory. She had married the most gifted of the Estignac boys; and during the holidays which she spent near Uzerche she had become a close friend of Madeleine's, and had known Pierre, who was later to meet her again in Paris.

Ordinary love stories struck me as very banal; and in any case Anne's piety and loyalty, not to mention Pierre's respect for her, debarred them from any vulgar liaison. I conceived them as having a relationship that was platonic, but of extraordinary depth. Morally and intellectually Anne was being quickened into life. But her husband forbade her to continue with this relationship. As in the previous novel, she died, torn between duty and happiness. Thus satire spilled over into tragedy, and bourgeois spiritual values were made to look not merely ridiculous, but lethal.

Meanwhile Madeleine had joined her brother in Paris, and was leading a cheerfully amoral existence. Since she could make men dance to her tune, she set about fleecing them with Pierre's assistance. Though she handled these frolics in an easy, self-assured way, she nevertheless had her problems: she was suffering from a complaint of which I was, I felt, only half cured myself—infatuation with another person. "How I wish I was Marguerite!" she used to say as a child, when she passed the tiny chatelaine with her impeccable ringlets. She really loved her brother; but she also fell violently for one of Pierre's comrades, a young Communist called Laborde, whose drive and self-assurance dazzled her. Henceforward her world revolved around this man, though he was himself a completely self-sufficient person: she became his satellite merely. But then he declared that he, too, was in love with her, that he needed her; and at this her illusions were shattered. Laborde was no longer the infallible be-all and end-all of existence, but a mere man, made from the same stuff as herself. So she turned away from him, and went proudly back to the life where her true roots lay.

This novel had one good quality: despite its numerous episodes and themes, I had constructed it along solid lines. None of the characters were dropped by the wayside, while external events and inner experience blended in a perfectly natural way. I had progressed in the art of telling a story, setting a scene, and constructing dialogue. But my failure was still basic, despite all this. Once again, by transposing the elements of Zaza's story, I had given the truth away. I had repeated the error of substituting a husband for a mother; and even though the husband's jealousy was somewhat more comprehensible than in my preceding novel, I had still not given any plausible explanation of Anne's despair. From the moment that she resigned herself to staying with her husband, the "salvation" which Pierre offered her was salvation no longer, and their break merely deprived her of a friendship, which I had not managed to endow with sufficiently burning intensity to justify Anne's subsequent death.

Madeleine's development was even less probable. Granted her character, it was unlikely that she would break with a man, for whom her feelings remained, in any case, exactly what they had been, simply because he turned out to be in love with her.

Finally, I had no firsthand knowledge of the background in which I placed Pierre, so that my minor characters lacked all depth and verisimilitude. After a promising start the novel dragged on as though it would never be finished. Seeing that the attempt was a failure, I scamped the final chapters. The most convincing passages, despite everything, were those describing Madeleine's difficulties. I had regained my peace of mind, it is true; but I was still scarred by the harsh transition I had brought about from pride to humility. And I still had not achieved any final resolution of my most serious problem: how was I to reconcile my longing for independence with the feelings that drove me so impetuously toward another person?

That year Mussolini had organized a so-called Fascist Exhibition, and in order to attract foreign tourists, the Italian railways agreed to a 70 per cent fare reduction. We took advantage of this without scruple. In contrast to Spain, which contained much that was ugly, not a single bare wall in Italy but possessed its own special charm: I was instantly captivated. Sartre, on the other hand, was not. Standing in a Pisan cloister he told me, sourly, that he found this country too *dry,* and didn't like it at all. The truth was that he hated passing black-shirted rank-and-file Fascists in the street.

We visited the most beautiful cities of Central Italy, and spent a fortnight in Florence. We had decided to keep Rome for another trip, and only stopped there four days. We put up in the Piazza della Rotonda, at a hotel which, according to the *Guide Bleu,* offered best value for money in the whole of Rome: the Albergo del Sole, where Cervantès had once stayed. We were bowled over by the squares and fountains and bewitching statues. It pleased me that the Forum should now be a vast garden, with oleanders growing along the Via Sacra, and scarlet roses blooming round the circular Temple of the Vestals; and to think that I was actually strolling up the Palatine! But Mussolini's presence lay over the city like a pall. Inscriptions covered the walls, and Black Shirts had the right of way along the sidewalks. After nightfall not a soul was to be seen on the streets. This city where the centuries, frozen in stone, stood proudly triumphant against the Void, was slipping back at last into the chasm of nonexistence. One evening we decided to stay out till dawn rose, lonely witnesses to this solitude. About midnight we were talking in the empty Piazza Navona, sitting beside the fountain. Not a single peep of light gleamed from behind the drawn shutters. Two Black Shirts came up and asked us what we were doing out so late. Our tourist status made them treat us with some indulgence, but they firmly insisted on our going home to bed. We took no notice of this order. It was a remarkable experience, walking along on those small, neat Roman flagstones without hearing anything except our own footsteps—as though we had been miraculously transported to one of those Mayan cities that the jungle guards so well from prying eyes. About three o'clock, in the Colosseum, a light was flashed on us. What were we doing? This time it seemed that—even for tourists—our behavior had passed the bounds of all decency. Sighing in recollection of those long nights in Madrid, we finally returned to our hotel. In order to obtain our cheap rail tickets, we had to visit the Fascist Exhibition, where we glanced over the glass cases where the pistols and cudgels of the "Fascist martyrs" were on display.

At Orvieto we saw Signorelli's famous fresco, and lingered several hours in red-bricked Bologna. Then we came to Venice. As we left the station I stared in amazement at the travelers who were giving various gondoliers the names of their hotels. They were going to settle in, unpack their luggage, and have a wash: I found myself hoping that such level-headed behavior would never be laid at *my* door. We dumped our bags in the checkroom office and simply walked, for hours. We saw Venice as you can only see it once: the first time. For the first time, we gazed at Tintoretto's "Crucifixion"; and it was in Venice, too, near the Rialto, that we had our first sight of S.S. men in their brown shirts. They were a wholly different species from those little black-clad Fascists, being very big men, with empty eyes, who marched along in a stiff, military fashion. Three hundred thousand Brown Shirts on parade at Nuremberg: it was frightening to think of it. Sartre had a sudden sinking feeling as he realized that in a month's time he would be passing them daily in the streets of Berlin.

By the time we reached Milan we were penniless. We wandered sadly along the Galleria: shops and restaurants, simply because we were debarred from them, seemed to attain unheard-of heights of luxury. We had to give up the three days we originally intended to spend on the Italian Lakes (I cried with rage at this: the least sacrifice drove me half out of my mind) and return to Paris instead.

After Sartre had left for Berlin, I lost all interest in public affairs. But clouds gathered in the sky, and burst, and the lightning struck. Hitler broke with the League of Nations, and the triumphant plebiscite that followed his much-publicized speech of November 11 was a proof that Germany welcomed these strong-arm policies with some enthusiasm. No one believed him when he declared that Germany wanted peace "with honor and equality of rights." Despite this, the French Left continued to assert that it lay with France to prevent an outbreak of war. "The price of peace," Alain wrote in 1934, "is to stand firm against these waves of terrorism." The verdict at the Leipzig Trials—all the accused were acquitted except Van der Lubbe, who received the death sentence and was executed in January—convinced the Left that the Nazis were far from sure of their power. What the Left feared above all else was the rise of a French Fascist movement. Right-wing organizations were using the international situation and the economic depression as an excuse for preaching an antidemocratic and bellicose brand of nationalism. The Stavisky scandal, which broke toward the end of December, was an unremarkable enough business at first; but it quickly blew up into a major issue, with the Right exploiting it vociferously against the left-wing coalition, the Third Republic, Parliament, and democracy in general. All through January there were street riots—on the Boulevard Raspail or the Boulevard Saint-Germain or outside the Chamber of Deputies itself—stirred up by organizations such as Action Française or the Jeunesses Patriotes groups, or Solidarité Française, or the Union Nationale des Combattants, or the Croix de Feu. Chiappe deliberately gave them a free hand. After the demonstration in the Place de l'Opéra, on January 26, when a crowd of about forty thousand assembled, the Cabinet resigned. Daladier formed a new government, and superseded Chiappe. It was on February 6, the day when the new ministers presented themselves to the Chamber of Deputies, that the riot broke out. I only followed the sequence of events from a distance, being convinced that it was no concern of mine. After the storm a lull would come; there seemed no point in my worrying about these agonized events, since there was absolutely nothing I could do about them. All over Europe Fascism was gaining strength and the time growing ripe for war; but I remained wrapped in eternal peace.

I must have been extremely stubborn to maintain this attitude of indifference: I had no lack of time at my disposal, so much so that I was sometimes uncertain how to employ it. I took refuge in provincial boredom. Not much could be expected of my new colleagues. Mademoiselle Lucas, the English mistress, looked like a vast mushroom; her black velvet dress hung down to her ankles, and under it a pink angora chemisette was visible. "I just *can't* bring myself to stop wearing my little-girl dresses!" she used to say. She loathed her pupils, who returned the sentiment with interest. Mademoiselle Aubin had just arrived from Sèvres, and pretended to be more artless than she was. She would pirouette round the staff room, sighing: "Peace and quiet—I must have peace and quiet." Simone Labourdin, certainly, was not quite so silly as this. She was the woman with whom Marco had had an affair, and she knew Madame Lemaire and Pagniez; she was dark-complexioned, had beautiful blue-gray eyes, a fresh, clean-cut profile, and the most appalling teeth. We did not especially take to one another, but she had been Colette Audry's friend in Sèvres, and we three often used to lunch in a crowded restaurant near the station. Our opinions brought us together. Colette Audry was the only one of us who was actively involved with politics, so that people regarded her as a Red; but Simone and I took more or less the same view of events as she did. Our youth and ideas and general demeanor singled us out as a kind of avant-garde at the *lycée*. We were also very concerned about our dress and make-up. Colette's usual garb consisted of Lacoste shirtwaists and daringly but successfully contrasted scarfs. She also owned a very attractive jacket (we thought it magnificent) of black leather, with white revers. Simone had a girl friend who bought her clothes in the *grandes maisons,* and who occasionally made her a present of some studiedly simple ensemble. My own single concession to elegance lay in my sweaters, which my mother knitted for me from very carefully chosen patterns, and which were often copied by my pupils. Our make-up and hair styling gave the lie to that odd ideal which a parent had once enthusiastically suggested to Colette Audry, that we should pursue a "secular nun" effect.

But what were we, really? No husband, no children, no home, no social polish, and twenty-six years old: when you reach this age you want to feel your feet on the ground. Colette had plunged into politics, choosing this as the field in which she would struggle to achieve consciousness of her own existence. Hitherto my zest for life, my literary projects, and the guarantee that Sartre represented to me had spared me worries of this sort. But now his absence, the weakness of the novel on which I had been working, and the depressing atmosphere of Rouen all helped to disorientate me during this particular year. At least, that is my explanation for the way I let myself become involved in various rather petty incidents.

Marco had just been appointed to a teaching post in Amiens, and I quite often dined with him in Paris. He took me to fashionable little dives where we ate heavily seasoned dishes and there were checked tablecloths. He put himself out to charm and flatter me; he told endless anecdotes, most of them untrue, but which I found entertaining; with a reckless abandon that didn't take me in for one moment he bared the secrets of his heart to me. I responded with my own elaborate confidences, which he no more believed than I did his; yet his physical beauty did give some value to these acts of feigned collusion. At the time I was trying hard to be really bitchy, and was quite happy to listen while he tore Simone Labourdin apart, tooth and claw. He had not only made her very unhappy, but boasted about it. Why, though, had he allowed himself to be touched, if only briefly, by the passion which he inspired in her? I never found the answer to this. In fact he was only really interested in men. Very soon he set up house with a good-looking blond boy, to whom he wrote very bad poems, praising his "cytisus-scented hair." They let Simone share their flat, but, as Marco said, tittering: "We make her sleep in a cupboard." She tried to seduce the blond boy, but this gambit failed. Then Marco left for Amiens, and she went off to Rouen. She still saw him occasionally, trying, at one and the same time and with equal lack of success, to win him back and get him out of her system. She lived only for his attention, and possessed inexhaustible defenses against his spite. He had abstracted one volume of her private diary, and read extracts out to me. *I want to dominate,* she wrote, *dominate! I will fashion myself beak and talons, and hold people and events helpless under my claws.* It was more deserving of pity than ridicule. Marco had humiliated her cruelly, and she was trying to regain her self-confidence with the help of clumsy phrase-making. Despite this it never occurred to me to feel sorry for her, and I repeated her thread-bare incantations to Colette, roaring with laughter as I did so. Her constant obsession with building herself so rich and various a life that Marco, even from the heights of his future fame, could not despise it—this I found incredibly irritating. She played hopscotch with the truth and exaggerated her own experiences; and though Marco, it must be admitted, did the same thing, he at least did it stylishly and, as far as one could judge, without ulterior motives, whereas she applied herself to the task with positively heartrending seriousness.

I would probably have judged her less harshly had she not shown a strongly marked hostility toward me. Certainly Marco had not concealed from her the fact that I jeered at her when I was with him; and this could hardly have been conducive to friendly feelings.

Sartre's absence had meant a renewal of my intimacy with Pagniez. During this year we frequently had dinner alone together: I used to tell him everything that had happened to me, and if I needed advice, it was to him that I turned. I placed great trust in his judgment, and he occupied a most important place in my life. I was vexed to find that Simone had repeated certain remarks—amiable comments, in fact, but she injected a note of bitchiness into them—which I had made about him. I got my own back by gossiping about her. Occasionally, when I was at loose ends, I used to have a drink with Mademoiselle Ponthieu, a youngish senior mistress with a purple birthmark on her face. Though unattractive in other respects, she had a good figure and dressed well. She was to some extent supported by a Parisian businessman, a minor industrialist, besides flirting with the young teachers at the boys' *lycée*. We talked clothes, and gossiped. At the end of a long hard afternoon I would sample the stale delights of scandalmongering. Outside lay the mist and darkness of a provincial night; but nothing existed for me any more apart from the light and warmth of the café in which I was sitting, the hot tea scalding my throat, and the sound of my own voice. With words I could slaughter the entire universe; and Simone was my favorite victim.

One Sunday I went to see Marco in Amiens. He showed me the cathedral and took me around the town; he was more attentive and cajoling than ever. He asked me insidious leading questions about Madame Lemaire and Pagniez, and my relationship with Sartre, but I avoided the traps he laid by a series of lies and deliberate naïvetés. The conversation was a series of skirmishes, interspersed with great bursts of laughter on his part. I spent a thoroughly enjoyable day. That evening Marco solemnly announced to me that he was going to let me in on a great secret. He took out from his wallet a snapshot of a good-looking, fair-haired child, and said: "That's my son." Three years earlier, it seemed, he had spent a holiday in an Algerian coastal resort. A yacht lay at anchor offshore, glittering with lights. He had swum out to it, hauled himself aboard, and there met a really gorgeous English girl—blonde, well-connected, and rich as Croesus. He had returned every night after this. The child had been born secretly.

I'm not sure what happened next, or how this idyl among the idle rich finally came to an end: the details of the legend didn't really interest me. Later Marco gave Sartre a different version of the story, and Pagniez a different one again. The truth was, the blond child was his nephew. Doubtless Marco congratulated himself on having deceived me; no one cherishes a more naive belief in other people's credulity than a fantasist of this sort. At any rate, later that evening I chalked up a definite victory. He had booked a room for me at his rooming house, and suggested that we should share the same bed "as brother and sister." I replied that as a general rule when brothers and sisters reached a certain age they had beds to themselves. He laughed at this, though somewhat sourly. I would in any case have declined so incongruous a proposal; but there was a special reason for doing so as well. He had told me that when Simone Labourdin came to visit him in Amiens, one way he amused himself was by spending the night with her without making love in any way. He would feign to be asleep, and then gently rub up against and half hug his bed companion;

he said he laughed inside fit to burst when he heard her beginning to pant with desire. Marco left me stone-cold personally, and I wasn't afraid of his wiles; but I *was* alarmed by his preening self-conceit. What a triumph it would be for him if I sighed or moaned in my sleep! His chagrin gave me great satisfaction. When I got back to Rouen I gleefully told Mademoiselle Ponthieu all about this weekend, adding that Marco couldn't stand Simone Labourdin any longer, and now had a decided thing about me. I heard through Pagniez that Simone laughed heartily to hear that I had boasted of supplanting her in Marco's affections—which was what Mademoiselle Ponthieu had passed on to her. I felt very crestfallen about this. I too, it appeared, could easily be slaughtered with words; this, as I was learning, was a game in which nobody won. If the fancy took me that way I would not refuse to get a little fun out of it; but I no longer looked to it for revenge or triumph.

Another, more serious contretemps befell me about the same time. I was supposed to spend the evening of Wednesday, February 7, with Marco; and then Madame Lemaire and Pagniez invited me to dinner on the same day. I had no wish to discuss my relationship with Marco in their company, since they exaggerated its intimacy and did not, in any case, very much approve of it. I was afraid of the glances that might pass between them if I told the truth, so I informed them that I had already arranged to go out with my sister. On February 6, I was in Rouen, and learned about events in Paris from the papers the following morning. After my dinner with Marco we both went for a stroll round the Place de la Concorde. There were still some overturned, half-burned cars lying there, with numerous people rubbernecking round them. Suddenly we found ourselves face to face with Pagniez and Simone Labourdin. Pagniez and Marco exchanged a few cheerful commonplaces; but I felt the words choke in my throat. I remembered the trap I had fallen into at the age of sixteen, when I copied out the translation of a Latin text: an inconsequential act, unexpectedly divulged, had become charged with vast implications. Madame Lemaire and Pagniez would severely criticize my act of concealment, and take it as proof that my relationship with Marco was totally suspect. How could I explain to them that I had merely wanted to avoid their knowing smiles? No, once again the only possible solution, it seemed to me, was to persist in my lie. The following week I had dinner with Pagniez, in a restaurant near the Halle Aux Vins. I told him that I had really meant to go out with my sister, and only modified my plans at the very last moment. I protested my innocence so fiercely that he almost believed me; but Madame Lemaire was only the more convinced of my duplicity, and took steps to let me see it. I felt desolate at having lost her confidence. Sartre got me out of this predicament when he came to Paris for the Easter holidays. He gave a true account of the affair to his friends, and explained my behavior to them in a most sympathetic way; he knew just how to make his sympathy catching. They may conceivably have gone so far as to doubt whether I was being quite open with Sartre himself; but in any case his cheerful attitude convinced them that they had taken the whole affair too seriously. They laughed about it in my company, without any private reservations. Nevertheless, this experience left me with one very vivid recollection. Nothing worse can happen to you, I thought, than to be regarded as guilty by those whose judgment you respect. To be condemned without the right of appeal would permanently warp a person's relationships with himself, his friends, and the world at large; it would leave a mark on you for life. Once again I found myself in an extremely lucky position: I would never have to carry the burden of a secret alone.

On the evening of February 9 the Communist Party organized an anti-Fascist demonstration which the police suppressed with great brutality, killing six workers. During the afternoon of February 12, for the first time in years, Socialist and Communist workers marched side by side in procession toward the Cours de Vincennes. The Confédération Générale de Travail declared a general strike for the same day, and the Confédération du Travail Universitaire rallied to it, "against the threat of Fascism and for the defense of political freedom." This watchword was followed by something like four and a half million workers. In the Rouen lycée only Colette Audry, Simone Labourdin, and one militant trade unionist obeyed it. For my own part, I was such a stranger to all practical political activities that it never occurred to me that I might join them. There was, too, another reason for my abstention. I shrank from any action that would have forced me to acknowledge my actual status; what I was refusing, now as on previous occasions, was to act as the teacher I was. I could no longer pretend that I was merely playing at giving lessons. I regarded my profession as a coercive restraint, which obliged me to live in Rouen, come to the lycée at fixed hours, and so on. It still, despite this, remained a role that had been imposed on me, and to which I adapted myself, but behind which, I thought, my true nature lay untouched. I was not concerned with the claims of bureaucratic unionists. I was only too willing to behave in class as one individual expressing personal ideas to other individuals, but not to assert my position as a member of the staff by any action whatsoever.

Nevertheless, because of what I discussed during my classes, I was eyed very much askance by the Rouen bourgeoisie: it was even rumored that I was kept by a wealthy senator. Could this have been because Pagniez, who had a very fine presence, often came to meet me at the Gare Saint-Lazare? He was, even so, rather young for a senator; and I had neither the appearance nor the way of life expected of a gold digger. But people did not consider the matter as closely as this; they were content to gossip. I now avoided such indiscretions as lending pupils scandalous books in class; and if a question of practical morality arose, I sent them to Cuvillier's handbook on the subject. Nevertheless, when I was obliged to discuss the problem of the family, I said that women were not exclusively intended for bringing children into the world. Some months earlier, in December, Marshal Pétain had made a speech proclaiming the need for closer ties between school and army, and a circular had come around to all teachers exhorting them to help spread propaganda for an increased birth rate: I made a sarcastic reference to this. The word got about that I had bragged of having wealthy lovers and had advised my pupils to follow my example, after which I imperiously demanded their individual approval, and only one or two girls "of high moral principle" had dared to protest. After the February riots Doumergue had come to power, and we were now witnessing a violent recrudescence of "public morality." It was this, no doubt, that encouraged the so-called Departmental Commission for Natal Increase and Child Care to send a report to the Prefect, denouncing the propaganda which a certain "unworthy teacher" was making against the sanctity of the family. With Pagniez's assistance I composed a reply that was all outraged innocence, and dispatched it to my superiors through the proper official channels. I accused the parents who were attacking me of themselves maintaining Hitlerian doctrines by their insistence that women should be relegated to the home. The schools inspector was a little old man who wore ill-fitting clothes and clearly had no great affection for the local *haute bourgeoisie*: he laughed, and backed me up. But my male opposite number at the Lycée Corneille, Monsieur Troude, hardly let a lesson pass without summoning me before his class, in imagination, and figuratively chopping me to bits.

The stories that got about concerning Colette, Simone, and myself merely whetted the interest displayed in us by all except the most bigoted of our pupils. Colette in particular inspired a large number of crushes. We attached little importance to such things, but we were still young enough to find it amusing that anyone should find us "marvelous." As I have remarked, Marco, like most homosexuals, was always finding "marvelous creatures." Simone Labourdin was eager to unearth some *lycéenne d'élite,* some adolescent of genius to set up in opposition to Marco's discoveries. Colette was primarily concerned to exercise a political influence on her older pupils, and many of them joined the Young Communists. For my part, I spun romances about some of the girls at the *lycée* to whom I taught Latin. There were three or four of them who already, at fourteen or so, had the interests and the physical charms of young women; the prettiest of them all—who later became an actress under Baty—found herself pregnant and was obliged to get married when only fifteen. The philosophy students had already acquired their future adult personalities, and I felt little sympathy with the women they would later become. (As it turned out, though, I had one or two surprises. I never guessed at the time that the well-behaved, studious Jacqueline Netter would escape the guillotine only by the skin of her teeth: she became that courageous woman Jacqueline Guerroudji, condemned to death by an Algiers court at the same time as her husband.) There was one boarder, however, whom Colette Audry drew my attention to during our first year. She was known as *la petite Russe,* being the daughter of a White Russian who had married a Frenchwoman, and all her teachers recognized the fact that she possessed "personality." Her pale face in its frame of blonde hair struck me as somewhat listless, and the essays she gave me were so brief that I had some difficulty in marking them. Yet when I gave back my pupils' papers after the second end-of-term exams,

I announced that the highest marks had, to my great surprise, been obtained by Olga D. Before the actual *baccalauréat* examination there was a preliminary test. It was extremely hot at the time, and the mere sight of my pupils struggling over their essays made me feel ready to drop with fatigue. One after another they deposited their papers on my desk—all except *la petite Russe,* who still sat hopelessly at her desk. I asked her to hand in what she had written, and she burst into tears. I asked her what the matter was, and she said everything was going wrong. I said, would she like to come out with me one Sunday afternoon? I took her for a walk down by the river, and bought her a drink at the Brasserie Victor. She talked to me about God and Baudelaire. She had always been an unbeliever, but was regarded as a mystic by her fellow boarders because she detested girls "who went in for radicalism or socialism." She passed her *baccalauréat* with flying colors, and this despite Monsieur Troude who, taking out his hatred of me on my pupils, laid every possible sort of trap for them.

Next term her parents, who lived at Beuzeville, sent her to work for a bachelor's degree in medicine in Rouen. At twelve she had wanted to be a dancer, and at seventeen an architect: the whole idea of medicine disgusted her. Her father was a Russian nobleman who had fled the country after the Revolution, and her mother read *L'Action Française*; but despite this she was still sickened by her fellow students in Rouen, most of whom were of the extreme Right. She took no interest in political matters, but found their platitudes intolerable. She joined a group of Polish and Romanian Jews, who had been driven from their own countries by anti-Semitism, and were studying in Rouen because the cost of living was less there than in Paris. The Romanians had a little money and did not take life very seriously; she developed a closer intimacy with the Poles, who led a miserable existence and were either passionate Zionists or passionate Communists. One of them played the violin, and they all adored music. Unlike young Frenchmen, they would often go without a meal in order to buy a ticket for a concert, or go and dance at the Royal. For a few months Olga stayed in a boarding house for young ladies, and then moved into a furnished room, which she shared with a Polish girl friend of hers. She sometimes saw former school friends, among others Lucie Vernon, who belonged to the Young Communists and took her along to meetings. One of these Olga told me about. On this particular evening there was a lecture on abortion, which at the time was legalized in the U.S.S.R. Since the subject was one of special interest to women, the greater part of the audience consisted of adolescent girls. There was an ex-student, at least thirty years old, and a leading light of the *Camelots du Roy,* who wore a floppy bow tie and carried a cane and made humorous interruptions during the discussion period. It was only too easy to disconcert the young girls there. They were serious-minded young rebels, whose reflections on the problems arising from their sex contained not the slightest hint of surreptitious licentiousness. This outburst of "national bitching" (*chiennerie française,* an expression coined by Julien Gracq) took their breath away, and brought blushes to their cheeks. The stewards had brought in several dock workers for this meeting, and one of them now strolled across to the group of *Camelots*. "I haven't had your sort of education, Monsieur," he said, "but *I* wouldn't talk to young girls like that." The ex-student slunk out at this, and his escort with him.

Olga kept me informed about her day-to-day life, and discussed her friends with me. One day she asked what it *really* meant to be a Jew. With absolute certainty I replied: "Nothing at all. There are no such things as 'Jews'; only human beings." Long afterward she told me what an impression she had created by marching into the violinist's room and announcing: "My friends, none of you exist! My philosophy teacher has told me so!"

On a great many subjects I—and Sartre to a lesser degree—was deplorably prone to abstraction. I recognized the actuality of social classes; but in reaction against my father's ideologies, I objected when people talked to me about Frenchmen, Germans, or Jews: for me there were only individuals. I was right to reject essentialism; I knew already what abuses could follow in the train of abstract concepts such as the "Slav soul," the "Jewish character," "primitive mentality," or *das ewige Weib*. But the universalist notions to which I turned bore me equally far from reality. What I lacked was the idea of "situation," which alone allows one to make some concrete definition of human groups without enslaving them to a timeless and deterministic pattern. But there was no one, outside the framework of the class struggle, who would give me what I needed.

I enjoyed listening to Olga, and liked both her way of thinking and her sensibility; but as far as I was concerned she was still a child, and I did not see her very often. Once a week I invited her to lunch with me at the Brasserie Paul. These meetings—as I found out later—she found irritating, since she believed eating and talking to be incompatible activities: her line therefore was to eat nothing and hardly speak. Three or four times I took her out for the evening. We saw the Opéra Russe do *Boris Godunov,* and I made her come to a recital given by Gilles and Julien, of whom I never tired. She also accompanied me to a meeting organized (for what purpose I forget) by Colette Audry's splinter group, where speakers from various parties were on the platform. The big attraction was Jacques Doriot, who had just been summoned to Moscow to answer for his political deviationism, and had refused to go. Colette Audry and Michel Collinet were also up there among the platform personalities, and Rouen's Communists had turned out in force. The moment Doriot opened his mouth the shout "To Moscow! To Moscow!" broke out from every corner of the hall. Chairs flew over people's heads. Colette and her friends stood at the front of the platform and shielded Doriot with their bodies; Colette herself was hurled down by a docker. Doriot left, and calm returned. The audience listened to a pale-faced little Socialist in respectful silence, even giving him occasional tepid applause. My liberal heart was bursting with indignation.

This sort of evening made a change from the daily monotony of life in Rouen. Another diversion was provided by Jacqueline Audry, who turned up on a flying visit, gave me a lesson in the use of cosmetics, and taught me how to pluck my eyebrows. In the evening, Colette, Jacqueline, and

I went out to Duclair by bus and dined on *canard au sang*. I saw little of Colette, who had her own interests and concerns. I worked, with scant enthusiasm, at my novel, and went on taking German lessons. With the aid of a dictionary I managed to read *Frau Sorge, Karl und Anna,* and some of Schnitzler's plays. This still left me with plenty of time to kill. The whole year would have foundered in a sea of dullness had it not been crossed by the tragic episode of Louise Perron.

Louise Perron taught at a secondary school in Rouen. She was a tall, dark, plain girl of about thirty, with sparkling eyes and an excellent figure, which she ruined by the appalling clothes she wore. She had an attic room in an old house near where I lived. When I arrived in Rouen she had been for the past year on intimate terms with Colette Audry; but one day, while Louise was unburdening to her, Colette unfortunately smiled at the wrong moment, and I was chosen to replace her as Louise's confidante. During a recent cultural congress at Pontigny Louise had met a well-known writer whom I shall call J.B. One evening she had announced, provocatively, that she was a Trotskyite, and he had glanced at her, she told me, with some curiosity. She made vigorous advances to him, and even claimed that once in the grounds of Pontigny Abbey she had bitten his neck. At any rate, she had got him into bed with her, and had then confessed that he was her first lover. "For heaven's sake, girl," J.B. retorted, somewhat abashed, but not daring to back out at this juncture, "they're all virgins here!" He was married, but Louise convinced herself that he would leave his wife for love of her. But once back in Paris, J.B. brought things to a head. This affair couldn't go on, he said, and suggested that he and Louise should be "just friends." Since this did not satisfy her, he wrote that it would be better to break off the relationship altogether. Louise refused to believe he meant what he said. Either he was playing some sort of cruel joke, or else he was lying out of compassion for his wife; but whichever it was, he still loved her. He refused to make appointments with her, but she knew a trick worth two of that: on Sunday she went to Paris and took a room in the luxury hotel opposite J.B.'s apartment. Here she watched the front door of his building till he emerged, and then rushed down to meet him, and what with one thing and another forced him to offer her a drink. While in Rouen she read and reread the books that he admired, and plastered her room with reproductions of his favorite pictures. She tried to guess what he would say, think, or feel in any given circumstances. One morning I was having coffee with Colette Audry at a bar in the Place de la Gare, La Métropole, when Louise rushed up to us. "J.B. has just had a daughter—Lux!" she exclaimed, and was off again like the wind. "Lux," Colette repeated. "What an odd name for a girl." In fact what Louise had meant was that light (*lux*) had entered her soul; it was because his wife was expecting a child that J.B. had not asked for a divorce. She sent Madame J.B. a bouquet of red roses and a greetings post card with a picture of Rouen harbor on the back. During the Easter holidays she went off to the Midi, but when she returned things did not improve at all. Telegrams, phone calls, special delivery letters—J.B. answered none. I tried to make her see reason. "He's decided to break it off," I told her. She shrugged. "You don't break off without any warning," she said. "He would have written." One day she got a new inspiration: he must be jealous. She explained why. She had sent him a post card from Provence, with the following message (or something like it): "Here is a souvenir of Provence for you. I am told this landscape is like me." "That 'I am told' means I have a lover," she said. "It isn't true, of course, but that's what he must have thought."

On another occasion she spent an evening at the theater with a friend of J.B.'s, whom she had also met at Pontigny, and according to her he behaved in the most peculiar way throughout the performance. He *said* his new shoes were pinching, but wasn't he really suspicious that Louise might be trying to seduce him? Wouldn't he have given a bad report of her to J.B.? She wrote J.B. a long letter to clear up this misunderstanding, but still got no reply. Then she thought of another brick she might have dropped. She had sent Madame J.B. *red* roses, and red was the color of blood and death; besides, there was a boat in the photograph of Rouen harbor. *They* thought she was telling her rival that she, Louise, would like to be rid of her. She drafted yet another letter clarifying the situation.

One afternoon in June I had gone to meet Sartre at the station, and we were walking across the square when I saw Louise coming toward me, with tears pouring down her face. She took me by the arm and drew me aside. "Read this," she said. She had received a curt, final note from J.B., which ended with the words: "If we meet in future, let it be by chance rather than arrangement." "Well," I told her, "*that's* a breaking-off letter all right." She shrugged in irritation. "Oh come: when you're going to break off with somebody *you don't write letters about it.*" She then plunged into her own theory, which was quite amazingly ingenious: every comma, it seemed, was eloquent proof of J.B.'s unfairness and dishonesty. *"By chance,"* she repeated. "Don't you see what that means? He wants me to go back to that hotel and watch out for him again, and then pretend to have met him accidentally in the street. But why all these tricks? Why?" She made arrangements to see J.B. again before the holidays, and no doubt he was polite enough to her in conversation. Then she went off into the mountains, having made up her mind to write a major article on his work which would prove her worthy of him. I was well aware that she was an unhappy woman; yet despite this I regarded the whole affair as broad comedy, a joke to be laughed at. Till that June day when I saw her weep, my own emotions had been untouched.

A few days after the beginning of term I ran into Louise near the *lycée.* She seized me by the hand and dragged me off to have a cup of tea with her. During her holidays, which she had spent in a little Alpine hotel, she had written her article on J.B., and had taken it along to him at the paper where he worked, just before the end of September. He had received her in a friendly enough fashion, but some of his actions had struck her as decidedly odd. He had, it seemed, turned his back on her and stood for a long moment with his forehead pressed against the window. Well, obviously he was trying to hide his emotions. But when he sat down at his desk again, he had rested his chin on his fist, revealing three clear tooth marks on the back of his hand. "The meaning of *that's* clear enough," Louise said: "he isn't sleeping with his wife any more. But why should he tell *me* that?" At this precise moment something clicked in my head, and the whole business lost its funny side once and for all. It was no longer possible either to reason with Louise, or to laugh at her. Often, during the weeks that followed, she would appear out of a doorway and grasp my arm. Was J.B. putting her to the proof or trying to get his revenge on her? If the latter, wouldn't her best course be to kill him? She had got the feeling that perhaps this was what he really wanted. As during the previous year, I tried to distract her with anecdotes about Marco and Simone Labourdin, or Camille and Dullin, but now she no longer listened; she was too busy raking through her memories. One evening the manager of the Hôtel La Rochefoucauld sent me up a bouquet of tea roses from her, with a message that read: "The misunderstanding has been smoothed out. I'm happy, so I bought you some roses." I put the flowers into a vase: the gesture wrung my heart. Next day Louise explained. Before she fell asleep at night there was always a long procession of images trailing across her mind, and one of these had suddenly provided her with a blinding illumination. The notepaper at her Alpine hotel had a little picture of a fountain printed on it. In the language of psychoanalysis a fountain possesses a very clearly defined symbolic meaning, and J.B. had therefore inferred that Louise was defiantly telling him she had a lover. His *amour-propre* had been wounded, and this was why he was tormenting her. She had immediately sent off a special delivery letter clearing everything up, and had bought me the roses on her way back from the post office. A few hours after this conversation she was in my room again, lying prostrate on my bed with a telegram beside her which read: *No misunderstanding: letter follows.* Her elaborate explanations were abandoned now; she admitted that this was the end of the affair. I said the vague conventional things that one does on such occasions.

Perhaps the shock had been a salutary one, because during November there were no more fantasies woven around the truth. Colette and I both saw more of her than before, and I introduced her to Olga. At my suggestion she began to write down her childhood memories, in a crude style which I did not find wholly displeasing. She had occasional bursts of cheerfulness and seemed determined to forget J.B. There had been someone else after her at Pontigny, a fifty-year-old Socialist: she wrote to him, they met, and he took her off for the night to a hotel near the Gare du Nord.

Two days later—it was a Monday—I was due to have tea at her place, together with Olga. I told Olga to go on alone, as I had work I wanted to do, and would come along later in the evening. As soon as I arrived, Olga vanished. Louise told me, fixing me with an unwavering stare that I found very hard to meet, that she had come out with a whole string of delightful stories about her childhood. Having said this, Louise fell silent, but continued to stare at me. I tried to make conversation, but couldn't think of anything to say. The hatred that I read in her expression scared me less than the brutal frankness with which she declared it. We had left the world of comforting conventions, and the terrain I was exploring was wholly unfamiliar to me. Suddenly Louise turned her head away and began to speak. For two hours, almost without drawing breath, she narrated the story of George Sand's *Consuelo* to me.

I went off to Paris, and snatched three unofficial days with Sartre, who was giving himself a long Christmas holiday. He came back to Rouen with me on Thursday evening. On Friday morning, as we were having coffee at La Métropole, Colette Audry came up, looking rather agitated. She was supposed to meet Louise that afternoon, but dared not go. Louise had asked her to dinner on Tuesday: there had been a table laid for twelve in her room. "Where are the others?" she asked Colette when she opened the door. "I thought there'd be a lot more of you!" She then picked a telegram off the mantlepiece and said: "Alexandre isn't coming." Alexandre, a former editor of *Libres Propos,* had been teaching in Rouen two years before, and now had a job in London. "London's a long way off," Colette said. Louise shrugged, and her face darkened. "There's nothing to eat," she announced, and added, abruptly: "I'll go and cook some pasta." They dined on a dish of noodles.

Two days later, that is on the Thursday, Louise rang the bell of the house where Colette lived, fell on her knees, and poured out a mixture of threats and supplications, swearing she wasn't to blame for anything. This time it was Colette's turn to be alarmed. She had just phoned the school where Louise taught, and heard that Louise had not put in an appearance that morning. Also, she had for some little while appeared to be suffering from extreme exhaustion. Since Colette was due back at the *lycée* we decided that Sartre and I should go and see Louise at her apartment.

On the way I ran into Olga, who was looking for me. The previous Wednesday evening she had stopped by Louise's with a book she had borrowed two nights before. Ordinarily, when anyone rang the front door bell Louise pressed a button which opened it from her room. On this occasion she came down. She grabbed the book, and exclaimed, "What about the dog whip? Haven't you brought the dog whip?" As she set off back up the stairs she muttered, "What a comedy! Ah, what a comedy!" Olga added that on the Monday, when she was trying to counteract that oppressive silence by breathlessly recounting her whole stock of childhood memories, she had included a quarrel between herself and her grandmother. She had been four years old at the time, and, furiously aware of her own impotence, had tried to threaten the old lady: "When Papa comes home he'll beat you with the dog whip!" she cried. Her Communist friend Lucie Vernon, to whom she recounted the incident, said, reassuringly, "That's the explanation, of course." Lucie, who always rationalized everything, had been of the opinion that Louise's behavior was quite normal. But Olga remained worried.

Sartre and I speculated about the night Louise had spent, the previous

Saturday, with her quinquegenarian Socialist. Sartre was later to use this theme for the first draft of a story: the story itself was abandoned, but later formed the basis of *La Chambre* (*The Room*).

Louise lived alone on the fourth, and highest, floor of her apartment house. I pressed the button belonging to her flat. Nothing happened. I tried another one, and the front door opened. We climbed the staircase, and when we reached the top we saw a white oblong on Louise's door; it turned out to be a piece of paper, held there with drawing pins, and inscribed in block capitals with the words: THE IMMORTAL CLOWN. Despite what I had heard from Colette and Olga, I got a shock. I knocked, but there was no answer. I peered through the keyhole: Louise was sitting there in front of her stove, wrapped in a shawl, her face waxen white, and as motionless as a corpse. What was to be done? We went down and argued the problem out in the street; then we climbed back to the fourth floor again. Once again I knocked at the door, and begged Louise, through the keyhole, to let us in. She did so. I held out my hand to her, and she quickly put her own hand behind her back. Papers were burning in the stove, and the room was full of smoke; other papers lay in heaps on the floor. Louise went down on her hands and knees, scooped up an armful, and threw them into the flames. "What are you doing?" I asked her. *"No!"* she said. "I won't say any more. I've said too much already." I put a hand on her shoulder. "Come along with us," I said. "Come and have something to eat." She shivered, and looked at me furiously. "Do you know what you're saying?" she cried. I said the first thing that came into my head: "You know very well that I'm your friend—" "Ah-ha!" she said, "a fine friend you are! Go on, get out! Leave me alone!" We did so; and then, because I felt matters were now desperate, I sent a telegram to her parents, who lived in a small town in Auvergne.

I had some lessons to give during the afternoon. About two o'clock Sartre went up to Louise's apartment with Colette Audry. The third-floor tenant stopped them on the staircase, and said that for three days now Louise had been pacing around her room from morning till night, making the floorboards creak overhead. Her charwoman added that for weeks she had been talking to herself out loud. When they entered her room, Louise fell into Colette's arms, sobbing that she was ill. She agreed to let Sartre go down and buy her some fruit. Colette caught up with him on the sidewalk outside: Louise had had a change of mood and thrown her out. Sartre went back, and pushed open the door, which Louise had not shut properly. She was still huddled in one corner of her sofa, her eyes shut, a hopeless expression on her face. Sartre set down the fruit beside her, and departed. Behind him a voice exclaimed, "I don't want this stuff!" There was a quick patter of feet, and then pears, oranges, and bananas went showering down the stairs. The lady on the next floor poked her head around her door and said, "Could I pick them up, like? Seems a pity for them to be wasted."

Rouen, with its drizzling sky and respectable streets, had never had a more depressing effect on me than it did late that afternoon. I was anxiously awaiting a telegram from the Perron family, and went down to check at the concierge's office, where I was told that a "dark lady" had come and left a message for me. It read: "I do not hate you. I *must* talk to you. Come quickly: I am waiting." What obsessional behavior, I thought: all the business of opening and shutting that door, clambering up and down that dim stairway, and all the time such a whirling turmoil in her poor head! But to be shut up, alone and at night, in Louise's apartment, under her burning gaze, and to breathe the sour smell of despair that infected the entire place—this I found a terrifying prospect. Once again Sartre accompanied me. Louise stretched out a hand to us, and smiled. "Well, now," she said, in a relaxed voice, "I've got you to come here to ask your advice, since you are my friends: ought I to go on living, or kill myself?"

"Go on living, of course," I said, with emphatic promptness.

"Very well. But how? How can I earn a living?"

I reminded her that she was a teacher. She shrugged her shoulders, irritated.

"Look, I've sent in my resignation. I can't spend the rest of my life messing about like a monkey on a stick." Like Karamazov *père,* she had played the roles of monkey and buffoon, but that was all over now. She wanted to regenerate herself, work with her hands—roadsweeping, maybe, or doing domestic chores. She put on her coat, and said she was going out to buy a paper and go through the small ads. All right, I said. What else could one say? She stared at us, her face distraught. "Look at me," she said. "Still playing the same old comedy." She took off her coat and threw it down on the sofa. "But this is just a comedy, too," she went on, hands pressed to her cheeks. "Isn't there any way out?" Finally she calmed down and managed another smile. "Ah well," she said, "it only remains now to thank you for all your help." Hurriedly I protested that I had done nothing. "Don't tell such lies!" she cried, in annoyed tones. I had, it is true, applied myself with some assiduity to the task of convincing her that this self-abasement of hers was a fact. I wanted to know whether she had sunk low enough to believe all the stories I told her about Simone Labourdin, Marco, and Camille: and it was. In the presence of other people she resembled some inanimate log slowly being engulfed. It was only when she was alone that she recovered a little independent judgment: this passive acceptance of other people's opinions was indeed one aspect of her self-abasement. Doubtless I had only worked so hard to plunge her into this mood with the intention of provoking a reaction from her that would let her snap out of it unaided. By advising her to set down her childhood memories I achieved half my purpose: this was a kind of psychoanalysis. I abandoned any idea of protesting against her disturbing gratitude.

This scene had been as close-knit as a good stretch of stage dialogue, and made a very vivid impression on us. We were struck by Louise's inability to detach herself from the "comedy": this completely confirmed the ideas we had formed on the subject. Louise's mistake, as we saw it, was her attempt to construct an image of herself that could be used as a weapon against an ill-starred love affair; while her most meritorious achievement was to have broken through to daylight again. The drama of her situation lay in the fact that the harder she struggled to achieve self-forgetfulness, the less successful she would be.

Louise's father arrived the following morning. He was a cooper from the Aveyron district, and questioned us somewhat suspiciously, asking just what had happened to "the girl." He obviously suspected that she had been seduced, with unfortunate consequences. The same evening Louise's brother descended on us. He was some six years her junior, a student at the Ecole Normale, and he too was very much on the defensive. He settled in with his sister for the whole of the Christmas holidays. Before she left Rouen, Colette went to see Louise's headmistress, intending to ask her if she would tear up Louise's letter of resignation. She was received by the senior mistress, who explained that the headmistress had called upon Louise in person, wishing to talk things over with her. Louise had driven her away, shrieking: "I must have purity of action!" This had so alarmed the headmistress that she took to her bed and was still there.

I saw Louise again early in January, at the Métropole café: she was haggard and yellow, with damp hands, and her whole body trembled. "I've been ill," she told me, "very ill." During the past two weeks she had suffered from a sort of psychological dissociation of personality, and she said how ghastly it was to *see oneself* the whole time, without respite. She wept; there was no more hostility in her. Instead she begged me to protect her against calumny. "My hand is innocent, I swear it," she cried, and stretched her hand out across the table. Yes, she had said in her article that J.B.'s characters were as alike as the fingers on one hand, but there was no hidden implication in this phrase. She had never wished any harm to befall J.B.'s child. She was determined to get better now. The doctor had advised her to go up into the mountains; her brother would take her there, and she would stay for two or three weeks.

From her first letter it sounded as though the snow and a healthy regimen had transformed her. She was going out skiing; she described her hotel and the surrounding landscape; she was busy knitting me a lovely all-white sweater. "I will thank the others another time," she wrote. It was only this remark, at the foot of the last page, that worried me: as it turned out, with good reason. The letters that followed were by no means so reassuring. Louise had sprained her ankle, and while she lay stretched out on her chaise longue, she had leisure to brood over the past again. Often when she woke up "someone" caused her to see stars and crosses on the walls of her room. Who, and why? Did we want to save her—or to destroy her? She sounded as though she were leaning toward the second hypothesis.

I was not feeling exactly cheerful when I went to meet her at the station. It was nine o'clock at night, and I decided I lacked sufficient courage to shut myself up alone with her in that flat. I was a bit afraid of her, and very much afraid of being afraid. Then I saw her, in the crowd surging toward me, carrying both her suitcases, her face bronzed and tough, radiating robust health. She did not smile at me. I insisted on our going and having a drink in the station buffet; the idea did not appeal to her much, but I persisted, and was glad I had done so. It was comforting to have people and noise around us while she was conducting her interrogation. She demanded clear-cut answers to her questions. Had the "conspirators" acted for her good, or in a spirit of revenge? She spoke in a cool, clear voice, and her improved physical health had allowed her to impose some sort of order on her lunatic notions: it was, indeed, a superb hypothesis she presented, harder to refute than anything in Leibniz or Spinoza. I denied the existence of any "conspiracy." "Come, come!" she said. "Who do you suppose turns up at the meetings? Shadows?" She now had "certain knowledge" that Colette was J.B.'s mistress: the previous summer she had gone to Norway, supposedly with friends; and J.B., for his part, had spoken ironically of a projected Norwegian cruise. Coincidence? No. Everybody knew about this liaison except Louise. Anyway she was kept systematically in the dark. Once in a restaurant, when Colette, Simone Labourdin, and myself were drinking cider, Louise had ordered wine, and I had said, jeeringly, "On your own, eh?"

I tried a counterattack to this. "You know perfectly well that you misinterpret everything," I told her. She had once declared that she spent hours stretched out on her sofa, searching for the hidden significance of gestures and words that she had noted during the day. "Yes, I know," she replied tranquilly. "But a fact is a fact." She cited "facts" to me in abundance: an insolent wink, a day when I cut her in the street, an exchange of smiles with Colette; an odd intonation of Olga's; phrases I had used taken out of context. Against evidence of this sort it was hopeless to put up any defense. As we came out of the station I carefully repeated the statement that there was no conspiracy. "Very well," she said, "since you refuse to help me, there's no point in our meeting again at the moment. I will make my own decisions." And with that she vanished into the darkness of the town.

I slept badly that night, and on the nights that followed. I dreamed that Louise came into my room, foaming at the mouth, and someone was helping me to shut her up in a violin case. I tried to go back to sleep, but the violin case still lay on my mantelpiece, and inside it there was a living thing, all twisted up with hatred and horror. I opened my eyes, and stayed awake. What would I do if Louise *did* knock at my door in the middle of the night? I could hardly refuse to let her in, and yet after our last conversation I believed her capable of anything. Even my daylight hours were made hideous by the fear of meeting her. The very thought that she was breathing and thinking a few hundred yards away from me was enough to arouse in me the same agony of mind I had experienced at the age of fifteen, when I saw Charles VI strutting across the stage at the Odéon.

About two weeks passed by. Colette and I received two identical letters, which read: "It will give me great pleasure if you will attend the large luncheon party I am organizing in Paris, at half past twelve on Sunday, February 11, in honor of my friends." This meal, the exact venue of which was not indicated, recalled that other phantom banquet in which Colette had been involved. Invitations also went out to Louise's parents, to Alexandre, to J.B., to her Socialist, and to several others. But before the date she had arranged, Louise paid a visit to Madame J.B., and swore to her, weeping, that she meant her no harm. Madame J.B. managed to persuade her to enter a clinic the very same day.

She came out in midsummer, and stayed with her parents till autumn. She made a trip to Paris in October, and arranged to meet me at the Dôme. I waited for her at the far end of the café, my throat tight with anxiety. She arrived in a friendly enough mood, but glanced somewhat suspiciously at the book I had put down in front of me: a translation of an English novel, done by Louis Guilloux. "Why Louis Guilloux?" she inquired. She talked bitterly of the clinic, where the doctors had subjected her to experiments in hypnotism and thought transmission, which had thrown her into a state of terrible anxiety. She had calmed down again, but she was still convinced that the "conspiracy" was by no means disbanded. Colette's last letter had been mailed on the Rue Singer, which was as much to say, "You are a monkey [*singe*]"; and the English watermark in the notepaper read "The strongest," meaning, "I was the strongest." As for me, there was even something equivocal about *my* attitude today. Louise admitted that she had a mania for interpreting events. When she reread *Cinna,* the idea had occurred to her that this story of conspiracy made allusions to her case; but, as she reasonably told herself, the tragedy happened to have been written three hundred years previously. On the other hand, when she heard provocative remarks on the radio or read them in a weekly, what reason was there for not supposing herself to be the subject of attack? The conspiracy had ample funds for financing broadcasts or articles. She launched into an astounding description of this world of hers. Psychoanalytical symbols, dream interpretations, numerology and floral signs, puns and anagrams— all served to invest the slightest object or most casual incident with infinite purposiveness, aimed directly at her. In this universe there were no casual moments, not an inch of neutral territory, not one detail left to chance: it was governed by iron necessity, and significant in all its parts. To me it seemed removed, far from the earth and its human weakness, to a paradise or a hell. Hell now, beyond any doubt: Louise's face was dark.

"I can only see two possible solutions," she said, weighing her words. "Either I join the Communist Party, or else I do the killing myself. The trouble is, I shall have to begin with the people I'm most attached to." All the time I was watching the movements of her hands. From time to time she gripped her bag: I knew from previous experience that she carried a razor, and was quite capable of using it. I told myself in order to calm my nerves that her first victim would be J.B., and that she was very unlikely to get the chance of dispatching a second; but this only half-reassured me. At the same time I was fascinated by the grim fantasy world in which Louise moved. I went off to join Sartre and Colette Audry at La Closerie des Lilas, but somehow could not get on their conversational wave length. It was the only time in my life that I found a discussion with Sartre dull. "It's true," I told him amusedly, in the train taking us back to Rouen, "you're not mad, not mad at all." Madness for me possessed its own metaphysical dignity: I saw in it both a refusal and a circumvention of the human condition.

Louise went back to her family in Aveyron. I wrote to her, suggesting that we correspond and assuring her of my friendship. She replied with a letter thanking me, and saying that she no longer hated me. "Unfortunately," she went on, "I am in no fit state for doing *anything* constructive at the moment. There's something inside me, something as hard an an iron bar, that crushes my will and stops every flicker of enthusiasm or desire. Besides, I feel that the whole relationship I would like to build with you would have a land mine buried deep in its foundations. With the best will in the world on both sides, this mine would probably blow up at a time when neither of us could foresee. . . . Let us admit that on occasion I behave in the most frightful way; that I strip my heart bare, and have a soul as black as any pitch. The thought that mine is not an isolated case offers me no consolation. It merely helps me to struggle clear of that masochistic self-abasement in which I have been wallowing for the past year and more—I admit, you see, that I have not been in thrall to it all my life—and enables me to see things in a slightly different way."

I never saw her again after this. She persisted in her delusions for a long while, but finally became sick of them, and returned to teaching. I know that she played an active part in the Resistance; and she did join the Communist Party.

I made up my mind to go to Berlin toward the end of February. I had the idea of using Louise Perron's case as a means of obtaining a medical certificate that would let me take some leave. Colette recommended me to a psychiatrist, that same Dr. D. who had advised one of her friends to let emotions detach themselves from her like dead leaves. I sat for nearly half an hour in a dingy mezzanine waiting room in the Latin Quarter, feeling rather anxious: might this doctor *not* prescribe a change of air for me? At last he opened the door. He was an old man, with a white mustache and an air of great dignity; but there was a large, fresh, quite unmistakable stain on the front of his trousers. It helped set me up: my timidity vanished, and I talked freely. I pretended to be consulting him about Louise's case (she was not yet in a clinic), and added that the whole thing had been a severe nervous strain on me personally. He readily prescribed up to two weeks' rest for me. When I climbed aboard the Berlin express, I felt myself assuming the character of some internationally famous woman traveler, a "Madonna of the Sleeping Cars" almost.

The students at the French Institute in Berlin regarded Nazism much in the same way as the bulk of the French Left did. They associated only with anti-Fascist students and intellectuals, who were all convinced that

Hitlerism was liable to collapse at any moment. They explained the Nuremberg Congress and the November plebiscite as being due to a temporary fit of collective hysteria. Anti-Semitism they considered too egregiously stupid an attitude to merit serious concern. Among the students at the Institute there was a tall, handsome, strapping young Jew, and a small, kinky-haired Corsican: German racialists always took the former for an Aryan and the latter for a Hebrew. Sartre and his friends derived much quiet fun from this persistent error. Nevertheless they were well aware that until it was finally crushed Nazi fanaticism contained a very real element of danger. A former friend of Sartre's had, a year or so previously, embarked on an affair with a wealthy and fairly well-known Jewess. He did not write to her direct, for fear that correspondence with a Frenchman might compromise her position. Instead he sent his letters to Sartre, who then passed them on. Sartre liked Berlin very much; but whenever he passed Brown Shirts in the street he experienced the same unpleasant feeling as he had felt that first time in Venice.

During my visit the Austrian Socialists attempted to exploit proletarian discontent as a way of opposing the rise of Nazism. They triggered off a rising, which Dollfuss crushed with much bloodshed. This setback disheartened us somewhat. We would not set our own shoulders to the wheel of history, but we wanted to believe that it was turning in the right direction; otherwise we would have had too many problems to rethink.

To the eye of a casual visitor, Berlin did not look as though it were crushed under a dictatorship. The streets were cheerful and animated, though their ugliness astounded me; I had been enchanted by the London scene, and never thought houses could be so unprepossessing. Only one district escaped this general criticism, a sort of garden-city that had recently been built on the outskirts, and was known as "Uncle Tom's Cabin." The Nazis had also put up "workers' blocks" in the suburbs: these were comfortable enough, though actually inhabited by *petit bourgeois* tenants. We walked a good deal between the Kurfürstendamm and the Alexanderplatz. It was extremely cold, only just above zero, so we moved fast, with plenty of stops for refreshment. I was not attracted by the *Konditorei,* which were rather like teashops; but the brasseries, with their big, solid tables and rich aroma of cooking, I found extremely comfortable, and we often lunched in them. I was very fond of German cooking, heavy though it was—red cabbage and smoked pork, or *Bauernfrühstück.* I appreciated rather less such things as game served *à la confiture,* or the cream-swamped dishes that they produced in the more expensive restaurants. I remember one such place, called Le Rêve: it was draped with velvet curtains, over which spotlights played *à la* Loïe Fuller. There were also colonnades, fountains, and—I think—birds. Sartre also took me to the Romanisches Café, which had formerly been a meeting place for intellectuals. But for the past year or two they had stopped going there, and all I saw was a large hall filled with little marble tables and straight-backed chairs.

Certain pleasure haunts had been closed down, among them the Silhouetten, where transvestites had been much in evidence. Nevertheless, respectability by no means reigned supreme everywhere. Either the first or second evening I was there we went out with a friend of Sartre's called Cantin, who specialized in low dives. On a street corner he went up to a tall and extremely elegant woman, who was wearing a chic little veil, silk stockings, and high-heeled shoes. Even though her voice was pitched a little on the low side I couldn't believe my eyes when I heard that "she" was actually a man. Cantin took us into some incredibly debauched nightspots round the Alexanderplatz. One notice hung on the wall amused me: *Das Animieren der Damen ist Verboten,* which means, "It is forbidden to encourage women."

During the next few days Sartre showed me some of the more respectable places. I drank German Bowle in a restaurant where the tables were arranged around a sort of tan-covered circus ring, in which an equestrienne was doing trick-riding stunts. I drank beer in huge beer halls, one of which contained a whole series of saloons, with three bands playing simultaneously. At eleven o'clock in the morning every table was full; people were embracing one another and rocking to and fro as they sang. "That," Sartre explained to me, "is *Stimmung.*" At the far end of the main saloon hung a kind of backcloth, depicting the banks of the Rhine. Suddenly, with much clashing of brass, a storm broke out: the painted scene changed from violet to deep purple, while lightning flashes zigzagged across it, and we heard the sound of thunder and rushing torrents. The company applauded vigorously.

We made a short tour round the area: at Hanover we stood in the pouring rain and saw Leibniz's house, a huge, opulent place, and very attractive with its bottled windows. I loved the old houses of Hildesheim, with their dark-red roofs that held garret upon garret, three times as high as the façades. The silent, deserted streets seemed to stand right outside time, and I felt as though I had walked into some weird film, that round the next corner I would find a man clad in black cape and top hat, who would turn out to be Dr. Caligari.

I had dinner on two or three occasions at the French Institute. Most of the resident students found relief from their studies by trafficking in currency. There was a great difference in value between the "frozen" marks allotted to tourists and ordinary Deutschmarks, which it was illegal to export from the country. Cantin, and several others, crossed the frontier once a month, packets of banknotes hidden in the lining of their overcoats. The French banks gave them a very high rate of exchange; and when they came back they could, as foreigners, redeem an equivalent number of marks for a quite modest outlay.

Sartre took no interest in little schemes of this sort. He was working hard: besides going on with the story of Roquantin, he was reading Husserl and writing his essay, "The Transcendence of the Ego," which appeared in 1936, in *Recherches philosophiques.* Here he outlined—in a Husserlian perspective, but contrary to some of Husserl's most recent theories—the relationship between the self and the conscious mind, and also established a distinction, which he was to maintain permanently, between the conscious mind and the psyche. While the conscious mind constitutes per se an obvious and immediately apprehensible entity, the psyche is a cluster of phenomena which must be grasped by a process of mental analysis and which further, like any object of perception, reveal themselves, as it were, in profile only. Hatred, for instance, is a transcendent quality: we apprehend it by way of *Erlebnissen,* individual experiences, but its actual existence is no more than a probability. My ego, on the other hand, like the ego of any other person, is by its nature a recognizable phenomenon. Herein lay the foundation of one of Sartre's earliest and most stubbornly held beliefs: the autonomy of the irrational mind. It is only in certain special circumstances that there appears that relationship to the self which, according to La Rochefoucauld and French traditional psychology, is liable to deflect even our most spontaneous actions. More important for Sartre, this theory—and in his opinion this theory alone—offered an escape from solipsism, with psyche and ego possessing, both for oneself and external observers, an equally objective existence. By abolishing solipsism one avoided the snares of idealism, and in his concluding section Sartre emphasized the practical implications of his thesis, both moral and political. I quote these final remarks here, since the essay, written in 1934 and published in 1936, is hard to come by, and they may serve to demonstrate the perennial nature of Sartre's special preoccupations:

> It has always seemed to me that any working hypothesis as prolific as historical materialism stands in no need whatsoever of so absurd a foundation as a materialist metaphysic. In fact it is not necessary that the "objective" should precede the "subjective" to dissolve all these spiritual pseudo values and bring the world back to a proper foundation, in the actual. All that is needed is for the self to be abreast of contemporary realities, and then the subject-object dualism, which is a matter of logical theory and nothing else, will finally vanish from the philosophical arena.

Such conditions, he adds, are sufficient

> to make it look to the world at large as though the individual self is in danger, and for the self (indirectly, and through the agency of special circumstances) to absorb its contents, in turn, from the world at large. That is all that is required to guarantee a philosophical basis for absolutely positive moral and political attitudes.

Sartre enjoyed himself at the Institute, where he rediscovered the freedom and, to some extent, the camaraderie which had made him so fond of the Ecole Normale. In addition, he formed there one of those relationships with a woman by which he set such store. One of the resident students, whose zest for philology was only equaled by his indifference to passion, had a wife whom everyone at the Institute found charming. Marie Girard had been around the Latin Quarter for ages; in those days she had lived in shabby little hotels, shut away in her room for weeks on end, smoking and dreaming. She had not the slightest notion of what the purpose of her existence on this earth might be; she lived from one day to the next, lost in a private fog which only a few stubbornly irrefragable realities could penetrate. She did not believe in misfortunes of the heart or the afflictions that spring from luxury and riches. In her eyes the only real misfortunes were misery, hunger, phsyical pain; and as for happiness, the word simply had no meaning for her. She was an attractive, graceful girl, with a slow smile, and her pensive, abstracted daydreaming aroused a sympathetic response in Sartre. She felt the same about him. They agreed that there could be no future in this relationship, but that its present reality sufficed: accordingly they saw a good deal of each other. I met her, and liked her; there was no feeling of jealousy on my part. Yet this was the first time since we had known one another that Sartre had taken a serious interest in another woman; and jealousy is far from being an emotion of which I am incapable, or which I underrate. But this affair neither took me by surprise nor upset any notions I had formed concerning our joint lives, since right from the outset Sartre had warned me that he was liable to embark on such adventures. I had accepted the principle, and now had no difficulty in accepting the fact. To know the world and give it expression, this was the aim that governed the whole of Sartre's existence; and I knew just how set he was on it. Besides, I felt so closely bound to him that no such episode in his life could disturb me.

Shortly after I arrived in Berlin I got a letter from Colette Audry, warning me that my absence from the *lycée* had not been taken at all well in official quarters. Sartre advised me to cut my visit short; but I refused, saying that I would be covered by my medical certificate. He insisted, saying that if it became known that I had gone off to Germany, I might get into serious trouble. This was quite true, but I shook with rage at the idea of being forced to make any concessions to prudence, and stayed where I was. When I got back to Rouen I was glad I had acted as I did, since nothing happened to me at all. Cheerfully I told my friends about my trip. "But didn't you *meet* anyone?" Marco asked. "No little *encounters?*" When I said no, I hadn't, he looked at me pityingly.

Sartre and I both continued to keep abreast of new writing. That year was notable, as far as we were concerned, for two names. The first was Faulkner, whose novels *As I Lay Dying* and *Sanctuary* were published almost simultaneously in French translation. There had been several earlier writers, Joyce, Virginia Woolf, and Hemingway among them, who had rejected the false objectivity of the realistic novel and chosen to interpret the world by means of a more subjective approach; but the novelty and effectiveness of Faulkner's technique amazed us. Not only did he show great skill in deploying and harmonizing multiple viewpoints, but he got inside each individual mind, setting forth its knowledge and ignorance, its moments of insincerity, its fantasies, the words it formed and the silences it kept. As a result the narrative was bathed in a chiaroscuro, which gave each event the greatest possible highlight and shadow. His stories appealed to us equally for their themes and for their artistic skill. In a way, that aggressively picaresque novel *As I Lay Dying* could be linked with surrealistic developments. The child remarks that his mother is a fish; and when her coffin, insecurely balanced on an old cart, topples over into the river and is borne away by the current, it looks as though his mother's corpse has, indeed, become a fish of sorts. In the cement with which the farmer plasters his hurt knee we can recognize one of those pseudo substances so popular both with Dali and the Marx Brothers, like edible china or lumps of marble sugar. But in Faulkner such ambiguities contained deep materialist implications. If objects or habits were presented to the reader in a preposterous light, the reason was that misery and want not only change man's attitude to things but transform the very appearance of such things. This was what we found most attractive about this novel which Valery Larbaud, to our surprise, described in his preface as being concerned with "country life and ways." *Sanctuary* we found even more interesting. We had not hitherto understood Freud, or sympathized with his approach; but the moment someone presented his discoveries in a form more accessible to us, we were all enthusiasm. We had rejected those tools which the psychoanalysts offered us to pierce the "dark impenetrable core" set in every human heart. Faulkner skillfully breached the defenses and offered us a glimpse of fascinating depths beyond. It was not enough for Faulkner to *say* that behind the face of innocence unspeakable horrors lurked; he *showed* us. He stripped the pure young American girl of her mask; he made us feel, behind that soothing ritual with which the world is camouflaged, the tragic violence of need and desire, and the perversities which the thwarting of these emotions are liable to engender. In Faulkner's work sex quite literally brings fire and blood to the world. The inner drama of the individual is symbolized, externally, by rape, murder, and arson. The flames that toward the end of *Sanctuary* transform a man into a living torch are only superficially due to a can of gasoline: their true source lies in those secret, shameful fires that rage in the bellies of men and women alike.

The second name was that of Kafka, who assumed even greater importance for us. We had read the French translation of *Die Verwandlung* (*Metamorphosis*) in the *N.R.F.*, and had realized that the essayist who set Kafka on a level with Joyce and Proust was not being merely ridiculous. *The Trial* appeared, but created little excitement at the time, the critics showing a marked preference for Hans Fallada; but for us it was one of the finest and best books we had read in a very long while. We perceived at once that it was pointless to reduce it to mere allegory, or search through it for symbolical interpretations. What it expressed was a totalitarian vision of the world. By confusing the relationship between ends and means, Kakfa called in question the purpose not only of man's artifacts, functions, and activities qua individual, but also of his relationship to the world at large, globally considered. Merely by presenting his image of human society upside down (an idea which Sartre further developed in 1943 in his study of Blanchot) he made it not only fantastic but unbearable. K.'s story differed considerably from that of Antoine Roquantin, being far more drastic and despairing; but in both cases the hero found himself so remote from the context of his familiar surroundings that as far as he was concerned all rational order vanished, and he wandered alone and benighted through a strange shadowy wilderness. We conceived an immediate and deep-rooted admiration for Kafka; without being quite sure why, we felt that his work had personal significance for us. Faulkner and the rest told us stories remote from our own experience, but Kafka described *ourselves* to us: he openly stated the problems *we* faced, in a world that was without God, yet where our salvation still remained at stake. No father had embodied the idea of Law for us, yet that Law was, none the less, unalterably inscribed upon our hearts. It could not be deciphered by the light of universal reason: it was so unique, so secret, that we failed to spell it out for ourselves—though we knew at the same time that once we ceased to pursue it we were lost. As lost and lonely as Joseph K. and the surveyor, we groped our way through a fog where no visible link existed between our road and our destination. A voice told us to write. We obeyed; we covered page after page with our writing— but to what end? What sort of people would read us? And what would they read? The rigorous path along which some accident of fate forced our steps led into endless darkness. Sometimes a moment of illumination revealed our goal to us. Such-and-such a novel or essay had to be finished: there it gleamed on the distant horizon, perfect and complete. But it proved impossible to find the right phrases which, page by page, brought us slowly thither; we would end up somewhere else, or nowhere at all. Already we were coming to guess a truth of which we were continually reminded later, that there was neither limit nor sanction to this blind undertaking. Death would loom up abruptly, as it did for Joseph K., without any verdict having been pronounced: everything would remain in suspense.

We talked a great deal about Kafka and Faulkner when Sartre came to Paris for the Easter holidays. He sketched out the broad principles of the Husserlian system for me, together with the concept of "intentionality." This notion provided him with just what he had hoped for: a chance to get over the contradictions that at this period divided his mind, and which I have already mentioned. He had always been repelled by the idea of *"la vie intérieure"*: according to him this faculty was wholly eliminated as soon as the rational mind came into existence, which it did by continually leapfrogging over itself toward some specific object. Everything possessed an external situation and actuality: physical objects, statements of truth, emotions, meaning, even the self; it followed that no subjective factor could modify the truth concerning the world as it was presented to our senses. Rational mind still had the sovereignty, and the universe retained that "real presence" which Sartre had always claimed to guarantee. This formed a starting point for a radical revision of psychology, and Sartre had already begun to attack this task with his essay on the ego.

Soon he was off again, and I made the most of my final term. I saw a lot of my sister. She still lived at home with the family (but had rented a little studio attic in the Rue Castagnary—freezing in winter, roasting in summer—where she painted. She made a little money by working afternoons as a secretary at the Galerie Bonjean. Occasionally she would go to the Bal des Anglais, or a party at some studio with Francis Grüber and his band; but such diversions were rare. Her life was hard and austere from a practical point of view, and she bore it in a good-humored fashion which I much admired. I often took her with me to the theater. We both saw John Ford's *Tis Pity She's a Whore* at the Atelier, and I enjoyed this production greatly: the actors wore the same gorgeous hand-painted costumes that Valentine Hugo had created for *Romeo and Juliet*. (The play was advertised as *Dommage qu'elle soit une prostituée* [rather than *putain*]; this verbal squeamishness misrepresented both the original title and the point of the play. Sartre had Ford in mind when he used the word *putain* in the title of one of his own plays.) We both emotionalized over *Little Women;* the performance of a young beginner, Katherine Hepburn, as Jo Marsh, achieved the same sort of poignant attractiveness as I had imagined in my own adolescent dreams. I felt ten years younger after seeing it.

We also trailed assiduously around all the new art exhibitions; it was with my sister that, toward the end of June, I went to see Dali's first big show at the Galerie Bonjean. I also recollect having seen a good number of his pictures with Sartre, but am not sure when. Fernando had spoken unenthusiastically of the detailed, finicking works that Dali was placing under Meissonier's patronage; these fake color prints appealed to us. Surrealist tricks hinging on the ambiguity of substance or artifact had always intrigued us, and we appreciated Dali's liquefying watches; but what struck me most, personally, was the glazed, transparent quality of his landscapes, in which—even more than in Chirico's street scenes— I found the vertiginous, agonizing poetry produced by naked space receding to infinity. Here form and color seemed pure modulations of the void. It was when he made a detailed painting of some rocky Spanish hillside, such as I had seen with my own eyes, that he transported me furthest from reality, with a revelation of the missing, the inaccessible elements that underlie all our experience. Other painters of the period were busy "returning to humanism"; I did not approve of this gambit, and its results failed to convince me.

While Sartre was away I gave philosophy lessons to Lionel de Roulet, who was now living in Paris. He and a few friends had founded a so-called Merovingian Party, which advocated, by means of posters and pamphlets, the return of Chilperic's descendants to the throne. I scolded him for giving up, as I found, far too much time to such nonsense; but he had a natural talent for philosophy, and I felt very warmly toward him. He also made the acquaintance of my sister, and the two of them became great friends.

I made fairly frequent visits to Camille and Dullin, who had a place not far from Paris. The first time I called on her at the Rue Gabrielle after Sartre's departure, Camille made a great fuss over me. She was wearing a magnificent black velvet dress, and there was a bouquet of little black flowers, with yellow centers, stuck in her belt. "I want to seduce you," she told me gaily, and went on to assert that her feelings about me were liable to become all-demanding, even to the point of jealousy. She seemed to take this little joke half seriously, and I found myself unable to enter into the spirit of the thing. By the time we next met she had abandoned it. I sensed that she regarded me with friendly condescension; but her narcissism and her coquettish tricks had somewhat depreciated her in my eyes, and she had lost all her former power over me. Now I simply enjoyed her company, without any ulterior motives to worry me.

Dullin had bought a house at Ferrolles, near Crécy-en-Brie. The journey by train was rather complicated; and as Mademoiselle Ponthieu had told me that her boy friend drove her around the countryside every weekend, I asked her if they couldn't perhaps take me to Ferrolles. I suspected—rightly, as it turned out—that the idea of seeing a celebrity at close quarters would tempt them. Late one Saturday afternoon we reached Crécy, and from there climbed up to a hillside village. Camille welcomed us with glasses of port. My companions gazed in stupefaction at her country disguise, which consisted of a long homespun dress and several oddly colored shawls. She set the final seal on their astonishment by introducing them, as seriously as any mother, to her two dolls Friedrich and Albrecht. Dullin, for his part, sat there in silence, puffing at his pipe, and thoughtfully examining this middle-class French couple. After they drove off I explored the house, an old farm that Dullin and Camille had converted themselves. They had preserved its rustic atmosphere: the rough-cast walls were pink-washed, exposed oak beams ran across the ceilings, and in the open hearth a log fire was burning. They had furnished and decorated it with a mixture of exquisite antiques and theatrical bric-a-brac; their taste, though bold, was impeccable.

I stayed a day and a night on this occasion, and made several return visits. Dullin used to meet me at Crécy station, with an old-fashioned trap: he groomed the horse himself, and took pride in the job. All the time he was driving he ate chocolates, since Camille, for some obscure reason, had suddenly forbidden him to smoke. Camille's dinners were as carefully planned as her clothes and make-up. She used to order thrush pies and *foie gras* from Toulouse, and prepare the most complicated and delicious dishes. In summer we would spend the evening sitting out in their small, luxuriant garden. Dullin would tell stories and hum old songs. He was obviously devoted to Camille, but it was very hard to deduce anything about the real nature of their relationship, since when any third party

was present Camille turned her life into a theatrical performance, and he
followed her cue. It was, indeed, a very amusing performance: a comedy
duologue full of coquetry, sulks, fury, and tenderness.

I was not very attracted to Normandy, but I went for a few walks
with Olga through the sparse woodland around Rouen, and was glad to
take advantage of the spring holiday and stretch out for a bit in the warm
grass. One Sunday I went to have a look at a hotel which someone had
recommended to me at Lyons-la-Forêt. It turned out to be far too expensive for me; but while I was strolling around in the area I spotted
a hut in the middle of a field, near the Château de Rosay, its windows
glinting in the sun, and the word CAFÉ painted in giant letters on the
roof. I went in for a drink, and asked the proprietor if he had rooms to
rent. He offered me a little cottage some fifty yards off, with a thatched
roof on which iris was in bloom. The following week I spent five days
there. There were red tiles on the floor of my room, and I slept in a
farmhouse bed under a plumped-out blue eiderdown: at five in the morning
I awoke to the sound of cocks crowing. Eyes still shut, I let myself drift
between sleeping and waking, between mornings long past and the light
now welling up behind my shutters. When I opened the cottage door,
there was the green grass, and trees all in blossom. I would go and have
coffee, and put a table up under an apple tree, and become once more
that little girl doing her holiday task under the catalpa tree at Meyrignac.
It was to her that I was now offering what, in various forms, she had
so often dreamed of: a little house to herself.

At the end of June I was sent to examine in the *baccalauréat* examinations at Caen. Many of the candidates came from the Military Academy
at La Flèche. They sweated big drops in their blue serge uniforms, and
had a hunted air. The part I was playing in this brutal ritual did not
appeal to me at all, and I got around it by giving everyone a passing mark.
Between orals my amusements were few. I could not stand forever staring
at the local monastery and nunnery, so I buried myself with a book inside
the Brasserie Chandivert: I found its provincial jollity most depressing.
One afternoon some of my colleagues and I went canoeing on the Orne:
a mournful experience. Aron, who had replaced Sartre at Le Havre,
was one of my fellow examiners, and we had some pleasant suppers
together. I also met Politzer, who at this period was teaching at Evreux,
and who boasted that no one could mention the word "idealism" in front
of his pupils without their bursting out laughing. He took me out to
lunch in a little restaurant set below street level in one of the oldest squares
of Caen. I told him indignantly about the meeting at which the Communists had prevented Doriot speaking, and he laughed unrestrainedly
at my *petit bourgeois* liberalism. He then explained his own character
to me, according to the findings of graphology, which he regarded as an
exact science. His handwriting, he said, revealed traces of an unstable
and emotional substructure, but also of a firm, sensible superstructure,
thanks to which he could keep himself under control. His aggressively
Marxist language irked me, but there was in point of fact a most striking

contrast between his dogmatic statements and the charm and mobility of his features. I did not enjoy his conversation half so much as his gestures, his voice, his quick blushes, and the superb mop of fiery hair which Sartre borrowed from him for the character of Antoine Roquantin.

The orals finished a few days before July 14, and—faithful to my resolution that I would explore every aspect of the world—I made a trip around Trouville and Deauville, which filled me with a kind of delighted horror. I stopped at Bayeux to see Queen Matilda's famous tapestry. I walked along the cliffs above Granville. Then I returned to Rouen, and sat between Colette Audry and Simone Labourdin on Prizegiving Day. Forty-eight hours later I caught a train for Hamburg, where I had arranged to meet Sartre.

Despite the night of June 30, despite even the dismissal of Hindenburg, German anti-Nazis were still predicting Hitler's imminent collapse. Sartre wanted to believe them, but even so he was glad to be leaving Germany. We intended to make a tour of the country during our summer holidays, after which he would say goodbye to it and resume his teaching post at Le Havre.

Hamburg might be German, and Nazi, but it remained, first and foremost, a great port. There were ships and more ships—sailing, dropping anchor, idle in dock; there were sailors' dives, and every kind of debauchery. A large part of the out-of-bounds area had actually been blown up and demolished on grounds of public morality; but a few streets still remained, cut off by piles of rubble, where girls with frizzed hair and heavily painted faces displayed themselves behind well-polished windows. Their expressions never altered, nor did they move; you might have been looking at the dummies in a hairdresser's shop. We strolled along the quais and around the docks, and had lunch on the banks of the Alster. In the evenings we explored the slums and trouble spots. All this moving around gave us great pleasure. We went on a boat up the Elbe as far as the rock of Heligoland, where not a single tree grows. A German got into conversation with us: a man of about forty, wearing a black peaked cap and a somewhat morose expression. He told us he had been a sergeant in the 1914-18 war, and his voice gradually rose as he went on talking.

"If there's another war," he said, "we shall not be defeated this time. We shall retrieve our honor."

Sartre replied that there was no need of a war; we all ought to want peace.

"Honor comes first," the sergeant said. "First we must retrieve our honor."

His fanatical tone alarmed me. I tried to reassure myself with the reflection that an ex-serviceman is bound to hold militaristic views; yet how many such were there, who lived only for the moment when the great day of revenge would come? Never had I seen hatred shine so nakedly from any human face. All through our journey I did my best to forget it, but without success.

Through the quiet streets of Lübeck, with its fine red-roofed churches, and in Stralsond, where a pleasant sea wind whipped in our faces, we saw battalions of Brown Shirts marching past with their implacable tread. Yet under the beamed ceilings of the rathskellers people looked peaceful enough, sitting elbow to elbow, drinking beer and singing. Is it, I wondered, possible to love human warmth so much and yet dream of massacres? The two things seemed irreconcilable.

In any case we found the coarse German sort of "humanity" singulariy unattractive. We crossed Berlin and saw Potsdam, and had tea on the Isle of Swans. Among all the people around us, busily tucking away their whipped cream, there was not one face which aroused liking, or even so much as curiosity. With sad nostalgia we recalled Spanish bodegas and open-air cafés in Italy where our eyes had wandered so eagerly from one table to the next.

Dresden struck me as even uglier than Berlin. I have forgotten everything about it apart from a big flight of steps, and a reasonably picturesque panorama spread out far below us, "the Saxon Switzerland," as it was called. And while I was repairing my make-up in a café toilet, the attendant interrupted me angrily, saying: "No lipstick; is bad! In Germany we not put red on lips!"

We breathed more freely once across the frontier. The Prague boulevards were lined with French-style cafés, where we found once more a gaiety and ease that we had almost forgotten. The streets and medieval squares of the so-called poor quarter, not to mention the Jewish cemetery, we found charming. At night we stood for ages leaning over the parapet of the old bridge, among the stone saints frozen there for centuries now above the black water. We went into an almost empty dance hall; and as soon as the manager found out that we were French, the band struck up the "Marseillaise." The few scattered couples began to smile at us, and much to our embarrassment let out a cheer for France, and Barthou, and the Little Entente. It was a most depressing moment.

We were intending to visit Vienna; but as we came out of our hotel one morning, we saw crowds gathered in the streets, and people fighting for the latest papers, which carried banner headlines. We recognized the name of Dollfuss, and also a word beginning with *M*, the meaning of which we could guess. A German-speaking passer-by told Sartre the news: Dollfuss had been assassinated. Today I feel this was one more good reason for our going to Vienna at once. But we were so imbued with the characteristic optimism of the period that, for us, the true condition of the world *had* to be peace. Vienna in mourning, bereft of its airy graces, would be Vienna no longer. I hesitated to change my plans, out of pure indecision; but Sartre flatly refused to submit himself to the tedium of staying in any town that had been spoiled by so absurd a drama. We refused to consider the possibility that this attack upon Dollfuss might, on the contrary, show us the true face of Austria—and indeed of all Europe. Or perhaps Sartre suspected the truth, but could not bring himself to face the sinister reality he had been unable to escape during his nine months in Berlin—that Nazism was spreading right across Central Europe, and was far less of a mere "straw fire" than the Communists asserted.

At all events, we turned our backs on this tragedy and set off for Munich. We saw the pictures in the Pinacothek, and visited beer halls that were even more monstrous than the Vaterland in Berlin. Bavaria was rather spoiled for me by its inhabitants; I found it hard to stomach vast Bavarians who displayed their great hairy thighs while wolfing sausages. We had looked forward to the picturesque splendors of Nuremberg; but when we got there thousands of swastikas were still fluttering from the windows, and the pictures we had previously seen superimposed themselves with a sort of intolerable arrogance upon the actual scene—the giant parade, arms outstretched in salute, staring eyes, a whole people hypnotized. We were relieved to get out of the place. Things were different at Rothenburg, where the passing centuries had left no mark of change: here we walked through a medieval world—carefully refurbished, perhaps, but still enchanting. I know of no lake which can compare with the sheer perfection of the Königsee. A rack railway took us up over nine thousand feet to a summit of the Zugspitze. As we walked around we pondered a rather thorny problem. I don't know how we managed when we crossed over into Czechoslovakia; but now we had to cross the frontier once more, in order to visit Innsbruck, and it was illegal to take German currency out with us. We had exchanged it all for one high-denomination banknote, and now we wanted to hide this—but where? Finally Sartre concealed it at the bottom of a box of matches. The following day the customs official went through our books and toilet cases, but didn't bother about the matches, which Sartre had taken out of his pocket and put down with a lot of other small objects.

Even in Austria the atmosphere seemed lighter to us than it had been in Germany. We liked Innsbruck, and completely fell in love with Salzburg—its eighteenth-century houses, its innumerable unshuttered diamond windows, the exquisite signs swinging above the street doors: bears, swans, eagles, or stags, all wrought in fine patinated copper. There was a tiny puppet-theater where a group of charming marionettes were performing Mozart's *The Abduction from the Seraglio*. After a bus trip through the Salzkammergut we returned to Munich.

Dullin and Camille, backed by general public opinion, had most strongly advised us to see the celebrated Passion Play at Oberammergau. Performances took place every ten years, the last having been in 1930; but we were in luck, since 1934 was a Jubilee Year. The village had been struck by plague in 1633, and it was in 1634, in fulfillment of their vow, that the inhabitants had for the first time solemnly acted out the death of Jesus. There was, therefore, a special éclat about this year's festival, and never before had the place seen so great an influx of tourists. Performances had taken place every day for the past two months, and yet the agency to which we applied had the greatest difficulty in finding us a room. We got out of the bus late at night, with the rain pouring down, and wandered around for some time before finding our lodgings. We had been put in a house on the very edge of the village, where a tailor and his family lived. We had dinner with them and a couple from Munich, whom they were also putting up. It was a very Germanic meal, with potatoes doing duty for bread, and I found it highly indigestible. The couple from Munich eyed Sartre suspiciously. "You speak extremely good German," they told him, and added, disapprovingyly: "You haven't the least trace of an accent." Sartre was both flattered and embarrassed: they obviously took him for a spy. The rain slackened off a little, and we strolled out through the streets, with their brightly painted and decorated houses: the façades were a riot of carved flowers and animals, with volutes, garland motifs, and *trompe-l'oeil* windows. Despite the lateness of the hour we could hear the noise of saws and planes in action. Nearly all the villagers were woodcarvers, and in their shop windows we could see masses of ghastly little figurines. The bars were all crammed full, and tourists found themselves rubbing shoulders with long-haired, bearded men: the actors themselves, who had been busy for years rehearsing their parts in the Passion Play. The Christus was the same as in 1930, and the son of the man who had taken the part in 1920 and 1910; his grandfather, too, had been the Christus, and indeed the part had never gone outside the family for very many years. Lights went out early here: the curtain was due to go up at eight o'clock the following morning. We went back to our lodgings. All the rooms had been taken and we were relegated to a lean-to shed, full of planks and shavings, with earwigs running about in it. A tailor's dummy stood guard in one corner, and we slept on the ground, on straw pailasses. Rainwater gathered in drops across the ceiling.

We had little taste for displays of traditional folk-culture, but the Oberammergau Passion Play was great theater. We went through various tunnel-like passages and emerged in a vast hall that held twenty thousand spectators. The performance ran from eight till midday, and from two till six in the afternoon; and not for one instant did our attention falter. The stage was both wide and deep enough to make vast crowd scenes possible, and each performer put such conviction into his part that one felt personally involved with the mob that acclaimed Christ, or jeered at him through the streets of Jerusalem. Scenes of action alternated with dumb, motionless *tableaux vivants*. A women's choir provided a commentary on the drama, to the accompaniment of some extremely pleasant eighteenth-century music: their long, wavy locks, falling over their shoulders, put me in mind of old-fashioned advertisements for shampoo. As for the style of acting, it would have delighted Dullin's heart, so sinewy and competent was it: the cast achieved a kind of truthfulness which had nothing to do with realism. For instance, Judas counted out all his thirty pieces of silver, one after the other; but the gesture was governed by so unexpected— and yet so inevitable—a rhythm that far from boring the audience, it held them breathless. The villagers of Oberammergau had anticipated Brecht's principles: the Passion Play's beautiful effects were achieved by a most remarkable blend of precision and "distancing."

All the same, we had had quite enough of Germany. The plebiscite of August 19 guaranteed Hitler absolutely unlimited dictatorial powers, and Austria too was going Nazi. We were enormously relieved to find ourselves back in France again, though disenchantment followed soon enough: Doumergue's paternalism was almost as tyrannical as a genuine dictatorship. Still, it did our hearts good to read the solemn cant that was printed in the papers—even if behind this smokescreen of pious moralizing the extremists of the Right were gradually consolidating their position. As I usually did, I put politics out of my mind, and gave my undivided attention to Strasbourg, with its Cathedral and "Little Paris." That evening we saw one of the first color films, *The Mystery of the Wax Museum,* which had drawn protests from Paris audiences. The frightful screams of poor Fay Wray, who had been stuck in horror films ever since *King Kong,* we found highly amusing. I loved the villages of Alsace, the châteaux and pine trees and lakes and gently sloping vineyards; we sat in the sunshine outside country inns drinking Riquewihr and Traminer. We ate *foie gras* and sauerkraut and *quiche Lorraine.* We visited Colmar. Sartre had often discussed Grünewald's pictures with me, and he had not fallen prey to a mere youthful illusion. Every time I have been back to see them again—the thorn-racked Christ, the livid, fainting Virgin, alive, yet petrified with sorrow—I have experienced the same deep emotional reaction.

Sartre was so taken with this countryside that he himself suggested following the line of the hills on foot. Three days' walking from Les Trois Epis brought us to Hohneck, Machstein, and Ballon d'Alsace. Such luggage as we had, we carried in our pockets. A colleague of Sartre's that we met near the Col de la Schlucht asked us where we were staying. "Nowhere," Sartre told him, "we're walking." His friend appeared disconcerted, Sartre made up songs as we went, and sang them with cheerful verve, though their words were inspired by the uncertain world situation. I remember one verse that went:

> Alas, alas, who would have thought it?
> All of us, all of us soon will have bought it,
> Mown down without mercy like dogs in the street:
> Isn't Progress sweet?

I believe it was then that he also composed *"La Rue des Blancs-Manteaux,"* which he afterward made Inès sing in *Huis Clos (No Exit).*

Sartre left me at Mulhouse, and went off to spend two weeks with his family. Pagniez, who was camping in Corsica with his sister and two cousins, had invited me to join them there. I embarked at Marseille just before nightfall. I had booked a deck passage, and made the crossing dozing in a deck chair. I found it an intoxicating experience to sleep out under the stars: I would half open my eyes, and there was the sky above me! As dawn broke, a faint scent reached the boat, a burnt, earthy smell: the smell of the maquis.

I now discovered the delights of camping. It always gave me a thrill to see the tents standing there in the evening, in some grassy meadow or on the soft mossy floor of a chestnut forest. They were so light and flimsy, yet at the same time so safe, so hospitable. Their material scarcely separated me from earth and sky; yet on two or three occasions it protected me against the violence of a storm. By sleeping in a movable house I had fulfilled another old childhood dream, inspired by gypsy caravans and Jules Verne's *La Maison à vapeur*. But there was something peculiarly charming about the way a tent was dismantled in the morning and reborn at nightfall. Although the last Corsican bandits had been arrested, the island attracted few visitors: we did not meet a single camper or tourist. The range and variety of scenery was quite astonishing. A day's journey on foot was enough to bring you down from chestnut forests such as can be found in Limousin to a wholly Mediterranean landscape. I left, with crimson, blue, and gold memories sparkling in my mind.

Chapter 4

B ETWEEN OCTOBER, 1934, AND MARCH, 1935, THE political situation became—as far as the general public was concerned, at least—increasingly confused. The economic crisis worsened: Salmson laid off workers, Citroën went bankrupt, and the number of unemployed rose to two million. A wave of xenophobia hit France: it was out of the question to employ Italian or Polish labor while Frenchmen were out of a job. Students of the extreme Right made furious demonstrations against foreign students, whom they accused of wanting to take the bread out of their mouths. The case of Inspector Bonny reminded people of the Stavisky scandal: during the libel action which he brought against the weekly paper *Gringoire,* Bonny was proved guilty—in particular by Mademoiselle Cotillon's testimony—of blackmail, bribery, and corruption. In January the Saar, by a ninety per cent majority, voted for secession to Germany. Anti-democratic propaganda became increasingly virulent. The Croix de Feu movement gained ground daily: the weekly *Candide* became its official organ, and Colonel de la Roque, with considerable publicity, brought out his program under the title of *La Révolution.* Carbuccia meanwhile was upholding a somewhat different sort of fascism in *Gringoire,* which, at the end of 1934, had a circulation of 650,000: it was my father's favorite periodical. All these right-wing Nationalists were hoping for the appearance of a French Hitler, and eager to fight against the German Führer; they demanded an extension of national service to two full years. But meanwhile Laval had been appointed Minister for Foreign Affairs, and we now saw the emergence and consolidation of a right-wing neopacifist movement. Mussolini was getting ready to invade Ethiopia, and Laval signed a treaty with him, giving him a free hand. He negotiated with Hitler. A certain number of intellectuals fell into step behind him. Drieu proclaimed his sympathy with the Nazi movement. Ramon Fernandez left the revolutionary organizations to which he had belonged, remarking that he preferred trains which actually left the station. The Radical-Socialist weekly *Marianne* backed Laval. Emmanuel Berl, Jew though he was, wrote: "When . . . one is determined to view Germany in as *just* and as *friendly* a light as possible, one cannot call this decision in question simply because Herr Hitler has announced legal sanctions against the Jews."

The Left, too, had its problems. In June, 1934, Alain, Langevin, Rivet, and Pierre Gérôme had formed the Anti-Fascist Committee, with the aim of stopping the drift toward reaction. They denounced German anti-Semitism, and protested against the system of imprisonment and deportation now rampant in Italy. On the crucial question of peace versus war they refused to support either Colonel de la Roque or Pierre Laval. All the anti-Fascists admitted that the time for "total pacifism" was now over. In 1932 Victor Margueritte had vigorously defended the conscientious objector's position against Communist opposition, but now he admitted the inadequacy of such an attitude. He supported Langevin's appeal in favor of action by the masses, who, as he also thought, alone were capable of checking the advance of Fascism. Nevertheless they unanimously asserted that war both could and must be avoided. On this point Alain, Rivet, and Langevin wrote in one of their joint manifestoes: "Let us beware of spreading the lies peddled by the reactionary press," while Guéhenno stubbornly repeated that it was essential to desire peace. As for the Communists, their position had grown steadily more ambiguous during these last six months. They voted against the two-year conscription law; and yet, when they were faced with the fact of German rearmament, they had no objection to supporting an increase in French military forces. These vacillations gave me a chance to preserve my own peace of mind. Since no one really understood what was happening, I argued, why not admit that it was nothing really serious? And so, tranquilly enough, I once more picked up the threads of my private life.

I knew that my last novel was worthless, and I had not the heart to risk another failure. It was better to read and improve my mind, I decided, while waiting for a favorable inspiration. History was one of my weak points, so I decided to study the French Revolution. I ordered Buchez and Roux's collection of primary sources from the Rouen Public Library. I read Aulard and Mathiez, and plunged into Jaurès's *Histoire de la Révolution*. I found this research work exciting in the extreme. The impenetrable events cluttering up the past suddenly became intelligible to me, and their sequence acquired a meaning. I worked at this subject as meticulously as I would have done for an examination. I also dipped into Husserl for the first time. Sartre had told me all he knew about Husserl: now he presented me with the German text of *Leçons sur la conscience interne du temps,* which I stumbled through without too much difficulty. Every time we met we would discuss various passages in it. The novelty and richness of phenomenology filled me with enthusiasm; I felt I had never come so close to the real truth.

These studies kept me busy enough. I saw no one in Rouen now apart from Colette Audry and Olga, who was having a second try at her preliminary medical examinations. The previous year she had worked very dutifully for one term, and her teachers were very pleased with her; then she had gotten mixed up with her Polish friends, and ceased to be a resident student.

Freedom had gone to her head. She now spent all day and night walking, dancing, listening to music, having discussions, and reading; she had completely given up working for her exams. The setback had annoyed her far too much for her to think of trying to make up for lost time during the vacation. At the moment her friends were scattered, some being in Paris and others in Italy; the only people she saw were French, and these she did not care for. She had lost all enthusiasm for her work, which bored her, and the prospect of a second failure, with trouble from her parents to follow, made her feel absolutely miserable. It was only in my company that she regained a little self-confidence and zest for life: I was touched by this, and went out with her fairly frequently. Louise Perron was convalescing in Auvergne; Simone Labourdin had been appointed to a post in Paris; and I had given up seeing Mademoiselle Ponthieu. I no longer felt the need to kill time, since once again I was spending nearly all my free time with Sartre.

He was working extraordinarily hard. The second version of his book had been finished in Berlin, and I liked it. At the same time I agreed with Madame Lemaire and Pagniez in feeling that Sartre had overdone his adjectives and comparisons; he now intended to make a scrupulous revision of every single page. But he had also been invited to write a work on the imaginative function, for a series published by the house of Alcan. This had been the subject of his *diplôme d'études,* with which he had won a prize and a special distinction. The problem interested him: he abandoned Antoine Roquantin and returned to psychology. Nevertheless, he hoped to get through this task quickly, and gave himself little respite.

We generally met in Le Havre, which struck us as being a more cheerful place than Rouen. I loved the old docks, and the quais with their sailors' dives and disreputable hotels, and the narrow houses, their slate roofs pulled down over their eyes: one façade was plastered from top to bottom with sea shells. The most attractive street in this area was the Rue des Galions, all lighted up at night with its multicolored signs— the Chat Noir, the Lanterne Rouge, the Moulin Rose, the Etoile Violette. Everyone in Le Havre knew it. Between two brothels, each guarded by a tough pimp, was that renowned restaurant, La Grosse Tonne; we went there occasionally to sample the *sole normande* and *soufflé au calvados.* Most of the time we ate in the big Brasserie Paillette, a quiet and commonplace establishment. We spent hours on end in the Café Guillaume Tell, where Sartre often settled down to write; with its red plush banquettes and plate-glass bay windows it was a very comfortable sort of place. The people with whom we rubbed elbows in the streets and public squares were a more animated and motley crowd than the good folk of Rouen. The reason for this was that Le Havre was a big port, where people from all parts of the world mingled. A lot of big business was handled there by up-to-date methods; the inhabitants lived in the present instead of burying themselves in the shadows of the past. When it was fine weather we sat out on the veranda of a little bistro near the beach, called Les Mouettes. I would eat plums in brandy and gaze at the green and choppy sea, far away in the middle distance. We strolled down the broad central boulevards, climbed up to Sainte-Adresse, and wandered through lanes high above the city, lined with wealthy villas. In Rouen there were always walls to block my vision; here one's eye could travel to the horizon, and a fresh wind blew in my face from the uttermost parts of the earth. Two or three times we took a boat across to Honfleur. This little slate-built port, where the past seemed to have survived in all its freshness, we found a charming place.

Sometimes, for a change, Sartre would come to Rouen. In October a fair was held, all along the boulevards that encircled the town, and we played each other at Russian billiards. We visited a tiny puppet theater and saw a performance that had all the elegance of a Méliès film: in one scene a vastly fat old woman was transformed into an aeronautical balloon, and floated off into the flies. One afternoon, at Colette Audry's suggestion, we decided to visit the Museum. Its proudest possession was a fine classical painting by David, which made no impression on us at all. What did amuse us was the collection of portraits by Jacques-Emile Blanche, which showed us the faces of our contemporaries, such as Drieu, Montherlant, Gide, or Giraudoux. I lingered in front of one picture which I had seen, as a child, reproduced on the cover of *Petit Français illustré,* and which had made a great impression on me—"Les énervés de Jumièges." I had been bothered by the paradoxical implications of the word *énervé,* which was the wrong word to use in the title, since the first meaning that came to my mind was an improper one, whereas it was the tendons of the two dying men which had been severed. They lay side by side on a flat barge; and as they drifted downstream, tormented by hunger and thirst, toward their dreadful end, their very inertia wore the appearance of beatitude. It mattered little to me that the painting as such was an abominable piece of work: for a long while afterward I remained conscious of the quiet horror it evoked.

We looked around for new places where it would be pleasant to sit and talk. Opposite a dance hall called Le Royal there was a little bar, L'Océanie, popular with a group of young middle-class people who affected Bohemianism, and called themselves "The Vagrants." In the evening the hostesses from Le Royal would drop in there for a drink and some gossip. We began to patronize the place regularly; we also abandoned the Brasserie Paul for a café-restaurant called Chez Alexandre, which Sartre took as a rough model for Chez Camille in *Nausea.* There were about half a dozen marble-topped tables, bathed winter and summer alike in an aquariumlike glow. The *patron,* a bald and melancholy man, acted as his own waiter, and the menu consisted almost entirely of egg dishes or stew out of cans. Being romantic by nature, we suspected Alexandre of trafficking in drugs. Apart from ourselves almost the only customers were three young "kept" women, quite attractive creatures, who as far as we could make out lived only for clothes. They displayed a wide range of emotions during their discussions; hope, despair, anger, jubilation, pride, chagrin, envy—all these stirred them, but solely with reference to some dress that had been offered or refused them, that was a success or a failure. In the middle of the saloon there stood a Russian billiard table, and we used to play a game or two before and after our meals. How much spare time we had in those days! Sartre also taught me the basic rules of chess. It was the most popular period for crossword puzzles, too, and every Wednesday we pored over the one in *Marianne,* besides solving the rebus. We enjoyed Dubout's early cartoons, and Jean Effel's first sketches of Academicians, and the comic-strip adventures of Soglow's "Little King."

From time to time we received visits from friends. Marco was expecting to be posted to Rouen the following year, so he made a somewhat suspicious inspection of the town. "Just like Bône," he announced, to our great astonishment. He had a new singing teacher now, far better than his last one, he said. In a very short while he would pass his audition before *Monsieur le Directeur de l'Opéra,* and without further delay be launched upon his triumphal career.

Fernando and Stépha were back in Paris again, living in a very pleasant studio near Montparnasse. Stépha had been to see her mother in Lvov, and had stayed on for a few days in Central Europe. She spent a day with us in Rouen, and we took her to the Brasserie de l'Opéra, where we occasionally treated ourselves—for fifteen francs—to a really first-class meal. Stépha's eyes widened in surprise. "These *enormous* steaks!" she exclaimed. "And strawberries and cream! Imagine *petits bourgeois* eating on this scale!" In Lvov or Vienna such a dinner would have cost a small fortune. It had never occurred to me that diet could vary so much between one country and the next; I found it very odd to hear Stépha muttering about how well-nourished the French were.

Madame Lemaire and Pagniez visited us several times. We split a *canard au sang* between us at the Hôtel de la Couronne, and they took us out in their car to see Caudebec, Saint-Wandrille, and Jumièges Abbey. We returned late at night by a road overlooking the Seine, and stopped to look at the Grand-Couronne factory buildings on the far side. They were all lit up in the darkness, and looked exactly like gigantic but motionless fireworks, a set piece under the black vault of the sky. "A beautiful sight," Pagniez said. Sartre rubbed his nose. "It's a factory," he said. "People work all night there." Pagniez maintained, somewhat impatiently, that this didn't affect its beauty. But according to Sartre, he was letting himself be taken in by a mere mirage. Where was the beauty in sweated labor and exhaustion? I was very struck by this argument, which left me in a state of some perplexity—and later inspired a similar discussion between Henri and Nadine in *The Mandarins,* when they are looking at the lights of Lisbon.

Our most unexpected guest was Nizan, who came down to speak at a meeting. He was dressed in a carefully casual style, and carried a splendid brand-new umbrella over the crook of his arm. "I bought it out of my traveling expenses," he told us; he loved giving himself little presents. In 1933 he had published his first novel, *Antoine Bloyé,* which had been well received by the critics; he was now regarded as a "promising young writer." (We misinterpreted this novel even more than *Aden Arabie*: we assumed it to be a Populist tract. In his preface to the new edition of Nizan's works Sartre has stated how false such a view appears to us today.) He had just spent a year in the U.S.S.R. and, together with Malraux, Aragon, and Jean-Richard Bloch, had attended the Congress of Revolutionary Writers. "It was a most corrupting period for me," he said, gnawing his nails with some complacency. He told us of vast banquets where the vodka flowed in rivers, and rhapsodized over Georgian wines; the *wagons-lits* were so comfortable, hotel rooms absolutely magnificent. His casual tone somehow contrived to suggest that this luxury reflected vast general Russian prosperity. He described a village down in the South, near the Turkish frontier: it was brimful of local color, it seemed, complete with veiled women, markets, and Oriental bazaars. His artful tricks delighted us. The friendly, almost confidential key in which his conversation was pitched excluded any suggestion of propaganda, and certainly he wasn't telling positive lies. But from the truths at his disposal he carefully chose those most likely to appeal to the anarchic-metaphysical element in his old friend Sartre. He talked to us about a writer called Olesha, who was still unknown in France. From a novel published in 1927 Olesha had extracted one section called "The Emotional Conspiracy," and this had proved a tremendous success in Moscow. It was an ambiguous work: although it attacked bureaucratic crimes and the dehumanized condition of Soviet society, it also, in a weird and roundabout way undertook the defense of the regime. (Was this conviction or discretion?) "Sartre *is* Olesha," Nizan said, and this whetted our curiosity. But Olesha's novel did not appear in France till 1936, when it was published in the "Feux Croisés" series as *L'Envie* (*Envy*), and turned out to be a genuinely seductive and disconcerting piece of work. But we found Nizan most intriguing when he approached anywhere near his pet obsession, the idea of death. Though he never openly alluded to the fact, we knew how anguished a state he could get into at the thought of one day vanishing for all eternity: he would trail round for days on end from one cheap bar to the next, drinking glass after glass of cheap red wine to keep this terrifying prospect at bay. He had asked himself whether the Socialist creed might not somehow help him to exorcise it, and felt quite optimistic as to the prospects; but his lengthy interrogation of young Russian Communists concerning this topic had elicited a unanimous reply—in the face of death, comradeship and solidarity were no help at all, and they were all scared of death themselves. Officially—as, for instance, when he was reporting on his trip abroad at some meeting— Nizan interpreted facts in an optimistic way. To the extent that progress was made in solving technical problems, he explained, love and death would regain their former importance in the U.S.S.R.: a new humanism was being born. But in private conversation with us he spoke very differently. It had been a great blow to him to discover that, in Russia as in France, the individual was alone when he died, and knew it.

The Christmas holidays were marked by one important new venture, in which I took the initiative—or at any rate, I thought so at the time: I have since come to realize that quite often my "discoveries" merely reflect a contemporary fashion. For some while winter sports, previously the privilege of the few, had been within reach of those with more modest incomes, who were beginning to go in for them with great enthusiasm. The previous year Lionel de Roulet, who had spent his childhood in the Alps and knew all there was to be known about Telemarks and Christies, took my sister and Gégé and various other friends to Val d'Isère. It was a small village, with little in the way of skiing aids; but they enjoyed themselves hugely nevertheless. I could not bear the idea of foregoing a pleasure once it was within my reach, and I persuaded Sartre to come with me. We borrowed the basic kit, some here, some there, and went off to a little *pension* at Montroc, above the Chamonix Valley. There we rented some old skis, which did not even have metal runners. Every morning and every afternoon we turned up at the same easy beginners slope, plodded to the summit, skied down to the bottom, and then began all over again. There were several other beginners, like us, feeling their way slowly. A ten-year-old peasant boy showed us how to make a turn. Despite its monotony, the sport amused us: we enjoyed the process of learning, irrespective of the end in view. Besides, I had never before experienced anything like this odorless, colorless, blindingly white landscape, its crystalline surface iridescent in the sunlight. We would trudge back to our *pension* at nightfall, skis on our shoulders, hands swollen with the cold. We drank tea and read a volume on human geography which taught us the differences between "ground-planned" and "elevated" houses. We had also brought along a massive textbook of physiology; we were particularly interested in the nervous system, and recent research work on chronaxia. How wonderful it was to venture forth each morning into this vast, cold world—and how wonderful to return every evening to the warmth and intimacy that lay behind those four walls! Those ten days were as smooth and sparkling as a snowfield under a blue sky.

One day in November we were sitting on the veranda of our seaside café in Le Havre, Les Mouettes, and complaining at length about the monotony of our future existence. Our two lives were bound up together; our friendships were fixed and determined to all eternity; our careers were traced out, and our world moving forward on its predestined track. We were both still the right side of thirty, and yet nothing new would ever happen to us! Ordinarily I did not take such complaints very seriously; but there were occasions when I slipped from my Mount Olympus. If I drank a little too much one evening I was liable to burst into floods of tears, and my old hankering after the Absolute would be aroused again. Once more I would become aware of the vanity of human endeavor and the imminence of death; I would reproach Sartre for allowing himself to be duped by that hateful mystification known as "life." The following day I would still be suffering from the effects of this revelation. One afternoon, when we were walking round that grass-patched, chalky hillside overlooking the Seine near Rouen, we became involved in a long argument. Sartre denied that the truth could be found in a flood of tears and wine; according to him alcohol depressed me physically, and it was a fallacy for me to explain my condition in terms of metaphysics. I maintained, on the other hand, that intoxication broke down those controls and defenses that normally protect us against unpalatable truths, and forced us to face reality. Today I believe that, under the specially privileged conditions in which I exist, life contains two main truths which we must face simultaneously, and between which there is no choice—the joy of being, the horror of being no more. At the time I vacillated between one and the other. It was only for brief moments that the second triumphed, but I had a suspicion it might be the more valuable of the two.

I had another worry besides this: I was getting old. Neither my general health nor my facial appearance bore witness to the fact, but from time to time I felt that everything was going gray and colorless around me, and began to lament the decrepitude of my senses. I was still capable of going into one of my "tranced" states, but I nevertheless had a feeling of irreparable loss. The excitement of all the discoveries I had made after leaving the Sorbonne had gradually ebbed away. My curiosity still found matter on which to feed, but there were no more fresh and blinding revelations. And yet reality was abundantly present all around me; the mistake I made was in not attempting to penetrate it. I boxed it up in more or less outworn systems or myths, such as the cult of the picturesque. It struck me that life was moving in a circle because I was. Even so, this depressed mood did not disturb my life very seriously.

Sartre had completed the critical chapters of the book on L'Imagination that Professor Delacroix had commissioned from him for the Alcan series, and was now embarked upon a second and far more original section. In this he followed the problem of the image back to its basic origins, utilizing for the purpose phenomenological concepts such as purposiveness [intentionalité] and hylism. It was now that he crystallized the first key concepts of his philosophy: the conscious mind as tabula rasa, and its capacity for annihilation [néantisation]. This line of research, where he had to formulate both method and content, drawing on personal experience for all his material, required considerable concentration. Since there were no formal considerations to hold him up, he wrote with incredible speed, breathlessly driving his pen in pursuit of his thoughts. This hasty yet sustained creative effort, in contrast to his more literary labors, drained him of energy.

He took a marked interest in dreams, dream-induced imagery, and anomalies of perception. In February one of his former fellow students, Dr. Lagache (who had passed his state examinations the year Sartre failed, qualified as a medical practitioner, and specialized in psychiatry) suggested that he should come to Sainte-Anne's Hospital and undergo a mescaline injection. This drug induced hallucinations, and Sartre would be able to observe the phenomenon in himself. Lagache warned him that it would be a mildly disagreeable experience, although not in the least dangerous. The worst that could happen was that Sartre might "behave rather oddly" for a few hours afterward.

I spent the appointed day with Madame Lemaire and Pagniez at their place on the Boulevard Raspail. Late that afternoon, as we had arranged, I telephoned Sainte-Anne's, to hear Sartre telling me, in a thick, blurred voice, that my phone call had rescued him from a battle with several devil-fish, which he would almost certainly have lost. Half an hour later he arrived. He had been made to lie down on a bed in a dimly lit room, he said. He had not exactly had hallucinations, but the objects he looked at changed their appearance in the most horrifying manner: umbrellas had become vultures, shoes turned into skeletons, and faces acquired monstrous characteristics, while behind him, just past the corner of his eye, swarmed crabs and polyps and grimacing Things. One of the internes was amazed at these reactions; on him, as he told Sartre when the session was over, mescaline had produced wholly different effects. *He* had gone romping through flowery meadows, full of exotic houris. Sartre reflected, a little regretfully, that if he had waited till his nightmares turned into some-thing more pleasant, he too might have gravitated toward such paradisaic visions. But he had been influenced by Lagache's predictions. He spoke listlessly, staring all the time in a distrustful way at the telephone cord that ran across the carpet. In the train he said very little. I was wearing a pair of crocodile-skin shoes, the laces of which ended in two acornlike objects; he expected to see them turn into gigantic dung beetles at any moment. There was also an orangutan, doubtless hanging on to the roof of the carriage by its feet, which kept its leering face glued to the window. The next day Sartre was quite himself again, and talked about Sainte-Anne's with cheerful detachment.

A Sunday or two later Colette Audry came with me to Le Havre. Normally with people he liked, Sartre put himself out to be pleasant, and I was amazed at his surliness on this occasion. We walked along the beach collecting starfish, and hardly a word was exchanged between us. Sartre looked as though he had no idea what Colette and I—or indeed he himself—were doing there. I was somewhat irritated when I left him.

The next time we met, he explained what had happened. For several days he had been in a state of deep depression, and the moods that came upon him recalled those that had been induced by mescaline. This frightened him. His visual faculties became distorted: houses had leering faces, all eyes and jaws, and he couldn't help looking at every clockface he passed, expecting it to display the features of an owl—which it always did. He knew perfectly well that such objects were in fact houses and clocks, and no one could say that he *believed* in their eyes and gaping maws—but a time might well come when he *would* believe in them; one day he would really be convinced that there was a lobster trotting along behind him. Already he had a black spot persistently dancing about in his line of vision, at eye level. One afternoon, as we were walking along the left bank of the Seine at Rouen through a wilderness of railway tracks, sidings, dump trucks, and patches of leprous grass, he said abruptly: "I know what the matter with me is: I'm on the edge of a chronic hallucinatory psychosis." As defined at the time, this was an illness which in ten years would inevitably produce total insanity. I disagreed violently—not, for once, because of my natural optimism, but through plain common sense. Sartre's symptoms were not in the least like those produced by the onset of psychotic hallucinations. Neither the black spot nor his obsession with houses that gnashed their jaws suggested the inception of an incurable psychosis. Besides, I knew how readily Sartre's imagination tended toward disaster. "Your only madness," I told him, 'is believing that you're mad." "You'll see," he replied gloomily.

I saw nothing, apart from this depression of his, which he had the greatest difficulty in shaking off. Sometimes, though, he managed to do so. At Easter we went down to the Italian Lakes; we took a canoe out on Lake Como, and one night we saw a torchlight procession in the narrow streets of Bellagio, and all the time Sartre seemed in very high spirits. But after our return to Paris he could not even pretend to be in a normal state. Fernando had an exhibition of paintings at the Galerie Bonjean; and all through the day of the *vernissage* Sartre sat huddled in a corner, his face expressionless, not saying a word. Whereas a short time ago he missed nothing, now he simply did not bother to look. Sometimes we would sit side by side in a café or walk down the street together without a word passing between us. Madame Lemaire, who thought he had been overworking, sent him to see one of her friends who was a doctor. The doctor, however, refused to grant him a certificate of leave; in his opinion what Sartre needed was as little solitude and leisure as possible. He did, however, prescribe a small dose of belladonna morning and evening. Sartre therefore went on with his teaching and writing; and it is true that he was less liable to fall a prey to his fears when there was someone with him. He began to go out a lot with two of his former pupils, of whom he was very fond, Albert Palle and Jacques Bost, who was Pierre Bost's youngest brother: their presence protected him from crabs and similar monsters. When I was busy teaching in Rouen, Olga kept him company, and became very attached to her role of nurse-companion. Sartre told her endless stories, which amused her and distracted him from his own problems.

Doctors have told me that the mescaline could not possibly have provoked this attack. All that his session at Sainte-Anne's did for Sartre was to furnish him with certain hallucinatory patterns. It was, beyond any doubt, the fatigue and tension engendered by his philosophical research work that brought his fears to the surface again. We afterward concluded that they were the physical expression of a deep emotional malaise: Sartre could not resign himself to going on to "the age of reason," to full manhood.

When he was in residence at the Ecole Normale, there was a fine old song and dance about the miserable future in store for students there, and I have already described how even then he loathed the prospect. But afterward he was so delighted to have finished his period of military service that he cheerfully put up with his first two years as a teacher: the novelty of this new existence helped him to endure it. In Berlin he had recaptured both the freedom and the gaiety of his life as a student, which made it all the harder for him to get back into the serious daily routine proper to an adult. The discussion we had had in Les Mouettes about the aridity of our future had by no means been a casual piece of chitchat as far as he was concerned. He liked his pupils, and enjoyed teaching; but he detested having to deal with headmaster, senior master, colleagues, and parents. The horror which *les salauds,* as he called them, inspired in him was not merely a theme for literature. He felt weighed down by this bourgeois world; it held him prisoner. He was not married, and he still had a certain measure of freedom, but all the same his life was bound up with mine. Now at the age of thirty he was setting out upon a fore-ordained road, and his only adventures would consist of the books he wrote. The first had been turned down; the second still needed work done on it. As for his book *L'Image,* Alcan had kept only the first part, which was published as *L'Imagination (The Psychology of Imagination);* and he foresaw that the second section, which interested him much more, would not be published for a very long time. We both had an absolute confidence in his future; but the future will not always suffice to brighten present prospects. Sartre had thrown himself so wholeheartedly into the business of being young that when his youth finally would leave him he would need strong enchantments indeed to afford him consolation.

As I have said already, despite appearances I was in a quite different position from his. To acquire a teacher's certificate and have a profession was something he took for granted. But when I stood at the top of that flight of steps in Marseille I had turned dizzy with sheer delight: it seemed to me that, far from enduring my destiny, I had deliberately chosen it. The career in which Sartre saw his freedom foundering still meant liberation to me. Besides, as Rilke wrote of Rodin, Sartre was "his own heaven," and consequently always doubtful, always surrounded by uncertainties. But for me there was no doubt at all where he was concerned; for me his mere existence justified the world—though there was nothing that could perform the same service for him.

My own experience, then, made it impossible for me to understand the causes of his depression. In any case, as should be clear by now, psychology was not my strong suit, and I was especially determined to avoid using it on Sartre. To me he stood for pure mind and radical freedom; I would not consider him as a sport of obscure circumstances, a mere passive object. I preferred to think that he produced these fears and delusions of his because of some perverse streak in his character, and his breakdown I found far more irksome than alarming. I argued and reasoned with him, and attacked him for the resigned way in which he accepted his fate as a fact. I regarded this as a kind of treachery: he had no right to indulge such whims when they threatened the fabric of our joint existence. There was a good deal of cowardice about this way of dodging the truth, but clear-mindedness would not have done me much good either. I could not have solved Sartre's actual difficulties for him; I lacked both the experience and the skill that were needed to cure him of these temporary worries. But if I had shared his anxiety I most certainly would have been no help at all to him; so no doubt my anger was a healthy reaction.

Sartre's crisis dragged on, with various ups and downs, until the holidays; its shadow lies across all my recollections of that term. As in previous years, however, I was at great pains to educate—and entertain—myself. There was an important art exhibition entitled "Painters of Reality" which introduced us to Georges de La Tour; the best works in the Grenoble Museum were brought to Paris for the occasion, and I came to appreciate Zurbaran, whom I had ignored when we were in Spain. I went to Mozart's *Don Giovanni,* which the Opéra had taken into their repertoire the previous year. At the Atelier I saw Copeau's production of *As You Like It,* and a play by Calderón called *Physician of His Own Honor,* in which Dullin had one of his best parts. I went to all the films starring Joan Crawford, Jean Harlow, Bette Davis, James Cagney, Ginger Rogers, Fred Astaire, and I also saw *Crime Without Passion* and *The Whole Town's Talking.*

My way of reading the papers remained decidedly frivolous. As I have said, I avoided all problems posed by Hitler's political activities, and regarded the rest of the world with an indifferent eye. Venizelos attempted an unsuccessful *coup d'état* in Greece, and Governor Huey Long wielded his weird dictatorship over Louisiana, but I cared nothing for such incidents. The only thing that did arouse my concern was the situation in Spain. The workers had staged uprisings in Catalonia and Asturias, but the right-wing government then in power suppressed them with savage brutality.

Among lesser events which made the headlines I recall the assassination of King Alexander I of Yugoslavia and Jean-Louis Barthou, in Marseille; the wedding of Princess Marina; the trial in Budapest of a train wrecker named Martuska, who asserted that not he but his hypnotist should be held responsible; and a series of mysterious deaths in the Galapagos Islands. There was nothing here to stir my interest. On the other hand, both Sartre and I read every word of Inspector Guillaume's report on the death of Counselor Prince: we had found the whole affair as fascinating as a Freeman Wills Crofts novel. Apropos of that lovely creature Arlette Stavisky, I found myself faced with a problem which I was to meet again later, in more agonizing circumstances. Are there any limits to the loyalty which a man and a woman bound by the ties of love owe one another? And if so, where are they set? One question which was causing a lot of spilled ink at the time was female suffrage: during the municipal election Maria Vérone and Louise Weiss were campaigning furiously, and were quite right to do so. But as I was apolitical and would not have availed myself of my voting privilege had I possessed it, it hardly mattered to me whether my rights were acknowledged or not.

But there was one phenomenon concerning which neither my concern nor my indignation slumbered: the scandalous role which repressive measures played in our society. In 1934 some young delinquents escaped from Belle-Ile. Kindly tourists joined with the police in hunting them down, placing their cars across roads as barriers and shining their headlights into ditches. All the youths were recaptured, and so horribly beaten up that their screams disturbed some of the local inhabitants. A press campaign laid bare the scandalous conditions prevailing in juvenile detention centers: arbitrary sentences, ill treatment, brutality. But despite the publicity given to these revelations, no action was taken, apart from disciplining a few of the most guilty officials: the system itself was not modified. During Violette Nozière's trial the Bench deliberately suppressed any evidence or testimony that might have "sullied her father's memory," and so the poor girl lost the benefit of any extenuating circumstances. Those guilty of physical cruelty to children generally got off with three or four years in jail, even if their victim died; but Violette was condemned to the guillotine as a parricide, and only escaped execution because for many years no woman in France had so perished. We were similarly sickened by those frenzied American crowds howling for blood outside the jail where Bruno Hauptmann, the Lindbergh child's presumed kidnaper, was incarcerated: after four hundred and sixty days' shilly-shallying he was executed without his guilt having ever been finally established.

By an ironical twist of fate which we appreciated to the full, Henriot, the public prosecutor, one of our social order's most zealous supporters—and so notorious for his severity that he was known as Old Maximum—about this time saw his own son in court on a murder charge. Michel Henriot was a degenerate and and epileptic, with a taste for cruelty to animals. His parents had married him off to a farmer's daughter: she was an invalid, and weak in the wits, but brought a very solid dowry with her. For a whole year, in their isolated home at Loch Guidel on the Atlantic seaboard, Michel beat and maltreated her. He bred silver foxes, and was never without a gun, even in bed. "He'll kill me," the girl wrote to her sister. Her letters gave a full account of her martyrdom, but no one took any notice. Then one night Michel took his carbine and put six shots into her. It was not this lunatic crime which outraged us so much as the connivance of the two families. For purely selfish motives, and to rid themselves of an embarrassment, they had put a half-wit at the mercy of a brute. Michel, who was a cousin of Philippe Henriot, the Fascist, was sent to jail for twenty years.

Another trial attracted our attention because of the personality of the accused, Malou Guérin, who had egged on her lover, Nathan, to murder and rob a wealthy old woman. In extenuation of her responsibility, Maître Henri Torrès pleaded that she had been involved in a serious accident two or three years before, and had suffered concussion and nervous shock as a result. Malou seemed an attractive girl, what could be seen of her—she wore an elegant hat which hid half her face—and her self-possession irritated the jury. She was said to have practiced various disgusting perversions with her lover, being addicted not only to maochism and algolagnia, but to coprophagy as well. From the glances which they exchanged they appeared to love each other passionately, and she stubbornly refused to abandon her support of him. The Brussels jury condemned the man to twenty years' forced labor, and the woman to fifteen—even though she had not been present at the murder. Then, abruptly, Maître Torrès tore off her hat, revealing an empty eye-socket, a seamed and concave forehead, a battered cranium. No doubt if she had displayed these ugly scars, the results of her accident, right from the beginning, she would have got off more lightly.

While discussing crimes, trials, and verdicts with Sartre, I found myself considering the question of the death sentence. It seemed to me unrealistic to attack the principle; what I found odious was the manner of its application. We had lengthy arguments on the subject, and I flew into a passion over it. But in the end all this rebelliousness and disgust and hope for a more justly ordered future began to be dated as an attitude. It is true that I would not have had the feeling of aging and marking time if I had gone out into the world instead of isolating myself within my own private routine; for the world was on the move, and history, far from repeating itself, was plunging forward. In March, 1935, Hitler reintroduced compulsory military service, and all France, Left and Right alike, went into a panic. The pact that we signed with the U.S.S.R. ushered in a new era: Stalin officially approved our national defense policy, and the barrier which separated the *petite bourgeoisie* from working-class socialists and Communists suddenly crumbled. Journals of every political shade, or very nearly, began to publish a spate of sympathetic articles on Moscow and the all-powerful Red Rrmy. The Communists gained some successes in the local elections, and this helped to bring about a *rapprochement* between them and the other two left-wing parties: the formation, toward the end of June, of a general left-wing coalition heralded the Popular Front. Thanks to this energetic countermeasure, peace seemed finally secure. Hitler was a megalomaniac, who was plunging into a rearmament plan that would ruin Germany. With Russia on one side and France on the other, Germany had no chance of winning a war. Hitler knew this, and whatever happened he would not be so mad as to commit an exhausted nation to an utterly hopeless venture; or even if he did, the German people would refuse to follow him.

The Left decided to celebrate its victory with a vast demonstration, and a committee set about organizing on an unprecedented scale for the July 14 celebrations. Sartre and I went along to the Bastille, where five hundred thousand people marched past, flourishing tricolor flags, singing, and shouting. The favorite slogans were "Death to La Roque!" and "Long live the Popular Front!" Up to a certain point we shared this enthusiasm, but we had no inclination to march in procession, or sing and shout with the rest. This more or less represented our attitude at the time: events could arouse strong emotions in us, whether anger, fear, or joy, but we did not participate in them. We remained spectators.

"You've seen Spain and Italy and Central Europe," Pagniez told us reproachfully, "but you still don't know your own country!" It was true that we were ignorant of great areas of it. Since we were too broke to go abroad this year, we decided to explore France. But first Sartre went off to join his parents on a Norwegian cruise. For my own part I got into a train one morning carrying a rucksack stuffed with clothes, bedding, an alarm clock, a *Guide Bleu,* and a set of Michelin maps. I got off at La Chaise-Dieu in the Haute-Loire, and walked solidly for three weeks, keeping away from main roads and taking short cuts through woods and fields. Every peak was a challenge. Eagerly my eyes drank in the magnificent scenery—lakes, waterfalls, hidden glades, and valleys. There was not a thought in my head: I simply walked and stared. I carried all my possessions on my back, I had no idea where I would sleep each night, and I was still on the move when the first star pricked out in the sky. The way in which flowers and the whole world folded up at dusk I found enchanting. Sometimes as I strode over the brow of a hill, to find it utterly deserted—no people there, and even the light draining away—I would feel as though I had brushed the edge of that ungraspable emptiness which every man-made embellishment is designed to conceal. Then panic would descend on me, the sort of panic I had experienced at the age of fourteen in that "landscaped park" where God no longer existed; and, as I had done then, I would hurry toward the sound of the nearest human voice, and a bowl of soup and a glass of red wine in some country inn. Often I could not bear the thought of being cut off from grass and trees and sky: at least I wanted to keep their scent with me. So instead of taking a room in the inn, I would trudge on another four or five miles and beg hospitality in some hamlet: I would sleep in a barn, and the smell of hay would drift through my dreams.

The night of which I retain the most vivid memory is the one I spent up on Mont Mézenc. I had counted on sleeping in the dismal little hamlet of Etaples, at the foot of the mountain; but when I arrived it was still daylight. I was told that I could get to the summit in under two hours, and that there was a rest hut up there; so I bought some bread, and a candle, and had my felt-covered waterbottle filled up with red wine, and began the ascent, plodding up through lush, flower-laden pastureland. Dusk fell, and presently night began to draw in. It was quite dark by the time I pushed open the door of the hut—a gray flint building furnished with a table, a bench, and two sloping boards for beds. I fixed my candle on the table, ate a few mouthfuls of bread, and drank all my wine—the latter to keep my courage up, since at this altitude loneliness became a little unnerving: the wind whistled fiercely through chinks in the stonework, and I slept very badly, with my rucksack as a pillow and a board in lieu of mattress, huddled up under a blanket which failed to keep out the cold. But even during my sleepless moments I liked to feel the vast emptiness of the night all about me; I could hardly have been more isolated if I had been cruising in an airplane. I woke at six to a bright morning sky and a grassy smell that recalled my childhood. Beneath my feet there lay an impenetrable sea of cloud, cutting me off from the ground: I alone stood above it, framed in azure spendor. The wind was still blowing, whipping through the blanket as I tried to wrap it around me. I waited there till the gray layers of cotton beneath me began to thin out, and through the gaps I made out patches of sunlit countryside. Then I went running down the slope, on the side opposite the one I had climbed. I had been foolish enough to go practically barefooted, wearing only a pair of canvas espadrilles, and the fierce heat of the sun burned the soles of my feet. By the time I reached Saint-Agrève I was beginning to suffer the agonies of the damned, and I had to stop there for twenty-four hours. Once I lay down it was so painful to get up again that I kept dragging myself to and fro across my room; and when I got on the move again every halt was torture. I bought some provisions in a grocery, and while the clerk served me I kept pacing up and down like a wild beast in its cage. Finally the pain lessened and I set out once more, my feet protected with anklets.

There was another night, in the Basse-Ardèche district, when the air was so mild that I could not bear to be cooped up indoors, and slept on the mossy floor of a chestnut grove, my head pillowed on my rucksack, my alarm clock beside me. I never stirred till dawn, and then how wonderful it was, when I opened my eyes, to see the blue sky above me! Sometimes on awaking I could sense that a storm was imminent: I could recognize that curious damp smell that trees give off from their foliage, announcing the approach of rain before the least hint of it appears in the sky. I would quicken my pace then, already prey to the commotion that would soon descend upon the peaceful landscape. Scents, patterns of light and shade, winds and hurricanes—all pulsed inwardly through my own sinews and veins: so much so, indeed, that the throb of my blood stream, the swarming growth of my cells, the whole mystery of life housed within me seemed to be echoed by the shrilling cicadas, the gusts of wind that shook the trees, and the faint crunch of the moss as I trod it underfoot.

But when I was surfeited with blue skies and chlorophyll, it was pleasant to linger in town or village, where the stones had been shaped and ordered by human hands. Solitude never oppressed me, nor did my sense of wonder at inanimate objects and my relationship to them ever pall. Doubtless this was the reason—though I did not work it out at the time—for my blissful condition. My exercise of freedom had triumphantly avoided both external constraint and willful capriciousness, since the world's resistance, far from harassing me, actually furnished the framework and substance of my plans. This persistent yet easygoing trek of mine gave a semblance of truth to my vast, crazy optimism. I was enjoying a taste of divine bliss, and yet was myself the begetter of the gifts showered so richly upon me.

One evening Sartre turned up on the platform at Sainte-Cécile-d'Andorge station. When he felt like it he was a good walker. He loved this countryside, with its bare uplands and colored mountains: he cheerfully joined me in exploring it on foot, and even resigned himself to picnics—we always lunched alfresco, on hardboiled eggs and sausages. We followed the mountain gorges of the Tarn, and climbed up to Aigoual, and walked for miles over high limestone plateaus. We got lost among the "false keeps" at Montpellier-le-Vieux and in order to get back on to the road were obliged to make a hair-raising descent, clambering from rock to rock. The Larzac plateau was alive with chirring crickets, busy eating one another alive: we crunched them underfoot at every step. Measured against the pace we kept up, Larzac was a veritable Sahara, and for a long day its dust clung to our feet. Dusk was falling as we approached La Couvertoirade, and the sudden appearance, amid that sparse scrub, of those centuries-old slumbering ramparts made a great impression on us. The fine medieval houses were half buried under brambles and creepers, and till it was dark we wandered through the city's ghostly, unreal streets.

We checked in at a good hotel in Rozier, outside the village; our rooms and the terrace where we had dinner looked out over the green waters of the Tarn. We had arranged for Pagniez to meet us here; he was walking through the district with his youngest cousin, Thérèse, whom I had met in Corsica and liked very much. She was an attractive, fresh-complexioned blonde girl, with a fine strapping figure, who adored life, the open air—and Pagniez. She was about twenty, a schoolteacher from Seine-et-Marne. Ever since that Corsican holiday, Pagniez had been very attached to her. He was not exactly bursting to set up house right away, but they did get along very well together, and thought of marrying some day. Together we climbed up to various rocky pinnacles, and scrambled from ledge to ledge on the Causse Méjean and the Causse Noir. We ate trout and *écrevisse,* and went paddling in the Tarn. One day, when Thérèse was absent, Pagniez asked us what we thought of her. "A wonderful girl," Sartre said, but added that she was still a little childish, and rather too ready to oblige with family anecdotes. This reservation annoyed Pagniez, and he was so attached to Thérèse that he could not help also holding her aggressive modesty against her. "Poor Thérèse," he told her, with somewhat forced jocularity, "they don't think you're very bright"—a remark which depressed her a little and embarrassed us a great deal. But we parted on very friendly terms.

Sartre preferred old stones to trees, and my itinerary took this inclination of his into account. Either on foot or by bus we visited a whole succession of towns, villages, abbeys, and châteaux. One evening, in a jolting, jam-packed little bus, we made our way to Castelnau de Montmirail: there was a pouring rain, and as we drove into the colonnaded main square, Sartre suddenly declared that he was tired of being mad. Throughout this trip the lobsters had been trying to trail along behind him, and that evening he finally sent them packing. He kept his word, too; henceforward he displayed an absolutely imperturable cheerfulness.

The previous year I had written nothing. I was determined to get back to some serious work now—but what was it to be? Why was I not tempted to try my hand at philosophical writing? Sartre had declared that my grasp of philosophical doctrines, including that held by Husserl, was quicker and more precise than his own. The truth was that he tended to interpret them according to his own hypotheses; he found great difficulty in jettisoning his own viewpoint and unreservedly adopting anyone else's. In my case there was no such resistance to break down: my thinking bent itself directly to the point I was attempting to master. I did not, however, accept it passively: the degree of my acceptance was always modified by the lacunae and muddled logic I perceived in any proposition, and which I emphasized no less than its potential development. If a theory convinced me, it did not remain an external, alien phenomenon; it altered my relationship with the world, and colored all my experience. In short, I possessed both considerable powers of assimilation and a well-developed critical sense; and philosophy was for me a living reality, which gave me never-failing satisfaction.

Yet I did not regard myself as a philosopher: I was well aware that the ease with which I penetrated to the heart of a text stemmed, precisely, from my lack of originality. In this field a genuinely creative talent is so rare that queries as to why I did not attempt to join the elite are surely otiose: it would be more useful to explain *how* certain individuals are capable of getting results from that conscious venture into lunacy known as a "philosophical system," from which they derive that obsessional attitude which endows their tentative patterns with universal insight and applicability. As I have remarked before, women are not by nature prone to obsessions of this type.

I might at least have undertaken a well-documented critical study—perhaps even aspiring to a degree of ingenuity—on some limited problem, involving an unknown or little-known author and a debatable point of logic. This did not attract me at all. When I talked philosophy with Sartre, and took the full measure of his patience and audacity, the idea of a philosophical career seemed wildly exciting—but only if one was bitten by a theory of one's own. Expounding other people's beliefs, developing, judging, collating, and criticizing them—no, I failed to see the attraction of this. When reading a work of Fink's I found myself wondering how anyone could bear to be someone else's follower, or disciple. Later I did, intermittently, come—for various reasons—to play such a role myself. But to begin with I possessed far too much intellectual ambition to let this satisfy me. I wanted to communicate the element of originality in my own experience. In order to do this successfully I knew it was literature toward which I must orientate myself.

I had written two long novels in which the opening chapters held up pretty well, but which then degenerated into a mere shapeless hodgepodge. This time I determined to compose some fairly brief stories, and to discipline them rigorously from beginning to end. I put a private ban on fantasy and shoddy romanticism. I renounced the idea of sketching intrigues which I didn't believe in, or backgrounds with which I was unfamiliar. I would restrict myself to people and things which I knew. I would attempt to express a truth of which I had personal experience, and which would give the book its unity. The theme was hinted at by my title, borrowed, somewhat ironically, from Jacques Maritain: *Primauté du spirituel* (The Ascendancy of the Spirit.)

The books and war films over which I had cried my eyes out as an adolescent had left a lasting mark upon me. All those lofty slogans and gestures, *Sursum corda, Debout les morts!,* and the rest, awoke the most frightful images in my mind—battlefields and charnel houses, wounded men with faces like calves' lungs (a phrase of Ellen Zena Smith's: her novel *Not So Quiet* had shattered me). Closer to home I had seen Zaza driven to madness and death by the puritan moral code of her environment. The most sincere thing in my last novel had been my loathing of bourgeois society. On this point, as on so many others, I found myself in agreement with current belief. Ideologically the Left was critical rather than constructive. The revolutionary spoke the same language as the rebel, and was not above attacking the morality, aesthetics, and philosophy of the ruling classes. All circumstances, therefore, favored the project I had in mind. Through the medium of individual characters and their affairs I wanted to convey something that lay beyond them: the multitude of crimes, both small and great, which hid behind a veil of spiritual hocuspocus.

The characters of my various stories were more or less loosely interlinked, but each possessed a separate, complete identity. I devoted the first to my old girl friend, Lisa. I sketched the slow atrophy of a young girl, timidly reaching out to life, overwhelmed by the mysticism and intrigues of the Institut Sainte-Marie: her vain struggle to be a pure soul among other pure souls, while all the while her body fought stubbornly against her. I gave my second heroine, Renée, the features—including the pallor and the high forehead—of Dr. A.'s sister, whom I had known in Marseille. I took cognizance of the fact that there had been a close connection between my piety and the masochistic elements in some of my games. I had also found out that my most devout aunt got her husband to whip her smartly every night. I amused myself by conceiving an adult figure in whom religiosity became degraded to mere gross indecency. I also drew a satirical picture of social welfare workers, and tried to bring out generally the equivocal nature of self-sacrifice. In these two tales I used a pseudo-objective tone and a certain concealed irony which I had borrowed from John Dos Passos.

For my next story I took Simone Labourdin as my model, renaming her Chantal. When she left Sèvres, she went to teach literature in Rouen. With laborious dishonesty she tried to project a version of herself and her life calculated to dazzle her friends. Her private diary and inner thoughts showed how she transformed each of her experiences, hunting avidly after fantasy, creating herself a new character, that of the Emancipated Woman, endowed with shimmering sensibilities. In fact, she was very concerned about her reputation. Her obsessional passion for acting a part led her to involve two young pupils, great admirers of hers, in disastrous trouble, and in the end she stripped off her mask for their benefit. This story marked an advance: Chantal's interior monologue showed her simultaneously as she dreamed of being and as she actually was; I had contrived to set down that split between two halves of the self which is the very essence of dishonesty. Chantal's interviews with her pupils were also done in a reasonably adroit fashion; the reader could catch the young woman's weaknesses as seen through the generous eyes of adolescence. I used a similar technique afterward in *L'Invitée* (*She Came To Stay*) to suggest Elisabeth's tricksiness.

If the bad habits which I attributed to Chantal irked me so much, that was not so much through having observed them in Simone Labourdin as because I had slipped into them myself: during the past two or three years I had more than once yielded to the temptation of embellishing my life history with false items of information. Alone in Marseille, I had more or less purged myself of this weakness, though I still reproached myself for it. The novel that Françoise writes in *She Came to Stay* turns on a similar theme: it was a favorite preoccupation of mine, and I enjoyed dealing with it. Yet today Chantal's story strikes me as being a mere exercise. My heroine might have held down a minor role in a novel, but she lacked the depth and solidity that would have made one *care* about her triumphs and setbacks.

Once again I attempted to resuscitate Zaza, and this time got rather nearer the truth: my Anne Vignon was a girl of twenty, who suffered from the same torments and doubts as Zaza had done. Nevertheless, I failed to make her story convincing. I didn't do too badly with the long prayer uttered by Madame Vignon, which formed the starting point of my narrative: in it she revealed both her lying assumptions and her true self. But I went wrong in the second half. I wanted everyone to be at fault where Anne was concerned, and thus gave her Chantal as a friend— Chantal who, being concerned only to act a part, pushed Anne into revolt without any genuine conviction, and without making the necessary effort to bring her out of her state of isolation. Chantal's attitude to the theater sprang directly from her own mediocrity; and without being aware of it, I debased Anne by assuming that she would accord her trust to anyone who deserved it so little. The denouement was approached by way of Pascal, for whom Anne had the same unhappy passion as Zaza did for Pradelles. The character of the young man was not badly done, but lacked depth. I had drawn a more plausible and attractive portrait of "Anne" than in my previous attempts; yet even so, neither her death nor the intensity of her affliction were at all credible. Perhaps the only way of convincing the reader was by telling the plain truth about what actually happened.

After I had written *The Mandarins* I made one further attempt to turn Zaza's tragic end into a long short story; yet though my technical skill was now far greater, I could not get to the end.

The last story in the book was a satirical piece about my childhood. I attributed to "Marguerite" both my childhood at the Cours Désir and the religious crisis I underwent during adolescence. Thereafter she was caught by the lure of fantasy; but her eyes were eventually unsealed, she jettisoned all myth, mirage, and mystery, and made up her mind to look the world straight in the face.

This was by far the best story: I wrote it in the first person, from the heroine's point of view, and in a vivid, lively style. My most successful achievement was in the autobiographical sequences; the events that brought about Marguerite's conversion to the truth were relatively unconvincing.

Over and above the faults attributable to each separate episode, the construction of the book as a whole was defective, being neither a collection of individual stories nor a continuous novel. My didactic and satirical aims were labored far too heavily, and once again I had avoided real self-exposure: this "I" was a manifestation from my past only, always at a considerable remove from my present self. These tales showed bloodless heroines moving through a pale, shadowy world, from which I had withheld all personal and living warmth. All the same, Sartre, who read my work as it progressed, approved of numerous passages. Throughout the two years that I spent writing these stories, I was sustained by the hope that a publisher would accept them.

Some important events took place during that summer. The Orders in Council promulgated by the Laval Government had provoked violent opposition, and rioting had broken out in most of the big ports, such as Brest, Cherbourg, and Lorient. At Le Havre and Toulon workers had been killed by the forces of law and order, and in the end their comrades were compelled to submit. Still, this defeat had not obliterated their hopes. The funeral of Barbusse provided a handy excuse for a demonstration which almost rivaled the Fourteenth of July in size and abandon. Certain writers— Chamson, André Viollis, Guéhenno—who hoped they might encourage the Popular Front both to clarify and publicize its various ideological attitudes, had just founded a new weekly called *Vendredi*. The Right was massing more energetically than ever against what it called "the Bolshies," and local Croix de Feu organizations gained increasing numbers of recruits. They also looked beyond the frontiers for support from Italian Fascism. When Mussolini refused all attempts at arbitration and was mounting his attack upon Haile Selassie, the League of Nations voted for sanctions against him; and when Italian troops actually crossed the borders of Ethiopia, the British Government decided to put such sanctions into operation. In the issue of *Le Temps* that appeared on October 4, sixty-four French intellectuals published a manifesto "in defense of Western civilization," attacking these sanctions—the very same day that Il Duce was bombarding the civilian population of Aduwa. The anti-Fascist intellectuals protested: there were some Catholics among them, and *Esprit,* edited by Emmanuel Mounier, found itself in line with *Commune.* The symbolic boycott practiced by certain left-wing writers we found merely ridiculous (for instance, their refusal to drink Cinzano), but Laval's maneuvers really did sicken us. His cautious advocacy of "long-term sanctions" made France a party to the atrocities that were being committed in Abyssinia by Italian airmen, with their slap-happy annihilation of women and children. Fortunately we anticipated a rapid reversal of French policy. The United Popular Front grew stronger every day, with more congresses, meetings, and processions; when militant members of Left and Right met in public brawls, it was the Left that came off best. The Popular Front seemed certain to gain an imminent victory at the Polls. The "cash barrier" would be pulled down, "feudal groups" broken up, and the "two hundred families" stripped of their power. The workers would enforce their claims, and get a large number of industries nationalized. From this point the future lay open before them.

It was in this sort of optimistic atmosphere and outlook that the new school year began. During the first term the Ustachi trial ran its course and the Stavisky trial began. The remains of little Nicole Marescot were discovered: her presumed murderer had already been languishing in jail for a year, while a host of water diviners vainly combed the Chaumont area with their hazel wands. The Abbé Lambert had made this a fashionable sport, and large numbers of people took it seriously. The Joliot-Curies received the Nobel Prize for their work on artificially produced radioactivity. There was much talk in the press about the new "norms of output" established in Soviet factories by someone called Stakhanov.

Now that Sartre had pronounced himself cured, there was nothing left to darken our private life together. I left the Hôtel La Rochefoucauld and moved into another place, recommended to me by Olga, called Le Petit Mouton; her Polish friends had once resided there, and she found it delightful. I too lost my heart to it: it was an old three-story building, in an alley just off the Rue de la République, and built in the Norman style, with exposed beams and numerous small leaded windows. It was divided into two wings, each with its separate front door and staircase, and the proprietress's private quarters in the middle. The right-hand wing was for transient guests, while the other one housed the regular tenants, most of them young couples: every night the corridors echoed to their amorous sighing. I lived next door to a sergeant major who used to beat his wife every night before making love to her. My chairs and table were rickety on their legs, but I loved the somewhat coarsely cheerful patterns of my bedspread, wallpaper, and curtains. I often brought home a piece of ham for supper, and several times at night, soon after my arrival, I was half-awakened by unusual rustlings and patterings: these turned out to be mice, dragging across the floor the greaseproof wrappings I had earlier consigned to the wastepaper basket. Occasionally I even felt tiny paws scampering over my face. The proprietress was a fat old procuress with frizzled hair, who wore pink cotton stockings. Marco, who had been appointed to a post in Rouen, also moved into the Petit Mouton, choosing the more bordello-like wing. He overwhelmed the *patronne* with lavish compliments for the pleasure of seeing her smirk and simper; he also played ball with his huge wolfhound right outside the front door.

During the holidays I had had some desperate letters from Olga. She had not even appeared for her medical exam in June, and instead of going straight back to Beuzeville, she spent a sleepless week walking around Rouen and dancing at the Royal. She reached home eight days late, with a haggard face and rings under her eyes, carrying on one shoulder an epileptic cat that she had picked out of the gutter. Her parents wanted to send her to boarding school in Caen: she could hardly have been more terrified if they had decided to consign her to a reformatory. Her distress touched me, and I was sad for my own sake that she was not coming back to Rouen: I had become deeply devoted to her.

This friendship of ours must have rested on solid foundations, for me as well as for her, since today, twenty-five years later, she still occupies a specially privileged place in my life. But at first it was Olga who wanted the relationship and brought it into being; nor could it have been otherwise. An attachment only develops any true strength if it has to assert itself *against* something. At eighteen Olga was anti practically everything, while I slid through life with the ease of a swimming fish: she had the weight of the whole world upon her, while I was as free as air. Her feelings toward me quickly reached a burning intensity, the full implications of which I took some time to appreciate.

As a young man, Olga's father had taken an engineering diploma in Munich, and after the Revolution he had contrived to make use of it, first in Strasbourg, then in Greece, and latterly at Beuzeville. The Greek marshes were unhealthy, and there was no *lycée* in Beuzeville, so for years on end Olga and her sister had been sent to boarding school at Angoulême and Rouen. Still, they had been with their parents as young children, and continued to spend long holidays in their company: Olga loved them both dearly. Madame D. was an intelligent, open-minded, and far from orthodox woman, who as a girl had shown enough independent drive to leave her uncongenial home for a job, teaching French in Russia. After her return to France, as the wife of a Russian exile, she had felt as much a stranger in her native land as he did, and mixed very little with her Alsatian or Norman neighbors. She had also used her own judgment in regard to her children's education. When they were still quite tiny she had read them books and told them stories that local opinion considered miles above their heads. She introduced them to mythology, and the Old Testament, and the Gospels, and the legends concerning the Buddha, all in such a way that they were enchanted, yet felt no need to believe what they heard. It was to this early training that Olga owed her precocious knowledge— which had charmed those who taught her literature, and irritated almost everyone else.

What with this somewhat unusual mother, and an exotically alien father who was always telling her tales of the fabulous country where she should, by rights, have been living, Olga felt herself set apart from ordinary children, and had always felt that the distinction indicated superiority on her part. She even got the impression of having strayed into a setting that lacked sufficient dignity for her condition. From the depths of a Russia that no longer existed, a little girl, brought up in the Institute for Young Ladies of the Nobility, looked with disdain at Olga D., schoolgirl, now lost in an anonymous mass of Rouen medical students. She distrusted this herd, she did not belong to it; yet there she was in its ranks, and nowhere else, a fact which she took very hard. The paradoxical quality about her education was due to her parents having first filled her up with hatred of all the traditional French virtues—conventional values, pious shibboleths, and general stupidity—and *then* being forced to abandon her to the ridiculous discipline, routine, and old-fashioned ideas prevalent in any girls' boarding school. There had been several quite serious clashes with authority as a result, but these had not affected Olga overmuch, as her parents had always taken her side. From time to time Madame D. experienced slight qualms of conscience, and expressed the wish that her daughters were "like the rest"; these stray impulses of hers triggered off domestic dramas which, fortunately, were always cut short by something or other diverting her from her purpose. When Olga left her *lycée* her parents were much concerned to steer her in the direction of "normality." They did not envisage marriage as a career; they believed in her talent, and wanted her to learn some profession. But which was it to be? Olga's dream of becoming a ballet dancer they had never taken very seriously, and in any case it was now too late for that. She was interested in architecture, but her father decided a woman had no chance of making a success in this field. They finally opted for medicine, ignoring Olga's almost complete lack of interest in the subject. The result was that Olga failed her medical exam twice, in June and October, 1935, and from her parents' point of view completely wasted the year she was supposed to spend revising for a further attempt. This made them feel violently resentful, and they lectured her constantly on her ways. When she was at Beuzeville they forbade her to smoke or stay up late—indeed, they practically stopped her reading—and laid down rules as to how she could occupy her time. They shook their heads over her dissipated habits and the low company she kept. The classic conflict between adolescent and parents was peculiarly agonizing in her case, since her mother and father were suddenly identified with the principles that they themselves, more or less consciously, had earlier taught her to despise: orderliness, worldly wisdom, established customs, and all the solemn paraphernalia of that grown-up world which now, to her horror, loomed ahead. She regretted having disappointed them, since she had always passionately longed for their approval; but their sudden change of attitude, what she felt to be their treachery, filled her with bitterness. She had spent the whole of the past year in a state of angry confusion, furious both with the world at large and with herself. Her sister, whom she loved dearly, was much younger than she, and with her various acquaintances she had superficial relationships only: there was no one to rescue her from the depressed state she was in.

No one, that is, except me. I was admirably placed to come to her aid, being nine years her senior, endowed with the authority of a teacher, and possessing the prestige conferred by culture and experience. I was at logger-heads with the staff of the *lycée* and the Rouen bourgeoisie, and my life took no account of conventional standards. In me Olga recognized her own hatreds and rejections, the same thirst for freedom: but all transfigured and magnified by age, and the wisdom which she attributed to me. I had traveled, and understood people; for her Rouen and Beuzeville were prisons to which I held the keys. It was through me that she pictured the infinite variety and novelty of the world lying hidden beyond her horizon; and it is true that during those two years much of what she absorbed—books, music, ideas—was due to me. Not only did I open up the future for her, but also—and this was still more important—I promised her she would blaze her own trail into it. Her parents' reproaches had driven her to a state very near embittered defeatism. I realized what a jolt failing her medical must have given her, and how her spirit of youthful independence had then gone to her head. So I took her wholly into my confidence, and this sort of encouragement—the sense of private solidarity, and everything else which, grudgingly at first, I gave her—was what she needed most of all. Of course, she herself did not identify the impulse underlying her enthusiasm for me, and supposed it was due to my merits as a person; but it was, to begin with, because of her own unhappy situation that I acquired a special, even a unique importance in her eyes.

I myself, on the other hand, had all I wanted. When I met new and attractive friends I established agreeable relationships with them, but did not allow them to penetrate my defenses. The veriest paragon, were he a compendium of every known human charm, could not have seduced me from my neutral attitude. Olga, because she *needed* me, touched my heart at its one vulnerable point. A few years earlier I would have found this bothersome; in those days I had thought only of my own emotional enrich-ment. But now I had more than enough myself, and the eagerness with which Olga received my first gifts revealed to me the pleasure to be got from *giving*. I had discovered the intoxicating delights of accepting favors, and the pleasures contained in a reciprocal relationship; but I did not yet know how touching it can be to feel that one is useful, and how utterly devastating to believe oneself indispensable. The smiles that I provoked on her countenance from time to time gave me a deep joy that I could not have foregone without regret.

Clearly they would not have moved me in the same way without that feeling of sympathy and regard which Olga had inspired in me from the first moment we met. I had savored the special charm of her features and gestures, her voice, speech, and special way of talking. Olga herself, though she might not fully understand them, was seldom mistaken about the basic quality of a person or a book. She possessed one virtue, genuineness, which we regarded as of the essence. She never faked her opinions or her impres-sions. I realized that she now bore very little resemblance to the pale, blonde, slightly washed-out girl whom I had once seen crying over an unfinished essay. There was an impetuous, whole-hogging streak in her that I found most disarming. As a small girl she had gone into even more violent temper tantrums than I had done, and even now she was liable to fits of rage so fierce that they almost knocked her unconscious. But the rebelliousness and disgust she felt were more often translated into terms of collapse than of fury: this apparent passivity, far from indicating weakness, was in fact a gesture of defiance against every sort of tyranny. To her pleasures Olga surrendered herself with unstinted enthusiasm: she would sometimes go on dancing till she passed out from sheer exhaustion. She had an eager and indiscriminate appetite for things and people, especially people; there was a fresh, childlike quality about her enthusiasms, and she would daydream over them for hours on end. I enjoyed talking to her, because she listened with passionate intensity to all I said. She told me about her past, and I acquainted her with much of mine: I could always reckon on her attention and understanding. I had more intimate discussions with her than with any woman of my own age. It pleased me, too, that her behavior and speech should always show such discretion, such reserve, when all the time beneath those well-disciplined manners a whole holocaust of passions was raging. I hoped I might help her to stop wasting her resources on barren preoccupations such as boredom or guilt, and turn them into more profitable channels. Nevertheless, I was a prudent person: it had not hitherto been my intention to take her life in hand quite openly and make it my particular concern.

But the only plan which her parents had conceived forced me, with Sartre's encouragement, to do just that. Sartre was very fond of Olga, and had found her a charming nurse-companion; it seemed out of the question to him that I should let her be immured in a Caen boarding school, and he made what I thought was an absolutely brilliant suggestion. Olga hated the natural sciences, but she had done very well indeed at philosophy: so why not steer her in *that* direction? Sartre was running an honors course at Le Havre for a group of students, both male and female, and would help me to coach Olga for her diploma. I wrote to her parents asking for an interview, and they invited me to visit them at Beuzeville. I got off the train at the previous station, long before the time appointed, and spent that afternoon with Olga, traipsing round the local countryside, which was chilly and depressing. We sought refuge in various village cafés, where we sat huddled up to the stove. Olga was not optimistic about the result of my *démarche*. Nevertheless, after a delicious Russian-style dinner I set forth our plan to Monsieur and Madame D., and actually persuaded them to let me take charge of Olga. When I was back in Rouen, Sartre and I drew up a detailed timetable of lessons we would give her, and the scheme of work, e.g., reading, essays, or exercises, that she would have to get through. I also rented her a room in the Petit Mouton.

She looked as though she enjoyed her new studies: she paid close attention to what we told her, and gave every sign of understanding it completely. Her table was conscientiously stacked with the books I obtained for her. But on the day that I asked her for a written précis of a certain chapter in Bergson, she ate a whole packet of gumdrops, which meant that she was in no fit condition to work. Something—her parents' reaction to those botched exams, or a more deep-rooted personal pride— had filled her with such a terror of failure that she would rather make no effort at all than run that risk. In any event, she did not manage to write so much as the first line of her first essay. Taken all in all, Sartre's scheme was perhaps not quite so brilliant after all. In order to read for a degree away from the Sorbonne, without the company of other students, one would need either great enthusiasm or considerable will power. Thanks to her natural intelligence, Olga had easily topped the class in philosophy, but in actual fact abstract speculation held little attraction for her, and she was quite incapable of buckling down to the tasks she had been set. I perceived that her defeatism during those two years of reading for the Bachelor of Medicine degree stemmed from less accidental causes than I had supposed. There are some people who thrive on difficulties; Olga simply gave up. Having been convinced since childhood that she did not belong to her society or environment, she could not envisage future time in such a context. For her, tomorrow scarcely existed, and next year not at all. She made little distinction between an actual plan and a dream, so had no hope to sustain her when at grips with some dry or boring task. I tried to fight against her indolence; but my reproaches, and her resultant guilt, far from stirring her to greater activity, simply made her drift into a state of inert despair. Sarrte very quickly gave up his efforts on her behalf, and I followed suit. After Christmas the philosophy lessons became a mere myth.

I was disappointed, but I got over it; and now that Olga was living a totally untrammeled life she began to bloom. As a student she had been sulky, but she turned out, on the other hand, to be a most agreeable companion. She flung herself into today's activities all the more enthusiastically for her indifference to tomorrow; she never tired of using her eyes, ears, and tongue, of dancing, walking, or simply listening to her own heartbeats. It was for her benefit that we shifted our stamping ground from Le Havre to Rouen. She dragged us off to the terrasse of the Café Victor to hear that fine gypsy violinist, Sacha Malo; he was followed by an all-female orchestra which reminded us of the one in the big café at Tours, and amused us so much with its airs and graces that Sartre later put it into Le Sursis (The Reprieve). In the normal course of things we were more curious about women than we were about men; we always cocked an attentive ear for the feminine chitchat at Alexander's, or the gossip of the "hostesses" in the Oceanic Bar. Down the Rue de la Grande-Horloge there was a Cintra Bar which was rather like the one in Marseille; I played poker dice there with Olga, and talked to Sartre over cups of coffee or glasses of orange juice. The directrix of an important fashion house often came there to discuss problems with wholesalers or clients, sitting around one of the barrels which served in lieu of tables. We watched her admiringly: women executives or heads of firms were far from common at this period, and we much appreciated both her un-self-

conscious elegance and her tartly authoritative air. When Colette Audry
went off to Paris she left us the keys of her studio. We cooked spaghetti
on her stove, listened to her records, and teased her turtledoves. She
often lent us her phonograph toward the end of the month so that we
could pawn it; I also used to pawn a gold brooch that had been a present
from my grandmother.

When Sartre was away I saw a great deal of Olga. I made her read
Stendhal, and Proust, and Conrad, and all the authors I enjoyed. Sometimes she raved over them, and sometimes she was furious: her relationships with these figures were so complicated and lively that they might
have been creatures of flesh and blood. Proust in particular inspired her
with the most ambiguous feelings, which veered to and fro between frantic
loathing and stunned admiration without ever stopping at some inter-
mediate point. When we wanted to talk we would go and sit in the
Oceanic or the Cintra, or frequently in a little dockside bar that was
decorated throughout in a most attractive shade of apricot—curtains,
cushions, and even the ice cream they served. We drank nothing but
cassis there. I set about teaching Olga chess, and we played several games
at the Brasserie de l'Opéra. But our ignorance of the game earned us
such indignant rebukes that we soon only dared to play privately. We
would shut ourselves up in my room and drink inordinate quantities of
cherry brandy—a tipple to which we were vastly attracted—while meditating
our moves. One night we drank so much of the stuff that Olga, after
leaving me, rolled head over heels down the stairs and slept there at the
bottom till one of the other tenants kicked her awake. We would often
go up to Marco's room and listen to records—Beethoven quartets, the
Brandenburgs, Stravinsky's *Octet;* I thus became familiar with a great
many works which previously I had known slightly or not at all. What
irritated me was that after each work Marco would give me an inquisitorial,
faintly mocking glance, and I was forced to rack my brains for some sort
of comment.

One afternoon Marco asked Olga, Sartre, and myself to the studio where
he practiced his singing. When he hummed snatches from a Bach
passacaglia or Beethoven's sublime "Cavatina" as we walked through the
streets of Rouen, Marco's voice enchanted me. Now he launched into the
great aria from *Boris Godunov.* The windows shook; I thought my ear-
drums would burst. I was stupified. Further sessions confirmed the melancholy truth. Marco's voice was getting stronger and stronger, but its quality
was steadily deteriorating. He himself had no idea of this; he was convinced that he would soon make his triumphant debut at the Opéra. On
the other hand he *was* conducting a desperate struggle against what
seemed to me a far less harmful misfortune: going bald. Every evening
he would massage his scalp with a lotion containing sulphur, which made
him feel as though he was being flayed alive; for about five minutes he
would stand gripping the window sill with both hands to stop himself
screaming out loud. But he had not as yet lost any of his good looks.
By now I knew him all too well and found his charm slightly stale. But

Olga was enchanted by him, and he felt strongly drawn toward her: they often went out together.

One evening, as they were strolling down the Rue Jeanne-d'Arc, Olga began to imitate the movement of a skater; Marco took her in his arms, and they whirled their way along the street, with Marco providing the music. Suddenly they noticed a small group on the opposite pavement, who were staring at them in astonishment—one of Marco's pupils, accompanied by his parents. *"Merde!"* said Marco, and added, without letting go of Olga: "The hell with it, let's keep on—too late now anyway." So the schoolboy was left to watch his teacher dancing away into the distance with a blonde.

In Marco's company the shortest walk became an adventure. He made up the most fabulous lies for Olga's amusement. He would go aboard small boats or coal barges and force his way into the crews' quarters. He would accost complete strangers, offer them a drink, and get them to tell him their life story. One evening, in the apricot-colored bar, Olga and I were approached by a ship's captain, an Englishman: he was extremely ugly, with the bottle-nose of a drunkard, but he told us tales of the sea, which we listened to, and complimented Olga on her English. A few days later, when Olga was in another bar with Marco, she met the Captain again. "Please introduce us," Marco said. And he added, in French and under his breath, "Tell him I have the honor of being related to you." The Captain, persuaded that Marco was Olga's brother, bought them both drinks and invited them to spend the evening aboard his ship. Marco hesitated: it was clear that the Captain had designs on Olga. "No, you come around to our place," Marco said. "But you'll have to bring a bottle," he added; "a young girl like Olga doesn't keep liquor in the house—I'm sure you understand." The Captain, who knew his way around, went off to buy some whisky, and Marco revealed his plan: they were going to fleece this sailor properly. Marco would leave him alone with Olga for a minute or two, and he would obviously try to rape her. Then Marco would burst in unexpectedly and threaten to make trouble. An essential preliminary would be to get their victim sozzled. Anyhow, off they all went up to Olga's room, and began to work their way through a bottle of Johnny Walker. The Captain knocked his off properly, but the other two surreptitiously emptied their glasses on the bed, which stank of whisky for about a month afterward. Despite this, the Captain kept a clear head. He asked Marco to go out on the landing with him for a moment, where he offered him money. In order to discourage his advances, Marco demanded a quite exorbitant sum, and the Captain lost his temper. In order to keep him sweet Marco finally explained, sobbing, that poverty had driven him to tout his young sister, but now he felt how ignominious such conduct was, and had changed his mind. This did not mollify the Captain, and Marco had to take him by the shoulders and steer him firmly toward the front door. Despite this, the Captain bore no grudge afterward. A few days later Olga and I were up in Marco's room listening to records, when a car drew up at the corner

of our alley. On second thought the Captain had felt sorry for the plight of
these young people, and had come by to invite us aboard his ship. We
went with him and he entertained us most charmingly.

What with Marco's presence, and the development of my friendship
with Olga, and Sartre's recovery, and my new enthusiasm for my work,
this was a particularly happy term. I was too busy to read as voraciously as
I used to do; yet even so I kept abreast of new work. The past year
could hardly be said to have enriched French literature. The Right had
scored a hit with the books of Robert Francis, who was Jean Maxence's
brother and, like him, a Fascist. *La Grange aux Trois Belles* and *Le
Bâteau-refuge* were pale imitations of Alain-Fournier. That winter Malraux
published his worst work, *Le Temps du mépris* (*Days of Wrath*), and
Nizan brought out *Le Cheval de Troie*. One of the main characters in
this latter work, Lange, was a provincial schoolmaster and an anarchist,
who spent his leisure time taking solitary walks round the town, his eyes
on the cobbles, his mind abandoned to dark metaphysical speculation.
There was an obvious resemblance between him and Sartre, though in the
final pages he plumped for Fascism. Nizan declared, nonchalantly but
firmly, that his actual model had been Brice Parain. Sartre said cheerfully
that he didn't believe a word of it.

The only book of note to be published that year was a translation of
Faulkner's *Light in August*. Sartre did not like the style, which he
criticized on the grounds of a certain Biblical prolixity that I found rather
attractive. But we both unanimously admired its originality and boldness. Never had the Faulknerian universe, with its gory and all-embracing
sexuality, achieved such tragic brilliance. I was amazed to find that the
events which brought Christmas into the hands of a lynching party conveyed not only the inevitability of death but also the poignancy of life.
Here was a South stripped of its future, possessing no kind of truth except
its own legend, where even the most catastrophic events were predetermined
by fate. Faulkner had contrived to give his narrative *durée* even though
he annihilated normal time-sequence: in the very center of the book he
set, as fulcrum and divider, the triumph of destiny, which held past and
future in equipoise, and left the present meaningless. For Christmas this
implied no more than a break between two linked sequences, the one
thing going back toward the day of his birth, the other moving forward
to the instant of his horrible end, yet both embodying the same fatal
heritage, the colored blood that flowed in his veins. This was the reason
for his crime being concealed. Faulkner's cavalier manipulation of time
enriched his technique. Highlights and shadows were more skillfully
distributed than in his previous novels; the narrative tension and sharp
portrayal of incident it achieved made *Light in August* an exemplary
work. Marco, who had a penchant for formulas, pronounced that henceforth the novel must be synchronous or nothing. At all events, we believed the traditional French novel had had its day, and that it was
impossible to ignore the new freedoms and limitations which these young
American writers were advocating.

We did not get to Paris very often, but we took full advantage of every visit. We went to the exhibitions of Italian and Flemish art. We also cast a somewhat nostalgic eye over the remains of the old Trocadero, which was in process of demolition. At the Casino de Paris Maurice Chevalier was singing *"Quand un vicomte rencontre un autre vicomte,"* and giving stunning imitations of his imitators. Films showing included *Carnival in Flanders, The Informer,* and *La Bandera.* We heard Madeleine Ozeray exclaim *"Le Petit Chat est mort!"* and went to see Marguerite Jamois in *Les Caprices de Marianne.* But the commonsensical perfection of Louis Jouvet's productions we found a trifle boring, and so we missed *La Guerre de Troie n'aura pas lieu.* We got seats for the dress rehearsal of *Faiseur* at the Atelier, a play which Camille had very successfully adapted from Balzac. Dullin, swathed in Mercadet's sumptuous dressing gown, seemed actually metamorphosed into the character he was portraying, while as Monsieur Violette—the lachrymose and seedy creditor who begs for his due in vain—Sokoloff gave an even more astonishing performance: there was something positively uncanny about it. It was the first time I had set foot in a green room on the night of a dress rehearsal: people crowded around Dullin and Camille, bleating, roaring, and cooing in a way that left me quite speechless. Luckily I did not need to make fine speeches for either Dullin's or Camille's benefit but when I told Camille how impressed I had been by Sokoloff's performance she said, "Well, go and congratulate him then," and pushed me in his direction. He was sitting on a sofa, looking vague and abstracted, with Monsieur Violette's moth-eaten topper resting on his knees. I stammered a few words, and he stared at me with narrowed eyes, ironically, but rather more in sheer astonishment. I felt my face turning scarlet, and drops of sweat ran down my forehead: I had, I decided, absolutely no gift for social chitchat.

I had preserved the brightest memories of my last Christmas holiday. This year Lionel was spending the winter with an old aunt of his, in a chalet at Gsteig, in Switzerland. They had invited my sister to stay with them. Sartre and I took rooms in a small and very pleasant hotel nearby: like every house in the village, it was built of wood and heated by an enormous tiled stove. The snow-covered streets smelled of damp pine-wood and log fires. We practiced on rather steeper slopes than at Montroc, but remained almost equally erratic, since though Lionel was an excellent skier himself, as an instructor he lacked inspiration. His aged aunt had ordered an English Christmas pudding to celebrate the occasion; it was doused with rum and set alight, and the flames looked very gay. But the moment they flickered out, Sartre knocked the pudding over on to the floor, with so firm a gesture that it seemed almost certainly deliberate. We ate it, just the same.

I got along very well with Olga, yet we were totally different types. I lived for my future plans, while she denied the future altogether. All striving she regarded as merely contemptible; in her eyes prudence was synonymous with pettiness, and perseverance with self-deceit. She only

valued her emotions; cerebral concerns left her cold. She enjoyed listening
to Bach or Beethoven, but when Marco put on the Stravinsky *Octet* for
us, she remarked wittily: "Music bores me; I only enjoy sounds." In the
language of Scheler, which we used freely at the time (although today
we regard Scheler as a Fascist lackey), Olga rated "life values" well above
"spiritual values"; neither art nor literature nor anything of that sort could
affect her so much as a physical presence, actual gestures, human expressions. She had a passion for Oscar Wilde, and I was somewhat less than
enthusiastic about her aesthetic views. Still, the attitudes she took up did
not worry me in the least; I put them down to her age, and got great fun
out of them—without its ever occurring to me that Olga might be right,
and I wrong. Her relationship with Sartre was equally uneventful: they
liked being together, and neither of them made demands on the other.
For Olga the present was all-sufficient, and words of definition, limitation,
promise, or anticipation—especially the last—seemed wholly irrelevant.

As often happens, it was the intervention of a third party that caused
trouble. Olga made no secret of the fact that she liked going out with
Marco, and Sartre got it into his head that she preferred Marco to him.
The moment anyone begins making calculations or comparisons, they cease
to live for the moment: the present becomes a mere pointer to the future,
and all sorts of questions tend to arise. Sartre put some of these to himself; then he put them to Olga, after which the two of them quarreled.
This jealousy and its subsequent developments operated on a wholly
platonic level. In his relationships with women Marco could easily have
hoodwinked the very angels. Olga was both childish and ethereal by
nature; she took fright easily, and men therefore tended to respect her.
Sartre, it was true, wanted to monopolize her, but in a purely sentimental
fashion.

Would he have asserted himself thus if Olga had shown no interest
in Marco? I suppose the answer is yes, and that Marco was only an excuse.
For a year now Sartre had stuck to Olga; he did not restrict her for long
to her role as nurse-companion. At first when he told her stories and made
up songs for her, his main object was not so much to charm Olga as to
distract himself. In my company he never made the slightest attempt to
act thus: I was too close to him for any falsification of what he regarded
as his personal view of truth. But he shrank from burdening a stranger
with the company of this pitiable neurotic (which was how he saw himself),
and for a few hours was transformed into a brilliant buffoon. The lobsters,
taken by surprise, abandoned him. He came to look forward to these
moments of respite with some impatience, and actively to desire Olga's
presence: she was no longer a means to an end but the end itself, and
henceforth his efforts to be pleasant were aimed at giving her pleasure.
When his mental symptoms vanished, Olga still retained the special position she had acquired in his eyes during those long afternoons devoted
to keeping him from himself. Sartre never stopped halfway in any enterprise; and having sketched the beginnings of a friendship with Olga, he
must needs bring it to a climax. Yet he had no intention of giving any

kind of physical embodiment, either by act or gesture, to the bonds he had begun to forge between them. Olga was sacred, and it was only in a negative way that the privileged character of his position vis-à-vis her could show itself. Sartre insisted on exclusive rights: no one should mean as much to Olga as he did.

From the moment they became symbols and emotional counters, Olga's smiles and glances and remarks assumed great importance. Moreover when the crustaceans withdrew they left a kind of vast empty beach behind them, all ready to be filled with new obsessional fancies. Instead of concentrating on a black spot that danced about at eye level, Sartre now began to devote the same sort of fanatical attention to Olga's every twitch or blink, from each of which he inferred whole volumes of meaning. He wisely refrained from overwhelming her with endless questions and theories, though he was not so considerate with me. Had he scored a point against Marco? Had Olga already granted him that absolute preference which he demanded of her, and if not, would she soon do so? We spent hours thrashing out such problems.

I did not mind this; I much preferred the idea of Sartre angling for Olga's emotional favors to his slow collapse from some hallucinatory psychosis. It was something quite different that worried me. His determination to conquer Olga meant that he set great store by her. Suddenly I found it impossible to take his opinions or tastes or dislikes casually, since they outlined a system of values, and that system contradicted my own. I did not contrive this change deliberately.

Sartre himself was by no means averse to this sort of dispute. In Berlin, his interest in Marie Girard had been largely due to the fact that she had no enthusiasms or desires, and hardly any beliefs—certainly not in the supreme importance of art and literature. No doubt could ever insinuate itself into Sartre's mind, nor anything sidetrack his determination to write; there was, therefore, no reason why he should not waste his time, succumb to various passions, or say and think exactly what he pleased. He ran no risk by so doing. He even found it to his advantage to play with fire when he was not liable to burn his fingers in it. He thus convinced himself that as far as his own schemes and aims were concerned, he remained a free man, untainted by that seriousness of mind which he so detested.

For my own part, the book on which I was now working absorbed all my interest. Yet during these two years I had only gone on writing out of loyalty to my past, and because Sartre pushed me into it. The less unshakable my resolve, the less willing I was to query the tasks I set myself. I therefore determined not to allow Olga too important a place in my life, since I could not cope with the disorder she would have sown there. I set about reducing her to what she had always been for me: I loved her wholeheartedly, I decided, and found her most charming, but the truth was not in her. Nor had I any intention of yielding up to her the sovereign position that *I* had always occupied, in the very center of the universe. Little by little, however, I began to compromise: my need to agree with Sartre on all subjects outweighed the desire to see Olga through eyes other than his.

The influence which this "mere gamine" had gained over us amused some of our friends and annoyed others; but all were equally surprised by it. It was primarily due to Olga's personal qualities. The character of Xavière in *She Came to Stay* was composed to some extent with her in mind, but even so underwent a systematic reconstruction. The conflict which set my two heroines against each other would have lacked all edge if I had not endowed Xavière, under her surface charm, with a streak of sly and indomitable egotism. If Françoise was one day to find herself driven by hatred to the point of murder, it was essential that Xavière's feelings for her should be merely a deceptive mirage. Olga certainly could be capricious and moody and inconsistent; but these qualities, far from being dominant, formed only a superficial aspect of her true nature. Her generosity (using the word, as we did, in its Cartesian sense) leapt to the eye; and there was obvious evidence—which future events amply bore out—to convince us of the depth, steadfastness, and constancy of her affections. She came very close to us in her contempt for the social vanities and her hankering after the absolute. We would not have found the characteristics which divided her from us so fascinating had she not satisfied our fundamental moral requirements. As far as we were concerned this conformity was self-evident; we passed over it in silence, restricting our comments to what surprised us. Yet it was the very foundation of our relationship with Olga. When I created Xavière, all I kept of Olga—and even that I darkened in tone—was the myth we had created around her; but her personality would never have attracted us so much, or, consequently, engendered a myth at all, had she not been an infinitely richer character than Xavière.

This was the aberration that most disconcerted our acquaintances, and not without reason: instead of peaceably enjoying a normal relationship with Olga, we invented a myth and put it in her place. This piece of eccentricity can only be explained in terms of the loathing which the adult world aroused in us; rather than compromise with *that,* Sartre had plunged into neurosis, and I frequently told myself, weeping, that growing older meant falling into decay. Day by day I found myself reminded of my own relative maturity in comparison with Olga. The fact that we too pursued the cult of youth, with all its rebellious upheavals and intransigent emphasis on freedom, made no difference at all. Her impetuous, whole-hogging nature made Olga the very epitome of adolescence. Not only her conversation, but her conduct also was in constant revolt against conventional behavior, social institutions, responsibilities, routine duties, and restraints of any sort. She took lack of food and sleep in her stride, and ridiculed rational argument; she claimed to be free of just that human condition to which we had shamefacedly resigned ourselves. This was why we loaded her with values and symbols. She became Rimbaud, Antigone, every *enfant terrible* that ever lived, a dark angel judging us from her diamond-bright heaven. She did nothing to provoke such a metamorphosis herself; on the contrary, it irritated her, and she detested the fantastic character who had usurped her place. But she was powerless to prevent herself being absorbed.

We admired the way in which she lived unreservedly for the moment, but our own first consideration was to build a future for her and for us. From now on we would be a trio rather than a couple. We believed that human relationships are a matter of constant fresh discovery, and that no particular kind is a priori either especially privileged or beyond the pale: our own seemed to have come about by itself. We had already dreamed of this possibility. During the period that Sartre was doing his military service, we met a young girl in Montparnasse one night—a delightful creature, half drunk, and in a somewhat distraught state. We invited her to have a drink with us, and listened to her tale of woe: we felt very sensible and grown-up. When we parted, Sartre and I derived much amusement from the idea of adopting her. But now we really *were* grown-up, and sensible too, and it struck us as being both opportune and flattering to our self-esteem to put ourselves out on behalf of a young person who might profit from our care. Her clumsy inability to cope with life gave Olga a claim on our assistance; and in return she gave our already stale world some much-needed freshening up. We organized a scheme for alternating tête-à-tête discussions with "plenary sessions," which, we thought, should satisfy all three of us.

Olga's enthusiasms swept away our provincial dust with a vengeance: Rouen began to take on a glimmering, iridescent appearance. She would open her door to us with great ceremony, offer us jasmine tea and sandwiches made from her own recipe, and tell us stories about her childhood and the Greek countryside in summer. We in turn told her about our travels, and Sartre went through his entire repertoire of songs. We made up plays and in general behaved as though we were twenty again. As soon as the first hint of spring appeared, we went off on Sunday to Saint-Adrien, at the foot of the chalk cliffs beside the Seine. There was outdoor dancing there, and at night they hung strings of colored lamps across from tree to tree. We discovered a place called the Aero Bar; this was beside the local airfield, with woods all around. It had a dance floor, and little booths where you could drink or dine. During the afternoon the place was deserted, and we often spent several hours there, with me working in one corner and Sartre and Olga chatting in another. Later I would join them. From time to time, but not very often, a small airplane would take off or land. Sartre had always been inclined to verbalize, and had got me into a similar habit; Olga, with her endless capacity for wonder, encouraged this mania. From time to time, though, I found it a little irritating. When we went on endlessly trying to describe the exact taste of a glass of cassis, or the precise way a cheek curved, I accused us of lapsing into mere "textual exegesis." But we had slender resources and were forced to exploit them to the limit.

Olga accompanied us to Paris for the Easter holidays. We took her to see *Modern Times,* and sat through two consecutive performances; we would

have liked to commit every single frame to memory. For the first time
Chaplin was using sound, though by no means in a realistic fashion. On
the contrary, he used it specifically to dehumanize certain characters. Mana-
gerial orders were passed on by microphone, and a phonograph kept endlessly repeating the inventor's gibberish. We carefully memorized the song
he sang to the tune of *"Je cherche après Titine"*:

> La spinach or la tacho
> Cigaretto torlo totto
> E rusho spagaletta
> Je le tu le tu le tava

We often hummed it, and Marco used to bellow it at the top of his voice.
We spent hours in the Dôme or the Vikings' Bar drinking, talking, and
watching the world go by. We had dinner in a Spanish restaurant where
there were some first-rate guitarists and a middle-aged *chanteuse* with a
pathetic voice; she danced, too, and when she did her bloated body acquired
a surprising lightness. From time to time she vanished, and when she
came back there would be a somehow triumphant expression on her
face: she was a heroin addict, Camille told us. As a pharmacist's daughter
Camille figured she was an expert on drugs. After a few days Olga had
to go off to Beuzeville, since her parents insisted on seeing her. Her moments
of despair were even more intense than her cheerful moods; and since for
her every single minute was a minute lost, she was convinced as she left
us that she would never see us again. For two whole hours the three of us
had sat in silent agony at the Dôme. When Olga came back to Rouen,
she was so amazed to find herself there and to have us meet her that in the
station her suitcase dropped from her hand. Sartre and I had concluded our
holiday with a brief trip to Belgium, taking in Brussels, Bruges, Anvers,
and Malines: crumbling stonework, a huge bustling port, and the most
beautiful paintings in the world.

During this final term various friends came to see us. Camille spent
a couple of days in Rouen, and as she was fond of provincial towns,
we took her through every nook and corner in the place. She enjoyed
canard au sang at the Hôtel de la Couronne, and drank port with us in
the Cintra. The Royal at night reminded her of the sleazy Toulouse
dance halls she had known as a young girl: the walls were adorned with
trellis-borne greenery, paper garlands hung looping across the ceiling, and
the dancers, mostly students and shop assistants, moved about in a weird
orange glow. Camille called for champagne, and then pulled Olga with
her onto the floor; when the orchestra struck up a *paso doble* she folded
her arms, threw back her head, and gave an exhibition in the grand style—
heels tapping, jewelry clashing, hair flying in all directions. Everybody
stared at her. As we walked back to the Petit Mouton, her voice, raised
in song, echoed through the slumbering streets. Sartre and I, she told us,
definitely belonged to the race of Abel, but Olga, like herself, was sealed
with a special demoniac sign, and she pronounced the girl her daughter
before Lucifer.

The previous year Sartre had made a friend of Jacques Bost, a student whom he was now coaching for a teacher's diploma in philosophy. He brought him to Rouen, and Bost made frequent visits thereafter. He was nineteen years old, with a dazzling smile and a most princely ease of bearing: as a good Protestant he believed that any man on this earth is a king in his own right. A democrat both by conviction and principle, he felt himself superior to nobody; but he found some difficulty in bringing himself to admit that anyone could possibly want to live through a personality other than his own—especially if this involved a change of age group. He too, in his way, personified youth for us. He possessed the casual grace of youth, so casual that it bordered on insolence, coupled with a certain narcissistic fragility: he spit up a little blood once after clearing his throat, and Sartre had to take him off to a doctor in order to convince him that he wasn't going to die at twenty. His need for security drove him to seek out the company of adults, though they all— with the possible exception of Sartre—moved him to a sort of compassionless astonishment. At some time during the past few years we had amused ourselves by inventing a character called Little Noddle, to whom we made frequent references. As I have mentioned, we loathed the whole idea of *la vie intérieure,* and Little Noddle was totally devoid of any such thing: all his interests were directed outward, toward objects or events. He was a modest, peaceable, but obstinate fellow, who, far from taking a pride in thinking for himself, always said and did the accepted thing. Jacques Bost—whom we called Little Bost to distinguish him from his brother Pierre—struck us as being the very embodiment of Little Noddle. (Boris, in Sartre's *The Age of Reason,* is a Russianized portrait of Little Bost, at least as he appeared to us at the time.) Like him, he fastened onto *objects,* whether the glass of pernod he was drinking or the story he was being told. He had no ambitions, but a number of small, obstinate desires instead, and was exceedingly delighted when he contrived to satisfy them. He never produced a word or a gesture that was out of place; on every occasion he reacted in just the right way—that is, it goes without saying, the way we would have reacted ourselves. He did not possess an original mind, and in any case he was so afraid of saying something stupid, as he put it, that even if an idea did pass through his head he made every effort to conceal the fact. On the other hand he was both quick-witted and droll. This drollness emerged in his manners no less than his speech, and sprang from the conflict between his natural spontaneity and the puritanical upbringing he had received. He would give himself orders and then break them practically in the same breath. I remember him coming into a café in Le Havre where Sartre, Marco, and I were awaiting him: he advanced with his stiff, jerky stride, that was at once quick-moving and held in, his face lit up yet sedulously under control. This blend of cheerful eagerness and calculated reserve made us smile. He stared at us suspiciously. "What are you all up to, catching each other's eye in that furtive way?" he asked. At this Marco suddenly exploded, and we both followed suit. Bost had made conquests everywhere in Rouen. Marco devoured him with his eyes.

Olga stayed out with him all one night; they drank a whole bottle of Cinzano as a special treat and woke up at dawn to find themselves lying in the gutter. The moment he pushed through the door of the Metropole, with that half-bashful, half-aggressive air, I myself felt drawn toward him. That afternoon Sartre went off with Olga and I had a walk with Bost. He told me a large number of anecdotes about Sartre which I found most amusing—the way he went about his lectures, his dislike of discipline, and his abrupt fits of anger, which were not so much those of a teacher as of a man suddenly shocked by the absurdity of life. One day, for instance, he suddenly broke off in the middle of expounding a point and stared round his class in defeated fury. "All these faces," he roared, "and not one single glimmer of intelligence!" Such outbursts terrorized half the class, but gave Bost an irresistible urge to giggle, which he had some difficulty in repressing.

My sister made a fairly long stay at the Petit Mouton: she was preparing for an exhibition that was to be held at the Galerie Bonjean. She undertook to paint Olga's portrait, but posing for any length of time made Olga feel miserable and depressed. Gégé turned up during the same period. We all piled into Olga's room and entertained each other in turn with our own specialties. Gégé did a belly dance, Marco sang, Bost struck matches with his toes, and Sartre dressed up as a woman. Oddly enough, drag suited him. During his Norwegian cruise he had gone to a fancy-dress ball in a black velvet dress of his mother's, and a blonde wig with long pigtails: an American lesbian had pursued him all night. The following morning she took one look at him and vanished in some consternation.

Rouen about this time was rocking with a vast scandal that gave my sister and me special pleasure. One prize-day at the Cours Désir we had piously kissed the amethyst ring of Monseigneur de La Villerabelle, who was presiding over the ceremony. Just recently the Vatican had taken stern measures against him after a case involving breach of trust and immoral conduct. A young girl had lost her life. Some nuns were compromised. There was frenzied whispering in the cathedral close; the Bishop's defenders put all the blame on his immediate deputy. But no one thought of denying the facts, which cast an unexpected light on the quiet convent-lined streets around the bishopric.

My sister had given up her secretarial job, which did not leave her enough time for painting; now she worked from morning till night. She had moved into a new studio on the Rue Santeuil, near the leather market: a big room, pleasant if rough-and-ready, but liable when the wind changed to smell of tanning and decayed meat. She had brought her own cooking utensils, and had meals there; to all intents and purposes she lived there nonstop, in a very austere style too, for paint was expensive and she hadn't a sou to her name. Her exhibition took place at the beginning of June: a lot of fashionable people came to the *vernissage,* and the critics were highly complimentary. Her landscapes and portraits did show definite talent. I was furious with Marco, who had been playing his usual complicated tricks on her. He started up with her one of his feigned "friendships" in Rouen (he was very good at this), and then invited her two or three times to lunch with him in fairly classy Parisian restaurants. He overwhelmed her with little attentions, opened his heart to her, gazed at her with spaniel eyes, and then, in a silky voice, said what a pity it was that Sartre and I failed to appreciate her properly. He gave no exact details, but his handsome face absolutely radiated sincerity: my sister was desolated. Luckily we were so close to one another that she felt able to ask me for an explanation. I told her just what Marco was, and she was furious at having fallen into his trap so easily.

He also interfered in our relationship with Pagniez, and here he scored a more lasting success. Pagniez was highly critical of our infatuation for Olga: as a friend he tended toward jealous exclusiveness, and in any case Olga did not appeal to him. We were tactless enough to let Olga know about his reservations, which hardly predisposed her in his favor. One evening when she was out with Marco the latter began to run Pagniez down in an offhand way. Olga took the bait and outdid him at his own game, telling him about Pagniez's semi-engagement to his cousin. Pagniez had no idea that Marco knew anything about this. Marco could hardly wait to mention the matter to Pagniez; he handled the situation so well, indeed, that Pagniez was convinced Olga hated him and had deliberately leaked the information out of spite. The result was that he felt resentment against both her and us. We for our part were irritated by his unfriendly attitude toward Olga. He and Thérèse came to Rouen and spent a night in the Petit Mouton. In the morning he told us how distressed he had been to hear a conversation going on in the next room between a male and a female voice. He had not been able to make out what was said, but felt that these alternating sounds, high against low pitch, had offered him an epitome of the universal and perennial mating duet. We protested sharply; he had, in fact, occupied a room next door to the sergeant major who beat his wife. That didn't matter, he declared: the "duet" still possessed a symbolic meaning of universal and breathtaking significance. There was nothing new about Pagniez and us having an argument of this sort; but we had lost our former liking for his views, and decided that his so-called humanism was creating a gulf between us.

We never managed, on the other hand, to get really annoyed with Marco: he laughed away our reproaches too disarmingly. His satanic sense of humor once led us to play a practical joke that was in somewhat doubtful taste, and which in retrospect I find singularly unfunny. He had it in for a colleague of his named Paul Guth, whom he criticized for excessive subservience to authority and unwarranted literary pretensions. Guth was writing a book and boasting about its merits in the most outrageous way; Marco was determined to bring him down a peg. Largely to amuse Olga, Sartre agreed to join in the fun. Marco told Guth that it would be to his advantage to get the opinion of a successful writer, and claimed acquaintance with Pierre Bost. Bost, he said, was shortly going to be in Rouen, and Marco suggested sending him Guth's manuscript and fixing up a meeting. Guth agreed.

The rendezvous was a little *café-tabac* near the Petit Mouton. On the appointed day I was the first there. Shortly afterward Marco arrived, accompanied by a fat little butterball of a man, who instantly began discussing his work with me. He explained that he found it both unfair and absurd how former school fellows of his—Brasillach, for example—had already made their mark, whereas he, who was worth far more than they, still remained in obscurity. Still, he had no doubt that very soon he would break through. He pulled Métro tickets and bits of string out of his pockets, explaining that such things were his source of inspiration, the material which guaranteed his remaining in contact with the realities of life. His book was to tell, in epic fashion, the story of a human being—the author himself, and Man in general—from the cradle to the grave. So far he had only written the first chapter. During this little lecture Olga entered the café and sat down at another table as though she didn't know me: she pretended to be a prostitute. A few moments later Sartre appeared, all muffled up in a scarf, and carrying under one arm a huge notebook that looked more like an accounts ledger. Marco introduced him to Guth as "Pierre Bost." Sartre spread out the manuscript in front of him and began to rip the writing to shreds. It was, he said, even grayer and more unpleasant than a Rouen sky, and chock-full of the most grotesque metaphors. There was only one phrase he had liked, *une fraise de sang* (a strawberry mark), and that was in every physiology textbook anyway. But apart from this, the *soi-disant* Pierre Bost was very severe on Guth for writing things like "The engine of my passion runs on the rails of your indifference." Having performed this just (if not justifiable) ax-job, Sartre took off, leaving Guth completely shattered, and Marco in the seventh heaven of delight.

The episode had one unfortunate repercussion. Guth wrote to the real Pierre Bost, who replied in a way that showed him what had happened. Bost also told his brother Jacques that he was most annoyed at his name having been used in such a way. This change of mood struck us as betraying a regrettable solemnity, which we held against him. But as a matter of fact both Sartre and I would have resented it highly if someone had usurped *our* identities in similar circumstances. Nevertheless, this rather tasteless farce has not left me with any feeling of remorse: the victim is doing very nicely indeed.

We remained as fascinated as ever with all the people who crossed our path: Olga, Bost, and Marco joined in our speculations on them with great enthusiasm. One incident that involved a member of Sartre's class made a deep impression on me. This pupil of his was brilliantly intelligent, but of a sullen disposition, and not only a Fascist but illegitimate into the bargain. He committed suicide by jumping off a rooftop. At eight o'clock in the morning he had drunk a bowl of *café au lait* and written two letters, one to his grandmother, the other to a girl. Then he had gone into the bathroom and cut his throat with a couple of razor blades. But he did not die. So then he climbed up onto the roof, shouted to the passers-by "Look out there below! Keep clear!" and jumped. For a long while afterward I pondered in deep concern over that bowl of *café au lait,* and the concern for others which he had preserved on the very brink of death.

There was a large mental hospital near Rouen which Sartre was anxious to visit. He obtained permission to take me along with him, and two students—Olga and Bost. The asylum was set in open country, and the director was waiting for us at the front gates. We walked through orchards and kitchen gardens where various men were working—inmates, all of them, the director told us, but quite harmless. It had a queer effect on me, seeing insane men pottering about freely, brandishing hoes, shovels, or rakes. The director escorted us as far as the main block, where he turned us over to a young doctor. We went into the first ward. There was a narrow central passageway between the two rows of beds, and a faint feral odor hung in the air, neither wholly human nor wholly animal. At the end of this open space there stood a group of men dressed in some blue material. One of them had opened his fly and exposed himself, and the others were scolding him and trying to hide him from us, smiling apologetically in our direction. I felt my gorge rise, and the other three seemed similarly ill at ease: just how ghastly was this tour of inspection going to be? The doctor alone wore a relaxed smile and spoke in a calm, unemphatic voice. "Those two," he remarked, pointing to a pair of bed-ridden patients, "have to be tube fed." He bent over one of them and murmured a few words. The man's eyes were open, but not a muscle flickered in his face. We passed on into a second ward, and then a third. Everywhere we found the same smell and the same motionless figures in their blue uniforms. A big dark-complexioned man rushed to the doctor. "The radio's gone crazy!" he roared, and went on shouting, in a transport of fury. Life, it seemed, was not much of a joke in this barrackslike place: how was one to kill time without a radio? The doctor gesticulated vaguely: radio maintenance was not his affair. It's true, I thought: even here time drags, and you have to kill it. The patients were stuck there from morning till night, with nothing to do and not even a corner they could call their own apart from their beds. The further we advanced, the thicker grew the atmosphere of misery around us.

In one little room, however, there were tables at which men were busy writing. They filled their notebooks with pages of fine script, the words following one another in a free association dictated by assonance or verbal similarity. At least these patients were not bored. The next room was noisy by contrast, with voices muttering aloud: here were the victims of paranoia or psychotic hallucinations. One of them took us aside and begged us to help him. They had installed a telephone inside his stomach, he said, and people were always ringing him up and gabbling nonsense at him. He spoke in a normal, if harassed, voice. His next-door neighbor winked at us and tapped his forehead. "He's nuts," he hissed, and then proceeded to tell us all about himself: there was a birthmark on his right thigh that proved he was the legitimate son of the South Sea Emperor.

Another patient embarked on a description of some machine he had invented, the patent of which had been stolen. I had seen similar cases at Sainte-Anne's, but the whole point was that there they remained cases and nothing else. Here we were brought up against real flesh-and-blood people, going about their daily lives, with the future lying interminably before them. This last was the worst thing of all. And while these men were talking to us, with normal voices and expressions, their minds still registering ordinary human feelings, I looked past them and saw other faces, behind barred windows: vacant, grimacing faces that had reached the very nadir of lunatic imbecility. Ten or twenty years from now the hallucinatory psychotics we met would inevitably sink into the same dark shadowy region, their eyes blank, their memories gone. I asked the doctor if any of them ever recovered. He shrugged his shoulders. There were two hundred and sixty male patients, and he had to cope with them single-handedly. He looked after their attacks of influenza and their liver complaints; no time to spare for mental illness. To tell the truth, he said, he didn't even know all the patients by sight. It was a regrettable state of affairs, as he freely admitted. I realized in some alarm that a person committed to an asylum for insufficient cause had no chance whatsoever of getting out again. Yet among these men there must have been some who were not altogether incurable, though no attempt was made to save them. Those who entered here had indeed to abandon all hope.

The doctor opened another door, and there, in the middle of a white-tiled cell, was a man tied to an iron bedstead, struggling and howling. The next cell was exactly the same, but here the occupant was asleep. Both of these were dangerous maniacs. Next we visited the quarters reserved for those with general paralysis, who were the only patients to receive therapeutic treatment. By inoculating them with malarial germs the disease was arrested in its euphoric stage; they were all grinning and babbling with beatific cheerfulness. Our last port of call was the block containing cases of total dementia; here were those tattered scraps of humanity that I had glimpsed through the barred windows. One, with emaciated face and mouth agape, hopped about on one foot; another twisted his fingers together, a third swayed backward and forward; endless repetition of gestures that had once been charged with meaning, but now were devoid of all sense. Had they once, in their far-off childhood, been as other men? How and why had they come where they now were? What were *we* doing here, staring at them and asking ourselves such questions? There was something insulting about our presence.

The director had invited us to lunch. He had a separate house of his own, where we were welcomed by his wife, a black-clad matron whose face proclaimed, with some arrogance, that no one had ever "gabbled nonsense" into *her* brain or heart. The maid who waited on table was an inmate of the asylum; she was liable to fits, but took care to warn her employers a day or two in advance when she felt them coming, and then another patient would fill in for her. The conversation at the table lacked gaiety: all four of us were still recovering from the effects of the morning we had just spent, and we found some difficulty in responding to the aggressively normal remarks of the director and his wife.

After coffee the director showed us a building reserved for fee-paying patients. They each had their own room: the windows had no catches, and there was a metal grille over the glass. A spy hole in the door enabled the staff to observe every corner of the cell. Patients must have felt more persecuted here than in the communal blocks.

We were not finished yet. An aged and mustachioed doctor now took us across to the women's quarters. Unlike the men, they had not been divided into various categories: cases of paranoia, depression, and manic aggression rubbed shoulders with one another, and their wards were so cluttered with beds, tables, and chairs that it was almost impossible to get through them. The women did not wear uniforms. Many of them had twisted flowers into their hair, or wound curious bits of cheap finery around themselves. The air was filled with a babel of singing, shrill screams, and dignified private monologues. I felt as though I was watching a messily produced burlesque show. Through it all some quietly dressed women sat silently doing embroidery in a corner. The doctor pointed out one who had tried to jump out of a window the previous evening: it was her seventh suicide attempt. He put one hand on her shoulder. "You've been at it again, eh?" he said. "That's naughty of you, isn't it? Come on now—life isn't all that bad! You must promise me to be sensible . . ." "Yes, doctor," the woman said, not looking up. This doctor had everything cut and dried, no unnecessary complications. The mad were mad, and that was that: the idea of curing, let alone understanding them never so much as occurred to him. Women held down on their beds in straitjackets eyed him with hatred or despair. If they promised to be reasonable, he told them in a scolding voice, their straitjackets would be removed. Olga and I paused near an extremely handsome old lady who sat on a chair knitting, while tears streamed quietly down her ivory-colored cheeks. We asked her why she was crying. "I cry the whole time," she said with a woebegone expression. "It was just too depressing for my husband and children, having to watch me cry day in, day out—so they brought me here." Her tears flowed faster than ever; she appeared to regard them as an unavoidable misfortune which neither she nor anyone else could do a thing to prevent. There they all lived side by side, from morning till night: some weeping and sobbing desperately, others singing in hoarse, strident tones or dancing about with their skirts pulled up—how could they have helped hating one another?

"Last week," the doctor told us, "one of them killed the woman in the next bed with a pair of scissors." By the time we got back to the *terrasse* of the Café Victor, and the ordinary everyday world, we were overwhelmed with disgust, exhaustion, and a curious feeling of shame.

Things turned out much as we had anticipated. Olga got to know our friends, and shared our experiences; we helped her to enrich her life, and her vision of the world put fresh color back into it for us. The

prejudices she entertained as an exiled aristocrat fitted in very well with
our own antibourgeois anarchism. We united in hating Sunday crowds,
fashionable ladies and gentlemen, the provinces, family life, children, and
any sort of "humanism." We liked exotic music; the *quais* along the Seine,
with their coal barges and dockside loafers; low, disreputable little bars;
and the silent loneliness of the night. We would park ourselves in some
dive or other and spin a silken cocoon of words and smiling glances to
protect us against Rouen and the outside world generally. Caught by the
magic that sparked from our eyes as they met, each of us felt himself
playing a double role—enchanter and enchanted at once. At such moments
the "trio" seemed a dazzling success; and yet cracks began to appear in the
splendid edifice almost immediately.

The edifice as such was Sartre's work, though he had not, one may say,
so much built it as called it into being, simply by virtue of his attachment
to Olga. For my own part, though I vainly tried to achieve satisfaction
from the relationship, I never felt at ease with it. I cared very much for
Sartre and for Olga, but in different and perhaps incompatible ways: the
relationships were mutually exclusive, and the feeling I had for each could
never amalgamate. My affection for Olga, though deep, had been a familiar,
day-to-day affair, with nothing star-struck about it; and when I tried to
see her through Sartre's eyes, I felt I was playing my own emotions false.
Her personality and her moods affected me more strongly than before,
and her own feeling for me had increased; but the vague sense of restraint
which governed my reactions where she was concerned in some way seemed
actually to turn me against her. Even when we were alone together I no
longer felt free to follow my natural bent, since I had forbidden myself
any expression of reserve or indifference; I no longer recognized her for
the easygoing companion of whom I had been so fond.

When the three of us went out together, the old Olga vanished completely, since it was a different aspect of her that Sartre craved. Sometimes
she responded to him as he hoped, behaving in a more feminine, coquettish,
and artificial way than she did with me; sometimes she found his expectations irksome, and then she would be sullen or actively bad-tempered.
But either way she could not ignore the situation. Sartre, too, was quite
different when he had his mind on Olga from what he was during our
private conversations together—so much so that during these meetings
à trois I felt myself doubly frustrated. They often developed a charming
atmosphere, to which I contributed as best I could; but whenever I thought
of the trio as a long-term project, stretching ahead for years, I was frankly
terrified. When Sartre and I went on our travels as we had planned, I had
not the slightest wish to see Olga tagging along with us too. On the other
hand, I was counting on a teaching job in Paris next year, and wanted
Olga to come with me: but if I admitted that her happiness depended on
Sartre as much as it did on me, and perhaps more, this spoiled my own
pleasure. I had no doubt that he would end up by supplanting me in
Olga's life; there was no question of fighting him for her, since I could

not bear any dissension between us. In any case he had earned such preferment by the sheer stubbornness with which he pursued it: I myself felt no similar urge. Since he gave Olga more time and consideration than I had ever done I had no right to complain; but this rational argument failed to curtail my resentment. Without putting my feelings into conscious terms, I was vexed with Sartre for having created this situation, and with Olga for taking advantage of it. There was something innately shameful about this obscure resentment on my part, and I consequently found it harder to endure than I was prepared to admit. Both in deed and word I zealously fostered the well-being of the trio; but I did not feel at all happy, either in myself or about the other two, and I looked forward to the future with apprehension.

Olga too was in a difficult position. At first her affair with Sartre had progressed without obstacles: he interested her, he amused her, she found him captivating. Besides, she was always attracted by the unusual: those walks they had taken together to throw the lobsters off his track had possessed a piquant, poetical quality in her eyes. Seen through his somber reveries—not to mention the manuscript of *Melancholia,* which she had had read with absorbed interest—Sartre struck her as a somewhat fantastic character, capable of carrying her far away from the dull tedium of this world. "That was a quite extraordinary time I had with you" was one of her frequent remarks to him. In the beginning he had been careful not to ask her too many questions, or demand too much of her. But now it was not enough that he had cut her out with Marco; the friendship he wanted of Olga was something as absolute and exclusive as love, and he felt the need for her to confirm it by some open sign—a word, a glance, a symbolic gesture. She had no wish to bind herself to any one man, and certainly not to someone already encumbered. But she was very fond of him, and possessed a flirtatious streak too: so quite often she gave him the glances or gestures he wanted, only to deny them the following day. He reproached her for capriciousness, she complained that he was tyrannical, and they would slide into a quarrel. Sometimes they were still at loggerheads when they parted: then Sartre would telephone me from Le Havre to find out whether Olga had got over her resentment yet. Marco walked in on one or two of these conversations: they made him laugh till he cried.

One day, when they had had a particularly stormy meeting, it was Olga who was summoned to the phone, some two hours after Sartre's departure. An unknown voice informed her that on getting out of the train at Rouen a choleric little man had attacked someone twice as big as himself, who had put out his eye in retaliation. The madman had been taken off to a hospital, and had asked for someone to tell Olga. She knocked at my door in a fine panic. I put on my hat and coat, determined to leave for Le Havre myself by the next train. Meanwhile I went up to see Marco. He suggested telephoning the Café Guillaume Tell to make sure Sartre wasn't peacefully working at his usual table. Sartre came to the phone, full of apologies: he had thought Olga would recognize his voice and guess from this little joke that he was pleading mental disturbance as an excuse for his furious bad temper. I was vastly relieved, Olga much put out, and Marco ecstatic with delight.

Not all their disputes had such a cheerful ending. Both Sartre and Olga in turn would pour out their complaints to me and solicit my alliance. I often took Olga's side, but she knew very well that my relationship with her was not the same as that I maintained with Sartre. Though we valued her youth more highly than our own experience, her role was, nevertheless, that of a child—a child up against an adult couple united by unfailing emotional bonds. However devotedly we consulted her interests, it was we who controlled the actual destiny of the trio. We had not established any real equality in our relationship with her, but had rather annexed her to ourselves. Even though I blamed Sartre on occasion, I remained so firmly behind him that Olga could fear the possibility of a quarrel with him jeopardizing my feelings for her. This idea infuriated her, because she was far fonder of me than she was of him: and her anger with him was, in a sense, directed against me too. His dogmatic behavior might well ruin our friendship, she told me, and I did nothing to stop it! She regarded my tact as plain indifference, and this bred resentment in her—which, in its turn, increased her fear of losing me. It was seldom that she quarreled with Sartre and did not involve me in her hostility as well. Sometimes, too, to get her own back for my lukewarmness, she would ostentatiously make it up with him and continue to cut me dead; then the enmity between us would suddenly scare her, and she would turn against Sartre once more.

Sartre himself could hardly be said to have got very much out of the whole business either: not only because Olga's hesitant tacking and veering drove him to distraction, but also since he had no real idea of what he expected from her. Since it was something that neither mind nor imagination could grasp, it seemed unobtainable. This was why Olga's personality, and even her physical attractions, although he found them charming enough, still failed to measure up to his expectations. Then he would fly into a rage, not so much for any specific reason as to camouflage the emptiness gnawing away at his desires and his joys: these unexpected tornadoes often dismayed Olga considerably. They both continued to tell me all about their meetings, in the most minute detail. At first I had welcomed these reports, not to mention the commentaries which they inspired; but by now I had come to feel an impatience I did not bother to conceal when Sartre speculated ad infinitum on the meaning of some frown or *moue* of Olga's. If I questioned his interpretations he became irritated, and if I took Olga's side against him, his irritation turned to fury. There was a phrase which we borrowed from phenomenology and much abused during these arguments: "self-evident truth." Emotions and all other "psychological entities" had only a *probable* existence; whereas the *Erlebnis* [experience] contained its own self-evident truth [*sa propre évidence*]. To stop any comeback on my part Sartre would say: "Olga was furious with me just now—*that's a self-evident truth.*" I would retort with other "self-evident truths," and criticize him for sliding from such individual instances to hypothetical generalities about Olga's friendship or hostility. On this subject we would wrangle indefinitely, and after a while I found it exhausting.

So all three of us found ourselves being led a terrible dance by this quietly infernal machine we had set in motion. In the last resort, however, we emerged unscathed from the ordeal: friendship triumphed. There was a lot of thoughtlessness and sheer folly in all these arguments between us, but at least we brought all the good will in the world to them, and none of us bore a really lasting grudge against either of the other two. All the same, each of us experienced some very black moments: the mere fact of our deep mutual attachment to one another meant that the least cloud was instantly magnified till it blotted out the entire sky. Such worries would have bothered us much less had we been living in Paris: what with our friends and all the amusements available there, distraction would have come easily enough. But the three of us were living in a kind of hothouse, under glass, hemmed in by the oppressive solitude of the provinces; when we suffered any trouble or distress, there was nothing to help us overcome it. Sartre had periods of morose gloom, which worried me less than those he had experienced the year before, but were by no means pleasant. Olga had momentary fits of aberration: during the Easter holidays in Paris, when we were visiting Camille, she burned her hand with a lighted cigarette, pressing it into the flesh with positively maniacal concentration. I brought this episode into *She Came to Stay*: it was a kind of self-defense against the confusion which so complex an adventure had brought about in her.

My own life, on the other hand—apart from brief mental crises induced by my horror of death—had so far been spent in the relentless light of unfailing cheerfulness: to learn what misery really felt like was for me a quite stupefying experience. I remember one afternoon when Olga and I were slouching through Rouen in the appalling summer heat, both of us equally depressed. Two children were chasing each other around inside a street urinal on the Rue Eau-de-Robec, roaring with laughter. From the first floor of one of the riverside houses came the screech of a violin. At the far end of the street a man sat on a campstool, singing tonelessly and accompanying himself on a saw:

> *Il pleut sur la route*
> *Dans la nuit j'écoute*
> *Le coeur en déroute*
> *Le bruit de ton pas.*

[It's raining out on the road; I can hear, in the still night, my hurrying, vanquished heart, and the sound of your footsteps.] Well, I could hear the sound of our footsteps; and my own heart was certainly *en déroute*.

I remember, too, a lunch I had once with Marco at the Brasserie de l'Opéra. Olga had said goodbye to me in an icy voice, and gone off, laughing, with Sartre. They were having one of their idyllic moments together, looking at the world in unison and sharing its enchantment, keeping it jealously to themselves. I was shut out from this world by Olga's spite, totally dispossessed, floating in the void. My throat was so tight that I couldn't swallow a single mouthful of my scrambled eggs, and Marco's words dwindled to nothing in an abyss of emptiness.

The fact is that at the time I was quite incapable of keeping Olga's moods in any kind of perspective. No, I thought, people's ideas were *not* harmless little puffs of smoke circulating inside their heads; they spread out over the whole earth, and I was disintegrating in them. Olga forced me to face a truth which hitherto, as I have said, I had been at considerable pains to avoid—that other people existed, exactly as I did, and with just as much *évidence* in their favor. Her natural temperament, together with the role assigned to her in the trio, made her stubbornly determined to preserve her independence. She could throw herself wholeheartedly into a friendship for a longer or shorter period, but in the end she always withdrew again: we did not share that community of interests which alone can guarantee the continued existence of any *entente*. When she stood apart from me she looked at me with alien eyes, and I was transformed into an *object* that might be either idol or enemy. What made her so alarming was the fact that she forgot the past, refused to consider the future, and upheld—with a violent emphasis from which there was no appeal—the truth of the here and now. If a word or gesture or decision of mine displeased her, I was made to feel an utter and loathsome outcast till all eternity. I once more acquired contours and boundaries to my existence, behavior which I had thought creditable was suddenly made to show up my deficiencies, and my right decisions were all proved wrong. In fact, of course, Olga's animosity lacked staying power, and I still retained some defenses: I raged against her to myself, accusing and condemning her in the privacy of my own head. I never, therefore, applied any radically severe criticism to myself, but I did lose a little of my self-assurance, and suffered as a result. On this plane I needed certainties, and the slightest flicker of doubt bewildered me.

What disturbed me even more was the way I sometimes found myself in opposition to Sartre. He always took great care not to say or do anything which might change our relationship; our discussions were extremely lively, as always, but free from any hint of rancor. Yet all the same I was led to revise certain postulates which hitherto I had thought we were agreed upon, and told myself it was wrong to bracket myself and another person in that equivocal and all-too-handy word "we." There were some experiences that each individual lived through alone. I had always maintained that words could not fully express the physical essence of reality, and now I must face the consequences. When I said "We are one person," I was dodging the issue. Harmony between two individuals is never a *donnée*; it must be worked for continually. This I was quite prepared to admit. But another, more painful question also posed itself: what was the true nature of such an achievement? We believed—and here phenomenology brought a long-standing tradition to our support—that time was something more than the sum of each separate instant, and that emotions existed above and beyond the heart's intermittent vagaries. But if they could be preserved only by promises and controls and passwords, would they not in the long run lose all their inward substance, and come to resemble the whited sepulchers of the Bible? Olga was furiously skeptical concerning all "voluntaristic" interpretations, which by itself was not enough to unsettle me; but in the face of her opposition Sartre, too, let himself go, to the great detriment of his emotional stability, and experienced feelings of alarm, frenzy, and ecstasy such as he had never known with me. The agony which this produced in me went far beyond mere jealousy: at times I asked myself whether the whole of my happiness did not rest upon a gigantic lie.

Toward the end of the school year, doubtless because what looked like a final parting between them was now imminent, Sartre and Olga were on rather strained terms. Then they had several serious quarrels and stopped seeing each other. Olga, having an instinctive need for emotional compensation, behaved twice as affectionately toward me as she had done before. I was tired of working, and decided to give myself a rest: for a few days we spent nearly all our time together. Sometimes Marco would accompany us in the evening: on these mild nights the narrow back streets behind the docks were full of foreign sailors on the prowl. Marco would pick some of them up, and take us all drinking in bars that were crowded with paid-off hands. We generally went home without him. Olga spoke English fluently, and we had long conversations with light-haired men from the four corners of the earth. There was one of these, an extremely good-looking Norwegian, whom we saw on several occasions and who asked us our names.

"She's called Castor The Beaver," said Olga, pointing to me.

"Ah then," exclaimed the sailor in cheerful triumph, "you must be Pollux." Henceforth whenever he saw us he ran up shouting, "Here's Castor and Pollux!" with great enthusiasm, and kissed us on both cheeks. We would finish our night out in a café-restaurant that stayed open till four in the morning and was popular with the *jeunesse dorée*; it was called Chez Nicod, and was the only place that you could get supper after midnight. I thoroughly enjoyed these slumming expeditions of ours, and the exclusive intimacy I had re-established with Olga. The only thing was, I knew Sartre felt considerable resentment about our reconciliation, since it had been achieved at his expense. Be that as it may, he no longer thought of me as an ally during this period, and such a rift between us poisoned the very air I breathed.

Olga had not even sat for her teacher's diploma, and her parents were writing her angry letters: she left for Beuzeville at the beginning of July, and I missed her. Nevertheless, the atmosphere bred by the trio in conflict had finally become so stifling that I found escape from it a blessed relief, and was only too glad to lose myself in frivolous and inconsequential relationships. Bost, with whom Marco had struck up a close friendship, came for a short stay at the Petit Mouton, and in the evenings the three of us made a round of the more or less shady dives that Marco ferreted out with such ingenuity. The Rue des Cordeliers lacked the special charm of the Rue des Galions in Le Havre, but here too the night was lit up with twinkling purple stars and red windmills and green cats. One night Marco went up to a procuress sitting in her doorway, and greeted her in the most lordly way imaginable; after the two of them had palavered for a while she showed us into a sort of shabby waiting room, where several women in evening dress were sitting on wooden benches. Marco offered a drink to an emaciated blonde, and with somewhat exaggerated politeness began to question her. Answering these questions seemed to embarrass the blonde, and I thought Marco showed himself lacking in tact. Ordinarily, though, his charm was such that he could get away with practically anything. Sartre found it easier to bear his estrangement from Olga now that she had returned to the bosom of her family: he was in excellent spirits during his visit to Rouen. One evening that we spent together ended with our going out for fried eggs at Nicod's, where round about midnight Marco made a highly public entry, with Bost riding on his shoulders, completely stewed after a couple of pernods, and laughing fit to burst.

His cheerful hilarity appealed to us, and all four of us kicked up a considerable row. It was high time that both Marco and I left Rouen: our reputations were beginning to suffer in no uncertain fashion. But we both nevertheless had been nominated to posts in Paris, and this promotion pleased me considerably. Sartre was due to leave Le Havre the following year. For some reason I cannot now remember—doubtless a matter of doubling up two appointments—a new philosophy instructor was being brought in. In exchange Sartre was offered a job in Lyon, preparing pupils for the Ecole Normale entrance. Both his parents and Madame Lemaire put strong pressure on him to accept; but Lyon was a long way off, and there was a danger that such a transfer might be regarded as promotion, which would mean his being kept there for a long time. He preferred to take a *baccalauréat* class in Laon: this meant that he remained within easy reach of Paris, and, considering the modest nature of the post he had chosen, was very likely to be transferred to a Paris post the following year. I backed him energetically in this.

My peace of mind began to reassert itself. Sartre seemed to have calmed down again, and I was going on a trip to Rome with him. During this year, too, throughout the upheavals of our private lives, we had kept a close eye on political developments, and gave an enthusiastic welcome to the victory of the Popular Front.

We had been expecting this for a long time, though right-wing factions had fought bitterly to prevent it. The Jèze affair was one of the more notorious episodes in the struggle. Jèze was a professor of law who had in the past frequently given tokens of his allegiance to the reactionaries; but in September he had agreed to deliver a speech before the League of Nations, on behalf of the Ethiopian delegation, publicly indicting Italian policy. His first open lecture took place in November and was greeted with such an uproar that he was forced to suspend the course. With Dean Allix at his side, he faced the students once more at the beginning of January, and the uproar broke out again. The Law School was closed, and young Fascists tried to whip up a general strike among the students in the Latin Quarter. The attempt failed, although the Chamber of Deputies passed a law authorizing the Government to dissolve seditious associations. In February, when the Italian armies captured Addis Ababa, and the French Right sent congratulatory telegrams to Mussolini, the Law School was reopened, but Jèze's lectures were once more sabotaged. The Dean was accused of giving him insufficient protection, and had to resign. In March, after a third unsuccessful attempt, Jèze finally gave up all plans for speaking in public.

A more serious attempt was made against Léon Blum. The so-called patriots had wanted to treat Bainville's funeral as an occasion for national mourning. On their way back from the ceremony they happened to meet the car taking Blum away from the Chamber: this was on the Boulevard Saint-Germain. They stopped it, molested the occupants, and managed to wound Blum seriously before the police intervened. Some arrests took place: Maurras, who had written some really bloodthirsty articles against Blum, was charged with provocation to murder and sentenced to several months in jail. The Popular Front organized a giant demonstration against Blum's assailants, where once more its strength was impressively deployed. Various meetings and processions confirmed the imminence of a victory which events in Spain appeared to foreshadow. La Pasionaria was whipping up Republican enthusiasm with her eloquence, and the Right was defeated at the polls. It was in vain that General Franco delivered his pronunciamento: victory remained with the *Frente popular*. Our more "respectable" papers rechristened it the *Frente crapular,* and set about describing its supposed atrocities. The left-wing press scored some facile but legitimate successes with excellent parodies of these accounts.

When Hitler occupied the Rhineland, our neopacifists were still advocating patience. "Resist and bargain," wrote Emmanuel Berl. But the Left, sure of its strength now, was taking a firmer line. Peace, it asserted, should not be an endless process of retreat. It was thanks to complicity on the part of the French Right that Hitler's bluffs came off: once confronted with a resolute adversary he would withdraw rapidly. The great mass of the French people did not want war, but in order to eliminate the threat of war they were putting their money on a tough-line policy.

All our friends, and indeed we ourselves, rallied to this position. We were relying on the Popular Front to save the peace abroad and to lend cohesion at home to a movement which one day would lead to true Socialism. Both Sartre and I had its victory very much at heart; and yet our individualism hampered our more progressive instincts, and we still maintained the attitude which had restricted us to the role of witnesses on July 14, 1935. I cannot now remember where we spent the night of May 3. It was out in a public square—somewhere in Rouen, no doubt—where loudspeakers were announcing results and figures that filled us with great satisfaction. Yet Sartre had not himself voted. The political aspirations of left-wing intellectuals made him shrug his shoulders. Jacques Bost had listened to the election results in Paris, together with his brother, Dabit, and Chamson. He told us how Chamson uttered exclamations of triumph, such as "What a beating we're giving them!" "Chamson never gave any sort of a beating to anyone," Sartre remarked impatiently. Talk, declamations, manifestoes, propaganda—what a lot of pointless fuss! Would it all have seemed so ridiculous to us, I wonder, if we had been given a chance of participating in it? I just don't know. On the other hand I am almost certain that if we had found ourselves in a position to take effective action we would have done so: our habit of abstention was largely due to our powerlessness, and we did not a priori object to participating in events. The proof of this is that when the strikes came and they went through the streets taking up collections for the strikers, we gave all we could. Pagniez reproached us for doing this: it was the first time there had been a serious divergence of political opinion between us. According to him, the strikes imperiled the "Blum experiment," whereas we saw in them the one chance to make it truly radical. We welcomed the picketing of factories with great enthusiasm: workers and employees astonished us, not only by the courage and solid unanimity with which they acted, but also by their skillful tactics, discipline, and cheerfulness. At last something new and significant and really revolutionary was being done. The signing of the Matignon Agreement filled us with joy: what with collective contracts, wage increases, a forty-hour week, and paid holidays, working-class conditions were beginning to look up. Defense industries were nationalized; a special Corn Marketing Board was set up, and the Government issued decrees dissolving all Fascist associations. Stupidity, injustice, and exploitation were losing ground, and this put fresh heart into us. Nevertheless—and all things considered, I see no inconsistency here—we still found conformity irritating, even when it changed the color of its coat. We had no liking whatsoever for the new-style chauvinism now sweeping over France. Aragon was writing jingoistic articles, while at the Alhambra Gilles and Julien got a rousing reception when they sang *"La Belle France."* The old blue and red boutonniere, cornflowers and poppies, began to appear; it was like the days of Déroulède again. The previous year we had joined in the celebrations on the Fourteenth of July, but this time we stayed away: Jacques Bost went along eagerly, and afterward we tried to convince him of the futility of his behavior. It had been wonderful to watch the masses marching toward victory; but now victory was theirs, and the spectacle of them commemorating their triumph seemed to us insipid.

That summer the beaches and countryside had their first wave of vacations-with-pay visitors. Two weeks is not very long; but all the same, the workers of Saint-Ouen or Aubervilliers did get a change of air from their factories and suburbs.

This cheerfully noisy exodus, however, and the whoopee associated with the Fourteenth, were both offset by some rather disturbing pieces of news. The press had printed accounts of a "mutiny in Spanish Morocco." On the night of July 12–13, General Franco landed in Spain. But the whole country had voted for the Republic, and the defeat of these rebels seemed absolutely inevitable. We packed our bags in a carefree mood.

The year before we had much enjoyed our exploration of France; and now, before going on to Italy, we stopped for a few days in Grenoble.

Every morning we caught a bus up into the mountains, and in the evening we drank port in a Cintra bar. We went for walks and discussed Stendhal, and Sartre sang a little ditty he had written about Grenoble and its *messieurs aux coeurs nobles,* not to mention the Place Grenette with its *demoiselles aux âmes nettes.* Pagniez was on holiday with his family at Guillestre, and we went to see him there: we took him with us by bus to Marseille.

We stayed for ten days in Rome, at the Albergo del Sole, and ate *porchetta* in the Piazza del Pantheon. Everything about Rome delighted me: its food, its noise, its public squares, its old brickwork and pines.

Naples intrigued us; the *Guide Bleu* boasted of its charms but failed to explain them. My sister, who had just been touring Italy herself, wrote: "It is far from attractive; it is a filthy place, and filthiness is not enough." The Piazza Garibaldi outside the Central Station, with its linear and dusty tram lines, we found a little unnerving. But very quickly we plunged into the network of tiny alleyways marked on our map just off the Via Roma. We must, unknown to ourselves, have been rabid humanists at heart; for conscientious bourgeois opinion (together with the hygienically minded, the Communists, and every sort of rationalist and progressive group) condemned this teeming warren, and had good reasons for doing so—not to mention the obscurantism that preserved it. If we compromised here, it at least showed we cared for mankind not as it *ought* to be, but as it *is.* At Naples the true South begins: the sun no longer seems a mere fiery body hung in the sky, but lowers over the earth like some gigantic shadow. In the depths of this sink no mineral substance remains: everything is swarming, fermenting. The very stones have a spongy, porous, sweaty appearance, and spawn mosses or lichens. Humanity stands revealed in its organic nakedness and visceral heat: it was this aspect of life here which dazed, disgusted, and bewitched us.

We felt something of Naples' frightfulness—the naked, scabby infants; the scrofulous and the crippled; the open, purulent sores and the livid, abscesslike faces; not to mention unsanitary slum apartments (with bills posted on them that said either CONDEMNED or FIT FOR HUMAN OCCUPATION) where innumerable families swarmed. Blows were exchanged over cabbage stalks or bits of rotten meat picked up in the gutter, while at every street corner stood a smiling, beatific image of the Virgin Mary, adorned with gilded drapery and surrounded by flowers and guttering candles. Yet we did not plumb the full depths of horror: in part at least we let ourselves be deceived by appearances. In the Via dei Tribunali, near the Capuan Gate, we were confronted by whole pyramids of watermelons, great piles of tomatoes and eggplants and lemons, figs and raisins, glittering heaps of fish, and those charming rococo display stands that the vendors of shellfish make from seaweed and mussels. But we did not realize that food is only exhibited with such violent emphasis when people are on the brink of starvation. Through misjudging the depths of misery that prevailed here, we were enabled to enjoy some of its consequences. It pleased us to find that common want had broken down all those barriers which isolate men from each other and diminish their stature. All these folk dwelled in the warmth of a common womb, where the words "inside" and "outside" had lost all meaning. The dim, cavelike dwellings, where icons glimmered by candlelight, formed an integral part of the street. In those great double beds the sick or the dead lay exposed for all to see. Moreover, the intimate life of the home spilled out onto the sidewalk. Tailors, cobblers, blacksmiths, makers of artificial flowers—every craftsman sat working in the doorway of his little shop. The women sat outside to delouse their children, do the washing, or gut fish, with one eye to the bowls of tomato pulp exposed to the far-off azure vault of the sky. From one end of the street to the other smiles, nods, gossip, and friendliness were the order of the day, and such natural generosity appealed to us. Round the Capuan Gate streamers and other decorations seemed to be up the whole time, with hucksters and showmen always in attendance. At dusk the candles would be lit, and hawkers and passers-by would argue, gesticulate, and praise their wares in a kind of nonstop fiesta. I remember one peasant who stood up in his cart, surrounded by a load of watermelons, and with a quick, flamboyant gesture cut a blood-red segment from the nearest melon and held it up on the point of his knife; having thus proved his fruit fresh and unblemished, he tossed the sample to a prospective purchaser, who caught it in midair; then, immediately, with breathtaking speed, he chopped out another chunk and flicked it after the first.

We had taken rooms at a hotel near the station, in the heart of the lower-class district, and we used to go out and listen to *canzonette* in a nearby dive. We kept clear of the fashionable bars and restaurants, and the splendid Marine Drive round the Bay; instead we would lunch comfortably in a shady, pleasant restaurant called the Papagallo, just off the Via Roma, where they had a real parakeet in a cage, and the walls were covered with framed photographs of stage artists, both Italian and foreign. For our supper we bought sandwiches or cold chicken in the same street, and ate it as we walked along. Occasionally we would have coffee in the Galleria, or nibble iced cakes at Cafflish's, the big pâtisserie, or sit outside the Café Gambrinus on the Piazza del Municipio, eating ices. We had escaped from the grim side of Naples, and were now discovering its more pleasant aspects. Yet wherever we were, at any hour, the dust and desolation and horrible stench of the docks could reach us on the breeze. And when we climbed up to Posilipo, the dazzling whiteness of Naples—as seen from a distance—did not deceive us.

Sartre, like myself, was a conscientious tourist, determined not to miss any major attraction. Every morning a small rack railway used to carry its load of Americans up to the summit of Vesuvius; but the price, some ninety francs a head or the equivalent, was beyond our means. We made the climb on foot, setting out from the nearest station on the narrow-gauge railway, the Circumvesuviana. At first we followed a stony track that cut through black-earth vineyards; then we began to climb over heaps of lava, slag, and cinders. The cinders grew thicker, and our feet slipped and sank in them, which made progress difficult. Finally we scrambled up over the ballast of the rack railway, which was constructed like a giant staircase;

getting from one "step" to the next required an effort that severely winded me. A peddler who had caught up with us kept making encouraging gestures and cheering me on. Two or three others followed us, and set out their meager wares near the terminus: old verdigris-covered coins, bits of lava, gimcrack souvenirs. One of them was selling grapes, and we bought an amber-colored bunch from him. Despite the suffocating and sulfurous fumes, we spent a long time sitting on the crater's edge, aware now, to our surprise, just how true that hackneyed phrase about "the earth's crust" was. This planet of ours was a sort of gigantic cake—badly baked, overdone, full of lumps and crevasses, split, cracked, blistered, pock-marked, smoky, steaming, and still boiling and bubbling! We were diverted from these reflections by the arrival of a horde of tourists, who charged toward the crater, shepherded by a guide who bombarded them with figures—width, breadth, depth, dates of most recent eruptions. They bought souvenirs and clicked their cameras busily; half an hour later they had vanished. We stayed a moment longer, relishing our solitary state; then we ran down the slope up which we had so laboriously climbed, feeling decidedly proud of ourselves.

I always enjoyed it when we overcame natural hazards by our own unaided physical exertions. On Capri we toiled up the ancient steps leading from the Marina to Anacapri. We had lunch up there, on a lonely terrace that looked out over the sea. The sun was bright yet kindly; a cool breeze caressed us; and what with the local wine, and those pale yellow omelettes, and the blue waters below us, and the sight of Naples on the horizon, my head was in a whirl. This occasion remains one of my most unforgettable memories.

We saw Pozzuoli, with its steam geysers, and also went by narrow-gauge train to Pompeii. Our visit to the Museo Nazionale in Naples had left Sartre slightly disturbed. He wrote to Olga:

> The thing I found most offensive was the passion these Pompeians had for making their rather cramped rooms look much larger. Artists pandered to them by covering their walls with false perspectives, like a backdrop: they painted in columns, and behind these columns sketched lines receding to a central point, in such a way that the room itself seemed of palatial dimensions. I don't know whether these vanity-ridden Pompeians allowed themselves to be taken in by such trompe-l'oeil effects; but I'm pretty sure they would have driven me half crazy—just the sort of irritating pattern that you can't take your eyes from when you've got a slight temperature.
>
> I was also very disappointed by the so-called best-period frescoes, with their portrayal of mythological scenes and characters. I had half hoped to find in Pompeii some revelation concerning Roman life as it really was—less staid and more brutal, perhaps, than what we had been taught at school. I felt these people must have at least a streak of barbarism about them: I held the eighteenth century responsible for all the conventional Greco-Roman platitudes that had so bored me in the class-

room. I thought I was going to rediscover Rome as she really was. Well, those frescoes very soon disillusioned me: my Greco-Roman platitudes were already well established before Pompeii's destruction. It was plain to me that no one for years past had believed in the gods and demigods they smothered their walls with. The religious motif had become a mere pretext for a picture, and yet they never abandoned it. As I went through these rooms, all of them chockablock with frescoes, I became hypnotized by this cliché-ridden classicism. I went back ten, no, twenty times to look at a scene from the life of Achilles (or was it Theseus?), and I found it quite terrifying to imagine a town whose inhabitants had nothing on their walls but *that* sort of stuff. It stamped their civilization as dead already; it was utterly remote from their real preoccupations as bankers or merchants or shipping magnates. I imagined how coldly distinguished these men must have been, how conventional in their approach to culture; I felt I had come a long way from the superb and enchanting statues we saw in Rome. (The Beaver will doubtless already have told you that a few days later we found a collection of equally enchanting statues, here in this same museum, on the first floor; their eyeballs were inlaid with copper. But they dated from an earlier period.)

When I came out of the Museum I had almost lost any desire to see Pompeii, and my feeling toward these Romans was an odd, rather disagreeable mixture of curiosity and repulsion. It seemed to me, if you like, that even in their own day they already represented Antiquity, that they might well have talked about "we Ancient Romans" like the knights in some farce or other who said, "We medieval knights just off to the Hundred Years' War . . ."

In any case, Pompeii, so miraculously preserved by its lightning-swift destruction, surpassed all we had imagined concerning it. At last we were strolling through ruins where the recognizable landmarks were not restricted to temples, palaces, and other public buildings, but included houses, villas, slum hovels, shops, taverns, and market arcades: a complete town, noisy and crowded, just like present-day Naples. The streets themselves, paved with heavy flagstones and receding toward the horizon between half-ruined walls, held my attention from one end to the other. Yet our imagination peopled them with ghosts; and caught between these phantoms and hard reality, I sensed here—better than anywhere else in the world—the mysterious quality of *absence*. We spent a whole day wandering through these ruins, only stopping to snatch a quick meal, and drink a wine that had absorbed the quintessence of all Vesuvian mud.

At Paestum we had our first sight of a Greek temple. Sartre was disconcerted because, as he said to me, "There was no stimulus to thought in it." I too found this beauty altogether oversmooth and oversimple: for me it contained no magic. The two days that followed, as I recall it, were much more exciting. Sartre went straight back to Naples, while I left the train at the next station after Salerno, and set out, rucksack on back, to cover the twelve or thirteen miles to Amalfi. A cab driver hailed me and offered to drive me all the way there for eight lire. Dazed by this windfall, I climbed aboard and sat down beside a taciturn young Italian wearing a plumed hat. I lolled back against the cushions and watched the glittering coast line slip past, while we drove through old, white-fronted Greek villages, their walls picked out with blue and gold faience squares. I walked through the streets of Amalfi and saw the cathedral; I put up for the night at the Albergo della Luna, which had once been a monastery, and sat late out on the terrace, watching the boats of the night fishermen, and the pearly glint of the sea beneath their lanterns. I would have stayed even longer if the porter had not made somewhat everenthusiastic attempts to beguile my solitude. The next day I discovered Ravello, with its gardens and villas and belvederes, and the balustrade topped by a row of marble busts, which all had their backs turned coyly to the sea and looked as though they had been nibbled by the ants in *L'Age d'or*. From Amalfi I went by bus to Sorrento, along the most glorious stretch of coast line in the whole world.

Sartre expressed no regrets about missing such delights when I described them to him, since he had had considerable fun on his own account. When he was prowling around by himself one evening a young man asked him to have a drink, took him on from one bar to another, and finally offered him a chance to see "something really special"—*tableaux vivants* inspired by the frescoes in the Villa of the Mysteries, at Pompeii. Sartre accompanied him to a *maison spécialisée* where, in return for a modest enough payment, the madam led him into a circular salon, the walls of which were lined with mirrors, and had a red plush banquette running the whole way around them. He sat there on his own, the madam having refused to let his companion in with him. Two women now appeared. The elder one, who had an ivory phallus in her hand, played the masculine role, and nonchalantly mimed the erotic postures which the frescoes portrayed. Next, the younger woman performed a dance, with tambourine accompaniment. For an extra consideration the client could retire in privacy with whichever of them he preferred. Sartre declined this privilege. He picked up his guide again in the street, outside the front door. The young man was clutching a bottle of wine, bought by Sartre at the last *bottiglieria* they had visited, and still only half empty: he was waiting till Sartre appeared so that they could finish it together. After this they parted. What had delighted Sartre, so he told me, was the feeling of *dépaysement* he had experienced on finding himself all alone in this garish salon, surrounded by his own reflections, while two women performed, on his behalf, an act that was at once comic and commonplace. The following year he attempted to describe this incident in a new story: he entitled it *Dépaysement*.

We slept on deck throughout our sea passage from Naples to Palermo. Having been inured to misery and want by Naples, I was able to take its counterpart—frightful though it was—in Palermo. Here too a lavish display of food concealed its actual scarcity. The place was dripping with picturesque local color, and I abandoned myself to it in delight: dark alleyways, threadbare washing, little workshops, pyramids of watermelons. And how I adored the picture sequences painted all round Sicilian carts, narrating legends of Robert Guiscard and the Crusades! There were lots of tiny marionette theaters about, and one afternoon we entered one of them, to find the place packed with children, squashed together on narrow wooden benches: we were the only adults there. We watched while Charlemagne, Roland, Robert Guiscard, and other knights, very stiff in their armor, split the skulls of various infidels. From time to time one of the children would begin to fidget, whereupon a man would tap him lightly with the end of a long switch. We ate bunches of sticky grapes and felt very happy.

In order to see all the churches and *palazzi,* from one end of the town to the other, we often took a horse-drawn fiacre. One evening, as we were strolling down the main thoroughfare, a vehicle of this type careered past, its horse bolting out of control. The peaceful dusk was shattered by the sound of clattering wheels and drumming hoofs, and people idling along the sidewalk ran for their lives. The whole thing was like some fantastic film, or the front page of *Domenica del Corriere.*

Once more we investigated some Greek temples; but we still could find nothing to say about them, and they certainly said nothing to us. Yet their very silence carried more weight than most loquacity. At Selinus we endured it for hours on end without wearying of it, sitting among those gigantic fallen column-drums. During our visit we did not see a single soul. We lunched on the water and bread and grapes we had brought with us, in the lizard-haunted shade of tumbled marble blocks, and Sartre tried to charm the lizards by whistling to them. At Segesta we began to understand the true nature of a Doric colonnade.

We gave up the idea of visiting Agrigento: the journey would have been too complicated. I hardly regretted this, so enchanted was I by Syracuse— the bare, bright texture of its stonework, spread like an amphitheater beside a metallic sea; its dusty roads, along which the "cattle of the sun," with their magnificent horns, plodded so heavily; the clearing of the land around the Fortress of Euryalus. We spent much time wandering through the city's subterranean grottoes, or along its ring roads, or out on the lonely sea-eroded dunes, away from everything. We went down into the Lautumiae, huge ancient limestone quarries, the only place I know where horror borders upon poetry. From Messina, its ugliness an irrefutable testimony to the cataclysm which overwhelmed the old town, we took the ferry across the Straits—a splendid view here. On the return trip, however, I was annoyed to see Sartre busy reading the papers while we were sailing into a rosy sunset, and to hear him talking of Spain and Germany, and of the future, which struck him as anything but rosy.

We returned from Messina to Naples aboard a miserable old tub of a boat, and I had an uncomfortable night: it was too cold to sleep on deck, and down below there was an intolerable stench. We stopped for a few more days in Rome. Quite abruptly Sartre's mood changed: the trip was nearly over, and all his worries were coming back—the political situation, his relationship with Olga. I felt scared. Were the lobsters going to stage a comeback?

He assured me they weren't, and when we reached Venice, which we were eager to revisit, I thought no more about the matter. We spent four or five days there, and decided to stay up all one night, as we had done in Rome two years before. To burn our bridges, and also as a measure of economy, we had settled our hotel bill and vacated our room: there was no longer any corner of the town in which we could hide. We trailed round the cafés till they closed; we sat on the steps of the Piazza San Marco; we strolled along the canals. Everything was quiet; as we crossed each little square we could hear the heavy breathing of sleepers through the open windows. We saw the sky begin to lighten behind the Fondamenta Nuova: between the quay and cemetery large flat-bottomed barges came gliding like shadows over the waters of the lagoon, with men sculling from the prow, bringing cargoes of fruit and vegetables from Murano and Burano, the islands, and the outlying countryside. We walked back toward the center of the town. As daylight grew and spread, the market arcades beside the Grand Canal began slowly to come to life, in a profusion of melons, oranges, and fish. The cafés opened; the streets began to fill up. Only now did we go and book ourselves a room, and get some sleep. Sartre told me later that all through that night a lobster had been following him.

Chapter 5

WE GOT BACK TO PARIS IN SEPTEMBER, AND were at once engulfed by the drama that for the next two and a half years was to dominate our lives: the Spanish Civil War. Franco's forces had not triumphed as quickly as the Right hoped they would; nor yet had they been wiped out with the speed that *we* had anticipated. The rebels' advance on Madrid had been halted, but they had won a footing in Seville, Saragossa, and Oviedo. Almost the entire army—some 95 per cent of it— together with the bulk of its state-owned equipment, had gone over to Franco, and the Republic could count on no support apart from that of the people.

But the people had rallied to the defenses of the Republic with immense enthusiasm. The accounts we read in the papers and the information that Fernando and his friends passed on fired our imagination. In Madrid and Barcelona workers had stormed the armories and supplied themselves with weapons; the citizens of Madrid had hoisted the red flag over Montana Barracks. Peasants brought down old guns and blunderbusses from their barns. In towns and villages recruits drilled with walking sticks for lack of rifles. There were large numbers of women in their ranks, all as eager to fight as the men. Franco's armored cars were met by *dinamiteros* hurling grenades and Molotov cocktails. Through sheer heroism, and with nothing but their bare hands, the common people of Spain were about to hold up the advance of the well-drilled, well-equipped forces launched against them by Private Ownership, Church, and Big Business in combination. It was an astonishing and epic struggle, in which we felt ourselves directly involved. No country was nearer to our hearts than Spain; and Fernando was one of our closest friends. We had shared in the rejoicings over the first year of the Republic, in sunny Madrid; we had mingled with the delirious crowds in Seville, after Sanjurjo's flight, when they set the aristocratic clubs on fire and the firemen failed to extinguish the flames. We had seen for ourselves the bloated insolence of priesthood and bourgeoisie, and the wretched poverty of the peasants, and had prayed that the Republic might speedily fulfill all its promises. In February the voice of La Pasionaria had raised these hopes to the highest pitch, and their frustration would have hit us like a personal disaster. Over and above all this, we knew that the Spanish Civil War would put our own future in jeopardy. The left-wing press gave it so wide a coverage that it might have been a French affair—and in effect it was: at all costs we had to prevent yet another Fascist state from establishing itself on our borders.

Such a thing would never come to pass, of that we were convinced: nobody in our camp had the least doubt that the Republicans would win. I remember one occasion when we were having dinner in the Spanish restaurant I have previously mentioned, and which was patronized exclusively by Republicans. A young Spanish girl suddenly stood up at her table and declaimed a poem in honor of freedom and her country. We did not understand the words—one of our neighbors gave us the general gist of what she said—but we found the girl's voice and expression most moving. All those present rose to their feet and shouted: "Long live the Spanish Republic!" Everyone believed in its imminent triumph. La Pasionaria had hurled a defiant slogan—"No pasaran!"—at the Fascist forces, and her words resounded throughout the length and breadth of Spain.

But there was another, angrier side to our enthusiasm. To insure a quick victory France should have at once flown to the succor of the Spanish people, and sent them the artillery, machine guns, aircraft, and rifles of which they were so desperately short. Yet despite the trade agreements between France and Spain, Blum opted, early in August, for nonintervention. He refused to let the Republic have French arms, and even closed the frontier to private gunrunning parties. On September 5 Irun fell because its defenders had nothing to fight with, two trains loaded with consignments of rifles for Spain having been held up by the French authorities a few hundred yards away. Because of this embargo Talavera de la Reina also fell, and Franco's forces advanced both in Estremadura and toward Guipúzcoa.

Blum's neutralism was all the more disgusting in that Hitler and Mussolini were openly supplying the rebels with both men and materiel. The first bomb dropped on Madrid, on August 28, was released by a German plane, a Junker. We had great admiration for Malraux and his squadron, who had volunteered for service with the Republic; but how could they possibly face up to the Nazi Air Force single-handed? At a big pacifist rally in Saint-Cloud Blum was received with shouts of "Planes for Spain!" The C.G.T., the Communists, and a large number of Socialists were demanding the reopening of the Franco-Spanish frontier. Other Socialists, however, together with the Radical-Socialists, were behind Blum, declaring that the first essential was to preserve the peace. But the truth was that though they had no love for Fascism, the revolutionary fervor animating the Frente Popular scared them even more. These disagreements were reflected in the papers we read. In Vendredi Guéhenno was still refusing "to sacrifice Peace to Revolution," while Andrée Viollis, and even the pacifist Romain Rolland, felt that any chance of peace depended on the fate of the Spanish Republic. Most of the contributors to the Canard enchaîné were in favor of intervention; Galtier-Boissière opposed it. We loathed the idea of war as much as anyone else, but we could not stomach the thought that with a few dozen machine guns and a few thousand rifles the Republicans could have finished Franco off—and that these supplies had been refused them. Blum's caution sickened us, and we were far from regarding it as a contribution to peace. At the beginning of October, we were agonized to learn, the rebels were at the gates of Madrid. In November they occupied the students' quarter by the University, and the Government was evacuated to Valencia; and still France made no move. Luckily the U.S.S.R. decided to weigh in now: tanks, aircraft, and machine guns were dispatched, and a citizens' army, supported by the International Brigades, saved Madrid.

When the battle for Madrid was joined, Fernando could not bear to stay in Paris any longer, and resolved to go off and fight. Once again we found ourselves at odds with Pagniez, who regarded Fernando's decision as a mere piece of empty braggadocio. Madame Lemaire, too, was of the opinion that he would have done better to think about his wife and son and stay with them instead of playing the hero. They both belonged to a section of opinion that, while supporting the Republic, had not the least wish to see the Civil War develop into a victorious revolution. We ourselves were wholeheartedly behind Fernando's decision: we went and saw him off at the station, together with Stépha and many of his friends. Bermann, the artist, went with him. Everyone on the platform felt deep concern about a Republican victory. Yes, it would happen all right—but when, and at how great a cost?

Franco's revolt had been largely fomented by Mussolini, and strengthened the hopes of the Axis still further. (Japan's treaty with Germany had lately provided them with an ally in the Far East.) French right-wing opinion was unanimous in applauding Franco's successes, and the so-called Western intellectuals, in particular—Maxence, Paul Chack, Miomandre, and Bonnard—acclaimed them with noisy enthusiasm. I was used to hearing my father extol the common-sense policy of *Gringoire* and Stéphane Lauzanne's enlightened patriotism, and never so much as raised an eyebrow over his views. But all my childhood fury revived, though I said nothing, when my parents and my Valleuse cousins regaled one another with the atrocities attributed by their right-wing papers to the *"Frente crapular"*—nuns raped by the thousand outside their own churches, choirboys disemboweled, cathedrals reduced to cinders—or when they praised the heroic conduct of the Alcazar cadets. I was hard put to it to see how, even from their own point of view, they could be pleased about successes scored by Nazi Stukas. The right-wing press became increasingly virulent: the slanderous campaign conducted by Carbuccia, in *Gringoire,* against Salengro, the Minister of the Interior, drove the latter to suicide. The employers began to reassert themselves, and attempted to go back on the concessions wrung out of them by the June strikes. Still, a certain general improvement of conditions in industry was discernible. Thanks to the forty-hour week, couples on tandem bicycles could now be seen pedaling out of Paris every Saturday morning; they came back on Sunday evening with bunches of flowers and foliage tied to their handlebars. Groups of young people sallied forth, rucksack on back, to camp in nearby woods. Something had been won, and remained as a permanent gain. The Left might be split over the question of intervention in Spain, but it kept its hopes intact.

I found myself teaching at the Lycée Molière. Obviously I had no intention of *living* out at Passy; I commuted there to give lessons, and left again immediately afterward. I took up residence in a very decent hotel on the Rue de la Gaîté, the Royal Bretagne. The previous year Simone Labourdin had moved into a three-room flat (Madame Lemaire said it was very attractive) and at the time I had felt vaguely inclined to rent a similar small apartment myself, and furnish it to suit my own taste. I was not a priori set on playing the Bohemian. But the idea of going the round of agents and setting up house terrified me; in any case, where was I to find the money for furniture? A hotel relieved me of all such worries. It mattered little to me that I had only one room, and that not a particularly attractive one, when all Paris was mine, its streets, its squares, its cafés.

Marco had a post at the Lycée Louis-le-Grand, and lived in a hotel at the far end of the Rue Delambre, a slightly more expensive one than mine. Bost was reading at the Sorbonne for his teacher's diploma, and had a little room to himself in his brother's apartment on the Place Saint-German-des-Prés. It was unthinkable that Olga should be left behind in Beuzeville; but her parents, who knew that she had made not the faintest pretense of working for her diploma, were opposed to her departure. So she went off by train without their permission, and rented a room in my hotel. Philosophy emphatically did *not* attract her, and she wondered with some anxiety just what she was to turn her hand to. For some time she had a job serving tea in a sort of combined cafeteria, bookshop, and record store on the Boulevard Saint-Michel; but this did not strike me as a final solution to her problem.

Twice a week I would go and meet Sartre at the Gare du Nord. His Venice attack had had no aftermath, and the lobsters seemed to have vanished for good. We usually had a drink in a café near the station (it no longer exists) which we found enchanting. There was a downstairs room which, with its imitation leather banquettes, marble-top tables, and dim lighting, reminded us of the Brasserie Paul; the walls were covered with dark fretted paneling, for all the world like a Neapolitan hearse. After exchanging the latest information about our private lives and discussing the news generally, we would make our way down toward Montparnasse. We had set up our GHQ, as it were, in the Dôme. On those mornings when I was not due at the *lycée* I used to have breakfast there. I never worked in my hotel room, but preferred one of the booths at the far end of the café. All around me were German refugees, reading the papers or playing chess, and other foreigners, of all nationalities, conducting passionate arguments in low voices. The murmur of their conversation did not bother me: to sit facing a blank sheet of paper all alone is an austere experience, whereas here I could always glance up and reassure myself that humanity existed. This encouraged me to write: one day, perhaps, my words would move some other person. When I was talking with Sartre or Olga I dearly loved to watch people coming and going. Thanks to Fernando and Stépha, we could now put a name to some of these faces. There was Rappoport, with his luxuriant beard, and Zadkine the sculptor, and huge Dominguez, and tiny Mané-Katz, and the Spanish painter Florès, and Francis Gruber (with whom my sister had a fairly intimate relationship), and Kisling, and Ilya Ehrenburg, his fleshy face crowned with a shock of thick hair, and a whole crowd of artists and writers, known or unknown. We were especially intrigued by one man, a handsome, chunky-faced fellow, with searching eyes and a wiry mop of hair, who used to wander along the sidewalk every evening, either by himself or with a very pretty woman. He had an air of being at one and the same time as solid as a rock and freer than an elf: the combination was too much for us. We knew that appearances were not to be trusted, and this particular setup looked so attractive that we could not but suspect a disappointment. The man was Swiss, a sculptor by occupation, and his name was Giacometti.

On the whole, just as in Rouen, we found the women more interesting and amusing than the men. Every night tall American girls could be seen getting themselves majestically stewed. There were women artists, artists' women, models, minor actresses from the Montparnasse theaters, pretty girls and those not so pretty, but all of them, more or less, kept by someone or other; and we derived much enjoyment from watching them dreaming over *cafés-crème,* gossiping with one another, and preening themselves in front of their menfolk. They dressed on the cheap side, but took some trouble over their clothes; some of them wore garments which possessed a certain outdated charm that had been bought at the flea market. I have a vivid memory of one such woman whom we called the Swiss Miss. She had very smooth blonde hair, which she tied up in a chignon bouffant that was pure 1900 style; she wore a puce taffeta blouse with leg-of-mutton sleeves, and she was always pushing a baby carriage. From time to time we would go and sit in the Sélect, among the crop-haired Lesbians, who wore ties and even monocles on occasion; but such exhibitionism struck us as affected. We preferred those less predictable forms of entertainment provided by one or two female eccentrics. One evening Olga and I discovered a dive on the Rue Monsier-le-Prince called Le Hoggar, which at that time was a cheap and decidedly shady sort of place. We were delighted by the cheap exoticism of the décor, by the nasal music that floated up from the basement, and especially by the glasses, decorated with a sculptured floral design, in which our mint tea was served by an Arab waiter wearing full native costume. Downstairs a phony Ouled-Naïl girl was doing a belly dance; the upper room was empty apart from a woman of about thirty, an unattractive creature with scraped-back hair who was sprawled out on a banquette and singing to herself. We saw her quite often afterward at the Dôme, always alone. She never sang again, but her lips moved as though she were inspired. There was another woman of about the same age, her coarse features fixed in a simpering smirk, who rolled her eyes heavenward and conversed with some unseen interlocutor whom we suspected of being God. The more bizarre and lost people seemed, the greater our sympathy with them. Nevertheless there were some of them who disturbed us, such as the exophthalmic character whose eyes bulged more and more every week, till they looked as though they would pop out of their sockets and roll across the tiled floor. There was also the man we nicknamed The Masochist. I was in the Coupole with Olga one day, having a drink: she was wearing an artificial leopardskin coat, while I had on a somewhat masculine felt hat. A man with prominent ears and a drooping mustache was sitting close by, his eyes fixed on us in a glassy stare. Then he dropped a newspaper on our table across which he had written "Slave or dog?" We finished our drinks with some speed. As we passed by him on our way out, he muttered: "Order me to go across the room on all fours, and I'd do it!" We saw him again a few weeks later, walking down the street with a woman who sported a stiff collar, a tie, and high-heeled shoes, and looked decidedly spiteful: he seemed in a sort of seventh heaven. A kind of silent familiarity developed between us and the other regulars at the Dôme. The word went around (how it began I'm not sure) that we were civil servants and therefore comparatively well off; so very often a drunk or a hard-luck type or a professional cadger would come up and beg a five-franc piece from us, and feel obliged, in exchange, to spin us some long, lying yarn or other. Chronic fantasy flourished in this setting. All these exiles, failures, fantasists, and déclassés made a change from our previous provincial monotony. It is said that nonconformism breeds its own conformity; it certainly produces more myth-making than its opposite. It gave me intense pleasure to work alone in the midst of these people—so near, yet so distant, so busy fumbling after the lost remnants of their lives.

Despite the resources that Paris offered us, our trio lost no time in falling back into the same sort of difficulties that had beset us in Rouen. Sartre had written several long letters to Olga during the holidays, among others the one which contained his description of Naples and produced the original idea for his story Dépaysement. Olga replied, and they came together again on terms of the warmest affection. They would often wander through the Paris streets till dawn, just for the pleasure of being together. Then, suddenly, Olga would turn sulky. Such rebuffs irritated Sartre all the more in that he felt their friendship to be progressing well; and Olga, for her part, found it increasingly difficult to put up with his fits of impatience. After hours spent serving tea she was often in a nervous state, and the emptiness of her future terrified her. Apart from Sartre and myself her only acquaintances were Marco and Bost; she would wander alone for hours, in a state of chronic boredom. A few months previously, in Rouen, she had conceived the idea of experimenting with alcohol. She had gone to a cheap bar and knocked back two pernods one after the other: the result had exceeded her wildest expectations, and she had not repeated the experiment. But now, in order to combat her boredom and depression, she resorted to pernod with a will, and sank into gloomy fantasies as a result.

When I returned to my room I would sometimes find a sheet of pink paper pushed under the door, covered with wild and straggling handwriting: Olga blowing off her self-hatred and her loathing for the entire world. Or else, rather like Louise Perron, she would pin up a sheet of paper on her own door, with barely legible phrases scribbled over it, very desperate and cryptic. I suffered tortures on her behalf, and found her occasional coolness toward me even unfairer than before. I had reckoned on Paris providing us with a natural way out of the labyrinth in which our isolated condition at Rouen had kept us imprisoned: but it was not to be. Sartre went on and on the whole time about Olga's extraordinary behavior; I lost hope of ever finding a solution to the problem, and began to get very tired of going round and round in circles. Far from improving, the situation had become increasingly intolerable for all three of us. The evenings I spent with Marco and Bost were doubly welcome as a means of escape. These two had become inseparable friends: they went to the cinema or concerts together, and Marco had given Bost the key to his room, so that he could go up and listen to records whenever he wanted. Bost responded to Marco's charm and droll wit and loving solicitude, taking the last for granted in the highhanded, direct way peculiar to youth, and remaining equally unsurprised when he saw Marco slip into one of his gloomy fits of depression. He imagined that Marco was worrying about his career. He had sung during the summer at the Casino in Vichy, and Lauri Volpi, who headed the bill there, happened to hear him one day and said, "What an amazing voice!" Famous singers seldom show themselves kindly disposed toward beginners, and this unlooked-for compliment went to Marco's head. in October he had an audition with *M. le Directeur de l'Opéra.* "My advice to you," that gentleman told him, "is to come back here when you can sing in time with the music." It was to this setback, which we found it very hard to comprehend, that Bost attributed Marco's sour moods. But little by little he was forced to face the true explanation, which was that Marco expected rather more from him than mere friendship, and had staked his life's happiness on obtaining his desire. Bost wanted to preserve his friendship with Marco, but was unwilling to acquiesce in the latter's passionate designs on him; thus he too found himself struggling in a trap. Marco no longer dissimulated his feelings: he raged and wept and suspected Bost of enlisting Sartre's aid against him. I was in the Dôme one morning, working, when Marco rushed up. "Come with me," he said, in a commanding yet half-choked voice. I walked back to the Rue Delambre with him, and saw to my astonishment that there were tears in his eyes. The previous evening, it seemed, he had come home about six in the evening to hear a faint sound of music and a murmur of voices coming from his room. He peeped through the keyhole and saw Olga and Bost locked in an embrace. That was all, but knowing Olga's capacity for self-restraint he had at once jumped to conclusions—conclusions with tragic implications as far as he was concerned.

I learned later that he had met Sartre and Olga at the Dôme that evening, and had made several sneering remarks which neither of them understood, since Sartre was ignorant of what Marco knew, and Olga had no idea that he knew it. Marco had spent the rest of the night in tears. He knew only too well what had happened. For a long while now these two young twenty-year-olds had been mutually attracted; and now they had sought refuge in one another's arms against the demands and complexities of the adult world.

Personally, I felt that Olga's decision to smash the circle we could not get out of was an extremely sane one. Sartre continued to put a good face on things, and showed himself an excellent loser. Marco tried desperately to make us break with both Olga and Bost, especially Bost. When we refused, his spleen embraced us too. He used to prowl about Montparnasse with a revolver in his pocket; he would march into the Dôme at unexpected times in order to catch us holding a secret confabulation; and he was convinced that the four of us met at my hotel to hatch plots against him. He used to watch one of the windows, and would flourish his revolver in the most hair-raising way when he saw shadowy profiles outlined against the glass. When I proved to him that I lived in a completely different room, he was most disconcerted and came down off his high horse. Instead he now piled on the tears and agony. He made us feel so sorry for him that we decided to take him with us to Chamonix.

Sartre was not too cheerful either. Quite apart from his setback over the trio, he suffered another rebuff which affected him even more. The manuscript of his book—entitled *Melancholia* because of the Dürer engraving which he loved so much—had been sent by Nizan to one of Gallimard's readers. Sartre received a note from Paulhan advising him that, despite certain qualities it possessed, the work had not been accepted. He had taken the refusal of *La Légende de la vérité* cheerfully enough; but he had put four years' work into *Melancholia,* and the book had come out exactly as he had planned it: in his own opinion, and in mine, he had achieved a success. Paulhan, it appeared, disapproved of Sartre's central purpose—that is, the expression in literary form of metaphysical truths and feelings. But the plan was too deeply rooted in Sartre's mind, and too long established, for him to accept this condemnation. All the same, it disconcerted us both.

Madame Lemaire and Pagniez were influenced by Gallimard's decision, and hinted that *Melancholia* might perhaps be a little tedious, and clumsily written. This defection set the final seal on our bewilderment: how could there be such a discrepancy between other people's views and our own? Sartre was all set to submit his manuscript to other publishers; but as every hostile argument found some echo in his own mind, instead of assuming a pose of self-protective arrogance he began to ask himself a number of disagreeable questions.

Our stay at Chamonix, therefore, was not as lively as it might have been. It was a very hard winter, and all the ski runs had been closed because of glaze. One young schoolboy, after only eight hours' instruction, wagered that he would make the run down from the Brévent peak; his

mangled body was picked up on the rocks. We took the ski lift up
to Planpraz, and Sartre and I went down some of the easier slopes. Marco,
who was scared stiff by even the gentlest gradient, took some private lessons,
and, on the pretext of "acquiring a decent style," went on practicing stem
turns ad infinitum. One afternoon Sartre and I went up the Col de
Voza, and took the beginners' trail down into Les Houches; it passed
through some woodland, and we didn't acquit ourselves particularly well.
Back in our hotel we found Marco waiting for us, getting steadily gloomier
as night drew on. He had dreamed of having Bost with him on this
winter sports holiday, and the boy's absence left him inconsolable. After
dinner he went out into the snow to massage his scalp with that stinking
sulphur lotion. He once made Sartre sample it; but all I would let him
do to me was pour three drops on to a wad of cotton and dab it on my
head, and even so I thought my scalp was peeling off in shreds.

Marco found it quite unbearable to sleep alone at night, and begged us to
let him share our room. This was a sort of bare, bleak barn of a place,
with three beds in it. As soon as he lay down Marco would begin to cry,
really cry, and his lamentations would continue in the darkness for a long
while. He had been in love before, he told us, he had even experienced
previous passionate attachments, but he had never met another person
with whom he wished to exchange an oath of eternal devotion. In July
he had believed that the chance lay open for him; now he had lost that
chance irretrievably, and he would never get over it. Sobbing, he evoked
the life he might have led with the companion of his choice, at whose
feet he would have laid his soon-to-be-achieved fame and fortune: they
would have journeyed together in long gleaming cars, from one palace
to the next. When we told him to go to sleep, he would fall silent, sigh,
and then once more start describing, aloud, all the images thronging his
mind: Bost's white scarf, the purity of his smile, his youth and charm
and unconscious cruelty; after an agonizing scene they would go off to the
cinema to see Chaplin or the Marx Brothers, and Marco had to sit there,
heartbroken, while Bost laughed his head off. There was something more
somber and obsessional about his ravings than those of Louise Perron:
it looked to me as though he were creating a hell for himself from which
he would never escape.

When the school term began again he renewed his tearful and furious
attentions to Bost, who found such scenes very wearisome. Neither Bost
nor Olga were very cheerful, in fact. Olga was still seeing Sartre, and
he made great efforts to keep their relationship amicable, though his
heart wasn't really in it any more. Olga was full of her usual qualms
about the future, and as a form of distraction lugged me off to little
Montparnasse dance halls, such as La Bohème or the Arc-en-Ciel, which
I found very boring. Our evenings together, therefore, tended to be somewhat glum. Luckily Sartre was taking a brighter view of life again: he
had become a little more hopeful about *Melancholia*. Dullin was an old
friend of Gaston Gallimard's, and had written asking him to take a look
at the rejected manuscript himself. Pierre Bost had also gone to see

Gallimard and recommended it. Sartre was now working on a story and finding it an enjoyable task. He had first tackled this genre during his Norwegian cruise, with a short piece entitled *Le Soleil de minuit,* which he lost somewhere in the Causses and never began again. This year he had written *Erostrate,* and now he was at work on *Dépaysement.* (A few fragments only have been published, a long time after *Le Mur* [*The Wall*], which appeared in 1939.) I once or twice went back with him to Laon, where he lived in a cosy, fusty-smelling old hotel. In Paris we went to the Gauguin exhibition and saw various films. We also read a good deal. Guérin's *Fascisme et Grand Capitalisme* helped us to understand our own age a little better. We got very enthusiastic about Stekel's *Frigidity in Women,* since it proposed a method of psychoanalysis that rejected the concept of the subconscious. Though we were far from sharing Bernanos's outlook, his *Journal d'un curé de campagne* (*The Diary of a Country Priest*) compelled our admiration; I reread it several times, astonished by the virtuosity concealed by its seeming simplicity. Two other authors whom we did not know aroused our sympathetic interest: one was Queneau, with *Les Derniers Jours,* the other Michel Leiris, with *L'Age d'homme.*

We watched several rehearsals of *Julius Caesar,* which Dullin was directing. Camille had done the adaptation, and took an active part in the production itself. Dullin was playing the somewhat unrewarding part of Cassius: his main talent was for coaxing lively performances from others. He had chosen as his Caesar an old barnstormer with a third-rate reputation, who partially made up for his lack of talent by a certain professional expertise, and who did, physically speaking, *look* the part. He built that man up, gesture by gesture, word by word, so well that in the end he could have passed for a great actor. Vandéric made a splendid Brutus, while Genika Athanasiou had great nobility of expression and, despite her strong accent, a most moving voice. As for Marchat, he got inside the personality of Mark Antony right from the beginning, and was quite superb in the part. I appreciated at its true worth all that Dullin and Camille and their entire company had put into the production; and on the first night I kept an anxious eye on the critics that Camille had pointed out to me. Most of them were elderly and seemed in a grumpy mood; it was winter, which meant they were coughing, and Lugné Poe was using a little silver box as a spittoon. The text, which Camille had carefully avoided toning down, appeared to shock them. All the same, the production was a resounding success. During the Lupercalian scene two young slaves had to run across the stage, almost naked, each with a flail in his hand. At every rehearsal they had nearly knocked over the bust of Caesar that stood in the center of the market place, but tonight they swerved round it most skillfully. One of them struck the whole audience with his remarkable good looks. Jean Cocteau inquired who he was. His name was Jean Marais.

I found myself putting less than my usual energy into work and leisure occupations alike about this time: indeed, I felt permanently fatigued.

What with Olga, and Sartre, or the two of them together, I tended to stay up late at night; Sartre could rest at Laon, and Olga had the daytime to recover in, but I never made up for the sleep I lost. I was working hard, and desperately anxious to finish my book. Every morning I got up early in order to get to the *lycée*. Often in the Métro I would anxiously reckon up the time to be got through between then and the following night. "Sixteen hours before I can go to bed again!" I used to think. I would have given anything to be able to fall asleep on the spot, forever. While waiting for Sartre in a café near the Gare du Nord I sometimes closed my eyes and lost consciousness for several minutes.

Sleep became an obsession with me. I had known real exhaustion during the year I spent cramming for my teacher's diploma, but when my head grew heavy in the evening, I made no attempt to struggle on: I simply went to bed. Now I had to draw on my reserves far into the night, and always woke up still tired. The reserves were never replaced. To always be hoping for a respite and never to get it was a peculiarly harassing experience. It was at this point that I realized the destructive power of sheer exhaustion. It is as deadly as any disease, and kills all joy in living.

On the other hand, I had followed the rise of the Popular Front with such delight that I could not but be saddened by its decline. Blum was in grave financial difficulties, and declared that it was necessary to "mark time" for a while. A secret society organized by the extreme right-wing fringe had been discovered, which was stockpiling arms and working in liaison with Hitler's espionage agents. When the conspiracy became known, far from publishing the names of those involved, the authorities hushed the whole thing up. England, like France, was quite willing to sit by and watch the intervention of German and Italian forces in Spain. The one country that was both capable of stopping the advance of Fascism and sincerely desired to do so was the U.S.S.R. Yet now we could no longer make head or tail of what was going on there, either. Both Gide's infatuation with Soviet Russia and his subsequent disenchantment had happened too quickly for us to take his *Retour d'U.R.S.S.* (*Back from the U.S.S.R.*) altogether seriously. (He had brought it out very soon after his return from Russia, and it had created a big stir.) But what was the meaning of the trials now taking place in Moscow? *Le Matin* informed us, quite seriously, that the confessions of the accused had been extracted from them by means of a "truth drug" that could be bought for a few cents in America. This was the merest imbecility; yet what explanation could one offer in its stead? Even Nizan, who had spent a blissful year in Russia, was deeply disconcerted. We had a long discussion with him at the Mahieu, and although ordinarily he was always highly circumspect about expressing his opinions, he did not conceal the fact that he was worried. We had never pictured the U.S.S.R. as a paradise, but we had never before seriously questioned the basis of the Socialist State, either. It was galling to be driven to do so just when the policy of the Western democracies had aroused such antipathy in us. Was there no corner of the world left on which we could pin our hopes?

Certainly Spain was no longer the Promised Land, but a field of battle; and the issue of that battle was becoming steadily more uncertain. In February Fernando got some leave: he was brimming over with enthusiasm, yet from what he said we inferred that the situation gave cause for alarm. He made us laugh by his account of how he had come to be regarded as a "responsible officer." During some skirmish or other, it appeared, he had found himself, together with a few comrades, on open ground and exposed to enemy fire; so he had very cleverly led them off behind a low wall, where they took shelter. He had been warmly congratulated for displaying such initiative, and was quickly promoted, first to captain, then to colonel. He ended up as a full-blown general. Yet while entertaining us with the saga of his rapid military advancement, he also made it clear what a desperate shortage of trained men, discipline, and organization there was in this Popular Army; and the socio-political confusion was greater still. Communists, Radicals, and Anarcho-Syndicalists were very far from serving identical interests. The Anarchists refused to recognize the fact that before making a revolution they had to win the war; in certain provinces, Catalonia included, the Syndicates were busy establishing local soviets when they ought rather to have been boosting output in the factories. Anarchist detachments embarrassed official Government strategy by their sudden and untimely surprise attacks, and took no notice of orders from GHQ. This lack of unity constituted the most frightful danger—especially when dealing with Franco's homogeneous army, now receiving ever more massive reinforcements in the form of German and Italian expeditionary forces.

Our hearts bled when Fernando talked to us of conditions in Madrid: the gutted houses on the Alcalá, shell holes all over the roads around the Puerta del Sol, a heap of rubble where the University students' quarter had once stood. He went back to Spain assuring us that despite all this the final victory would still go to the Republicans; and events seemed to confirm his prediction. Both at Jarama and Guadalajara the Popular Army held up the offensive that Franco had launched against Madrid. Despite this, the *dinamiteros* failed in their attempt to recapture Oviedo, and in the south Malaga fell.

The reason for these setbacks was always the same: lack of arms. The farce of "nonintervention" struck us daily as more criminal. For the first time in our lives, because the fate of Spain concerned us so deeply, indignation per se was no longer a sufficient outlet for us: our political impotence, far from furnishing us with an alibi, left us feeling hopeless and desolate. And it was so absolute: we were mere isolated nobodies. Nothing we could say or do in favor of intervention would carry the very slightest weight. There was no question of our going off to Spain ourselves; nothing in our previous background inclined us to such headstrong action. In any case, unless one got into some clearly defined technical or political job, there was a danger of being a nuisance rather than a help. Simone Weil had crossed the frontier determined to serve with the infantry; but when she asked for a gun they put her in the kitchens, where she spilled a bowl of boiling oil all over her feet. Colette Audry met the P.O.U.M. leaders in Barcelona and spoke at their meetings; but though she came back in a cheerfully elated frame of mind, we doubted whether her speeches had done much good.

Bost longed to go: he wanted to shake himself free of the stagnating depression in which the scenes with Marco and the breakup of a long-established relationship had plunged him. The frontier had been closed since February, not only for shipments of arms, but for volunteers as well. He asked Sartre whether Nizan might not be able to help him get through illegally. Sartre pondered this request with some anxiety: should he agree to Bost's request or not? In theory individual freedom of choice should always be respected; but if something happened to Bost, he, Sartre, would feel directly responsible. In the end he mentioned the matter casually to Nizan, and the latter put Bost in touch with Malraux, who explained that what the Republic needed was trained men, specialists, and military equipment, not raw recruits. Could Bost handle a machine gun? No, he had to admit he couldn't. "Perhaps," Malraux said, in a quite serious voice, "you could get some practice at Gastine-Reinette's." Bost's project quickly foundered.

One evening about ten o'clock I was chatting with Bost in the Sélect when a shiver ran through me. I generally took scant notice of such things as influenza, tonsillitis, or high temperature; but on this occasion the attack was so severe that I felt immediately I had to get home. I passed a disturbed night, woke dripping with sweat, and spent the whole day in bed. When Sartre arrived from Laon that evening we both felt quite certain that this prompt treatment had cured me. In any case, Camille had been wanting to meet Madame Lemaire for some time now, and had invited both her and us to dinner; this was a meeting I was determined not to miss. Dressing was a difficult business, since I could hardly stand up straight; but I had no intention of letting a mere microbe get the better of me. It was extremely cold outside, and when we reached Camille's place I was in a decidedly poor state. She had moved to a large studio on the Rue Navarin, and had furnished it in the same way as the house at Ferrolles, with theatrical gewgaws, odds and ends picked up in antique shops, and special creations of her own. The room was heated with a gigantic tiled stove, which was both an attractive and essential part of the décor, and yet contrived to produce a genuine hearth-and-home intimacy. Camille's ideas of entertaining were both sumptuous and elegant. But I scarcely glanced at the flowers and decanters and multi-colored hors-d'oeuvres; I lay down on a couch covered with an old silken bedspread, and while the others ate and drank and talked, I was doing my best to breathe. Finally Madame Lemaire and Sartre took me out. Halfway down the stairs my legs gave under me; a chill mist had settled in the street, and I felt it reaching down into my lungs as I stood waiting at the front door for Sartre to come back with a taxi. When I got to bed I was in a feverish, trancelike state, and all through the night I lay there sweating and shivering. Next morning, before he caught his train, Sartre got a doctor to come and see me. He prescribed mustard plasters. For two days my sister and Olga and Madame Lemaire looked after me. They brought me invalid tidbits such as caramel cream and stewed apricots, but I could not touch a thing. At the least movement I made, a sharp pain went ripping through my left side. A nurse was called and did several wet-cuppings on me; but I still sweated feverishly all night, and soaked two pairs of pajamas. In the morning the doctor became alarmed and said it was essential to get me into the hospital forthwith. When Sartre got back from Laon and told me that Madame Lemaire had arranged everything—an ambulance would take me to Saint-Cloud that same afternoon—I burst into tears: I felt as though I were being torn away from my own life, forever. When a pair of male nurses put me on a stretcher and carried me head first down the stairs, all that remained in my mind was a vast feeling of surprise. There was a group of loafers watching outside the street door, and as they loaded me into the ambulance I thought, in consternation: "This is really happening, and it's happening to *me*." I couldn't have been more astonished if I'd awakened and found myself on the moon. Anything, it was clear, could happen to me, just as it could to any other person. Now here was a revolution. To be oneself, simply oneself, is so amazing and utterly unique an experience that it's hard to convince oneself so singular a thing happens to everybody in the world, and is amenable to statistics. Sickness, accidents, and misfortunes were things that happened only to other people; but in the eyes of those curious bystanders *I* had abruptly become "other people," and, like all such, I was to all "other people" just "another person" myself. I had been stripped of my personal existence and security, and flung into a no man's land where literally anything was possible. I no longer had any protection; I was exposed to every danger there was. At the time I did not put all this into words; but it was the direct cause of the stupor in which I lay throughout my ambulance trip. "This patient they're taking away is *me*," I thought.

But afterward I ceased even to think, abandoning myself instead to the peace of fresh sheets. I was put to bed and given injections: someone had taken me in charge. For me, who lived with hands constantly clenched, in a permanent state of tension, this was rest indeed. I learned afterward that when I was admitted one of my lungs resembled a chunk of liver, and the other was beginning to go the same way. At the time there was no known method of checking the infection, and they restricted themselves to giving me injections that boosted my heart. If the second lung failed, I was done for. This idea never even occurred to me; I lay there confidently waiting to be cured. I slept with my torso propped up on pillows; during the day I remained in the same position, and was hardly ever awake, so that the passage of time became confused. When I recovered consciousness I was aware of little apart from my own feverish condition, which intensified the faintest sound or slightest glimmer of light a thousandfold. The singing of a bird in the early morning filled the whole universe to all eternity. I lay and stared at the basket of flowers my pupils had sent me, or the carafe of orangeade on my bedside table, and had no wish for anything else. Everything sufficed me as it was.

Little by little I came round. My mother visited me almost every morning, and Sartre came on any afternoon he was not in Laon. My sister, Olga, Madame Lemaire, and Bost all took turns to sit with me, and I was able to talk to them. The day came when I was able to read. Through Thyde Monnier's first novel, *La Rue courte,* I rediscovered Provence. The doctor was anxious to find out whether my lungs were seriously affected, and had X rays taken. It was agony for me to stand up straight, and I nearly fainted. For two days I awaited the results, with a good deal more curiosity than apprehension. I had wept on leaving my hotel room, but the idea of going off to a sanatorium did not alarm me at all: it would, I told myself, be a new experience. I remained faithful to my declared intention of turning all that life imposed upon me to my own purposes. I had complained that life was wearisomely repetitive: well, now it was going to change. The trio, with all its upsets and obsessions, had become so burdensome to me in the end that exile seemed restful by comparison. It may be that this detached attitude was only a precarious essay in self-protection: if I had in fact been forced to undergo a lengthy stay in some distant sanatorium, would I have stayed in so tranquil a mood? However, I was spared this ordeal: permission was granted me to complete my period of convalescence in Paris.

Sartre had gotten me a room in Marco's hotel which was more spacious and comfortable than the one I occupied in the Royal Bretagne. I was still bedridden, but how pleased to be out of the hospital! The Easter holidays had come; at lunch time Sartre would go and get me a helping of the *plat du jour* from the Coupole, and bring it back to my room, taking short steps so as not to spill anything. In the evening I ate ham and fruit and my energies rallied. The tiresome thing was that I was at the mercy of everyone who took it into their head to visit me. Besides, this close confinement was beginning to irk me. I tried to walk across the room, and my head spun; I had to learn to stand up straight again. Since Sartre had by now departed for Laon again, it was Marco and Bost— now superficially reconciled—who together took me on my first outing. They walked me as far as the Luxembourg Gardens, each supporting me by one arm. The fresh air and sunlight were quite overwhelming, and I could hardly keep my balance.

I was reading the papers again now: the same ones as previously, with the addition of *Ce soir,* which had begun publication in March under Aragon's editorship, with Nizan in charge of foreign affairs. Although Blum had proclaimed his "marking time" period, the world of high finance was systematically bent upon ruining his government. The right-wing societies might have been dissolved, but immediately after their dissolution La Rocque had founded the Parti Social Français, and a little later Doriot formed the Parti Populaire Français, which was supported by Ramon Fernandez. The workers of Clichy staged a vigorous counter-demonstration during one P.S.F. meeting, and were broken up by the police, which cost them the death of five in the process. The Spanish War was going badly now. Franco's troops were bombarding Madrid and the Basque country, and had slaughtered countless women and children at Durango; while Bilbao had taken a heavy hammering from German planes in an air attack. Toward the end of April the massacre at Guernica aroused the indignation of certain Catholics: Mauriac, Madaule, Bernanos, and Maritain all protested. In France a new press campaign opened against juvenile prisons. A nineteen-year-old convict had died at Eysses as the result of ill treatment. The Government promised that everything would be changed for the better; but at Eysses, and Amiane, and Mettray things remained exactly as before. Being powerless to fight the world's evils, I asked nothing better than to forget them, and happily obeyed the advice of my doctor, who had prescribed a three-week rest in the Midi.

Olga saw me off on the train. My compartment was overheated, and I could not sleep. I spent the night reading André Baillon's *Le Perce-oreille de Luxembourg*. In the early morning air Toulon smelled of fish and mimosa. I changed there to a diesel car that followed a tortuous in-and-out route along the coast, rocking perilously as it went: I felt it was going to jump the rails at each successive bend. My doctor had forbidden me the seaside, long walks, and fatiguing exercise of any sort; I had accordingly settled for Bormes-les-Mimosas. The station was a deserted shack, and I was the only person who got off there. Not a porter or ticket collector anywhere in sight. It was midday; I was sluiced with Provençal sunlight and all the scents of the Midi. It was a glorious resurrection from the foggy atmosphere of my convalescence. There was a man setting off up the steep path to the village just as I appeared, and he relieved me of my bag. From the village square I could see the sea quite close below me, and the Iles d'Hyères too; but I decided that the distance separating us was just about adequate. I no longer felt in the least ill, anyway. It was the first time in my life that I had gotten away for a rest in the country, and at first I enjoyed it. I put up at the best hotel (full *pension* for thirty francs) and stuffed myself full of good food, and as I ate I watched the old girls playing *belote* down under the veranda. I walked over the hills, through pinewoods that were intersected by beautiful sandy paths known to the inhabitants, somewhat pretentiously, as "the boulevards." Here I rediscovered those heavy, hairy, brightly colored yet scentless flowers, and the pungent-smelling herbs I had once loved to rub between my fingers. I read some of Faulkner's short stories, and basked in the sun for hours on end. But after three days of this I found I couldn't stand seeing the same faces at every meal; so I slung my rucksack over my back and moved on. Despite my doctor's advice I spent some time at Porquerolles and Port-Cros. Then I turned inland toward the mountains. At Collobrière it was raining, and I spent two days in a hotel where I was the only guest. In its red-tiled dining room I read *Catherine-soldat*, Mazo de la Roche's *Jalna*, which I found very tedious, Moravia's *Les Ambitions déçues,* which struck me as mildly boring, and a tome by Morgan on embryology and genetics which I found hardly more amusing. I had been told to fatten myself up, so I gorged myself on *crème de marrons*—the natural specialty of an area whose great chestnut groves I remembered from my childhood. I went to bed at ten o'clock, and generally coddled myself. It was a new kind of game. I had also been told not to walk too far each day; but little by little I slipped back into the long treks to which I was accustomed. I climbed the Monts des Maures, and tramped through petrified forests, under a stormy sky, to get to La Chartreuse de La Verne. I discovered the little peninsula of Saint-Tropez, with its cliff-top villages and wild headlands, reached by coast guard tracks or through the thorny undergrowth of the maquis. My reading adapted itself somewhat capriciously to various backgrounds. It was among the red rocks of the Estérel massif, among those *gorges d'enfer* where there was, indeed, a most hellish degree of heat, that I was first captivated by Orwell's *Animal Farm*. I climbed to the summit of Mont Vinaigre, and breathed the scent of flowering mimosa in the Tanneron valley. Health and joy once more flooded through my veins.

In various village post offices I found letters from Sartre awaiting me, each of them like some unexpected gift. He told me about Jean-Louis Barrault's production of *Numance,* based on Cervantes' play *Numancia,* with décor by Masson: it was a truly new kind of theatrical presentation, with many fine moments. He also passed on some news which made me jump for joy. He had been summoned to Gallimard's: *Melancholia* had been accepted. Here is his own account of the episode:

> I reached the Gare du Nord at twenty to three. Bost was waiting for me there. We hailed a taxi and I went to the hotel to pick up *Erostratus*. From there we went on to the Dôme, where we found Poupette correcting the other two stories, *Dépaysement* and *The Wall*. All three of us got down to the job, and it was finished by four o'clock precisely. I left Bost in the same little café where I waited for you, the day you went off to pick up that pamphlet of mine the N.R.F. had turned down. Very depressed you were, too. Anyway, I made my magnificent entry. There were seven chaps already waiting up in the outer office, some for Brice Parain, some for Hirsch, others for Seligmann. I gave my name to an amiable sort of woman who sat at a table answering several telephones. She picked up one of them and announced me. I was told to wait for five minutes. I sat down in one corner on a little kitchen chair, and waited. I saw Brice Parain go past; he gave me a vague glance, but didn't appear to recognize me. I began to reread *The Wall*—partly to pass the time, and also, just a little, to reassure myself, since I found *Dépaysement* a shoddy piece of work. Then a dapper little man arrived—spotless linen, tie pin, black waistcoat, striped trousers, spats, and a bowler hat pushed back on his head. He had a reddish face, a big hooked nose, and very hard eyes. It was Jules Romains—yes, it really *was* he, don't worry, and not just someone rather like him. In the first place he was as liable to turn up there as anywhere; and in the second, he told them his

name. Just like that. A moment or so later, when everyone had forgotten about me, the telephone girl came out of her corner and asked one of the four chaps who were still there for a light. Not one of them could oblige her. She stood there and said, with coquettish impertinence: "What, four men and not a match between them?" I raised my head at this; she glanced in my direction and said hesitantly: "Well, five." Then she asked me what I was doing there.

"I want to see M. Parent—I mean, Paulhan."

"Well go on up then," she said.

I climbed two stories and found myself facing a tall, swarthy man with a soft black mustache going discreetly gray. He was a somewhat large man, wearing a light-toned suit, and looked like a Brazilian to me. This was Paulhan. He took me into his private office, talking all the time in a refined, high-pitched, almost feminine voice: there was something caressing about it. I sat down gingerly on the very edge of a leather armchair.

Without any preliminaries he said to me: "What's all this misunderstanding about letters? I don't get it."

I told him: "The misunderstanding originated with me in the first instance. I never anticipated appearing in your review at all."

He said: "Well, it *was* impossible—to begin with, what you sent us was far too long; it would have lasted us for six months, and the reader would have been lost after the second installment. But it's an admirable piece of work." This was followed by several laudatory phrases of the sort you can imagine for yourself—"remarkably individual tone," that kind of thing. I sat there, very ill at ease, thinking that after this he would find my stories poor stuff by comparison. You will tell me that Paulhan's judgment is unimportant. But insofar as I was capable of being flattered by his good opinion of *Melancholia,* I found the prospect of his dismissing my stories decidedly unpalatable.

Meanwhile he was saying to me: "Do you know Kafka? Despite the differences between you, Kafka is the only modern writer who comes to mind when I consider this work of yours." Then he got up, gave me a copy of *Mesure,* and said: "I'm going to give one of your stories to *Mesure,* and keep one myself for the *N.R.F.*"

I said: "They're a bit . . . er . . . outspoken. I deal with what might be described as, hmm, sexual problems."

He smiled with an indulgent air. "In matters of that sort *Mesure* is very strict," he told me. "But we at the *N.R.F.* are prepared to publish anything."

Then I revealed to him that I had two others. He seemed delighted. "Fine, fine!" he said. "Give them to me. Then I can pick and choose for something that'll suit the issue, eh?" So within eight days I am to take him my two remaining stories—if I'm not too busy commuting to finish *The Room.* Finally he said: "Your manuscript is with Brice Parain at the moment. He doesn't see quite eye to eye with me about it: he finds parts of it dull and full of *longueurs.* But I disagree with him here: in my opinion such shadows are essential, in order to throw the brilliant passages into clearer relief." I was caught like a rat in a trap.

Then he added: "But your book will certainly be accepted. Gallimard simply *cannot fail* to take it on. Anyway, I shall now take you along to see Parain yourself."

So we went down one floor and found Parain, who nowadays looks as though he might be mistaken for Constant Rémy, except that he's rather more hirsute. "Here's Sartre," said Paulhan. Parain was all cordiality. "I thought it must be. There's only one Sartre, after all." He addressed me in the familiar second person right from the start. Paulhan went back to his own office, and Parain took me through a smoking room full of leather armchairs and odd characters, out onto a sunlit garden terrace. We sat down in white-enameled chairs, by a polished wooden table, and he began to talk to me about *Melancholia*. It's hard to tell you his words in detail, but here is the gist of what he said. He read the first thirty pages, and thought: Here's a character drawn like something out of Dostoevsky. He'll have to go on as he begins, and undergo all sorts of extraordinary experiences, simply because he's outside the normal social pattern. But from page 30 onward disappointment and impatience set in: too much dull heavy stuff with a Populist slant. He found the night scene in the hotel (the bit involving the two servant girls) far too long-drawn-out, since, as he said, any modern writer can do that sort of thing standing on his head. The scene on the Boulevard Victor-Noir struck him as over-lengthy, too, though the argument between the man and the woman there he regarded as "tip-top." He wasn't particularly impressed with the Autodidact, who he thinks is both dull *and* over-caricatured. On the other hand, he confesses himself most impressed with my nausea motif, and the looking-glass episode (when the fellow catches sight of himself in a mirror), and the intrigue itself, and the scene where all those solid respectable citizens are raising their hats to one another and making conversation in the brasserie. That's as far as he's gone: he hasn't read any more yet. He thinks the form I've chosen (i.e., the diary) a mistake, and feels it would be less obtrusive if I were not so determined to "weld" chunks of Populism onto the sections he regards as "fantasy." He wants me to cut as much of the Populism as possible—the dull passages about town life, and phrases such as "I've eaten too heavy a dinner at the Brasserie Vézelise"—and all the botched-up linking passages [*soudages*]. He is very impressed with M. de Rollebon. I told him that in any case there was no more *soudage* after Sunday's entry. (All that remains are the sections entitled "Fear," "The Museum," "The Discovery of Existence," "Conversation with the Autodidact," "Contingency," and so to the conclusion.) He said: "If we think a young author's book could profitably be changed in any respect, we usually return it to him—in his own best interests— so that he can touch it up here and there. All the same, I know how difficult revising a book can be. You have a look and see what you can do. If it's impossible, well, we'll come to some sort of decision just the same." He was a bit the benevolent patron and very much the *jeune aîné*.

As he had things to do, I left him at this point, but he invited me to take a drink with him when he was through. So off I went and played a little joke on Little Bost. As I had inadvertently walked out still clutching the manuscript of *Melancholia*, I entered the café and threw the book on the table without saying a word. He stared at me, and turned a little pale.

"Rejected," I told him, in a pathetic voice, trying to sound as though I didn't care.

"Oh *no!*" he exclaimed. "But why?"

"They found it dull and tiresome."

He was absolutely dumfounded by this. Then I told him the whole story, and he showed vast delight. I filled up his glass and then went off for my drink with Brice Parain. We met in a little café down the Rue du Bac; I'll spare you an account of our conversation. B.P. is reasonably intelligent, but nothing more. He's the sort of chap who speculates about language, like Paulhan: that's their business. You know the old line: dialectic is only a battle of words, because the meaning of words is infinite and inexhaustible. Therefore everything is dialectic, and so on. He wants to write a thesis on the subject. At this point I left him. He's going to write to me in a week or so. As far as the alterations to *Melancholia* are concerned, I shall of course, wait till I see you, and we can then decide jointly what is feasible . . .

On my return to Paris Sartre gave me further details concerning the *Melancholia* episode. Paulhan had merely refused to publish it in the *N.R.F.;* as regards possible publication in book form, the reader commissioned to report on it had felt himself finally baffled. Knowing that Sartre had been recommended by Pierre Bost, he noted on his report: "Inquire of Pierre Bost if this author has talent." Afterward Gallimard read the book himself, and apparently liked it: the only criticism he had to make concerned its title. He suggested an alternative one, *Nausea,* which I was against—wrongly, as I realized afterward; but I was afraid the public might take a book called *Nausea* for a naturalistic novel. It was agreed that the work should be published at some time during 1938. In July Paulhan published *The Wall* in the *N.R.F.,* and this story by an unknown author proved a real sensation. Sartre received numerous letters about it. Over and above this, he had just been offered a post at the Lycée Pasteur, in Neuilly. I myself had just completed the revision of *Primauté du spirituel,* which my sister was typing, and which Sartre recommended to Brice Parain that October, just after the beginning of the term.

I had recovered all my normal gaiety and got the most I could out of Paris. I saw the Negro dancers from New York's Cotton Club, who stirred up fresh visions of America in my mind. The Exposition opened its doors to us; we spent hours contemplating masterpieces of French art, especially in the salons devoted to Van Gogh. It was the first time we had seen a conspectus of his work, from the first grim youthful sketches to the irises and ravens of Auvers. The Spanish Pavilion was opened in mid-July, and it was in its brand-new surroundings that we received the initial shock of Picasso's "Guernica."

Nizan was back from the Writers' Congress that had been held in Madrid during the bombardment. He gave us a most entertaining account of how the various participants had reacted to bombs and artillery fire— some were calm, and others scared, and one character in particular used to go on all fours under the table at the very slightest explosion outside. He told us that morale in the battered city was unwaveringly high. Yet the situation was critical. At the beginning of May there had been an Anarcho-Syndicalist insurrection, which caused bloody slaughter in Barcelona and came within an ace of letting Catalonia pass into Fascist hands. Negrin had formed a new Cabinet and undertaken to stamp out all these Anarchist and Trotskyite outbreaks that were disorganizing the struggle against Franco. The Communists denounced the P.O.U.M. as a nest of traitors, and the leaders of the organization were arrested. On the other hand, both the Anarchists and a Socialist splinter group accused Negrin and the Stalinists of assassinating both the proletarian movement and the Republic itself. These dissensions augured ill for the future. Nazi squadrons were stepping up their raids on Madrid and Barcelona, and Franco's offensive in the North was pushed forward with redoubled violence. On June 19 Bilbao fell, and the French left-wing neutralists began to realize the mistake they had made. Guéhenno, writing in *Vendredi,* delivered himself of a self-critical palinode that began: "Men of my generation have a whole mass of paralyzing memories at the back of their minds," and ended: "We must accept the possibility of war in order to preserve the peace." Many people were changing their attitude in a similar fashion. But the Government had no intention of modifying its policy. For all its excessive prudence, Blum's Cabinet fell, brought down by the banks, railway companies, and big insurance groups. There was no chance of Chautemps opting for intervention. This new Government still meant a majority for the Left; but *Le Canard enchaîné* was by no means altogether joking when it announced the imminent formation of a new sort of Popular Front— with no Communists, no Socialists, and no Radicals.

On the night of the Fourteenth of July we went the rounds of the small local balls held in Montparnasse and near the Bastille; after which I left Paris, and Sartre stayed on for a few days, having things to settle. I had made up my mind to explore some higher-lying area than I had ever dared to tackle on foot hitherto. Pagniez suggested the parts around the Col d'Allos. I set out from Lauzet at midday, and slept in a rest hut at the foot of the Trois-Evêchés, which I attempted to scale the following morning. The track referred to in the *Guide Bleu* was practically invisible, and very soon I became terrified by the sheer drop below me. In an effort to get away from it I climbed higher and higher, which merely increased the void yawning under my feet. Eventually I came to a halt. The way I was going I could not possibly reach the summit; and yet, I thought, I was bound to break my neck if I tried to retrace my steps. So there I stuck, pressed into the rock face, heart beating madly. I made an effort to shift one foot, but exhaustion and fear made me stumble, and to recover my balance I jettisoned my rucksack, which went plummeting down into the valley below. How was I to follow it without being dashed to pieces? Once again I moved a foot forward, and struggled on very slowly, yard by yard. I felt as though I would never reach level ground again. Suddenly I lost my footing, slipped, grabbed frantically at some loose stones, and brought them tumbling down with me. "Well," I thought, "it's happened, and it's happened to me: this is the end." But I found myself at the bottom of the ravine with nothing worse than some skin abrasures on my thigh—not a single bone broken. It astonished me that I had felt so little emotional reaction when I believed myself on the very brink of death. I picked up my rucksack, ran back all the way to Lauzet, and thumbed a lift from a car, which took me across the mountains as far as my chalet-hotel on the Col d'Allos. As I fell asleep I remember telling myself crossly that I'd wasted twenty-four hours.

I caught up with lost time during the next few days, however. I strode across high mountain ranges all gleaming with pure white snow, and over plateaus where all the villages had long been abandoned to brambles and vipers. My last night I spent in Riez, on a park bench, while the town slumbered around me. About the time when the roof tiles became visible against the morning sky, I caught a bus to Marseille. Sartre and Bost and I were due to embark here for Piraeus at noon the following day.

We had planned this trip to Greece a long while back; as on so many other occasions, if we were not exactly following the fashion, at least we were carried along by circumstance. Many impecunious intellectuals made great efforts to visit this country at bargain rates; though it was a long way off, the exchange rate was all in our favor. Gégé had been there the year before, and returned brimful of enthusiasm, despite having caught a dose of malaria. She also gave us some very valuable tips. Bost was dying to accompany us, and it had been arranged that he should join our party for two or three weeks.

I found Sartre and Bost waiting for me at the station, and we went off to buy provisions. The deck passage we had bought entitled us to traveling room only; it did not include meals. Thanks to this measure of economy we found ourselves with plenty of cash on hand, and so we went the rounds of the well-stocked food shops on the Rue Paradis, buying everything that took our fancy. I felt, in an elated sort of way, that it wasn't so much a shopping expedition as a freebooters' raid. When we went aboard the *Cairo City* one fact immediately struck us. A kind of spontaneous segregation was in force among the deck passengers. The poor immigrants returning home gathered forward, with all their bundles and packages; the few tourists there were huddled together in the stern. We hired deck chairs, and spread out our blankets and rucksacks (we hadn't even brought sleeping bags) while Bost, our technical expert, produced a small portable stove. Two couples in their thirties made up another party. We had come across one of the women in Montparnasse— a dark-skinned, lively brunette with short, powerful thighs, whose husband was tall and good-looking and heavily tanned under his fair hair. We nicknamed him *le grand sympathique*. His back was already flayed into strips from sunburn, and his wife was rubbing oil into the sore patches. When the deckhands hosed down the deck at six o'clock in the morning, these two were already up, in bathing costumes, capering about under the icy jets of water. They seemed extremely happy.

So, indeed, were we. Bost's stove went wrong almost at once, but the ship's cooks let us heat up our sauerkraut and canned stew in the galley, and gave us grapes and peaches as well. We ate, slept, read, and chatted. Rocked by the motion of the boat, and half stupefied with sun-bathing, I felt a pleasant vagueness invading me, a kind of mental torpor. I had my second glimpse of the Straits of Messina, and saw flames belching from Stromboli in the darkness. Time and the boat moved smoothly on till we passed through the Corinth Canal and dropped anchor at Piraeus. A taxi whisked us into Athens, along a heavily potholed road.

Since 1936 Metaxas had ruled Greece as dictator. Occasionally we saw ceremonial troops in their pleated skirts parading in some public square, but Athens did not look in the least like the capital of a military state. It was a dismal, chaotic, and unbelievably poverty-stricken city. At first I found the warren of lower-class streets round the Acropolis very at-tractive—little squat houses, pink- or blue-washed, with flat roofs and outside staircases. Then one day, as we were strolling through, some chil-dren threw stones at us. Well, well, we thought placidly, they're not very fond of foreigners, are they? When, some time afterward, I traveled through another poor country and felt myself the object of hatred, I took it very much to heart. But during the thirties, though we waxed indignant enough against the world's injustices, we tended—especially on the sort of trip where a picturesque background was apt to sidetrack us—to take such things for granted, as part of the natural order. Against these Greek urchins' stones we had employed our usual defensive subter-fuge: these tourists who formed the target for their anger were not really *us*. We were never prepared to acknowledge the status which circumstances objectively assigned to us. Through thoughtlessness and self-deception we managed to defend ourselves against any harsh realities that might have spoiled our holidays. All the same, we did feel some qualms about certain quarters of Piraeus, where the houses—mere shacks—were gaily painted, but betrayed the most filthy and abject poverty. The wretched folk squatting here were far from embracing the squalor of their city with that natural warmth that Naples evoked in the Neapolitans; they were a feckless lot—down-and-outs, emigrants, resident aliens, sub-Bohemian flotsam, subhumans. They were starving, ragged, and full of sores, without either the Italian's kindliness or his gaiety. The place was swarming with beggars, who sat mechanically scratching their scabs. A terrifying proportion of the children were crippled, misshapen, blind, or mutilated. On the dockside at Piraeus I saw a hydrocephalous infant, whose head was a kind of monstrous protuberance, the features barely recognizable as a face. Taken by and large, though, *all* the Athenians looked miserable, even the *petite bourgeoisie* and the prosperous middle classes. All one saw outside the cafés were fattish men in dark suits, sitting there in gloomy silence and playing with their strings of amber beads. When a shopkeeper was asked for a commodity he did not possess, or a news vendor for a paper that had not yet arrived, his face would assume an expression of disdain and alarm, and he would jerk his head up with a gesture which to a Frenchman signifies assent, but here suggested all the woes of the world.

We had taken a room in a somewhat seedy hotel off Omonia Square. The proprietor had agreed to let Bost sleep out on the roof for nothing: sometimes, however, he preferred to spend the night under the pine trees of the Pnyx. For breakfast we went off to the (relatively) luxurious atmosphere of Stadium Street. By nine o'clock the temperature was already approaching 95°; we would sit, sweating, on the *terrasse* outside some well-known pâtisserie, where I would drink a cup of hot chocolate with creamy milk, thickened still further by the addition of an egg yolk. This was the best meal of the day. The smart French restaurants were not within our means, and the food in the *tavernas* around Omonia Square was very bad. The menu announced, in French, *"indestins de mouton à la broache"*; the rice clung soggily to one's palate and had a distinct flavor of perspiration. In every neighboring street *intestins de mouton* were being spit-roasted, but failed to tempt us. In any case I had taken an active dislike to the sheep themselves after seeing them in the Athenian markets, with their idiotic profiles, and their penchant, as wretched as it was indecent, for displaying their sourly anemic bodies. I remember how once we were looking for a restaurant along Stadium Street, in the grilling midday sun; Sartre turned them all down, and flew into one of those sudden, brief tempers to which the dog days made him more than usually liable. He laughed at himself afterward, but somewhat ruefully. "July twenty-eighth, 1937: Poulou in a bad mood all day," he muttered, parodying a ship's log. (We didn't keep a diary at all as a matter of fact.) It was either then or later that we found a small, shady German restaurant: henceforth we lived almost entirely on *Bauernfrühstück*. In the cafés we drank tiny cups of a black syrupy substance that was, in fact, coffee, and which I liked very much. We drank from large glasses quantities of water, iced and chlorinated, with which there came on a saucer, a dab of cherry jam.

Our days were very full. We walked round the streets and the markets and the port area, and climbed Lycabettus, and visited the museums. But our favorite targets were the Acropolis and the Pnyx—from which we could get a view of the Acropolis. Beauty is no more amenable to words than happiness. If I say "I saw the Acropolis," or "I went to the Museum and saw the statues," either I have to leave it at that or write a

whole extra book on the subject. I am not concerned here to draw a picture
of Greece, but simply of the life we led there. We were no longer struck
dumb when brought face to face with Greek temples; we had learned to
express our reactions to them verbally. Standing on the Pnyx we conjured
up bygone ages—the crowded, noisy, bustling assemblies of ancient Athens.
But most often we were so moved that we remained silent. As the sun
went down we observed that Hymettus really *was* purple; after which we
were shooed out of the Acropolis by the attendants. Sartre and Bost raced
each other down the marble steps, beside which a notice stood proclaiming
NO RUBBISH TO BE SHOT HERE. This inspired Sartre to an extempore strophe
à la Claudel:

> Little Bost stood lost in thought on the flight
> Of marble steps. Yet, being well aware
> That rubbish was not (repeat *not*) to be shot here, he moved on
> With some celerity.

We organized a carefully planned tour through the Cyclades, taking in
Mykonos, Delos, Syra, and Santorin. We would travel on diminutive old
tubs, sleeping on deck as we had done aboard the *Cairo City*. The night we
sailed from Piraeus a vast reddish moon was rising, and the air was so
warm and mild that it made my heart turn over. Several times I woke
up out of sheer blissful happiness, and opened my eyes to look at the
Great Bear. On Mykonos we drank coffee and looked at the windmills.
A caique took us across to Delos; the sea began to get choppy, and I
heaved my very guts up. "Are we," Sartre inquired, "staying on Delos for
four hours or three days?" He remained quite unmoved by my spasms of
retching, which he ascribed to deliberate malice on my part. "Four
hours or three days? Come on, make up your mind." I didn't give a
damn which in my present state: I felt mindless as well as bodiless. But
he kept nagging at me. "You've got to decide *now*," he repeated. "Three
days," I muttered, and half passed out.

I came to, still very giddy, on the way to the Tourist Pavilion. The two
rooms were already occupied by a couple of young Englishmen, wearing
impeccably laundered white shorts; but the manager helped us stow our
gear out on the terrace. Sartre stayed there while Bost and I went off
for a swim in the sea, which settled my stomach, and a session of sun-
bathing, which played hell with my back. Still, I was so pleased to be
where I was that I bore the pain with stoical resignation. We were deeply
impressed by the sight of those brooding stone lions, against a background
of shattered marble temple columns; and glad that, as in Pompeii, the
ruins were largely those of a real living city—a port complete with shops
and warehouses and craftsmen's booths and sailors' dives. Later that morning some women in local costume landed from Mykonos, and spread out
a collection of tourist souvenirs on the jetty: shawls, rugs, peasant headdresses, gimcrack jewelry, a whole mass of stuff. About eleven o'clock a
boat doing a Hellenic cruise dropped anchor, and the tourists came ashore,
firmly shepherded by a guide, as at the summit of Vesuvius. They stayed

scarcely three hours, and most of them had lunch at the hotel: they "did" the ruins in double-quick time. One or two bolder spirits set off to climb Mt. Cynthus, but were brought back to the jetty by a few blasts on a whistle, where they bought various trinkets. We watched them re-embark with a delicious feeling of superiority. The traveling hawkers likewise cast off in their caique once more, and the island became our own private property again. A little later we climbed to the top of Mt. Cynthus ourselves, and stood watching the distant islands gleam and fade in the purplish evening haze. Delos was one of the places where I had a taste of Paradise.

On the steamer that took us to Syra we slept surrounded by cages full of stinking poultry. The next morning we spent ambling up and down flights of steps between ancient whitewashed houses. In the afternoon I went swimming with Bost on the other side of the island, some six or seven miles away. We had to catch the boat for Santorin at three o'clock in the morning, and all three of us spent the night under the lee of a big sand dune near the harbor—I myself slept like a log. We weighed anchor at dawn, and when we woke the following morning there above us were the cliffs of Santorin. The steamer was moored some way out from the shore, and surrounded by shrill-voiced rowboatmen. Three young bearded Frenchmen, anxious not to be "had," were chaffering over the price of their passage in an arrogant way that ill-concealed their avarice. When in a poor country they would have felt exploited themselves if they didn't exploit the populace. We criticized them, but among ourselves, as was only proper. Speaking for myself, I felt sorry for them, too: how silly they were to spoil that radiant morning scene! The blood-red cliff fell sheer into the blue of the sea, and on its summit houses gleamed, white and diminutive. We were rowed ashore, and then followed a stepped pathway up to the village. Here we asked for the Hotel Vulcan, where we intended to stay. People shook their heads despondently or smiled at our inquiries. Someone pointed toward a hole in the wall which turned out to be a *taverna*. The proprietor served us with thick Turkish coffee and also brought us a narghile, or hookah, which Bost and Sartre, taking turns, smoked with great diligence. Once again we made inquiries concerning the Hotel Vulcan; somehow the proprietor both grasped what we meant and managed to explain to us that we had got the wrong village; we had landed not at Thira, the "capital," but at Oia, on the northernmost tip of the island. This mattered very little, since from one place to the other took less than three hours by foot along a clifftop path. I observed that the cliffs themselves were not really red, but rather resembled those layer cakes which contain superimposed strata of red, chocolate, ocher, strawberry, orange, and lemon. Westward across the strait the three Burnt Islands gleamed like anthracite. We found the Hotel Vulcan; as an economic measure, and also through fear of bedbugs, we asked the proprietor whether we might sleep out on the roof, and he agreed. Once more I enjoyed some paradisiacal nights, and was not at all bothered by the hard cement surface. We lay rolled up in our blankets, listening to the whispers and soft footsteps that were audible away above us—the town was stepped

up in terraces, and both dogs and men prowled about on the rooftops
at night. The hotelkeeper's daughter woke us in the morning, and brought
us a jug of water and a basin. Below us we saw a vista of white lime-
washed cupolas, crisp starched terrace roofs, and, across the dazzling water,
the sulfurous, lava-built bulk of the Burnt Islands. From the instant I
blinked my eyes open I was sluiced with so achingly lovely a panorama
that I felt as though something inside me might burst.

We had our morning coffee in the hotel, and dined there at night, when
they served us with the same sort of bony, scrawny fowls that I had
observed in the markets of Piraeus, and which had depressed me just as
much as the sheep. At lunch time we were always out on some excursion.
The longest trip we made was to the ruins of Thera and the sanctuary
of Stavrós. We walked through the vineyards, along cinder tracks that
sank underfoot as we trod on them, so that each step cost us the effort
of three. It was really exhausting; we followed the line of those little white
walls, broken every so often by a stunted fig tree, and all the time the
sun blazed down on us. As a sort of last straw, we strayed a little from
the path we should have taken. Sartre lost his temper. "This is a fine sort
of lark," he grumbled, and added, not unreasonably: "I came out here to
make the Grand Tour, and now you've got me playing at Boy Scouts."
He calmed down after a while, but by the time we reached Emborio, where
we intended to have lunch, we were all three pretty well exhausted. There
was not a soul about in those baking streets, and all the houses were barred
and shuttered. The one black-clad woman we found, and tried to approach,
fled from us. (Sartre had Emborio in mind when he described Argos in
the first act of _Les Mouches_ [_The Flies_].) We prowled around for a
while in this furnace, and eventually found a café, thick with buzzing
flies, where they produced a tomato salad for us. The tomatoes were dotted
with dead flies, and swimming in an even more nauseous oil than the
stuff we were offered at Tarifa. To quench our thirst we had the choice
of resinated wine, which none of us could stand, or muddy, brackish cistern
water. I tried to swallow alternate mouthfuls of the two, but was soon
forced to give up. (A year later, however, Pagniez described Emborio to
us as a "charming village": he and Thérèse had found a nearby inn where
they got a magnificent lunch.)

We also made a trip by boat to the Kaïméni Islands. The ground was
sulfurous, and so hot that it burned our feet. We saw the black, yellow-
streaked crater, an astonishing spectacle when viewed against that intensely
blue sky. When we were offshore from the islands Sartre and Bost dived
in and swam round the boat. Here and there the water was practically at
boiling point, and the immense depths beneath them they found rather
worrying; at all events, they very quickly climbed aboard again.

From Santorin we returned directly to Athens. Sartre and Bost squatted
on deck playing Greek music on a recorder: they produced just the right
sort of nasal twang. When we dropped anchor, Bost would plunge in
and swim round the boat. He parted from us at Piraeus, where he re-em-
barked for France. He told us afterward that his last night on Greek soil

had been spent in some awful flophouse, where his inquiry of the landlady as to the whereabouts of what we called "the john" elicited a flamboyant gesture seaward, and Xenophon's cry of *"Thalassa! Thalassa!"*

Sartre and I visited Delphi together. Here marble and olive blended exquisitely, with the sea in the distant background, to form the loveliest landscape in all Greece. We spent our first night out of doors, in the Stadium; but the wind blew so strongly that next morning we booked a room in the hotel. This was fortunate, since toward evening a really savage storm broke, lashing down on trees and ruins. We stood with our noses pressed to the window, thinking how lucky we were to be there when Zeus was roaring in anger over the Phaedriades. We made our way down to Itéa, and slept for a few hours in a ramshackle little *xenodokeion*. When I was awakened in the middle of the night to catch the boat, I caught a glimpse through an open door of a woman wearing a long black dress, and combing out her long black hair. But when she turned toward me, I saw that "she" was really a bearded man, a Greek Orthodox priest: there was a whole group of them going through the Canal with us. I had worked out a most ingenious itinerary by which we could reach Olympia across the mountains. A rack railway took us as far as the monastery of Megas Pilaion—a famous place, though three years later it was gutted by fire—and thence to a village with very bad water, where we had lunch. From here we traveled twenty-five miles or so by hired car, finally stopping when a mountain torrent barred any further advance, and continuing the trek on foot. The path wound through hills that modulated in color between amethyst and plum, and were carpeted with low, dark-green undergrowth. Sartre had our joint rucksack slung on his back; he was wearing a wide-brimmed straw hat, and carried a stick. I had a cardboard box under one arm. We did not meet a living soul, though from time to time we came across yellowish curs that Sartre drove off with showers of stones: he was scared of dogs. After we had been walking for some four hours it struck me that we were at an altitude of about 3,500 feet, and that even in Greece we would need camping equipment if we intended to sleep outdoors. I watched the darkening sky somewhat uneasily. Suddenly we turned a bend and saw the lights of a village twinkling in front of us: on one wooden balcony I read the magic word *xenodokeion*. The sheets were snowy white, and next morning I found that there was a bus leaving for Olympia. The fields we drove past were covered with fruit trays on which black grapes were drying out in the sun.

We spent three days wandering around the terraced slopes of Olympia, among the gigantic fallen column-drums; these placid ruins, however, moved us less than Delos or Delphi had done. When night came, we settled down under the pines on the flank of Mt. Kronion, which is hardly more than a hill. We burned greenish, strong-smelling twists of paper close to our "beds": this was supposed to keep off mosquitoes. We changed into pajamas and rolled ourselves up in our blankets. A stream of oaths burst out in the darkness: Sartre had gone rolling right down the slope, over the pine needles. The return journey made his bare feet extremely sore.

A little later I heard voices, and saw the wink of a light. A few yards above us, we discovered, our old friend *le grand sympathique* and his party were also encamped for the night. We had noticed them down in the village, drinking under an arbor in somebody's private garden, and as heartily cheerful as ever.

The afternoon heat was so intense that walking could only be done in the morning or evening. We set off for Andritsaena at 5 P.M., and among the reeds we passed a couple of young Englishmen coming back from our destination. They were accompanied by a guide, and a donkey to carry their luggage: this struck us as decidedly fussy. We slept under a tree, and set off again at dawn. According to our calculations, we ought to have got there about ten o'clock, before the heat of the day set in—"there" being Monsieur Kristopoulos's hotel, which Gégé had so warmly recommended to us. The *Guide Bleu* gave no indication that crossing the Alpheus was a difficult operation; but the fact was this river turned out to be a sort of Hydra, with innumerable arms, into which we plunged waist-high. It took us over two hours to reach the further bank, and in addition I had underestimated the distance involved. At one o'clock, with the temperature at something like 105°, we found ourselves at the foot of a stony hillside, with not a scrap of shade in sight. Sartre's feet were stuck full of thorns, and our throats felt as though bars of red-hot iron had been thrust down them. For an instant, as we slipped and slithered among the pebbles, we felt utter despair. Then we pulled ourselves together and went on climbing. I spotted a house and went and asked for water, which I gulped down with great avidity. When I returned to Sartre he was flourishing his stick defensively at one of those yellowish mongrels, a particularly fierce specimen, and looking rather apoplectic under his straw hat. He felt better after a drink. An hour later we struck a road and came to a village, where we collapsed in the cool shade of a *taverna,* got on the phone to Monsieur Kristopoulos, and asked him to come and pick us up in his car. While we waited for him we lunched on hard-boiled eggs: there was nothing else to eat, not even bread. When we got to Andritsaena both the hotel and its cuisine seemed exquisitely luxurious to us.

We rode up on muleback to the temple of Bassae, and took a bus to Sparta, where there was nothing to see, and visited Mistra, where we slept on the floor of a ruined palace. When we woke up it was to find five or six faces, framed in black kerchiefs, bending over us with somewhat perplexed expressions. We explored all the churches and examined every fresco, spellbound and ravished by the stunning impact of Byzantine art. Sartre stole a skull from the ossuary, and we took it away as a souvenir. It was while we were sitting in the cool of the Despot's Palace that we had one of our few really memorable spats. I had planned to climb Mt. Taygetus: nine and a half hours up, five and a half hours down, the *Guide* said, and added that there was a rest house, and several springs. Sartre flatly refused, saying that he valued his skin; and I certainly think, looking back, that we would beyond doubt have ended up half-dead with sunstroke, in a stony wilderness where it was all too easy to lose your way. Yet could we forego the wonderful spectacle of watching the sun rise over Taygetus? We could and we did.

Mycenae. In the shaft graves and before the Lion Gate we experienced—as we had done on the Acropolis—that prickling of the scalp which Breton describes so well, and which comes from an encounter with beauty sheer and absolute. The most wonderful landscape on earth is perhaps that which Clytemnestra surveyed as she leaned out over her castle wall and searched the distant sea for a sign of Agamemnon's homecoming. We spent two days in an enchantingly named hotel: The Fair Helen and King Menelaus.

We reached the coast at Nauplia. Above the bay there was a hill covered with Barbary fig trees; their rotted windfalls filled the air with a faint, sourish tang. On the hilltop a prison stood, with a sentry marching up and down between clumps of cactus and a rusty barbed-wire fence. Proudly he jerked his thumb toward a barred window and said, in French: "Every Communist in Greece is locked up there!" It was then that we remembered Metaxas. But we forgot him again when we fell asleep, and when we woke, in the theater of Epidaurus, with those tiered stone seats above us, and the whole round sky for our ceiling. That is one of the memories I will cherish till my dying day, and I hate the thought of its perishing with me.

From here we moved on to Corinth, which we found boring; then back to Athens again, and a trip to Aegina, with its tiny well-built port, and its temple rising so gracefully among the scented pines. After this we went north to Macedonia. It was the end of August, and our funds were running out. Bost was supposed to draw our salaries and wire the entire sum to us at Salonika; but the day we embarked we had so little money left that all I bought to feed us for the next twenty-four hours was some bread, a pot of jam, and some big onions. When we arrived, the draft had not yet come through. The only solution was to stay at a hotel *en pension*, and pay for our meals and board at the same time—a week later. But as ill luck would have it, there was no hotel with a restaurant attached. So we went to the most comfortable one, and insisted so vehemently on full board that the astonished proprietor finally made a special arrangement with the best *taverna* in town, down by the harbor. We were now assured of our meals and a roof over our heads. But we had to ration our entertainment severely. All the same we saw two films in the local open-air cinema: *Mayerling*, about which we were unenthusiastic, and *The Thirty-nine Steps*, which we enjoyed greatly. It was made by a man called Hitchcock, whose name then meant nothing to us. But what pacing to and fro there was before Sartre bought a packet of cigarettes or I treated myself to one of those crumbling, succulent shortbreads known as *kourabiethes*, which I so enjoyed! Twice a day we went to the post office: still nothing. The situation was becoming critical; we literally hadn't a sou left. We once passed Jean Prévost in the street: he was a friend of Pierre Bost's, and almost certainly would not have refused us a loan, but we lacked the courage to approach him. We had not reckoned on staying so long in Salonika. After a while we grew weary of its graceful basilicas, the dewy charm of its domes and pleasure gardens.

The moment the draft arrived, we were on our way. I wanted to see the Meteora: a fourteen-hour round trip by train, leaving from Volos. Sartre, whom curiosities of nature left completely cold, rebelled at this. He said yes so often to please me that when he *did* refuse, my divided mind felt obliged to yield the point, though not without a struggle: alone in my cabin, I shed tears of pure rage. The boat was threading its way past pumice-stone reefs and clusters of giant sponges, and as I gazed out at the coast of Euboea, I told myself that all manner of marvels were awaiting me, and yet I would not be there to see them.

Back in Athens we had a celebratory meal in a French restaurant before setting up camp aboard the *Théophile Gautier*. This big mailboat lacked the pleasant atmosphere of the *Cairo City,* though here too a spontaneous segregation movement divided tourists from emigrants. The tourists were more numerous, while the emigrants were dirtier and even less well off. I brought only the most meager provisions aboard; the ship's cooks were not allowed to sell us anything, but they gave us large supplies of fruit and cakes. Despite this we were still hungry, and it turned cold for mid-September; the sea became rough, and the miserable depression characteristic of a homecoming ran right through me from top to toe.

But two days with Sartre in Marseille reinvigorated me. After this he went on to Paris, while I left for a short tour of Alsace with Olga. She showed me the haunts of her childhood in Strasbourg, and that evening we went to a dance hall and were astounded by the spectacle of Alsatians dancing the tango. We saw Bar, and Obernai, and a motley collection of little villages all colored like something out of a Silly Symphony. We were especially attracted by those pink granite castles, perched in solitary splendor above the pine forests. Olga strode purposefully across soft hill-country, and through thick woodland. We had little money, and our main diet consisted of onion pie and thick slices of *quiche Lorraine*. At night I would drink white wine, and we would sleep in chalets, forest huts, or youth hostels. But the cold weather rather spoiled our excursions, and we were not altogether sorry to be back in Paris again.

Lionel de Roulet had left Le Havre for Paris, but then became ill, and had continued so for a year: the diagnosis was renal TB, which put an end to his studies for the time being. He had spent months in the clinic at Saint-Cloud, where I got over my attack of pulmonary congestion; then he went back to the small flat he had taken on the Rue Broca. He underwent some very unpleasant treatment and had an agonizing operation. Sometimes the disease appeared to have been removed altogether; then it would manifest itself again. Lionel bore both the uncertainty and what were often really excruciating pains with stoic fortitude. He had begun an essay in which he analyzed his own reactions to his complaint. His experience corroborated Sartre's ideas: when the sharpest agony laid hold of him, he became conscious of a sort of void, an emptiness, which made it impossible for him to grasp or isolate the exact quality of the pain. He threw himself into all he did with passionate enthusiasm, and it was this work that helped him to endure his condition. But about June he had a relapse. He found that he was suffering from tuberculosis of the bones, and his doctors sent him to Berck. Before we returned to our teaching jobs, about the end of September, we went and spent a couple of days with him there. Despite all I had read about Berck, the place itself made a more sinister impression on me. A fierce, icy wind was blowing, and both sky and sea were of a strange bituminous hue. The clinic was an unusual sort of place: hardly any furniture in the rooms, and not even a table in the dining room, where at various set times the nurses would line up the patients in their wheel chairs. Yet Lionel did not appear depressed. He took a keen interest in everything that went on around him—he seemed to find it almost amusing—and this curiosity bred a kind of detachment in him. He described the customs of this strange world to us, and told us endless anecdotes, in particular ones concerning the patients' love affairs, either with each other or their nurses. These stories, which were fiercely realistic, together with the over-all atmosphere of Berck, formed the inspiration of an episode in Sartre's *The Reprieve* for which he was especially criticized among "decent people."

We were done with the provinces at last. Now we both lived in Paris: no more train journeys, no more hanging about on station platforms. We moved into a hotel that Sartre had discovered while I was convalescing in Provence, and which was a great improvement on the Royal Bretagne. It stood between the Avenue du Maine and the Montparnasse cemetery. I had a divan, and bookshelves, and a really comfortable working desk. I also got into a new daily routine: every morning I had coffee and *croissants* standing at the counter of a bright, noisy brasserie called Les Trois Mousquetaires. Also I often now worked at home. Sartre lived on the floor above me; thus we had all the advantages of a shared life, without any of its inconveniences.

What was I to write, now that my stories were finished? Certain themes had been going around in my head for a long time now, but I had no idea how to tackle them. One evening, shortly after the beginning of the school term, Sartre and I were sitting inside the Dôme, discussing my work, and he criticized me for my timidity. In my last book, he said, I had dealt with questions that concerned me, but through the medium of persons for whom I felt either active distaste or else a qualified sympathy only: it was, for instance, a pity that I had observed Anne through Chantal's eyes. "Look," he said, with sudden vehemence, "why don't you put *yourself* into your writing? You're more interesting than all these Renées and Lisas." The blood flushed up in my cheeks; it was a hot day, and as usual the place was full of smoke and noise. I felt as though someone had banged me hard on the head. "I'd never dare to do that," I said. To put my raw, undigested self into a book, to lose perspective, compromise myself—no, I couldn't do it, I found the whole idea terrifying. "Screw up your courage," Sartre told me, and kept pressing the point. I had my own individual emotions and reactions; it was these that I ought to express in my writings. As happened whenever he put himself behind a plan, his words conjured up a host of possibilities and hopes; but I was still afraid. What in fact was I afraid of? It seemed to me that from the moment I began to nourish literature with the stuff of my own personality, it would become something as serious as happiness or death.

During the days that followed I thought over Sartre's advice. He gave me courage to devote myself seriously to a theme which I had been considering, in brief spasms, for at least three years. I have already alluded to it, but I must come back to it again now. Like death, which we discuss without ever having actually faced it, so rational awareness in other people [*la conscience d'autrui*] remained for me a mere hypothesis; when I came to realize its actuality, I felt that I was at grips with as shocking and unacceptable a fact as death. Absurdly enough, the one could complement the other; by depriving the Other of life, he lost all power over the world and me. (I did not then know Hegel's phrase about all awareness seeking the death of the Other; I did not read it till 1940.) An incident that took place in 1934 had made a great impression on me: a young man had murdered a taxi driver, and said in explanation that he had no money to pay his fare. He had chosen to commit a crime rather than be put to shame. In a way I understood him. This news item stuck in my mind: it had affinities with a whole linked group of problems that preoccupied me. I could not resign myself to the idea of death, and when I thought about death by violence I became quite breathless. In an instant my awareness could burst into nothingness, like those blistered strips of bladder wrack that I used to stamp on as a child. With equal speed I could explode another person's existence, too: the metaphysical aspect of murder fascinated me. Besides, for various ethical reasons, crime figured regularly as an element in my dreams and fantasies. I saw myself in the dock, facing judge, prosecutor, jury, and a crowd of spectators, bearing the consequences of an act which I recognized as my handiwork, and bearing it alone. Ever since Sartre and I had met, I had shoved off the responsibility for justifying my existence onto him. I felt that this was an immoral attitude, but I could not envisage any practical way of changing it. The only solution would have been to accomplish some deed for which I alone, and no one else, must bear the consequences; but this would have meant society as a whole taking charge of the matter, since otherwise Sartre would have shared the responsibility with me. Nothing, in fact, short of an aggravated crime could bring me true independence. I often amused myself by a more or less close interweaving of these related themes. An alien personality revealed itself to me, in all its irreducible actuality. Through jealousy and envy I committed some crime which put me at this person's mercy, and achieved my own safety by destroying the Other. Because of the awed admiration she inspired in me at a distance, I had thought of using Simone

Weil as a model for the protagonist I aimed to set up against me. But when I suggested this to Sartre, he objected that a woman devoted to the art of communication, through the medium of universal reason and the world at large, could not possibly be presented as an exclusively inward-turned personality. Surely Olga, separated from me as she was by her youth, and her sulky silences, and the moods which the clumsy efforts of the trio tended to produce in her, would suit my purpose far better? I was convinced on the spot. But the pattern of *She Came to Stay* had crystallized *before* she came to play an important part in my life.

I lacked the courage to plunge straight into the heart of my chosen subject and make a frank study of the thirty-year-old woman I then was. I came at it obliquely, partly at least through sheer technical incompetence. I was determined that my heroine, to borrow a phrase from D. H. Lawrence that had much impressed me, should have "roots." I also admired the way in which Faulkner contrived to play tag with the time scheme of *Light in August*; but his technique was designed for a novel constructed on a fatalistic basis, whereas I was concerned with free and unpredictable decisions. Besides, I was aware that breaking up the flow of a narrative with episodes in flashback tended to make it rather heavy going. I therefore decided to take the character based on myself (I gave her my mother's name, Françoise) and tell the story of her childhood and youth in their natural sequence. I did not put my own real recollections into her mouth; and my description of her, at one remove, was couched in a style that I had once again borrowed from John Dos Passos. I took up a theme that I had already explored through the medium of Chantal, in *Primauté du spirituel*: I tried to suggest the sort of deceptive trickery that young girls so readily adopt in their efforts to acquire status. I provided Françoise with a friend whom I called Elisabeth—and who had not the slightest connection with Zaza. I gave her instead the physical attributes of one of my fifteen-year-old pupils, whose mass of ash-blonde hair and black, clinging dresses made her look a complete vamp. Elisabeth was embarking upon life with a provocative self-confidence that her school friend Françoise found quite overwhelming. Once again I was concerned to present the miragelike aspects of an alien personality: in actuality Elisabeth was a mere slavish reflection of her brother Pierre, whom at first Françoise had scarcely even met. I drew, at length and in detail, a picture of Françoise's uncertain relationship with a young lecturer on art history, who somewhat resembled Herbaud. Finally she became acquainted with Pierre Labrousse, and they formed a close relationship. Elisabeth, who felt a violent—but unreciprocated—love for her brother, became jealous of Françoise, and then herself succumbed to her charms. I spent the whole year working on this first part of the book.

Meanwhile Sartre was writing a treatise on phenomenological psychology which he entitled *La Psyché,* and of which in the end he published an extract only, calling it *Esquisse d'une théorie phénoménologique des émotions* (*The Emotions: Outline of a Theory*). Here he developed his theory of "physic objectivity," which had been sketched out in the essay on *The Transcendence of the Ego*. But to his way of thinking this was little more than an exercise, and after writing four hundred pages he broke off to complete his collection of stories.

Olga had achieved a reconciliation with her parents, and spent her vacation in Beuzeville. They had proved broadminded enough to agree that she should try her luck in Paris rather than vegetate in a provincial town. In June I had suggested to her that she might go in for theatrical work. Camille, who always referred to her as "my child," encouraged this idea. She joined the Atelier Drama School in October, and for her audition before Dullin delivered Mérimée's monologue *"L'Occasion,"* which I helped her to prepare. Though she collapsed in tears at the end of this ordeal, Dullin congratulated her, and for several weeks she took great pleasure in her studies. Dullin gave her another part to rehearse, and she learned it by heart. But she knew no one at the School, and stuck in her corner, never exchanging a word with the other students, and not even daring to ask one of them to cue her. When Dullin called her out for her audition, she was forced to make the pathetic confession that she had no one to give her her cues, at which Dullin raised eyes and arms to heaven, and picked a partner for her, telling them to work on the piece together for the next few days and present it in a week's time. Olga was so scared that she didn't set foot in the Atelier again for months. This was a wrench for her, since she found Dullin's methods of teaching most attractive. She made no mention of this setback to me; such silent restraint weighed heavily on her, and her life was not made any easier by the endless reproaches she directed at herself. Lionel, now exiled at Berck, had lent her his flat for the time being; she more or less shut herself up there, chain smoking, lost in gloomy revery and surrounded by considerable disorder. Her moodiness was most marked in her attitude to me; during this period our relationship reached its nadir.

Indeed, I now passed through one of the most depressing periods of my whole life. I refused to admit that war was even possible, let alone imminent. But it was no use my playing the ostrich; the growing perils all around crushed me beneath their weight.

In France the Popular Front struggled on for a few more months, but collapsed when the Socialists withdrew from the Chautemps Government. While the Left was foundering, the Fascist threat grew apace. Time bombs were planted in the Rue Presbourg, and blew up a couple of apartment houses belonging to the Confédération Générale du Patronat Français, killing two policemen in the process. It was a deliberate act of provocation, carried out by a secret society which Action Française had christened "The Hoods"; subsequent inquiries revealed just how widespread and powerful this organization was. It had been behind several murders where the killer had never been caught: there was Navachine the engineer, whose body had been found in the Bois de Boulogne, and Laetitia Toureaux, killed in a Métro train near the Porte Dorée, and the Rosselli brothers, who had founded the anti-Fascist movement known as "Justice and Liberty." By the end of January, however, forty Hoods found themselves behind bars. The disappearance of General Miller indicated the existence of a Fascist conspiracy extending right across Europe and America, and involving a large number of White Russians. Such activities did not per se constitute a very serious danger; but they did demonstrate the growth of a world-wide international Fascist organization, which operated quite openly. The Axis had recently sparked off a new war in the Far East: after the incident of the Marco Polo bridge, the Japanese had occupied Peking, and were determined to subdue the whole of China. Chinese Communists and Nationalists united in defense of their country—but the price was appalling. Nanking was shelled into rubble, and Chapei—a vast, thickly populated suburb to the north of Shanghai—destroyed by fire. The papers published ghastly pictures of heaped-up corpses—women and children who had fallen victim to Japanese bombing raids.

On our very doorstep Mussolini and Hitler were busy reducing Spain. On August 26 Italian troops entered Santander; Gijon fell at the end of October. Henceforth the Fascists were masters of the Asturias coal mines and the Biscay steelworks; they held all northern Spain, and every attempt to dislodge them failed. The Government moved to Barcelona in October, and the city was devastated by frightful air attacks. Valencia, Madrid, and Lérida were also bombarded, and the bodies of women and children lay in heaps along the sidewalks. At a vast rally in Paris, La Pasionaria once more made the promise, *"No pasaran,"* and the Republicans won a victory at Teruel: they encircled the town and occupied it. But afterward they were forced to withdraw again; and now Franco was threatening Catalonia. If France and England persisted in their neutrality, Spain was lost. And neutral they remained: not a single gun or plane did the Republic receive, while both Italy and Germany continued to send an ever-increasing stream of supplies to Franco. In March the Fascists broke through on the Eastern front. Their aircraft flattened every town along the Catalan coast, while liquid-air bombs pulverized the poorer quarters of Barcelona and did heavy damage in the heart of the city: in two days there was a death toll of thirteen hundred, and some four thousand wounded. Vast hordes of miserable refugees streamed over the Col de Perthus. Resistance stiffened in Barcelona, but production was practically reduced to nothing by the bombing, and Catalonia, cut off now both from eastern and central Spain, was in a desperate plight. Fernando came to Paris on leave again, but now he was a very different person, no longer his old smiling self. *"Salauds de Fran-çais!"* he snarled, and seemed to include Sartre and me in his rancorous attack. This struck me as unfair, since we hoped with all our hearts that France would come to his country's aid; but his wrath took small heed of such subtle distinctions.

If the Spanish tragedy dismayed us, events in Germany scared us stiff. In September, at Nuremberg, before an audience of 300,000 Nazis and something like a million visitors, Hitler delivered his most aggressive speech yet. Mussolini had traveled to Munich and Berlin and sealed an alliance between the two dictators. The defeat of a military *coup d'état* had brought the German armed forces under Hitler's direct command, and Himmler had been made Minister of the Interior. It was a triumph for the Gestapo. In Vienna a supporter of Hitler, Seyss-Inquart, had come to power. After another speech that made world headlines, Hitler sent his troops into Austria, and the *Anschluss* was an accomplished fact. Panic reigned in Vienna, and the Sudeten Germans in Czechoslovakia began to clamor aggressively for their independence. Sartre no longer could deceive himself: the chances of peace were now very slender indeed. Bost was convinced that he would soon be off to the front, and he thought it very much on the cards that he would lose his life there.

For my own part I was still trying to delude myself, and refusing to face the facts. But the future had begun to open up under my very feet, and produced in me a sick feeling akin to real anguish. No doubt that is why I retain only a misty recollection of this entire year. Nor can I remember anything of outstanding interest in my private life. I took greater care of myself than I had done the year before, going to bed earlier and staying out less frequently. In October or November Sartre, Olga, and I went to the recital that Marianne Oswald gave in the Salle Gaveau, after her suicide attempt. Draped in black, her hair dyed an outrageous red, she recited Cocteau's *"Anna la bonne"* in a voice of muted fury which seemed to suggest the Papin sisters' frantic revolt. She sang a lot of Prévert's songs, among others the one inspired by the abortive jail break of the young convicts on Belle-Ile:

> *Bandits, voyous, voleurs, chenapans!*
> *C'est la meute des honnêtes gens*
> *Qui fait la chasse à l'enfant.*

[Bandits, riff-raff, thieves, and scoundrels! The pack that hunts down children is composed of decent people.]

There was a virulent quality about Prévert's anarchism which I found most satisfying; and I adored Marianne Oswald's warm, harsh voice, her tortured features, and the subtle relationship she established between gesture, expression, and the words of the songs she sang.

It was in the Salle Gaveau, too, that Sartre and I first heard the whole of the Beethoven quartets, given as a series. We saw Camille there; during passages which bored her she would scribble on bits of paper—noting down ideas for her novel, she told us. This double activity left me in a thoughtful mood.

During the Christmas holidays we went to Mégève, where we stayed at a small *pension.* My sister and Gégé were staying with friends in a nearby chalet, and Bost tagged along with us. We made up our minds to take skiing lessons: and despite my lack of both courage and agility, I made gradual progress. We had some enjoyable moments on the slopes of Mont d'Arbois and of Rochebrune. In the evenings we read Pepy's *Diary* and Swift's *Journal to Stella,* both of which had just appeared in translation.

It was either now or immediately after our return to Paris that we read Malraux's *L'Espoir* (*Man's Hope*), with an excitement that far outstripped any purely literary emotion. As in his previous novels, Malraux's characters lacked human solidity, but this mattered little, since the action was far more important than its protagonists, and Malraux narrated it brilliantly. He stood very near to us both as regards his apocalyptic predilections and his resentment of the inherent contradiction between enthusiasm and discipline. He was tackling themes hitherto ignored in literature, such as the relationship between individual morality and practical politics, or the possibility of maintaining humanist standards in the thick of war—for those who fought in the People's Army were men and civilians first, soldiers second, and never forgot it. We were intensely interested in their dilemmas, but never guessed how soon they would seem completely out of date. Total war was utterly to abolish the whole pattern of humane relationships which so concerned Malraux, and by which we ourselves set such great store.

All the things that had once stirred my curiosity paled into insignificance beside the Madrid bombardments and each engagement lost or won. I hardly bothered to read the ordinary news at all, and remained indifferent to the Weidmann Trial—though the press gave it enormous coverage, obviously for its entertainment value. It diverted me less than it had once done to study people who passed by me in the street.

In January we attended rehearsals of *Plutus* at the Atelier, very freely adapted by Camille from Aristophanes. With the aid of Coutaud's décor, and a score by Darius Milhaud, she had turned it into a kind of revue. The total effect was not particularly impressive, but many individual scenes were most entertaining. Dullin played the lead, and Marie-Hélène Dasté's beauty and graceful bearing overcame her affectation in the role of Poverty. What gave the production an extra piquancy in our eyes was the fact that Marco had a part: he was anxious to practice singing on a stage, and thought that Dullin's patronage might stand him in good stead. There he was, barelegged, wearing a short tunic and sandals, as leader of the "peasant" chorus. But it was difficult to rehearse him, since he had, as the *Director de l'Opéra* once unkindly told him, no sense of time or rhythm whatsoever. He sang out of time with the music, and when he moved across the stage, his footwork bore no relation to the rhythm of the orchestra. Despite this, his voice, in the Atelier's small auditorium, had enormous impact.

I saw only one other play with Sartre that year: Marcel Achard's *Le Corsaire,* in a production by Jouvet. It was a weak piece of writing, and the trick of playing some scenes at two levels—the play-within-a-play technique exemplified in *Hamlet* by the Players' performance before the Court—had nothing original to recommend it; yet we still delighted in this intrusion of the imaginary into a world that was itself the product of imagination.

On the other hand, we still went regularly to the cinema. The work of Prévert and Vigo apart—we made another exception in favor of *Carnival in Flanders*—French films bored us: flat dialogue, insipid photography, and actors talking in artificial voices. As on top of this we did not care

for war films, we even went so far as to miss Renoir's *The Grand Illusion.*
But we greatly enjoyed American comedies such as *Outward Bound, My
Man Godfrey, Mr. Deeds Goes to Town, Bluebeard's Eighth Wife,* and
many others. The stories they told seldom had much significance, but
they were most beautifully constructed: there was not a single incident
that—in accord with Valéry's ideal requirement—failed to have
multiple relationships to the over-all pattern and we relished the technical
expertise of their construction as we might have appreciated a classical
sonata. On the other hand, their realism was hidden from us by their
exoticism: a street, a staircase, a doorbell, each tiny detail of background
or custom reminded us that this was abroad. The antagonism that generally existed between the lovers struck us as a piquant novelty, and we
were unaware that it corresponded to an established American phenomenon,
the Battle of the Sexes. In one of these comedies the hero was carrying
the heroine across a stretch of flooded countryside. Finding her too much
of a weight, he dropped her in a puddle. We thought this a most daring
sequence, whereas in fact it merely indicated the American male's latent
feelings of hostility toward women. And so it went on. True and false
became confused while crossing the Atlantic, and from this confusion sprang
fantasies which we found most agreeable. Many of these films, in any case,
contained genuine discoveries. This was the year that Hollywood sent us
one of its happiest—and, as we were concerned, completely unexpected—
successes, *Green Pastures,* based on Marc Connolly's play of the same name:
the Bible story told and enacted by Negroes. God the Father, black and
bearded, smoked huge cigars and was surrounded by a choir of black angels
who sang Negro spirituals. His Divine Abode was swept out by house-
maid-angels, their wings encased in checked dust covers. Cain's children
shot it out with revolvers. The denizens of Heaven went angling and held
fish frys. It seemed to us that this film had the freshness of some long-lost
paradise, without ever lapsing into *fausse naïveté.*

Since 1933 we had been watching the Silly Symphonies, in color, appear
on our screens, and Sartre used to do imitations of Donald Duck. I had
delightedly renewed my acquaintances with a favorite childhood fairy tale,
"The Three Little Pigs," and for years we, like everyone else, went round
humming "Who's Afraid of the Big Bad Wolf?"

The most remarkable event that winter was the Surrealist Exhibition,
which opened on January 17, 1938, at the Galerie des Beaux-Arts in the
Faubourg Saint-Honoré. In the entrance hall stood one of Dali's special
creations: a taxi cab, rain streaming off it, with a blonde, swooning female
dummy posed inside, surrounded by a sort of lettuce-and-chicory salad all
smothered with snails. The "Rue Surréaliste" contained other similar lay
figures, clothed or nude, by Man Ray, Max Ernst, Dominguez, and Maurice
Henry: we were particularly drawn to Masson's, that of a face imprisoned
in a cage and gagged with pansy. The main salon had been arranged by
Marcel Duchamp to look like a grotto: it contained, among other things,
a pond and four beds grouped round a brazier, while the ceiling was
covered with coal bags. The whole place smelled of Brazilian coffee, and

various objects loomed up out of the carefully contrived semidarkness: a fur-lined dish, an occasional table with the legs of a woman. On all sides ordinary things like walls and doors and flower vases were breaking free from human restraint. I don't think surrealism had any direct influence on us, but it had impregnated the very air we breathed. It was the surrealists, for instance, who made it fashionable to frequent the flea market where Sartre and Olga and I often spent our Sunday afternoons.

Thus we were not short of entertainment; but our circle of friends had somewhat diminished. Marco made no secret of his hostility toward us; I saw him very seldom, and got little pleasure from our meetings. Pagniez too had faded out of our lives. He had been irked by Sartre's political extremism, and our attachment to Olga; he also felt, quite wrongly, that we were less than amiably disposed toward his cousin Thérèse. We did not actually quarrel, but we simply ceased to meet. One afternoon in the Dôme I spotted Thérèse wearing a wedding ring; she told me she had recently got married to "one of her colleagues." She was waiting for Pagniez, I was expecting Sartre; all four of us finally spent an hour or two together. Sartre and I were both wondering privately why Pagniez and Thérèse had given each other up; they offered no explanation, and our mutual embarrassment grew more intense every moment. A few days later Madame Lemaire informed us that in fact they had married one another, and Marco had acted as their witness. Shortly afterward good relations were restored between us; but we never learned the exact reason for their playing this miserable joke on us. My relationship with Olga was in a sad state, and my sister was suffering agonies over Lionel's health: almost every time I saw her she kept bursting into tears. There is no doubt that these dark gaps and shadows contributed to my state of depression. I suppose a literary success might have spurred me into cheerfulness, but this seemed a remote prospect. One afternoon Sartre told me he was dropping in at Gallimard's, and would make inquiries about my manuscript. I waited for him in the Dôme; I was busy working, and not particularly impatient to hear his news. The book had been turned down. Brice Parain found its general construction clumsy, and made specific charges of heaviness and tedium. "We'll try another publisher," Sartre said, and sent the manuscript off to Grasset's. I felt little disappointment—at least, not immediately—but it may well be that this setback helped to plunge me yet deeper in my slough of depression. I got little comfort from what I was writing at the time, either; this story of Françoise's childhood and adolescence failed even to convince me. Apart from anything else, my health still remained uncertain. Just before the Easter holidays I had a relapse—not a serious one, but I had to spend several days in bed.

As soon as I was up again we left Paris. We had originally intended to visit Algeria, but now there was not enough time, so instead we took a train to Bayonne and made a tour of the Basque country. It was springtime, and the flowers were out: I began to blossom myself. At Itxassou our room had a tree as annex, with a ropewalk leading to it; a platform had been constructed, high among the branches, and here Sartre settled down to work while I roamed the neighboring hills. I strode through miles of bracken, my eyes adazzle with sunlight and pink plum blossom. On our way home we stopped at Saintes, and at La Rochelle, where Sartre spent his childhood. We walked round the harbor fortifications and street arcades discussing the outcome of *L'Enfance d'un chef* (*The Childhood of a Leader*), which he was then writing. He was wondering whether his narrative could not be broken off at its *de facto* conclusion, with Lucien's emergence from the adolescent state into full manhood. I, on the other hand, felt that he ought to extend it somewhat further; otherwise the reader would be left with his appetite unsatisfied. Today I think he was right and I was wrong.

Fresh air, exercise, and the excitement of travel did me so much good that late in the spring I went off again, rucksack on back, alone this time, for a walking holiday in Auvergne. I particularly recall one afternoon in a shimmering hot gorge near Saint-Flour. I was thinking about my childhood, and one of my earliest memories returned to me: the flower I was accused of picking in Aunt Alice's garden. I thought how much I would love, one day, to write a book that evoked the shade of this little girl from the distant past—never dreaming that I would get the chance to do so.

Sartre and I also made a pilgrimage into our more recent past, at Rouen. Nothing had changed, and oh, the things we remembered! Yet we felt a sense of frustration, too: instead of the hothouse we had once inhabited, we found a neat, scentless herbarium. The fact was that the future—today itself fulfilled—had broken loose from those past moments whose living flesh it once was; and all that remained, whether in those streets or our own memories, was a collection of skeletons.

And what future lay in store for the days we were then living? I can recall sitting talking with Sartre in that tomblike café near the Gare du Nord, to which we returned from time to time. I was delightedly discussing the success of *La Nausée,* which the critics had hailed as a major literary event, and also the letters he had received about *Intimité* (*Intimacy*) and *La Chambre,* which had appeared respectively in the *N.R.F.* and *Mesure.* "It might prove amusing if we got to be really well-known writers," I said, and that was the first time the idea of public success, with all its attendant temptations, actually entered my mind. One would make new acquaintances, I thought vaguely, learn new ideas: it would be a sort of self-renewal. Hitherto I had relied upon no one but myself to ensure my happiness, and asked nothing of tomorrow but that it repeat today. Now, suddenly, I wanted something to happen to me from outside, as it were, something new and different. All we had lived through during the past nine years began to look rather threadbare. To console myself for this thought I planned rather more concrete objectives than my vague dreams of glory. Very soon our joint salaries would be enough for us to buy a car. It seemed a waste to spend your money furnishing a flat rather than getting the means of transport. I would learn to drive, I decided, and then think what glorious freedom would be ours when we went on our travels! We also toyed with the idea of one day flying from Paris to London. We looked forward—not this year, but in 1939 perhaps—to visiting the U.S.S.R. with Intourist, despite our loathing for organized tours. America gleamed on the horizon, more enticing than any other country, but it seemed extremely unlikely that we should ever have sufficient means to get there, and for the present, at any rate, it was out of the question.

Grasset turned down my manuscript, as I had expected. The reader, Henry Müller, wrote:

> This description of postwar young women, variously influenced by the intellectual currents of their day, certainly possesses good qualities: intelligence, the ability both to observe and to analyze. I found the account here given of certain contemporary milieus an extremely accurate one; nevertheless my main criticism is that the novel is lacking in any originality at a deeper level. To put it another way: the social picture you create has been painted countless times already over the past twenty years. You are content to describe a disintegrating world, and then to abandon your readers on the very threshold of the new order, without giving any very precise indication of what its benefits will be . . . But *La Primauté du spirituel* displays qualities which give reason to hope that you will one day write a successful book . . .

This surprised me. I had had no intention of painting a social picture; I thought I had achieved a series of subtle psychological studies. To be criticized for lack of originality I found disconcerting: I had known the real-life models for my heroines, and no one prior to myself had ever mentioned them. Each was a unique individual. Many years later I myself aroused a similar astonishment in other beginners, who thought they had given expression to an "original" experience, whereas I could find nothing but banal platitudes in their manuscripts. Yet even the most commonplace truths can be transmuted by the pen of a real writer, and shine with a hitherto unsuspected light. Herein lies the whole problem of turning life into literature, the crux of the art of letters. But in any case, I told myself, if people had failed to understand me, that was because I hadn't made my meaning sufficiently clear. I was not discouraged. Next time, I felt sure, I would make a better job of it. The approach of the holidays, with all their alluring prospects, helped me to bury *La Primauté du spirituel* in a fairly cheerful mood.

Since Sartre had to stay in Paris, I went off for a holiday in the Alps. Looking back, I admire my own stamina: after a night on the train I started out at once, over hill and dale, and walked for nine solid hours. Nor did this rhythm slacken. I climbed every single peak between Chamonix and Tigne that was within the competence of an unaccompanied climber.

At Tigne I found a letter from Sartre awaiting me. He had finished *The Childhood of a Leader* at the beginning of July, and was thinking about a new novel. He wrote: "I have, quite suddenly, found the theme, scope, and title of this book: as you will probably guess, the theme is freedom." The title, which he printed in capital letters, was *Lucifer*. Volume I was to be called *The Revolt,* and Volume II *The Oath.* The epigraph read: "The pity of it is, we are free."

We were supposed to embark at Marseille for our trip to Morocco; we had third-class tickets, but an old friend of Sartre's who worked for the shipping company concerned had arranged second-class reservations for us. I was determined to do nothing to spoil such good fortune, and reached the Gare Saint-Charles, where we had arranged to meet, well before time. But as bad luck would have it, the Paris train which theoretically connected with the mailboat, and was due in at 10 A.M., happened to be running very late. There was no sign of it at midday, nor yet at 2 P.M.; I gnawed my nails with impatience, and latterly in despair. Sartre finally arrived at four o'clock, by which time I had given up all hope. "Let's go down to the docks anyway," he said. When our taxi drew up at the quayside, they were just about to haul up the gangplank. I flung myself onto it, while Sartre was grabbed by a couple of sailors and hauled across the rapidly widening gap between ship and shore. When I recalled our trips on the *Cairo City* and those little Greek tubs, the comfort of this crossing struck me as something quite fabulous. I relaxed in the sun on a comfortable deck chair and watched the flying fish flit by. I had not, I decided, grown any older; indeed, I felt like a twenty-year-old, and could not conceive a more delightful age to be.

In Casablanca we soon became bored with the European quarter, and went off in search of the native shantytown, which we found only too easily. Conditions here were more frightful than in the very worst of the Athens slums, and the French were responsible for it. We picked our way through this wilderness hurriedly, feeling very ashamed of ourselves. Faithful to the traditions established by Gide, Larbaud, Morand, and their numerous successors—of which I have already spoken—we decided to visit Bous-bir. It was divided into two quarters, Jewish and Arab, and in the listless afternoon air seemed like one of those model villages you occasionally find in exhibitions; I was amazed to find cafés and grocery shops there. We met an Arab woman who was heavily tattooed and swathed in long flowing robes, over which she wore masses of heavy, clashing jewelry. She took us to a bistro, and then to her room, where she undressed, did a belly dance, and smoked a cigarette through her vagina.

My most vivid memory of Rabat is the storks that perched, flapping, on biscuit-brown and crenellated towers set among oleanders. It was dark when we reached Fez. We had decided to put up at the Djalnai Palace Hotel, and boarded a fiacre which set off along a lonely road, flanked by whitewashed walls. There was not a sound to be heard except the regular clop-clop-clop of the horse's hoofs. The journey seemed as though it would never end, and the darkness and stillness unnerved us: what sort of cut-throat den were we being taken to? After traveling three or four miles, the cabby pulled up in front of a locked and barred door, his face registering broken-hearted disappointment. Quite obviously he must have known the hotel was shut, but he had not been able to forego so profitable a trip. Back we went to the European town, disappointed, but with the brilliant starry night as some sort of consolation. Here we were, two dusty, torrid miles away from the native quarter—a distance we resentfully trudged every morning. But once we got there, all manner of delights awaited us. We adored Fez: it combined extremes of secrecy and riotous extroversion— on the one hand veiled women, shuttered palaces, and impenetrable *medersa* and mosques; on the other, lavish displays of goods, with hawkers and shopkeepers shouting and gesticulating fit to beat the band. But secrecy won out over openhandedness; as we walked back up the main street at dusk, with torches flaring, on both sides we observed police officers barricading the dark alleyways with chains; first the gates of the *souks,* then those of the town itself were closed behind us. One evening we got lost in the labyrinthine back streets around the market, and a young man offered to be our guide. After following him for a short time we soon got the feeling that he was leading us out of our way. An elderly Moslem suddenly shouted out, "Don't go with him!" whereupon our guide abruptly took to his heels. Had he been hoping to rob us? Even during the day the air was almost unbreathable in this warren, so laden was it with the odors of decaying gutter refuse, cloves, freshly tanned leather, and of course, all the perfumes of Arabia. Overhead lattice work shut out the sky, and it was rather like walking through a series of subterranean passages. The place was chockablock with small donkeys, prancing about or obstinately refusing to budge, and holding up the traffic either way; sometimes a *caïd* would ride past on his big horse with its ornamental trappings, and the common folk would make way for him. When I thought of the panic that would be let loose in these choked-up tunnels if the place caught fire, I went into a cold sweat of fright. Yet such impalpable uneasiness merely heightened the smell and savor and colorfulness of it all for me. If ever the word bewitchment had a real meaning for me, it was in Fez. We had to stay in our cheap European hotel two days longer than we had planned, however: one evening we went to a restaurant—pleasant enough, despite its tourist atmosphere, and practically deserted at this time of year—determined to have a native meal. With great conscientiousness we squatted on the ground, eating with our fingers, and worked our way through *pastilla,* chicken *au citron, mechoui, couscous,* and the marrow of gazelles' horns. As we walked out we congratulated ourselves on feeling so sprightly still, and came to the conclusion that this was because we hadn't drunk any wine. But almost the moment we were back in our room Sartre had a liver attack, and had to stay in bed for two days.

Meknes was an altogether quieter place than Fez, less splendidly garish but less oppressive too. We left it, aboard a native bus, for a visit to the Roman remains at Volubilis and Moulay Idris. The holy city we found somewhat tedious; its only attraction lay in its mosques, and these were all barred to visitors, with much pompous paraphernalia such as chain barriers, fences, and posters publicizing the "Lyautey Plan." You couldn't get within a hundred yards of them. What pleased us, though, was the fact that because of the August heat there wasn't a single European in the place apart from ourselves.

It was in a tiny little Moorish café—no more than a hole in the wall—that we experienced one of those uncomfortable jolts that formed the most important part of our travels. We were squatting on mats, and about to drink some mint tea: there was a crowd of poverty-stricken Moroccans all around us. But just as we raised our glasses to our lips we both thought of all the diseased, pock-marked mouths that had touched them previously; and we decided to pass up the mint tea. The proprietor gave Sartre a pipe with a long stem and tiny bowl, full of a fine dusty substance that turned out to be kief; he and his cronies stood there laughing sympathetically as Sartre inhaled the acrid smoke. He didn't experience the dizzy ecstasy which the onlookers predicted he would, but it certainly made him very cheerful. On our return journey the bus driver was a virtuoso performer, who unfortunately didn't believe in braking; as a result the bus, which was carrying an all-native passenger load, swerved so violently that one person sitting immediately behind me spewed up large quantities of vomit all over my blouse and Sartre's sweater.

In Marrakech we were determined not to be exiled miles from the native quarter, as we had been in Fez. Here, too, all the best hotels were shut, and we put up in a squalid Arab establishment that did, however, command a view of Djelma el Fna Square; it was so roasting hot inside at night that people dragged their beds out into the miserable little garden flanking the guests' rooms. I found this open-air dormitory decidedly charming—apart, that is, from the latrine, which was practically unusable. We spent the hottest part of the day in a café at the far end of the square. It possessed a sidewalk *terrasse* where we used to have dinner; we never tired of watching the seething bazaarlike activity that went on day and night in that vast flat arena. Here one could see men who were very different from the coastal Arabs—tall, gaunt, muscular, bronzed fellows who looked like John the Baptist and doubtless lived on a diet of locusts: these were the desert nomads. They were as astonished as we were by the snake charmers and sword swallowers; they would gather round in a circle, standing or squatting, and listen to the musically cadenced voices—allegro and andante by turn—of the bazaar storytellers. In the shadow of their tents great haunches of mutton were roasting, and vast yellowish stews bubbled away in iron cooking pots. The air resounded to a babel of voices, with people buying, selling, exchanging gossip, admiring goods, or haggling over prices. In the evening, when the heat of the day had finally abated, little lamps cast a feeble glow over the hawkers' trays, and Arab chanting wound its slow way to the stars. I had already seen camels in the North; but it was at Marrakech, beneath the baked-mud ramparts, among the palm trees and the fountains, that I came to recognize their nobility and grace. I never wearied of watching them kneel, get up again, and pad along with their balanced gait. The *souks* were larger and more open to the light than those in Fez; we were less conscious here of the merchants' wealthy display, and more of individual craftsmanship. I was particularly fascinated by the Street of the Dyers. Color here was not an attribute of other objects, but a substance in its own right; just as water can become snow, hail, ice, frost, or steam, so it too had its metamorphoses. Violet and red ran liquid along channels, but took on the consistency of thick cream when collected in bowls; at a later stage, drying out on trays in twisted hanks, they possessed the soft, spongy quality of wool. Confronted with all these simple, basic substances—wool, copper, leather, wood—and the elementary skills which fashioned them, I felt as though I were back in the rich and fertile apprenticeship of childhood.

Equipped with maps, guides, provisions, and much local information, we went on a walking tour in the Atlas Mountains. A bus dropped us at the head of a pass, and picked us up at the same point three days later. We spent the intervening period tramping along lonely paths over those lush red ranges, sleeping in rest huts below the Berber villages. We bargained with blue-eyed peasants for the flat unleavened loaves that served them in lieu of bread; this homely fare we ate with slices of cold sausage, standing at the window of our shelter, elbows propped on the sill. I particularly remember our first night, in a hut that looked out toward a lofty mountain chain: Sartre sat there trying to work out whether the line of peaks went up or down, and to our way of looking it was clearly *up,* though it could also be regarded as a sort of landslide, and for a long while we conscientiously tried to see it that way.

We went to the South by long-distance bus. We were the only European passengers, and the driver, a European himself, made us sit beside him. We got the hot blast of the engine and the stink of gasoline straight in our faces, and more than once I felt I was going to choke. If I put my arm through the open window, the red-hazed air burned my skin: we were driving through a regular furnace. This was a region where drought and famine were endemic, and the inhabitants never had enough to eat: we had arrived during one of the worst years. Desperate starving hordes had tried to migrate northward, but the authorities had blocked the roads; they were given a bowl of soup apiece and forced to return home. People died like flies, and even the survivors looked as though they were at death's door. During our very occasional village halts we would make for the local bar-grocery, invariably run by a young Jew wearing a black skullcap, and down large glassfuls of cold water. I did not like watching the ragged, gaunt villagers who crowded around the bus, anxiously asking for the goods they had ordered in town—manure as often as not. The driver played the petty tyrant, hurling parcels out as though scattering alms; their distribution appeared to depend on nothing but his benevolent whim. Often he passed the motionless little groups under the palm trees without actually stopping at all: he would slacken speed a fraction while the native boy who acted as his Number Two hurled sacks and packages off the roof of the bus.

For hours on end we drove across a landscape scoured bare by the hot sirocco, where not a blade of grass grew. We stopped at a phosphorus mine; the earth all around it was veined with the most fantastic colors— green, gray-green, lemon, orange, sickly pink. We drank anisette and had lunch with the mine engineers in their canteen. Every township seemed as dreary as the last. Our longest stay was at Ouarzazate; the heat was so unbearable that we did not go out in the afternoon at all. After lunch we tried to sleep, despite the clouds of tiny greenish mosquitoes, so small as to be almost invisible, that sucked away at our blood. Later we sat in the hotel dining room, where the shutters were tightly closed, and drank cassis-and-water. After dusk we ventured out of doors along a dried-up wadi, past clumps of withered palm trees; this vast flat expanse matched the night sky's immensity, and we found ourselves caught and moved by its absolute stillness. We took a great liking to the hotel proprietor, who wore baggy trousers and went around coughing his lungs up; he gave us a graphic description of the typhus epidemic that had devastated the country some while before. (Sartre took this account as the basis for his film script, *Typhus,* which was later distorted to make *Les Orgueilleux.*) Every day at noon he made a free distribution of boiled rice to the local children; these urchins came from six or seven miles around, and I had never in my life seen such appalling cases of disease and malnutrition. Scarcely one of them had unblemished eyesight; some were suffering from trachoma, while others had inverted eyelids that had grown down till they pierced the cornea. They were either blind, or one-eyed, or else had cataracts of greater or lesser thickness growing over their pupils. Others again had feet that were turned back to front: this was the most spectacular deformity, and the one which I found the hardest sight to bear. These tiny spectral figures squatted in a courtyard around several huge bowls, and dipped into them with their bare hands—all together, keeping time, so that no one should get an unfair advantage.

A great weight was lifted from our hearts when we finally left this southern inferno. We returned to Casablanca by the coastal road; at Safi and Mostaganem we filled our lungs with fresh sea air. Finally we made the return crossing to France.

All through this trip Sartre had been keeping an uneasy eye on the negotiations then being carried on in Czechoslovakia. Ever since the Anschluss the pro-German faction among the Sudetens had been up in arms, agitating for the abolition of the National State in favor of a federal system that would guarantee the German minority complete independence. After the municipal elections, in which the Sudeten party voted by plebiscite, Heinlein, the chief of the Czech Nazi Party, demanded that this would-be autonomous community should be made part of Greater Germany. As Hitler had begun to mass troops at the frontier, Prague ordered partial mobilization. At the beginning of August Lord Runciman came to Prague on a peacemaking mission; he declared that the Sudeten districts had a right of self-determination, which merely encouraged them in their demands. The situation was becoming increasingly tense, and the non-co-operative attitude of the Sudeten delegates ruled out any chance of agreement between them and the authorities in Prague. On August 31 the negotiations were within a hairbreadth of being broken off:

Lord Runciman patched them up at the eleventh hour. Throughout the first half of September England was conducting intense diplomatic activities: Chamberlain and Lord Halifax held meeting after meeting. On September 13, the day before I met Olga again in Marseille, a state of siege was proclaimed in Prague, and Heinlein rejected the Czech Government's final offers. War seemed imminent, and I was on the point of returning to Paris with Sartre. Next day the news was slightly more reassuring: Chamberlain was flying to Berchtesgaden for personal discussions with Hitler. Sartre encouraged me to stick to my original plans. He said he would wire me *poste restante* if the situation worsened. My divided mind easily triumphed over my disquiet, and I let him catch the train without me.

It was a strange period. Olga had spent the larger part of her vacation with Bost, in a small lower-class hotel that looked over the Old Port of Marseille. She had a room with a red-tiled floor, a seedy, threadbare place, but full of sunlight and cheerful noise: it was here that I picked her up again. I spent forty-eight hours in Marseille, after which we set off together, carrying rucksacks, across the Basses-Alpes. The first lap was traveled by bus, but thereafter we walked. When we were toiling up a mountainside Olga sometimes got so irritated that she would hammer the ground with her stick; but like me, she loved these sweeping landscapes of white limestone rock and red soil. She enjoyed picking ripe figs along the wayside, the air redolent with the scent of the maquis, and climbing the stepped streets of old villages perched on some high mountain spur. She picked strong-scented herbs as she walked, and when we reached the inn where we proposed to spend the night, she would boil up the most curious concoctions from them. At every stage of our journey, however, I would hurry to the nearest *poste restante*. At Puget-Théniers, on September 20, I found a fairly optimistic telegram from Sartre awaiting me. Five days later, at Gap, there was another, telling me to come back to Paris immediately. The Préfecture was a dismal building, made doubly oppressive by the sluggish heat that presaged a storm: I well remember how panic-stricken I felt at that moment. All the way in the train I reproached myself furiously for my blind optimism and my obsessional preoccupation with my own private affairs. When I got out at the Paris terminus there were newspaper headlines talking about a "period of crisis." Reservists of both the second and third draft categories had been recalled. Hitler had issued an ultimatum demanding Prague's surrender within the next six days, and Prague was stiffening its defenses against the worst. This time war really did seem inevitable. I faced this prospect with furious incredulity; so lunatic a catastrophe could not possibly happen to *me*. I remember running into Merleau-Ponty in the Dôme; I had hardly seen him since our probationary period together at Janson-de-Sailly, but that day I had a lengthy discussion with him. I told him that Czechoslovakia was perfectly justified in her indignation against the betrayal of her interests by Britain and France; but anything, even the cruelest injustice, was better than war. My attitude struck him as shortsighted, and Sartre thought the same: "We can't go on appeasing Hitler indefinitely," he told me. But even though his rational mind inclined him to accept the prospect of war, he still rebelled at the thought of seeing it actually break out. Our next few days were grim ones: we went to the cinema a lot and read every edition of the daily papers. Sartre was making a fiercely valiant effort to reconcile his political ideas with his private inclinations, while I was fundamentally all at sea. Then the storm abruptly passed over without having broken, and the Munich Pact was signed; I was delighted, and felt not the faintest pang of conscience at my reaction. I felt I had escaped death, now and forever. There was even an element of triumph in my relief. Decidedly, I thought, I was born lucky: no misfortune would ever touch me.

My eyes were not opened immediately after the Munich crisis, far from it: the threat of war had receded, and I recovered confidence in the future. Left-wing opinions were divided on the value of the peace concessions we had gained. Despite the fact that part of its staff had recently been attacking nonintervention, *Le Canard enchaîné* was elated. *L'Oeuvre* remained undecided, while *Vendredi* was so radically split over this issue that it abandoned politics altogether, changed its title to *Reflets,* and restricted itself to purely cultural matters. Giono and Alain persisted in their out-and-out pacifism. A large number of intellectuals went about repeating their assertion that "the democracies have just declared peace in the world." There was another slogan in circulation, which ran: "Peace is working on the side of democracy." The Communists had voted against the Munich agreements, but they could not chew the cud of their wrath indefinitely; they had to advance, and, whatever their private convictions, do so with a show of vigorous optimism in the Party as a whole. So they exhorted the French Government to reverse their home policy, ratify a pact with Soviet Russia, step up the national defense program, and counter Hitler's bluff with rousing demonstrations of firmness. They advocated these measures so enthusiastically that hope flickered up once more. Thus while one faction regarded the peace as already saved, the other was proclaiming ways by which it *could* be saved; certainly no one forbade me to believe in the possibility.

Once my mind had been set at rest, I resumed work. I had sent Brice Parain a typed version of the first hundred pages of my novel—that is, the section dealing with Françoise's childhood. In his opinion this did not measure up to my stories, and Sartre agreed with him. I now decided to omit not only my heroine's past life, but also her meeting with Pierre and the eight years they spent together. These would be assumed in the background, and the actual narrative would begin with the entry of a stranger into their lives. I sketched out a rough plan: the beginnings of the trio, Xavière's progress toward rational self-understanding, incipient jealousy in Françoise, leading to crime: she was to intervene treacherously between Pierre and Xavière in their relationship, Xavière would make violent and contemptuous recriminations, and in self-defense Françoise would kill her. It was all rather two-dimensional. Sartre made a suggestion: in order to emphasize the importance Françoise attached to the happiness she and Pierre had built together, it would be a good idea if she gave up something for his sake in the first chapter. So I introduced Gerbert, and let Françoise be tempted by his youth and charm, only to renounce them. Later, when he had won Xavière's love, she fell into his arms, and it was this betrayal that she expunged by murder. Extra complexity made the intrigue more closely knit, and I could now give Elisabeth, whose character interested me per se, a more precise role to fulfill.

I was working by one rule which both Sartre and I regarded as fundamental, and which he expounded shortly afterward in an article on Mauriac and the French novel. In each successive chapter I identified myself with one of my characters, and excluded any knowledge or notion beyond what he or she would have had. Most often the viewpoint I adopted was that of Françoise, whom I endowed with my own experiences, though making various important changes and transpositions. She regarded herself as conscious mind *et praeterea nihil,* the only such in existence; she had allowed Pierre to share her sovereign position, and now they both stood together at the center of a world which it was her compelling mission in life to explore and reveal. But there was a price to pay for this privilege: by merging her identity with everything she saw she lost all sharply defined individualism in her own eyes. I had become aware of this shortcoming earlier, when I made comparisons between myself and Zaza. In my first book, Madame de Préliane looked regretfully, from her position of superior wisdom, at the salty tears streaming down Geneviève's face; similarly Françoise, in a dance hall, found herself vaguely envying Elisabeth's misery-wracked expression, and Xavière's transports of ecstasy. There was a strain of sadness in her pride when she told herself, during a party to celebrate the hundredth performance of *Julius Caesar,* that she was nobody, nobody at all. (Anne was to say the same thing in *The Mandarins,* during the post-Liberation festivities, but tranquilly, neither in pride nor with resentment.) One afternoon, finding herself "exiled," with Pierre and Xavière both far away, she tried to draw on her own inner resources for support—but in vain. She had, literally, no real self [*moi*]. She was an utterly transparent creature, without features or individuality. When she let herself slip into the clinging hell of passion, there was one thing which consoled her for her fall from grace: her very limitations and vulnerability made a human being of her, with precisely mapped contours, existing at one particular spot on earth.

Such was Françoise's first transformation: from a position of absolute and all-embracing authority she was suddenly reduced to an infinitely tiny particle in the external universe. This misfortune succeeded in convincing her, as it had done me, that she was an individual among other individuals, no matter who they might be. Now another danger threatened her, one which I myself had been endeavoring to exorcise ever since my adolescence. Other people [*autrui*] could not only steal the world from her, but also invade her personality and bewitch it. Xavière, with her outbursts of temper and spitefulness, was disfiguring Françoise's inner self, and the more she struggled, the more hopelessly she became entangled in the snare. Her own image became so loathsome to Françoise that she was faced with two alternatives: a lifetime of self-disgust, or to shatter the spell by destroying her who cast it. This latter course she took, and thus remained, triumphantly, true to herself.

I have often been criticized for this conclusion, and it is beyond any doubt the weakest aspect of the book. One part I do feel is good, on the other hand, is the scene at night with its contrasting implications for Françoise and Gerbert, and for Xavière. For the former, since it has brought them together, it is all gaiety and innocence. To Xavière it represents the darkness of betrayal. Because of the mutual antagonism that lurks in individual lives, happiness, beauty, and the bloom of youth often carry ugliness or evil as their obverse: this is a truth we meet at all the crossroads of life. But to make this the motive for murder is quite another matter. Novelists are rather apt to forget that in real life there is a great difference between dreaming of murder and actually committing it: to kill is not a commonplace action. Françoise, as I have depicted her, is just as incapable of murder as I am. On the other hand, I think the reader is made to believe in Xavière's ability to make Françoise lose her temper—or her self-confidence. But however much I labored, in the final chapters, to heighten the egotism and devious guile with which I had endowed her at the outset, she still lacked that extra degree of malice and consistency of purpose necessary for the hatred between Françoise and herself to assume really obsessional proportions. Childish and capricious as she was, she could never pierce Françoise's inner defenses and turn her into a monster; there was only one character who possessed the necessary strength, and that was Pierre. It has also been stated as an objection that in fact this act of violence does *not* save Françoise; Xavière's damning verdict against her remains unexpunged. This criticism I find unconvincing. Françoise has given up looking for an ethical solution to the problem of coexistence. She endures the Other as an inevitable burden, and then defends herself against this invasion by accomplishing an equally brutal and irrational act herself: murder. The rights and wrongs of her individual case do not concern me: *She Came to Stay* is not in any sense a *roman à thèse*. I would rest content if those who challenge her decision would at least believe this.

On second thoughts, no. From a literary viewpoint my error is all the more flagrant in that I failed to achieve a properly balanced integration between daily life and tragedy. Yet insofar as literature is a living activity, it was essential that I should end with this denouement, which possessed a cathartic quality for me personally. In the first place, by killing Olga on paper I purged every twinge of irritation and resentment I had previously felt toward her, and cleansed our friendship of all the unpleasant memories that lurked among those of a happier nature. But above all, by releasing Françoise, through the agency of a crime, from the dependent position in which her love for Pierre kept her, I regained my own personal autonomy. The paradoxical thing is that to do so did not require any unpardonable action on my part, but merely the description of such an action in a book. However attentive the encouragement and advice one receives, writing remains an act for which the responsibility cannot be shared with any other person. In this novel I exposed myself so dangerously that at times the gap between my emotions and the words to express them seemed insurmountable. But such an abstract victory, projected onto an imaginary situation, would not, by itself, have carried sufficient weight of reality. If I was to overcome *on my own account* that solitary wilderness into which I had flung Françoise, I must work my fantasy through to the bitter end, and not water my version of it down in any way. And in any event, the process of self-identification came off. Rereading the final pages, today so contrived and dead, I can hardly believe that when I wrote them my throat was as tight as though I had the burden of a real murder on my shoulders. Yet so it was; and sitting there, pen in hand, I felt a weird sort of terror as I set down Françoise's experience of mental isolation. Xavière's murder may look like the abrupt and clumsy conclusion of a drama I had no idea how to finish; but in fact it was the motive force and *raison d'être* behind the entire novel.

In Xavière I wanted to portray the opacity of a human mind turned in upon itself, and therefore never examined her from the inside. On the other hand, I did, for several chapters, make Elisabeth the focal center of my narrative. Prejudice, far from lessening her insight, merely served to sharpen it; she reduced the adventures of the trio to those derisory proportions which human passion normally attains in the eyes of a third party. I hinted, qua author, that this emotional ambiguity was something I never forgot, that Françoise's experiences (albeit from *her* viewpoint they were enacted on the tragic level) could also be treated as something to be smiled at.

But Elisabeth was not merely a convenient device: I attached far too much importance to her character as such. One of the problems which obsessed me was the relationship between honesty and the will. Elisabeth's artful deceit over facial make-up extended to every aspect of her life; Françoise, on the other hand, tried to achieve over-all consistency in her life without cheating or trickery; she was therefore led to ask herself, through observing her friend's behavior, just where the dividing line is set between a true and a false construction. Though Xavière was frequently made to bracket both women as targets for her contempt, there was one difference between them which struck me as fundamental. Françoise very seldom bothered herself about the void that lurks in every human creature's heart; she loved Pierre, she took an active interest in ideas and the world at large, and people, and her work. Elisabeth's misfortune, which I connected with her childhood, was that no person or event could make a warm, living impression on her: she took nothing for granted, and masked this inner indifference with feigned enthusiasms for things like politics or painting which in fact left her quite unmoved. Though she went hunting after emotions and beliefs, she felt she could hold none of them permanently: she reproached herself for this disability of hers, and her self-contempt spread devastatingly outward till it embraced the whole world. She denied all value or importance to the background or incidents of her life; everything she touched turned to cardboard. She yielded to the dizzying conviction that I had known in Zaza's company, and for a few moments when confronted by Camille: that universal truth—indeed, the very essence of the universe as we know it—belonged to *other people*— in this case to Pierre and Françoise. It was to protect herself against this belief that she clung to phantoms. In my portrait of her—especially the interior monologues—I borrowed many of the failings that I had previously attributed to Chantal, including her insincerity and her verbal hyperbole. But I blackened this previous picture considerably. Elisabeth knew—as had Louise Perron during her breakdown—that her obsessions were imaginary, but her efforts to shake them off merely plunged her in deeper. Françoise felt compassionate sympathy for her friend, whose condition she saw as a parody of her own; but there were times when this quality of caricature seemed to cast doubts on Elisabeth's own sincerity. (I may add here that in most of my novels there is a foil to the main heroine. Denise and Hélène are thus balanced in *Le Sang des autres, The Blood of Others,* as are Anne and Paula in *The Mandarins.* But the relationship of Françoise and Elisabeth is more close-knit, the latter standing as a disturbing challenge to the former.)

In order to offset Elisabeth's view of the trio by a more charitable opinion, which still came from an outsider, I let Gerbert take over the narrative for one chapter. Nevertheless, since his role was a purely sub-ordinate one, I drew no more than a superficial sketch here. There were several reasons that stopped me from looking at the story through Pierre's eyes: in the first place, I had endowed him with a sensibility and intelli-gence at least equal to those of my heroine, and if I had drawn these qualities in all their prolific liveliness, the novel would have become lopsided—after all, it was Françoise's story that I had chosen to tell. Secondly, I wanted to establish a symmetrical balance between Xavière's lack of forthrightness and Pierre's apparent transparency: both these bastions had to be breached by means of Françoise. What I *do* regret is failing to give him that three-dimensional quality which was the main thing that drew Françoise to him. I had put too much of myself into Françoise to link her with a man who would have been a stranger to me; my imagination balked at this switch of partners. But equally, I was loath to offer the public a portrait of Sartre as I knew him. In the end I compromised. Pierre kept the name of the hero in my second novel, together with his type of ambitiousness. I borrowed one or two super-ficial traits from Dullin, and based the rest of the character on Sartre, though individual features were much toned down, and some I invented to meet the requirements of my plot. Since my free invention was shackled by a combination of mental blocks and self-criticism, I could neither create an original character nor draw an accurate portrait. The upshot was that Pierre—on whom the entire story hinges, since Françoise's choice of action is, *au fond,* always made with reference to him—possesses less depth or truthful characterization than any of the novel's other protagonists.

She Came to Stay testifies both to the advantages and the inconveniences of what is known as "fictionalized fact." It was more amusing and pleasant to describe Paris—the theatrical world, Montparnasse, the flea market, and other parts of the city that I loved—than Rouen; but with its background shifted to Paris the story of the trio lost much of its probability and significance. The obsessional attachment of two grown people to a child of nineteen could hardly be explained otherwise than in a context of provincial life. This stifling atmosphere was an essential ingredient: only thus could the least desire or regret turn into an obsession, every emotion acquire a violent and tragic intensity, a smile embrace the very heavens. I turned two young and unknown teachers into a pair of highly Parisian characters, whose lives were packed with friends and relations, who were always fully occupied, never at a loss for entertainment. As a result, the story of this isolated trio—a story as poignant as it was agonizing, with moments of sheer wonder about it—became unreal, falsified.

When I began *She Came to Stay,* I intended Xavière's murder to take place while Pierre was away, and doubtless this is how it would have turned out had it not been for the war. But the war furnished me with an excellent excuse for removing him to a distance. It struck me that in a town where all the men were absent, a close intimacy between two women would reach a climax of tenseness more easily than in normal times. But it is impossible that Françoise, as I drew her, should not have been lifted out of her private worries by the vast impact of this more general tragedy; and this being so, her relationship with Xavière would lack all real intensity—certainly it would not achieve the conviction necessary for murder. The denouement would look more plausible if it had taken place in the provinces, in time of peace. In this respect, at all events, the transposition of scene and period did me a disservice.

I have already set down the main aesthetic principle governing the construction of *She Came to Stay,* and I congratulate myself on having stuck to it, since it is responsible for the best things in the novel. Because of each character's limited knowledge, the plot development is often as enigmatic as that of a good Agatha Christie thriller, and the reader does not at once grasp its implications. Little by little fresh incidents and discussions reveal unexpected facets of the story. Pierre can go on analyzing a certain gesture of Xavière's indefinitely, though Françoise scarcely notices it; and no definitive interpretation of it can ever be made, since no character is the repository of absolute truth. In the novel's more successful sequences I achieved a situational ambivalence corresponding to the kind of thing one meets in real life. I also tried to insure that that events I described should not develop in terms of some cut-and-dried causal pattern, but should be, just as in real life, simultaneously comprehensible and contingent. Françoise sleeps with Gerbert to revenge herself on Xavière, but also because she has wanted him for ages, because her moral scruples have collapsed, and because she feels old (or, alternatively, young), and for a number of reasons over and above those that could be set down here. Since I refused to examine my characters' various outlooks with an all-seeing author's eye, I refrained likewise from intervening in the natural time sequence they followed. Each successive chapter represented an excised segment of time, but each was presented unabridged in itself, with no abbreviation of dialogue or incident.

There was another, less demanding rule, the effectiveness of which I had learned from Dashiell Hammett no less than Dostoevsky, and which I now endeavored to follow in my own work. All dialogue must be dynamic, that is, it must modify or develop the characters' relationships and the plot as a whole. Furthermore, during any such discussion, important events must be taking place off-stage, as it were, so that the reader strains eagerly forward through those thick-bulking pages of text toward a denouement, and shares the characters' own awareness of the resistance and passage of time.

The most obvious influence on my writing is Hemingway's, as several critical articles have pointed out. One of the features in his stories which I most admired was his rejection of would-be "objective" descriptions: landscapes, interiors, or artifacts are always shown us through the central character's eyes, and in the limiting perspective of the action. I tried to do the same thing. I also attempted to imitate, as he did, the tones and rhythms of the spoken vernacular, without being afraid of pointlessness or repetition. (I say *imitate* rather than *copy,* since there can be no question of transcribing in a novel the fragmented babble of an actual conversation.)

With these provisos I accepted, as did the Americans, a certain number of traditional conventions. I know the arguments that can be brought against such usages, but I know, too, the ways in which they justify themselves. I will discuss them more fully when I come to *The Mandarins,* since during the period that I was writing *She Came to Stay* they did not concern me at all as a problem. All I wanted to do was write a novel, and that was quite a tall order in itself.

At last I was embarked on a book with the firm conviction not only that I would finish it, but also that it would find a publisher. So Sartre assured me, as chapter succeeded chapter, and I came to believe it myself. Once again I experienced the joyful feeling which had come over me that fine autumn day beside the pond at Berre; I wrenched myself free of the common clay of everyday life, and plunged heart and soul into the wonders of my imaginary world. In a year or two this novel would have a permanent form. It embodied my future, and I moved toward this goal with effortless speed; I no longer thought of myself as old at all. That winter I took special pains over my personal appearance. I had a dress made of a fine-quality eggshell wool. I bought a black pleated skirt and a collection of shirtwaists, some black, some yellow, with which I wore contrasting yellow or black scarves. I changed my hair style to conform to the current fashion, wearing it piled on top of my head. In the spring I bought a black straw hat which I wore with a little veil. I felt very chic, and was proud of the fact.

Sartre too was full of zest for life. He was working on the novel he had told me about in one of his letters; its title was no longer *Lucifer* but *Les Chemins de la liberté* (*Roads to Freedom*). The success of *Nausea* showed no signs of abating, and *The Wall*, which appeared at the beginning of 1939, made a great stir. Paulhan and Cassou invited him to review for the *N.R.F.* and *Europe,* which he was delighted to do. He had articles written about him, and readers sent him letters; he had become acquainted with several other writers, Paulhan in particular. Yet he did not make any new friends; our old ones were quite sufficient. Marco was still sulking, and wouldn't come near us, but we were back on an intimate footing again with Pagniez and his wife. Nizan had just published his best book, *La Conspiration,* which we admired very much and for which he won the Prix Interallié.

We regretted Bost's absence. He was doing his military service at Amiens, as a buck private. As a good Protestant he was ultrademocratic, and rather than command others he preferred to work himself up into a white-hot fury about the swine who assumed they had the right to give *him* orders. His officers, irritated by his obvious education and culture, impatiently exhorted him to take various military courses leading to promotion; his obstinate refusal to do so vexed them mightily, a fact from which he derived considerable satisfaction. His associates were roughhewn Picardy peasants: he got along very well indeed with them, though this did not prevent him from loathing barracks life. Fortunately he could very often get up to Paris on Sundays.

My own profession was tolerable enough. Teachers' meetings were a bore, but I did not resent the discipline which my timetable imposed on me: it gave some framework to my daily life. Besides, I only had sixteen hours of classwork a week, which was hardly excessive. But I still persisted in my refusal to form any close relationships with my colleagues; and considering the high regard which I have for the teaching profession as a body today, I cannot but regret this attitude a little. The truth of the matter is that if I kept my distance from *them* it was really to keep *myself* at arm's length. I discharged the duties of a philosophy teacher without really being one. I was not even the grown woman that my fellow teachers saw; I was living out a private and individual adventure to which no categories had permanent relevance. As for my classes, I enjoyed them actively, since they were discussions between individuals rather than work. I read books on philosophy, discussed them with Sartre, and let my pupils profit by these personal discoveries: in this way I contrived to avoid rehashing the same lessons, except on certain particularly boring subjects. Besides, my audience changed from one year to the next: each class had its own individual features and set me fresh problems. For the first few days I used to stare in some perplexity at these forty adolescent girls, in whose minds I had to try and establish my own methods of thinking. Which of them would follow me, and how far? I had learned to be wary of eyes that lit up too quickly, lips that framed too intelligent a smile. Little by little a hierarchy would establish itself, likes and dislikes crystallize. As I took few pains to conceal my own prejudices, I tended to inspire positive sentiments, one way or the other, in my class. Contrary to the predictions of my colleagues in Marseille, after seven years' teaching I still enjoyed discussions with some of my pupils. They were at the "metaphysical age"; life for them existed solely in terms of ideas, and that is why their ideas were so very much alive. I made them talk a lot in class, and these discussions went on after the lesson had officially ended. Even when they had taken their *baccalauréat,* I still continued to have occasional meetings with those who had specialized in philosophy. One such was Bianca Bienenfeld, who had been at the top of her class the preceding year, went on to the Sorbonne, and there joined up with a group of Sartre's former pupils, among whom was Jean Kanapa. In their essays and exercises this group was trying to win acceptance for phenomenological methods. Bianca brought a great deal of passion to her work, and reacted violently to events in the world at large. We became good friends.

There was a colony of White Russians at Passy, and that year my best pupil was a White Rusisan girl called Lise Oblanoff. She was seventeen, blonde (though with a dark streak running through her hair which made her look older), and wore large, heavy shoes. Her skirts were too long, as well. Right from the first I was amused by her aggressive attitude. She would interrupt what I was saying with an abrupt cry of "I don't understand!" Sometimes she held out against my explanations so long and so stubbornly that I was obliged to bypass her objections; on these occasions she would ostentatiously fold her arms and stare at me in a really murderous way. One morning I ran into her in the Métro, as I was changing lines at Trocadéro Station. She greeted me with a broad smile and said, "I wanted to tell you, mademoiselle, that by and large I find your classes most interesting." We went on chatting till we reached the *lycée* gate. A few mornings later I met her again, on the same platform, and realized that this encounter was no accident. She was watching out for me, determined to use these private conversations as a means of getting the answers I had failed to give her in class. She would have liked to go on with her philosophical studies the following year; but her parents were not naturalized, and as a stateless person she was debarred from teaching as a career. Her father wanted her to become a chemical engineer. She had been attending the Lycée Molière for years, but made only one friend there, a Russian girl like herself, who had left three years earlier to take a job. Her other classmates she found stupid and dull. She judged the entire world by extremely severe standards, and did not feel in any way a part of the society in which she lived, preferring to observe it at arm's length, with detached irony. It was this detachment of hers that made her so intellectually demanding. She would take no part of this foreign civilization on trust; the only truths she would accept were those that could be demonstrated by the light of universal reason. To her condition of exile she also owed a vision of people and things as droll as it was exotic.

I did not spend my leisure time quite as I had done in previous years. For one thing, I forsook Montparnasse. Olga had unobtrusively gone back to attending classes at the Atelier. Mainly in order to cue a friend of hers, she had studied the part of Olivia in Shakespeare's *Twelfth Night*; and when the two of them went up for their audition, it was Olga who caught Dullin's attention, and received his unstinted praise. This at once made everyone else in the class seek her company, and, what was more important, gave her self-confidence. She became regular in her attendance, and at that time there was no more conscientious student at the Atelier. She was working hard to perfect her diction, repeating tongue-twisters such as, *"Dis-moi gros gras grain d'orge, quand te dé-gro-gra-graindorgeras-tu?"* followed by, *"Je me dé-gro-gra-graindorangerai quand tous les gros gras grains d'orge se dé-gro-gra-graindorgeront."* She took lessons in extempore playing from various teachers, and studied mime under Jean-Louis Barrault, whose work Dullin appreciated, and whom he pointed out to her; he often spoke of her to me in warmly appreciative tones.

Olga took rooms in a hotel on the Place Dancourt; I often used to meet her for dinner near the theater in a small restaurant much frequented by Atelier actors and students. She used to tell me no end of scandalous stories about them all. That lovely actress Madeleine Robinson had already by then played several parts both on the stage and the screen, but she went on learning more about her profession. Her life was chaotic and frenzied; she used to toss money out of windows, and dress in the most gorgeous clothes that were always more or less threadbare. For decency, caution, and keeping up appearances she had nothing but contempt, and Olga admired her for it. Of the beginners, Dullin predicted that Berthe Tissen was destined for the most successful career: she was a petite Luxembourger, with no looks but a quite phenomenal personality, and as Mara in *L'Annonce fait à Marie* (*The Tidings Brought to Mary*) she had reduced her fellow students to tears. Much was also expected of a dark girl with long pigtails and an impassioned face, who was known, pseudonymously, as Andrée Clement, and seriously involved with a droll and talented young man called Dufilho. I made the acquaintance of Célia Bertin, who was simultaneously training for a theatrical career and reading for a degree in philosophy. With her brilliant eyes, high cheekbones, and dark skin—not to mention her habit of draping herself in bright colored shawls—she looked just like a gypsy. She had considerable charm, but lacked natural ease of manner. Olga also struck up a close friendship with a Yugoslav girl, a raven-haired creature I had often seen around Montparnasse, and whose name was Olga, too. But out of all the Atelier students, of either sex, her favorite was little Mouloudji, already a celebrity after making two or three films. At sixteen he still contrived to avoid the gawkiness of adolescence, and preserved something of a child's freshness and seriousness. He had been taken up by Jacques Prévert and his gang—in particular by Marcel Duhamel—and contact with them had given him a weirdly uneven cultural background: both his knowledge and his ignorance were quite astonishing in their range. He had been long familiar with surrealist poetry and modern American fiction, but was only now discovering Alexandre Dumas, who enchanted him. Both his background and his success brought him into marginal contact with Paris society, which he judged with a blend of childish intransigence and proletarian austerity: "Among the workers," he often used to say reprovingly, "that is *not done.*" Both the bourgeoisie and Left Bank Bohemianism seemed to him equally corrupt. Reserved to the point of surliness yet exuberant in his cordiality, with cut-and-dried views about good and evil that masked perplexity amounting to total bewilderment; sensitive, openhearted, liable to sudden fits of obstinacy; kindly in the extreme, yet capable of spitefulness and occasional downright treachery— Mouloudji was a fascinating little monster. He got along very well with Olga, since in her, too, some element of childhood had survived.

Olga often went down from Montmartre to Saint-Germain-des-Prés. It was she, I fancy, who first took me to the Café de Flore, where she and I and Sartre got into the habit of spending our evenings. This place had become a regular rendezvous for film people, ranging from directors and actors to script girls and cutters. In the Café Flore we rubbed shoulders with people such as Jacques and Pierre Prévert, Grémillon, Aurenche, Chavanne the scriptwriter, and the members of the old "October" group— Sylvain Itkine, Roger Blin, Fabien Lorris, Bussière, Baquet, Yves Deniaud, Marcel Duhamel. There were also some extremely attractive girls to be seen there. The most striking of these was Sonia Mossé whose superb features and body—though perhaps a little overblown for a girl of twenty—had inspired many painters and sculptors, Derain among them. She had gorgeous blonde hair, which she brushed back over the nape of her neck in artfully arranged coils; the quiet originality of her clothes and jewels I found utterly entrancing. Among other things I particularly admired one dress, which was of a most severe cut, but made out of old and extremely precious cashmere brocade. She was generally accompanied by an attractive brunette with cropped hair and a boyish stride. Sometimes Jacqueline Breton put in an appearance, shell pendants at her ears, eyelashes pointed with mascara, bracelets clashing as she waved her hands to show off those long, alluring fingernails. But the most common type of woman was what we nicknamed the Shock Brigade: pale-haired creatures, all to a greater or lesser extent ravaged by drugs (or alcohol, or just life), with sad mouths and shifty, restless eyes.

The Flore had its own mores, its private ideology; the little band of regulars who met there daily were neither wholly Bohemian nor wholly bourgeois, but belonged for the most part, in a vague sort of way, to the world of films or the theater. They lived on unspecified private incomes, from hand to mouth, or on their expectations. Their God and oracle, the source of all their opinions, was Jacques Prévert: they worshiped his films and poetry, doing their best to ape his language and attitudes. We too found Prévert's verses and lyrics very much to our taste: his dreamy, somewhat inconsequential anarchism suited us perfectly. We had been enchanted by *L'Affaire est dans le sac,* and, more recently, by *Drôle de drame,* directed by Carné, and which featured Barrault, Jouvet, and Françoise Rosay. But it was *Quai des brumes* that impressed us most. There were admirable performances by Gabin, Brasseur, Michel Simon, and a remarkable unknown actress called Michèle Morgan; Prévert's dialogue and Carné's visual imagery, the fog of despair enveloping the entire film—these we found deeply moving. In this we saw eye to eye with current thought, which regarded *Quai des brumes* as the French cinema's crowning achievement. But the sympathy we felt for the young idlers in the Flore was tinged with impatience: the main object of their nonconformism was to justify their inactivity, and they were very, very bored. Their chief means of distraction was the Shock Brigade, with each member of which they all in turn had an affair of varying length— generally pretty short. Once they had gone the rounds they started off again at the beginning, which induced a certain monotony after a while. They spent the whole day venting their spleen with blasé little aphorisms, uttered in between yawns. They were forever complaining about *la connerie humaine.*

On Sunday evenings we would abandon the chic, if bitter, haunts of skepticism, and let ourselves be elated by the splendid animal zest of the Negroes on the Rue Blomet. I several times accompanied Olga to the dance hall there, which was popular with Sonia and her friends, too. Here I met Marie Girard, who had changed little since her Berlin days; she loafed around in Montparnasse and any other places the Montparnasse crowd frequented. We were very much in a minority, since at this time very few white people mingled with the colored crowd, and fewer still risked dancing on the same floor: when set beside these sinuous Africans and shimmying West Indians, their stiffness was quite appalling, and if they tried to shed it, they tended to look like cases of hysteria under hypnotism. I never shared the snobbish attitude of the Flore regulars, or imagined that I was participating in some grand African erotic mystery. But I enjoyed watching the dancers, and I drank rum punch, and what with the noise and the smoke and the fumes of alcohol, and the violent rhythms banged out by the orchestra, my mind would become quite dazed. Through this fog a sequence of handsome, laughing faces passed by me. My heart beat a little faster when the uproarious final quadrille burst upon us. This explosion of cheerful, festive bodies seemed to be closely bound up with my own urge to live.

The Café de Flore spirit was very much to the fore in the cabaret which (thanks to the efforts of Sonia Mossé, together with her copartner Agnès Capri, a former pupil of Dullin's) was opened on the Rue Molière at the beginning of 1939. It was housed in a small but well-appointed room, and the tiny stage at the far end had a crimson curtain. Agnès Capri,

her pointed features taking on a most ingenuous expression, would sing
songs by Prévert, and recite his poems, or Apollinaire's. I loved the fresh
yet acidulous quality of her voice, and never tired of hearing her render
"La Pêche à la baleine," nor of watching her lips give shape, Medea-
like, to those witching poisons of hers. Yves Deniaud gave a stunning
performance as a street hawker proclaiming the merits of a tie-knotting
machine. There was a number called "Beards" which he did with Fabien
Lorris, and which made us laugh till we cried. They had a remarkable
repertoire of songs dating from 1900 or thereabout; the most popular of
these concerned a German officer whose new-born child, through some
obscure combination of circumstances, was starving to death. He offered
a small fortune to a young Alsatian mother if she would agree to wet-
nurse the infant; to which the bearded lady from Alsace replied, in a
deep thrilling voice, hand upon bosom:

> No no, never! My breast is French,
> I shall never give suck to a German child. . . .

Irony and parody held pride of place in Agnès Capri's programs. When
we mocked bygone generations we experienced the delicate pleasure produced by collective narcissism: we felt that *we* were clear-headed, well-
informed, critical, and oh-so-intelligent. When, a year later, I realized how
blind and ignorant I had been, I conceived a dislike for smart-aleck witti-
cisms of this sort.

We had not completely abandoned the Dôme, however. Its regulars
were seedier and less predictable than those at the Flore. One evening
the giant Dominguez, with whom we had scraped up an acquaintance
by some trick or other, asked Olga and me around to his studio. Those
present included Roma, the half-Greek, half-Romanian woman he was
then living with, Florès the painter, and a dozen or so more. For the
first and only time in my life I played the truth game so popular among
the surrealists. Almost all the questions were of a sexual, indeed a positively obscene, nature. Roma was asked why she enjoyed Dominguez's
love-making; with a most delightful sweeping gesture she sketched a
vast body in air, and replied, "Because there's so *much* of him!" But for
the most part questions and answers alike were both crude and banal.
We put a good face on it, though to do so cost us quite an effort.
Gradually the atmosphere became what *Le Canard enchaîné* might have
described as *"nettement ambiante,"* since some of the players seemed ready
to turn from words to deeds. We slipped away.

The new French films were not of a caliber that could stand up to
Quai des brumes. Nevertheless Mouloudji was delightful in *L'Enfer des
anges.* American pictures were becoming rather tedious; they all went over
to the side of the police at the expense of the gangsters. In *Angels with
Dirty Faces* James Cagney let himself die a coward's death in order to
keep a gang of young boys from crime. Both *Mr. Smith Goes to Washington* and *You Can't Take It With You* were most amusing comedies, well

acted and well constructed; but they also presumed to put over a message, to the effect that capitalism is the only true humanism.

Ever since Jean Zay had invited the Cartel directors to stage shows there, the Comédie-Française had offered some excellent entertainment. Fifteen years before, I had seen *Chacun sa vérité* at the Atelier; now I saw it once again, in the more lavish production that Dullin presented at the Comédie-Française. When Ledoux and Berthe Bovy appeared at the end of a long corridor (which by a trick of perspective was made to seem even longer), and stood there, stiff and awkward in their mourning clothes, both their fellow actors and the audience seemed struck dumb with anguish. With *The Marriage of Figaro* Dullin aroused the most lively controversy, however. Cherubino was played by a boy called Claudio, who looked scarcely twelve years old, and was regarded as being really *too* young for the part. Dullin was also criticized for failing to place sufficient emphasis on the play's sociopolitical side, though in my opinion he removed none of its virulence through treating it lightly. I was present at the first night of Salacrou's *La Terre est ronde,* which struck me, rightly or wrongly, as a most fashionable social occasion. I thought Lucienne Salacrou looked quite splendid in her silk evening dress, hair piled high and adorned with a valuable ornamental comb. And how attractive Sylvia Bataille was when seen in the flesh, under that chic little bonnet trimmed with scarlet feathers! I had not the least desire to become part of fashionable Paris society myself, or to parade dressed to the nines; but this close-up view of celebrities in their gorgeous clothes I did find most entertaining.

Dullin handed over the Atelier to Barrault for the latter's production of *La Faim (Hunger),* a play in which Olga had several minor parts. The evening began with Granval's version of Laforgue's adaptation of *Hamlet,* in which Barrault offered the audience a sort of one-man show. But in *Hunger* he tried, for the first time, to carry his idea of "total theater" to its logical conclusion. He had preserved little of Knut Hamsun's novel apart from the central idea—the hopeless loneliness of a starving man in the very heart of a great city. To this theme he had added another which much preoccupied him: that of the alter ego. The hero, played by Barrault, had an "inner brother" at his elbow, the latter being endowed with the disturbing features of Roger Blin. In this play dialogue was only of secondary importance, and often replaced by the montage technique known as *fatrasie,* a new device with which Barrault achieved some excellent effects; but his own favorite mode of expression was mime. Though a pupil of Decroux, who had devoted his whole life to reviving the art of mime, Barrault did not regard it as an adequate independent medium, preferring to use its resources as an adjunct to the development of the drama. He could not resist the temptation to introduce several bravura touches into *Hunger*: at one point, for instance, he climbed an imaginary staircase by "marking time," an exercise which stuck out from the over-all pattern of the production and disrupted its rhythm. I was far more appreciative of those moments when gesture per se became a genuine mode of dramatic self-expression. There was one scene conducted wholly in dumb show, where the hero, through sheer physical debility, failed to possess the woman he desired: this was strikingly successful, and though daring, contained not the slightest hint of coarseness. The play was a success, and achieved a run of over fifty performances. After *Numance* and *As I Lay Dying,* this production of *Hunger* suggested that Barrault might well give the theater just that fresh lease on life which it so badly needed. The Cartel had outlived its usefulness, and was now wholly devoid of original drive. Now that the cinema was moving in the direction of realism, we all hoped that some new approach to production would revolutionize the legitimate stage, too: the relationships between actor and text, text and production, and production and audience had all to be redefined from scratch. Perhaps Barrault would bring it off.

We went back to Mégève during the Christmas holidays, and our performance on skis began to reach a standard that satisfied our unambitious needs. At Easter we made a trip through Provence, traveling by train and bus from one town or village to the next. I would leave Sartre behind at each stop, while I tramped across the Lubéron slopes, or climbed the still snow-capped mountains near Digne. All the bookshops and stalls in Manosque had Giono's novels on display. He had begun preaching his back-to-the-land theory, and once, when I was walking along a track somewhere near Contadour, rucksack on back, some local peasants asked me whether I belonged to the "colony." Sartre had been busy since the beginning of the year reading Heidegger, both in Corbin's translation and the German text. It was at Sisteron that he first discussed Heidegger seriously with me. I can still see the stone bench we sat on while Sartre explained what the definition of man as "a creature of distances" meant, and just how "the world stands revealed in the viewfinders of maladjusted instruments"; but I was hard put to it to understand how much actuality Heidegger attributed to the future. Sartre, whose main preoccupation had always been to preserve the reality of the world, realized that Heidegger's philosophy embodied a method of reconciling objective with subjective; it was not, in his opinion, very closely argued, but packed with suggestive ideas.

Whenever I had a few free days I got out of Paris. During spring vacation I went walking in the Morvan area, visiting Dijon, Auxerre, and Vézelay. In June, during the *baccalauréat* exams, which lasted a week, I was away in the Jura, and climbed every peak in sight. I got so exhausted that my knee swelled up and walking became sheer agony; I caught a train to Geneva, and limped my way around the city for a day or two. The Spanish Government had moved the Prado art collections there, to protect them from the bombardments, and I spent an afternoon surrounded by Goyas, El Grecos, and the works of Velasquez. My heart was aching with the knowledge that it would be a long time, now, before I went back to Spain.

All that year I had gone on trying to live exclusively in the present, to grasp each flying minute. Yet I had not, even so, managed to forget the world about me. The hopes raised in June, 1936, had finally guttered out. The working classes failed to reverse the Orders in Council that docked them of the major part of their concessions, and the employers successfully countered the strike on November 30 with a massive lockout. I lacked the imagination to be stirred by the burning of Canton or the fall of Hankow; but the defeats that the Spanish Republicans endured touched us like some personal misfortune. Their internal dissensions, especially the P.O.U.M. trial now taking place in Barcelona, sowed the seeds of doubt in our hearts. Was it true that the Stalinists had "assassinated the Revolution," or should we rather believe that it was the Anarchists who played ball with Franco's rebels? At all events, the rebels were winning, and Barcelona enduring the last agonies before collapse. Fernando, back on leave, told us about the bombardments and the famine: nothing to eat except for the odd handful of dried peas, not even any tobacco to appease one's hunger, not even a fag-end to be picked up in the streets. The children were haggard and emaciated, with swollen bellies. In January, after being devastated by liquid-air bombs, the city fell. An ever-increasing number of gaunt and ragged refugees streamed toward the frontier. Madrid was still holding out, but already England had given recognition of the Franco Government, and France was sending out Pétain as Ambassador to Burgos. After a prolonged final struggle Madrid, too, fell, and the whole of the French Left mourned its loss, for which they felt in some sense responsible. Blum admitted that in 1936 promptly dispatched shipments of arms could have saved the Republic, and that non-intervention had been an idiotic policy: why, then, had public opinion failed to make him change it? I was coming to realize that my political inertia did not guarantee me a certificate of innocence; nowadays when Fernando muttered about "bastard Frenchmen" I felt personally involved.

But could I still opt for a passive role when confronted with the tragic events going on beyond the Rhine? The Nazis had organized a reign of terror both in Bohemia and Austria. The press made known to us the existence of Dachau, where millions of Jews and anti-Fascists were interned. Bianco Bienenfeld was visited by one of her cousins, who had managed ot get away from Vienna after being held for a night by the Gestapo. He had been beaten up for hours on end, and his face was still puffy and blue-scarred with cigarette burns. He said that the night after Von Rath's murder, in a small town where he had some relations, they got all the Jews out of bed, herded them into the main square, made them undress, and then branded them with red-hot irons. Throughout the Reich this assassination had been made an excuse for the most ghastly pogroms. The last surviving synagogues had been burned, Jewish shops gutted, and thousands of Jews interned. "How can anyone still work and play and carry on his life as usual when things like *that* are being done?" Bianca asked me, weeping. And I, who was so obstinately determined to stake everything on happiness, felt ashamed of my egocentricity.

Yet despite my shame I still did not abandon my position, still tried hard to believe that there would be no war. Now Italy in her turn was demanding *Lebensraum*—repudiating her pact with France, stirring up trouble in Tunisia, threatening Djibouti. The day the Italian troops entered Barcelona beside Franco's soldiers the crowds in Rome staged a noisy demonstration, celebrating the dictators' victory with shouts of "Tunisia for Italy!" and "Corsica for Italy!" I meanwhile was comforting myself with the latest pacifist slogan: "In the last resort we wouldn't go to war over Djibouti." And indeed it looked as though things would not come to a showdown. Hitler's support of Mussolini was only lukewarm, and Roosevelt had promised that in the event of an attack he would intervene on behalf of the democracies. But Slovakia and the Ukraine placed themselves under the "protection" of the Reich, and on March 16 Hitler entered Prague. In England the Government introduced conscription, while Daladier in France obtained full emergency powers: gas masks began to be distributed, and the forty-hour week was sacrificed in the interests of national defense. Peace daily receded further. Mussolini attacked Albania, Hitler threatened Memel and laid claim to Danzig; while England, committed now to a strong-line policy, signed a mutual-assistance pact with Poland. There was a chance, it seemed, that an Anglo-Soviet-French treaty might scare Hitler off; but negotiations with the U.S.S.R. finally came to nothing. Very soon there would be no alternative but war—or yet another backing-down. Déat wrote a piece in *L'Oeuvre* that caused a considerable rumpus: it was entitled "Dying for Danzig," and suggested that the French should resign all claims on Danzig's behalf. The bulk of left-wing opinion, from the Radicals to the Communists, almost unanimously attacked this proposal.

In this connection I remember a discussion that took place between Colette Audry and Sartre. She had been so shaken by the Spanish disaster that politically speaking she no longer had any beliefs at all. "Anything is preferable to war," she said, to which Sartre replied: "No, not *anything*—not Fascism, for instance." He was not naturally bellicose, and at the time, on September 30, he had not been sorry to pick up the threads of his civilian life again; but he still regarded Munich as a bad mistake, and believed that any further retreat would be criminal. Appeasement, he argued, made us accessories to all of Hitler's persecutions and exterminations—a notion which I too found repugnant. There were tens of thousands of Jews wandering over the face of the globe in order to escape the torture chamber or the concentration camp. The episode of the *St. Louis* brought home to us the horror of their situation. Nine hundred and eighteen Jews had embarked at Hamburg for Cuba; but the Cuban Government turned them away, and the captain set course for Germany again. All the passengers took a collective oath to die together rather than return to Hamburg. They wandered about for weeks on end, but eventually Holland, France, and England agreed to give them asylum. There were numbers of other boats, similarly shipping wretched human cargoes (that no country would accept) from one port of call to the next. Our egotism had put up with these atrocities for far too long, and it was high time to have done with them.

But visions of the first World War kept recurring in my mind: what a

contradiction in terms it was to condemn a million Frenchmen to death
for the sake of humanity! Sartre retorted to this that it was not a matter
of humanitarianism or any other such moral abstraction: we ourselves were
in peril, and if Hitler was not crushed, France would suffer more or less
the same fate as Austria. Like Colette Audry, and many of Alain's disciples,
I said: "Surely France at war would be worse than France under the
Nazis?" But Sartre shook his head. "I have no wish," he said, "to be
made to eat my manuscripts. I don't want Nizan to have his eyes gouged
out with teaspoons." Fair enough: it was clear that Nazi domination would
remove all meaning from life as far as intellectuals like ourselves were
concerned. But if the decision had lain in our hands, would we have dared
to send shepherds from the Basses-Alpes or Douarnenez fishermen to die
in the defense of our liberties? But they, too, were involved, Sartre told
me; if they would not take up arms against Hitler, one day, no doubt,
they would be compelled to fight *for* him. In an occupied or satellite
France workers, peasants, and bourgeoisie would all suffer alike, would
all be treated as defeated persons, a subhuman rabble to be ruthlessly
sacrificed to the glory of the Reich.

He convinced me; war could no longer be avoided. But why had such
a position ever been reached? I had no right to complain, since I had
not so much as stirred my little finger to stop it. I felt guilty about this.
If only I had been able to say: Very well, I will pay the penalty. I will
redeem my blindness and obstinacy, and accept the consequences. But then
I thought of Bost and all the young men of his age who had never had
the slightest chance to influence events; they were fully justified in accusing
their elders. We are twenty years old, they could say, and we are going
to die; and it is your fault. Nizan had been right in his contention that
there is no way of avoiding political engagement; to abstain from politics
is in itself a political attitude. I was gripped by remorse.

It is impossible to assign any particular day, week, or even month to
the conversion that took place in me about this time. But there is no doubt
that the spring of 1939 marked a watershed in my life. I renounced my
individualistic, antihumanist way of life. I learned the value of solidarity.
But before I embark on the account of this new period, I would like to
make a rapid summing-up of what the ten previous years had brought me.

To divide one's life up into sections is an arbitrary process. But the year
1929 obviously opened a new era for me: from it date the end of my formal
education, my economic emancipation, my departure from home, the
breaking up of old friendships, and my first meeting with Sartre. In 1939
my existence was upset in an equally radical fashion. History took hold
of me, and never let go thereafter; and I threw myself totally and permanently into a life of literature. An epoch was ending. This period which
I have just described took me from youth to maturity. It was dominated
by two preoccupations: to live fully, and to achieve my still theoretical
vocation as a writer—that is to say, to find the point at which literature
could best enter my life.

A full life, above all. Whatever one does, naturally, one is alive; but there is more than one way of unifying the moments in time through which one passes: by subordinating them to some specific action, for instance, or projecting them into a work of art. My own particular enterprise was the development of my life, which I believed lay in my own hands. It had to satisfy two requirements, which in my optimism I treated as identical: it must make me happy, and put the whole world at my disposal. Unhappiness, I thought, would have given me a contaminated view of reality. Since my intimacy with Sartre guaranteed my happiness, I was mainly concerned to cram in as rich a harvest of experience as I could. My discoveries did not follow a straight, clear line, as they had done during my childhood, and I did not get that feeling of steady day-by-day progress; but in their muddled, disorderly way they quite overwhelmed me. I was facing up to real flesh-and-blood *things,* and found unsuspected qualities about them besides those I had anticipated while still shut away in my cage. We have seen how earnestly I pursued my investigations. I long cherished the illusion that *my* rational mind could grasp the absolute truth of things, and mine alone—with a possible exception in favor of Sartre. Obviously I was aware that people existed who could understand a picture or a sonata better than I could; but in a confused way it seemed to me that the moment any object became absorbed into my own life, it took on a specially privileged sort of luminosity. A landscape was virgin of all mortal gaze till *I* had set eyes on it.

Until I was thirty I felt myself to be better informed than the young, and younger than the old, the first being too scatterbrained and the second too staid. In me alone did existence organize itself in truly exemplary fashion, with every little detail profiting from such perfection. As a consequence it was as important for the universe as it was for me that I should know all of it. Enjoyment took second place to this self-perpetuating mandate that was laid upon me. I accepted it willingly enough, but I did not actively seek it out. I preferred to familiarize myself with Stravinsky's *Octet—* which at that time gave me no pleasure—than to listen to the overfamiliar strains of the "Cavatina." There was something rather frivolous about my curiosity. As during my childhood, I fancied that my first analysis of a piece of music, or a town, or a novel, would enable me to grasp its essentials. I preferred diversity to repetition, and would rather see Naples for the first time than pay a return visit to Venice. Up to a point, indeed, this avidity justified itself. In order to understand any specific object, you have to place it in its proper context: the "Cavatina" sends one back to the entire corpus of Beethoven's work, and thence to Haydn, to the origins of music, and even to its ultimate premusical antecedents. This I knew not only through having read Spinoza, but because the whole idea of synthesis, as I have said elsewhere, dominated both Sartre's way of thinking and my own. I had to aim at the universe in its totality if I was to possess the least grain of dust upon it. Contradiction, we have seen, presented no terrors for us. We pruned and trimmed and cut bits off, consigning Murillo and Brahms to the abyss; and yet at the same time we refused to choose, to select, since everything in existence must thereby exist for us.

Granted the infinite immensity of such a task, it is not surprising that I was ceaselessly caught up by various projects: each conquest was one stage further on my journey. This characteristic is not, however, wholly explicable in terms of the vast field I had set myself to cover, since today, though I have given up all hope of exhausting it, I am very little changed in myself, and still full of projects. The idea of contingency terrifies me; by filling the future with demands and appeals and expectations, I inject an element of determinism into the present. Yet, as I have said, I knew moments of respite, when scheming was replaced by contemplation. Such occasions, when the cares of my existence were lost in the fullness of that universal state with which I merged myself, offered priceless recompense.

The working plan which Sartre and I were pursuing for the annexation of the world around us did not fit in with those patterns and taboos established by society. Very well, then; we rejected the latter, on the supposition that man would have to create his world over again from scratch. Colette Audry's politically committed friends reproached her for wasting time in our company; but she would reply, cheerfully: "I'm working on the Man of Tomorrow." We smiled at this joke with her, but it didn't seem to us that farfetched. One day people would shake off their paralysis and build their lives freely, for themselves; such, at all events, was our claim. As a matter of fact we ourselves were generally carried along by the stream of current opinion—witness our winter sports holidays, and our trip to Greece, and our liking for jazz concerts and American films and Gilles and Julien. All the same, we did approach each new situation in the belief that it was up to us to tackle it for ourselves, without adapting ourselves to any model. We had pioneered our own relationship—its freedom, intimacy, and frankness. We had also, rather less successfully, thought up the idea of the "trio." There was an original quality about our way of traveling which stemmed, at least in part, from our carelessness in matters of organization; yet even this blundering attitude reflected our a priori assumption of independence. We toured Greece in our own fashion, and whether in Italy, Spain, or Morocco, we attained our own casual *ad hoc* blend of comfort and frugality, activity and idleness. Above all we created our own attitudes, theories, and ideas, though we refused to be tied down to any one of them, preferring to live in a state of permanent revolution. This was embarrassing for our close friends, who believed themselves to be following our "line" faithfully when we ourselves had already moved on to something else. "What I find exhausting about you two," Bost told us one day, "is that one has to share your opinions *at the same time as you do*." The truth was that the contradictions we piled up between ourselves appealed to us much less when presented by an outsider; so we blasted our friends with irrefutable arguments one day, only to pulverize these same arguments ourselves forty-eight hours later.

These constant switches of opinion, coupled with our close interest in public events, gave us the feeling that we were sticking close to reality. It made us laugh when Jean Wahl or Raymond Aron used to speak, in their writings or conversation, about "getting down to brass tacks" or "facing up to reality"; we were convinced that *we* had a thorough grip on reality already. And yet our life, like that of all *petits bourgeois* intellectuals, was in fact mainly characterized by its *lack* of reality. We had a profession, which we pursued in the correct manner, but which did not detach us from our own verbal universe. On an intellectual plane we were both honest and conscientious: as Sartre said to me one day, we had a genuine sense of the truth (as opposed to the bulk of the bourgeoisie and the entire fashionable world, whose approach to truth is utterly unreal); though this was a step in the right direction, it did not in any way imply that we possessed *a true sense of reality*. Like every bourgeois, we were sheltered from want; like every civil servant, we were guaranteed against insecurity. Furthermore, we had no children, no families, no responsibilities: we were like elves. There was no intelligible connection between the work we did (which was on the whole enjoyable and not in the least exhausting) and the money we got for it, which seemed to lack all proper substance. Since we had no position to keep up, we spent it in a capricious fashion: sometimes it lasted us till the end of the month, sometimes not. Such mishaps did not tell us the truth about our economic position, which we contrived to ignore; we flourished, in fact, like the lilies of the field, and circumstances fostered our illusions. We were bursting with good health, and our bodies objected to no demands we made on them unless we pushed things to extremes: the fact that we could ask a lot in this quarter compensated us for the slenderness of our resources. We had seen as much of the world as any rich person might do—simply because we were quite prepared to sleep out of doors, eat in cheap cafés, and travel on foot. In one sense we earned our pleasures, by paying a price for them which other people would have found intolerable; but the fact that we *could* earn them in this fashion was one of our lucky breaks. We were lucky in other ways, too. I don't know why it was, but our illegitimate relationship was regarded almost as respectfully as though it were a marriage. Monsieur Parodi, the Inspector General, knew all about it, and took it into account in the most considerate fashion when he sent me to Rouen after moving Sartre to Le Havre. One could, it appeared, defy the conventions with impunity. This served to increase our feeling of personal freedom. Such evidence as we had in this field concealed the fact of the world's adversity from us. We had each in our own way been pursuing a dream. I still wanted my life to be "a lovely story that became true as I told it to myself," and touched it up improvingly here and there in the telling. Like my unhappy heroine Chantal, I loaded my life for two or three years with symbols and myths. Afterward I gave up fantasy, though I failed to shake off those puritanical and moralizing tendencies which prevented me from seeing people as they really are. Nor could I break free from my universalist abstractions; I remained riddled with bourgeois idealism and aestheticism. Above all, my emotionally ambivalent obsession with happiness blinded me to political realities. This blindness, however, was not peculiar to me; it was a characteristic and almost universal failing of the period. It is significant that after Munich the staff of *Vendredi* (which was genuinely and unanimously left wing) found itself split and confused over its policy. As Sartre has suggested in *The Reprieve,* we were all living an unreal life centered upon the preservation of the peace. No one possessed the necessary equipment to grasp the over-all pattern of this new world then coming about, which could not be understood at all except in its totality. Nevertheless I carried my rejection of History and its dangers to extraordinary lengths.

In that case, it might be asked, what value is there in the experiences I have now related? Sometimes they seem wrapped in such layers of ignorance and dishonesty that I can feel nothing but contempt for this part of my past life. When I looked at the Umbrian landscape, it gave me a unique and unforgettable moment; but in fact Umbria itself eluded me. What I contemplated were mere tricks of light and shade, what I told myself was the old myth: I failed to see the harshness of the soil, and the joyless lives of the peasants who work it. Doubtless there is such a thing as the truth of appearances—granted, that is, that one recognizes appearances as such, which was not so in my case. I was greedy for knowledge, but let myself be satisfied with false lures. At times I suspected the truth, which is why, I think, I became so hotly involved in the argument which Pagniez and Sartre had as we stood looking over toward the lights of Grand-Couronne. But I contrived to forget such moments.

All the same, any balanced reckoning of these years shows, I think, a vast amount on the credit side: so many books and pictures, so many new towns, new faces, new ideas, such a wealth of feelings and emotions! Not everything was false. If error is marred truth, and truth can only be realized through the development of its imperfect manifestations, it becomes clear that reality can reach us even through a fog of obscurity and muddle. Such culture as I had acquired, inadequate though it might be, was essential for this filtering process. The fact that we had very little idea what to do with the information we amassed did not make its collection any the less valuable per se. What leads me to treat our divagations with a certain degree of indulgence is the fact that not even our firmest convictions ever held us back: the future remained open, truth still enjoyed a reprieve.

In any case, even if we had been more clear-headed than we were, our lives would hardly have differed, since we were less concerned to plot our exact position than to move forward. The very confusion against which I struggled goaded me on irresistibly toward the goal I had long since set myself: the writing of books.

Here, then, was the second of my problems, inextricably bound up with the first. In order to lead a satisfying life I *had* to give pride of place in it to literature. During my adolescence and early maturity my vocation, though sincere, had lacked fulfillment: I had contented myself with the statement that I wanted to be a writer. Now the problem was to find out both *what* I wanted to write about, and to what extent I could actually do so: action was called for. This took me some time. Long ago I had sworn to complete my great, all-revealing work at the age of twenty-two;

yet when I embarked upon the first of my published novels, *She Came to Stay,* I was already thirty. In the family and among my childhood friends the whisper went around that I was a *fruit sec;* my father remarked irritably that if I had something inside me, why couldn't I hurry up and get it out? But I wasn't impatient myself. I knew that creating a first book out of nothing—or at least entirely from one's own resources—and making it stand up against anything, was a task that, exceptional luck apart, demanded endless time and labor, a long process of trial and error. Writing, I told myself, is a profession that can only be learned by writing. All the same, ten years is a long time, and during that period I covered reams of paper with my handwriting. I do not believe that my lack of experience can suffice to explain so prolonged a failure: I was hardly more professional when I began writing *She Came to Stay.* Must I, then, admit that whereas previously I had nothing to say, I had now "found a subject"? But the world is always there around one: what does that word "nothing" *mean* then? How, why, and in what circumstances does a situation present itself to the writer as "something to say"?

Literature is born when something in life goes slightly adrift. In order to write—as Blanchot showed so well in the paradoxical case of Aytré— the first essential condition is that *reality should no longer be taken for granted*; only then can one both perceive it, and make others do so. When I struggled free of the boredom and slavery of my childhood years, I was overwhelmed, stunned, blinded with sheer happiness. How could I ever have found in this blissful condition the urge to escape from it? My schemes of work remained futile dreams till the day came when that happiness was threatened, and I rediscovered a certain kind of solitude in anxiety. The unfortunate episode of the trio did much more than supply me with a subject for a novel; it enabled me to deal with it. (Everything that I subsequently wrote confirms the importance of this "revised perspective" idea. There are many journeys and countries which meant a great deal to me, but about which I scarcely bothered to write, so closely did I identify myself with them. In Portugal I found myself investigating both the pleasures and the more disgraceful aspects of the tourist industry: I threw light on many tricks of the trade, and felt the impulse to set my findings down on paper. There was a wide gap between my idea of America and actual conditions there; this discrepancy gave me the impulse to recount my experiences in that country. Finally China confronted me with a number of problems and gave me something of a bad conscience: my reaction was an attempt to set down what I had seen. But Italy, Spain, Greece, Morocco, and many other countries I plunged into without a second thought; when I left them I had no reason to write about them, nothing to report concerning them—and so I remained silent.)

Despite my helpless position and the setbacks I faced, I still remained convinced that one day I would write books that someone would publish. They would, I thought, be novels and nothing else: in my opinion this medium surpassed all others, so much so that when Sartre started writing notes and news items for the *N.R.F.* and *Europe,* I felt he was frittering

away his talents. I passionately wanted the public to like my work; therefore like George Eliot, who had become identified in my mind with Maggie
Tulliver, I would myself become an imaginary character, endowed with
beauty, desirability, and a sort of shimmering transparent loveliness. It
was this metamorphosis that my ambition sought. I was alive, and still
am, to reflections everywhere, in windows, rippling over water, and would
watch them for minutes on end, in a state of charmed fascination. I
dreamed of splitting into two selves, and of having a shadowy alter ego that
would pierce and haunt people's hearts. It would have been no good if
this phantom had had overt connections with a person of flesh and blood;
anonymity would have suited me perfectly. It was only in 1938, as I have
said, that for a brief moment I wanted to become well known—simply
in order to make the acquaintance of some new people myself.

The way in which my universe altered was somewhat different; but
before discussing this there are one or two observations I would like to
make. I know that when certain critics read this autobiography they will
point out, triumphantly, that it flatly contradicts my thesis in *The Second
Sex*, a suggestion they have already made with regard to *Memoirs of a
Dutiful Daughter*. The fact is that they have failed to grasp the point of
The Second Sex, and probably even refer to it without having read it.
Have I ever written that women were the same as men? Have I ever
claimed that I, personally, was not a woman? On the contrary, my main
purpose has been to isolate and identify my own particular brand of
femininity. I received a young lady's education, and when my studies were
finished, my position was still that of any woman in a society where the
sexes are divided into two embattled castes. In a great many ways I reacted
like the woman I was: what distinguishes my thesis from the traditional
one is that, as far as I am concerned, femininity is neither a natural nor
an innate entity, but rather a condition brought about by society, on the
basis of certain physiological characteristics. For reasons which I have set
forth in some detail in *The Second Sex*, women experience a greater need
for a stable firmament above their heads than men do; they are not endowed
with the temper that makes explorers, in the sense that Freud used the
word. They are averse to questioning the fundamental premises of existence,
or to organizing and controlling the world. Therefore it suited me to live
with a man whom I regarded as my superior; my ambitions, though stubbornly held, were nevertheless timid; and though public affairs might
interest me, I could not regard them as my personal concern. Yet as I have
made clear, I attached small importance to the actual conditions of my
life: nothing, I believed, could impede my will. I did not deny my femininity, any more than I took it for granted: I simply ignored it. I had the
same freedoms and responsibilities as men did. I was spared the curse
that weighs upon most women, that of dependence—and whether they are
afflicted by it, adapt themselves to it, or treat it as a subject for self-con-
gratulation, in the last resort it still remains a curse; since I wrote *The
Second Sex* my conviction on this point has merely been strengthened. To
earn one's living is not an end in itself, but it is the only way to achieve

securely based inner independence. It moves me to recall my arrival in
Marseille precisely because I felt, standing at the top of that high flight
of steps, just how great a strength I derived from my chosen profession,
and even from the very obstacles which it obliged me to surmount. Material self-sufficiency enables one to realize oneself fully as an individual;
with this achievement behind me I was able to reject a life of moral
parasitism and all the dangerous conveniences it had to offer. On the
other hand, neither Sartre nor any of my other male friends ever showed
a superiority complex where I was concerned; so it never occurred to me
that I was in a disadvantageous position. Today I know that the first thing
I have to say if I want to describe myself is that I am a woman; but my
feminine status has been for me neither an embarrassment nor an alibi.
In any case, it is a given condition of my life, not an explanation of it.

It is precisely this kind of detailed explanation which I most mistrust.
I have attempted to set out the facts in as frank a way as possible, neither
simplifying their ambiguities nor swaddling them in false syntheses, but
offering them for the reader's own interpretation. Nevertheless, I reject
the crude sort of yardstick against which our more elementary psychoanalysts will in all likelihood attempt to measure them: no doubt it will
be asserted that Sartre was a substitute father figure for me, and that Olga
took the place of the child I never had. In the eyes of such doctrinaires,
adult relationships are nonexistent: they take no note of that dialectic
process which from childhood to maturity—starting with roots the deep
importance of which I am very far from misconceiving—works a slow
transformation upon one's emotional ties with other people. It preserves
them, but achieves this preservation through a by-passing process which
incapsulates the object of one's feelings, and lets one re-examine it afresh.
Certainly my attachment to Sartre could, in one sense, be traced back to
my childhood; but it also was a result of the sort of person *he* was.
Doubtless a prior condition of my taking an interest in Olga was the fact
that I was free to do so, that my need to exert myself on another person's
behalf had not yet been assuaged; but it was Olga's personality that gave
our friendship its genuine and individual characteristics. With these reservations, I still believe to this day in the theory of the "transcendental ego."
The self [*moi*] has only a probable objectivity, and anyone saying "I" only
grasps the outer edge of it; an outsider can get a clearer and more accurate
picture. Let me repeat that this personal account is not offered in any
sense as an "explanation." Indeed, one of my main reasons for undertaking
it is my realization that self-knowledge is impossible, and the best one can
hope for is self-revelation.

Part 2

THE annoying thing about settling down to a lengthy, carefully constructed piece of writing is that long before finishing it one is no longer in step with it: the here-and-now cannot affect its development. I began *She Came to Stay* in October, 1938, and ended it in the late spring of 1941. During the intervening period events and characters modified one another, the final chapters led me to revise the opening ones, and each episode was revised in the light of the narrative as a whole. These modifications, however, were made to satisfy the book's internal requirements, and did not reflect my own personal development; any facts I borrowed from real life were purely subordinate. The novel had been conceived and executed to express a period of my past life which I was now leaving behind me; it was precisely because of the divergence between my new self and the one I drew in those pages that the truth *as I now saw it* had no place there. There were weeks, months on end when I was incapable of working; but once I sat down to my manuscript my mind jumped back into the past, resuscitating a vanished world. When I look through those printed pages I can find no hint of the days I spent writing them—the color of the morning and the evening sky, the trembling bred of fear or antici- pation: all is gone.

But while I was so laboriously conjuring this novel from the void, the weather broke, the sun moved on, and I became a different person. Hitherto my sole concern had been to enrich my personal life and learn the art of converting it into words. Little by little I had abandoned the quasi solipsism and illusory autonomy I cherished as a girl of twenty; though I had come to recognize the fact of other people's existence, it was still my individual relationships with separate people that mattered most to me, and I still yearned fiercely for happiness. Then, suddenly, History burst over me, and I dissolved into fragments. I woke to find myself scattered over the four quarters of the globe, linked by every nerve in me to each and every other individual. All my ideas and values were turned upside down; even the pursuit of happiness lost its importance. In September, 1939, I wrote: "For me, happiness was, above all, a privileged way of apprehending the world; if the world changes to such a degree that it can no longer be apprehended in this fashion, then happiness is no longer of any value." Again, in January, 1941, I wrote: "How shortsighted my old idea of happiness now seems! It dominated ten whole years of my life, but I think I am almost completely rid of it now." In actuality I never discarded it altogether. Later, when I ceased to regard my life as an autonomous and self-sufficient project, I was obliged to rediscover my links with a universe the very face of which I had forgotten. It is this metamorphosis that I now propose to relate.

Chapter 6

DURING THE EARLY SUMMER OF 1939 I HAD NOT yet wholly given up hope. An obstinate voice still whispered inside my head: "It can't happen to me; not a war, not to me." Hitler would never dare to attack Poland; the Tripartite Agreement would finally be ratified, and this would scare him off. I was still busy working out plans for a peaceful holiday. This was not exactly the right time to explore the U.S.S.R. with Intourist's assistance, as we had originally planned. However, if the international situation was sorted out all right, we could go for a trip to Portugal. Sartre agreed to this, adding, however, that the situation almost certainly would *not* be "sorted out all right." He was only warning me for my own good, he said: it was better to face the facts. Otherwise when the storm broke I would not be prepared to weather it, and would go under. But how, I asked myself, does one prepare to face a horror of this sort? Any attempt to reduce it to familiar proportions would be a waste of time and drain my energies pointlessly. Whatever happened, I should have to improvise; so I deliberately clamped down on my imagination.

Madame Lemaire had invited us to spend the first part of August with her in her villa at Juan-les-Pins. On July 15 I set off alone for Provence, my rucksack on my back. I went by way of Mont Ventoux, the Lure hills, the Basses-Alpes, Queyras Valley, and the Alpes-Maritimes: it was the most delightful of all my walking tours. Fernando, who was in Nice with Stépha, had the idea of going along with me for a few days. He joined me at Puget-Théniers, wearing magnificent studded walking shoes. The first day we tramped cheerfully for eight hours at a stretch over those reddish hills. The next day we did a nine-hour stint over the mountains, from Guillaume to Saint-Etienne-de-Tiné. Fernando retired to bed that evening shivering feverishly. The following morning I went out on a long climbing expedition without him, and when I got back in the evening, he had decided to go back to Nice. I went on my way without him. I climbed to a height of some nine thousand feet up above Saint-Véran, clambering over deserted spurs where I startled a herd of chamois. When I was moving close to the

Italian frontier I ran into some soldiers on maneuvers, and twice had my
papers examined, somewhat suspiciously, by their officers. Larche, which
I reached one evening after a particularly long day's trek, was literally
occupied by these troops, and to find a bed was an impossibility. In the
end I slept with the local policeman's wife, a small, neat, elderly woman.
I had not a thought in my head apart from flowers and beasts and stony
tracks and wide horizons, the pleasurable sensation of possessing legs and
lungs and a stomach, and the determination to break some of my own
records.

In Marseille I found Sartre and Bost, the latter being on leave. Both
considered war inevitable. The Germans were already infiltrating into
Danzig; there was no question of Hitler giving up his plans, nor of
England going back on her undertakings with regard to Poland. In any
case, the last thing Sartre wanted was another Munich. But it was with
a far from elated heart that he contemplated the prospect of mobilization.
We went off for a bouillabaisse lunch at Martigues; the sun was blazing
down on the nets and their owners' gaily painted boats. We sat down at
the water's edge on large, sharp-groined boulders: not very comfortable,
but Sartre throve on discomfort. We sat with our faces turned up to the
blue of the sky, nonchalantly musing out loud. Was it preferable to come
back from the front blinded, or with your face bashed in? without arms,
or without legs? Would Paris be bombed? Would they use poison gas?
Two days later Bost left us, and we spent another two or three days in
Marseille. One afternoon we were sitting on the pavement outside the
Brûleur de Loups, down at the Old Port, when Nizan strolled past,
carrying an enormous India-rubber swan under one arm. He was sailing
for Corsica that evening with his wife and children, where he was to join
Laurent Casanova. He had a drink with us and declared, confidentially
yet triumphantly, that the Tripartite Agreement was in the process of ratifi-
cation. Normally the most reserved of men, he now spoke in a voice of
positively feverish jubilation. "Germany will be on her knees!" he asserted.
His views on the situation were very different from those that appeared
in *Ce Soir;* he obviously was privy to secrets in high places, and his optimism
gave us a great feeling of reassurance. We wished one another a peaceful and
pleasant holiday, and then he left us, his swan under his arm. We never
saw him again.

Madame Lemaire's father had built the villa known as Puerta del Sol
at a time when this stretch of coast was still deserted. The house was surrounded with a big garden and pine grove, which ran right down to the
sea, at the far end of the Plage du Provençal. We ate our breakfast out
on the terrace, watching the water-skiers skimming over the blue surface
of the bay, speedboats roaring ahead. One morning we watched a water-
slalom display and found it most amusing. While Sartre wrote, I read:
at that period I had little notion of how to blend work and pleasure.
About midday we would go down to the beach, where Sartre was giving
me swimming lessons. I managed to keep afloat, but could never progress
more than ten yards or so. Sartre could do half a mile and more; the only

trouble was that when he found himself alone in open water, he became convinced that an enormous octopus was about to emerge from the depths and drag him down, with the result that he would swim back to terra firma at a fast crawl. I liked to get back to the shade of the villa about two o'clock: all the shutters were closed for the afternoon. We used to eat *salade niçoise* and cold fish, and occasionally a dish of garlic mayonnaise, which put us to sleep. There were always guests dropping in for lunch and dinner; the Lemaire children brought their friends along, and they had a large number of them. Marco, too, was staying at Puerta del Sol. He had just, again, failed the audition that would surely have set him on the road to the Opéra; he was smarting from fresh disappointments in love; and the threat of war scared him stiff. He was going bald and fleshy and ugly, too, so his temper was somewhat sour. He got it into his head that Madame Lemaire and Sartre and I were criticizing him behind his back, so he took to eavesdropping on our conversations. Once we caught him behind the door, and another time lurking under a window. He apologized, with his old hearty laugh, but now it sounded cracked and false. He went around seeking allies and fomenting intrigues. Some members of the household were at loggerheads with each other, and as usual we took a passionate interest in their problems; we discussed them with Madame Lemaire, constructing hypotheses and distributing censure with eager partiality. Marco used to amuse himself by sowing discord between us, for the sheer pleasure of maliciously annoying everyone, indiscriminately. He gave Jacqueline Lemaire a completely false account of various disobliging things that Sartre was supposed to have said about her; she taxed Sartre with this, and a fine hassle developed. Sartre often flew off the handle in a harmless sort of way, but I have seldom seen him lose his temper properly, and when he did his face was by no means a pleasant sight. He could on such occasions flay his adversary alive with a few well-chosen words, and Marco actually wept. To set the seal on our reconciliation he took us and Madame Lemaire to Cannes to make a round of the transvestite *boîtes*. Yet, despite all this, the fact that I was not working made the days seem rather slow and idle to me. There were times when the blue sky and the blue sea got altogether too much for me. Like Sartre, I had the feeling that something was lurking beneath the surface of the water—not an octopus, but some sort of poison. This sunlit calm was deceptive: the whole thing was liable to be suddenly ripped apart.

And so it turned out; everything *was* ripped apart. One morning we opened our papers and read the news of the German-Soviet treaty. This came as a terrible blow. Stalin was leaving Hitler free to attack Europe: there was no hope whatsoever of peace now. It was this self-evident fact which struck home to us first; but other thoughts followed. Though we had plenty of reservations about goings-on inside the U.S.S.R., we nevertheless had believed hitherto that the Soviet Government served the cause of world revolution. This treaty proved, in the most brutal way, that Colette Audry and the Trotskyites and every left-wing opposition group were right after all: that Russia had become an imperialist power like any other, obstinately pursuing her own selfish interests. Stalin didn't give a damn for the proletariat of Europe. Through the dark gathering clouds one great gleam of hope had shone till now; but the morning's news had extinguished it. Night was falling over the earth, and entering our very bones.

Sartre and I wanted to spend a few days alone together, so we left Juan-les-Pins. There was no point in going straight back to Paris, so we went off for a trip into the Pyrenees. We felt a twinge of distress when we said goodbye to Madame Lemaire and even to Marco: what would happen before we all met again? The train from Juan to Carcassonne was packed with troops summoned back from leave, and who were already claiming the privileges of seasoned veterans. "We'll all be killed soon enough," they said, as they moved in on the reserved seats. I found the ramparts of Carcassonne hideously ugly, but the tiny streets of the city delighted me. We sat drinking white wine under the arbor of a deserted restaurant garden, talking about the war and what would happen after the war, glad that we could face up to this disaster together. We took bus trips, visited little towns nearby, wandered through churches and cloisters. At Montlouis it was raining, and we saw the first mobilization posters. We decided to go back to Paris, but spent one more day in Foix first. At the Hôtel de la Barbacane we treated ourselves to a really enormous lunch—hors-d'oeuvre, trout, *cassoulet, foie gras,* cheese, and fruit, together with a local wine—and Sartre told me how, in the third volume of *Roads to Freedom,* Brunet, disgusted by the German-Soviet pact, would resign from the Communist Party and go to seek help from Mathieu: an essential reversal, he said, of the situation described in the first volume. Afterward we went for a walk along the bank of a clear-flowing river, telling each other that whatever happened this countryside, with its quiet little town, would remain untouched by the war, and we would find both of them just as they had been, afterward. This gave us something to hang on to. We said that the die was cast, and our participation in this war already an established fact; we strolled along nonchalantly, trying to convince ourselves that the calmness of our gestures and the serenity of the surrounding landscape corresponded to an equally tranquil state of mind. But this pretense lasted only a little while. At half past seven that evening we caught a train to Toulouse, where we should have connected immediately with the Paris express. But the express was crammed full, and we spent two and a half hours in a dark and crowded station, lit only by a few feebly glowing violet lamps. The darkness and that uneasy crowd heralded a cataclysm: I could no longer avoid the truth, it pierced to my very marrow. Another express drew in, and the crowd surged aboard; by dint of prompt action and considerable shoving we managed to get a couple of corner seats.

Since it was August, everything in Paris was closed—restaurants theaters, shops, and all. None of our friends had come back yet. Olga was at Beuzeville, Bost in barracks at Amiens, Pagniez in the country with his wife's family, my sister at La Grillère with my parents, and Nizan in Corsica. It was Nizan especially that we wanted to talk to; we couldn't understand how his intelligence had proved so faulty. He had told us of important people on *Ce Soir* who disliked him; but surely these enmities should have gone by the board in so serious a situation? How had he reacted to the news? Neither in his private nor in his more militant public life was he the sort of man to swallow any affront: for him Communism meant something that was in direct conflict with this treaty.

We thought about him a lot, and the fate of Communists generally was very much in our minds: some of the more militant Party members had been arrested, and both *L'Humanité* and *Ce Soir* had been banned. It was a paradoxical and infuriating situation, since it was the French Communists who had been in the spearhead of the attack against Fascism. There were a lot of other things that annoyed us, both in the papers and in conversations we overheard at café tables. The press had been perfectly justified in its long-standing denunciations of what it called the Fifth Column: beyond any doubt this constituted a very real danger. All the same, we guessed that this might serve as the excuse for an outbreak of spy hysteria worse than anything in the 1914–18 war. The mixture of braggadocio and cowardice, hoplessness and panic, that we smelled in the air made us feel highly uneasy.

The hours passed slowly. There was nothing for us to do, and we did nothing, except traipse through the blank streets and seize every edition of the daily papers. In the evening we would go to the cinema and see the latest American films; among others we saw Ford's masterpiece *Stagecoach,* which revived in modern idiom everything we had enjoyed about the old-style Westerns. But this was a brief respite; we would emerge from the auditorium on to the Champs Elysées and grab the late-night final edition of *Paris-Soir.* As we fell asleep each night our last question would be: "What will happen tomorrow?" And when we awoke it was to the same mood of agonized anxiety. Why had we been landed in this position? We were scarcely over thirty, our lives were beginning to take shape, and now, brutally, this existence was snatched from us. Would we get it back? And if so, at what cost? That peaceful afternoon near Foix had been a mere lull before the storm; but we were too firmly attached to too many things, and could not give them up as easily as all that. Each of us kept his alarm and inner struggle to himself, but neither was deceived by the other's outward appearance of calm. I recalled Sartre's furious outbursts of temper during his period of military service, the hatred he felt for useless discipline and the sheer waste of time. Today, on the contrary, he refrained from any display of anger, even of bitterness; yet I knew that though he might be more capable of self-control than the next man, the effort cost him more, too. He had paid a pretty price for submitting to the Age of Reason's categorical imperatives. Now he accepted the necessity of his joining up stoically, without complaint; but internally he was stretched to the breaking point.

We had no doubt that war was imminent. French foreign correspondents in Berlin claimed that Hitler, having announced the German-Soviet pact on Friday, originally intended to invade Poland at 5 A.M. on Saturday morning, but had missed his opportunity somehow, and that this was the reason why he had summoned Henderson to Berchtesgaden. Perhaps he would decide to negotiate with the Polish government, using Italy as an intermediary. Sartre attached no importance to such rumors. On the other hand, he, like everyone else, was convinced that the war would not last long, and that the democracies would win it. The papers recalled Schacht's remark: "In a pinch one may end a war with bread-rationing, but never begin one." Germany was short of food, steel, gasoline, indeed of everything. The German populace had no wish to gegt themselves wiped out; they couldn't stand a war; the Reich would collapse. Seen in this perspective, the war began to make some sense. We met Fernando at the Dôme, and listened to the discussions of pro-Communists at the Flore. If the U.S.S.R. *was* letting Germany unleash this war, they asserted, that was because the Russian government was anticipating a world revolution. This justification of the treaty seemed to us the merest moonshine; but at least we hoped that the destruction of Fascism would bring about an upsurge of socialism both in France and all over Europe. This was why Sartre did not rebel against his fate, though he had to put in some doggedly persistent work on himself to achieve this condition of resignation.

During the latter half of August I met Merleau-Ponty, and acquainted him with our present attitude, i.e., that all things considered this was was an acceptable means of putting an end to a number of scandalous abominations. He asked me, with a touch of irony, why I welcomed it so calmly now, when only a year before I had dreaded it. What made him smile, I think, was the fire with which I defended these brand-new convictions of mine; but—as so often happened—my reversal of attitude coincided with nearly everybody else's. During the last twelve months the idea of war had gradually imposed itself upon most of those who had still believed they could reject it at the time of Munich. Speaking for myself, the main reason why I accepted the war was because I knew it to be inevitable, and decided, in order to preserve my peace of mind, to subdue my own inclinations rather than fight fate. As long as it remained possible, right up to May 11, 1940, I did my best to put up with this Cartesian precept. Besides, I was far less calm than I pretended: I was afraid. Not for my own skin, though: I never for one moment thought of fleeing from Paris. It was Sartre I was afraid for. He assured me he would remain stuck in the rear on some airfield or other, and was far more scared of boredom than actual danger; but I only half believed him. Both of us, though, were anxious about Bost. There is no more likely cannon fodder than your buck private infantryman, and Bost was only twenty-one. People said that this war would be different from its predecessors: maybe. We would very much have liked to know in advance both how it would turn out and what was going to happen *after* it. But as long as we were together, and talking, our curiosity, coupled with a kind of feverish excitement, outweighed the misery of approaching separation.

Then one morning it happened. It was now, in an agony of loneliness, that I began to keep a diary. Its entries strike me as more vivid and accurate than any narrative I could piece together out of them, so I give them here, omitting only certain boring or overintimate details, and a mass of tedious repetition.

September 1

10 A.M.: the papers print Hitler's demands, without comment. The disturbing nature of the news is not overemphasized, but no one any longer takes a hopeful line, either. I go to the Dôme, unsettled and at loose ends. Not many people there. Have hardly ordered a coffee before a waiter announces: "They've declared war on Poland." A customer inside has a copy of *Paris-Midi*. Others make a rush for him, and also for nearby newsstands, but *Paris-Midi* hasn't come in. I get up and go back to my hotel. People in the street don't know anything yet, they're still as cheerful as they were a while ago. One or two people along the Avenue du Maine are carrying copies of *Paris-Midi,* and passers-by stop them to read the headlines. I find Sartre, and travel out to Passy with him, where he has to see his parents. Wait for him in the Viaduct Café below the Métro. Passy absolutely deserted, nobody about in the streets, but along the *quai* an endless procession of cars crammed with luggage and children—I even noticed some motorcycles and sidecars. I am incapable of thought, absolutely exhausted. Sartre comes back. Mobilization has been ordered. The papers announce that it will take place starting tomorrow, which gives us a bit of time. Back to the hotel to hunt for the kit bag and army boots from the cellar. Sartre afraid of getting to the assembly center late, so we take a taxi to the Place Hébert, a small square near the Porte de la Chapelle. It is deserted. In the middle stands a post with a placard on it that reads ASSEMBLY CENTER NO. 4, and there are a couple of policemen standing by it. Various posters have just been stuck up on the wall: an "urgent appeal" to the people of Paris (this one has red, white, and blue stripes across it), and the rather less garish Mobilization Decree, operative from 0001 hours September 2. Sartre goes up to the policemen and shows them his mobilization instructions: he has to report in Nancy. "Turn up at 0001 hours if you feel like it," says the gendarme, "but don't expect us to put on a special train just for you." We walk back to the Flore: Sonia and Agnès Capri there, Sonia looking marvelous, hair done up in a red silk handkerchief, and Agnès very springlike, wearing a shepherdess hat with a huge white ribbon. A hard-faced woman sobbing to herself. One waiter observes that it looks like the real thing this time. But people still seem cheerful. I've given up trying to think altogether, but I've still got a headache. There's a gorgeous moon rising above Saint-Germain-des-Prés, making it look like a country church. Everywhere, underlying everything, a feeling of unfathomable horror. You can't foresee anything, or imagine what it will be like, or grasp the situation at any point.

Though I'm so desperately tired I get scared at night. I can't sleep for the moonlight flooding into my room. A sudden loud shout brings me to the window. It was a woman screaming. People gather, clatter of feet on the sidewalk, gleam of a flashlight. Then I fall asleep.

September 2

The alarm clock goes off at 3 A.M. We walk down to the Dôme: night air very mild. Both the Dôme and the Rotonde are feebly lit, and the Dôme is noisy, packed with figures in uniform. Out on the *terrasse* two tarts are sitting with their arms around a couple of officers. One of the tarts is singing, as though from sheer habit. The officers take no notice of them. Loud shouts and laughter from inside. We take a taxi to the Place Hébert through this mild and empty night. Find the square bathed in moonlight, but deserted except for the two gendarmes. It's like something out of a Kafka novel: Sartre's decisive action looks completely free and voluntary, yet obeys the dictates of an inflexible and self-generated compulsion that operates quite independently of human will. The gendarmes greet him with a friendly but indifferent air. "Go to the Gare de l'Est," they tell him, as though addressing a lunatic. We march over the big iron bridges spanning the tracks: the sky is turning red, a lovely sight. The station is deserted. There's a train at 6:24, but we decide that Sartre will catch the 7:50. We sit down outside a café, and Sartre repeats that as a meteorologist he won't be in any danger. We talk a little longer in the station, across a barrier. Then he's gone. I walk back to Montparnasse. A wonderful autumn morning: the fresh smell of carrots and cabbages along the Boulevard Sébastopol . . .

When I come out of the cinema at five o'clock the air is heavy and there's an extraordinary silence in the streets. *L'Intransigeant* hints at unspecified diplomatic maneuvers, says Poland is resisting and the Reich is losing its nerve: an instant's joyless hope, more distressing than mere apathy. On the Avenue de l'Opéra people are queuing up for gas masks. Tchuntz's bookshop on the Boulevard Montparnasse has a handwritten notice stuck up in its window: "French family. One son called up in 1914, etc. Subject to ninth-day mobilization."

I go up to see Fernando. He welcomes me with a great display of pathos. "Ehrenburg's a finished man," he says. "Doesn't it break your heart?" Ehrenburg, it seems, can't eat or sleep any more because of the German-Soviet pact; he's even toying with the idea of suicide! This leaves me fairly unmoved. We go out for dinner to the Breton *crêperie* on the Rue Montparnasse. Blacked-out streets, very dark. Just make out the big sign SHELTER on the wall opposite, tarts lounging along the sidewalk, one or two blue-tinted lights. The *crêperie* is short of supplies: no bread or flour. I eat very little. Tonight the café are shutting at 11 P.M., and the night clubs not opening at all. Find the idea of going back to my room unbearable, so go and sleep at Fernando's place—on the downstairs couch, after putting a sheet on it. Take a long time dropping off, but eventually do so.

September 3

Awake at 8:30 to find it raining. My first thought: "It's really true, then." I'm not exactly miserable or unhappy, and I can't discern any feeling of resentment inside *me*: it's the world outside that's so horrible. Someone turns on the radio. No reply to the Final Notes from France and England; fighting still going on in Poland. Unthinkable prospect: another day after this, and another, and another—much worse, too, for then *we* shall be fighting. Only stopped from crying by the feeling that there would be just as many tears left to shed afterward.

I read Gide's *Journal*. Time passes slowly. Eleven o'clock brings news of last-minute efforts in Berlin. The result will be known today. Hope is nonexistent. I can't conceive the joy I would feel if someone told me, "There isn't going to be any war"; perhaps I wouldn't feel anything.

Phone call from Gégé, I go over to see her on foot. This cuts actual distances everywhere considerably: to go half a mile or so still takes about ten minutes of one's time. The police have all got magnificent new tin helmets, and carry their gas masks slung in little snuff-colored satchels. Some civilians have got the same equipment. Many Métro stations are shut and barricaded, with notices announcing the nearest one available. Car headlights, painted blue, look like large precious stones. I have lunch at the Dôme with Pardo [Gégé's second husband, whom she had married after her first marriage was annulled], Gégé herself, and an Englishman who has very striking blue eyes. Pardo takes a bet, against Gégé and me, that there won't be a war, and the Englishman agrees with him. All the same, there's a rumor going around that England has declared war already. Gégé tells us about her trip from Limoges back to Paris: all the way an endless stream of taxis and cars going in the opposite direction, piled high with bedding. Very few cars in the vicinity of Paris: nothing but unaccompanied men, mobilized reservists. Workmen busy blacking out the windows of the Dôme with thick blue curtains. Then the sudden announcemeant at 3:30 in *Paris-Soir*: "Great Britain declared war at 11 A.M. France to follow suit at five this afternoon." Despite everything, the shock is still tremendous . . .

A scuffle on the Place Montparnasse. Some woman mistook a man for a foreigner, and he slapped her face. Bystanders protested, and a military policeman grabbed the man by his hair. Fresh objections from the crowd. Policeman seemed somewhat confused and told people to move along. By and large they seemed to blame the atmosphere of hosility on the "foreigner."

This evening, with Gégé, at the Flore. People still saying they don't believe in the war, but they look pretty panic-stricken all the same. A man who works for Hachette says all his trucks have been requisitioned and the Métro bookstalls emptied out on the sidewalk, just like that. We walk back along the Rue de Rennes: lovely effect of violet or blue headlights in the darkness. At the Dôme we find a policeman arguing with the manager, who finally has extra-thick blue curtains put over the windows. I catch a glimpse of Pozner, in uniform, and the Hungarian. At eleven o'clock they clear the café. People hang around on the pavement; nobody wants to go home. I spend the night at Gégé's place. Pardo gives me a pill, and I am able to sleep.

September 4

I ring up the Lycée Molière from the post office; you have to show your identity card before they let you use the phone. Difficult to find a taxi; you have to watch for someone getting out of one. Finally find one at the Gare Montparnasse. The headmistress personally takes my measurements and gives me a small gas mask, explaining how to use it. I leave with my little cylinder slung from one shoulder. Pick up Gégé at the Gare Saint-Lazare and go home by Métro. Vast queues; trains going straight through lots of stations; all most odd. I get out at Solférino and go to the Flore to write letters. Pardo and his friend from Hachette turn up. He tells me the story of the *"volontaires de la mort."* This is something thought up by Péricart, the *"Debout les morts!"* man: he's launched an appeal to all the cripples, and those suffering from incurable diseases who'd have nothing to lose if they died anyway, begging them to volunteer to serve their country. He quotes us one of the letters Péricart has received: "I am thirty-two years old, one-eyed and one-armed. I thought my life had lost all purpose. But by restoring that word 'service' to me, in all its splendor, you have made me live again." The author of this letter wants to see the half-witted enrolled as well. Meanwhile the manager announces that the Flore will be closed tomorrow. Too bad; it was a nice little refuge. Amusing to see people one knows in uniform: at the Flore there was André Breton dressed as an officer; at the Dôme, Mané Katz in a private's uniform of the other war.

The Hungarian sits down opposite me and stammers out his formal intention of joining the armed forces. When I ask why, he just gestures vaguely. A half-drunken airman, well around the bend by the look of him, says in lofty tones: "Sir, let me offer you a drink." The two of them drink *fines* and discuss the Foreign Legion; the Hungarian declares he wouldn't care to be mixed up with such riffraff. The airman moves on to the subject of raids. No, he says, they won't use poison gas, but liquid-air bombs, yes; best to get down in a shelter. Everyone talking about the likelihood of a night alert; Paris has never been so dark. Go back to sleep at the Pardos' place again.

In the middle of the night Gégé comes into my room: the sirens have gone off. We peer out of the window, and see people running for the shelters. It's a fine starlit night. We go down as far as the concierge's cubbyhole and find that the concierge has got his gas mask on already. Then back upstairs again: almost certainly a false alarm. The time: 4 A.M. I go back to sleep again till seven, when the all-clear wakes me. People come up out of the shelters again; two women in flowered housecoats wear their underwear wrapped round their heads, doubtless as makeshift gas masks. A man rides past on a bicycle, mask slung over his shoulder, shouting, "Ah! The bastards!"

September 5

In the papers it says "contact is being developed at various points along the front." How clean and antiseptic that sounds! Pardo and Gégé pack their bags. A little script girl they're taking with them shows up, very tousled, saying that women aren't making up or bothering about their hair any more. Something in this. She tells us there's been a frightful rail accident a couple of days ago at Les Aubrais, with a hundred and twenty dead. Also that countless cars are breaking down on every major road.

Letters from Sartre, mailed in Nancy late on September 2. Kisling turns up at the Dôme in uniform, is hailed by Fujita's ex-wife Fernande Barrey with the remark: "You poor old thing, you: imagine having to put that stuff on *again.*" Tabouis still staunchly optimistic in *L'Oeuvre*: there won't be a war after all.

Decree promulgated concerning Germans residing in France: they're all to be shoved into concentration camps.

Notice stuck up in all Uniprix shops: "French firm; French directors; French capital."

The Flore is shut, so I sit out on the *terrasse* at the Deux Magots and read Gide's *Journal* for 1914; plentiful analogies with the present situation. Agnès Capri, Sonia, and her dark-haired girl friend are at the next table, all intent on getting out of Paris as soon as possible. Agnès is thinking of going to New York. Everyone talks in a nervous way about last night's alert. German reconnaissance aircraft are supposed to have crossed the frontier. All this is singularly lacking in interest: hardly even a touch of the picturesque about it. We don't feel the war's really begun yet. We're wait-ing—but for what? The horrors of the first battle? For the moment, the whole business looks farcical, with self-important citizens lugging gas masks around and all the café windows blacked out. The communiqués tell us nothing: "Military operations proceeding normally." Has anyone been killed yet?

Slowly, imperceptibly, from dawn to dusk our days move nearer the edge of disaster. The Place Saint-Germain-des-Prés is empty and dead in the sunlight. Men in dungarees are filling sandbags. One fellow is playing a little flute, and a hawker is selling peanuts.

I dine with the Hungarian, on a *terrasse* along the Boulevard Montpar-nasse. Drink a lot of red wine, and follow it up with aquavit at the Vikings' Bar, which now has the air of a mortuary. The Hungarian explains that he's volunteering for the services because he can neither go back to Hungary nor keep any sort of civilian status in France. He starts confiding in me about his sexual peculiarities, and in the end becomes a frightful bore, so I go back home. Tarts now wear gas masks on their beat.

Am awakened by explosions, and dash out to the landing. "That's machine-gun fire!" someone exclaims. The sirens sounded an hour earlier. I get dressed and go down, but no one hears anything else, so I return to bed.

September 6

I read the papers at the Trois Mousquetaires. No more crossword puzzles in *Marianne*: all amusements of this sort have been banned for fear of their being used to pass on coded information. Then suddenly the steel shutters clang down and people hurry out: the sirens have gone off. Little groups hang about in the street, very calm and collected. I go back to the hotel. The proprietress continues her washing up, while I read Gide in my room, and go on with him at the Dôme after the all-clear. According to *Paris-Midi* there haven't been any proper battles on our front yet. Fernando says this war looks to him like a hoax, an illusory affair that resembles the real thing but has nothing inside it. Can this situation continue?

September 7

I have a close and affectionate regard for this little Montparnasse square. I love its half-empty sidewalk cafés, and the expression of the switchboard girl at the Dôme; I feel part of the family, as it were, and that protects me against depression. While reading Gide over my coffee am interrupted by a character with somewhat protruding eyes, whom we've often seen at the Dôme: "Imagine," he remarks, "finding someone reading André Gide! You might almost think this stupendous nonsense wasn't happening at all." He tells me that Breton's wife created a scandal at the Dôme last night by shouting "That bastard General Gamelin!" at the top of her voice, out on the *terrasse*. His name is Adamov, and he is vaguely connected with the surrealists.

Another letter from Sartre, who is still in training at Nancy.

Bought a copy of *Marie-Claire*. The word war is never mentioned once, and yet the issue is perfectly slanted for present conditions. A tart repairing her make-up in the ladies' room at the Dôme explains, somewhat mystifyingly, that she's "stopped using mascara in case there might be a gas attack."

September 8

Fernando turns up in the restaurant on the Rue Vavin, and joins me for coffee. He saw Ehrenburg and Malraux yesterday. Malraux is trying to organize help for those foreigners who are being forcibly conscripted into the Legion. A Czechoslovak Brigade has been formed, and 150,000 American Jews have volunteered for an expeditionary force; but it looks as though the neutrality laws will be strictly applied, which means the Americans won't be able to come over. The papers announce "an improvement in our positions," and speak of "fierce fighting between the Rhine and the Moselle." Fernando asserts that several strongholds in the Siegfried Line have already been captured. I go back to the hotel, where the chambermaid talks to me about her young man who just finished his military service, like Monsieur Bost, and now is up in the front line under fire. I feel afraid for Bost—and despite everything, for Sartre too.

Eight days' mental struggle, and to what purpose? It's as though I were expecting a miracle. But eight days haven't put me a step forward. *It's just beginning*. That's what I ought to get into my head, and can't— or won't. I don't know how to come to grips with this war. Nothing clear-cut, as Lionel used to say about disease: just a constant threat. At times I regard the condition of fear as a crisis merely, which must be accepted, indeed, but minimized as far as possible; but occasionally I feel that fear represents the moment of truth, and all else is escapism. No emotional reaction when I revisit places where I have known happiness: it would be very different if I were making a clean break myself. When you make a break, go away, you give up a world that's still *there,* that clings to you on every side, and the parting is terrible. But when the world you know is itself destroyed, once and for all, nothing remains but a shapeless universe. You are debarred from any sad regrets, even from the pangs of actual separation. For these at least a shadow of hope is essential.

On the Place Edgar Quinet people look up to watch the great gray barrage balloons going up against a gray, red-streaked sky. I settle down in the Dôme to write this entry. You have to pay right away in the cafés now so that you can get out quickly in the event of an alert.

Get back at midnight to find a note waiting for me: "I'm here, in No. 20, at the other end of the corridor. Olga." I knock at No. 20, and a coarse male voice answers. Then, with my candle (no electricity in the hotel for the past two days) I wander up and down the corridor, listening. The redhead from the room opposite comes out of her room and looks at me suspiciously. In the end I tap on the door of No. 17, where I find Olga half asleep. We go on talking till three in the morning.

September 9

Olga tells me that Bost is out of harm's way for the time being. The mail brings a letter from Sartre, who seems very calm and cheerful. Fear drops away from me: the relief is almost physical. Suddenly I find myself if not with memories, at least with a future.

I go to the Dôme with Olga. There are two little Lesbians sitting next to us; one of them starts a row with the waiter. "I'm not in the habit of talking for the benefit of *waiters,*" she says, to which the waiter—a large, smooth, menacing man with a heavy mustache—replies: "But waiters have ears to hear, my girl, and they can repeat what they've heard, and Vincennes Prison isn't that far away." Olga tells me how Beuzeville has been trans-formed by the war: elegant lady refugees taking the air in the streets, and endless rail convoys, the trucks crammed with neighing horses and silent troops. Only the Negroes, she says, ever sing. There were trainloads of refugees, too: apparently the local boy scouts pounce fiercely on any child among them and gorge it with condensed milk. Fernando drops by, and tells us that things are going badly in Poland: it looks as though Warsaw has fallen. Olga and I move into Gégé's empty apartment.

September 10

I spend the morning at my grandmother's. Find her arguing with some good lady in Civil Defense who's trying to persuade her to leave, ex-plaining that first priority for evacuation goes to children and old people. My grandmother folds her hands over her small round paunch and re-

marks, in a stubbornly mutinous sort of voice: "But *I* am *not* a child."
She has had a letter from my mother: at Saint-Germain-les-Belles, a spy
has been arrested who, they claim, was trying to derail the Paris-Toulouse
express.

Back home, I find a letter from Sartre and a notice that a telegram is
awaiting collection. This is doubtless from Bianca. But in order to get the
telegram it is necessary to have the notice countersigned at the police station,
which in its turn requires a certificate of residence; only after that can you
go and collect the telegram itself at the post office.

About eleven at night, while in bed reading Pearl Buck's *The Mother,*
an insipid book, I hear raucous voices in the street yelling, "Light! Light!"
I try to argue, but someone yells: "Put a bullet through their lousy shutters,
then! And you go somewhere else if you want to play at espionage!" I
decide to turn the light off.

Short alert at 4 A.M. We go down to the shelter, and find a boarded
floor, and some chairs. Several tenants turn up carrying little campstools.
The concierge tells us that the chairs belong to some "gentlemen opposite,"
and we can't sit on them. We go back upstairs on the excuse of looking
for something to sit on, and talk till the all-clear.

In the restaurant this morning a soldier told us, weeping and sobbing,
that two other soldiers from his barracks had hanged themselves rather
than leave for the front, and that one of them had been desperate at the
thought of abandoning his four children.

September 11

An impression of boundless leisure; time no longer means anything.
I go and collect Bianca's telegram. She wants me to come and see her in
Quimper. Decide I'll go, and write some letters. Am beginning to feel
like work again, but must go on waiting. The mustachioed waiter in the
Dôme recounts his memories of the previous war: "My first Boche was
so big that when they brought him in they shoved him in a wheelbarrow,
and he wouldn't sit, they had to keep hold of his legs. And I was in such a
state that when I was wounded my blood wouldn't clot."

We buy lots of blue powder, which Olga mixes with water, with olive
oil, and even with Gégé's suntan lotion. This solution she daubs over the
windows while I sit playing records and writing a stack of letters. At nine
o'clock we go out. Our windows are a wonderful shade of blue. We go
through the thick blackout to the Dôme, stumbling against the curb all
the way. We sit down at Fernando's table. Also present: a very handsome
Greek, some Spaniards, and a rather vague surrealist poetess, as fat as
butter, but with very nice skin and eyes and teeth. She is apoplectic with
rage because a friend introduced two men to her whom she'd never met
before, and then asked her for news of her husband (who, as she points
out, isn't her husband at all). She made some vague reply, and one of these
characters said: "I do not care for Madame's line of conversation." They
turned out to be *agents provocateurs.* She tells her story over and over
again, and is obviously scared out of her wits. All these foreign residents

are being persecuted, and many of them want to get out of the country. Fernando toyed with the idea of asking us all up to his place for a drink, but he's scared of the noise and the scandal.

September 12

A gray morning. The Sita buses only run at 10 A.M. now. There's a plaster statuette lying in the middle of the street. The news is still the same: local advances on our front, and Warsaw holding out. A letter from Sartre which worries me intensely: he's not with the Air Force, but the Artillery, and he hasn't heard from me yet. Fear descends once more: everything is poisonous, horrible.

September 14

News from the various fronts remains unchanged. The Poles continue to resist, and rain is holding up the German advance. Severe restrictions inside Germany, and, so it is said, considerable discontent. Little movement on the French front, but reserves are being built up with an eye to the future. All in all, the war hasn't really begun yet as far as we are concerned. When we are actually fighting, and Paris has been bombarded, the whole thing will look quite different. We can't yet believe that this will ever happen, which is the reason for the weird sort of betwixt-and-between atmosphere that characterizes the present period. Cinemas, bars, and dance halls are going to stay open till eleven at night again. Everything is moving back toward normality.

Walked through the Luxembourg, and found the place quiet as death. The lake is drained and foul, and sandbags are piled high round the Sénat. A flimsy barricade of chairs blocks off the area by the Petit Luxembourg: there are some troops behind it, digging in a desultory way, and a heap of cut-down branches. Wonder what the hell they're fiddling at.

Evening at cinema. Read Henry James's *Portrait of a Lady* in bed.

September 15

We make up huge parcels of books and tobacco for Sartre and Bost. Outside the post office we run into Levillain [a former Rouen student who belonged to Action Française], all dolled up as a cavalry officer, very easy and elegant, slapping his fine riding boots with his swagger stick while he talks to us. A perfect officer type, and the joke of it is that Sartre and Bost are obliged to *respect* such creatures. A long line inside the post office. The landlady of Marco's old hotel is there, quarreling with a man. The slightest dispute these days at once becomes a kind of national argument, and those who use their good offices to reconcile those who have fallen out feel that they embody some sacred idea of unity.

We go to see *Blanche-Neige*: very dull.

September 16

Letter from Sartre; he's in a quiet Alsatian village and getting on with his work.

I help Olga pack her bags and see her off at the Gare Montparnasse, then make for the Gare de l'Est and my own train. Alone again now, and once more sucked back into the war, a mere fragment of suffering humanity. This café in Esbly, where I'm sitting waiting for the Grécy train, is a heartbreaking sort of place. I sit outside on the *terrasse* in the twilight, with conversation going on inside, close to the open window. Someone mentions a woman who's received a telegram: "Husband honorably fallen on field of battle," and there's a rustle of indignation; generally the mayor comes around and says something like: "Now, dear lady, I'm afraid I've got bad news for you; your husband's seriously wounded"—or words to that effect. This is less chilly and impersonal than a telegram. They say that there's a mayor in some little hole or other who's got fifteen such telegrams, and daren't deliver them. Talk turns to the postmen on their rounds, and how worried the women are as they watch out for them, and how they're always going to the post office. Someone says, "Fifteen thousand Germans killed: how many Frenchmen, then?" They're drinking port and pernod. One man exclaims angrily, "It's forbidden to wear mourning—you get sent to a concentration camp if you do!" Some women reply that mourning doesn't signify anything. Night comes on, and cars go by. One woman says, "It's loving them, and not being able to do anything for them . . ." Several trains go through, crammed with silent troops. The war is all around me here, and has once more entered the very depths of my being.

I was counting on reaching Crécy in an hour, but the trains aren't running on time. By seven o'clock we have only got as far as Esbly (I having spent the trip half-dozing in the corridor), and I feel detached from things; if it were in my power to annihilate myself altogether I'd do it without turning a hair. Yet I can clearly recall just what it was like to be happy. At Esbly station someone told me there would be an hour's delay. I've already been moved on from two cafés, and am writing these words in the third. I like this halt, and the night, and the noise of trains. It isn't a halt in the true sense, and somehow this brings me close to reality—with no home, no friends, no purpose, no horizon, a tiny speck of suffering in the heart of this tragic night.

Continued my journey in a small dark train, equipped with dim blue ceiling lights that illuminated precisely nothing. So I stayed out in the corridor and watched the square of light we cast on the embankment. At each tiny station a porter would cry out the name of the place and wave his lamp. When we reached Crécy I found Dullin waiting for me at the exit, all swathed in shawls. He embraced me, and made me climb into his ancient trap; he had a black dog in there as well, which was a great encumbrance. The vehicle was not equipped with regulation lights, and Dullin drove through Crécy with a fine conspiratorial air. It wasn't too cold, with a blanket wrapped around our legs, and the leisurely motion of the horse through the night was most pleasant. It was quite impossible to see anything. Outside the village some men asked to see our papers. Dullin kept saying "It's dreadful, dreadful!" in his most hammily tragic voice. He's sick of rear-line heroes, especially Giraudoux, with his little clique of official censors and other draft dodgers, and of Jouvet, whom Giraudoux has turned into a big film tycoon, and who now wears a monocle and gives himself such airs he might be a general. As he has several films under way he declares: "The first essential is to finish films already begun. Afterward we can think of boosting production generally." Jouvet is also responsible for this statement: "On the radio we must have items that raise morale—cheerful, easily understood things, like Claudel's *Le Soulier de satin* or Péguy's *La Jeanne d'Arc*. No foreign authors."

Baty apparently had a long discussion with Dullin: they considered the possibility of touring America and the neutral countries, but the idea of America didn't appeal to Dullin, and he felt that such a plan would be a great come-down for him. He decided that he would rather try to organize some sort of mobile theater in France; but this sounds hard to get going.

So on we jog into Ferrolles, and there is the shadowy figure of Camille, with a small blue lamp casting its faint light on her. She guides our vehicle ahead, and a couple of soldiers join us, making jokes about "the old boneshaker." There are troops everywhere; Madame J.'s house—Madame J. is Camille's mother—is also an infirmary, and she has only one room to herself. Even the w.c. she shares with the sergeant. At street corners there are notices up, saying "Section X" or "Section Y." Dullin led the horse around to the stable and unharnessed it, taking great care not to let any light filter through: blackout precautions are just as thorough here as in Paris. Then we trooped into the dining room, where Madame J. eyed us severely, obviously all set to pick on Dullin for something done wrong.

All the same, she did kiss me on both cheeks. She's a somewhat alarming woman, with dyed red hair showing white at the roots, exophthalmic eyes, a drooping mouth, puckered features, and a hard, cutting voice. Over the dinner table she had a very fierce argument with Dullin about a slice of sausage; despite this she addresses him as Lolo and kissed him goodnight before going off to bed. When Camille was left alone with me she told me that her mother was an ether drinker, and the cause of considerable scandal in the village. Apparently things became really bad when Camille's father was laid low with some kind of sleeping sickness or encephalitis, and was cared for by this drugged creature who tossed about the floor and cut her head open on the andirons. In the end Camille's father was taken away to a clinic at Lagny, where Camille herself stayed with him for the eight days it took him to die. She's lent me the prologue and first act of her play about the Princesse des Ursins, and I read them in bed, after which I fell asleep and didn't wake up till eleven o'clock in the morning.

September 17

Awake feeling depressed. Bright cheerful light is streaming through my little green-curtained window, and I feel horribly depressed. In the old days the worst part of my depression used to be the astonishment it caused me, the scandalized way in which I fought against it. Nowadays, on the other hand, I accept it cheerfully enough, like an old familiar friend.

Camille says a few words through the door: they're off to do the shopping. I wash, dress, go downstairs. I like this house. The piratical living room has had yet further embellishments added, including a magnificent antique trunk, and a crimson quilt embroidered with wonderful ships. Mariette brings me coffee out in the garden, on a little wooden table. Flowers and sunlight. From the kitchen there comes the clink of casseroles and a sound of boiling water: everything seems so cheerful. I finish Camille's play and write some letters. Soldiers about outside the garden; soldiers everywhere, in fact. The village is completely transformed by them.

Camille and Dullin come back, the provisions are unpacked, and we have lunch out in the loggia: a delicious meal, with excellent wine and marc to follow. Dullin's relationship with Madame J. is always a joy to watch. A young, rather ugly female relative turns up: after embracing Dullin and exchanging a round of greetings she announces that the Russians have crossed the Polish frontier, claiming that this step does not prejudice their neutrality in respect to other countries. It seems they are also negotiating treaties with Japan and Turkey. This may mean a war lasting three or five years at least. I had never envisaged the possibility of a *long* war. Dullin begins talking about the first war again: he joined up and spent three years in the trenches without once being wounded, and what he emphasizes is the sheer physical discomfort, the frightful cold. He also gives a most vivid picture of what the infantryman has to face: gas, flame throwers, bombardments, grenade and bayonet charges. He sounds as though he admires what Céline describes as "the heroic and shrinking soul" characteristic of certain leaders. I find this irritating.

A walk through the fields with Camille under a beautiful sky full of clouds; the orchards laden with apples; sleepy red-roofed villages where clusters of beans are hung out on the house fronts to dry. We stop at the side of the main road, near a small railroad station, and drink lemonade out on the terrace of a hotel. There are two soldiers on guard at the crossing. One has a beard and is a painter from Crécy. The other carries a policeman's stick. Cars go by, often full of officers. We make our way home across fields and through villages.

A memorable moment, this: it recalls to my mind something Sartre said to me once in Avignon—and how true it is: that it's possible to live in great tranquillity even at a time when your life is hedged about with danger. I don't forget for the moment all the grim actuality of war and separation and death; I know the future is barred against me. Yet nothing can efface the luminous softness of this countryside; it's as though one had been overcome by a feeling sufficient to itself, that had no past history, as if one had been torn out of context, suddenly without a sense of involvement.

On our return we listen to the radio. The news is vague; they're trying to conceal the importance of this Russia intervention. For a long moment we brood in alarm over this ominous, uncertain prospect before us. But over dinner Dullin perks up and tells amusing stories about Gide and Ghéon.

September 18

I come down at eleven o'clock and sit beside the kitchen stove. Dullin, with an air of great absorption, is busy writing away—page after page of manuscript: I believe he's working on some new project of his. I read Shakespeare's *Henry IV*, Part I, which I once began in English, but never finished. About midday Camille appears in her negligee. The radio, after a brief snatch of Couperin, gives us the latest news: a quiet night on most of the front, but Poland is caught between two fires, and suffering utter devastation. Outside we can hear loud military voices: every shouted order or blast on a whistle carries sinister overtones. Camille comes to Crécy with me, bringing the dog on a lead, and looking very young and graceful. We drink bottled cider. Crécy is full of troops and requisitioned vehicles. I catch a train at five o'clock, an estimated two-and-a-half-hour journey to Paris, with another half-hour's wait at Esbly. Long trains go through, empty, moving eastward, and another one loaded with troops and cannons. Far away over there is another world, something unimaginable. The Gare de l'Est is completely blacked out, and so are the passageways in the Métro, with just a few faint blue bulbs for guidance. This blue lighting makes my room look like a mortuary. I read late into the night. Tomorrow I leave for Quimper.

September 19

I sit waiting for Colette Audry outside the Dôme. A beautiful day. Feel glad I'm having a change of air, and pleased with this lovely autumn weather and the letters I got yesterday evening. You might also call it joy, this feeling: no future to it—but how I love being alive, despite everything!

Colette Audry turns up on a magnificent bicycle, its chromium fittings glinting in the sunlight. She bought it as soon as war was declared; it cost her 900 francs, and swallowed up all her savings. She's back after a spell in the Seine-et-Oise district, and married to Minder, who is a reformed character now. Her sister carries a lot of influence these days, being the wife of a general. It appears you can do quite a lot if you have someone to put in a word for you, such as get a pass to go and visit your husband; but how do you find a friend at court in the first place? Colette tells me about Katia Landau: her husband has been taken away and never seen again, and she herself, as a German Jewess, is having a terribly rough time of it. We have five minutes' chat with Rabaud, who says that the troops' morale is very low, and that all they talk of is putting out one eye to stop themselves being sent up to the front line. Alfredo, Fernando's brother, stops at our table and tells me in a low voice that Fernando has been arrested. I go and see Stépha, whom I find in tears: apparently some men came for Fernando yesterday and he hasn't been heard of since,

Then Billiger turns up, very miserable, and announces that he's spent the night with Fernando. As he, Billiger, was coming out of the Rotonde yesterday he was stopped and asked for his papers. He had an Austrian citizen's passport, and had already spent some time in the concentration camp at Colombes, where he was given a document authorizing him to return to Paris. Despite this the *flic* who picked him up took him along to the police station, where an inspector furiously tore up his passport. From here he was taken to the Préfecture, where to his astonishment he spotted Fernando, in the middle of a group of Spaniards. They were thrown a few hunks of bread and shut up for the night in a sort of cellar, full of coal. All the Spaniards in Paris had been arrested, even businessmen who had been residents in France for months. Next morning Billiger was released, but the poor devil had to go to Colombes, and Stépha was busy packing him a grip and searching around for a mess kit. Fernando must be in the same place still, he thought. Stépha got in touch with her neighbor, a luscious little tart who is the mistress of a Socialist Deputy, to see what could be done.

I advise Alfrero to go see Colette Audry [she knew both Stépha and Fernando well], who will doubtless be able to do something. Lunch with Stépha at the Breton *crêperie*: she's terribly worried about her mother, who was in Lvov, but calms down a bit afterward.

I keep an appointment at the Dôme with Raoul Lévy [a former pupil of Sartre's, and a friend of Bianca and Jean Kanapa], whose actions are entirely dictated by the Theory of Probabilities: he estimates the odds are very heavy on his being killed in the war, but this doesn't worry him overmuch—nor Kanapa either, he says. He tells me about German propaganda in France: how the soldiers on the Siegfried Line stick up notices that read: "We have nothing against the French; we won't shoot unless you do," and a German mother has addressed all French mothers in a radio talk, saying that the whole thing is England's fault, and young Frenchmen shouldn't let themselves be killed on its behalf. He also talks about an article by Massis, which asserts that German philosophy is a philosophy of *becoming,* and that this is the reason for the Germans ignoring or breaking their promises. Also a piece entitled "The Boche is not intelligent." He supports my belief that one man or five million come to the same thing in the end, since there's no one whose mind can embrace the sum of things.

I catch my train, a very long one, from the open-air station overlooking the Avenue du Maine. What I find most striking is not so much the number of passengers as the amount of luggage piled up in the racks. The lighting is so feeble that I can't see to read, and sit dozing instead. I think about my life, with which I'm profoundly satisfied. I think about happiness. For me it was, primarily, a privileged way of apprehending the world; and if the world is changing to such a degree that it can no longer be apprehended in this, fashion, then happiness loses its importance.

Seven women and one man in my compartment. The man and two

of the women have got suitcases stuffed full of silverware. One smelly little girl keeps prattling on about spies, and points out the least gleam of light in a disapproving voice. General atmosphere of panic. You'd think there were bomb-laden conspirators hanging onto the undercarriage and crawling all over the roof. Everyone watches for "signs." One says, "I saw a light!" and another, trembling: "I *smelled something*." A third will claim to have heard a noise. This noise, in point of fact, is a lavatory seat banging up and down; but my traveling companions' minds are haring off after explosions. The train tends to pull up in a frightfully abrupt way; apparently the drivers and firemen are now elderly retired railroadmen recalled for the emergency. At one stop a woman decides she feels rather unwell (she's shivering with fright) and the rest fill her up with tea. Everyone thinks the train is liable to be derailed. One thing that *did* happen was a case falling off the rack in a nearby compartment and laying the man below out cold; he was carted away on a stretcher. A long, uneventful night, with no trouble of any sort. The dawn comes up slowly, and I recognize the quiet landscape of Brittany, with its squat gray church towers.

September 20

Bianca is waiting for me on the platform. She takes me to my hotel, the Relais Saint-Corentin, which used to be a very chic establishment, and where I now get a room—a very small one, it's true—for 12 francs. It reminds me rather of the Petit Mouton; I and one officer are the only guests. The old Breton proprietress keeps the front door shut almost all the time, so we go around to the back, by way of a coal yard and a stinking back yard. But the hotel itself is extremely pleasant, and I'm delighted to be there. It's a day for peace and forgetfulness. The weather's wonderful: Bianca and I walk down toward the Odet, over heath and moorland, past delightful farms with white roses trailing over their gray walls—but inside are blank-eyed idiots, frightened children, ailing invalids. Bianca talks about the anti-British German propaganda, and says a lot of the people round these parts are affected by it. She goes home for dinner, and I hunt around for a cheap restaurant, since I'm very hard up. I find a slovenly sort of bistro where I have bread and soup and listen to the radio announcing a fierce battle between the Germans and the Poles. At eight o'clock I go to the Brasserie de l'Epée to write some letters. At eight-thirty they draw those thick blue curtains, and then move me to a table almost on top of the cashier's desk: most of the lights are put out. The effect is too funereal for words. Two tables only, and the other one's occupied by a man with a couple of prostitutes. I go home and turn in.

September 21

Walk along the banks of the Odet, which smells of mud and seaweed. Much gossip. In the evening reread *Tête d'or,* which I think a fine piece of work, especially the passages describing the death of Cebes; but it's

Fascist stuff, Nazi almost. Find a café slightly less dismal than the one I went to last night. Even though they lower the steel shutters, there's at least some light, and two tables are occupied.

September 22

Trip out to Concarneau. The old medieval city, entirely surrounded by ramparts, juts out into the sea like a miniature Saint-Malo. From our vantage point on the top of the wall we can see blue fishing nets spread out to dry over the boats below us.

September 23

At the post office I find a card from Madame Lemaire inviting me to La Pouèze, which pleases me very much. Marco is in Constantine, and Pagniez at Dijon. See some Canadian troops going through the Place du Marché on huge khaki-colored motorcycles: everybody stares at them. In the bistro where I have lunch the radio is blaring out news about Poland. Some Breton women, wearing those starched white headdresses, turn toward the set and thoughtfully register Poland's disasters on their weather-beaten faces. The news is followed by an address to the "peasants of France" which very quickly drives me out of the café. We go to Beg-Meil: the beach is magnificent—all rocks and white sand—and absolutely deserted. The icy water stings my body voluptuously.

September 24

Another walk over the moorlands: I love these pines, these sad stretches of gorse, these little gray tarns. I drink milk and eat some pancakes at the *crêperie*. Chic refugees cruise around in cars and complain about the lack of entertainment: what a mad, twittering world they inhabit! No change in the situation. Germany and Russia have divided Poland between them, and there have been a few "engagements" on our front.

September 25

Am curious to find out how I shall spend these three days of solitary traveling. Haven't dared to bring my rucksack; instead am clutching a ridiculous sort of bundle, containing my swimming suit, my alarm clock, and a couple of books: it keeps coming undone the whole time. The annoying thing is that I've practically no cash whatsoever. A two-hour bus ride takes me to Morgat. Find this little port an enchanting place. Feel hungry already, but don't eat anything for the sake of economizing. Set off along the coast. In one or two of the villages people look at me as though I were a spy, and old women mutter to each other in Breton dialect as I pass by; no one here speaks French. Make for Cap de la Chèvre, but find that the military authorities have wired off the surrounding area within a radius of about five hundred yards. Manage to reach Cap de Dinan by a cliff path. In a baker's shop I eat some bread and chocolate and very bad buns.

The delicate hues of this Breton landscape make a very pleasing impression when viewed against a dull gray background of sky and sea and rocks. The sea is somehow ubiquitous, you can't get away from it, even up on the moors or among the granite houses and the windmills. I take the bus to Locronan, dazed with wind and sun and suffering from a headache, no doubt because I haven't been eating anything. I remember the place very clearly, and our hotel, where I was hoping to stay again; but they've turned it into a *crêperie,* which is closed anyway. The hotel has moved across the road to a splendid Renaissance mansion. Have dinner there: the dining room is most attractive, with its beams and magnificent china and its view out over the bay, but it's quite empty. Proprietress busy packing up, say she's closing tomorrow because it isn't paying her to stay open. I catch a bus to Douarnenez: there is the port still, and the fishermen in their red trousers, and the boats, and the blue nets. The moon comes up full as the sun goes down, and the moon is finally victorious. Out on the jetty a group of laughing girls, and some boys singing: it looks like a peacetime evening, and I burst into tears.

September 26

Still dark at six-thirty. I take a small road along the coast. No cafés in the villages, but grocers' shops with a counter to drink at, and no tables. It isn't the impersonal ruggedness of the hills that freezes one's heart so much as the air of human desolation. Lots of aircraft flying over the coast, and a large number of cruisers out at sea. One meets only women, children, and cripples: all the men have gone. I walk fifteen miles, and then climb down the crumbling, indented cliff face and go for a swim. Water a beautiful blue, merging into violet. Follow a path up to the Pointe du Raz, where I sit and rest for a while. I think of all the life lying behind me that the future can never take away. This makes me less afraid of dying.

There are four hotels near the signal tower: three are closed, the fourth, just barely alive. A little room all cluttered up with files is found and cleared for me. The lighting is provided by hurricane lamps, and I read the *Mémoires de Gramont* over dinner: mildly amusing. Out for a stroll in the moonlight, I am accosted by two men in naval uniform. "You local?" I tell them no. "Out for a walk?" "Yes." "At this hour of night? You can't see a thing." "You can see the moonlight." "Moonlight," retorts one of them, "you can see just as well in Quimper or Landernau." His tone has become openly insulting. I show them my papers, which they examine by the light of a pocket flashlight. Then they make vague apologies and go. My room is on the first floor, looking out over the moors and the sea; I almost feel as though I were sleeping out in the open.

September 27

I get up at six 'clock, in the dark. There is a candle lit downstairs and I go on reading the *Mémoires de Gramont* while I'm waiting for the bus. It's decidedly cold. The sun comes up over the heath as we're approaching Audierne. I drank a *cassis* in the combined grocery-bar-excise office while waiting for my coach. Walk from Pont-l'Abbé to Saint-Guénolé across the dunes. Return to Quimper by bus. See some Breton women wearing make-up under their sugar-loaf headdresses. Very odd.

Catch a crowded train to Angers. Darkness falls; the landscape is flat, but the moonlight embellishes it. "Like something in a film," one woman exclaims ecstatically. A discussion takes place concerning the merits of Breton butter. Reading under that dim blue nightlight is out of the question, but I feel endowed with infinite patience, as though it were a state of grace that the war had brought me to.

I arrive at two in the morning. A man in army uniform addresses me by name outside the station, and mumbles something about Mademoiselle S. [a friend of Madame Lemaire's] having telephoned him. He takes my suitcase—and my arm—telling me he's old enough to be my father, and conducts me to a hotel room that he's reserved for me. Then off he goes and comes back with beer, bananas, and sandwiches. I'm enchanted by this reception, and highly amused to find myself in an unknown town, at 3 A.M., shut up in a hotel bedroom with a soldier I've never met before; it all strikes me as quite unreal. On the other hand, his intentions seem dubious, to say the least. First he puts on a most peculiar expression and asks if he can stay a while. Then, when I remain standing through embarrassment at his fixed stare, he tells me to sit down. I pull up a chair. "No, sit on the bed," he says. I take the chair, and offer him a drink. "I shall have to drink from the same glass as you then—are you sure that doesn't worry you? Really?" We indulge in casual conversation for a while. In the end he goes, saying that he'll have breakfast sent up to me.

September 28

Here I sit writing letters in a big café on the Place du Ralliement, a little worried because I haven't a sou on me. Madame Lemaire and her daughter arrive in a car, and I'm overjoyed to see them. They leave me in Angers for an hour or so, and I look around the place: so very pleasant in this cool autumn sunlight. Then we drive through some rather unattractive countryside and arrive in a tumbledown village. The house is charming. There are three big cupboards in the attic stuffed full of books, and I make a preliminary selection from them. Am told that Pagniez is a switchboard operator at H.Q. somewhere, and Marco still in Constantine. They give me a couch in the dining room; there's a large fire blazing in the open hearth, and I feel so good that I read till one o'clock.

September 29

I bring an armful of books down from the attic and read all day. Warsaw has surrendered, and a treaty is signed between the U.S.S.R. and Germany. Germany announces her intention of offering the Allies peace terms. We shall refuse them, and then things will start in earnest. I tell myself this, and read books on the last war, but I still can't really believe it.

September 30

Monsieur Lemaire has found me some bound numbers of *Crapouillot* covering the period of the 1914–18 war. I read these, and also a book by Rathenau, and one by Kautsky. The fire burns brightly, and Jacqueline Lemaire pecks away at her typewriter. It's raining. A long time since I've enjoyed this sort of leisure.

October 1

Hitler's "peace offensive." One knows nothing of what is happening, or liable to happen. I live like a fighting cock. Before every meal Madame Lemaire takes me down to the cellar to choose a bottle of vintage wine. I'm glutted with food and reading.

October 2

What beautiful weather it is! I do my reading in the meadow now, stretched out in the sun under the poplars. This place reminds me of Limousin: there are big apples gleaming on the apple trees. Pleasant autumn abundance.

October 3

This is a weird moment in history. No one can accept Hitler's peace proposals; but what sort of a war will there be instead? What does this word "war" really mean? A month ago, when all the papers printed it boldly across their headlines, it meant a shapeless horror, something undefined but very real. Now it lacks all substance and identity. I feel vaguely deflated; I'm waiting for something, I know not what. A feeling in the air that the whole world is waiting. Besides, the first thing that strikes one about the 1914–18 war on going through the volumes of Pierrefeu is that it meant *four years'* waiting, punctuated by completely useless massacres. You might think the only real work was done by Time.

October 4

Up to now I've been vacationing. Now I am about to adapt myself to a "wartime existence," and it seems ominous to me. Yet this morning I was seized by an almost panicky urge to get away from all this tranquillity, to come to grips with something again. On top of this was the vague hope, after Sartre's last letter, of being able to visit him, coupled with a fresh upsurge of fear and impatience. Made up my mind to go today, and they took me in to Angers at seven o'clock. Am writing this in a café near the station, a most depressing place. Wanted to go to the cinema, and wandered through a quarter that was full of military barracks with tarts picking up soldiers and bistros crammed with troops. The cinema turned out to be closed, so I had to walk back through those terrifying streets. The war is back again, in me and around me, together with an anguish that knows no resting place.

October 5

Paris. I go to the local police station and say, like a fool, that I've a fiancé in the army and want to go and see him. They tell me that applications of this sort are refused on principle, and that *he* would be punished if I managed to join him. I decide to try another police station and play it more craftily. Go to the Bon Marché to get myself photographed, and eat a dish of pork and lentils at the bar next door to the Photomaton. My photos are horrible. The hardest job is to get a new certificate of residence. I try the Rue de Rennes, but Madame Martand refuses me one: "You don't live here any longer, it would be under false pretenses." This in a very curt voice. I realize that here, too, there's a war on, with a firing squad lurking at the back of every concierge's mind. I go to the Lycée Camille-Sée—a beautiful building—and see the headmistress, a slim, elegant, youngish creature, with a bluish chin showing through her heavy powder. She's determinedly playing lively-whimsical-gay act: "I'm a very *gay* sort of person, you know," she says, quite openly and without shame. I won't be overworked; only two hundred pupils in the whole lycée, of whom I shall have a mere twenty; they've got more women teachers than they know what to do with.

I go back to the Rue d'Assas, and find Gégé's concierge busy with a sewing machine. No, she can't let me have a certificate of residence since I only sublet. I continue standing in front of her, she goes on with her sewing. Nothing much more is said. This goes on for some time. Suddenly she gets up and writes me a certificate as from September 14. I slip her 50 francs which she refuses indignantly at first, afterward softening— "Well, only half that"—and finally taking it all. Things go excellently at the police station; I tell them about my sister, who's got a bone disease, and is in Marmoutiers; can I go and see her there? The clerk is very fatherly, and writes me a chit in his finest script. During all this someone else is choking off a blonde girl who wants to go and see her husband in Seine-et-Marne. "You can't go for *that,*" she's told. "But you can for some other purpose?" "You have to have a valid reason," they reply. I'm promised the safe-conduct for Monday or Tuesday. I go up and have a drink with Fernando and Stépha. Fernando was held four days in prison. He had been denounced for "propaganda designed to prevent foreigners enlisting in the Legion." Some character had told him he was a White Russian and asked if it was possible to get into Spain. "Sure it is," Fernando said. "But I haven't a passport," was the reply. Fernando advised, "You just get to the frontier and walk." The man turned out to be an *agent provocateur.* Fernando was bundled off to the Préfecture, and then to a camp, where the guards and NCO's treated him with great consideration. One of them gave him some tobacco when he heard that Fernando had fought in Spain, and threw in an extra packet when told that he had been a general. Fernando's friends were astonished by his speedy release, he tells us, and a little distrustful of him as a result. He has the feeling that the police are watching his movements, and doesn't dare go and see Ehrenburg. It seems that Malraux wants to enlist in the Tank Corps, but has been rejected because of his nervous tics.

Nizan has sent Duclos a very brief letter of resignation: "I am sending you herewith my resignation from the French Communist Party. My status as a soldier on active service dispenses with the need to add any more." I have dinner at the Coupole, and find it full: Montparnasse has been invaded both by the military and an entirely new clientele, so that the old habitués look mildly troglodytic. In a dazed way I ask the waiter for a *demi munich;* he laughs and says, "Wait till we're through the Siegfried Line." Paris at night makes a powerful impression on me: I'd forgotten just what it was like. The Great Bear is twinkling above the Carrefour Vavin, a beautiful and unusual sight. Almost no one out on the café *terrasses* now: it's beginning to get too cold. The whole place is even more deserted than it was last month. Go back to my room through streets as dark as tunnels.

October 6

Gégé comes back at midnight and wakes me up. She's been to Castel Novel, where there was a horde of women and Spanish refugees. About six-thirty we hear the fluctuating note of a siren, though somewhat muted: people peer out of windows, wondering if it's an alert. It isn't; merely a mechanical defect. The post comes: one of Sartre's letters has been opened by the censor. It's the first time this has happened. Misery! On October 3 he was posted "to an unknown destination," and all my scheming has come to nothing. I go on teaching, with a lump in my throat. These past three weeks have proved an unreal respite, and now distress and terror close in once more. I'm sick of thinking how long all this may go on. It no longer concerns me, and what's more to the point, I'm no longer concerned with *it*. This ticket carries no option out. I buy *The Idiot* and Julien Green's *Journal* for Sartre. The *N.R.F.* is no longer on sale and can only be got by subscribers.

October 7

Miserable day. Have an afternoon appointment with Colette Audry and her husband at the Marignan, but this café has been closed down by the military authorities because it stayed open after eleven at night. I find a table at the Colisée, just opposite. The place is a public scandal: nothing but high-class tarts, the sort of officers who, as they say, only die in bed, and various other draft dodgers. It's the public of 1916 all over again, seen through the pages of *Crapouillot*. Colette and her husband speak in disgusted tones of the propaganda films they have begun to produce. A misty night, tragic and beautiful, with already a hint in it of the coming winter. In Paris the cataclysm has already struck, is everywhere. Merely to become aware of that fact is sufficient occupation for anyone.

October 10

Pardo back today, and my last night in Gégé's apartment. Move to a hotel on the Rue Vavin. I like my room: it has thicks red curtains and I can keep the light on in the evening. Lise Oblanoff has returned to Paris, and is bewailing her unhappy lot: she can't be accepted by the Sorbonne if she hasn't an identity card, and she can't get an identity card if the Sorbonne hasn't taken her. It's always the same old story. Her father has retired, her mother isn't allowed to work by law. She asks me, weeping: "Why is it that N. is allowed to do everything, and I'm not?"

Adamov sits down opposite me in the Dôme, looking haggard. He's no longer earning anything either; he has his call-up papers and is waiting to go. The Dôme's like that at the moment, full of strays.

Fernando claims that a thousand soldiers in the front lines took over a train by main force and came back on illegal leave, without anyone daring to arrest them.

October 11

I want to get down to work again. Spent the day rereading my novel. Much to do still.

October 12

Working. Meet Marie Girard in the evening at the Dôme. There's a weird old man in blue overalls next to us who's reading *Science and Health,* a black book that looks like a missal. A drunk tries to start a conversation with him, and they very nearly come to blows. The drunk turns and addresses us. "I may have narrow shoulders," he tells us, "but I've a good high forehead." "The hell with your shoulders," says Marie. Two of the drunk's friends tear him away from our table. We have dinner at the *crêperie,* and then move on to the downstairs room at the Schubert. It's empty, but there's a pianist in there playing jazz, which improves the scenery a bit. "Now I wonder where everyone can have gone?" says Marie in a loud voice, which makes the waiter mutter something to himself. They chuck us out at eleven, and we go for a stroll along the Seine. Lots of policemen on night patrol, all big capes and shiny helmets, some on foot, some on bicycles, turning flashlights on the passers-by, stopping all the men to examine their papers. They even go marching into the urinals. Marie tells me about her love affair with a twenty-two-year-old Spanish refugee, who is as handsome as a god, and at present leading a hunted existence in some mountain hideout, with scarcely a rag to his back. She, Marie, intends to go back and find him. The village folk loathe these refugees; Marie even asserts that they beat some of them to death with their fists because they wouldn't join up. Therefore she will have to go very carefully. One night up there she got lost, lost her shoes, and walked three miles barefoot through rough maquis. The Spanish boy doesn't know more than a dozen words of French. Her one thought is to go and find him again. She's convinced that Daladier asked Hitler to bring about the war so that he, Daladier, could crush the Popular Front. She makes defeatist remarks. Once in a train she tried to make some soldiers feel sorry for what had happened to Giono. "You shouldn't say such things to young soldiers," one of them told her severely. She asks nothing better than to be sent to prison; it's a good way of saving some money, she says. She's given me much amusement.

October 13

Marie suggested that I should accompany her to Yuki Desnos's place tonight, and I said I would. We find the dining room full of smoke, people, and glasses of red wine. On the walls hang pictures by Fujita, one of which shows Yuki naked, with a lion. They're in color, because she asked him to prove that he could do something other than black-and-white washes. I don't find them particularly attractive. Yuki presiding, wrapped in a Japanese kimono which leaves her throat and beautiful arms bare; she's blonde and passably pretty. There's an ex-mistress of Pascin's there, who is beginning to drift into mysticism, and talks, with swimming eyes, of all she has suffered at various men's hands. Her husband, an exhibitionistic person with a long, dismal face, is in the next room telling fortunes by cards. His predictions are being made on behalf of humanity at large, and he doesn't foresee anything good for it. Other guests include a ravaged actress, a small Lesbian smoking a pipe, two other women, some silent young men, and a soldier on leave who looks like Buster Keaton. Yuki reads out a letter from Desnos, which gives a placid enough account of the life he's leading at the front. Everyone gets most indignant: he isn't nearly rebellious enough, they say. The soldier protests wearily. It's just like a scene from a play: on the one hand cynical anarchism, on the other a fighting man sickened by the civilian mentality. Four-letter words fly to and fro. "Shit!" they exclaim, and "You make me vomit"—emphasizing the words and saying them in the most unnatural way imaginable. Everyone looks as though they're permanently in heat. The soldier says: "Fuck all women! Tell your girl friends we can take care of ourselves, we don't need to wait for them!" And *you* tell your mates," a woman replies, "that we're not waiting for them, either—and there's no need for us to take care of ourselves." They all start singing patriotic songs from the first war, very derisively, and follow these up with antimilitary ballads, which last them till 4 A.M.

October 16

School begins again. At Camille-Sée I spend two periods confronted with nine well-behaved little girls in blue blouses: this strikes me as both unreal and ridiculous. Then I move over to the Lycée Henri IV, which now also houses the Lycée Fénelon. Classes held in an extremely ugly modern wing. Narrow corridors with notices up saying SHELTER No. 1, SHELTER No. 5, and full of black-clad women carrying those putty-colored gas-mask containers slung from one shoulder. I have twenty-four pupils, all well groomed and made-up and wearing ordinary town clothes: too Latin Quarter for words. They bring their gas masks into class with them and put them down beside their desks.

Olga back last night, with news of Bost, whose life at present sounds as though it's no joke.

German activity on the Western Front—and a new peace offensive by Hitler.

October 17

It looks as though serious fighting is really beginning at last. A German attack, followed by a French counterattack. German air raid on the Scottish coast. What will Stalin do? I read all this in the papers with vague feeling of indifference. My mind is anaesthetized.

To get to the Lycée Henri IV I have to walk through the Luxembourg Gardens—all mud and golden leaves now—after which I have a coffee in the Capoulade, standing up at the counter. Two and a half hours of teaching, interrupted by an air-raid exercise. The headmistress scuttles through the corridors in her tin hat, whistle in mouth, emitting strident blasts as she goes. We all troop down, Indian file, to a superbly well-appointed shelter, where we sit on garden chairs. A gas mask exercise follows. She whips off her hat and shouts, from inside her mask, "Teachers too!" but I haven't got mine with me. The pupils giggle at the sight of themselves in masks, and she says, snappishly, that it's no laughing matter. She also explains that all talking and movement should be avoided down in the shelter so as to conserve the oxygen supply.

Spend the evening with Olga in the Flore, which has just reopened. It's now fitted out with thick blue curtains and crimson banquettes—a splendid sight. Café managers have now learned the art of blacking out their premises efficiently, so that they can switch all their lights on. Coming in from the darkness it's quite dazzling.

October 18

I go to meet my sister at the Gare d'Austerlitz. Find the station most depressing. Crowds of troops milling round, held up by some *flic* who wants to see their leave papers. Take Poupette to the Milk-Bar. She tells me that in Saint-Germain-les-Belles they've been expecting the refugees from Haguenau for six weeks now, and the town crier goes through the streets exhorting people not to forget that Alsatians are still Frenchmen, despite everything.

A letter from Sartre, with the coded information that he's stationed at Brumath.

October 21

Go to the Jockey Bar this evening with Olga and my sister. Find it deserted. Very attractive room, bigger than before, with the same old cinema poster on the walls, though cleaner now, and a dance floor in the middle. A redheaded *chanteuse* is at the piano going through her numbers. The owner comes up and tells us that as of Monday there will be dinner, with cabaret, for 25 francs. Guests can dine in any of the booths, it's a new arrangement. He explains that he's had the place redesigned along the lines of the Seville dance halls, and I find myself recalling the Alaméda —what changes there have been for Spain, and for us! It's the first occasion on which the march of time has thrust me back unanswerably into past history. The place slowly fills up: middle-aged couples, servicemen in navy-blue uniform with no regiment number showing. The redhead sings a few numbers, but because it's wartime nobody dances. At eleven o'clock a warning bell sounds, and the band plays "Lights Out." Outside on the pavement a few groups stand about undecidedly. I read Koestler's *Spanish Testament* till about one-thirty, when I hear loud shouts and running feet on the staircase and the sound of a woman screaming. I peer out of my door, but the woman has such a thick accent that you can't understand a word she says. I believe it's the attractive blonde Norwegian, and she seemingly wants to pack up and get out: she keeps shrieking, "Coward! Coward!" The proprietress comes up and gives her a quiet scolding.

October 23

New moves toward acquiring a safe-conduct pass. Get my application filed at the police station in the 15th *arrondissement,* so that they won't pick up my previous tracks.

At nine o'clock I go with my sister and Gégé to Agnès Capri's. Whole place in a terrible disorder, rather like an unlit theater on the night when a rehearsal's due. At one table La Capri herself, in a white fur stole, Sonia in a black ditto, together with Marie-Hélène, and Germaine Montero in a funny little red-veiled hat. Deniaud, one of the original "Beards," is there having dinner, wearing a smoking jacket. Leduc, also in a smoking jacket, is waiting on the guests. See Tony at another table, with some ravishing unknown girl. Two more elegant couples that I don't recognize. Deniaud sings *"La Marchande de violettes"*—an overfacile performance, which I find irritating. La Capri quite charming in a red-and-black dress, with black shoes; their soles are gilded and about three handbreadths' high. A lot of her songs have been censored, but she's still got some excellent ones in her repertoire.

It's being said that nothing will happen on the Western Front till next spring. There's talk of the troops getting ten days' leave every four months.

October 25

Olga feels pleased because it looks as though the classes at the Atelier may be resumed. She sees a coat she wants in a shop on the Boulevard Saint-Germain, but finds when she gets inside that the one she picked from the window display is actually a military cape. The salesgirl laughs at us. Olga's sister has turned up from Beuzeville, and is staying in our hotel.

Go to the cinema in the evening and see *Knock.* Fernando says the papers are full of tall stories, and the war's going to last a long time. No longer react to all these prophecies. Work at my novel, take classes, live in a kind of stupor. Can't conceive of a future that contains any reality.

October 27

Twice a day, every day of the week, the headmistress at the Lycée Fénelon circulates little memoranda listing girls who have volunteered for various chores, and which monitors are to shut the windows if there's alert, etc.

Apparently the dictatorship of Haiti is offering asylum to 100,000 refugees, and especially welcomes intellectuals. Fernando and Stépha are thinking of emigrating there. We discuss the manifesto advocating "immediate peace terms" to which Giono, Alain, and Déat signed their names. They are now protesting that their good faith has been exploited; Alain is reported to have said that when he saw the word "peace" he signed without bothering to read any further.

October 29

The occupant of room No. 7 in our hotel is a Viennese hermaphrodite, legally male, with breasts, a beard, both male and female sexual organs, and hair on the chest. In the good old days of Dr. Magnus Hirschfeld this creature was well known in Vienna, but, as she explained to us, had to emigrate after the Anschluss, since Hitler had declared that he didn't want any of *that* sort around. She has a tiresome time of it emotionally, since she only goes for masculine men, and only attracts queers. But this is not the worst of her troubles. Germany laid claim on her for military service, and she was put in a French concentration camp, where the revelation of her sexual peculiarities (her clothes being forcibly removed) horrified the staff. She cries the whole time. As for the Norwegian girl who was screaming the other night, she turns out to be a drunk, whose lover beats her to make her shut up when she's had one too many.

October 30

Lise accompanies me to the police station. I sit waiting for a while. When I give my name, the clerk assumes an encouraging expression. Yes, I've got my permit. The news gives me a tremendous fillip of joy. It's valid till next Monday. I can't travel outside Nancy, but even so that'll mean five full days if the doctor gives me a certificate in time. Do some shopping, take my classes, go home to bed, and send for a local G.P. I read while I wait, beginning to feel as though I'm really ill. At 8:30 he arrives: a man with brushed-back gray hair, tortoise-shell glasses, and a watchful expression. He examines me, and to my disappointment diagnoses a common or garden-variety strained muscle. He keeps shooting questions at me, rather like Knock: "You haven't been rope-climbing in the gym, I suppose? Or lifting a heavy trunk? Most peculiar." He also gives me a sharp glance and says: "You don't sometimes feel as though you were sitting on a pebble, by any chance?" Despite this he gets out his little instruments to make quite sure I haven't got appendicitis. He pricks my finger, sucks some blood out into a small pipette, and dilutes it with a quantity of greenish liquid. He finds that my white corpuscle count is 11,000: high, but not high enough for acute appendicitis. He goes over me with a stethoscope and talks learnedly about the effects of cold on the feet, at the same time pulling up his trouser legs to show me his long underwear. He also holds forth on the circulatory system of Negroes and Eskimos. "When the

Negro comes out of his hut and puts his feet on the damp grass he has an instant reflex motion of the intestines," he tells me. Finally he signs a certificate authorizing me to stay away from school till the following Monday.

Get up very cheerfully and pack a suitcase.

October 31

Six-thirty. The Dôme and the Rotonde are scarcely stirring. I catch precisely the same train from the Gare de l'Est as Sartre took two months ago, on the same platform. Find it packed with troops. The man next to me has fingers like horses' hoofs and a great red stupid face; the others are reasonably bright for peasants. They're coming back from harvesting leave: they say very little, and pass the time playing *belote*. Though I tell myself that very soon they may be mashed to a pulp, I can't really believe it—the whole thing has the air of a field exercise, a mock battle. The countryside is flooded, and there's something both poetic and cataclysmic about these woods and hedges standing up from vast lakes of water.

Reach Nancy at one in the afternoon. No one so much as asks if I've got a permit. I walk down a broad street with my little suitcase in my hand. Deathly silence. The shops are open all right; there are confectioners' windows crammed with candy and giant caramels that look freshly made, but not a human being in sight. It might be an evacuated town. This makes a very strong impression on me. Reach the Place Stanislas, which always sounded so attractive from the account of it in Barrès's book *Les Déracinés*—all those mysterious gilded grilles. Find it completely deserted under a blue sky, with the reddening leaves of the park visible behind it like a backdrop: all very beautiful in the stilly silence. Walk on to another square, find Army HQ and am redirected to the gendarmerie, which is still closed. Decide to go and have lunch first, and stroll across the park, a vast and richly red autumnal expanse. Suddenly the iron-throated sirens start up. No sign of panic; on the contrary, in fact: lots more people are around than there were before. I decide that this must be some sort of civil-defense exercise that the inhabitants of Nancy have got used to, but I still find it a little surprising. Finally the truth occurs to me: I must have arrived in the middle of an alert, and this was the all-clear! Anyway the town is now swarming with people. I find the main thoroughfare lined with cinemas, restaurants, and Uniprix stores: it looks like a less attractive version of Strasbourg. Almost all the houses are barricaded with wooden planking; the town looks like one vast encampment. "Makes me feel I'm back in Paris, looking at you, lady," someone calls out to me—meaning my yellow turban, high heels, and earrings, I suppose. I have lunch in a brasserie and go back to the police station. Inside there's a crowd of people treading on each other's feet, with one good lady complaining about her varicose veins and another in tears because she's just heard her son's dead. No safe-conducts to Mulhouse are being issued: the general's orders. Everyone speaks German, even the troops. After half an hour I get to the front of the queue, where a clerk takes my documents, nods when he

sees the name Brumath, and goes off to find his lieutenant, with me hurrying after him. The lieutenant stares at me through his spectacles. "You're
not just trying to see your boy friend, are you?" "Oh *no!*" I say, from
the bottom of my heart. He allows twenty-four hours, and I make my
escape, bitterly disappointed and put out. Only twenty-four hours. Will
anyone possibly extend it? I go for a walk along the canal bank in a state
of great depression.

At six o'clock I'm waiting on the station platform. It's very cold, and
my feet are hurting from walking so far in high heels. There's a large
crowd of people, both servicemen and civilians, waiting for the train. It's
a very dark night. Various lights, blue, red, and white, can be seen
flickering over the tracks, but these aren't the train, just ordinary lamps.
When a train *does* come in it's never ours. Seven o'clock. Seven-thirty.
Cold and exhausted. Everything seems unreal. At last the train appears.
General rush for it. Every carriage crammed, but somehow I manage to
find a corner. Lots of Alsatians aboard; no one speaks French. One huge
woman is snoring so violently that it makes the whole compartment
snicker. Everyone very calm, you wouldn't know the train was making for
the front—very different from all those panic-stricken Parisians fleeing to
Quimper with their bagfuls of silverware! Bright moonlight outside,
illuminating a flat, frosty landscape. The train stops at every station and
I keep an eye out for their names. We pass through Sarrebourg and Saverne,
and the train empties out till there's only one soldier and me left in the
compartment. Begin to feel this is a real adventure. Five more stations only:
the story is merging into reality.

Brumath. I get out on a deserted platform. I'm the only passenger who
does. No one asks me anything at the gate. There are some soldiers there,
but they don't stop me. Near the station I see the lights of an inn; then I'm
walking across a deserted stretch of countryside in the moonlight. I realize,
with vaguely incredulous astonishment, that Sartre is somewhere near here.
Pass the Taverne du Cerf, where according to his letters he has breakfast.
I knock at the door of the Lion d'Or Hotel. No one answers, but a light is
flashed in my direction: a patrol. No one's allowed out after midnight.
Show my papers, and two soldiers kindly offer to escort me: they're both
Parisians themselves. They bang on the shutters of the Ecrevisse with their
rifle butts, but get no response. We wander around for half an hour or so.
Finally try the Ville de Paris, going from back shed to back yard and
finally into the main building. Find a door with PROPRIETOR written on it.
I knock and a large blond Alsatian appears and gives me an icy-cold bedroom. My teeth are chattering as I wash, undress, and slip between those
freezing sheets, having first set my alarm clock for 7 A.M.

November 1

The alarm goes off. A gray dawn. All the houses are shut, and there's
no one to be seen on the streets apart from one or two soldiers. Much
blowing of bugles. Feel worried rather than happy: how can I let Sartre
know I'm here? How can I get my permit extended? Feel hedged about

by threats and menaces: dependent on some officer's caprice, the casual whim of a gendarme. But watching the village come to life is still a romantic sight. Some trucks pull up under my window. Sounds of footsteps and voices, people climbing aboard. Suppose they shipped Sartre off like that today? I hurry off to the Taverne du Cerf. Long wooden tables, wickerwork chairs, and a huge tile stove. The place is still half asleep, and the windows are open. There's a nip in the air, and I feel decidedly uneasy. The two women in charge have a simple-minded look about them. Ask the address of the training school, but all I can get out of them is "Ask at headquarters." I write a note for Sartre which reads: "You left your pipe behind at the Taverne du Cerf. It's waiting there for you." Then I make off down the muddy street. Past a big gate, over a bit of wasteland, and there's a big modern red-brick building, all its windows painted blue like stained glass. Outside there a group of soldiers lounging around; I ask one of them if he'll deliver my note. "Must be one of the fellows in the office," the soldier says, looking rather baffled. But he promises to get my message to Sartre within the next few minutes. I go back to the Cerf, and see Sartre's figure coming down the street—I recognize him at once from his walk and his pipe and his size, though he's grown a horrible scrubby beard which makes him look simply awful. He hasn't received my telegram and wasn't expecting me. We can't go into a café, so I take him back to my room, where we talk for an hour, after which he has to get back. I go back to the Cerf. Sartre says the police are being very tough, and I still feel most uneasy. He comes back at eleven o'clock, clean-shaven. He and his assistants are the only ones here in air force blue: like everyone up at the front, he has no regiment number on his uniform. Many of the soldiers are wearing khaki, and a beret or police-style cap with a pompom: these are the *chasseurs*. Not many civilians about. But the tavern is packed—no doubt on account of its being the first of the month. We have lunch at a table at the far end, and decide to drop my story of a sick sister in favor of some female cousin that Sartre wants me to find. The two women running the place eye us in a friendly fashion, and I begin to feel a bit less hunted.

When Sartre leaves me I go back to bed absolutely dead with exhaustion, and sleep like a log for three hours. My alarm clocks gets me up again, and then the proprietress comes and tells me, in Alsatian, that she's promised my room to a lady who's traveling a long way to see her husband at the front. The local residents find all this perfectly natural and do what they can to help; the only people one needs to look out for are the police. I pack my bag and try unsuccessfully for a room at the Ecrevisse and the Lion d'Or. Meet Sartre again, who says he'll find me somewhere to stay while I go to the police station. The police pass me on to the town hall, where the mayor argues, in Alsatian, with a sergeant and two fat civilians. It looks like it's going on forever. Finally he examines my permit, but can't make head or tail of my request for an extension, so stamps the document at random. A gendarme, who is called in to sort things out, and seems much impressed by the Paris seals on my pass, declares it valid till Sunday

evening. What a relief! I go back to the Cerf and find it full of troops. I
sit down at the bar. A tall, quite good-looking *chasseur,* with a small
moustache, slides up to me, smelling of alcohol. "What? You still here?"
he says. "They were expecting you at the Ecrevisse." I remember two characters calling out "See you soon in the Ecrevisse" as I went into the police
station, but I didn't pay any attention at the time. I tell the *chasseur* I'm
waiting for someone. "Why not me?" he says, clasping me to him and
rubbing away at himself. He must think I'm a pro. "I know *you* aren't
here with any warlike intentions," he says. My position being somewhat
irregular, the last thing I want is a row. A big, burly fellow asks impatiently: "Well, are you coming or aren't you?" Yet another runs his
hand over me. "Oh stop it," I tell him despairingly. "I wish to God you'd
all leave me alone." The drunken *chasseur* threatens me one moment and
offers me his protection the next. He looks into my eyes and says, "Look,
are you with us or against us?" "Neither." "Well, are you Alsatian or
French?" "I'm French," I tell him. "That's all I wanted to know," he says,
in a satisfied and mysterious voice. He offers me his stick, an extraordinary
clublike affair which I decline. Sartre turns up at this point with the news
that I can stay at his landlady's place—though not with him. When he told
her his wife was coming, she said in a shocked voice, "But you aren't
married," and he had to amend it to "my fiancée." We have dinner at the
Lion d'Or. Very crowded. There's even a married woman there who's
obviously come up to see her husband. The contrast between all my
nervous traipsing around in the cold and the dark and this atmosphere of
gross Alsatian plenty is really extraordinary. Thick, comfortable voices,
tobacco smoke, warmth, the smell of sauerkraut. Sartre points out that
people are now using the polite *vous* to him, treating him like a civilian
because he's with a woman. This gives him a feeling of being an individual
again. We say goodnight early: troops aren't allowed on the streets after
9 P.M. My room has some rudimentary form of heating, but the sheets are
icy cold. On the walls are various samplers embroidered with inscriptions
in German, one of which tells me to have a peaceful night.

November 2
I get up at six to have breakfast with Sartre. It's dark and freezing,
with just an occasional light visible. The Taverne du Cerf is very gloomy:
all the lights are swathed in blue paper, and only one of them is on.
Hardly a soul there. The two women in charge are still half asleep,
and busy poking the stove into life. Dawn is breaking. Sartre comes in a
moment or so later. "He's laughing and talking this morning," one of the
women remarks, as though discussing a mechanical doll. "Never does anything but read ordinarily." She pushes away the books I'd brought with me
and says in a conspiratorial voice, "No reading today, see." Then she brings
us two cups of horrible Alsatian coffee, worse than the stuff you'd get in a
third-class French inn. We chat for an hour, after which Sartre goes off to
take some unspecified meteorological observations, while I remain sitting
here in this big, empty room, and watch the light get steadily brighter.

Soldiers are marching past outside, with shovels on their shoulders. One of the servant girls, a redhead, puts out a coffee and a glass of rum on the window sill for the M.P. controlling the traffic at the intersection; he comes over and knocks them back, still with one eye on the moving vehicles. He's wearing heavy fleece-lined gauntlets, and his breath steams in the morning air. I read a hundred pages of Sartre's novel—the first time I've read so much of it straight through—and find it excellent. Note down one or two criticisms, especially concerning the character of Marcelle. Then move on to the café, where Sartre meets me for lunch. Two of his subordinates come looking for him there, and they all go off together to look for a room. They eventually find one, for Sartre and me, at the Boeuf Noir. The local inhabitants are glad to oblige the troops, who provide them with a living and therefore receive much more consideration than civilians. Now everything is settled. Long discussions with Sartre, who also thinks that there won't be any real fighting: this will be a modern war, without slaughter, just as a modern painting has no subject, modern music no melody, and modern physics no solid matter.

November 3

A familiar, reminiscent feeling that I couldn't quite pin down yesterday morning—memories of winter sports holidays. Same sort of night, same cold weather, same screwing up of one's courage to plunge out in the icy morning (but done willingly, for the sake of pleasures to come)—even the same smell of damp wood in the hotel corridors. The soldiers rest their elbows on the bar counter, like skiing instructors in Chamonix tossing off a quick one before early lessons—a moment of fleeting comfort in the winter dawn. I'm on holiday again, alone with Sartre in a village. The illusion fades as morning wears on, but during the first hour or so it's very potent. The lounge of the Boeuf Noir is a pleasant room, adorned with mounted butterflies, stags' heads, and stuffed birds. Read Sartre's notebooks [He was jotting down day-to-day events and drawing up a sort of balance sheet of his past life.] with passionate interest; we discuss them on his return.

This afternoon, in a grocer's shop, I see two soldiers contemplating a gigantic jar full of mustard. Have never before seen so much mustard in one place. They want to have it all, but the grocer's wife won't lend them the jar. "I can't very well carry mustard in my hands," one of the soldiers grumbles, adding spitefully, "No one in Alsace has got any business sense." You feel this atmosphere of hostility everywhere. People from these parts refuse to be evacuated because in the rest of France they're treated like Boches. Nevertheless they remain very calm, even though they're only six or seven miles from the front line.

I show Sartre my diary. He tells me I ought to expand my analysis of myself. I would like to do so. I feel that my character has now set into a well-defined mold: I shall soon be thirty-two, and feel myself a mature woman—but what *sort* of woman? I wish I knew. For instance, in what ways am I typically "feminine," and in what ways not? Generally speaking, what do I ask of life today, what expectations do I have of my intellect, where do I stand with regard to the world at large? If time permits, I shall study such problems in this notebook.

November 5

Very mild yesterday, and a thaw today. Take advantage of this to explore the village, which is charming. One group of soldiers playing ball on a street corner, others sunning themselves on a bench. Almost everyone you see is in uniform. All the cars are camouflaged. Endless stream of horses and trucks going through. Yet peace still thrusts up through this blanket of war; down by the canal there are still some blue signposts showing the way to various places, and never suggesting that these routes are now closed. There's an unusually thick growth of moss on the roofs here; the very trees seem to lead an indolent, self-centered sort of existence. Brumath is, very shyly, hanging on to its own individual quality; it is not a mere anonymous military cantonment. And yet— Here comes an ancient country bus, all camouflaged now, its driver in uniform, and the word *Vaguemestre* [Baggagemaster] stuck on its front window instead of the name of some village; while the muddy lanes are all fenced in with barbed-wire entanglements.

In the Boeuf Noir get to talking with a soldier who has an office job. He says that Strasbourg's almost completely evacuated apart from a skeleton staff of administrators. Civilians can come in to look for their possessions, but are not allowed to sleep there. The tobacconists' shops have gone out of business and the whole place is dead. Yet people there are expecting peace by Christmas. My informant, too, believes in a "diplomatic" war where there won't be any real fighting. The nearer the front you get, the more intangible the war becomes. Paris reassures those arriving from Beuzeville or Quimper; Brumath in turn reassures those arriving from Paris.

When Sartre rejoins me at four o'clock we're put in a back room, since the café proper isn't yet open for troops. We sit at one corner of a long table covered in blue-and-white oilcloth: very comfortable for talking. From time to time someone opens the door and then backs out quickly, with an apologetic expression. I tell Sartre I've decided not to undertake the task of self-analysis we discussed two days ago: I want to finish my novel. Feel the urge to live actively, not sit down and take stock of myself. At five o'clock we move through to the main room, and eat a dish of black pudding and potatoes. Sartre walks with me as far as the station yard, under a great starry sky; then he vanishes into the night.

The waiting room is a gloomy place: lots of soldiers, and some civilians loaded down with bundles. Many of them are carrying rucksacks. Out on the platform there's a strong smell of kirsch. The train pulls in, so crowded that it's almost impossible to get the carriage doors open. I push my way to the front, latch on to a group of soldiers, and am lucky enough to find a place. We stop at every station before Saverne, which we reach at nine o'clock: a vast, black, crowded station. There's nothing but a buffet-waiting room, and no drinks are being served there. I walk out of the station, and an airman attaches himself to me. We cross a square in total darkness, and he knocks at the main entrance of a hotel. A diplomatic discussion with the proprietress ensues: he seems to know her well, and she lets us in. Sit in a dreary dining room drinking lemonade, with the airman opposite me teasing the waitress. But they shoo us out again almost immediately. The express doesn't leave till midnight, and I'm feeling a bit hunted. The waiting room stinks of war: the tables are pushed together and stacked high with dismal luggage—mattresses, blankets, evacuees' baggage—while the evacuees themselves huddle on chairs, surrounded by a thick, smoky atmosphere, and absorbing the unhealthy heat of a stove that gives off abundant carbon monoxide fumes. I stand in one corner for a while, reading, then go out again. Find some soldiers who have piled up their kit bags in the underground passage and are sitting on them having a meal; others are resting on the stairs, and the entire platform is so swamped with troops that it's impossible to move a step. I remain standing, like a sort of Simeon Stylites, so absorbed in my own thoughts that I hardly notice the last hour of waiting. As Sartre would say, the reason why this war is so "undiscoverable" is because it's everywhere: this station platform *is* the war.

A relief train pulls in and swallows up all the soldiers; this is followed by the express. I walk into a comfortable compartment with green leather seats. "You alone?" a big Alsatian serviceman inquires. "All right, you can come in, then." I sit down in one corner. There's a civilian who's exchanged his bowler hat for a tin one, and two soldiers, peasants from Les Deux-Sèvres, who are going back home for three days on special leave. The Alsatian is a Class 10 man, who's going back home and leaving his son behind on the Rhine. He makes clumsy jokes about the pleasure of traveling with a lady, and, having observed that I'm trying to read, climbs up on the seat and scrapes some of the blue paint off the light bulb with his penknife. This sheds some light on my nose, eyes, and chin, and makes it possible to read. Later, when I feel like going to sleep, the Alsatian wraps me up in his cape, and the civilian, fired with the urge to emulate him, lends me a beautiful plump cushion. I stretch out at full length, and my feet push into the Alsatian; when I pull them back he remarks, "Please leave them where they are; this is the first contact I've had with a woman in twelve weeks." Someone passes around a bottle of Alsatian marc, and I drink half a mugful of it. Very good stuff: makes me nice and drowsy. Lie there half asleep, listening to their anecdotes. More tales about the Peace Offensive: stories of French and Germans both fishing from opposite banks of the Rhine, and how once, when a German machine gun went off unexpectedly, a notice was held up almost immediately that read: "French soldiers, please forgive us: it was just a clumsy idiot who fired then—we don't want to shoot at you." They talk about Strasbourg, and the hardships of the evacuation: one man came back from his home in tears, having found it gutted. The soldiers, too, are full of indignation. They recount how in one house occupied by their platoon someone nailed

a rabbit to a mirror-wardrobe in order to skin it: the spoiling of so lovely
a piece of furniture absolutely shattered them. They appear to be devoted
to their officers: the captain, it would appear, goes down to the bistro every
night in person to buy liquor for his men. All the same, these peasants
from Les Deux-Sèvres have only the haziest notions about the war. The
Alsatian is holding forth at length and making jokes: "Two nanny goats
and two billy goats; you're the two billy goats," after which he bursts out
laughing. He pulls off my shoes, and lays my stockinged feet on his knees,
asking me whether this is all right. Drowsily I tell him he can do what he
likes with my feet, but during the night am awakened by his tenderly
squeezing my ankles. I pull my feet away and he makes no protest.

When I got back to Paris I continued to keep this diary, but without
any sense of urgency. I had settled down into the war; and the war had
settled down in Paris. It was a very different city now. To begin with,
you saw far more women, children, and old people about than young
men. Above all, though, the place had lost that fascinating air of depth
and mystery which Caillois had described a year or two before in a work
entitled *Le Mythe de la grande ville*. The unknown people I passed in
the street looked forward to the same future—the end of the war—as I did;
and this narrow perspective transformed our erstwhile "jungle" into a
familiar, predictable domain; I felt I no longer belonged to a city, but
rather to a village. On fine nights the Milky Way shone in the sky, and
during the evening from behind the railings of the Luxembourg Gardens
the sound of soldiers' voices was mingled with the hooting of the owls.

My parents had returned to Paris, but my sister stayed on in Limousin:
she could never have continued with her painting on the Rue Santeuil,
what with the cold and the blackout. Lionel, too, remained away; he was
a sick man still, and needed country air. He and his aunt moved to Saint-
Germain-les-Belles and took lodgings with a doctor. I saw almost nobody
but other women: Bianca, who was still reading for her philosophy degree,
and Olga, who was once again working with Dullin. We slipped back into
the previous year's routine. There were some new faces at the Flore: Simone
Signoret, very young then, looking like a schoolgirl, with close-cropped
black hair and wearing a beret; or Lola the redhead, who sat dreaming at
her table for hours on end, mouth drooping, eyes lost in the distance,
without, apparently, ever suspecting how attractive she was. As for the
men, they were all put in the shade by a newcomer called Nicod, a half-
Greek, half-Ethiopian twenty-year-old, who danced at the Bal Nègre, in a
way that blended supreme grace and utter lack of self-consciousness. By
and large the crowd at the Flore remained very much in character; I enjoyed rubbing elbows with them, but had no urge to make their closer
acquaintance.

In order to fill my all too ample leisure hours, I took to listening to
music and, true to form, set about the business with obsessional intensity.
I got a great deal out of it, too: as in the most formative moments of my

childhood, pleasure and knowledge coincided. Someone lent me a phonograph, and I borrowed records from various people; I felt the same elation at the sight of these silent yet sound-laden disks as I did when confronted by my new books at the beginning of the term. I lost no time in listening to them, but mere aural titillation was not enough for me: I wanted both to be intoxicated by music and to understand it intellectually. So I played each work ten times in succession, analyzing every phrase, trying to grasp it in its unity. I read a number of works on musical history and studies of various individual composers. I became a regular visitor at Chantecler's on Boulevard Saint-Michel: I would settle down in an armchair and don a ' pair of headphones, and even though the music reached me through the most frightful crackling and interference, the pleasure of freely choosing my own programs was ample compensation for this disadvantage, and I filled numerous gaps in my musical knowledge. I went to a great many concerts, particularly those under the direction of Charles Munch at the Conservatoire, which I attended regularly: he brought such passion and fire to his conducting that he was obliged to change his shirt between each number. I often went to the Saturday morning final rehearsal, and never missed a Sunday afternoon performance. Various celebrities turned up for these, including Cocteau and Colette, the latter wearing sandals and no stockings. I also heard Gluck's *Alceste* at the Opéra. Evening dress was not now obligatory, even in the orchestra, and the price of seats had been considerably reduced: the original figure on my ticket, 33 francs, had been struck out and "12 francs" stamped there instead. I took a special interest in modern music—though this, as far as I was concerned, stopped short with Stravinsky—and my favorite composer was Ravel, of whose work I made as exhaustive a study as lay in my power. For two years music occupied a large part of my time.

Occasionally, very occasionally, I would have a drink at the Jockey Bar with Olga. From December 9 dancing was resumed in the night clubs: the strip-tease girls wore a red-white-and-blue *cache-sexe* or skirts striped like the Union Jack. Police raids were frequent, with *flics* in shiny tin helmets examining customers' papers, using a flashlight strapped to their chest. The sirens would occasionally sound an alert at night, but I no longer took any notice of them. Olga and her sister, together with one or two women neighbors, would get together during an alert to drink tea and gossip; but I didn't want to be tired the next day, so I simply plugged my ears and slept in peace.

Such a life was monotonous to the point of austerity, and so the slightest diversion assumed an exaggerated importance for me. The following two incidents are transcribed direct from my diary.

December 3

Pleasant day with Olga at Ferrolles. We now have a luxurious diesel car on the run from Esbly to Crécy instead of the slow, old local train. But at the exit we find two militiamen stationed, who threaten to send us back to Paris because we haven't got permits. I argue the point, till one of them softens a bit and takes me along, in some indecision, to see his superior officer. The latter starts by bawling me out. I show him my passport and talk in a steady stream. There's a woman there whose mother is ill, and since they're letting her out of the station they include us as well. They go through Olga's passport very meticulously because of her foreign name, but can't find anything wrong with it; so off we go, colors flying.

It's so sunny as we trudge up the slope that I take my coat off. We reach Ferrolles, and I point out Madame J.'s house to Olga. See a man shoeing a horse; when he turns around, I see that it's Dullin, wearing corduroy trousers and a large apron made out of sacking. He greets us and tells us to go on up and see Camille, who's calling to us from an upstairs window. We go inside to find a brand-new small divan and, at the far end of the drawing room, a sort of winter garden constructed with artificial flowers. Delightful pictures of birds now adorn the walls. Camille comes down, resplendent in a housecoat of several different shades of purple, with her hair braided and caught up by a purple, bejeweled ribbon; she's wearing a necklace and bracelets, and has a Berber ring on one finger. Her small bitch and the cat are playing together quite amicably. Dullin comes in and we all drink Advocat mixed with port, a delectable concoction. Madame J. is somewhat less alarming than last time, but her hair is now emulating the tricolor: white in front, red in the middle, and a gray bun behind. After lunch Dullin gets to work on the décor for his new production of *Richard III,* with fretsaw and glue and plywood, building a small model of the Tower of London. Madame J. watches this process with a disapproving eye. "Well," she says. "Never knew making a stage set was so complicated. I always thought you just shoved some furniture on and that was that." Meanwhile Olga is copying out a scene from the play and Camille busily knitting a pair of white-and-purple shoes. Soon the afternoon's over, and we plunge out into the night, guided by a small blue-tinted pocket flashlight that Camille has lent us.

December 8

While I'm working in the Mahieu a hawker comes past selling comic composite pictures of gorillas, pigs, and elephants, each with Hitler's head instead of its own. Haven't seen anything in this line before. Cécilia Bertin comes over to my table. [She had taken her diploma in philosophy and given up attending lectures at the Atelier in order to work with Jouvet.] She is wearing a red velvet dress, and her complexion is waxy pale, with two reddish patches on her cheekbones. Tells me that without knowing it she must have come in here to see me. She's been teaching literature in a boys' school at Saint-Quentin, where she had to expound Horace to third-year classes. "When I got home," she tells me, "I used to burst into tears and beg Corneille to forgive me!" She also had a *baccalauréat* class: "I began by reading them Verlaine and Baudelaire. They didn't understand a word, but they felt I was *really suffering* as I read, and that made a big impression on them." She took a day off, with permission, to present herself at the Conservatoire. Jouvet wrote and said he'd do something about her case, but has in fact done nothing at all. The fantasy she has woven around Jouvet is as exaggerated as anything Louise Perron ever produced. She explains to me that he is scared of love because when he falls for a woman he's bound to her hand and foot, her slave, her chattel. "So it's got to the point where he'll only see me in the corridor or on the landing! Ah, how we make each other suffer!" Every sign of indifference is to her proof positive of passion. She is convinced of his jealousy: when he turns up her coat collar to keep her from getting cold, she thinks he wants her to wear a mask, so that no other man can see her. She imagines he follows her, and is convinced she's seen him in the Mahieu. On Saturday morning she missed her class, and in the afternoon he said to her, very brusquely, "Why didn't you turn up this morning? Go on, be off with you!" And to get revenge, she said, he kissed another girl, a decidedly attractive one, while she was still there. When she's playing Hermione, and speaks the line "Ah, cruel one, I loved thee not! What have I done?" he hides his face to conceal his emotion; and he's never paid her a single compliment. She goes on about loneliness and sorrow fostering his genius. She herself has had a "sudden spell of solitariness" and thereby acquired some quite remarkable effects—*inner* effects, she specifies—for her interpretation of the part of Phèdre. She is very proud of the fact that she hasn't offered herself to Jouvet, who anyway has made no demands whatever upon her. She lives in a hotel, and sees no one. She is also writing: "Poems at first, to free words from their social context and implications; then novels, using this purged vocabulary." The day she was refused admission to the Conservatoire she went to see Jouvet in the evening. She was, she says, "calm and serene." He took her hands and said, looking into her eyes, "Are you sure you don't mind about this?" She told him yes, she was quite sure. He kissed her hands and gave her the most extraordinary and penetrating glance, "the look of someone who has at last found what he has been searching for all his life." She adds, "Having had that moment makes me not care about being rejected." Jouvet, she explains, cares only for one woman in the whole world, needs Cécilia alone. But he knows himself, and has come to the conclusion that his difficult character debars him from making a liaison with any woman. Accordingly he prefers to break off the relationship. Her eyes burning and eager, she says, "Now tell me *your* opinion of me." I manage to avoid doing so.

Nizan got some leave at the end of November and came to Paris; but I didn't see him, and regretted it later. We had had news of him, however. As we had guessed, the German-Soviet pact had completely upset him. His comrades in Corsica hadn't breathed a word to him of what was in the wind: he thought they had been deliberately keeping him in the dark, and was cut to the quick as a result. We therefore possessed a very clear idea about the reasons for his resignation; but we would have liked him to explain all his motives to us in greater detail. He had written Sartre a brief note which told us very little; Sartre replied, and got another letter back dated December 8, since when we had not heard from him. This letter ran as follows:

> *Mon petit camarade*: Thanks for your card, which I've just found waiting for me on my return from Paris, where I managed to go for a while. Paris is very odd nowadays, and the people I saw decidedly queer customers. You and I and about five other writers are the only ones who remain too naive to join the Censor's office or Giraudoux's crowd. No one can mention us without an ironic smile. We've got to write our novels. I'm facing up to the challenge again, but meteorological reports can't occupy quite as much of your time as the Pioneer Corps does of mine—and I'm only a buck private! Not that we'll be able to publish any of this for ages. Even novels are censured in a way that'd make your brain reel, and I most certainly couldn't tell you, here and now, the reasons for my resignation from the Communist Party. Saw Petitjean recently—wounded, a scratch merely, but very much the hero, seeing that he's in the commandos and now reckons he's a tough one as well as a thinker. It'll take him ten years to explain *that* one to us. Aron and he are becoming rivals in the philosophical field. Between a neo-Péguy and a neo-Dilthey we won't have much to laugh about; but I suppose they'll regard us as incurably frivolous. Didn't have much time in Paris and so failed to see the Beaver as I would have liked to do. Please give her my regards—and drop me a line from Sector 108. Regards, Nizan.

I got frequent news of Bost via Olga: he was in no sort of danger, and merely complained that his life was stultifying in the extreme. As for Sartre, he continued to make weather observations and hang out at the Brumath bars. He wrote to me almost every day, but this correspondence got lost during the mass exodus. In a letter to Paulhan he gave the following desciption of his existence:

> My work here consists of sending up balloons and then watching them through a pair of field glasses: this is called "making a meteorological observation." Afterward I phone the battery artillery officers and tell them the wind direction: what they do with this information is their affair. The young ones make some use of intelligence reports; the old school just shove them straight in the waste-paper basket. Since there isn't any shooting either course is equally effective. It's extremely peaceful work (I can't think of any branch of the services that has a quieter, more poetic job, apart from the pigeon breeders, that is, always supposing there are any of them left nowadays) and I'm left with a large amount of spare time, which I'm using to finish my novel. I hope it'll be out in a few months' time—I can't really see anything the censors could object to in it, apart from a lack of "moral health," and anyway I can't rewrite it.

(Paulhan sent this letter on to Adrienne Monnier, who wanted to publish the fragment I quote in some bulletin or other; she sent a typed copy of it back to Sartre, with a request for his permission to use it, which he refused.)

So this curious war dragged on, and at the front no less than in the rear the main problem was one of killing time, of patiently sitting out this interim period whose right name we found it so hard to decipher—was it fear, or hope? My first wartime term drew to its close and I thought of going skiing during the Christmas holidays: why not? The annoying thing was that I couldn't find anyone to go with me: you need competition on a ski run, and solitary excursions can be dangerous. Bianca told me that Kanapa was in a similar dilemma; so, though we were barely acquainted, the two of us went off together to Mégève. We stayed at the Chalet Idéal Sport, at the top of Mont d'Arbois. During this period the comforts the Idéal Sport offered were somewhat sketchy, and despite the splendid view, prices were moderate. There were very few skiers that winter. You had to stand in line on Sundays for the Rochebrune ski lift, but for the rest of the week I felt as though the snow slopes belonged to me alone. I got along very well with Kanapa, in a curiously negative way; ten days went by without our making the slightest attempt at conversation, and even when we were sitting opposite one another at the table we read books without the slightest embarrassment. The things that I found amusing—our fellow guests, their private habits and tricks of speech—did not interest him, and I never succeeded in finding out what did. We were both about the same standard as skiers, and went down side by side, in silence: we made one particularly good descent, across virgin snow, from the Prarion peak above Saint-Gervais-les-Bains. This arrangement suited me very well; I had someone at hand in case of accidents, and in the normal way of things there wasn't a soul about. When I got back, about five o'clock, I would sit down at the table in the main lounge, beside the radio, of which I had undisputed control, and twist the knobs in search of an interesting concert. I was often lucky, and enjoyed combing the dial. My pleasure in music and snow and everything else was enlivened by the prospect of Sartre being due for leave in January.

Back in Paris I began to count the days. The only noteworthy event during this month was a rehearsal of *Richard III* at the Atelier.

January 10

Rehearsal of *Richard III*. Beautiful décor and costumes. Marie-Hélène Dasté looks magnificent in her black dress and white sugar-loaf headdress; Blin resplendent in Buckingham's white robes. Only Dullin is still wearing his own clothes, complete with a Basque beret, which gives him a mischievous air. The women do very well, and Dullin himself is terrific; the other men, even Blin, don't seem to me quite so good. Mouloudji goes prancing around the auditorium in a ghost's shroud. Dullin does a series of what Mouloudji describes as his "vignettes": he puts on a particularly disdainful and enraged hauteur when he has to harangue the crowd from the balcony. He greets me afterward, remarking, "*She* is suffering from bronchitis," in the solemn and somehow devious voice he always puts on when discussing Camille.

One day early in February I went off to meet Sartre at the Gare de l'Est, and we spent a week walking and talking. Sartre was thinking a good deal about the postwar period; he had firmly made up his mind to hold aloof from politics no longer. His new morality was based on the notion of "genuineness," and he was determined to make a practical application of it to himself. It required every man to shoulder the responsibility of his situation in life; and the only way in which he could do so was to transcend that situation by engaging upon some course of action. Any other attitude was mere escapist pretense, a masquerade based upon insincerity. It will be clear that a radical change had taken place in him—and in me too, since I rallied to his point of view immediately; for not so long ago our first concern had been to keep our situation in life at arm's length by means of fantasy, deception, and plain lies. As for the detailed development of this theory, it has been so widely expounded since that I will not dwell on it here. Sartre as yet did not know the exact nature of his future political commitments (he could hardly predict them in advance, and anyway did not want to prejudge the issue); but one thing of which he was convinced was that he had a duty to the younger generation. He did not want them to feel after the war, as the young veterans of the 1914–18 war had done, that they were a "lost generation." He had a very brisk discussion concerning this idea of the generations with Brice Parain, who was very quick to take up the cudgels whenever any of his contemporaries were attacked. For example, we detested Drieu's *Gilles,* and Parain felt himself personally impugned by our criticisms. Sartre wrote a letter to him (which never actually got mailed) containing the following remarks:

> I would not dream of denying that Drieu happens to possess an outlook very differently constituted from my own, and formed in a context with which I am unfamiliar. Any such denial would be merely childish. But you mustn't whisk Drieu away when I want to judge him, and put his "generation" up for me instead in that highhanded way of yours, with the assurance that the two are identical. Drieu as an individual is *of* his generation, agreed, and he has been faced with his generation's problems. But you can't say he *is* his generation. One's generation forms part of one's given situation, like one's social class or nationality; it is not equatable with a personal attitude of mind.
>
> As for the political side of the business, you have no cause for alarm: I shall go into this rough-and-tumble on my own. I shall follow no leader, and if anyone wants to follow me, that's up to them. But the most urgent thing is to stop the young men who got into this war at the same age you went into the last one from coming out of it with "sick

consciences." (Not that this isn't a good thing in itself; but it's most disagreeable for them.) No one, I believe, will be able to do this for them except those members of the older generation who have gone through the war side by side with them.

Sartre's leave was soon over. In my diary for February 15 I wrote: Sartre gets into uniform again. We reach the station just before 9:15. Large notice up announcing that all trains for men going back from leave will depart at 9:25. Crowds of soldiers and their womenfolk making for the underground passage. Am reasonably calm, but the idea of this departure as part of a collective move I find distressing. The scene on the platform brings a lump to my throat—all these men and women with their awkward handshakes! There are two crowded trains, one on either side. The right-hand one pulls out, and a long line of women—some mothers, but mostly wives or girl friends—drift away, eyes glassy and red-rimmed: some of them are sobbing. A few elderly fathers among them, a dozen at most: this separation of the sexes is a primitive business, with the men being carried off and the women returning to town. There are very few tearful ones among those waiting for the departure of the second train, though some cling desperately around their lovers' necks; you can sense a warm, passionate night behind them, and the lack of sleep, and the nervous exhaustion that morning has brought. The soldiers make joking little remarks like, "Look at the waterworks!" but you can feel their closeness and solidarity. Just as the train is about to leave, a crowd of them jam the door of the carriage, and all I can see of Sartre in a dark corner of the compartment is his garrison cap, and his glasses, and an intermittently waving hand. The fellow in front at the door steps back and lets another take his place. The newcomer embraces a woman, then calls out, "Who's next?" The women line up and each takes her turn on the step, me among them. Then Sartre vanishes inside again. Violent feeling of collective tension in the air: this train's departure is really like a physical severance. Then the break comes, and it's gone. I'm the first to leave, walking very fast.

The day after Sartre left, a snowstorm hit Paris. Labor was in such short supply that the streets were not swept, and even the big boulevards were a snowy carpet underfoot. If you wanted to cross the road you had to struggle through the high drifts piled up against the sidewalk, and the road itself was a muddy swamp into which you sank ankle-deep. The passers-by had a dazed and somewhat nervous air about them: Nature had made a tumultuous invasion of the city, and human hands could no longer restrain her. It looked as though vast cataclysms were impending. It was on one of these glacial days that Bost arrived home on leave. Even in the front line, he told us, this seemed the most insubstantial and elusive of wars; they hadn't so much as seen the shadow of a German anywhere. He liked some of his comrades very much, but was horribly bored. He played cards and slept; once, out of sheer desperation, he spent sixty hours in bed at a stretch. The idea of rotting away in barns for another two or three years didn't appeal to him at all. He was most intrigued when I told him of Sartre's plan to go into politics after the war.

Winter drew to a close, and the first rationing began. Very soon we were going to be issued bread coupons. All fancy breads were prohibited, and the pâtisseries stayed shut three days a week. No more luxury chocolates; three "dry" days when the sale of alcohol was prohibited; only two courses available in restaurants, one of which could be a meat dish. None of this was a serious annoyance. The war continued to be elusive. A peace treaty was signed between Russia and Finland, in Moscow. Hitler announced at the beginning of April that he would enter Paris on June 15, but no one took this piece of braggadocio seriously. There were ghastly stories circulating about the occupation of Poland: the Germans rounded up all patriots, put them in concentration camps, and quite deliberately left them to starve to death. Some accounts even mentioned sealed trains, which were filled with prisoners and then had asphyxiant gases released in them. One hesitated to believe such rumors, remembering the fantastic stories that had got about during the first war. Equally, one distrusted all optimistic eyewash.

I continued to work, teach, see my friends, and pine for Sartre; my heart was empty, and loneliness weighed heavily on me. This was why I put up only a token resistance against the efforts that Lise made to infiltrate into my life. Often when I left the hotel at eight o'clock in the morning she would be waiting outside my door, silk scarf knotted at her throat and eyes full of tears. "I had to get out of the house," she would sob, sniffling a bit as she uttered the words. "My father was all set to kill me!" Or else her mother had boxed her ears, or her father had beaten her mother; whichever it was, she, Lise, was entitled to consolation. I would soften at this point, and she would talk with me through the desolate Luxembourg Gardens, as far as the *lycée*. When my classes were over, I would find her back there, waiting on the sidewalk, and she would beg me to have a drink with her. Once again she would be full of complaints. She was studying chemistry as her father had insisted on her doing. The lectures on theory bored her stiff, laboratory work scared her—she broke test tubes and cut her fingers. She was certain to fail the course. She gave me detailed descriptions of her parents, in all their meanness, malice, and brutality. Sometimes she would interrupt her lamentations to tell me anecdotes of her childhood, and on such occasions she could be quite charming. When she was fourteen, she and her friend Tania had practiced systematic and regular shoplifting in the Galeries Lafayette. She had carried out a series of most profitable hauls; and then one day, at the street corner, a woman in black had put a hand on her shoulder and marched her off to the police station. Lise had wept, her parents had pleaded on her behalf, and she had been released; but when she was home again she had received a really topnotch beating. "It wasn't fair," she told me. "When my mother told me to buy her something, and I swiped it, I was saving her money!" About the same period, while she was spending her summer holiday in a youth camp, she seduced a scoutmaster, a quinquegenarian White Russian. He arranged nocturnal meetings, and made love to her with great enthusiasm; but he had a wife and a reputation, and on his return to Paris he dropped her in the most craven manner.

To be quite honest, I can see why he was scared. This infant martyr was by no means wholly lacking in the wherewithal to defend herself. There was a violent quality about her expression and features generally that belied the timid softness of her mouth. She still kept up the stubbornness, temper tantrums, untidiness, and demanding nature that had been characteristic of her childhood. I found her need for me rather touching. She marked off her private calendar with the days when she *did* see me ringed in red, and those from which I was absent shaded gray: black was reserved for really catastrophic events. I got into the habit of spending a few hours with her each week, though she found this far too short a ration. "I've been working it out," she told me once. "You give up slightly less than a hundred and fortieth part of your life to me!" I explained that I had work to do, that I was writing a novel. "Is *that* the reason you refuse to see me?" she exclaimed indignantly. "To write down stories that haven't even happened!" I told her a little about Sartre, and she was frankly delighted at his absence on active service: if he hadn't been away, she said, I would never have any time for her at all. One day she went so far as to say, furiously: "I hope he gets himself killed!"

There were days when I longed to be alone; when the news was bad, and I lapsed into a state of chronic misery or depression, and would beg Lise not to hang around outside the gates of the *lycée* for me. But she still came. I would tell her to leave me alone, say I wasn't in the mood for talking, only to have her tag along beside me talking enough for both of us. She strained my patience severely: I would get irritable, she would mock me, till in the end she would burst into tears, whereupon I would relent again. She seemed so utterly vulnerable that I felt myself altogether disarmed when dealing with her.

The frequency of leave periods began to increase. Sartre came back to Paris again in mid-April, and we picked up the threads of our earlier discussions. We talked about the books we had read, simultaneously though at a distance. He much admired Saint-Exupéry's *Terre des hommes* (*Wind, Sand and Stars*), which he linked with Heidegger's philosophy, and discussed later in *Qu'est-ce que la littérature?* (*What Is Literature?*). In describing the flier's world, Saint-Exupéry also transcended the opposition between subjective and objective; he showed how diverse truths are made manifest by means of diverse techniques, yet each expresses the whole of reality, and no single one is specially privileged over the rest. He took us every step of the way through that metamorphosis of earth and sky which a pilot experiences while sitting at the controls; it would have been hard to conceive a better, more concrete, or more convincing illustration of Heidegger's theories. In a somewhat different field of ideas, we had developed a passionate interest in the works of Rauschning: *Hitler Told Me* and in particular *The Revolution of Nihilism* enlightened us a great deal concerning the history of Nazism. *The Castle* had just appeared in French, and turned out to be an even more extraordinary book than *The Trial*: among other problems which it touched on—via the story of that temptingly fallacious messenger in whom K. puts his trust—was one that had a burning interest for us, that of communication. We were also much taken with the portrait that Kafka draws of the surveyor's two "assistants": so enthusiastic, so muddle-headed, so liable in their zeal to compromise whatever slim chance of success he might have. In his own two subordinates Sartre recognized just such "assistants," and we were to meet many others during the course of our life.

We went to the cinema regularly, and saw one or two plays. The theme of Cocteau's *Monstres sacrés* moved me, since it had much in common with *She Came to Stay*: it too dealt with a couple bound together by a lengthy association and common aims, whose relationship is suddenly jeopardized by the temptations of youth.

L'Imaginaire had at long last been published by Gallimard: in it Sartre sketched out the theory of "annihilation" [*néantisation*] that he was now developing. In those imitation-leather notebooks which acted as receptacles both for notes about his everyday life as well as a mass of reflections concerning himself and his past, he was now drafting a whole philosophy. He drew the main outlines of it for my benefit one evening when we were strolling around near the Gare du Nord. The streets were dark and damp, and the impression I got was one of unutterable desolation. I had longed for the Absolute too much, and suffered too acutely from its absence, not to recognize in myself that futile drive toward "being" which *L'Etre et le néant (Being and Nothingness)* describes. But what a miserable illusion it is, this search—futile, endless, infinitely repetitive, consuming one's entire life! During the days that followed we discussed certain specific problems, in particular the relationship between "situation" and freedom. I maintained that from the angle of freedom as Sartre defined it—that is, an active transcendence of some given context rather than mere stoic resignation— not every situation was equally valid: what sort of transcendence could a woman shut up in a harem achieve? Sartre replied that even such a cloistered existence could be lived in several quite different ways. I stuck to my point for a long time, and in the end made only a token submission. Basically I was right. But to defend my attitude I should have had to abandon the plane of individual, and therefore idealistic, morality on which we had set ourselves.

Once again we parted, and the horizon daily grew grimmer. The United States decided not to enter the war. The Germans attacked Scandinavia, and as the battle for Narvik began, Reynaud declared emphatically over the air that "the rail link is cut, and will remain cut." It was not. The Allied Expeditionary Force withdrew again by sea. Hitler remained master of Norway, with all its mineral wealth.

On the morning of May 10 I bought a paper at the corner of the Rue Vavin and unfolded it as I walked down the Boulevard Raspail. The front-page lead instantly caught my eye. "This morning," I read, "in the early hours, Germany invaded Holland and attacked Belgium and Luxembourg. French and British forces have crossed the Belgian frontier." I sat down on one of the benches along the boulevard and began to cry. "Somebody saw you howling this morning," Fernando remarked to me, in a patronizing voice. Since the Spanish Civil War he had had it in for all Frenchmen, and was not in the least put out by our distress. The next day, and throughout the days that followed, my heart was pounding as I opened my paper. German columns had made immediate deep penetration at several points, and there was talk of a "pocket" that would soon be nipped off. But on May 14 rumors were already circulating that the entire Corap Army had folded up, that seventy thousand men had thrown down their rifles and run from the enemy. Had there been treachery? No other explanation seemed possible.

The frontiers were sealed, but correspondence with neutral countries had not been suspended. I got a letter from my sister. Lionel had left Limousin some weeks earlier to go and live with his mother, who had married again, to a Portuguese painter, and was living in Faro; they had invited my sister to go and spend two or three weeks with them there. She spent three days traveling across Spain, in a third-class carriage, and was quite exhausted by the time she reached Lisbon. She sat down outside a café: there was no other woman there, and the waiter spotted her right away. As he served her a coffee he asked her if she was French. Yes, she said. "Well, madame," the waiter told her, "the Germans have just invaded Holland and Belgium." She ran out into the square, and there was the news on the posters, in a language which was almost wholly incomprehensive as far as she was concerned. But she understood enough, and burst into tears. People pressed around her. "She's a Frenchwoman!" they told each other. She found herself exiled for the duration of the war.

One evening late in May I met Olga in the Capoulade Bar: she looked very upset. "Bost has been wounded," she told me. She had received a short note from him which said he'd been hit in the abdomen by flying shrapnel, and was being evacuated to the rear, somewhere near Beaune. He was out of the game for good, he said. In that case, his wound had turned out a blessing in disguise: but could one believe him? In less than a week his regiment had been wiped out, and the cream of his comrades slaughtered. Death stalked among us daily, and it was impossible to think of anything else. Sartre continued to send me reassuring letters; but he was up at the front too, and anything might happen.

Everything happened, the worst. Day by day the German Army drew nearer. We heard Paul Reynaud say over the radio: "If I were to be told one day that only a miracle could save France, I would say, 'I believe in that miracle, for I believe in France.'" That clearly meant everything was lost. I no longer had the strength to write, and scarcely to read: I spent my time in the cinema, or listening to music. The Opéra put on Darius Milhaud's *Médée,* produced by Dullin, with Masson's décor. The music struck me as very fine, and the over-all presentation quite remarkable. Over and above the singing chorus—masked, motionless, imprisoned in what looked like sacks—there was a nonspeaking chorus, which emphasized certain dramatic moments by gestures that were mime rather than dance: I believe it was Barrault himself who had been responsible for this, and it was certainly most effective. For a few hours I forgot the world. I was quickly brought back to it again. On May 29 I opened *L'Oeuvre* and read, in huge letters, KING LEOPOLD A TRAITOR. Then came Dunkirk. Perhaps Hitler had not been bluffing after all, then. Could he possibly enter Paris on June 15? What was I to do? Sartre would obviously retreat southward, and I had no wish to find myself cut off from him. I toyed with the idea of leaving for La Pouèze; from there I would easily be able to cross the Loire if, as rumor had it, the French army was regrouping on the far side of the river. But I could not abandon my teaching post.

On June 4 the Paris area was bombed, and there were many victims. Olga's parents begged her and her sister to come back to Beuzeville, and after some firmness on my part, they duly left. Stépha and Fernando traveled down toward the Spanish frontier, with the idea of slipping through secretly and making their way to America or Mexico. (In the end they found asylum in New York.) I had to supervise a *baccalauréat* examination on June 10, so I was kept in Paris. I sat on the *terrasse* outside the Dôme and thought with agony about the arrival of the Germans, of what their presence would mean. No, I had not the least desire to be shut up in this city turned fortress till the end of the war; nor to live for months, perhaps longer, as a prisoner. But I was under both a material and a moral obligation to stay there: life had finally ceased to adapt itself to my will.

The collapse was sudden and complete. Toward the end of June I composed an account of this period, and I print it here, though, as in the case of my war diary, I have made a few cuts.

June 9, 1940, *et seq.*

It was a Sunday; there had been some bad news about five o'clock in the evening—an unspecified retreat somewhere along the Aisne. Spent the evening with Bianca, at the Opéra; they were playing *Ariane et Barbe-Bleue* to a near-empty house. Got the impression of a last symbolical, swashbuckling gesture against the enemy. The weather was stormy, and both of us nervous: I remember the grand staircase, and Bianca in her charming red dress. We returned home on foot, talking about the defeat. She said one could always kill oneself, and I replied that people usually don't. Got back to my hotel in a taut, strung-up mood. This Sunday was like any other day in my life during the last two weeks: reading in the morning, a music session at Chantecler's from one till three, then on to the cinema to see *Fantôme à vendre* (for the second time) and *L'Etrange Visiteur.* Afterward went to the Mahieu and wrote a letter to Sartre. Antiaircraft guns were blasting away; little puffs of white smoke hung in the sky, and those drinking outside the cafés moved elsewhere. I felt the German advance as a personal threat. There was only one idea in my head: not to be cut off from Sartre, not to be caught like a rat in occupied Paris. I listened to a little more music, and went back to my hotel about ten o'clock. Here I found a note from Bianca saying she had been looking for me all day, that she was in the Flore, and had some very serious news to give me, and might be going to leave Paris in the course of the night. I looked around for a taxi, but they were all off the streets by now, so I went by Métro. Bianca was sitting there outside the Flore with some friends: we all left together. She told me her father had heard from some friend of his at GHQ that a big withdrawal would almost certainly take place the following day: all examinations were canceled and teachers released from duty. My heart froze. This was the end, and no mistake: the Germans would enter Paris within the next two days, and there was nothing for me to do but leave with her for Angers. In addition Bianca told me that the Maginot Line was obviously going to be by-passed. I realized that Sartre would be a prisoner indefinitely; that he would suffer the most appalling sort of existence, and that I would have no real news of him. For the first time in my life I had a kind of hysterical fit; this, as far as I was concerned, was the most awful moment in the whole course of the war. I packed my bags, taking only the essentials—including all of Sartre's letters: I have no idea where or when they were lost—and accompanied Bianca to her hotel on the Rue Royer-Collard. Here we found her Sorbonne colleagues and a couple of Swiss friends, and we all talked till four in the morning. It helped a lot to be surrounded by people, lapped in noisy conversation. We still thought victory possible if only we could hold out outside Paris until American troops came on the scene.

The next day, June 10, I got up at seven o'clock, and was lucky enough to find a taxi which took me to the Lycée Camille-Sée; a few pupils had turned up to make sure the exams weren't being held after all. The headmistress sent on to me an evacuation order that had come in; the *lycée* was moving to Nantes. I went back to the Latin Quarter, where I met some pupils from the Lycée Henri IV, all very hilarious. For a lot of young people this exam day without exams, all confusion and free time, seemed like a holiday. They were wandering gaily along the Rue Soufflot, apparently enjoying themselves to the full. But the tables outside the cafés were already almost deserted, and the great stream of traffic along the boulevards had begun in earnest. I was in a frightful state. Before leaving the Hotel Royer-Collard, I joined the Swiss pair in drinking a bottle of cheap champagne left behind by some Austrian woman who had been sent to a concentration camp: this restored my strength somewhat. Afterward I had lunch with Bianca at a Savoyard restaurant; the proprietor told us he was leaving that evening. Everyone was leaving. The old woman in charge of the washrooms at the Mahieu was packing her bags, the grocer on the Rue Claude-Bernard was shutting up shop; the whole quarter was being evacuated.

We waited for Bianca's father outside the Mahieu. It was a long and nerve-racking business. He had said he would get there between two and five, and we wondered if he would make it on time, if he might not be too late to get out of Paris at all. Above all I was itching to have done with the whole business; I couldn't stand this endlessly prolonged fare-well to Paris. The stream of retreating cars never slackened. People were watching for taxis, and commandeered them by assault; but hardly any more came along now. About midday I had my first glimpse of one of those tumbrel-like wagonloads of refugees that I was to see so often after-ward. About a dozen big carts came by, each one harnessed to four or five horses and loaded high with hay, over which a protective green tarpaulin was lashed. Bicycles and trunks were stacked against the tilt at either end, while in the middle sat motionless groups of folk, crouched under large umbrellas. It was all composed with a careful eye to detail that made me think of a Breughel picture, and had the air of a festival procession, at once solemn and attractive. Bianca began to cry, and I had tears in my eyes myself. The atmosphere was hot and heavy, and we were constantly on the point of dropping off to sleep: drowsiness stung our eyelids. The past kept returning to my mind in isolated flashes, with quite unbearable vividness. There was a man across the way, peacefully cleaning the street-lamps on the sidewalk: his calm gestures sketched a future in which one could no longer believe.

The car finally arrived. Monsieur B. had brought one of his women employees with him: she was sitting at the back, surrounded by piles of cases. We got in the front. Just as we were clambering aboard, the hotel proprietress shouted excitedly, "The Russians and English have just landed at Hamburg." It was a soldier from the Val-de-Grâce Hospital who was spreading this rumor; I heard later that the story of Russia's entry into the war had been both widespread and persistent in Paris during the next few days. (Sartre told me later that it had also spread to the armed forces.) It gave me a quite ridiculous fillip, but I soon knew it was false, since there was no mention of it on the four-thirty news. Nevertheless we went off with the vague feeling that all was not yet lost. There were plenty of cars at the Porte d'Orléans, but it wasn't overcongested as yet: only a few bicycles, and no pedestrians. We got away ahead of the main rush. At Croix-de-Berny we had to wait a quarter of an hour to let a convoy of trucks go through: they were packed with worried-looking young soldiers. After this we took minor roads across country, in the direction of the Chevreuse Val-ley. It was beautiful weather, and as we sped past flowery gardens and rural villas we could almost imagine ourselves going off on a weekend holiday. Near Chartre we lost our way, and also began to encounter various obstacles that tended to build up a bottleneck. At one point we were held up by a long queue of immobilized cars, whose occupants were spread about the surrounding fields. It took us a moment to realize what was happening: then a young soldier came running from car to car, warning us that there had been an alert. We got out like the rest, and sat by the edge of a little grove of trees while we had something to eat. Afterward we crawled along for an hour behind a slow-moving column of vehicles, and then at last had a clear road. As we drove through one village a soldier was going around blowing a little trumpet and shouting, "Alert's on! Get out of the village and take cover!" However, we kept straight on. At a railroad crossing we heard from a young sentry that Italy had come into the war: this was an expected move. Night fell. There was no point in turning the headlights on since there was a bicycle strapped across them. We stopped for the night at Iliers, a tiny village, where we were lucky enough to find a couple of rooms right away in the house of an old man suffering from goiter. We went to the café for a drink, just before they put up the shutters. The patrons were arguing about street lighting and other local government affairs, and asked us suspiciously what part of Paris we were from. We left to go to bed. Bianca slept on a mattress in her father's room, and I shared a vast bed with Monsieur B.'s employee. There was a large and noisy clock, which threatened to keep us awake, but we immobilized the pendulum.

At eight o'clock next morning I looked out of the window to see a gray sky, a rectangular garden, and a horrible flat landscape stretching away behind it. I hurried down to the café to write to Sartre, though without any real hope. The news was coming over the radio in the back of the shop. There was a woman there who burst into tears as she listened to the communiqué, as did I: it was impossible that morning not to recognize the fact of defeat. You came up against it everywhere—in the announcer's voice no less than in what he said, and throughout the village. "Does that mean it's finished?" people asked us, and, "Has Paris fallen?" A man was going around Iliers sticking up posters about the Italians. Refugees' cars were parked at every street corner.

We set off again at nine o'clock. The journey this time was easy. We passed various carts like those we had seen on the Boulevard Saint-Michel; but by now they were already in a decidedly rickety state, much of their hay eaten, and their owners trudging along on foot. The previous evening we had seen similar parties eating supper by the roadside, their horses untethered, and preparing for a night under the stars. Le Mans was full of English troops. When we reached Laval, we found it swarming with refugees. We came across a car with completely blackened tires: it had driven through Evreux when the town was a mass of flames, and I began to tremble with fear on Olga's behalf. Many of the refugees came from Normandy. All the sidewalks in Laval were lined with cars, and every square as well as the tree-lined strips down the boulevards were swamped with a mass of people sitting among their possessions. The cafés were packed inside, and their sidewalk *terrasses* now extended endlessly. At the station word was going around that trains coming from Paris were lost en route, but there was, I found out, a diesel car leaving for Angers at five-thirty. We went off to look for a restaurant. At the Grand Hotel they laughed in our faces: there wasn't so much as a slice of ham left. We tried a brasserie next, a place with tiled walls and tables for checkers and backgammon up against a window. It must have been a quiet little place a few days earlier; now it looked more like a station buffet. All its black-topped tables were set end to end, and there was only one dish available— veal and peas. We had it too. Then I collected my bags, said goodbye to Bianca, thanked her father for the ride, dumped my luggage in the

checkroom, and went across to the post office to put a call through to
La Pouèze. There was a milling crowd there and I had to wait more than
an hour to make my call. One wretched refugee went up to the switchboard operator and said, "Would you telephone for me, please?" The girl
just roared with laughter. For lack of anything to do I busied myself
with this good woman's problem. She told me the place she wanted to get
through to, and I went through the list of subscribers in the directory.
None of them would do for her: this one had gone away, that one would
be out in the fields, and so on. Finally I forsook her. I was so nervous and
exhausted that when I got through to Madame Lemaire my voice began
to tremble and my heart was pounding like mad. She told me that the
house was all at sixes and sevens and crammed full, but someone would
come and pick me up from Angers after dinner. I caught the diesel car,
but had to make the journey standing. I met an ex-pupil of mine from
Rouen on the car; she was getting away as fast as she could, rucksack on
back, changing from one diesel car to another. We stood and talked about
old times.

In Angers, at eight o'clock that night, I found the station yard packed
with refugees who had no idea what to do with themselves, since all
accommodations were taken. There was a sort of madwoman, wrapped
in a blanket, who kept pushing a baby carriage loaded with suitcases
round and round the square, going on desperately, never stopping. I sat
down outside a café. Night came on, and it began to rain a little. Slowly
time went by: I was dead tired. At last a car pulled up. In it were Jacqueline
Lemaire and one of her sisters-in-law, a German by derivation, who spent
the entire trip criticizing French troops for their lack of idealism. I had
a pick-up supper and spent the night in a curious bed, totally innocent of
box springs; the mattress slipped down between the wooden slats, and I felt
as though I were at the bottom of a canoe.

For three days I did nothing but read detective novels and wallow in
despair. Madame Lemaire never left her husband's bedside: he had
ghastly nightmares about the war every night, and she sacrificed her own
sleep in order to sit up with him. The village was full of relatives and
friends. We listened to every news bulletin with feverish intensity. One
evening the doorbell rang about nine o'clock: someone had seen parachutists about, and would Madame Lemaire drive down to notify them at
the police station, three miles away? The next day we heard that these
supposed parachutists had been ordinary weather balloons.

At this point my account breaks off. I have given a more or less accurate
description of the days that followed in *The Blood of Others*, making
Hélène go through the experiences that I did. Every day trucks from
Alençon and Laigle would drive through the village. Some of Madame
Lemaire's numerous guests were very scared indeed, and wanted to move
still farther away, in the direction of Bordeaux. They frightened the villagers by telling them the Germans would cut off the hands of all the
boys. But there was no question of moving Monsieur Lemaire outside the

house, and flight of any sort seemed pointless. From my own point of view, convinced as I was that Sartre had been taken prisoner, I saw no reason for being in Bordeaux rather than La Pouèze. Insofar as it served as some slight reminder that the Lycée Camille-Sée was now evacuated to Nantes, I might as well remain in the latter vicinity. The upshot was that nobody moved at all. Men patrolled the streets at night, rifle on shoulder, but the reason for this activity was not very clear. One evening someone shouted from a truck, "They've reached Le Mans." The following morning the villagers fled by pickup truck, horse-drawn carriage, bicycle, or else vanished across the fields. No one now paraded through the streets with a gun: the village was deserted—every door bolted, every shutter barred. We could hear the sound of guns, and then several big explosions as the gasoline storage tanks at Angers went up. Down the silent main street came several trucks full of French troops. They were singing. Four officers, very cool and elegant, got out of a car. One of them, a lieutenant, asked Jacqueline Lemaire if they were on the right road for Cholet. She told him they were. They hesitated indecisively, and then explained that they were going to try some "delaying tactics" along the line of the Loire. But they wanted very much to know whether or not the Germans were in Angers yet. They asked to be taken to the post office. The phone was ringing inside the building, but the door was locked. Jacqueline went away and found an axe, and they burst the lock. After they had telephoned they advised us to go home and stay put. Then they pulled out. A few soldiers still came straggling down the street, without helmets or rifles, leaning on sticks. They were followed by a column of tanks moving away from the enemy. Then nothing more. Most of those in the house had settled themselves down at the far end of the garden. Monsieur Lemaire was in bed in his room, which I had never entered, and Madame Lemaire went to join him there, after first closing all the Venetian blinds. I was left by myself, standing behind a window and staring through the slats at the deserted road. The sun was shining brightly. I felt as though I were a character in some futurist novel: it was still the same familiar village, but time had gone haywire. I had been projected into a moment of time which had no connection with my own life. This was no longer France, not yet Germany, but betwixt and between, a no man's land. Then something exploded under our windows, the plate glass in the restaurant across the way flew into slivers, a gutteral voice barked out some words in an incomprehensible language, and they were upon us—all very tall and blond, with pink complexions. They marched in step and looked straight ahead; it took a long time for the column to pass. Behind them came horses, tanks, trucks, artillery, and field kitchens.

A fairly sizable detachment stayed behind in the village. As evening drew on the peasants crept timidly back to their houses, and the cafés opened. The Germans did not cut off children's hands; they paid for their drinks and the eggs they bought on the farms, and spoke politely; all the shopkeepers smiled at them invitingly. They started in on their propaganda straight away. As I was reading in a field two soldiers approached me. They spoke a little clumsy French, and assured me of their friendly feelings toward the French people: it was the English and the Jews who had brought us to this sorry pass. This little conversation did not surprise me; what *was* disconcerting was to pass these green-uniformed men in the street and find them just like soldiers anywhere the world over. About the second or third night one of them vaulted clumsily over the garden wall, and whispered—in German, which Madame Lemaire understood— that the curfew had begun, and he was afraid of being brought up on charges by his adjutant. He appeared to have had a few drinks, and was quite obviously scared. He stayed hidden there for several minutes, and then vanished again.

From the moment I woke up till far into the night I listened to every radio bulletin. On the morning of June 17 the announcer told us that Reynaud had resigned, and Lebrun had called upon Pétain to form a new government. At twelve-thirty a fatherly military voice echoed around the dining room: "I am giving myself personally to France that her misfortunes may thereby be lessened . . . It is with a heavy heart I tell you today that we must give up the struggle." Pétain: the hero of Verdun, the ambassador who had hastened to congratulate Franco on his victory, an intimate friend of the Cagoulards. The tone of his homily made my gorge rise. All the same, I was relieved to learn that the shedding of French blood would cease at last: how absurd and ghastly these so-called rearguard actions were, in which men died to maintain a mere pale shadow of resistance! I misconstrued the meaning of Pétain's words at one point, however. When he spoke of "the military on both sides seeking a way, after the struggle and by honorable means, of putting an end to hostilities," I thought he was referring to a purely military capitulation. It took me several days to realize the true significance of the armistice. When its clauses were published, on June 21 what concerned me most was anything relevant to prisoners of war. The clause was not very clear, or perhaps I wanted to read it in an ambiguous sense. It stipulated that troops interned in Germany would stay there until the end of hostilities. Yet the Germans would hardly take this course with the hundreds of thousands of men they had been rounding up along the highways. If they sent *them* to Germany they would be obliged to feed them, and there was small profit in that. No, they would be sent home beyond a doubt. Endless rumors circulated. Some soldiers had hidden in cellars or sheds and contrived to avoid falling into the hands of the occupying power; they were liable to turn up out of the blue at their farm or in their village wearing civilian clothes. Perhaps Sartre had managed to make his way back to Paris, but how could I find out? No telephone, no mail delivery, no way of discovering what was going on in the capital. The only answer was to return there myself. Among the refugees at La Pouèze was a Dutchman, accompanied by his young wife and his mother-in-law: the latter owned a dye works near the Gare de Lyon. They were driving back, and agreed to take me with them. Once again I feel it best to give here the account of this return journey which I set down at the time.

June 28, *et seq.*

For four days I had been restless, unable to sit still. I had convinced myself that Sartre might well have returned to Paris unexpectedly, and that in any case I should pick up some news of him there. Besides, I wanted to see Paris under the Occupation, and I was getting bored. The Dutch family made up their minds to go back, too, and said they'd give me a lift. Got up at five o'clock, and made my farewells. I was upset at going, agonized by the thought of the emptiness awaiting me in Paris, but glad to be *doing* something. The Dutchman took an hour to load the car. His calm, unhurried movements made me want to murder him. He put a mattress on the roof and a pile of cases in the back. His young wife stacked up a hoard of little packages, not forgetting a jar of green beans left over from dinner the night before, which she had no intention of letting go to waste. On what remained of the rear seat went the mother-in-law and me while the wife sat beside her husband: both women wore hats and white satin blouses.

All the roads were thick with traffic. Here and there I saw traces of a bombardment; along the way we passed an overturned tank, a truck, a German grave with a cross and the man's helmet on it, and any number of burned-out vehicles. When we reached La Flèche I found out that we had started with only 10 liters of gasoline: the Dutchman was relying on the Germans, who had promised to distribute gasoline all along the route. A few days earlier he could have had 25 liters, but he got tired of waiting in line, and had given up with only another half-hour or so to wait. So at La Flèche he went off to the Kommandantur, which had been set up in a splendid riverside house. It was here that I first saw field-gray uniforms; the Germans in La Pouèze had all been wearing green. I took a turn around the town with the other two women: we bought a copy of *La Sarthe* and read the conditions of the armistice. I had already heard them over the air, and the only one I didn't know was that concerning the extradition of German refugees, which revolted me. I read the paragraph concerning prisoners with close attention, and it seemed certain to me that they would only hold those who were in Germany already. This conviction sustained me throughout the two days of my return journey, and made it possible for me to take some interest in it.

The Dutchman returned with the news that no one would be allowed more than 5 liters, and not before two o'clock anyway: it was now eleven. He decided to try for Le Mans, saying he "thought" he had enough gasoline to make it. About six miles short of our destination we were turned back: there was no gasoline in Le Mans, and three hundred cars had already formed a solid jam there. We had scarcely a drop left, and were really in the lurch; but we were lucky enough to try a farm, where there was a 5-liter can of reddish stuff that had been abandoned by the British.

At midday our car pulled up in Le Mans, between two large squares. In one of these stood the Kommandantur, and in the other the Préfecture. The entrance gates of the latter were still closed; about two hundred people were pressed up against them, clutching jugs, gasoline cans, or watering cans. Around the statue of some comically small public figure in a plumed hat (Levasseur, I guess) a whole mass of cars had halted, not to mention some trucks loaded with mattresses and kitchenware. Refugees sat about, eating or dozing or just waiting for something to happen, very dirty and shabby-looking, surrounded by children and bundles, and grumbling away like mad. Someone said they'd been waiting eight days now, shuttled to and fro indefinitely between Préfecture and Kommandantur; there was also a rumor going about that Paris had no food supplies whatsoever. The Dutchman stood there in the midday sun and grinned in that idiotic way of his; he didn't want to stand in line at all, but his wife, with me supporting her, forced him to stay where he was. "Want eaties," she said, in a childish voice. She complained that the crowd smelled nasty, and made a paper hat to protect her husband's head. We were told that you first had to get a queue number; when you had this you could obtain a voucher; and once in possession of the voucher you could get some fuel—that is, on the day the gasoline arrived. At two-thirty the iron gates were opened, and the crowd surged forward; but an official shooed everyone out again, telling them that at three o'clock a tanker was coming that held 10,000 liters, and there would be enough and to spare for everyone. Some people nevertheless stayed on, and obtained vouchers which entitled them to buy 5 liters from a nearby garage. The Dutchman, however, decided he was hungry. So we made our way to the main square, the atmosphere of which somewhat resembled a country fair, being dusty, overcrowded, and exposed to a killingly fierce sun. There were mobs of soldiers in field gray, numerous German cars, plus hundreds of trucks and other vehicles belonging to the refugees. All the cafés were packed with Germans. It was depressing to see them there, so well-groomed, cheerful, and courteous, while France was only represented by this miserable rabble. Military trucks, sound trucks, and motorcycles charged noisily around the island in the center of the square; a loud-speaker was blaring out some ear-splitting military march, and also a series of communiqués in French and German. It was absolutely hellish. Victory was written across every German face, while every French face proclaimed defeat aloud.

Nothing to eat in the cafés. We went back for our provisions and divided them among us. The Germans came and went, and saluted with much clicking of heels, and drank, and laughed. They also were very much on their best and most courteous behavior. When I dropped some small object one of them instantly picked it up for me. Then we sat down on the sidewalk beside our car, while the procession continued to and fro between Préfecture and Kommandantur, with people still clutching their empty watering cans. Some of them simply sat down on their gasoline cans and waited for a miracle, in the shape of that truck with its 10,000 liters of gasoline. An hour or two passed. Once again the Dutchman got tired of waiting in line and came back empty-handed. We found a small shop with a little bread and some pork for sale: the pâtisseries were crammed with young Germans, stuffing themselves on candy and ices. Further waiting.

By eight o'clock the Dutchman had managed to get hold of 5 liters of gasoline. It was a relief to get clear of this baking caravanserai and be driving through open countryside. We found a farm, and slept in the hayloft.

The women woke up whining and complaining; the older one was having twinges in her sciatic nerve. "Those villainous Germans!" the younger one said, in that crappy voice of hers. "If we only had them in our power, we'd machine gun every nasty little Boche in sight." Her husband started complaining because the straw had been pricking his knees. The farmer's wife sold us milk and eggs at a very reasonable price.

Once more we joined the procession of cars, wagons loaded with peasants and bales of hay, bicyclists, and the occasional footslogger. At La Ferté-Bernard there was a crowd of refugees who had got that far on German trucks, but had been put off and left just as night was drawing in. Now they were waiting for more trucks. Once again we saw empty watering cans and heard the rumor that there would be "no gasoline today." I was sick and tired of the whole business, and decided to get home under my own steam. There was a train in the station leaving for Paris, but it was reserved for railway employees who were being repatriated, and though there were plenty of empty compartments, no one else was allowed aboard. Orders were that no travelers bound for Paris should be let on, only those bound for Chartres, and even then you had to prove you were domiciled there. Some people told me that they had been coming there every morning for the last few days, but it was never any use. Paris was desperately short of food, they said, and this was why refugees were not being repatriated. Yet, despite this, the papers and the radio exhorted them constantly to do so, and German trucks gave them lifts home. In any case there was no food at La Ferté either, and we were quite liable to sit there till we starved to death. I walked back to the car in a disheartened mood and sat down on the running board. Later I tried to buy some food, but found nothing except a chunk of coarse, oversalty bread which I swallowed with misery. No gasoline for three days at least, someone said. My heart sank into my boots. I left my suitcase with the Dutch couple, determined to get out of this place, no matter how.

It was nearly 110 miles to Paris. It's easy enough to say you'll go on foot if you have to, but the thought of that distance on a tarred road, with that sun blazing down on me, was decidedly discouraging. So I went on sitting there on the sidewalk. I had a thousand francs in my pocket, which was quite a lot—or nothing at all; last night people had paid 1,500 francs for a seat in a car, and today you couldn't get a seat at all, even at that price. Two men had put on armbands and stood in the middle of the road, stopping any car which looked as though it had a little room left in it; but in reality they could never squeeze another body in. Finally a German truck pulled up, and I, together with two other women, made a dash for it. I climbed aboard behind them, to find that the truck was going as far as Mantes, only twenty-five miles short of Paris. This got me well on the way to my objective. It was horribly hot under the tarpaulin roof: there was a crowd of people aboard, and a strong smell of gasoline. I was sitting near the back, on a suitcase, and shot up every time we went over a bump. To cap it all I was sitting facing the wrong way. Miserably I felt my stomach begin to rebel, and presently I brought up all the bread I had eaten. No one seemed so much as to notice this.

When the truck stopped I lay down on the embankment while the others were eating: a German tapped me on the shoulder and asked me if I would like some food. I said I wouldn't. Shortly afterward he woke me up, very politely. An old woman said that for the past two days the truck drivers had been showering cigarettes, food, and champagne on them. They were genuinely kind, she said; they seemed not to be obeying orders but rather possessed of a spontaneous urge to be helpful. Nogent-le-Rotrou looked as though it had been heavily damaged, Chartres seemed scarcely touched, and Dreux more or less intact too, though we passed a few shell holes along the road. We met large numbers of military trucks; the troops often shouted *"Heil!"* at us, and in one or two trucks they had all pinned the most gorgeous red roses to their gray uniforms. And still the long procession of refugees trailed on.

At Mantes I looked around, slightly bewildered, and finally approached a Red Cross car which seemed about to move off. I got in the back and found myself sitting between a really ultra-chic nurse—a certain Mademoiselle de Hérédia, and she didn't ever forget it, either—and some sort of senior Red Cross woman officer wearing glasses. In front we had another nurse, and a gentleman, whose name I've forgotten but who was driving. The women told me that all over France doctors had been among the first to flee, leaving the nurses at clinics and hospitals completely in the lurch. They described the fires that had raged around Paris, and the scene at Etampes, where two columns of jammed traffic had gone up in flames, and the great exodus, and the lack of proper first-aid, and the ridiculous inadequacy of the Civil Defense system; apparently the Germans split themselves laughing when they saw our slit trenches. These women were rabidly anti-British. One of them said she hadn't let her revolver out of her sight for three weeks now because of French and English soldiers trying to commandeer her car for a speedier get-away. We stopped for a while at Saint-Germain; my head was splitting, and when I looked in a glass I saw that my face was black with dust. We all drank peppermint cordial, and around us the town was absolutely dead. Not a sign of life from now onward, all the way to Paris. I spotted some blown-up bridges across the Seine, and a little farther on some bomb craters and ruined houses; and everywhere that lunar silence reigned. On the Rue François I there was a queue outside the Red Cross: people coming to get news of prisoners. One or two people were waiting outside butcher shops, too, but almost all other establishments were closed. How empty the streets were! I had never expected to find such a deserted wilderness.

On the Rue Vavin the landlady went into exclamations of despair because she had thrown out all my belongings: I couldn't have cared less. She gave me a letter from Sartre dated June 9, still optimistic in tone.

I cleaned myself up a bit and decided to go and try to telephone from the post office. Spotted my father sitting outside the Dumesnil, and had a sandwich and a beer with him. There were a few Germans about, but one was far less aware of them than in La Pouèze. My father told me they were very polite, that as was to be expected Paris now had German news bulletins only, that all foreign currency had been frozen. He also expressed the opinion that POWs were most unlikely to be released before the end of the war, and that there were vast camps at Garches, Antony, etc., where they were starving to death on a diet of "dead dog," as he put it. Occupied France, he told me, had been "assimilated" into Germany, and therefore they would all be held indefinitely.

The post office turned out to be closed. I went to see my mother. When I left her, at eight-thirty, she told me to hurry because of the curfew. I don't think I have ever felt so utterly depressed as I did during that walk back through the deserted streets, under a stormy sky: my eyes were burning, my head on fire, and the one thought in my mind was of Sartre, literally and physically starving to death. The houses and shops and the trees in the Luxembourg Gardens were all still standing; but there were no men left, there never would be any men again, and I had no idea why I myself so absurdly continued to survive. Went to bed in the grip of absolute despair.

June 30

Will they or won't they come home? Stories go around about soldiers turning up when they're least expected, dressed in civilian clothes. To tell the truth I was still half expecting to find Sartre waiting for me, all smiles, outside the Dôme; but no, there's the same feeling of loneliness there as at La Pouèze, only this time more hopeless. Still, there's one piece of slight consolation in *Le Matin*, where they're asking if families couldn't be allowed to communicate with their relatives in the forces before the latter are demobilized. It now occurs to me that perhaps the camps are holding our troops prior to releasing them by stages. I can't give up hope.

It's lovely weather. I resume my usual table at the Dôme, close to the now almost deserted *terrasse*. There's a notice up with information about the *plats du jour,* and I've seen shops displaying magnificent fruit and good fresh ham; there's an apparent air of prosperity abroad, very different from conditions in Chartres or Le Mans. Almost no one about on the boulevard. Two trucks full of young Germans in gray go past: this has become so common a sight that now it hardly strikes me as odd. Quite suddenly, and with my whole heart and soul, I find myself believing the war will end, that there will be an "afterward." The proof of this is my purchase of a bottle of ink and the notebook in which I'm writing an account of the past few days. For three weeks now I have been in a sort of limbo: vast public events brought their own individual, physiological agony, but I wanted to become a *person* again, with a past and future of my own. Perhaps here in Paris I shall achieve this aim. If I can draw my salary, I shall stay put for a long while.

Paris is quite extraordinarily deserted, even more so than in September. The weather is more or less the same, the air as mild and calm as ever. Not many food stores are still open, and those that are have queues outside them. We see a few Germans around. But the real difference is of another sort. In September something was *beginning*—something terrible perhaps, but nevertheless of all-absorbing interest. Now that's all vanished, and the future stretches out before me in unremitting stagnancy. I shall sit here and rot for years. Passy and Auteuil are utterly dead; there's a smell of lime blossom and leafy greenness about them that reminds me both of the coming holidays and of time past. Even the concierges have packed up and gone. Down the Boulevard de Grenelle I walk past the former concentration camp for women. By the terms of the armistice all German refugees have to be returned to Germany. No clause in the whole document fills me with greater horror. I come back through the Latin Quarter and find it deserted. But the cafés are open, and one or two people can be seen sitting outside them. Hardly any Germans here.

I return to the Dôme. Now there are people around: a Swiss sculptor, Hoggar's wife, a former beauty who wears odd golfing plus fours and a funny little hood. And the Germans are in evidence again: this strikes me as strange, but only in an abstract sort of way. They have dull faces, and look like tourists. One isn't, as one was at Le Mans, conscious of their collective power; and individually they are boring to look at. I observe them but register nothing. Airplanes have been passing over the city at rooftop level all day, with large black crosses painted on their gleaming wings. Only three or four tarts out on the *terrasse,* busy soliciting German clients—not without some success.

July 1

Today the tarts have invaded the whole front part of the café—so much so, indeed, that it's like walking into a brothel. One of them's crying, and some of the others offer her consolation: "So he hasn't written—nobody's written; don't take on so." It's the same old story everywhere, in the Métro, on doorsteps, with women exchanging virtually identical lines: "Any news?" "No, he must be a prisoner." "When will the lists come out?" and so on. None of them, it now seems clear, will be released before peace is concluded; but still the stories keep circulating: "He got all the way to Paris before he was arrested. The Germans give them civilian clothes." So there is always the possibility of a miracle; and though it's as illusory and nerve-racking and irresistible as any lottery ticket, it provides every woman in Paris with one all-engrossing obsession. I used to think that this sort of uncertainty was quite unbearable, but even here patience can be acquired. In a week, perhaps, there will be some news, or a letter, or the lists will be published. So you prepare to wait for a week; time has little value.

Took a long walk through the suburbs to kill some time. People were coming back home. All the way I heard the same thing everywhere: "Just back from Montauban—if I'd known what things were like I'd never have

gone!" A cyclist stopped by one group: "Your mother is back already!"—
and then they all crowded around to give him the latest news about his
mother and his house. Much milling around and greetings between neighbors. There are gardens full of roses and currant bushes, cornfields dappled
with red poppies, and sweet-smelling clover along the embankments—all
the elements of country living spread out around prim suburban villas.
Certain of these carry a sign reading *"Maison habitée"* or, more often,
"Bewohnt." I thumb a lift back, get picked up by a small and ancient car,
the driver of which was just making the return trip from Agen. He too
was saying, "If only I'd known!" He'd driven nearly five hundred miles
with his wife aboard, she having a fractured spine at the time. He tells
me how frightful this was for both of them: "I can tell you, madame,
you're a mature woman;"—here gesturing toward his private parts—"I
feel it *there,* I feel it really badly!" The authorities in the nonoccupied
départements were preventing people leaving, and some said we'd be
arrested at Vierzon, but Vierzon came and went without our being stopped.
Followed the Seine most of the way back. People swimming and boating
in the Grand-Jatte: holiday atmosphere, though somewhat oppressive. When
the car stopped close to a bridge a German soldier threw us a bar of
chocolate from a truck. Some of them standing beside the road, chatting
very cheerfully with a group of pretty girls. "There'll be plenty of little
Germans on the way soon," the driver remarked to me. I've heard this
phrase a dozen times, never with any hint of censure attached to it. "It's
just human nature," said the driver. "You don't need to talk the same
language for *that.*" I haven't seen the symptoms of real hatred in anyone
yet, only a wave of panicky fear among the country villagers, followed by
a wide and wary eye when that first alarm had worn off.

I meet Lise again. She tried to get out of Paris by bicycle last Thursday,
and found herself pedaling along beside a German car. Afterward she
was held up in a long line of crawling trucks and told to turn back. She
and her bicycle were both bundled into the back of a truck and given a
ride. Now she wants to teach me to ride a bicycle.

My parents complain about the dearth of adequate food. Dinner con-
sists of soup and macaroni: I haven't had a good square meal for days.
Seems that Paris really is short of supplies. My father tells me of the
menu offered by one big restaurant on the Place Gaillon: cucumber salad,
8 fr., cheese omelette, 12 fr., crab pilaf, 20 fr., noodles, 8 fr., strawberries,
18 fr. No other dishes. I think of Magny's dinners at Braibant's during
the siege of Paris.

July 2

A gray day, with a chill in the air. Everywhere deserted. Just six people
around the newsstand by the Métro station. I bought two papers. What a
wasteland—sentimental pro-German propaganda—a "compassionate" tone,
a mixture of sorrow, superiority, and brotherly regard for the wretched
population of France. And promises: the railways will be running again,
postal service will be resumed.

Telephoned Camille's house. Madame J. told me she and Zina left on foot, with rucksacks, since when nothing has been heard of them. Dullin too has had some adventures: am going to see him tomorrow. Also phoned one of Bost's sisters, who says he's been evacuated to Avignon, and his brother is a prisoner.

I went to the Sorbonne to find out about my salary. Was filling in some forms when a schools inspector pounced on me. "Teacher of philosophy? Exactly what we need." He put a call through to Duruy, and I'm to report there tomorrow. Eight hours of work a week; it might be much worse.

July 3

Have had a bicycling lesson with Lise through the small quiet back streets around the Rue Vavin. Kept my balance on the seat right away. Have even learned to mount by myself and to turn corners. Start classes at Duruy.

At 4:15 I go see Dullin at the Atelier. Find Montmartre depressingly dead. The concierge wouldn't let me in at first, saying that Monsieur Dullin was "not in a state to receive visitors"; but then she came back, visibly astonished, with the information that I was lucky—he was expecting me right away. I found him in his shirt sleeves, with an apron tied around him, surrounded by a mass of old papers and torn photographs, and looking rather haggard. He shook hands with me effusively, and said how worried he was about Camille. He had left on Tuesday to see old Madame J. at Ferrolles, and about the same time Camille and Zina were to have caught a train down from the Gare d'Orsay. They had arranged to meet in Tours, but Dullin had been unable to get there, and now had no idea of Camille's whereabouts. Crécy was already completely evacuated by the time Madame J. climbed into his trap. They set off in the direction of the Loire, but got caught up in a flood of refugees and wandered around for thirteen days, sleeping in the trap, eating practically nothing, and on several occasions being machine-gunned from the air—all without ever managing to get across the river. He had also taken an old servant-woman with him, who proceeded to go crazy. She spent all one day wandering vaguely round in search of food, and finally vanished into a wood, saying she was looking for eggs. He never saw her again. Finally the Germans picked them up and made them turn back. He was very scared of being recognized by the Germans, and tried to pass himself off as a peasant. Once he passed a convoy of prisoners who greeted him by name: this caused him great annoyance.

July 5

The newspapers are quite unspeakable: it turns my stomach to read them and they put me in a black mood. Lise and I went to the Palais-Royal to check through the lists of prisoners. Found the place closed, with a fantastic queue outside, and in any case information is available only about camps in the Paris area. Anyway I know Sartre is a prisoner: the only thing I'm interested in is the date of his release. Afterward we had a drink in the Café de la Paix: full of extremely dandified German officers, and no one else there at all. Most depressing. Have moved into my grandmother's flat, she being at present with my parents. The postal services have been restored, and I've written some letters, but still feel a desperate sense of isolation.

July 6

Notice posted up in the Dôme saying the place is out of bounds to Germans: I wonder why? Anyway it's a relief not to have to look at those uniforms any longer.

I went to the Bibliothèque National and took a reader's ticket. I have embarked upon Hegel's *Phenomenology of Mind*; at present can scarcely make head or tail of a word of it. Have decided to work at Hegel every afternoon from two till five; it's the most soothing occupation I can imagine.

I telephoned Dullin. When he reached Crécy he found there had been widespread looting—by Frenchmen. Someone told him Camille was in the Tours area, and he's determined to get a lift down there in a truck.

After this year's events the thought of dying no longer seems quite so frightful. Anyway I know only too well that all life is nothing but a brief reprieve from death.

July 7

A bicycle ride around Paris with Lise. I passed a column of armored cars, full of black-uniformed Germans, their heavy berets blowing in the breeze: a fine yet depressing spectacle. Back to the Bibliothèque Nationale, and read more Hegel. Still find him extremely hard to understand. Have come across one passage that would make a wonderful epigraph for my novel. Copied it out.

Potatoes are once more available, albeit intermittently, in Paris, and meat, and even butter. Meals are back to normal at the Dôme; there's no feeling of scarcity at all. What I really miss is the cinema, but they're only putting on quite impossible films.

What with the clocks being set to German time, and a curfew at eleven o'clock, find myself cooped up in my room while it's still quite light. Most peculiar. I stand outside on my balcony for a long while, unable to believe my eyes.

July 11

A penciled note from Sartre, in an open envelope that's been canceled twice—once by the postal authorities and once by the Government of Paris. For a moment I don't recognize the handwriting; then I stare uncomprehendingly at the letter itself, which looks as though it's been delivered by hand. He says he may, repeat *may,* be home before the end of the month; he asks for news of me (though I'm by no means sure a letter will reach him); he says he's not badly treated, and that's about all he's allowed to say. I have no real idea of *how* he is. This note is of unbelievable importance, yet its content is nil. All the same, I breathe a little easier now.

July 14

Paris in the rain: most depressing. Felt an overwhelming need to talk to someone, anyone, so phoned Dullin. To my amazement Camille answered: went over to see her at six o'clock. Found her wearing indoor clothes; a little puffy around the eyes, but otherwise flourishing. Dullin was there too, similarly dressed and all in black, very cheerful and expansive. Madame J. and Vandéric were also present. Vandéric had served with the Belgian Army: he told us they were sent up to the front line completely unarmed, and left there. Three days later they were told to move out again, still without having been issued any arms. Camille told me about her own exodus: on Tuesday she forwarded her luggage to Tours—it has almost certainly been lost, and there was a mass of manuscript material and notes in it—after which she and Zina set off together, each of them wearing a rucksack, and Camille herself also carrying the two dolls, Friedrich and Albrecht, in a suitcase. They reached Nevers in two days, by train. After that they tried to go on to Tours by truck; it was a tough job, but they managed it. Tours was deserted. The bridges were being mined, and air raids took place every night. Their rendezvous with Dullin was at the *poste restante,* and the post office was closed. Accordingly, they moved out into the country, where they found an engineless train that had been standing in a siding for days, and climbed aboard it. Everyone was very disturbed, expecting the Germans to arrive during the night. Camille and Zina finally sought refuge with the railroad-crossing attendant, who rented them a room. There they stayed, dressed as peasant women and bored stiff. Meanwhile the occupants of the train gradually drifted away. One evening a colonel turned up and warned them that there would be a "small artillery battle" next day, and they should all take shelter. They accordingly went into a cave, and when the "small battle" was over, they returned home. Camille passed herself off as the gatekeeper's sister-in-law, being improbably convinced that the Germans had some dreadful fate in store for all refugees. She contrived to send a letter off to Dullin; and when Dullin learned about this letter, he dropped all the parcels he was holding, and began to tremble so violently that Madame J. thought he was on the point of passing out. It all ended with Camille getting a lift back on a track.

Here my diary breaks off once more. There was nothing further for me to note down. I became used to the gray and green uniforms, and the swastika flag flying over the Sénat. I continued to teach at Duruy, and to read Hegel in the Bibliothèque Nationale, which now opened in the morning. Hegel I found a tranquillizing influence. Just as at the age of twenty, my heart bleeding because of my cousin Jacques, I read Homer "to set all humanity between myself and my private grief," so now I endeavored to sink this present experience of mine in the "trend of world-development." All about me, embalmed in countless thousands of volumes, the past lay sleeping, and the present seemed to me like a past that was yet to come. I was abolishing my individualistic self altogether. Yet such reveries in no way tempted me to acquiesce to Fascism. If one was an optimist, one might regard it as the necessary antithesis to bourgeois liberalism, and therefore a step in the direction of that final synthesis to which we all aspired, i.e., socialism; but to hope for its eventual supersession one had to begin by rejecting it. No philosophy on earth could have persuaded me to accept it; it ran counter to all the basic values on which my life had been built. Every day, moreover, brought me fresh cause for hating it. How nauseating it was to pick up *Le Matin* or *La Victoire* each morning and read these self-righteous apologias for Germany, or the minatory lectures which our conquerors insisted on reading us! From the end of July onward, too, the notice "Out of Bounds to Jews" began to appear in the windows of certain shops. *Le Matin* published a muckraking article on "the Ghetto," demanding its abolition. Vichy Radio was busy denouncing the "renegade Jews" who had left France in the lurch, and Pétain repealed the law forbidding anti-Semitic propaganda. Anti-Jewish demonstrations were whipped up in Vichy, Toulouse, Marseille, Lyon, and on the Champs Elysées, while a large number of factories fired all "Jews and foreigners" among their workers. The violent nature of this campaign, right from the start, was something I found terrifying. Where would they draw the line? I found myself wishing there was someone with whom I could share my fear and, more particularly, my rage. Sartre's letters from Baccarat were the only things that kept me going: he maintained, persistently, that our ideas and hopes would triumph in the end. He also said there was a chance of his being set free at the beginning of September: civil servants in certain categories were being repatriated. I sat outside the Dôme and gazed at Rodin's "Balzac," the unveiling of which had caused such an uproar two years before, and it seemed to me as though Sartre was going to appear at any moment, smiling, walking toward me with that quick step of his. At other times I told myself I wouldn't see him again for another three or four years, and wished I could fall asleep till they had elapsed. During this period, indeed, I never envisaged peace in the immediate future. A quick showdown would have implied victory for Nazism, and this one sincerely and passionately refused to accept: one couldn't believe in the possibility even, at least not quite so soon. Russia and America would surely intervene, and one day Hitler would be beaten: this implied a lengthy war. A lengthy separation.

As soon as the trains were running again, Olga came to see me. She spent six hours standing in a corridor: even the w.c.'s were packed full, so that children relieved themselves out of the window, and old ladies on the floor. Beuzeville station had been bombed to bits. Olga's family lived over twenty miles away, and had stayed with some friends of theirs during this raid: when they got home they found every window in the house shattered by blast. Olga spent a few days in my grandmother's flat and then went back to her parents. Bianca came across Paris to see me: she had spent a fortnight pea-picking on a Breton farm, and now she was going off with her mother and sister to finish her holiday in the Yonne area. Her father had made arrangements for one of his friends, an Aryan, to take charge of his affairs: both he and Bianca feared the worst. Bianca was in a state of extreme anxiety and depression, and despite all my efforts to comfort her, I could sense her feeling of complete isloation, even when she was with me. I remembered how once I had said to Olga that there was no such thing as "a Jew," there were only human beings: how head-in-the-clouds I had been! Much earlier in 1939, when Bianca had talked to me about her Viennese cousins, I had foreseen, with a twinge of private shame, that her life was destined to be very different from mine. There was no getting away from the truth of that premonition now. She was in positive danger, whereas I had nothing specific to fear: neither friendship nor affinity could succeed in bridging the gulf that yawned between us. Neither of us measured the size of that gulf, and her generous nature shied away from plumbing its depths even more than I did. But though she allowed herself no bitterness, I could not escape an uncomfortable feeling very much akin to remorse.

When she was gone I once again had no one to talk to. My parents lived in a state of permanent bewilderment. My father could never understand how *Le Matin,* which he regarded as the most clear-sighted and patriotic paper in Paris, had been the first to sell out to the Germans, whom he regarded, with loathing, as "the Boches." I could never bring myself to use this term, which I found insufferably chauvinistic; it was as Nazis that I detested the Germans. But at least, thanks to this verbal equivocation, I managed to avoid falling out with my parents. I often saw Lise: after her ill treatment by the French, she regarded the German occupation with indifference. All the same I found her a godsend: she was as tough and daring and enterprising as a boy, and I had great fun in her company. She presented me with a bicycle, which I had no qualms about accepting, even though she had come by it illegally. We used to go for rides around Paris, and farther afield after August had come and my classes were at an end. I saw the Ile-de-France, with its forests and châteaux and abbeys. I rode through Compiègne, Beauvais, and Normandy, and it seemed almost natural to me that they should all lie in ruins. I pedaled on, and the sheer physical exertion kept me occupied. Besides, Lise's ways were a source of endless amusement to me. At times, indeed, despite my own indifference to public opinion, I actually found them a little embarrassing: she courted scandal so deliberately. When we visited a church in Evreux she washed her hands in the holy water basin. At Louviers there was a washstand in the passage leading to the hotel dining room: Lise vigorously soaped her face at it, under the astonished eyes of waitresses and our fellow guests. "Why not?" she used to ask me, with a touch of defiance; and as every reply would have had to be based on the most rigorous logical foundations, I would have been forced to deploy a whole philosophical system merely to stop her blowing her nose in her table napkin.

Quite apart from this, though, she was genuinely interested in philosophy, and I gave her a few lessons on the subject. She developed a great passion for Descartes, because he made a clean sweep of everything and began from scratch, building strictly on evidence. But she refused to read him by the paragraph, or even phrase by phrase: she dwelled on every single word, which often made these working sessions rather stormy. I disliked storms, but Lise seemed positively to enjoy them. She cheerfully admitted that most of the family quarrels she had made the excuse to waylay me outside my hotel last year had been her own invention—but this did not affect her belief that by comforting her so assiduously I had given her certain rights over me, which she was now exercising. She reproached me most vehemently for having left Paris without her in June. She would not admit the fact that I preferred my own company to hers; when I took that long walk through the suburbs which I describe in my diary, she followed me as far as the Porte d'Orléans, stubbornly repeating the words, "I want to come with you." On this occasion my anger intimidated her; but often neither prayers nor threats could make any headway against her determination. When we were working or talking in my room, late at night, she had to leave at a reasonable hour because of the curfew. I used to keep one eye on the clock and tell her when it was time. One evening she calmly announced that she wasn't going. Her voice rose: it wasn't polite to throw her out like this, she could sleep here, the flat was quite big enough, and anyway I had put Olga up in it. My one argument was that I didn't want her to stay, and this she refused to consider. Furiously I saw the curfew hour drawing nearer and nearer, till in the end I was forced to give her a bed in my grandmother's room. This success emboldened her, and she tried the same thing again. This time tears of sheer rage sprang to my eyes, and somehow—heaven knows how, since she was much stronger than I—I managed to shove her out onto the landing. Doubtless her resolution wavered for a moment at this point; but she quickly returned to the attack and began to ring the bell, continuously. I wouldn't budge. When I fell asleep, my ears plugged with wax, she was still pealing away every now and again. In the morning I found her lying on the doormat, her face all befouled with tears and dust. The apartment was on the top floor, with no other door on the same landing; she had slept there without anyone disturbing her. I hoped this lesson would do the trick, but not at all: she was incorrigible. We continued as before: great mutual understanding and endless bickering.

August declined into September, and about the fifteenth I got a letter from Sartre telling me he was being transferred to Germany. As usual he said he was in good health and very cheerful. But I had been so much counting on his return that I collapsed at the news. I find the following note scribbled in a notebook where I was trying to resuscitate my diary:

> This time I really am miserable. Last year the world around me had become a tragic world, and I lived accordingly: this was not real misery. I recall very clearly how in September I felt myself to be just one fragment of a vast collective episode, and found that episode interesting. But for the past week it's been different. The world is chaotic. Misery sits within me like some intimate personal illness, a

sequence of insomnia, nightmares, and migraines . . . I have a vague picture of a map of Germany, its frontier a black tangle of barbed wire, and somewhere I read the name Silesia, and hear words that sound like "They're starving to death."

I hadn't the heart to go on with this: even to think aloud on paper had become unbearable.

Nevertheless, I took advantage of these last bright September days: Bianca had come back to Paris, and now suggested our going off on a cycling tour together. Since I was now no longer waiting for Sartre, I accepted. We took a train as far as a small town in the Brière region, which I was anxious to explore. The villages, with their spotless whitewashed cottages and thatched roofs, had an almost artificial air about them: they stood in the midst of desolate, thickly reeded swamps which I found, on the whole, unattractive. I visited Guérande, slumbering peacefully behind its ancient ramparts; I followed the gently sun-warmed coast line of southern Brittany, with its pine woods and dunes and creeks and heathland all glowing under the autumn sky; I came to Rochefort-en-Terre, where the houses are built of gray granite and decorated with scarlet geraniums. We ate lobster and pancakes and delicious pastries. We met no Germans on the road, but heard a good deal about them in country inns. They wolfed down five-egg omelettes and tucked away whole bowls of cream: no one had even seen such enormous appetites before. "They certainly like good food, those boys," a waiter in a Rennes café told us. Yet during this fortnight I managed to forget them almost completely: a faint flicker of the old peacetime *douceur de vivre* glowed into transient life. Then we returned to Paris.

Chapter 7

N O, TIME HAD NOT TURNED TOPSY-TURVY AFTER all; the seasons continued to revolve, and a new school year was beginning. It began badly, too. At the Lycée Camille-Sée—as was the case in every *lycée*—I was made to sign a document affirming upon oath that I was neither a Freemason nor a Jew. I found putting my name to this most repugnant, but no one refused to do so; the majority of my colleagues, like myself, had no possible alternative.

I left my grandmother's flat and moved back to the Hôtel du Danemark on the Rue Vavin. Paris was a dismal place now. No more gasoline, so no cars on the streets; the few buses operating were running on fuel oil. Almost the only means of transport was by bicycle; many Métro stations were still barricaded. The curfew had been extended till midnight, though places of public entertainment still closed at eleven. I no longer went anywhere near a cinema: nothing was being shown except German films and the very worst sort of French features. The Germans had forbidden any applause during the newsreels, on the grounds that such demonstrations were intended to be insulting. A large number of cinemas, incuding the Rex, had been turned into troops' cinemas, or *Soldaten-Kino.* I took my meals in various little restaurants which still got by quite nicely; but in the markets and food shops there was a real shortage. Ration cards had been brought in toward the end of September, though this step did nothing to improve supplies. At my parents' dinner table I found vegetables served up that had been popular during the previous war, such as rutabagas and Jerusalem artichokes.

Nevertheless, people came drifting back to town again. I ran into Marco at the Dôme; he had resumed his old job at the Lycée Louis-le-Grand. He told me, mysteriously, "I have Philippe Pétain's ear," which probably meant he knew someone who was very vaguely acquainted with Alibert. Anyway, I thought, it was hardly something to boast about. I was far more pleased to see Pagniez again; he had gone through the retreat as a colonel's driver, and had stayed at the wheel for nearly forty-eight hours without sleep. He disconcerted me by refusing to join in my fulminations against the Vichy Government. To disparage Pétain, he assured me, was to play straight into the hands of those who wanted to put all France under some Gauleiter's heel. "And what about afterward?" I asked him.

At all events, Vichy did what the Germans commanded. On October 2 a German edict had been promulgated ordering all Jews to declare themselves as such, and all Jewish firms to notify the authorities of their nationality. On October 19 Vichy published its own "Jewish statute," debarring all Jews from public office or the liberal professions. The crawling hypocrisy of the man who had the nerve to assert his loathing for "the lies which have done us such terrible harm" put me in a blazing temper. Under the specious pretext of moral improvement he was preaching a back-to-the-land policy (as my father's friend Monsieur Jeannot had previously done in his sponsored plays), the real point of which was to reduce France, at her conquerors' insistence, to be a mere German granary. They were all lying: these generals and other notabilities who had sabotaged the war because they preferred Hitler to the Popular Front were now proclaiming that it was because of our "frivolous spirit" that we had lost. These ultrapatriotic characters were turning the defeat of France into a sort of pedestal on which they could stand, the better to insult Frenchmen. In a mealy-mouthed way they protested that they were working for the good of France—but which France? They took advantage of the German occupation to impose a really tyrannous program on the people, something that might have been thought up by a bunch of former Cagoulards. The Marshal's "messages" attacked everything which I felt to be of value, liberty in particular. Henceforth the family would be the sovereign unit, the reign of virtue was at hand, and God would be spoken of respectfully in the schools. This was something I knew only too well, the same violent prejudice and stupidity that had darkened my childhood—only now it extended over the entire country, an official and repressive blanket. Hitler and Nazism had been worlds apart from me; I hated them at a distance, almost calmly. But Pétain and the Révolution Nationale aroused my active personal loathing, and the anger they kindled in me flared up afresh daily. The details of what was going on in Vichy, the various transactions and concessions, never aroused my interest at all, since I regarded the whole idea of Vichy as a shameful scandal.

Olga came back to Paris—for good, this time—and moved into a hotel on the Rue Jules-Chaplain, together with her sister. Bost joined her there. He had spent a long and weary convalescence at Montpellier, and now he was entirely cured. After so many months exclusively in female company, it was wonderful to pick up a friendship with a man again. We were in agreement about everything, but he could see no further ahead than I could. The future was restricted, and even the present lay beyond our grasp; our only source of information was the German press. I had absolutely no political contacts: Aron had got away to London, Fernando and Stépha had left France for America, Colette Audry had settled down in Grenoble with her husband, and Bost's brother was a prisoner. Who was left for me to extract information from? I felt terribly isolated. There were one or two clandestine news sheets in circulation already, such as *Pantagruel* or Jean Texier's *Les Conseils à l'occupant,* but I was unaware of their existence. I went round to the *N.R.F.* and had a talk with Brice Parain. He told me that the review was going to recommence publication: Paulhan had refused to edit it under Greman control, and Drieu was taking over. Parain also talked to me about the "Otto List," a list of books which publishers and booksellers were required to withdraw from sale: Heine, Thomas Mann, Freud, Stekel, Maurois, the works of General de Gaulle, and various others. There was only one important piece of information he passed on to me: Nizan had been killed. Where, and the precise circumstances of his death, remained uncertain, but there was no doubt that he *was* dead. His wife and children had fled to America. My heart turned over at the news. Had Nizan, who so loathed the very thought of death, foreseen his own demise? He had finished his best and finest book, *La Conspiration.* Shortly afterward the ground had quaked beneath his feet, forcing him to reappraise his position, and in the very instant of deciding afresh where he stood, he had died. It struck me as particularly absurd that he should have been robbed of his future now, of all times. Several days went by before I discovered, to my stupefied amazement, that he was gradually being robbed of his past, too.

Sartre had informed me in one letter that a fellow prisoner of his, a Communist, had just been repatriated—on what grounds I cannot recall. He gave me the address of this man, B., and I at once rang up and made an appointment to meet him. We knew very little of what was going on among the Communists. Some of them were bringing out clandestine numbers of *Humanité* which took an anti-imperialist line but observed a sort of neutral attitude toward Germany; there were also supposedly Communist pamphlets in circulation that spoke of collaboration. Nevertheless it was rumored that a considerable proportion of them were organizing anti-German propaganda. Anyway, if Sartre had told me to go and see B., that meant they were in fundamental agreement. When I entered B.'s comfortable study, therefore, I had high hopes of learning some interesting facts. He welcomed me in a most friendly fashion, and gave me news of Sartre which made me sit up and take a fresh interest in life. The conditions of life as a POW, in the Stalags at any rate, were far from intolerable. Rations were short, but prisoners did no work. Sartre had taken advantage of this leisure to get on with his writing. He had made numerous friends, and found his way of life most intriguing. This was exactly what he had told me in his letters, but I had only half dared to believe it. Then I asked B. if he could shed any light on the general situation. Where did we stand? What could we hope for? What should we most fear? He spoke contemptuously of Gaullisme, which according to him only appealed to sentimental old women, and hinted that rescue would come from quite another quarter. I did not ask him for further details, which in any case he could not supply. But I did say that the German-Soviet pact, as far as I and many other people were concerned, had severely shaken our previous sympathy toward the U.S.S.R., and did not encourage us to place our trust in the Communist Party. He roared with laughter at this, saying that only *petits bourgeois* without any political education could possibly mistrust Stalin's diplomatic skill. I retorted that some dyed-in-the-wool Communists had likewise been shaken by the pact, and mentioned Nizan's name. B.'s face became stern at this: Nizan, he said, must have been a traitor to resign from the Party after the signing of the pact. I replied that Nizan most certainly was not a traitor. He shrugged. There were, he informed me, in an arrogantly cool way, only two Party members who had resigned. One of these was a militant young woman who had fallen afoul of the police over a little matter involving abortion; the other was Nizan, who, it had been known for some time, was in the pay of the Ministry of the Interior. Indignation fairly took my breath away at this. *Who* knew? *How* did they know? They just knew, B. said; and anyway, the man had resigned, hadn't he? I made further protestations, but all in vain, and took myself away, feeling utterly disgusted. Yet I still had not fully measured the implications of this slanderous story; I regarded it as a mere aberration on B.'s part. Doubtless he had been misinformed by people or never knew Nizan. It never occurred to me that I was up against a smear campaign, conducted with utter cynicism by those who *had* known him.

Brice Parain had mentioned the names of two writers who had, by some mysterious means, managed to get prisoners repatriated. Either these tips were ill-founded, or else I went about following them up in the wrong way, because my efforts yielded no results. I went for some time without any news from Sartre, but this did not worry me: my interview with B. had at least benefited me in one way—I no longer felt any anxiety on Sartre's behalf. I decided to begin writing again: this, it seemed to me, was an act of faith and hope. There were no grounds for supposing that Germany would be beaten. Hitler had not as yet sustained a single defeat, London was being battered by the frightful air attacks, and Nazi troops might soon force a landing on British soil. The U.S.A. still refused to budge, and the U.S.S.R. remained inactive. But I made a kind of wager with myself. If everything was doomed, then hours vainly spent writing didn't matter anyway. But if ever the world, and my life, and literature became meaningful again, then I would reproach myself for the months and years I had wasted in inactivity. So every morning and evening I settled down in the Dôme and worked at the last chapters of my novel; when they were completed I revised the entire manuscript. It was not an exciting task; this book expressed an aspect of my life now gone forever. But, quite rightly, I wanted to get it over and done with, which made me tackle the job in a most zealous fashion.

I went on reading Hegel, and was now beginning to understand him rather better. His amplitude of detail dazzled me, and his system as a whole made me feel giddy. It was, indeed, tempting to abolish one's individual self and merge with Universal Being, to observe one's own life in the perspective of Historical Necessity, with a detachment that also carried implications concerning one's attitude to death. How ludicrous did this brief instant of time then appear, viewed against the world's long history, and how small a speck was this individual, myself! Why should I concern myself with my present surroundings, with what was happening to me *now,* at this precise moment? But the least flutter of my heart gave such speculations the lie. Hate, anger, expectation, or misery would assert themselves against all my efforts to by-pass them, and this "flight into the Universal" merely formed one further episode in my private development. I turned back to Kierkegaard and began to read him with passionate interest. The type of "truth" that he postulated defied doubt no less triumphantly than Descartes' use of "evidence." Neither History nor the Hegelian System could, any more than the Devil in person, upset the living certainty of "I am, I exist, here and now, I am myself." This conflict recalled my own adolescent doubts and uncertainties, when I read Spinoza and Dostoevsky alternately; at one moment I was convinced that literature was mere meaningless sound and fury; at the next, that metaphysics was nothing but idle speculation and logic-chopping. Now I had learned of philosophical systems that stuck to the fact of existence and gave my presence on this earth its proper significance: to these I could adhere without reservation. Nevertheless, because of the difficult period I was going through, I was occasionally tempted by dreams of that calm and neutral state in which being and nothingness coincide. From an intellectual viewpoint this confrontation of the individual and the universal was the merest cliché; but for me it was as original and actual an experience as my revelation concerning the existence of rational awareness in others. I considered making it the theme of my next novel.

The further I went, the more I diverged from Hegel, without ever losing my admiration for him. I knew already that in the very marrow of my being I was bound up with my contemporaries; now I was learning that this dependent condition carried a complementary burden of responsibility. Heidegger had convinced me that "human reality" is accomplished and expressed in each separate living entity. Conversely, each person also commits and jeopardizes that reality *as a whole.* The individual's concept of himself, either as a man among men or an ant on an anthill, will depend on whether his society is aiming at the achievement of freedom, or content to endure mere passive bondage; yet each one of us has the power to challenge that collective decision, to reject or confirm it. Every day I had experience of this ambiguous solidarity. In Occupied France the mere fact of being alive implied acquiescence in oppression. Not even suicide would have freed me from this dilemma; on the contrary, it would have set the final seal on my defeat. My salvation was bound up with that of my country as a whole. But I myself, as I learned from my guilt and remorse, had been partially responsible for creating the situation now forced upon me. No individual can lose himself in the circumambient universe; though it supports him, it also influences his behavior—if only by its very immutability. These truths took deep root in me: the pity of it was that I saw no way of putting them to practical use. I could think of nothing better to do than live, survive, and hope for better days. My old natural inertia took the blame for this.

The theaters had opened their doors again: performances now began at eight and ended at eleven because of the curfew. Dullin moved to the Théâtre de Paris, where he put on a revival of *Plutus*. Marco had given up his old role; Dullin gave Olga a small but pleasant part, which she played admirably. Tissen, the little Luxembourg girl, gave a piquant performance which was picked out by the critics. Shortly afterward, about the middle of November, Dullin put on another play, Ben Jonson's *The Silent Woman*, which formed part of the Atelier's repertoire. Olga and Wanda and I were supposed to be going to the dress rehearsal. I got dressed, and was just walking out of the hotel when I found a note in my pigeonhole. It was from the wife of one of Sartre's fellow prisoners, and contained his new address. I turned pale as I read it: Krankenrevier, Stalag XII D. I had stopped worrying about him and now there he was in sick quarters, perhaps suffering from typhus or on the brink of death. Despite this I went on to the theater, and left a message there that they weren't to expect me. Tissen, who spoke German, confirmed that *Krankenrevier* did mean sick quarters, and that this was where Sartre was. I decided to try and see the woman who had passed on his new address, and went off by Métro, trembling inwardly, conjuring up the most ghastly visions. When the woman opened the door to me she was taken aback by the anguish which my voice and expression all too clearly revealed. Yes indeed, both her husband and Sartre were in sick quarters, and found it a splendid sort of hide-out. They were supposed to be helping the staff, and had better accommodation and heating than the barracks provided. So back I hurried to the theater, arriving toward the end of the first act. The lights and the red-plush seats and the chattering crowds in the foyer contrasted sharply with the images still teeming through my brain—pallet beds, bodies all twisted and emaciated with fever, corpses. . . . From May 10 onward, two worlds—the one familiar and even, on occasion, amusing, the other sheer horror—had coexisted in my mind. It was impossible to envisage them both at once, and the continual abrupt transitions I had to make between them were a sore trial to heart and nerves alike.

The letters I got from Sartre managed to calm me down a little. He sent me two different sorts. There were official ones, written in pencil and restricted by the form on which they were inscribed to a mere score or so of lines. But there were other, longer ones, very similar to an ordinary letter, which friends of his on working parties in the town undertook to stamp and mail. He was very contented with his lot, and extremely busy. He had been having discussions with some Jesuits about the Mystery of the Virgin Birth. He was banking on a fairly quick return to Paris, but not right away, since he was rehearsing a play he'd written for Christmas. Once that was over he wouldn't delay any longer. The date of his return might, from what he said, have depended on nothing but his own say-so. Was he thinking of trying to escape? I thought of such an escape as a terribly risky business—he would have sentries shooting at him and be pursued by bloodhounds. I took fright again. But he also talked about the forthcoming repatriation of various civilians, as though he was one of them. No doubt he was in the middle of wangling something or other. I decided not to worry any more.

I had managed to regain some sort of a shaky equilibrium, but I still suffered from my sense of isolation. On November 11 the students gathered in the Champs Elysées defied German regulations so blatantly that the Germans, by way of reprisal, closed down the University. It was not re-opened till December 20. This episode formed an apt rejoinder to the mummery that was supposed to set the seal on Franco-German friendship— the restoration to France of the Duc de Reichstadt's ashes. But I knew none of these young people who had openly said No to Nazism. All I could see around me were people as helpless as myself. None of them owned a radio; I couldn't even listen to the B.B.C. How was one to sift facts and events from the lying propaganda in the papers? Apart from *La Victoire* and *Le Matin* two other dailies were now being published— *L'Oeuvre* and *Temps nouveaux*. All of them explained, with some gusto, that it was Gide, Cocteau, our schoolteachers, the Jews, and films like *Quai des brumes* that had between them brought about our downfall. Certain journalists whom I had much admired in the palmy days of *Le Canard enchaîné,* such as Henri Jeanson and Galtier-Boissière, were still attempting to preserve some independence of judgment in the pages of *Aujourd'hui,* although they had to print German communiqués and a large number of pro-German articles. Such compromises carried a good deal more weight than their own brief essays in *double entendre.* Even so, some of Jeanson's pieces were regarded as overcritical of authority: he himself was jailed for some weeks, and his staff broken up. Suarez took over the editorship, and brought the paper into line with the others. Drieu's first number of the *N.R.F.* came out in December. Alain was so obstinately committed a paci-fist that his participation in this venture scarcely surprised me. But why had Gide consented to publish extracts from his diary in it? I met Jean Wahl at the Dôme, and found him just as flabbergasted by this as I was. It afforded me some relief to be able to share my indignation with someone outside my immediate circle of friends.

On the other hand, I had a most disagreeable surprise a few days later. The last few times I had seen Dullin he had held forth at length about the shortcomings of the "Boches," no doubt inspired by the chauvinistic patriotism proper to an old soldier. But one night I was dining with him and Camille in the grillroom of the Théâtre de Paris, and halfway through the meal Camille made a most categorical declaration of her views, which he listened to without uttering so much as a word. Since Nazism was in the ascendant, she said, we should rally to it; if she, Camille, was ever to make a real name for herself it was now or never, and how could she use her own epoch as a pedestal if she rejected it? She was convinced that her hour had struck, and stuck to this position with passionate intensity. I interrupted her with what seemed to me an unanswerable argument: the persecution of the Jews. "Oh, that," she said. "Well, Bernstein's been running the theater for quite long enough—time to give someone else a chance." At this I really started to let loose, but she put on her haughtiest expression and said, hands fluttering, a delicate smile on her lips, "People with something inside them will always get it out, persecutions or no persecutions." In our present situation I found the futility of this infantile Nietzscheism quite intolerable, and I nearly left the table. In the end Dullin's kindness and embarrassment prevented my doing so, but I got up and went the moment I had swallowed my last mouthful, feeling both hurt and angry. It was a long time before I saw them again.

On December 28, as I was walking down the Boulevard Saint-Michel, I saw a crowd standing in front of a fence on which the following notice in red print had been posted:

WARNING

Jacques Bonsergent, engineer, of Paris, having been condemned to death by a German Military Tribunal for an act of violence against a member of the German Armed Forces, was executed by shooting this morning.

Who was he? What had he done? I had no idea. (I found out later that he had in fact suffered for one of his friends, who was guilty of accidently jostling a German officer on the Rue du Havre.) But for the first time these "correct" Occupation authorities were telling us, officially, that they had executed a Frenchman for failing to bow before them in the approved manner.

The kowtowers were far from being in total agreement even among themselves. The Paris press supported Laval's policy; but Pétain was demanding his resignation, and replaced him first by Flandin and then by Darlan. The Rassemblement National Populaire, created by Déat in January, 1941, was opposed over certain matters both to Doriot's Parti Populaire Français and to Bucard's ultranationalistic movement; but they all criticized Vichy for too craven a subservience to the German authorities. Yet in the Free Zone the Legion backed the Révolution Nationale, and banned André Gide from giving a lecture in Nice on Michaux. Such dissensions and subtle distinctions and confused ideas were not of the slightest importance in the eyes of those who rejected collaboration out of hand: they regarded anyone who leaned in that direction with equal disgust. Even so I got a shock when the weekly *Je suis partout* reappeared in February: its editorial staff seemed to have been smitten with group paranoia. Not only were they after the blood of all those who had served the Third Republic, not to mention every Communist and Jew, but they also let go against those writers in the other zone who were trying, within the extremely narrow limits open to them, to express their opinions without wholly surrendering their independence. They piled one denunciation on another, frenziedly.

"There is another right which we demand," Brasillach wrote: "the right to expose the traitors in our midst." They were not slow to avail themselves of the privilege.

That winter was even colder than the previous one; for days on end the thermometer stood below freezing point. There was a shortage of coal, and my room was not heated; I inserted myself between icy sheets wearing ski trousers and a sweater, and shivered horribly while washing. Because the clocks had to keep German time, it was still dark in the streets when I went out. I would hurry over to the Dôme in search of a little warmth: the place was no longer out of bounds to the Germans, and while I gulped down my ersatz coffee, various "gray mice" would be putting out butter and jam on their tables, or handing over a packet of real tea to the waiter. As in the old days, I used to work in one of the booths at the back, but now there were no more refugees reading the papers or playing chess; most of the foreigners had disappeared, together with practically all the familiar faces I knew. Occasionally Adamov would appear at my table, more pop-eyed than ever, and embark on one of his endless interrogations. "How's it going?" he would ask me, emphasizing each word separately, fixing me with that questioning gaze. "Have you been *thinking* lately? Have you decided on the true nature of such-and-such? Are you sure who's in and who's out?" He was too obsessed by symbols and etymologies during this period for my liking. Olga, who had made his acquaintance, said he was wonderful at telling Irish folk tales, and had an inexhaustible repertoire of these and similar stories. No doubt this was how he acquired the women one saw him with—regular grade A beauties, every one of them. Unfortunately what he wanted from me was deep intellectual conversation, and we never really clicked on this level. He was always eyeing my papers. "What *are* you writing?" he once asked me. "A novel," I admitted, courageously. "A novel?" he repeated, "*a real novel,* with a beginning, a middle, and an end?" He had the same air of flabbergasted bewilderment about him as my father's friends used to have when confronted with the poems of Max Jacob. He made me read the rough draft of *L'Aveu,* scribbled in school notebooks; it dismayed me at the time, and later it dismayed him, too.

Most evenings I spent in the Flore, where no member of the occupation forces ever set foot. I no longer went to night clubs, since they were all packed with Germans. The Bal Nègre was shut. Being deprived of the cinema, I fell back on the theater. I find myself wondering how it came about that I had never before seen Dullin play *L'Avare* (*The Miser*), since he gave by far his most extraordinary performance in it. His gray locks disordered, his voice cracking, his face haggard and wan, he went crying after his lost treasure chest like some lovelorn dotard whose wits had turned: he had the air of a sorcerer bewitched. I also saw Feydeau's *La Main passe* at the Mathurins; this was played in too chilly a style, and failed to make me laugh. There was much talk about Cocteau's production of *Britannicus* at the Bouffes-Parisiens. It is true that Dorziat played Agrippina like a fashionable milliner; but thanks to Jean Marais's youth and spirit, Nero became a hero of our time, and Racine regained all his freshness and immediacy. The part of Britannicus was taken by a beginner from whom, it seemed, we might expect much—Serge Reggiani. I saw him again during rehearsals of Andreyev's play *The Life of Man* which was being produced by Rouleau, and in which Olga had a part; there was another young actor, Parédès by name, who also distinguished himself during this production, and for whom a great future in comedy was predicted. But by and large I went out very seldom. My main amusements were reading, listening to music, and discussions with Olga, Bost, Bianca, and Lise.

Despite the childish attitude she adopted toward me, Lise had by now emerged from the awkward age. She walked and moved with the heavy gait of a *muzhik,* but her face had become really lovely under that smooth blonde hair. When she walked into the Flore she created a sensation. Everywhere she went her brilliant good looks and unorthodox behavior made people notice her. She was not used to cafés; at first she used to hold out her hand to the waiters and address them as "monsieur." I was beginning to understand her more fully now. As a stateless person, reared without affection by quarreling parents, she was suffering from a general sense of frustration, and reacted by believing that she possessed absolute rights over everything, in the teeth of the entire world. Her attitude to other people was a priori both hostile and demanding, though she could be generous with her friend Tania, who was, like her, both stateless and poverty-stricken. But the French as a whole she regarded as privileged bastards, to be exploited as far as possible; no one could ever give her enough. She got herself accepted by the Sorbonne, and tried to collect some friends while she was reading for her philosophy degree. She would approach any girls or young men who took her fancy in an abrupt fashion which generally scared them off. Either they failed to turn up where and when she told them to, or else they ditched her after one such meeting. Finally she succeeded in getting her hooks into a twenty-year-old student, a good-looking, well-dressed boy who came from a wealthy, propertied family. He had a comfortable bachelor establishment, and suggested her coming to live with him there. As the one thing she wanted was a chance to get away from her parents, she jumped at his offer.

One morning, as I was on my way to the Dôme, she darted out in front of me.

"I've got something to tell you," she said. "I've been to bed with André Moreau. It was *most* amusing."

But she soon came to detest André: he fussed over his money and his health, he bowed before every custom and convention, in short he was a Frenchman to his fingertips. He wanted to make love all the time, an activity which she eventually found somewhat wearisome; she discussed their sexual relationships as coarsely and as frankly as any old trooper might have done. Her mother begged her to stay with André: he was a good catch, and might marry her in the end. This aiding and abetting drove her wild; if only I would give her a small monthly allowance, she told me, she would give both of them their walking papers. But it was quite impossible for me to do this, and she more or less accused me of forcing her out on the streets as a result. She also continued to reproach me for sparing her so little of my time: "You're nothing but a clock in a refrigerator!" she sobbed. She did not get along at all well with Olga, but she had some sort of common ground with Wanda, and the two of them sometimes went out together. One evening they turned up at some theater for a dress rehearsal, and in the intermission Lise unwrapped a large chunk of garlic sausage, which she proceeded to eat without leaving her seat in the orchestra. Wanda found this rather embarrassing. Lise was reasonably well-disposed toward Bost, but we all exasperated her by our references to Sartre. "This Sartre of yours," she would say to me. "Fancies himself as a phony genius." The news of his capture delighted her. "I'm sure you'd have dropped me otherwise," she said, and added, grinning: "I'm not altogether averse to your having a few bits of trouble now and then." This hostile feeling she had toward people who were integrated with their society explained both her taste for scandal and also the skepticism I mentioned earlier: she put her trust in no one—only in reason and experience. She was not a brave person; if she thought she was in danger, she ran for it. All the same, I never managed to convince her that, despite her physical vigor, a man was stronger than she was. One afternoon three young fellows passed her in a deserted street, somewhere in the Latin Quarter, and one of them pinched her bottom. She promptly lashed out at him, and was shattered to find herself lying on the ground with a bloody nose and one tooth broken. After this she avoided squaring up to any male adversaries; but despite all my warnings, she cheerfully had recourse to violence when she was sure of getting the upper hand. One of her former classmates, Geneviève Noullet, who was almost deaf, and so mentally retarded that I can't imagine how she got as far as she did in school, used sometimes to wait for me outside the Lycée Camille-Sée. I refused to talk to her, but she still trotted along behind me, through the streets and even down into the Métro. She would tug at my sleeve and say, "Mademoiselle, I *do* want to be your friend!" Then I would drive her away. She used to send me tiny stilted letters: "Might we perhaps visit the Louvre together, tomorrow afternoon? I shall be waiting at the Sèvres-Croix-Rouge Métro station at 3 P.M." I never replied, but next time I emerged from the *lycée,* there she would be again, waiting for me. Sometimes I had arranged to meet Lise, and Lise would march up to Geneviève Noullet and tell her to get the hell out of there. "I've got a perfect right to be here!" the deaf girl would exclaim, but generally she took fright and fled. On one occasion, however, she took a leaf out of Lise's own book and dogged our footsteps for quite a way; whereupon Lise sprang at her and beat her half silly before I had time to intervene. She ran off howling. That evening she rang at my parents' door and offered my mother a big bouquet of roses, in which she had inserted a card, with her apologies. Shortly afterward I got a letter from her, which ran: "Mademoiselle: Being a general, both in my family circle and elsewhere, is really too tough a job. I've had enough of it; I'm resigning. Henceforth I am devoting myself to you. My charms are all yours, and I shall adore your own in turn. Pass on the good news."

I never heard from her again. Lise, however, took far too great a pleasure in hating the poor girl to admit that she was not quite right in the head; indeed, Lise was constitutionally blind to anything which she found it advantageous or more pleasant to ignore. On the other hand, if she *wanted* to understand anything, she grasped it at once; her intellectual powers were quite remarkable. Her teachers at the Sorbonne took considerable interest in her; one essay she wrote for Etienne Gilson won her golden opinions. The sight of me writing irritated her, but she was fired to do likewise herself, and embarked on an account of her childhood and family, and her love affair with the scoutmaster. The result was a vivid, staccato, and most entertaining narrative. She also amused herself by drawing the most charming and curious pictures. In my eyes her vitality and natural gifts far outweighed her shortcomings.

One evening, toward the end of March, I returned to my hotel after dinner to find a note from Sartre in my pigeonhole. It merely said: "I'm at the Café des Trois Mousquetaires." I ran all the way back up the Rue Delambre and the Rue de la Gaieté, and reached the café (a reddish glow behind its thick blue curtains) completely out of breath. In I went: nobody there. I collapsed on to the nearest banquette, and then one of the waiters who knew me came over with a piece of paper. Sartre had waited two hours and then gone out to take a turn around the block and calm his nerves. He would be back shortly.

Never before had we felt any difficulty when we met after an absence; yet that evening, and the next day, and for several days thereafter, Sartre completely baffled me. He had emerged from a world of which I had no more real idea than he did of *my* life during the past few months; we both felt that the other one was speaking in a completely different language. First he told me how he had escaped. The Luxembourg frontier was quite close, and a fair number of prisoners managed to cross it. An organization had been set up inside the camp to procure them identity cards and clothes, and to work out various ingenious schemes for getting them through the perimeter. The members of this organization were risking their lives the whole time, whereas would-be escapers ran no risk at all: if they were recaptured their punishment was very slight. Sartre had at first thought of joining a small group who intended to reach Luxembourg on foot. But for some while before that he had been mulling over another possible solution; and suddenly a chance to try it out presented itself. There were considerable numbers of civilians in the Stalag who had been picked up on the road or in various villages; the Germans had promised to repatriate them, and one fine day they decided to do so. You proved your civilian status by showing your reservist's pay book. If you were too young or too old for military service, or had been discharged as unfit, the Germans released you. Faking the pay books was easy enough; there was a group of specialists who faked most convincing official stamps. The trouble was that the Germans were a suspicious lot, and interrogated those who claimed to have got their discharge. All the same, they didn't take their investigations overseriously. It was understood that a certain quota of men would be sent home as "civilians," and if the selection was not strictly fair, this mattered little to them. The medical examination was therefore perfunctory, and the doctor's verdict capricious. The prisoner in front of Sartre lacked know-how; when he was asked what illness he suffered from, he replied: "Cardiac palpitation." This was a worthless excuse, since the symptoms were only too easy to simulate, and the disease could not be verified on the spot. The stupid oaf was booted straight back inside the camp. When Sartre's turn came he tugged at his eyelid, exposing his near-blind eye in a most pathetic manner, and said: "Dizzy spells." This evidence satisfied the doctor, and Sartre joined the group of "civilians." If he had failed here, he was intending to wait a week and then go on foot, as he had planned to do at first. In any case he had never believed for one moment that his captivity could possibly last for a matter of years. Events had not destroyed or diminished his optimism.

This did not surprise me, any more than did the activities with which he had passed the last nine months, indeed the curiosity that had marked his attitude to camp life. What *did* disorientate me rather was the stringency of his moral standards. Did I buy things on the black market? A little tea occasionally, I told him. Even this was too much. I had been wrong to sign the paper stating I was neither a Freemason nor a Jew. Sartre had always asserted his ideas, not to mention his likes and dislikes, in a most dogmatic fashion, whether verbally or through his personal actions. Yet he never formulated them as universal maxims; the abstract concept of duty repelled him. I had been prepared to find him full of convictions and plans for the future and bursts of bad temper, but not armored with principles. Gradually I began to understand how this state of affairs had come about. Since they were daily confronted with Germans, collaborators, and quietists, the anti-Fascists in the Stalag formed a sort of small, tight-knit fraternity, whose members were bound by an unspoken oath—never to compromise, to reject all concessions. Each member swore to keep rigorously to this rule when separated from the others. But the position in the Stalag was easier than that in Paris, where simply to be alive implied some sort of compromise. It was with some regret that Sartre now abandoned the tense atmosphere and clear-cut simplicity of his life as a prisoner. But in civilian life his intransigence would have become mere formalism, and gradually he adapted himself to these new conditions.

The first evening he gave me yet another surprise. He had not come back to Paris to enjoy the sweets of freedom, he told me, but to *act*. How? I inquired, taken aback. We were so isolated, so powerless! It was precisely this isolation that had to be broken down, he said. We had to unite, to organize a resistance movement. I remained skeptical. I had already seen Sartre open up unlooked-for possibilities with a few well-chosen words, but I feared that this time he was nursing an illusion.

Before embarking on any course of action, however, he gave himself
a break, during which he strolled round Paris and revisited his friends.
He made Lise's acquaintance in circumstances which he found highly
amusing. She had been furious when she heard he was back. The day
he went to lunch for the first time with his parents, he arranged to meet
me in their district, at Passy. It was beautiful weather, and we set off to
walk back to Montparnasse. I spotted Lise in a doorway: she quickly
dropped back behind us. The whole way she dogged our footsteps, clumsily
hiding behind the pillars of the elevated railway. When we sat down outside a café, Lise took up a position on the opposite sidewalk and stared
at us balefully. I beckoned to her, and she came striding over, with her
awkward walk. Sartre smiled at her, and invited her to sit down; in the end
she smiled back and took the chair next to his. She told Sartre, however,
that if he hadn't been so pleasant, or if she hadn't liked the look of him,
she would have stabbed him with a large safety pin she had brought for
this precise purpose. She was extremely vexed when she realized that he
seemed not in the least put out by this threat.

But she was not to be quieted down that easily. A few days later I
was waiting for Sartre in the Dôme, and after a little while began to feel
worried: usually Sartre was as punctual as I was. Over an hour went by.
Had he run into some sort of trouble? His position was most irregular,
and by now I was thoroughly panicky. Then he appeared, followed by
Lise, who was hanging her head and trying to hide her face behind a
curtain of hair. "Now don't be cross with her," Sartre told me. It seemed
she had stopped him outside the Dôme with the information that Marco
was inside, and had gone there with the deliberate intention of bothering
us for hours; I had asked her to tell him to go to the Trois Mousquetaires
instead, where I would join him once I had managed to get rid of Marco.
She tagged along with him, and they had a talk. When Sartre had begun
to show signs of surprise at my delay, she had calmly remarked, "She
won't turn up at all. The rendezvous was somewhere else." Flabbergasted,
Sartre asked her why she had told such a lie. "I wanted to have a chat
with you and find out what sort of person I was up against," she said.
It took Sartre considerable time and effort to extract the truth from her.
Thenceforth she was prepared to accept the fact of his existence, and in
fact became very devoted to him.

If Sartre had wanted to regularize his status, he would have had to get
himself demobilized in the Free Zone, at Bourg. But the University was
not overconcerned with such details, and he was given back his job in
the Lycée Pasteur right away. Shortly afterward he had a long talk with
Davy, the Inspector General, on such topics as the Germans, Vichy, collaboration, and so on: without saying anything directly they came to a tacit
understanding, and Davy promised Sartre the Ecole Normale entrance
class at the Lycée Condorcet for the following year.

So Sartre went back to teaching after the Easter holidays, and began
to look around for good political contacts. He sought out former pupils
of his; he also met Merleau-Ponty, who had fought as an infantry lieu-

tenant, and was now writing a thesis on Perception. He knew various philosophy students at the Ecole Normale who were violently anti-German, including Cuzin and Desanti, whose interests embraced both phenomenology and Marxism. Our first meeting took place one afternoon in my room at the Hôtel Mistral, where we were now living again. Those present included Cuzin, Desanti, three or four of their friends, Bost, Jean Pouillon, Merleau-Ponty, Sartre, and myself. Desanti, with cheerful ferocity, proposed organizing attacks upon various individuals—Déat, for instance. But none of us felt qualified to manufacture bombs or hurl grenades. Our main activity for the time being, we decided, apart from recruiting further support, would be the compiling of information, which we would then circulate in the form of a news bulletin and various pamphlets. We very soon discovered that many other groups analogous to ours were already in existence. Although those running the so-called Pentagon were all right-wingers, Sartre got in touch with them: he had a meeting with one of his boyhood friends, Alfred Péron, an English teacher who was now acting as a British intelligence agent. He also had several interviews with Cavaillès, who had started the "Deuxième Colonne" movement at Clermont, and kept on the move between Paris and Auvergne. I went along with Sartre to one of these sessions, in the Closerie des Lilas; it was always here or in the gardens of the Petit Luxembourg that Cavaillès arranged his rendezvous. All these groups had two things in common: a very limited effective strength, and extraordinary lack of common caution. We held our meetings in hotel rooms or someone's study at the Ecole Normale, where walls might well have ears. Bost walked through the streets carrying a duplicating machine, and Pouillon went around with his briefcase stuffed full of pamphlets.

Over and above making contacts and collecting intelligence, we had a long-term objective: we believed it was vital to make preparations for the future. If the democracies won, it would be essential for the Left to have a new program; it was our job, by pooling our ideas and discussions and research, to bring such a program into being. Its basic aims could be summed up in two words—though their reconciliation posed vast problems—which also served as a watchword for our movement: "Socialism and Liberty." But the possibility of eventual defeat also had to be envisaged, and in his first news bulletin Sartre showed that if Germany won the war, our task would be to see that she lost the peace. Objectively speaking, indeed, there were scarcely any grounds for a belief in victory. The "desert war" had veered in favor of the Axis; German troops under Rommel, together with the Italians, had advanced as far as Mersa Matrûh in Egypt. The Italians held the whole of Greece; after their retreat from the Balkans the British no longer had any foothold in Europe. The collaborators were in the ascendant, and anti-Semitic persecutions becoming more frequent and intense. Henceforth Jews were forbidden to own, manage, or direct any sort of business. Vichy ordered a census of all Jews, and laid down a special *numerus clausus* for students. Thousands of foreign Jews were interned in a camp at Pithiviers, and from here deported, bit by bit, to Germany. In order to justify such measures, those in charge of German propaganda had *Jew Süss* shown in all the cinemas. I heard that when this film was on the auditorium remained empty; like many other Parisians, I never went to see a German film. We tried hard to keep on hoping, but the horizon looked dark.

All the same, we laughed heartily when we heard about Rudolph Hess landing in Scotland by parachute. The efforts the Germans made to keep this episode quiet, and their discomfiture when the truth broke, kept us amused for two or three days at least. Then rumors began to circulate about an attempted landing by the Reichswehr on the English coast. It had been beaten off, we heard, and people had seen various wounded Germans in hospitals, suffering from frightful burns. In any case Hitler had been bluffing when he had announced the "imminent occupation" of England a year before. In June he launched his attack on the U.S.S.R., and it looked unpleasantly as though this new blitzkrieg of his might well be successful: the Red Army was driven back, the Stalin Line breached, Kiev captured, and Leningrad besieged. Even so, taking the vast size of Russia into account, it seemed certain that this would prove a tougher nut to crack than either France or Poland. If the Russians could hold out for a few months, the famous Russian winter might well defeat the Germans, just as it had defeated Napoleon.

In France, Russia's entry into the war brought about the creation of the Ligue des Volontaires Français en Allemagne, which was organized by Déat, Deloncle, and other ex-Cagoulards. It also, in the most tragic way, removed all doubt concerning the position of the Communists. For some time now the press had been accusing them of pro-English sympathies, even of Gaullist leanings, and their clandestine organization of the Resistance movement was by no means a secret. Now all ambiguity vanished from their status, and they became public enemies: in the Paris area alone twelve hundred of them were arrested at once.

It was about now that the V sign, the English symbol of victory, began to appear all over Paris, daubed on walls, or along the tiled subways in the Métro. Since the Germans were unable to check this rash of V's they countered it by themselves adopting the motto "Victoria," and covering the whole city with V's of their own—in particular the Eiffel Tower and the façade of the Chamber of Deputies. The Gaullist emblem, the Cross of Lorraine, also became increasingly noticeable.

Sartre had settled down to work again. Before sitting down to write out the philosophical opus he had planned, bit by bit, during his time in Alsace, and latterly in the Stalag, he decided to finish off *The Age of Reason*. An old journalist called Delange, whom he regarded with some sympathy, offered him a regular literary column in *Comoedia,* a weekly that was being revived under Delange's editorship. It dealt exclusively with literature and the arts, and the old man swore it did not come under any sort of German censorship. Sartre accepted. The French translation of *Moby Dick* had just come out, and he wanted to discuss this extraordinary book somewhere. He devoted the whole of his first column to it—his last, too, since when the number actually appeared Sartre realized that

Comoedia was less independent than Delange had said and, doubtless, hoped. All the same, Delange did manage to give his weekly a tone sharply at variance with that of the rest of the press. He protested against the delations to which *Je suis partout* was so attached; he defended works that opposed Fascist values and Vichy-type morality. But despite this, the first rule on which all the intellectuals of the Resistance were agreed was: "No writing for Occupied Zone papers."

Since Sartre's return I had been relaxed and contented—but quite differently from before. Events had changed me; what Sartre used to call my "divided mind" had finally yielded before the unanswerable arguments that reality had brought against it. I was at last prepared to admit that my life was not a story of my own telling, but a compromise between myself and the world at large. By the same token, setbacks and adversities no longer struck me as instances of injustice. There was no point in rebelling against them; you had either to find a way to get around them, or else put up with your lot. I knew the future might hold some exceedingly dark hours for me, and that I might even become engulfed in that darkness forever; yet the prospect did not daunt me. This quasi-renunciatory spirit gave me a freedom from worry such as I had never before experienced. Throughout the spring and summer I took advantage of every spare moment: I finished my novel, and began taking notes for another book.

We paid occasional visits to the theater. Marguerite Jamois was far from convincing in her role as a "tamed Fury," and Cocteau's *La Machine à écrire* (*The Infernal Machine*), as a play, did not come up to his other work in this field. When Laubreaux grossly insulted Cocteau in *Je suis partout,* Jean Marais went around and beat him up, which gave us great satisfaction. The Margariti brothers, two former members of the October Group, put on a revue called *Les Chesterfollies*; both its general tone and some of the individual numbers were nostalgically reminiscent of the period immediately before the war—even down to Deniaud's performance as a bearded street hawker. Barrault put on *The Suppliant Maidens* at the Roland-Garros stadium, with incidental music by Honegger and settings by Labisse. The actors wore costumes designed by Marie-Hélène Dasté, complete with masks and buskins; there was an immense crowd of extras. As a curtain raiser we had a short piece by Obey, *Huit Cent Mètres,* an insipid little paean to the glories of athletics. Still, it gave us a chance to appreciate the technical skill of Barrault, Cuny, Dufilho, and Legentil—not to mention Jean Marais's good looks. It was during this production of *The Suppliant Maidens* that Sartre conceived the idea of writing a play himself. Both Olgas had parts in it: Barrault was very fond of them. During rehearsals they asked him how to go about getting a really first-rate part. "The best way," he replied, "would be to get someone to write a play for you." And Sartre thought: "Why shouldn't I be the one?" He had written and produced a play in the Stalag, called *Bariona*: ostensibly the theme of this "mystery play" was the birth of Christ, but in fact the drama centered on the Roman occupation of Palestine, and his fellow prisoners were quick to take the allusion. What they applauded on Christmas Eve was Resistance propaganda. The real function of the theater, Sartre thought at the time, is to appeal to those who share a common predicament with the playwright. This "common predicament" was one that faced Frenchmen everywhere, assailed daily as they were by German and Vichy propaganda exhorting them to repent and submit; the theater might provide a medium through which to remind them of rebellion and freedom. He began to cast around for a plot that would be at once technically unobjectionable and transparent in its implications.

During this spring we acquired a new friend. It was thanks to Lise that we made the acquaintance of Giacometti: though as I have already remarked, we had long been aware of his fine, hard-chiseled features and unkempt hair, and his characteristic prowling gait. I had found out that he was a Swiss sculptor; I also knew he had once been knocked down by a car, which explained his limp and the way he supported himself on a stick. He was often to be seen in the company of pretty women; he had noticed Lise in the Dôme, and got into conversation with her. She amused him, and he became very fond of her. She said he wasn't very intelligent: when she asked him if he liked Descartes, he had made some idiotic reply or other, and she had then decided he bored her. On the other hand he bought her dinner very often at the Dôme, and these meals she found absolutely marvelous, she said. She was a strong young girl with healthy appetites, and never got enough to eat in the student restaurants she normally frequented. So she was only too ready to accept his invitations; but the moment she had swallowed the last mouthful, she would wipe her mouth, get up, and go. In order to keep her there longer, Giacometti had the idea of ordering a second meal on top of the first, which she bolted with equal pleasure; but as soon as she was through it, nothing would stop her leaving. "What a little brute she is!" he would exclaim, with grudging admiration, and by way of revenge used to whack her lightly around the legs with his stick. She once complained that he'd invited her to the Palette bar and saddled her with a pair of awful old bores; she'd yawned all through the evening's conversation, she told us. We afterward found out that the tedious characters in question were Dora Marr and Picasso. The sculptor's studio opened onto a courtyard that Lise found very handy when she wanted to do some camouflage work on the bicycles she used to steal all over Paris. I asked her what she thought of Giacometti's work, and she laughed in a baffled sort of way and said, "I don't know; it's all so *small*!" She swore his sculptures were no bigger than a pin head, so how could one judge them? He had a queer way of working, too, she added: whatever he did during the day he smashed up at night, and vice versa. One day he piled all the sculptures in his studio onto a handcart, and went off and tipped them into the Seine.

I no longer recall the exact circumstances of our first meeting, though I rather think it took place at Lipp's. We saw at once that Lise had been completely mistaken about Giacometti's intelligence: he had brains and to spare, a really first-class mind, the sort that sticks to hard facts and shakes the meaning out of them. He was never satisfied with hearsay or approximations; he went straight to the heart of a subject and teased it out with unbounded patience. Sometimes when he was in form he could turn it inside out, like a glove. Everything interested him; curiosity was the special shape that his passionate love of life assumed. When he was run down by the car, he had thought, with detached amusement, "Is this the way one dies? I wonder what'll happen to me?" Death itself he regarded as a most lively experience. Every moment of his stay in the hospital had brought him some fresh and unlooked-for revelation; he was almost sorry when the time came for him to leave. This insatiable attitude I found most heart-warming.

Giacometti used words in a masterly fashion to evoke a picture of people or their background, to quicken them into life; he was also one of those very rare characters who can enrich your understanding simply by listening to what you say. There was a deep bond of understanding between him and Sartre: they had both staked everything on one obsession— literature in Sartre's case, art in Giacometti's—and it was hard to decide which of them was more fanatical. Giacometti did not give a damn for success or reputation or money; all he wanted was to carry through his own ideas. What was he aiming at, precisely? His sculptures took me somewhat aback, too, the first time I saw them; it was a fact that the biggest of them was scarcely the size of a pea. In the course of our numerous discussions he explained his ideas to me. He had formerly been connected with the surrealists, and I remembered having seen his name and a reproduction of one of his works in *L'Amour fou*. At that time he was making "objects" of the sort which appealed to Breton and his cronies, and which had only a tenuous suggestion of reality about them. But for two or three years now he had been convinced this method was getting him absolutely nowhere; he wanted to return to what he regarded as contemporary sculpture's real problem—the re-creation of the human face. Breton had been shocked by this. "Everyone knows what a head is!" he exclaimed, a remark which Giacometti, in turn, repeated as something shocking. In his opinion no one had yet succeeded in modeling or portraying a valid representation of the human countenance: the whole thing had to be started again from scratch. A face, he told us, is an indivisible whole, a meaningful and expressive unity; but the inert material of the artist, whether marble, bronze, or clay, is, on the contrary, capable of infinite subdivision—each little separate bit contradicts and destroys the over-all pattern by the fact of its isolation. Giacometti was trying to reduce matter to its furthest viable limits; this was how he had come to model these minuscule, almost non-existent heads, which, he thought, conveyed the unity of the human face as it presents itself to the intelligent eye. Perhaps one day he would find some other way of counteracting the dizzying centrifugal effect of space; but for the time being this was all he could think up.

Sartre, who ever since his youth had been striving to view the truth behind "reality" in terms of a synthesis, was particularly struck by Giacometti's line of inquiry: his attitude was comparable to that of the phenomenologists, since he claimed to sculpture a face *in its context*, as it existed for other people removed from it, and by so doing to avoid the pitfalls both of subjective idealism and pseudo-objectivity. Giacometti had never supposed that art should limit itself to enhancing appearances; on the other hand, the influence of the cubists and surrealists had led him, like many artists of the period, to confuse the real with the imaginary. For quite a while his work had aimed at creating "objects" rather than illuminating reality through the medium of a material "equivalent." Now, however, he criticized this attitude, both in himself and others, as an aberration. He spoke of Mondrian, who, because his canvas was two-dimensional, refused to create any false perspectives in depth on it. "But," Giacometti remarked, with a cruel smile, "when two lines cross each other one of them has to go above the other, notwithstanding; his paintings aren't really 'flat' at all!"

No one had explored this impasse quite so deeply as Marcel Duchamp, for whom Giacometti had a great affection. To begin with, he had painted pictures—among others the well-known "Bride stripped bare by her Bachelors even." But a picture only exists by virtue of the animating eye of the observer, and Duchamp wanted his works to exist in their own right, unassisted. So first he began to copy lumps of sugar in marble, but these imitations didn't satisfy him, and he set about making ordinary and completely real objects, including a chessboard. Next he contented himself with buying plates or glasses and signing his name on them. Finally he just folded his arms and did nothing. (I have set down the sequence just as, to the best of my recollection, Giacometti himself told it.)

In Giacometti's opinion these were false problems, and served no very profound purpose. His real concern was to defend himself against the infinite and terrifying emptiness of space. There was a long period when he could not walk down a street without putting out a hand and touching the solid bulk of a wall in order to arm himself against the gulf that yawned all around him. At another time he fancied everything was weightless, and that passers-by went floating through space over the roads and squares. When he was designing the mural decorations at Lipp's he kept saying happily, "Not a hole or a blank space anywhere! Absolute plenitude!" I never wearied of listening to him. For once Nature had played fair; Giacometti fulfilled all that his face promised, and when you examined him close up you couldn't miss the fact that these features belonged to no ordinary man. It was impossible to predict whether he would "wring sculpture's neck" or fail in his attempt to master space; but his struggling endeavors were per se more exciting than most other men's successes.

My sister had got news of her activities through to us during the year by way of the Red Cross. She was having a difficult time in Faro, scraping a living by giving French lessons; but she was painting, and Lionel's health got steadily better. She would have been very happy if her head had not been full of romantic notions about the dangers we were facing. We did our best to reassure her in the post cards we sent, but distance is apt to breed alarm, and she was tormented by the most ghastly visions.

She was never to see our father again, since he died that July. He had been operated on for prostate trouble, and at first he was thought to have made a good recovery. But months of undernourishment had weakened him, and the defeat and subsequent occupation had given him a grievous shock, so that the onset of senile tuberculosis carried him off in a few days. He faced death with an indifference that amazed me, though he had often said it mattered little to him whether he died on one day rather than another, since death was in any case inevitable. Besides, he had little in common with this new world of ours, and very few reasons for continuing to stay alive in it. He did not struggle: I was amazed at the peaceful way he returned to nothingness. He had no illusions, either: he asked me if I could, without causing my mother distress, see to it that no priest attended his deathbed. (She did, in fact, conform to this wish of his.) I sat with him through his last moments, and watched the grim, protracted struggle with which life finally extinguishes itself, vainly trying to grasp the mystery of this departure to no destination. I stayed a long while alone with him when he had breathed his last: at first, though dead, he was still *there,* it was my father, but then he receded dizzily from me as I watched, and I found myself bent over a mere corpse.

It was not so very difficult to cross the border between zones if you sauntered through without luggage, hands in pockets. Sartre decided that we would spend our holidays in the Free Zone: this would enable him to obtain his demobilization. His main purpose, however, was to establish some sort of liaison between "Socialism and Liberty" and certain people in the other zone. Lise presented him with one of her ill-gotten bicycles, which he hadn't the heart to refuse: especially since, as she pointed out, she wouldn't restore it to its owner even if he did. Bost lent us a tent and basic camping equipment. It was permissible to send parcels from one zone to the other, so we forwarded our bicycles and luggage to a priest in Roanne, who had escaped on foot a week after Sartre. Then we booked tickets to Montceau-les-Mines; we had been given the address of a café there where we could find someone to get us through the border.

This particular character had been arrested a few days earlier, the café proprietor informed us; but no doubt some arrangement could be made with another guide. We stayed in the café all that afternoon, watching people come and go, feeling pleasantly adventurous. Toward evening a woman in black, about forty years old, sat down at our table, and offered, for a very reasonable fee, to take us through across country that same night. We were not risking much, but for her it was a more serious affair, and she took every precaution. We followed her silently across fields and through woods that had that fresh night-smell about them; she tore her stockings on some barbed wire and kept grouching about it. From time to time she would signal us to stop and stay quite still. Suddenly she informed us that we were over the border, and we walked quickly toward a nearby village. The inn was full of people who had just slipped through as we had done; we slept on mattresses in a room where six people, plus a wailing baby, were already settled down for the night. But how lighthearted we felt the following morning as we strolled down the road, killing time till we caught our train to Roanne! Because I had defied one German prohibition, I felt as though I had regained my freedom.

We went into a café in Roanne and read through the Free Zone's papers, which weren't much better than ours. Then we picked up our gear from the Abbé P.'s place: he himself was out when we called. It took me some time to secure the stuff to our bicycles. The bicycles themselves caused me considerable anxiety. It was almost impossible to get hold of new tires; and our present ones were heavily patched and bulging with weird hernia-like growths, while the inner tubes were almost worn out. We were hardly clear of the town before Sartre's front tire went flat. I can't think how I ever came to embark upon this adventure without having learned about repairing punctures, but the fact remains that I didn't know how to. Luckily a mechanic turned up who instructed me in the art of getting a tire off and applying rubber patches. We set off again. It was years since Sartre had been for a bicycle ride of any length, and after twenty-five miles or so he was in very poor shape. We spent the night in a hotel. He pedaled along more vigorously the following day, and that evening we pitched our tent in a large meadow just outside Mâcon. This operation was not without its hazards, either, since both of us were rather clumsy. Nevertheless, after a few days we could pitch and strike that tent in no time at all. We normally camped near a town or village, since after a long day in the open air Sartre was longing to plunge back into the smoky atmosphere of a bistro. He got himself demobilized at Bourg; the officer who looked at his faked service book winced and said, "You shouldn't falsify your military record." "You mean I ought to have stayed in Germany?" Sartre asked. "A soldier's service book is not there to be messed with," the officer insisted. "So I ought to have remained a prisoner?" Sartre repeated. The officer shrugged; he hardly dared follow his idea through to its logical conclusion, but the gesture clearly said, "And why not?" Nevertheless he gave Sartre his certificate of demobilization.

We went for walks over the russet hills around Lyon; they were showing American films in the cinemas, and we made a beeline for them. We went through Saint-Etienne, where Sartre showed me his family's old house, and made our way down to Le Puy. Sartre far preferred bicycling to walking; the monotony of the latter bored him, whereas on a bicycle both one's intensity of effort and the rhythm of the journey were constantly changing. He enjoyed sprinting on hills, and left me puffing along far behind him; but on the flat he pedaled so indolently that several times he toppled off into the ditch. "My mind was elsewhere," he remarked on these occasions. Like me, he enjoyed the fun of whizzing downhill; besides, the scenery shifted faster than it did when we were on foot. I too was glad to exchange my former passion for these new delights.

But the great difference between this trip and its predecessors, as far as I was concerned, related to my inner state of mind. I no longer obsessionally pursued my old quasi-schizophrenic dreams, and indeed felt a delicious sense of freedom; it was already extraordinary enough that Sartre and I should be riding peacefully along these hill roads in the Cévennes. I had been so afraid of losing everything—not only Sartre himself, but all the happiness I had known. In one sense I *had* lost everything, only to have it given back to me again; now every pleasure I experienced seemed not a right but a godsend. I was more vividly aware of that carefree, detached mood I have spoken of than I had been in Paris; one tiny factual incident afforded me proof of this. When we reached Le Puy, Sartre's front tire finally collapsed. If we couldn't find some way of replacing it, we would be forced to give up our tour before it was well begun. Sartre trudged off to the town while I sat outside a café keeping an eye on our luggage. Previously the idea that this trip could be brought to an abrupt halt, against my express wishes, would have filled me with rage; now I had a smile on my lips as I waited. This didn't stop my heart jumping for joy when I saw Sartre coming back, riding a bicycle the front tire of which was a startling orange color and looked almost brand-new. He could never work out what lucky chance had persuaded the mechanic to let him have it. Now we were good for a couple of hundred miles at least.

Cavaillès had given Sartre the address of a former fellow student at the Ecole Normale, called Kahn, who was a member of the Resistance. We followed various small winding lanes till we reached a village that was hidden among chestnut trees. Kahn was spending his holiday there, with a charming, placid wife and some very cheerful children; they were also taking care of a blue-eyed little girl with brown pigtails, who turned out to be Cavaillès daughter. We had a delicious meal in their big, red-tiled kitchen, with big platefuls of bilberries for dessert. Sartre and Kahn talked for hours, sitting on the moss-grown ground among the trees. I could hear what they were saying; but it was hard to believe, with the summer sunlight bathing us and that delightful house close by, that action and its attendant dangers had any real existence. Children's laughter, the fresh scent of wild berries, the friendly atmosphere of the occasion—all these defied any kind of threatening situation. Despite all that these past two years had taught me, I was incapable of surmising that soon Kahn would be torn from the bosom of his family forever, or that one morning the father of that little brown-haired girl would be stood up against a wall and shot.

From the upper reaches of the Ardèche down to the Rhône Valley, a full day's journey, I was intoxicated by the swift transformation of the landscape: the sky became a clearer blue, the sun's heat grew drier, the scent of heather was replaced by that of lavender, and the earth itself took on richer, fiercer colors—ocher, red, purple. The first cypress trees appeared, and the first olives; all my life I have felt the same intense emotion on coming down from high mountain country into the Mediterranean basin. Sartre too was affected by the beauties of this descent; and the only blemish on our day was occasioned by our halt at Largentière. This little village on the border of Central France and the Midi I knew and loved of old. But today was the Legion's special holiday; the streets were all garlanded with red-white-and-blue flags, and a horde of men, young and old, surged through them, sporting Basque berets, together with tricolor ribbons and rosettes. Thirst and exhaustion forced us to stop, and unhealthy curiosity made us linger for a while.

We pitched camp up above Montélimar; when Sartre got on his bicycle next morning he was still so fast asleep, even though his eyes were open, that he pitched right over the handlebars. All along the roads in the Tricastin district the wind lent us wings, and we floated up hills almost without pedaling. We came down by the longest route into Arles, and from there made for Marseille.

In Marseille we found modest but very pretty rooms looking out over the Old Port. Sentimentally we repeated the walks we had made on previous visits, when the world was at peace, and again when war was threatening. The cinemas on the Cannbière were showing American films, and some of them opened at ten o'clock in the morning. We once saw three shows in the same day. We watched Bette Davis, Edward G. Robinson, and James Cagney in *Dark Victory,* hailing them like very dear, long-lost friends. We went to literally anything, from the sheer joy of seeing an American picture again. The past came surging back into our hearts.

Sartre met Daniel Mayer in Marseille, and talked to him about "Socialism and Liberty." Had he any broad policy to suggest to the group, or any specific tasks to give to them? Daniel Mayer asked us to address a letter to Léon Blum on the occasion of his birthday. Sartre left him, somewhat disappointed.

We ate much worse in the Midi than we had done in Paris or Central France. The staple item of diet was the tomato; and since Sartre loathed tomatoes, he had some trouble in getting a square meal. When we stopped off at Porquerolles, we found not a single restaurant open, so lunched on grapes, bread, and wine. I went off for a walk along the Grand-Langoustier road, while Sartre stayed behind in the café, working on the opening dialogue of a play about the Atridae. Almost all his new ideas took a mythic form initially, and I imagined he would soon eliminate Orestes, Electra, and the rest of their family from his play.

Sartre had written André Gide's name down on his list, with an indecipherable address scribbled beside it: Caloris? Valoris? Surely this must be Vallauris. We made our way there, riding ecstatically along the Mediterranean coast road. We called in at the Town Hall to ask for André Gide's address. "M. Gide the photographer?" said the clerk. This was the only one he knew. I stared at the illegible address yet again, and hunted over my Michelin map, trying to find anything remotely resembling it. Light suddenly dawned; Cabris. It was a stiff climb up the steep country lane under that blazing sun; but from the summit we could see the olive trees sloping away, terrace after terrace of them, to the blue sea below, with the same faintly solemn grace about them as you find in their counterparts between Delphi and Itea. We had lunch in the vine-shaded arbor of a local inn, and then Sartre went off and rang at Gide's front door. The door opened, and to his astonishment he was confronted by Gide's features—but attached to the body of a young girl. This turned out to be Catherine Gide, who told Sartre that her father had left Cabris for Grasse. So back we went down the way we had come, and by the time we reached Grasse I had a flat tire. I settled down beside a fountain to repair it. Meanwhile Sartre went off to try and find Gide at his hotel, but spotted him on the way there, and as he drew level with him braked abruptly, one foot scraping loudly along the sidewalk with a noise of tortured leather. "Well, now! Well, now!" Gide exclaimed, with a soothing gesture. They went into a café. "Gide," Sartre told me afterward, "kept a very suspicious eye on our fellow customers, and changed his table three times. He didn't really see what he could do himself. 'I'll have a word with Herbard,' he said, waving one hand vaguely. 'Yes, Herbard, perhaps . . .' " Sartre told him he had an appointment to see Malraux the following day. "Well," Gide said as they parted, "I hope you find him in a good mood—un bon Malraux, eh?"

Malraux received Sartre in a magnificent villa at Saint-Jean-Cap-Ferrat, where he was living with Josette Clotis. They lunched on Chicken Maryland, exquisitely prepared and served. Malraux heard Sartre out very courteously, but said that, for the time being at any rate, action of any sort would in his opinion be quite useless. He was relying on Russian tanks and American planes to win the war.

From Nice we went back up over the Alpes Maritimes, which we crossed by the Col d'Allos. It was a beautiful sunny morning when we set off on the next lap of our journey, to Colette Audry's house in Grenoble. We had lunch at the top of a pass, and I drank some white wine: not very much, but in this blazing sun even that was enough to make me a little dizzy. We began the descent, with Sartre freewheeling down about twenty yards in front of me. Suddenly I came face to face with two other cyclists, like me riding on the crown of the road, and indeed a little to the left of it. In order to pass them, I swerved to their free side—at the same time as they shifted back to the right-hand half of road, so that once more we were approaching each other head-on. My brakes were hardly working at all, and it was quite impossible to pull up; I swerved still further to the left, and went skidding across the fine gravel on the shoulder, a few inches only from the edge of the precipice. It flashed through my mind that one really ought to pass on the right, not the left; and then, "So this is death," I thought, and died. When I opened my eyes again I was on my feet, and Sartre was supporting me by one arm. I recognized him, but otherwise my mind was a complete blank. We staggered on as far as the nearest house, where I was given a glass of marc, and someone sponged my face while Sartre cycled up to the village and found a doctor, who refused to come back with him. When he returned I had more or less collected my wits again; at least I remembered that we were on a cycling holiday, and going to see Colette Audry. Sartre suggested that we might try to make the last ten miles by bicycle, since it was all downhill. But I felt as though all the cells in my body were jarring and grinding against each other, and couldn't even face the idea of hoisting myself into the saddle. Instead we went by train, on a little rack railway. Our fellow passengers averted their eyes from me in a startled way. When Colette Audry came to the door she uttered a little gasp of horror and completely failed to recognize me. I looked at myself in a mirror, and found that I had lost a tooth, one of my eyes was closed, my face had swollen up to twice its normal size, and the skin was all scraped raw. I couldn't get so much as a grape between my lips, so puffy were they. I went to bed without eating anything, more or less convinced that my face would never regain its normal proportions again.

I still looked just as hideous the following morning, but plucked up courage and mounted my bicycle. It was Sunday, and there were numerous other cyclists on the road to Chambéry: most of those who passed me either whistled in astonishment or burst into loud guffaws. During the next few days, whenever I walked into a shop everybody stared at me. One woman asked me, anxiously, "Was—was it an accident?" I have long regretted not replying, "No, I was born that way." One afternoon I had ridden on ahead of Sartre and was waiting for him at a crossroads. A man called out to me, roaring with laughter, "Still waiting for him after all he's done to you?"

Autumn was in the air along the roads through the Jura. When we emerged from our hotel in the morning the landscape was shrouded in mist, and the smell of dead leaves already abroad. But gradually the sun came shining through, the mist disappeared, and heat flooded our bodies again: my whole skin tingled with a childish sensation of well-being. One evening, sitting at table in an inn, Sartre turned to his play again. No, he wasn't abandoning the Atridae; he had thought of a way to put their story to good use. He would make it an instrument with which to attack official morality, purge the guilt with which Vichy and Germany were trying to poison us, and give freedom utterance again. The first act was inspired by Emborio, the village on Santorin which had presented so sinister an atmosphere to us when we first reached it—all those blank, shuttered houses under the blazing noonday sun.

Colette Audry had told us of a village near Châlons where it was very easy to arrange a border-crossing. Heaven knows how many of us there were next morning, all strung out along the main road, obviously bent on the same purpose. By the afternoon twenty of us, all on bicycles, were grouped around one of the local *passeurs*. I recognized a couple whom we had often seen at the Dôme: a good-looking, fair-haired boy with a small golden beard, and a pretty Czech girl, blonde also. We took narrow woodland tracks which eventually brought us out by a road with barbed wire fencing all along it; we wriggled under the wire and dispersed as quickly as possible. The *passeur* had taken no special precautions, so presumably he had some arrangement with the German sentries.

I found Burgundy very beautiful, with its vineyards now richly tinted in autumnal colors; but we hadn't so much as a sou in our pockets by now, and were gnawed by hunger all the way to Auxerre, where a money draft was awaiting us. As soon as we laid hands on the cash we shot straight off to a restaurant—where they served us with plates of spinach, and nothing else. We returned to Paris by train.

I had had several weeks of considerable happiness; I had also undergone an experience the effects of which were to last over the next two or three years. I had had a close brush with death. Considering the terror which death had always aroused in me, to have come so very near to it was, for me, a highly significant event. "I might never have wakened again," I told myself, and suddenly the business of dying seemed easy out of all proportion. It was at this moment that I emotionally accepted the truth of what I had once read in *Lucrèce,* and to which my rational mind had long since assented—that, in the most literal and precise sense, death is *nothing.* A *person* never is dead; there is no longer a "person" to sustain the concept of "death." I felt I had finally exorcised my fears on this score.

We spent the end of our holiday with Madame Lemaire, and returned to Paris at the beginning of the school term. The political climate had altered during the course of the summer. On August 13 the Communists had organized a riot in the neighborhood of the Porte Saint-Denis, and on the 19th two of the demonstrators had been shot. On August 23 a German soldier was killed. On August 28, after the ceremony to celebrate the departure of the Ligue des Volontaires Française for the Russian front, Paul Colette had tried to shoot Laval and Déat. There were numerous cases of sabotage on the railways. The French authorities promised a million-franc reward to anyone volunteering information that resulted in the arrest of a person responsible for "criminal outrages" of this sort. Pucheu had launched a vast police drive against Communists, in both zones. The Germans no longer talked of friendship; they were openly threatening. They had promulgated a decree imposing the death penalty on any person convicted of disseminating Communist propaganda, and had set up a special tribunal to judge those charged with anti-German activities. A proclamation posted up on August 22 inaugurated a reprisal system: for every member of the Reichswehr killed, they in turn would shoot a certain number of hostages. On August 30 they announced the execution of five Communists and three "spies." Since then the walls of Paris had seen quite a few black-bordered posters, in red or yellow, similar to the one that had moved me some ten months previously: the hostages shot in this way were nearly all Communists or Jews. In October two German officers were assassinated, one in Nantes and the other at Bordeaux. As a result of this, ninety-eight Frenchmen were put up against the wall, and twenty-seven consigned to the concentration camp at Châteaubriant.

On orders from London individual attacks against German military personnel were stopped; but during November grenades were tossed into restaurants and hotels occupied by the Germans; and despite severe counter-measures, "terrorist" activities increased and spread. The collaborators unleashed much furious rhetoric against this Resistance movement, and the Paris papers were demanding bloody reprisals, waxing indignant over the slow process of the Riom trial and the incompetence of the police. "No

mercy on these murderers who sagotage their own country," wrote Brasillach. Their cantankerousness was still riding high and arrogant, since they
were convinced of Hitler's ultimate victory. In Russia, the Germans began
the battle for Moscow at the beginning of October; their advance was
checked, but the Red Army's counteroffensives failed to budge them. The
attack on Pearl Harbor brought America into the war, but the Japanese
gained some shattering victories in the Pacific, invading Borneo, Malaya,
Hong Kong, the Philippines, the Malacca peninsula, Sumatra, and Java.

For those of us who were unwilling to acquiesce in the triumph of the
Reich, and who yet hardly dared to bank on its defeat, this was so doubtful
a period that my very memories of it are highly confused. I have often
felt, since the restoration of peace, how difficult it was to speak of those
days to anyone who had not lived through them. (It is my own feelings
I am expressing in *The Mandarins* when I make Anne say, during her
attempt to discuss the subject with Scriassine: "Everything had been either
worse or more unbearable than he imagined. The real tragedies hadn't
happened to me, and yet they haunted my life.") Now, after an interval
of nearly twenty years, I cannot recall the truth, even for my own benefit.
All I can do is to dredge up a few features of the times, one or two
isolated episodes.

Politically, we found ourselves reduced to a condition of total impotence.
When Sartre started "Socialism and Liberty" he hoped this group would
attach itself to a much larger central body; but our trip had produced no
very important results, and our return to Paris proved no less disappointing. Already the various movements that had sprung up right at the
beginning were disbanded or in the process of breaking up. Like ours,
they had come into being through individual initiative, and consisted
mainly of middle-class intellectuals without any experience of underground
action—or indeed of action in any form. It was far more difficult to establish communications or amalgamate the groups here than in the Free Zone;
such enterprises remained sporadic, and their lack of cohesion doomed
them to the most discouraging ineffectuality. The Communists, on the
other hand, were well organized, well disciplined, and possessed an excellent administrative machine, with the result that from the moment they
decided to intervene they obtained spectacular results. Right-wing patriotic
groups refused to co-operate with them, though the non-Communist Left
was not opposed to a *rapprochement*. Its members did not regard the
German-Soviet pact quite so severely as they had done in 1939: perhaps the
U.S.S.R. would have been powerless to resist a German invasion without
guaranteeing themselves a temporary respite, by any means whatsoever. So
though the Left still was chary of regarding Stalin's diplomacy with
wholehearted approval, radical condemnation of it was no longer desirable.
In any case, Sartre calculated that it was vital to establish a common front
in France at this juncture, and tried to make contact with the Communists.
They, however, distrusted any group formed outside the auspices of the
Party, and in particular those of the *"petit-bourgeois* intellectuals." They
told one of our friends that Sartre's release by the Germans could only

mean he had agreed to work for them as an *agent provocateur*. Whether they really believed this or not I cannot tell; but in any case they thus set up an absolutely impenetrable barrier between us and them. The isolation to which we saw ourselves condemned dampened our enthusiasm, and there were numerous defections from the group; on top of this Cuzin, the young philosopher who was our most brilliant and reliable member, came down with renal tuberculosis, and had to move to the Midi for a cure. Sartre made no attempt to check the progress of this debacle; by June he had already fallen a prey to tormenting scruples and doubts. The Gestapo had arrested numerous members of the "Pentagon"; Sartre's boyhood friend Péron had been deported, and so too, from a group operating in the close vicinity of ours, had one of my most brilliant former philosophy students, Yvonne Picard. Would they ever come back? (They did not return.) How absurd it would be if they died! They had not yet done anything of the slightest possible use. Hitherto we had been lucky; none of our members had been bothered by the authorities. But Sartre could now see just what risks, and all to no purpose, the continued existence of "Socialism and Liberty" would have meant for our friends. All through October we had interminable discussions on this subject—or, to be more precise, Sartre argued it over with himself, since I agreed with his view that to make yourself responsible for someone's death out of sheer obstinacy is not a thing lightly to be forgiven. Sartre had brooded over this plan of his for months in the Stalag, and had devoted weeks of his time and energy to it after his release, so it hit him hard to abandon it; but abandon it he did, though his heart told him otherwise. Then he obstinately settled down to the play he had begun, which represented the one form of resistance work still open to him.

We were both writing busily. Besides his play, Sartre was working on his philosophical treatise, while *Confluences* and *Les Cahiers du Sud* both asked him for critical articles, which he sent them. He dispatched the manuscript of my first novel to Brice Parain, and I began another one. It dealt with the Resistance among other things, and I knew it could never be published till the end of the Occupation. But we had decided to conduct our lives as though ultimate victory was a certainty. This resolution sustained us, though it was not enough to give us peace of mind. To bet on the future, even to hope, is not the same as to *know*—or even to believe. At times my imagination wavered horrifyingly. If Nazism was here to stay for ten or even twenty years, and we still refused to submit to it, we should undergo the same fate as Péron and Yvonne Picard. I had not the faintest suspicion what a concentration camp was really like; to me deportation signified above all separation and silence, but how could I survive these? Hitherto I had always said that there is always one last resort in the face of extreme misfortune: suicide; now, suddenly, this was snatched from me. For ten or fifteen years I would be thinking at every moment of the day that perhaps Sartre was dead, and I would not dare to kill myself for fear he might still be alive. I imagined myself already caught in this dilemma, and half choked at the thought. Then I firmly banished such fancies, and tried to convince myself—sometimes with a modicum of success—that I would stand the worst that might befall. I calmed down again, and lived wholly in the present. But the present had previously meant a happy proliferation of new schemes, in which the future bulked large; reduced to itself alone, it crumbled away into dust. Not only time but space had contracted. Two years before, Paris had occupied the center of a world which for the larger part lay open to my curiosity; but now France was Occupied Territory, and cut off from the rest of the globe. Italy and Spain, which we had loved so dearly, were now our enemies. Between us and America dark, fiery storm clouds lay, and the only voice which reached us from beyond our frontiers was that of the B.B.C. We were stifling under a blanket of ignorance.

At least, as the year went by, I no longer found myself an isolated case. My emotions and expectations and anxieties and rebellious instincts were all shared with a multitude of people. They were anonymous and faceless, but present all about me, both externally and within my own mind: it was they who, through the beating of my heart, were stirred to passion or hatred. Never before, I realized, had I known what hatred really was: the objects of my rage had been more or less abstract entities. But now I recognized its flavor, and focused it with especial violence against those of our enemies whom I knew most about. Pétain's speeches had a more inflammatory effect on me than Hitler's; and while I condemned all collaborators, I felt a sharply defined and quite excruciating personal loathing for those of my own kind who joined their ranks—intellectuals, journalists, writers. When artists or men of letters went to Germany to assure the conquerors of our spiritual loyalty, I felt I had been personally betrayed. Articles by men like Déat and Brasillach, with their denunciations and incitement to murder, I considered as crimes no less unforgivable than the actions of a Darlan.

Fear, rage, and blind impotence: these were the foundations on which my life now developed. But there were also flickers of hope, and so far I had not suffered directly from the war: I had not, for instance, lost one of my nearest or dearest. Sartre had returned from captivity, with neither his health nor his good spirits impaired; it was impossible to be depressed for long in his company. However restricted the area in which we found ourselves enclosed, his inquisitiveness and enthusiasm would animate every last corner of it. Here we were in Paris, with its village-like streets and great country skies, and so many people all around us— so many faces, so many adventures, such a lot still to see and understand and love! I no longer experienced any feeling of security, any overwhelming sensations of elated joy; but my day-to-day mood was one of gayness, and I often reflected that, despite everything, this obstinate gaiety was still a kind of happiness.

Materially, life was much harder than it had been the previous winter; and on top of this Sartre and I were burdened with certain responsibilities. Lise had decided to leave André Moreau, and would not return to her family either; she was now living in a seedy little hotel on the Rue Delambre, and we were partially supporting her. We were also helping Olga, Wanda, and Bost, who were struggling along in a state of dire poverty. Even the Category D restaurants, where strange meats were dished up under the name of "kid," still cost too much for our pockets. I moved to a room with a kitchen attached, still in the Hôtel Mistral, borrowed a saucepan, casseroles, and crockery from my sister's studio, and from then on cooked all our meals myself, with Bost as a frequent guest. I had little natural liking for domestic chores, and in order to adapt myself to the situation I had recourse to a familiar proceeding: I turned my culinary worries into a full-blown obsession, and stuck to it for the next three years. I watched while the coupons were clipped from my ration book, and never parted with one too many. I wandered through the streets, rummaging behind the dummy window displays for unrationed foodstuffs, a sort of treasure hunt, and I thoroughly enjoyed it; what a windfall it was if I stumbled on a beet or a cabbage! The first lunch we had in my room consisted of "turnip sauerkraut," which I tried to improve by pouring canned soup over it. Sartre said it wasn't at all bad. He could eat practically anything, and on occasion went without food altogether. This cost him little effort; I was less stoical. I often felt ravenous, which annoyed me; that was partly why I put so much energy and enthusiasm into collecting provisions, though they might only include a few packets of pasta and dried vegetables, or a handful or two of oatmeal. I resurrected one of my favorite childhood games—organizing a strict economy for a very poor household. I would glance over my treasures, and reckon at a glance how many days they would last; it was the future itself I kept shut up in my larder. Not one grain to waste: I began to understand the joys of miserliness and hoarding. I did not complain about the time this took up; while I was talking to Bost or to Lise, who often helped me with such tasks, I often spent hours slicing green beans or sorting out maggotty dried beans from the sound ones. I took as little time as possible in preparing a meal, but nevertheless found the alchemy of cookery fascinating. I remember one evening early in December, when I was kept at home by the curfew, now set back to 6 P.M. as the result of some new "outrage." I was writing away; everything outside was still with the utter silence of the desert, and on the stove a savory-smelling vegetable soup stood cooking. That delectable odor and the faint hissing of the gas kept me company; and though I was not in the true sense of the word a housewife, I had a glimpse of a housewife's joys.

Yet I was not really more up against the hard facts of life than I had ever been. Since we were young and healthy, I saw no reason why the austerity of our diet should have any serious effects on us; the pangs of hunger I felt were disagreeable, but not liable to produce any harmful consequences. I found no difficulty in giving up smoking, which I did not really enjoy; I used to light one cigarette after another when I was working, but this was more to mark the passage of time than anything else, since I didn't even inhale. Sartre was far harder hit in this respect; he used to search the gutters and the banquettes of the Trois Mousquetaires for cigarette butts to fill his pipe with. He never sank to using those weird mixtures which some fanatical pipe smokers affected, and which made the Café Flore smell like a herbalist's shop.

Clothes were a problem, too. The black market both offended our consciences and was far beyond the reach of our purse; but the official ration of clothing coupons was stingy in the extreme. I got hold of some after my father's death, enough to let me get a dress and overcoat made, which I took great care of. Toward the end of autumn many women exchanged their skirts for slacks, which kept one much warmer, and I followed their example; except when I was going to the *lycée,* my outdoor costume consisted of skiing rig, complete with boots. I had enjoyed keeping up my personal appearance in the days when such activities formed a pleasurable diversion; but I had no wish now to burden my existence with pointless complications of this sort, and so I stopped bothering. It already demanded considerable effort to keep up a decent minimum of appearances. You needed coupons for shoe repairs, so I made do with those wooden-soled clogs which were coming on the market about then; dry cleaners were charging exorbitant prices, and if you decided to clean your own garments, it was extremely difficult to get hold of any gasoline. Because of electricity cuts the hairdressers worked at odd and irregular hours, and an ordinary set became a hazardous ordeal, with the result that turbans came into fashion; they formed a simultaneous substitute for a hat and a permanent. I had worn them occasionally myself, both for convenience and because they suited me; now I adopted them as a regular thing. I aimed at simplification in every sphere. The swellings on my face gradually subsided, and my scrapes and scratches healed over; but I never bothered to replace the tooth I had lost on the way to Grenoble. I also had a nasty boil on my chin, which grew and grew, with slight suppuration; for a long while I took no notice of it, and then one morning, growing irked with the wretched thing, I went to the mirror and began squeezing it. Something white appeared; I pressed harder—and then for a fraction of a second I seemed to be acting out one of those surrealist nightmares in which cheeks suddenly sprout eyes. A tooth was protruding from my flesh, the very tooth that had been broken during my fall: it had remained embedded in my chin for weeks. When I told my friends this story they roared with laughter.

I bothered all the less with my appearance since I now saw so few people. Giacometti went back to Switzerland. We occasionally dined with Pagniez, who now had two children, and lived in a fifth floor on the Boulevard Saint-Michel, with a wonderful panoramic view of the Luxembourg Gardens and most of Paris. He had very quickly stopped defending Vichy; we now shared the same opinions, and his wife was a charming person. But the fierce humility that characterized him at twenty had now turned sour and morose. In the early days of his marriage he used to tell us cheerfully: "You two are writers; well, I've succeeded in another way, I've got a home and happiness, and that's not to be sniffed at, either." Very soon, however, he came to the conclusion that we found him a bore, and in order to prove his point set about boring us; he deliberately talked at great length on subjects which did not interest us in the least, such as cooking, or how to bring up children. Sometimes, though only intermittently, there would be a flicker of our old intimacy. With Marco, on the other hand, we now avoided any close relationship. He used to slouch round the Montparnasse markets, with his bald head and vast backside and lackluster expression, in search of illicit love. Now and then he would join us for a drink, and introduce some young guttersnipe or other, with an ecstatic aside to the effect that this one was "a *real* tough customer," or a burglar, or, once, a murderer. We saw hardly anyone outside the little group we referred to as "the family": Olga, Wanda, Bost, and Lise. They had highly subtle relationships with each of us and with one another, and we took great care to respect their individual quirks. Bost I generally saw in Sartre's company, but with this one exception twosomes were the general rule. When I was chatting in the Flore with Olga or Lise, when Sartre and Wanda went out together, when Lise and Wanda were having a tête-à-tête, none of us would have dreamed of joining their table. People found this behavior preposterous, but to us it seemed both natural and obvious. It was partly justified by the members of "the family" being very young, which meant that each of them was still shut up in his own individual self and required undivided attention; but we had always possessed—and were always to keep—the taste for conversation *à deux*. We would enjoy ourselves over the most idiotic topics—always provided that the two of us remained uninterrupted by any third party. Points of contact and disagreement would differ from one partner to the next, as would one's range of memories and interests; but when you have to discuss things with several people at once, conversation, except in very special circumstances, tends to become mundane—an amusing way of killing time, liable to become insipid or even exhausting, and far from the genuine sort of communication at which we aimed.

We had forsaken Montparnasse. We used to have breakfast in the Café des Trois Mousquetaires, and sometimes I would work there, with a great hubbub of voices and rattling crockery all about me, loud enough to drown the radio, which was always turned on full blast. In the evening we would meet at the Flore, where you could now drink nothing but ersatz beer and coffee. Some of the regulars had gone off to Marseille, where according to report they had started a small dried-fruit business. Anyway there were these blackish confections on sale in Paris, made out of the leftover figs and dates still shipped over from Africa. But on the whole the clientele had altered very little. Sonia still queened it over her small feminine court, as lovely and elegant as ever. We also saw the fair-haired lovers who had slipped across the zonal border with us: the boy's name was Jausion, and he was a writer, while his girl friend was a Czechoslovakian Jew. They were on intimate terms with another couple of about the same age. The girl, Bella, was Jewish too—a small ravishing brunette, with a creamy complexion, who was always laughing. Among the newcomers we noticed a very pretty and ethereal blonde named Joëlle le Feuve, who sat alone at her table, scarcely ever exchanging a word with anyone. We found her mildly consumptive charms most appealing. We still took a keen interest in those stunning or seductive creatures who came to the Flore in search of a future: we watched their gambits and speculated on their past lives and weighed up their chances. Public and national disasters had not diminished the interest we took in individual human beings.

We went to La Pouèze for Christmas. Madame Lemaire no longer had her car running, so we took our bicycles on the train, and rode them the fourteen miles or so from Angers to the Lemaires' village. Even in this fertile countryside austerity was abroad; but nevertheless we had a turkey on Christmas Eve, and there was often meat at lunch. We asked for the same dinner every night: apple fritters, which we found most filling. Afterward Madame Lemaire would fill us up with good rough brandy, which warmed our blood. In any case our bedrooms had great log fires burning in them and were far from cold. This comfortable existence appealed to us so much that we hardly ever put our noses out of doors. We worked and read and chatted with Madame Lemaire, who no longer came on visits to Paris now.

I say we read; but with no more English or American novels available there was little enough to catch our eye in bookshop windows, and few new books appeared. In *Quand vient la fin* Raymond Guérin, who was at the time a prisoner of war, described brilliantly and with great wealth of detail his father's protracted last illness, cancer of the anus. I found this terrible narrative most gripping. I also became very interested in Dumézil's work on myths and mythology, and continued to study history, going back now to ancient times. A book on the Etruscans I found especially remarkable; I told Sartre about Etruscan funeral ceremonies, and this information lent him inspiration for the second act of *The Flies*.

The theater had nothing very attractive to offer us, either. A revival of Cocteau's *Les Parents terribles* was banned, as a result of Alain Laubreaux taking the matter up. We saw *Jupiter*—a somewhat vulgar comedy, partly redeemed by the airy presence of Jacqueline Bouvier, who was later to marry Marcel Pagnol—and Crommelynck's *Le Cocu magnifique* (*The Magnificent Cuckold*). *The Playboy of the Western World* had supplied us, in our youth, with our myth of "predilection"; but the mediocre production put on at the Théâtre des Mathurins we found a great disappointment. In January, 1942, Vermorel staged his first play, *Jeanne avec nous,* which dealt with Joan of Arc. The part of Joan of Arc was first assigned to Joëlle le Feuve; it was her theatrical debut, and the papers gave her a great deal of publicity. Then they announced that owing to her poor state of health she would be unable to go on with rehearsals; the rumor went around the Flore that she really hadn't been up to the part. We saw her again, back at her usual table, alone as always, a frozen expression on her face. It hurt us to picture her humiliation and disappointment. Perhaps this blow aggravated her physical disabilities, because her health was indeed failing, and a few months later she died of pulmonary TB. We knew practically nothing about her, and yet there was an element of absurdity about her fate that wrung our hearts.

It was Berthe Tissen who actually played Joan of Arc; despite her slight stature and Luxembourg accent she proved a tremendous hit with the public. Vermorel had written a very clever play. It attacked the English, true; but they were presented as the occupying power, while Cauchon and his clique were their collaborators. So well was the point made that applause at Joan's proud retorts to them was quite clearly and unequivocally an anti-German and anti-Vichy demonstration.

Dullin, at Camille's insistence, had undertaken the management of the Théâtre Sarah Bernhardt, now renamed the Théâtre de la Cité. The first play he put on there was one by her, called *La Princesse des Ursins,* which was not a success. At the Comédie-Française, Barrault was playing Hamlet— a seductive interpretation, but this lean, bony, neurotic Prince was nearer to Laforgue's pastiche than the character Shakespeare conceived. At the Théâtre Montparnasse Jean Darcante's company put on *La Célestine,* in an unfortunately rather tasteless adaptation.

As we were coming out of *La Célestine,* on the night of March 3, we saw some lights in the sky, and heard what I recognized as antiaircraft gunfire. The sirens wailed out, but people remained standing about on the sidewalks, peering skyward and asking what exactly was happening: were the English bombing Paris? Or had the Germans staged a practice alert? We went to sleep with the problems unsolved. Next day the papers were jubilant: the English had shed French blood. Their target had been the Renault works at Billancourt, and they had claimed a large number of victims in the surrounding area. German propaganda exploited this raid for all it was worth.

One of Sartre's favorite fellow prisoners was repatriated about March, a dilettante called Courbeau, who had done a bit of journalism, painted when he felt like it, and had married the daughter of one of the biggest lawyers in Le Havre. He had also done the décor for *Bariona,* besides playing the part of Pilate. He was wondering, somewhat anxiously, what to do with himself now; there was something about his subtle, essentially bourgeois features that reminded me of my cousin Jacques. He and his wife lived in his father-in-law's vast house and invited us down for a couple of days. We left Paris by bicycle on the first day of the Easter holidays. We passed through Rouen, to find the old part of the town burned down, and Caudebec, which was reduced to rubble. A lot of houses had been wiped out in the suburbs of Le Havre itself. But Monsieur Vernadet, Courbeau's father-in-law, said with a sort of pride that he'd show us something better than *that.* His house stood on high ground near the port, and any night there was a raid he had a grandstand view. He gave us a lengthy description of the magnificent spectacle he could observe from his window, and the jubilation he felt when an important objective was hit. I asked him if he wasn't afraid. "You get used to it," he told me. He took us on a tour of the ruins: numerous houses in the neighborhood had been destroyed or damaged by the R.A.F., and lower down whole areas had been laid waste. "There was a gasoline refinery here," he would remark. "Nothing left of it now, as you can see. Over there it was warehouses . . ." and so on. To listen to his complacent voice you'd have thought he was the proprietor of some château, showing his guests over the estate. Afterward Courbeau took us to see the old Quartier Saint-François, which was now no more than a grass-grown wilderness. The Rue des Galions no longer existed, nor did the sailors' dives, nor the slate-fronted houses we had liked so much. I remembered that day in 1933 when we sat in the Café des Mouettes and agreed, in a melancholy way, that nothing further of importance could happen to us: how stupefied we would have been if anyone had showed us in a crystal ball how things would be in this spring of 1942! Yet I did not regret those days of peace and ignorance. I was too enamored of truth ever to mourn lost illusions, and such insipid ones at that.

After a dinner of rutabagas, but served in the most luxurious dishes, we listened to the B.B.C. news, and broke up about midnight. I had just gone to bed when I heard the sirens, and immediately afterward some loud explosions, and the sound of A.A. guns opening up. This time I was consciously aware of possible danger, and hesitated, on the very brink of fear. But I was so drowsy that I couldn't face the prospect of staying awake, all on edge, listening. What will be will be, I told myself, and inserted the ear plugs that I now kept handy every night. Today I find this attitude of indifference most astonishing; no doubt the harmless alerts I had already experienced and all the various adventures I had undergone had hardened me to such alarms. But the fact is I slept right through till morning. Courbeau showed us fragments of shrapnel in the garden; a few hundred yards away some houses had been blown to smithereens.

Sartre and Courbeau talked a good deal about their camp life and the friends they had made there: in particular about one young priest, the Abbé Page, who had won Sartre's sympathy both by his personal charm and the rigorous way in which he made his conduct match his beliefs. Eighteen months earlier, when his fellow priests had jumped at the chance of release, which anyway proved to be unfounded, he refused to accept any such offer, on the grounds that the priesthood conferred no special privileges upon him. Nor did he contemplate escaping; his place was in the camp. He always went for the most difficult assignments; he was previously the curé of some rural hell-hole in the Cévennes that he had picked for its wearisome primitivism. He had a keen sense of what freedom meant; in his eyes Fascism, by reducing man to bondage, was defying God's will: "God," he said, "has so great a respect for liberty that He willed His creatures to be free rather than incapable of sin." This conviction, coupled with his profound humanity, endeared him to Sartre. During endless discussions, for which Sartre showed an insatiable appetite, he affirmed his belief in the full humanity of Christ, a point over which he differed from the Jesuits in the camp. Jesus, like any child, was born in filth and suffering;

the Virgin had been granted no miraculous delivery. Sartre agreed with this: the myth of the Incarnation lost all its beauty if it failed to burden Christ with *all* the ills of our human condition. The Abbé Page did not oppose the celibacy of the clergy, but he could not accept the proposition that half the human race was taboo to him, and had various friendships with women—completely platonic, but full of tenderness and intimacy— which his superiors looked somewhat askance at. He opened his mind willingly to Sartre, and was so fond of him that he once declared emphatically, "If God were to damn you, I should not accept His heaven." He remained a prisoner till the end of the war. After his release he came to Paris. I had lunch with him and Sartre in a little flat above the Place du Tertre where Courbeau was living at the time; he was not wearing a soutane, and had very considerable charm. Then he went off, back to his dreary Cévennes parish.

We crossed the Seine by the nearest ferry, to find the flowers beginning to bloom in Normandy, and made our way via Pont-Audemer, Lisieux, and Flers to La Pouèze, where we spent the rest of our holidays. We returned by train, bringing some eggs with us, and Madame Lemaire now got into the habit of sending us two or three food parcels every month, which kept heaven knows how many people from hunger. The trouble was that the parcels took so long to arrive. The first one I received contained a large joint of pork, cooked to a turn and done brown: it looked highly appetizing to me. But when I examined it more closely, I found tiny whitish maggots crawling over it. Pity, I thought. I had got it into my head that we had to eat meat if we weren't to die of anemia; so I cut out the infected bits and scraped and cleaned the rest. Lise caught me at this occupation, but in her case, like mine, hunger was far stronger than disgust. As for Sartre, we hid the truth from him. Later parcels often arrived stinking to high heaven; I would extract cuts of malodorous beef and rinse them thoroughly in vinegar, after which I boiled them for hours, and seasoned the resultant *pot-au-feu* with strong-flavored herbs. Ordinarily I got away with this minor deception, and was mortified if Sartre pushed his plate away unfinished. Once he was there when I unwrapped half a rabbit; he grabbed it instantly and ran downstairs to deposit it in the garbage.

Lise had moved from the Rue Delambre to the Hôtel Mistral, and now shared all my domestic problems. This greater intimacy had made no very great difference to our relationship. We still went through interminable rows and reconciliations, with me veering from laughter to sheer fury. There were numerous alerts during that term, and Lise would come hammering on my door, yelling: "I'm afraid! I want to go down to the shelter —you come with me!" The central area of Paris was never made a target, and I refused to get up. "Go on your own," I'd yell back. "No!" she'd scream, and then she'd begin tugging at the door and reproaching me for being so selfish. But I never gave way, and she eventually got used to trotting off without me down to the Métro station, which was our nearest shelter.

We welcomed these raids with somewhat mixed feelings. We had very great sympathy for the young pilots who, at the risk of their lives, ran the gauntlet of the German barrage; and yet men, women, and children died under their bombs, and our attitude was all the more embarrassing because we ran no direct risk ourselves. All the same, when we heard the rattle of antiaircraft fire, and the distant *crump* of explosions, it was hope that ran uppermost in our minds. It was rumored that the R.A.F. had successfully raided targets in Germany, that Cologne and Hamburg and the Ruhr had been seriously damaged. If the English could win the battle for air supremacy, an Allied victory became far less unlikely.

But at this period there was a heavy price to pay for everything, even for hope. England was holding firm, and the German attitude toughening, while conditions inside France steadily deteriorated. Laval was appointed Prime Minister, and his ultra-collaborationist policy held the field. In the Occupied Zone the most extreme measures yet known were taken against the Jews. With effect from February 2, a decree forbade them to change their place of residence or to go out after eight o'clock in the evening. On June 17 they were ordered to wear the yellow Star of David. In Paris this news produced as much stupefaction as indignation, so convinced had we been that certain things, despite all, could not come about in *our* country. Indeed, optimism remained so obstinately rooted in French hearts that a certain number of Jews, particularly small folk without adequate resources, naively supposed that by observing the regulations they would escape the worst of what was happening. In fact, few of those identifiable by the yellow star survived. Others, equally ingenuous, thought they could flout all the decrees with impunity: I never saw anyone wearing a star in Montparnasse or Saint-Germain-des-Prés. Neither Sonia nor the pretty Czech girl nor Bella nor any of their friends changed their way of life in the slightest degree, even when from July 15 they were forbidden to enter any public building, such as restaurants, cinemas, or libraries. They still turned up at the Flore and chattered away till closing time. Yet the Gestapo, aided and abetted by the French police, was rumored to be rounding them all up in a series of raids: children were separated from their mothers and packed off to Drancy and other, unknown, destinations. Jews of French nationality were shut up in the camp at Pithiviers, and others, very many others, deported to Germany. Many finally admitted that their lives were in danger, and decided to cross the zonal border and go into hiding. Bianca, whose parents were already concealed somewhere in the Free Zone, and who had not so much as set foot in the Sorbonne this year because of her disgust at the *numerus clausus,* now made an arrangement with a *passeur*: in return for an exorbitant fee he took her to Moulins, booked her in at a hotel, and promised to come back for her in a few hours' time. In fact he never showed up again: this kind of swindle was rife at the time. Nevertheless she managed to get down to Aix, where several of her friends had settled. They had worked out an ingenious scheme for obtaining false papers. On some pretext or other they would obtain access to the faculty enrollment register, from which they excerpted the name and birthplace of some student, whether male or female, who was roughly their own age. Assuming his or her identity, they would then write to whatever local record office held this student's birth certificate, and demand a copy of it, which they had sent to them—a little simple collusion here—in the same name as that they intended to use. Once you had this document, all you needed was a couple of witnesses, who could be anyone you liked; and then the local police station would issue you a genuine identity card, bearing a false name but your own photograph and fingerprints.

At the end of May we learned that Politzer had been tortured and subsequently shot. Feldmann was executed in July. A large number of Communists had suffered the same fate, and the yellow-and-red "Warning" notices succeeded each other ever more rapidly on the tiled walls of the Métro. In July a proclamation signed "Oberg" was posted, announcing that henceforth reprisals would be extended to terrorists' families: their closest male relations would be shot, their wives deported, and their children interned. Despite this, there was no sign of the killings and acts of sabotage decreasing. Laval began to preach the "working levies for Germany" scheme, and we found this blackmailing of prisoners peculiarly sickening; but the French workers wouldn't budge. The Germans made great efforts to create an intellectuals' collaboration movement, but without success. A grenade was thrown into the Left Bank Bookshop they had opened in the Latin Quarter, on the Emplacement du d'Harcourt, and did considerable damage to it. Almost the entire French intelligentsia boycotted the Arno Breker exhibition which they organized, with great publicity, in the Orangerie. Abel Bonnard, on his appointment as Minister of Education, criticized the lukewarm attitude of his predecessors, and demanded that the University should be "committed." No one followed his lead. Sartre and I were both left to teach our classes exactly as we pleased, and no one ever called us to account. The students used to stage anti-German demonstrations in the Latin Quarter; they weren't very serious, but they annoyed the occupying power. A certain group of young people showed their disgust with *"la Révolution nationale"* in a rather more preposterous manner, which nevertheless exasperated staunch upholders of the "new morality." They wore their hair long, Oxford fashion, and carefully curled, and carried umbrellas, and dressed in zoot suits: thus attired they used to throw parties at which they went crazy over swing music. Their Anglophile and anarchic attitude did stand for a kind of opposition to the regime. We saw some of them in the Flore, and despite their affected airs, we rather liked them.

What with anti-Semitic persecutions, repressive police measures, and near-famine, the atmosphere in Paris was decidedly oppressive. At Vichy, however, the grim goings-on had their comic side too, which sometimes gave us a laugh. It was with jubilant delight that we heard *Tartuffe* had been banned in the Free Zone; and the embarrassed position in which Giraud put Pétain by coming to surrender to him after his escape we found highly entertaining.

The writers on our side of the zonal border had tacitly formulated certain rules and stuck to them. No one was to write for any journal or magazine in the Occupied Zone, nor to broadcast from Radio Paris. On the other hand, it was permissible to work for the press in the Free Zone and to speak on Radio Vichy: here it all depended on the content of the article or broadcast in question. To publish a book on the other side of the border was quite all right, but in the Occupied Zone it raised various problems. In the end it was decided that here, too, the content of the work was what mattered. Sartre kept *The Age of Reason* locked away in a drawer, since no publisher would have dared to bring out so "scandalous" a novel; but he had taken mine to Gallimard's. As for the theater, could Vermorel be blamed for having put on *Jeanne avec nous?* No one was in a position to decide. In *The Flies* Sartre had a message for the French: let them throw off their guilt and assert their right to freedom, in the teeth of the present regime. He wanted this play to reach the public, and without a moment's hesitation suggested that Barrault should put it on: after all, it was at his prompting that the play had been written in the first place. But it needed considerable nerve to stage a production in which the two leading female parts were to be played by a couple of beginners, and Barrault backed out. Sartre next discussed his proposition with Dullin, who had a very high opinion of both Olgas, blonde and brunette alike. The only thing was, he had certain financial difficulties just then, since the productions he had put on at the Théâtre de la Cité had failed to pay their way. *The Flies,* with the vast crowd of extras it required, would be an enormously expensive production, and he would need to find a backer for it. None of our friends could possibly supply the sum he needed; and we felt a miracle had taken place when Merleu-Ponty, whom we had kept informed of these negotiations, let us know that he had just unearthed a positively Maecenas-like couple, loaded with wealth, and filled with an ardent desire to meet Sartre and finance his play.

The meeting took place at the Flore. The man answered to the splendid name of Néron, and looked to be about thirty-five. He had a waxy-pale face, of somewhat degenerate appearance, with a chin like Philip II's, very bad teeth, and piercing eyes. He wore a most expensive suit, with a long waistcoat and high collar, and a cashmere tie knotted very tightly, as was the fashion then. There was a faint air of zootishness about his get-up which was out of key with the serious cast of his features. On one of his fingers there gleamed a huge signet ring. His girl friend, Renée Martinaud, a dark and attractive girl, was so elegantly attired that she took my breath away—all the more so since very few women at the time took the trouble to dress well. We either went around bareheaded, or wearing a turban; the vast flower-trimmed hats which had recently appeared in the milliners' shops not only cost a small fortune but frequently made people laugh. Renée wore one of these, covered with roses, but with such an un-self-conscious air that, far from making her look ridiculous, it actually enhanced her beauty. Néron dominated the discussion; his manner of speaking combined weight and preciosity. The only reason he was interested in money was because it enabled him to seek the company of writers and artists. He said he was passionately addicted to philosophy, and had a detailed knowledge of Hegel and phenomenology. He was especially fascinated by the problem of time. He had undertaken a monograph on fraud, regarded as a perversion of normal time concepts; according to him, the swindler was suffering from a kind of "foreshortening of the *durée*." He had read the manuscript of *The Flies,* approved of it, and was prepared to place at Dullin's disposal the sum he required to put it on. His intellectual fatuity irked us; but you can't expect too much from a Maecenas, and when he left us we rubbed our hands with satisfaction.

I saw him at the Flore every day after that, writing away absorbedly. He told me, with an air of mystery, that he had got hold of an unpublished tract by Hegel, which anticipated Heidegger's philosophy in a rather disturbing fashion; but he refused to divulge any more about it before he had finished the study he was preparing on the subject. On the other hand he did, one evening, confide in us about his private life. He had two mistresses, one fair, one dark, both of whom he called Renée. Neither knew of the other's existence. He gave them identical presents, and saw to it that they dressed very much alike; he had even set them up in near-duplicate apartments. He himself occupied a third one, at Passy, which neither of the two women knew about; it was here that he took us. There were Spanish chairs, I recall, with pointed backs that seemed to threaten the sky, and armchairs covered in vellum, and a riot of glassware, carpets, and chandeliers. The library was filled with row upon row of extremely valuable books, all bound in full calf. Despite its air of unstinted luxury, the whole place was astonishingly ugly, and so clean that it struck a note of impersonal chilliness. No one, clearly, ever sat on these chairs, these ash trays had never been sullied by a cigarette, and no hand had ever turned the pages of these books.

Despite what he said, Néron could not have treated both his girl friends in quite the same way, since Renée Martinaud was the only one we met. She had a flat in Montparnasse; like his, it was somewhat overluxurious, but not extravagantly so. She invited me and Olga there, and plied us with cakes and black-market liquor. When I pointed her out to Lise one day, in the Flore, Lise swore she'd known the woman a few months previously: she'd been living with three children then, in a shabby little room in Lise's own modest hotel on the Rue Delambre. Had she only recently met Néron, then? Yet she looked as though she'd been accustomed to every convenience in life for years.

Dullin invited Renée and Néron out to Ferrolles one fine day in May, and Sartre, Olga, and I went, too. We had lunch out in the little colonnade, and Camille really surpassed herself. Néron talked abundantly, treating us to an all-embracing flow of cultural expertise. He was even prepared to put the specialists right, as when he produced much detailed information for Dullin's benefit about the Chinese theater, information of which our host was wholly ignorant. He revealed the existence, in Bologna, of a theater built by Palladio, even more beautiful than that at Vicenza. A meeting was arranged, to be held in the presence of a notary, between Dullin, Sartre, and Néron, the latter having agreed to put up a million francs in cash.

On the appointed morning I was working in my room when a phone call came through for me. It was Sartre on the line. "A fine thing's happened," he said, and told me that Néron had tried to drown himself early that morning, in the lake by the Bois de Boulogne, but had been fished out by a German officer and was now in the hospital. The reason for his attempted suicide, it seemed, was that he hadn't a penny in the world.

He made a rapid recovery and, not without a certain air of complacency, told us the whole truth of the matter. His story had been that he was writing about fraud; in fact he practiced it. Six months previously he had been a junior bank employee, with nothing but a diploma to his name. But he had read a great deal, and dreamed more. His knowledge of the business world was extensive. He had a confident manner and the gift of gab. So he took some official notepaper with the bank's heading on it, and used this to arrange meetings between himself and various fairly shady financiers, to whom he proposed various investments which carried such a high rate of interest that they preferred not to inquire too closely into them. Obviously somewhat irregular speculations were involved. When they got their initial dividends their confidence increased and they entrusted Néron with ever larger capital sums. He payed X with the money he took from Y, and Y with what he extracted from Z, skimming off from all these funds enough to pay for his various luxuries. It was obvious that so elementary a scheme must very soon be found out, but he couldn't care less about this. He'd always wanted to have a taste of high living, and now he'd done it. If he ever got into really serious trouble, he told us, suicide was a way out which he'd always envisaged with equanimity, and to tell the truth, this wasn't his first attempt. As for his background of culture, that was all bluff. The unpublished Hegelian tract had never existed, nor had the Palladio theater in Bologna, and the details he had given Dullin about the Chinese theater he had made up himself. I listened, dumfounded, to all this; the potent Maecenas had vanished, and his place was now taken by a junior bank clerk with delusions of grandeur. Then, suddenly, we warmed to him. When he had played the rich backer, his haughtiness had put us off; but in fact what we had to deal with was a quite extraordinary piece of "conning." When he displayed all his supposed erudition, Néron had struck us as a fool; but what astuteness he must have possessed to camouflage his ignorance as well as he did! We far preferred a case of mythomania to endless snobbish pedantries. It was irritating to think of him using his "millions" to buy intellectual friends; but we admired the boldness and ingenuity which he had deployed to realize his life's ambition, if only for a brief period. I understood how it was that Lise had run across Renée in a third-rate hotel; in her, too, there was a touch of the adventurer, and this merely served to increase my interest in her. Shortly afterward Néron was consigned to Fresnes Prison, but his victims had more or less compromised themselves by accepting extraordinary financial returns with their eyes shut, and none of them pressed the matter seriously. On top of this, Néron contracted TB; he was released from jail very quickly, and went off for a cure in the country.

Sartre and Dullin had a good laugh together over the trap they had fallen into; but they sighed regretfully after that vanished million. "I'll put the play on anyway," Dullin said. We were certain he'd keep his promise, but it was necessary to bide our time patiently.

As for my own affairs, Brice Parain had discussed with me my novel, *Légitime Défense,* in January, and surprised me very much by remarking that Françoise could be summed up as an "isolated" character, especially since I had endowed her with the same urge and need to communicate as I found in myself. He also made what I regarded as a fairer criticism, namely, that she was not the stuff of which murderers are made. He thought the novel was worth publishing, but wanted to hear what Paulhan thought about it. The latter kept the manuscript for a long time. In June Sartre and I went to see him, in the apartment he occupied opposite the Lutetian amphitheater, on the Ile de la Cité. It was a fine day, and I felt rather on edge. Paulhan asked me, with an intrigued air, if Dullin *really* resembled my character Pierre. He regarded my style as too neutral, he said, and generously suggested that it *might* not be too much of a bore for me to rewrite the whole book from cover to cover. I told him this would be out of the question, as I'd already spent four years on it. "I see," Paulhan said. "In that case we'll publish it as it stands. It's an excellent novel." I couldn't decide if he was paying me a compliment, or if my novel was the sort that's regarded as a "good commercial risk." But the essential thing was that it had been accepted: they would publish it early the following spring. I felt not so much happy as immensely relieved. I was told firmly that my title, *Légitime Défense,* wouldn't do at all, and after turning various words and phrases over in my mind, I suggested *L'Invitée,* to which they agreed.

We wanted to get back to the Free Zone for a change of air; it was particularly easy to cross the border in the Basque country, we were told, and someone volunteered an address in Sauveterre. Bost came with us. About midday a guide, also with a bicycle, took us along a narrow lane, and after some five hundred yards told us we were there. We had lunch at Navarrenx, and found the inn crowded with refugees, who certainly hadn't crossed the border for the fun of it. They were mostly Jews, and had a hunted look about them. We did a lengthy tour of the Pyrenees: the high mountain country was less exciting than that in the Alpes Maritimes, and I preferred the lowlands by far—the cloistered peace of Saint-Bernard-de-Comminges, and Montségur, that famous stronghold where the Albigensians so long defied the northern Crusaders. I took Bost to Lourdes, and his Protestant eyes bulged in his head at the "Palace of the Rosary," the musical Virgins, the phosphorescent grottoes, and miraculous lozenges. Sartre did not come with us; there were certain trips which he left us to make by ourselves while he worked. For instance, one morning Bost and I went up on foot from the Col du Tourmalet to the summit of the Midi de Bigorre, leaving Sartre sitting in a meadow, with a writing pad on his knees and a strong wind blowing. When we came back he had knocked off heaven knows how many pages, wind or no wind, and felt very pleased with himself. The trip was a pretty tiring one, though, what with the steepness of the hills and the bad condition of our inner tubes, which needed constant repairing. In addition to this we didn't get enough to eat. Our lunch consisted of fruit and tomatoes bought in some village, and we usually dined on clear soup and an unappetizing vegetable dish. Meat was so rare that my record of the trip, which only notes the distance we traveled each day and where we got to, actually adds under one entry, "Two meat dishes at lunch!" It was not easy to find accommodations in hotels, and we often slept in barns. We revisited Foix and recalled the conversation we had had by that mountain tarn, on the eve of war: *this* was not the "afterward" we had bargained for. At Foix, too, Bost left us; he was going to see some friends in Lyon, and then returning to Paris. He got caught trying to slip across the border and spent two weeks fretting and fuming in Châlons Prison. When he came out he was tottering with hunger and ate two lunches, one right after the other.

We made our way by circuitous route from the eastern Pyrenees to Provence. Every day it became harder to find lodgings or food. When the road ran alongside some vineyards we dismounted and carried off a large haul of grapes: these literally saved us from starving.

In Marseille food was even scarcer than it had been the year before; but we were so fond of this town, and as usual, so delighted to see American films again, that we spent several days there. Our diet consisted of moldy bread, on which we spread a sort of garlic mayonnaise made without eggs: this was so strong it nearly took the roof off your mouth, but was just about the only commodity sold unrationed in the groceries. We soothed our palates by sucking green or red ices, which were simply colored water and quite tasteless. We found plenty of those dried-fruit slabs which the former Café Flore crowd now produced, but they were more indigestible than the famous shoelaces in *The Gold Rush*. I told Sartre I knew now what William James meant by his remark about the proof of the pudding being in the eating. The way our stomachs rebelled was proof that much of the goods marketed as foodstuffs was in fact nothing of the sort. Like Charlie Chaplin I saw visions, or very nearly, when I passed by the restaurants where once I had eaten sea perch with fennel or tuna cooked in Chartreuse, or *real* garlic mayonnaise, and saw well-dressed ladies and gentlemen walking in; we hadn't enough cash on us for even one such meal.

Despite our hunger, which was rapidly becoming an obsession, I was determined to push on with this trip, and Sartre, anxious not to deprive me of my pleasure, raised no objections. We went back through the Aigoual and Couvertoirade districts, and confirmed for ourselves what we had learned from Heidegger and Saint-Exupéry—that is, the different ways in which the world will reveal itself under different conditions of observation. The Larzac plateau over which we cycled was not the same as it had been when we tramped across it squashing crickets underfoot; yet both versions possessed an equally valid aspect of the truth.

We decided that we didn't need any help to get back into the Occupied Zone: we would return by the same route as we had come. We caught the first train to Pau, but our bicycles didn't arrive at the same time as we did, and we were forced to wait a whole day for them. By now we hadn't a bean left; at midday we sat on a bench and ate some fruit, and in the evening we had nothing at all. The next day we reached Navarrenx, where we couldn't find a single scrap of bread, let alone a tomato. If we got across the border without mishap, we were relying on being able to wire Paris for some more money; it was forbidden to do so from the Free Zone. Our situation was becoming critical. A woman who was a friend of my family lived about twelve miles away, on the banks of the Adour: I paid a call on her, borrowed some money, and was invited to lunch, at which I stuffed myself with roast duck and green beans. But Sartre had refused to come with me, and by the time we reached Dax that evening he was absolutely starving. All he could get for dinner was a dish of lentils. We bought tickets for Angers, but this involved spending a night in Bordeaux, where there wasn't a single hotel room to be had. We slept in the waiting room. The journey took all day, and it was blazing hot. We bought anything available on each station platform we stopped at: ersatz coffee, a few tough biscuits. I can't think how we mustered sufficient strength to ride over twelve miles on top of everything else. When we finally reached La Pouèze the first thing we did was have a shower, after which we hurried down to the dining room. But Sartre had only eaten a few spoonfuls of soup when he went pale, got to his feet, wavered a moment, and then collapsed on a sofa and passed out. He stayed in bed for three days. Occasionally someone would take him up some soup or fruit salad, whereupon he would blink his eyes open, obediently empty his bowl or plate, and then go to sleep again. Madame Lemaire was thinking of calling in a doctor when he suddenly woke up with a snort and announced that he was feeling fine. It was true, too: from that moment he returned to a normal existence. I myself had lost over sixteen pounds in weight and was covered with spots.

We stayed there a month, building up our strength and generally coddling ourselves. These visits—whose pleasures were never to pall during the next ten years—were moments of respite for us, and the best of them, to our minds, were those that lasted longest. Neither the countryside nor the village nor even the garden attached to the house was particularly attractive, nor was there anything in this big, commonplace residence itself which particularly appealed to the eye. But here in the country as in Paris, Madame Lemaire had a special gift of making you feel comfortable when she was around. She occupied a big room on the first floor, with a red-tiled floor and soft whitewashed walls and exposed beams running across the ceiling. Bed, chairs, tables, and chests of drawers were littered with a wild profusion of clothes, books, and other objects, so that the room was not so much a background for her as an extension of her personality. An elegently convex door linked her room and Sartre's, which was also extremely large: I had my worktable in it, and only used my room for sleeping. (Why was the accommodation arranged like this instead of the other way around? I can't now recall. In any case it came to the same thing. On reflection I supect it was because Sartre habitually refused even the slightest special privileges.) Jacqueline Lemaire was on a camp bed behind a screen, close to her mother's bed. On the same floor there also lived a eighty-two-year-old hunchbacked woman, whom Madame Lemaire had taken in; we used to meet her shuffling down the corridor wearing a corset and a pair of knee-length bloomers. On the ground floor a Russian princess was installed. She was ancient, haughty, stone-deaf, and never left her room; she shared it with a small, long-haired white dog, as arrogant as it was stupid, and which she loved to distraction. Madame Lemaire owned a large Briard collie bitch, which had been driven half mad at the beginning of the war by a journey inside a dark truck lasting three days and three nights. This beast was liable to make unprovoked attacks on children and small animals, so it was kept chained up. But one evening, despite this, it contrived to disembowel the white dog. The princess howled for hours.

The two old ladies ate in their rooms; we took lunch and dinner with Madame Lemaire and Jacqueline, after which all four of us went on talking till after midnight, generally in Sartre's room. These discussions would be punctuated by an imperiously shrilling bell. Ever since the outbreak of war Monsieur Lemaire had kept to his bed; he was liable to sudden attacks which brought him out in a lather of sweat, and when he called, his wife or daughter would hurry to his room and often stay with him for hours, comforting him. He insisted on being kept in complete darkness, broken only by the feeble glimmer of a night light. Some days he lay absolutely motionless, not even taking his hands out from under the blanket. On occasion, however, he would sit up and take an interest in world affairs, reading newspapers and even books; village people used to come up to ask his advice on various matters. I never went near him. The Lemaires had a fiercely devoted old maid called Joséphine, who served him like a slave and tyrannized the rest of the family. For all practical purposes it was she who made the decisions, and she eyed both Sartre and me with some distrust. On the other hand, we enjoyed the approval of Nanette, a bald octogenarian who had formerly been Madame Lemaire's Paris housekeeper, and who once declared solemnly, apropos of us: "They're very fair-minded—their advice is worth taking!"

Over and above their nursing duties, Madame Lemaire and Jacqueline went to much trouble to amass food supplies, parcel them up, and send them to their friends in Paris: they scarcely got any sleep and never took a holiday. Sartre and I spent our time reading and writing; sometimes I managed to drag him out of doors, and we would go off on bicycles or walking—preferably the latter, since it was easier to talk this way. When the weather was fine I would linger in the fields: I read *The Seven Pillars of*

THE PRIME OF LIFE 415

Wisdom lying in deep grass with apple boughs overhead and a scent in
my nostrils remembered from childhood. We used to listen regularly to
the B.B.C., and from time to time also heard a little music. Toward the
end of September Sartre wrote an article for *Les Cahiers du sud* on a
novel which most critics regarded as something quite out of the ordinary:
Albert Camus's *L'Etranger* (*The Stranger*). We had read the first few
lines of this book In *Comoedia's* page devoted to literary news, and our
interest had instantly been aroused; the tone of the narrative, the Stranger's
attitude, including his rejection of sentimental conventions delighted us.
In his piece Sartre did not praise the novel unreservedly, but he accorded
it considerable importance. It had been a long time since any new French
writer had moved us so strongly.

The press had made triumphant capital out of the unsuccessful British
landing at Dieppe, which took place on August 20. Yet from October onward it was easy to see, reading between the lines in the news reports,
that things were not developing as Hitler had anticipated. It was a long
while now since he had announced the Axis troops' "imminent victories"
at El Alamein and on the Russian front at Stalingrad. Now we were
told these these troops were "holding their own well" and "fighting heroi-
cally": they had obviously passed to the defensive. In France itself a close
link had now been established between the Resistance and London; terrorist
activities multiplied, and reprisals became more violent than ever. After
the Dieppe business a great number of Frenchmen—not only in Normandy,
but throughout the Occupied Zone—were accused of supplying intelligence
to Britain, and either interned or executed. Threatening notices were posted,
warning the population against collusion with the "enemy," and declaring
that all operations by parachute must be reported immediately, on pain
of death. The time bombs that exploded in the Garenne-Palace and Rex
cinemas, together with the grenade attack on a German detachment
marching down the Rue d'Hautpoul, produced a savage crop of reprisals. Forty-six Communist hostages were shot in the fortress at Romain-
ville, and seventy more at Bordeaux. Despite this, two other bombs were
exploded, at the Gare Montparnasse and the Gare de l'Est, killing three
German soldiers. By now the vast majority of Frenchmen were impatiently
looking forward to a German defeat. It was in vain that German propaganda tried to whip up public opinion against the British raids. The
country had suffered too much during these past two years; neither soft
words nor terrorist methods could paralyze its resentments now. Laval's
reiterated appeals for volunteers to join the "working levies for Germany"
movement, and the blackmailing technique used on prisoners, produced
such meager results that the Germans decided to conscript recruits by
force; but the bulk of the workers chosen by the S.T.O., Service du
Travail Obligatoire, did their best to get out of it, and some of the younger
ones now joined the Maquis, which was beginning to organize a Resistance
Army in the Free Zone.

Then, suddenly, on November 8, news came that sent us into a seventh heaven of excitement. British troops had landed in North Africa; Giraud, who had been living under house arrest since his escape, had managed to get away to Algeria; and even Darlan himself was rallying the French in Africa against the Germans. The German communiqués, Vichy's declarations, and the frantic vituperations of the collaborators—all served to increase our delight. The Germans at once crossed the zonal decarcatioᴙ line in order to "defend" the Mediterranean coast; but the destruction of the "Free Zone" myth mattered little to us. From now on it was a real pleasure to open a paper. We learned that the fleet at Toulon had scuttled itself rather than fall into German hands; that Delattre de Tassigny had taken over the Maquis; that despite his opportune switch of allegiance, Darlan had nevertheless lost his life. Vichy, together with press and radio, fulminated against "the traitors." We were informed, with grinding of teeth, that things were far from harmonious among the dissident elements, that Giraud and De Gaulle were at daggers point. This mattered little to us. The Allied armies held North Africa; that was the main thing. By feverishly informing us, over and over again, that any Anglo-American landings in Italy or France were doomed to failure, the Nazi propagandists merely convinced us of their imminence.

The price of this victory was a fresh wave of arrests. The warning notices informing French citizens of the execution of terrorists and hostages now dwindled away and finally vanished altogether. The Gestapo no longer desired this sort of publicity. But the prisons were crammed with detainees, and the most frightful tortures were practiced in the Rue des Saussaies and Rue Lauriston headquarters. At German instigation Vichy transformed the Legion into a militia, under Darnand's command, which was to suppress all "disaffections on the home front," and which hunted down members of the Resistance even more ruthlessly than the S.S. did. Trainloads of deportees were daily dispatched to Germany, crammed with Jews and "political suspects" picked up by the police all over France. There was no distinction made now between French Jews and those of foreign extraction: all were to be eliminated. Hitherto the "Free Zone" had offered them an uneasy refuge; now they lacked even this last resort. Many preferred to commit suicide. The sheer horror of their fate continually obsessed us. But this obsession was mild in comparison with the horror itself, as literally millions of men and women lived it out, body and soul, till death claimed them. Yet, though their suffering remained alien to us, it is also true that it poisoned the very air we breathed.

We had taken our last stroll round the old quarters of Marseille that I loved so much; it nearly broke my heart when I heard that Hitler ordered their destruction after an attack on a brothel that German soldiers frequented. Pétain's police gave the inhabitants only a few hours in which to evacuate the area, and about twenty thousand people found themselves homeless. They were dumped in camps at Fréjus and Compiègne, and their houses razed.

But the news transmitted by the B.B.C. cheered us up a great deal. The future was ours once more: all we needed now was a little patience, and we had plenty of that and to spare. I was accustomed by now to discomfort, and cheerfully put up with ever-increasing material difficulties. When I first got back to Paris I had one most disagreeable surprise: the proprietress of my hotel had not kept my room for me. It was a hard job finding a furnished room with a kitchen attached, and I spent several days traipsing around to every hotel in Montparnasse and Saint-Germain-des-Prés. Finally I found what I was looking for, at a place on the Rue Dauphine; but it was a wretched sort of room, with peeling walls and one dim yellow bulb in the ceiling. There was an iron bedstead, a wardrobe, a table, a couple of wooden chairs, and a kitchen which also did duty as a w.c. The hotel itself was a filthy dump, with an icy stone staircase that reeked of damp and innumerable other odors; but I had no choice in the matter.

In order to shift my belongings I hired a sort of handcart, with shafts. I had never been one to stand on my dignity, yet even so, before the Occupation I should never have dreamed of going between the shafts myself. But at present very few people could indulge in the luxury of caring what anyone thought of them; and I was not among the few. With Lise's assistance I cheerfully hauled my suitcases and a few bundles of books across Paris. No one found this an improbable sight; I would not even have been embarrassed to meet people I knew in Saint-Germain. People had to make what arrangements they could these days. That was one of the good things about this period: a whole mass of conventions, hesitations, and ceremonial observances had been swept away; one's needs were reduced to their true proportions. This pleased me, as did the quasi equality imposed upon us; I had never been in favor of special privileges. I decided that if a socialist regime, even one of extreme austerity, were to be established on a sound basis, I would have no trouble in adapting myself to it, and would certainly feel more at ease under such a dispensation than in an atmosphere of bourgeois injustice. The only thing it would be a real sacrifice to give up were the lengthy travels that had yearly so enriched my life: they were the one luxury I would really miss. The rest I could take or leave; it made no difference.

The hotel into which I moved was, nevertheless, more sordid an establishment than I could have wished. On the same floor as mine there lived a woman whose income was derived from men, and who also had a four-year-old son. She knocked this child about a good deal, and he was always crying; when she entertained a client, she put him outside, and he would sit on the staircase for hours, sobbing, in a sort of daze. The year I moved in, too, a most curious scandal occurred two floors above me. One of the tenants, a young woman, used to help the proprietress tidy up the place, after a fashion, and therefore looked after her own room. No one even went into it, and it gave off so alarming a smell that the neighbors complained. The proprietress, using her master key, went in there one day unannounced, to find the floor deep in excrement, and rows of dried turds laid out on the cupboard shelves, like cakes in a bakery.

This caused a fine hullabaloo. The tenant was thrown out on the spot, and left sobbing under the sting of some choice expletives.

I have already said how carefully I eked out the provisions I managed to acquire. I was heartbroken and furious if I opened a packet of noodles and found maggots swarming inside: many shopkeepers were unloading their old, unsellable stock quite unscrupulously. One day I was amazed to find my bags of lentils and dried peas ripped open, and what remained of the contents all befouled with mouse droppings: the mice had gnawed through the wooden partition in order to get inside the cupboard. I managed to obtain some tin biscuit boxes, and thus protect my supplies: but very often during the night I would hear scuttling sounds and metallic scrapings and know the enemy was launching an attack. It was said that rats were breeding vastly, all over Paris; and they worried me a good deal more than the relatively inoffensive intruders I had had at the Hôtel du Petit Mouton. In the end, indeed, they really made me loathe my new quarters.

Even so, I didn't realize quite how decayed a place it was till Courbeau paid me a visit. Since he and his wife were up in Paris on a visit, I invited them to dinner. I made a special effort over the meal, putting two eggs in the potato pie and an ounce or two of butter over the carrots. When they walked in they exchanged such incredulous glances that I suddenly saw how remote this slummy hovel of mine was from their house in Le Havre, and felt terribly embarrassed as I laid out the dishes I had prepared. We discussed the occasion later, and they admitted how dumfounded they had been at the time.

I continued to live in this state of isolated squalor, nevertheless. At the same time the "family" was increased by the addition of a new member called Bourla, a young Spanish Jew who was in Sartre's class at the Lycée Pasteur during the spring of 1941. They met occasionally at the Flore or the Deux Magots. His father handled a lot of big business and thought he had no need to be afraid of the Germans: the Spanish Consul would see him through. The boy was eighteen, with a face that some found attractive, others plain. He had very thick, black curly hair, and his dark eyes were asparkle with life; his nature combined passion and gentleness, and we found him quite delightful. He approached the world in a clumsy, childish, excited fashion, with inexhaustible enthusiasm. He was tearing through Spinoza and Kant, and intended later to take a teacher's diploma in philosophy. One day Sartre was discussing the future with him, and asked him what he would do in the event of a German victory. "A German victory does not figure in my scheme of things," he replied decisively. He wrote poetry, too; reading some of his verse we thought he might well, with luck, mature into a real poet. He once tried to explain to me the simultaneous ease and difficulty which he found in setting words down on a blank page. "What I need," he said, "is to *put my trust in the void.*" The phrase impressed me. I always took what he said seriously, since he never advanced any proposition without first testing its truth himself.

He met Lise, and soon became involved with her. The two of them decided to live together, and moved into my hotel on the Rue Dauphine. They had continual quarrels, but were tremendously fond of each other. Bourla had a good influence on her. He did not regard himself as possessing any private rights, and all he had he made available to her: his chocolate ration, his sweaters, the allowance he got from his father, not to mention the extra money he pinched. Monsieur Bourla senior kept some paper twists full of gold pieces in a private drawer, and on several occasions Bourla quietly extracted one of these coins. This would be followed by a vast black-market feast for Lise's benefit: they would wolf down ice cream, oysters, sausages, and other delicacies all higgledy-piggledy. Lise found his generosity so fascinating that she was almost tempted to imitate it. It was charming to see the two of them walking along side by side: Lise so tall and blonde, a majestic peasant, and Bourla so dark and lithe, eyes and hands perpetually moving, alert. He found me somewhat overrational, but liked me very much all the same. Lise insisted on my going and chatting to them when they were in bed at night. I would kiss her; whereupon he would put his own forehead up for my attention, saying, "What about me? Don't I get a kiss?" So I would kiss him as well.

It was a hard winter. There was a shortage of coal, and of electricity too. A large number of Métro stations were closed, and cinemas no longer had afternoon shows. Power cutoffs were frequent, and during them we had to get what light we could from candles, which were themselves very hard to come by. The damp and icy atmosphere of my room precluded any possibility of work. At the Flore, at least, it wasn't cold, and they had acetylene lamps there that gave quite a decent light when the electricity failed. It was during this period that we got into the habit of spending all our leisure time in the Flore; and not only because we found it offered us comparative comfort. It was our own special resort. We felt at home there; it sheltered us from the outside world.

During the winter especially I tried to arrive as soon as the doors were opened, in order to get the best and warmest table, right beside the stovepipe. I loved the moment when Boubal, a blue apron tied around him, came bustling into the still empty café and began to bring his little world to life again. He lived in a flat over the premises, which was reached by an inside staircase from the first-floor landing. Down this he would march just before eight o'clock and unbolt the doors in person. A pair of bloodshot eyes would blink at one from that tough, solid Auvergne face; for the first hour or two he would remain in a perfectly filthy temper. He would shout out orders, irritably, to the kitchen hand, who sent up bottles and boxes through an open trap door near the cashier's desk; he would also discuss the previous night's goings-on with the waiters, Jean and Pascal, and send back a stinking cup of ersatz coffee, the same stuff his customers drank without raising an eyebrow, with a burst of tigerish laughter and the contemptuous comment: "Give them shit, they'd still eat it." He received and got rid of salesmen in the same cantankerous fashion.

Meanwhile the charwoman would be down on her knees, vigorously scrubbing away at the tiled floor. She took a pride in her job. "I never needed men to help me," she told the kitchen hand one day; "I succeeded by myself." Little by little Boubal would calm down and eventually remove his apron. Then his wife would appear, beautifully turned out, with her pink-and-white complexion and blonde curly hair, and enthrone herself at the cash desk. The first customers would drift in; I used to stare enviously at a certain bookseller from the Rue Bonaparte, a horse-faced character with a thatch of russet hair, who was always accompanied by a good-looking young boy, and who ordered tea and little pots of jam, which cost the earth. Most people made do, as I did, with a cup of black pseudo-coffee. A little dark-haired creature, a girl friend of Sonia's and Agnès Capri's who had vanished for a couple of years, walked in one morning, sat down at a table, and with disarming ingenuousness ordered coffee with cream. Everyone burst out laughing, not altogether kindly. It astonished me that these three words should have become such an extravagance; it astonished me even more that I was able to take this state of affairs for granted. When people told me in 1938 and 1939 that the Germans were drinking curious concoctions brewed from acorns in lieu of coffee, I was flabbergasted: this seemed to make them a species as remote as those tribes that subsist on cockchafers' grubs. And yet today it required a deliberate effort to recall that once upon a time at the Flore one had been able to drink orange juice and eat fried eggs.

A certain number of regulars, like myself, used to settle down at the marble-topped tables to read or work, among them Thierry Maulnier, Dominique Aury, Audiberti, who lived in the Hôtel Taranne opposite, and Adamov, his bare, sandaled feet blue with cold. One of the most constant in attendance was Mouloudji. He had been writing poetry for ages, and also kept a sketchy, intermittent journal. He had shown me both poems and journal, and I had encouraged him, convinced as I was during this period that writing was the most important possible activity imaginable, and that Mouloudji possessed undoubted talent. Now he had begun to sketch out a thinly fictionalized version of his childhood memories. Occasionally I would correct some faults of spelling or construction, or give him some advice; but I was cautious in this respect, since I didn't want to spoil the artful naïveté of his style. Boubal loathed him for being ill-clad and unkempt, and because he occupied a table for hours on end without ever ordering a second drink. Sometimes he would get a part in a film; but as soon as he laid hands on any money he would give it away to his father and brother and friends; he never had a penny himself. He had made the acquaintance in Marseille of Lola, the gorgeous redhead whose drooping mouth and big, deep eyes had so often aroused my admiration in the Flore. Now he was more or less living with her, and she had no more money than he had. He did not exactly belong to the "family," and we did not maintain regular contact with him, but he wasn't far from such a relationship. He had been friends with Olga for a long while, and got along well with Wanda; he also saw quite a lot of Lise, who in turn became very friendly with Lola.

Every day about ten o'clock two journalists came in, sat down side by side on the banquette at the far end, and unfolded *Le Matin*. One of them was bald, and wrote for *Le Pilori;* the other was on *La Gerbe*. They used to discuss the news in a cynical, disillusioned manner. "What we ought to do," the bald character observed one day, "is to ship the whole lot of them on one immense boat and fix it to break in two in mid-ocean. These Yids—the way things are going we'll never be rid of 'em!" His companion nodded approvingly. I felt no rancor at this conversation; there was something so ridiculous about their expressions and the way they talked that, for a moment, the whole business of collaboration, Fascism, anti-Semitism, and the rest of it seemed to me a kind of farce, designed to entertain a simple-minded audience. Then, dazedly, I came to my senses again, in the knowledge that they not only could but did cause grave harm to people. Their colleagues on *Je suis partout* published the secret whereabouts of people like Tzara or Waldemar George, and were clamoring for their arrest. They were also calling for the deportation of Cardinal Liénart, who had been expressing anti-German opinions ex cathedra. It was the very nullity of these people that made them dangerous.

No one had anything to do with these two collaborators, apart from one little dark-skinned man, with frizzy hair, who said he was Laval's private secretary. He spoke little, and his eyes kept darting to and fro: we were surprised that his job left him with so much free time to waste in a café. It was possible—though she never did anything openly to confirm this—that Zizi Dugommier also belonged to the same group. She was a lean, angular old maid, very oddly dressed, who spent the whole time from morning till night drawing and coloring pictures of Saint Teresa of Lisieux and of the Immaculate Conception. One day she came up to me and said she was a copyist by profession, and was there any work she could do for me? Rumor had it that she was in league with the Gestapo; she used to pay frequent visits to the w.c. and stay shut in for a very considerable time, so that people suspected her of writing her reports in there. But reports on whom? and about what? Some people guessed that she listened to telephone conversations. It is true that in 1941 some customers made such compromising remarks on the phone and so loudly and clearly at that, that Boubal broke the glass panels in the cubicle, and the careless talkers, robbed of their illusory protection, henceforth kept more of a guard on their tongues. Zizi therefore could overhear nothing now which might be of interest to the police. The most likely explanation in my opinion is that she acted as an informer, for the love of the thing rather than with an eye to making a profit. She vanished in June, 1944, and no one ever saw her again.

Were there any other such stool pigeons? At the beginning of the Occupation two or three of the Flore's regulars were arrested: who had given them away? No one ever knew. In any case, there were no more harebrained *ad hoc* conspiracies being hatched there now, and those Resistance fighters who hung around cafés did so for cover-up purposes. About eleven o'clock in the morning Pierre Bénard would come in and sit down, always at the same table, between the entrance and the staircase, and enjoy a solitary drink. There was nothing to indicate that this portly character with the ruddy complexion had other very different ways of occupying his time. There were also a number of young men who whiled away the time drinking, smoking, flirting, with every appearance of listless boredom; I was quite taken in by this act, and only later found out what they were really up to. For by and large the customers at the Flore were firmly opposed both to Fascism and to collaboration, and made no secret of it. The Occupation forces no doubt knew it too, because they never came near the place. On one occasion a young German officer pushed open the door and settled down in one corner with a book. Nobody moved a muscle, but he must have felt the silent atmosphere, because he very quickly shut his book, paid, and walked out again.

Little by little, as the morning passed, the room would fill up, till by apéritif time it was packed. You would see Picasso there, smiling at Dora Marr, who had her big dog with her on the lead; Léon-Paul Fargue would be sitting quietly in a corner, and Jacques Prévert holding forth to a circle of acquaintances; while a noisy discussion would always be going on at the *cinéastes* table—they had been meeting there almost daily since 1939. Here and there in this mob you might find one or two old gentlemen who were local residents. I remember one such, who was afflicted with a disease of the prostate, and wore some kind of apparatus that bulged inside one of his trouser legs. There was another, known as "the Marquis" or "the Gaullist," who used to play dominoes with two young girl friends of his, whom, it was said, he maintained in fine style. He was a stoop-shouldered man, with down-thrust head and drooping mustachios; he would murmur in Jean's or Pascal's ear the news items he had just heard on the latest B.B.C. broadcast, and these would promptly be passed on from table to table. Throughout all this the two journalists still sat there and brooded, out loud, upon the possibility of exterminating the Jews.

I would return to my hotel for lunch, after which, unless I had a class at the *lycée,* I resumed my table at the Flore. I went out for dinner, and then returned again till closing time. It always gave me a thrill of pleasure at night to walk in out of the icy darkness and find myself in this warm, well-lit, snug retreat, with its charming blue-and-red wallpaper. Frequently the entire "family" was to be found at the Flore, but with its members, according to our principles of behavior, scattered in every corner of the room. For instance, Sartre might be chatting with Wanda at one table, Lise and Bourla at another, and Olga and I sitting together at a third. Yet Sartre and I were the only two who turned up regularly every night. "When they die," Bourla remarked of us, faintly irritated, "you'll have to dig them a grave under the floor."

One evening, just as we were arriving at the Flore, we saw a flash and heard a tremendous explosion. Windows rattled, people cried out in alarm: a grenade, it transpired, had gone off in a hotel that was being used as a *Soldatenheim,* at the end of the Rue Saint-Benoît. This produced a hubbub of speculation in all the cafés round about, since an "outrage" in these parts was something very unusual.

The sirens used to sound very frequently, both in the afternoon and at night. Boubal would shoo the customers out posthaste and bolt the doors; Sartre and I and one or two others, however, he allowed, as a special favor, to come up to the first floor and remain there till the all-clear sounded. In order to avoid this upheaval, and also to get away from the noise on the ground floor, I got into the habit of going straight up the stairs after lunch anyway. One or two other writers did likewise, doubtless for very similar reasons. Our pens scratched away over the paper; we might have been in some extremely well-behaved classroom. With a curiosity less malign in its purpose than Zizi Dugommier's was supposed to be, but keen enough notwithstanding, I too used to cock one ear for phone conversations. One day I latched on to an end-of-the-affair conversation, involving a professional actress of uncertain years who was decidedly plain into the bargain. She was distant, urgent, haughty, pathetic, and sarcastic by turns, intermingling invective, irony, and tremulous pleas with a skill that all too obviously was getting her nowhere; I could almost hear the bored impatience of the man on the other end of the line, waiting for an opportune moment to hang up. Rubbing shoulders daily as we did, we were bound to know a good deal about one another; even if we had never exchanged a single word, we felt a bond existed between us. Normally we did not greet each other; but if a couple of Flore regulars happened to meet in the Deux Magots, then mutual recogniton would be acknowledged by a smile and a nod. This very seldom, in fact, happened; between the two establishments an invisible but impenetrable barrier appeared to exist. If a customer at the Flore, whether male or female, was deceiving his or her accredited partner, any illicit meetings would take place at the Deux Magots, or so the legend ran.

Despite restrictions and air raids, we still found an atmosphere that was reminiscent of peacetime conditions; yet the war did penetrate our private snuggery on occasion. We were told one morning that Sonia had just been arrested; she had apparently been made the victim of another woman's jealousy—someone, at any rate, had certainly denounced her. She sent a message from Drancy, asking for a sweater and some silk stockings to be forwarded; this was the last request received from her. The blonde Czech girl who lived with Jausion vanished; and a few days afterward, when Bella was asleep in her boy friend's arms, the Gestapo came knocking on their door at dawn and took her away, too. Another girl, a friend of theirs, was living with a well-connected young man who wanted to marry her; she was denounced by her future father-in-law. Our knowledge of the camps was still very incomplete; but the way these gay and beautiful girls simply vanished into the blue, without a word, was terrifying enough in itself. Jausion and his friends still came to the Flore, and even went on sitting at the same table, where they talked among themselves in an agitated, hectic sort of way. But there was no mark on the red banquette to indicate the empty place at their side. This was what seemed the most unbearable thing about any absence to me: that it was, precisely, a *nothingness.* Yet the faces of Bella and the blonde Czech girl were never erased from my memory: they symbolized millions of others besides. Hope was beginning to stir once more, but I knew the illusive innocence of the past was gone beyond recall.

We spent the Christmas holidays at La Pouèze, listening daily to the B.B.C.'s bulletins on the fighting around Stalingrad. Von Paulus's army was encircled, and all its efforts to break out had failed. On February 4 we read in the papers: "The heroic resistance of our European forces in Stalingrad is at an end." They made no attempt to conceal the fact that in Berlin and throughout Germany the news had been greeted with several days of national mourning.

Press and radio, even Hitler's speeches, now took on a quite different tone. We were no longer exhorted to "build a new Europe" but besought to save the existing one. The "Bolshevik meance" was brought to the fore together with all the disasters that would befall the world "if Germany was defeated." Even a year earlier such a hypothesis would have been utter sacrilege; now it was mentioned by every journalistic scribbler. Hitler ordered a general mobilization of the whole German people—to front line, field, and factory—and wanted to extend this to the occupied territories. On February 16 Laval promulgated a law making young men who reached the call-up age between 1940 and 1942 liable for two years' duty with the Service du Travail Obligatoire. Posters were stuck up which read: "They are giving their blood. Give *your* labor to save Europe from Bolshevism." Many refused to answer the summons; they faked their identity cards, went into hiding, or joined the Maquis, the strength of which had grown considerably—an increase due in large part to the demobilization of the regular forces after the armistice. About this time a strange news item appeared in some Swiss and British papers: "Armed rebellion in Haute-Savoie," it ran. This was something of an exaggeration. But it is true that such armies were in the process of formation, both in Savoie and Central France; that they were obtaining arms and equipment, and training for guerilla warfare. Déat, writing in, *L'Oeuvre,* called France "the Vendée of Europe," on the grounds that, just as in olden times the Vendée had refused to accept the French Revolution, so France today was rising against the "European Revolution."

The intellectuals' part in the Resistance was now being organized. Early in 1943 certain members of the Communist intelligentsia invited Sartre to join the Comité National des Ecrivains. He asked if they wanted a spy in their ranks, but they all assured him they knew nothing about the rumors they had been circulating at his expense in 1941. So he took part in various meetings under Eluard's presidency, and contributed to *Lettres françaises.* I had not yet had a book published, and did not accompany him on these occasions. I regretted this slightly, since I should have liked to meet some new people; but Sartre discussed them all with me in such minute detail that I almost felt I had seen them with my own eyes, and very quickly ceased to envy him. I had thrown myself heart and soul into "Socialism and Liberty," because this was an improvised and hazardous undertaking; but to judge from Sartre's account of what went on there, the C.N.E.'s sessions had an official, indeed a routine, flavor about them which I found something less than attractive. I was always a bit worried when he was going to a meeting, and all the time that he was actually away; but nevertheless I was very glad we had emerged from our isolation, all the more so since I had often felt how tedious Sartre found a life of passive inaction.

Everyone we knew at all closely was on the same side as we were, though Marie Girard reproached us once for not looking further than the ends of our noses. "A German defeat will mean the triumph of Anglo-American imperialism," she said. Her view typified that of most Trotskyite intellectuals, who held equally aloof from collaboration and resistance alike—though in the last resort they were far less scared of American domination than they were of any increase in the Stalinists' power and prestige. In our opinion, anyway, they totally mistook the order and urgency of the problems confronting us: the prime essential was for Europe to cleanse herself of Fascism. By now we no longer had any doubt that Fascism *would* be destroyed, and in the very near future. The R.A.F. was bombing French ports and industrial centers, and pounding the Rhineland, the Ruhr, Hamburg, and Berlin itself. On May 14 the Axis Powers lost the battle for Tunisia. The Germans were feverishly building up their Atlantic Wall, and on both sides a landing was regarded as imminent.

Literature was in a flourishing state. Raymond Queneau published *Pierrot mon ami,* the humor of which struck me as rather overcontrived. There were several passages in Blanchot's *Aminadab* which I found impressive, among others—perhaps because it echoed my own obsession of the moment—that describing the unwilling executioner; but taken over-all, Blanchot's novel appeared to be a Kafka pastiche. In *L'Eau et les rêves* Bachelard investigated the imaginative processes in terms of something very much like existential psychoanalysis; hitherto hardly anyone had risked exporing this particular field, and the book interested us as a result. A great stir was created by Saint-Exupéry's latest work, *Pilot de Guerre* (*Flight to Arras*). He gave a brilliant description in it of his experiences as a pilot during the fall of France; but to this narrative he had added a lengthy, nebulous dissertation, supposedly humanistic, but ambiguous enough for the book to be praised by critics in papers such as *Paris-Midi, Aujourd'hui,* and *Les Nouveaux Temps;* even Maxence liked it. Almost the only attack it received was in the columns of *Je suis partout.*

The French cinema was waking up again with the appearance of some new directors. Delannoy came up with *Pontcarral* and *L'Enfer du jeu;* Becker produced *Goupi mains rouges,* and Clouzot *L'Assassin habite au 21;* while Daquin's *Voyageur de la Toussaint* gave us a brief glimpse of Simone Signoret, making us wonder why so attractive a girl had not yet landed a star part. The most interesting film, however, was *La Nuit fantastique,* directed by L'Herbier and written by Chavance: this shook the public considerably. Raimu gave a remarkable performance in *Les Inconnus dans la maison,* though the script made some nasty concessions to racial prejudice; the murderer, played by Mouloudji, was not actually described as a Jew, but his alien status was subtly emphasized. Carné's *Les Visiteurs du soir,* with a Prévert script, was a lush, almost edible production, with gorgeous visual affects and an overdose of literary dialogue. The dazzling new château didn't look in the least like a real, recently built castle but an enormous chunk of nougat; it ruined the landscape. I far preferred *Lumière d'été,* in which Prévert collaborated with Grémillon.

Dullin kept his promise; he put *The Flies* into rehearsal in the spring, with both Olgas playing leading roles. I knew the text almost by heart, and I found its gradual transformation into a living play immensely exciting: I was fired with the urge to write a play too. Nevertheless things didn't go altogether without a hitch. There was a great deal of discussion before the settings and costumes were finally decided. Since the statues of Jupiter and Apollo played a considerable part in the action, Dullin decided to bring in a sculptor for the job. His choice fell on Adam, a placid and most likeable giant of a man, with a wife who had masses of black frizzy hair that gnawed at the edges of her face, and a small, pleasantly plump body which she put into clinging black dresses and adorned with gaudy jewelry. They had an apartment on the Rue Christine, which was as attractive as Camille's, though its style was wholly different. The dining room had a red-tiled floor, and its windows were curtained with Turkey-red cotton; it contained a long refectory table, heavy wooden benches, various copper pots, and earthenware bowls laden with gleaming fruit and vegetables, while strings of onions and corncobs hung from the beams on the ceiling near an old-fashioned open hearth. Adam took us up to his studio and showed us an old hand press, together with the collection of precise and complex little instruments he used for etching and engraving. Great blocks of stone stood about on the floor. He created settings, masks, and statues for *The Flies,* all very bold and aggressive in style.

There were large numbers of extras involved: women, children, old men, a whole population had somehow to be deployed across the vast stage of the Théâtre Sarah Bernhardt. Dullin found himself less at ease here than in the Atelier. The actor playing Orestes lacked experience, and so did Olga; the part of Electra was quite overwhelming, and though she interpreted it well enough, neither she nor her leading man really got their performances across. Dullin lost his temper violently several times, and remarked in a scathing voice that perhaps they imagined this was drawing-room comedy. Olga would burst into tears of rage, whereupon Dullin would soften for a while; then there would come a fresh explosion, followed by further bridling on Olga's part, and both of them would go at it hammer and tongs in a manner halfway between a family quarrel and a lovers' tiff. Her fellow pupils from the Atelier used to watch these *corridas* in the hope that Olga would come a cropper during one of them; but they were doomed to disappointment. Olga's natural gifts, Dullin's hard work, and their joint determination to succeed brought triumph in the end. During the final rehearsals she acted like a veteran; she stood alone on the stage and filled it with her mere presence.

The dress rehearsal took place in the afternoon, since at night it might well have been interrupted by an electricity cut. Sartre was standing in the foyer, near the box office, when a dark-skinned young man came up and introduced himself: it was Albert Camus. How tense I was when the curtain went up! It was impossible to mistake the play's implications; the word Liberty, dropped from Orestes' mouth, burst on us like a bomb. The German critic of *Pariser Zeitung* saw this very clearly, and said so, though at the same time taking the credit for giving the play a favorable notice. Michel Leiris praised *The Flies* in a clandestine edition of *Les Lettres françaises,* and emphasized its political significance. Most reviewers pretended not to have noticed any such allusion; they pitched into the play viciously, but, so they alleged, on purely literary grounds: it was an unsuccessful imitation of Giraudoux, it was wordy, obscure, and plain dull. They acclaimed Olga's performance, however: for her personally the occasion was a smash hit. On the other hand, they damned the production, the sets, and the costumes. The public did not flock to see *The Flies;* it was June by now, and the theater had to close anyway. Dullin put the play on again in October, together with several others, for a season of repertory.

I enjoyed teaching nowadays somewhat less than I had in the past. At Camille-Sée I was preparing pupils for the entrance examination to the women's training college at Sèvres, which meant that I could deal more thoroughly with certain subjects. But for these grown-up young ladies philosophy was no longer an awakening, a revelation; I even had to rid them of certain preconceived ideas which I regarded as erroneous. Besides, they had such a heavy program that there wasn't a minute to waste, and I had to be as brief as possible. This atmosphere of anxiety I found most depressing. It was not only their work that overtaxed them, but their whole way of life: their mothers needed them to overcome material difficulties, which could be extremely pressing in families where there were several children. They were undernourished and often fell ill; my most promising pupil that year went down with Pott's disease. They hardly ever smiled, and our discussions lacked enthusiasm. Besides, I had been teaching for twelve years now and was beginning to tire of it.

Yet it was not my decision that removed me from the rolls of the Université. Lise's mother, furious that her daughter had thrown aside a highly eligible suitor and was now living with Bourla, told me to use my influence and get her back to her previous lover. When I refused, she accused me of corrupting a minor. Before the war the affair would have gone no further; but with Abel Bonnard and his clique in charge, things turned out somewhat differently. At the end of the academic year the blue-chinned headmistress informed me that I had been expelled from the Université. My name was restored after the Liberation; but I never went back to teaching.

This break with an old familiar routine did not disturb me unduly. The only problem was how to make a living. I can't remember how I managed to wangle a job as a features producer on the national radio network. As I remarked earlier, our unwritten code allowed us to work for this organization: it all depended what you did there. I suggested a neutral, colorless program: reconstructions of traditional festivals, from the Middle Ages to modern times, complete with speech, music, and background effects. This idea was accepted.

I had finished *She Came to Stay* during the summer of 1941; but the novel had belonged to past history as far as I was concerned ever since January of that year. I was anxious to move on and discuss the problems which were now foremost in my mind. The chief of these was still my relationship to the Other; but I understood its complexity better than I had previously. My new hero, Jean Blomart, did not insist, as Françoise had done, on remaining the one sentient personality when confronted with other people. He refused to be a mere *object* where they were concerned, intervening in their lives with the brutal opacity of some inanimate thing; his problem was to get around this stumbling block and establish a clear relationship with them, involving freedom on both sides.

I began with his childhood. He was the son of a rich printer and lived in a house the atmosphere of which I borrowed from that of the Laiguillons'. He was in rebellion against his privileged position, and this led him to sign on as a worker in a rival firm. Having thus eliminated the chance injustice of this birth, he thought that henceforth he would be able to implement his own personal choice of action. He very soon lost this illusion, however. He involved his best friend in a political brawl and saw him killed as a result: his responsibilities far outstripped his desired ends. After this he sought refuge in passivity: political neutrality, avoidance of all emotional involvement. But this retreat of his and the silence he embraced carried as weighty an implication as any words or actions: both the general march of history and his own private life convinced him of this. He put up a struggle. He refused to accept the attitude of passive guilt which was his lot; yet he could not steel himself to act, either, since all action involves a choice, and every choice seemed quite arbitrary to him. Men are not mere units, to be added, multiplied, or subtracted. They do not figure in any kind of equation, because each individual life is an incommensurable quantity; to sacrifice one man for the sake of ten means acquiescing in a sheer absurdity. Finally, however, the defeat and the Occupation forced him to a decision; he discovered certain absolute imperatives and refusals in his nature, which lay beyond the reach of all reason and calculation. He gave up trying to untie the Gordian knot, and slashed it through. After years of pacifism, he now accepted violence and organized guerilla "outrages" in the teeth of possible reprisals. This resolution did not bring him peace of mind, but peace of mind he no longer aspired to; he resigned himself now to a life of mental agony. (I had been very struck by Kierke-gaard's idea that a *genuinely* moral person could never have an easy conscience, and only pledges his liberty in "fear and trembling.") However, in the last few pages, the woman whom Blomart loved, now dying beside him and because of him, was to release him from his scruples. You are never any more than an instrument in another person's destiny, she told him. No external factor could possibly encroach upon freedom of choice: I willed my own death. From this Blomart concluded that each individual has the right to follow his bent, if it leads to a worthwhile goal.

The story of this dying woman, Hélène, was to occupy a large part of the book. As a girl, Hélène's position had been diametrically opposed to Blomart's: she regarded herself as altogether independent of humanity in the mass, and cared for nothing but her personal salvation. What she was to learn in the course of her development was the meaning of solidarity.

I made the same mistake as I had done when beginning *She Came to Stay*: I felt compelled to describe Hélène's childhood, which I based on my own. Later I decided to restrict any account of this past life of hers to a few brief allusions. At the beginning of the novel Hélène was eighteen, and trying to compensate for the absence of God by an intense interest in herself. This, however, proved unsuccessful. In isolation, without an audience, her existence seemed to her a mere rank vegetable growth, wholly lacking in purpose; and even when a friend fell in love with her—a nice man, but sadly deficient in glamour—she continued to stagnate regardless. When she met Blomart, however, she found him fascinating, because of the strength and certainty of mind she discerned in him. She wanted a love that would, she believed, have provided her with an absolute justifi-cation for her existence; but Blomart shied at this and withdrew. In furious despair she took shelter behind a mask of utter indifference, both to her own life and the world at large. She affected to regard the defeat and Occupation with the calm impartiality of History. But friendship, revulsion, and anger drew her away from this false assumption of wisdom. In the generous atmosphere bred by comradeship and action she finally won through to that "recognition," in the Hegelian sense of the word, which preserves men from mere immanence and contingency. She died as a result; but only after reaching a point where death itself could not prevail against her.

I gave a considerable part in the narrative to a third character, based on Giacometti and his descriptions of Duchamp. Marcel was a painter and sculptor, whose researches on the aesthetic plane bore comparison with those Blomart was conducting in the field of ethics: he wanted to attain a condition of absolute creation. I had once had a predilection for those pictures and statues which I felt broke through the frontiers of human normality; Marcel insisted that his work should hold up by itself without any "seeing eye" to assist it. In this he showed a similarity to Hélène, who for a short while had supposed she could guarantee her own happi-ness by retreating into total isolation. Like her, he failed in his attempt, and sank into a state of neurotic depression. Later he fought in the war and was taken prisoner. In the Stalag he painted the sets for a play his comrades were putting on, and learned to appreciate the warmth of human friendship. His view of men and art changed; he accepted the fact that all creativity requires the collaboration of others.

I provided Marcel with a wife, Denise, whom I used as a foil, just as I had done with Elisabeth in *She Came to Stay*. Alone among his friends Denise had no aspirations toward the Absolute, and set her trust in worldly values. The hostility that she aroused in Marcel drove him to the very brink of madness. I had not as yet had much experience of the subject, but I could guess the risks an ordinary, unremarkable woman runs by linking her life to that of an obsessional creative artist. (I returned to this theme more emphatically in *The Mandarins*.) Since Marcel held in contempt those moderate satisfactions with which the bulk of mankind is satisfied, he forbade his wife to indulge in them, and deprived her of the wherewithal to achieve her own sort of happiness. Frustrated, humiliated, always an outsider, her heart bursting with resentment, Denise found herself floundering in a sea of inconsistencies that bid fair to derange her wits altogether.

I did not want this novel to resemble its predecessor, so I altered my tactics. I wrote from two viewpoints, those of Hélène and Blomart, in alternate chapters. The parts of the narrative centered on Hélène I wrote in the third person, observing the same rules as I had in *She Came to Stay*. But for Blomart I proceeded rather differently. I placed him at the dying Hélène's bedside, and made him reflect in retrospect on his past life. When he spoke of himself, his own bygone activities, I made him use the first person, changing to the third when he was required to survey, at a distance, the impression he had made upon other people. By pretending to follow the thread of his memories I could take far more liberties than had been possible in *She Came to Stay*: I could slow down or speed up the tempo of the narrative, use foreshortening and ellipses, and fade in or out as I chose. I also reduced the amount of dialogue. I retained a normal chronological sequence, though now and then present events broke in on the evocation of bygone time. I also inserted here and there, in italics, the thoughts and emotions which Blomart experienced during the night. In order to prevent his ruminations from becoming otiose, I introduced an element of suspense: would he or would he not, when dawn broke, give the signal for a fresh "operation"? All the dimensions of time were united in this deathbed vigil; the hero lived through it in the present, while searching his past for clues to a decision that would affect the course of his future. This constructional method suited my theme. My intention was to reveal the way every individual looks at the fact of his coexistence with the rest of mankind—as an inborn curse. Events per se mattered less to Blomart than the haunting way they had of all pointing, with tragic unanimity, in an identical direction; this being so, it was right that yesterday and tomorrow should both be encapsulated in the now of today.

My second novel, then, was composed with greater technical subtlety than my first; it expresses a broader and truer picture of human relationships. Although in 1945, owing to fortuitous external circumstances, it was warmly acclaimed, today not only public opinion but also those whose judgment I value assure me it is a lesser work than *She Came to Stay*. Even my own critical sense concurs. What is the reason for this?

In his essay on the *roman à thèse* Blanchot observes, with perfect justice, that to criticize a book for suggesting some ulterior idea is ridiculous. But, he adds, there is a great difference between *suggesting* and *demonstrating*; every facet of life is always rich in suggestion, yet this never proves anything conclusively. The writer's aim is to *make people see* the world, by re-creating it in words; he betrays and impoverishes it if he does not respect its essential ambiguity. Blanchot does not class *She Came to Stay* as a *roman à thèse,* because it has an open ending, and no lesson could be drawn from it. On the other hand, he does put *Le Sang des autres* (*The Blood of Others*) in this category: it reaches a clear-cut, definite conclusion, which can be reduced to terms of maxims and concepts. I agree with his finding. But the fault that he criticizes does not only mar the novel's final pages: it is inherent in the text from beginning to end.

Rereading the book today I find myself most struck by my characters' lack of depth. They are distinguished by their various moral attitudes, the living roots of which I never sought to grasp. I endowed Blomart with some of my own childhood emotions; yet these do not suffice to explain the feeling of guilt that clouds the whole course of his life. I realized this, and decided that he should have accidentally caused the death of his best friend when he was twenty. But no accident is ever enough to determine the whole course of anyone's life; Blomart conforms far too exactly to the character I assigned him. I knew nothing about union battles; the world in which I set Blomart lacks the complexity it would have possessed for any genuine militant radical. The character and background which I gave him are built up from ideas in the abstract, they lack immediate truth. Hélène, in whom I put more of myself, is nearer to a flesh-and-blood creation; the chapters written from her viewpoint displease me less than the others. In the scenes of the mass evacuation and return to Paris narrative gets the upper hand for once over theory. The best sequence, I think, is that in which Hélène makes the painful decision to renounce her stubbornly held attitudes. She abandons the meaningless symbols and illusions and pretenses by which she set such store, and finally cuts herself off from happiness itself. Here I make my meaning clear without any nudging overemphasis. Even so, her portrait is too slight, too diagrammatic.

Marcel, on the other hand, is always viewed externally, through the eyes of his perplexed friends, and therefore I was entitled to draw him in perspective. As a result I find more depth to his character than is the case with my other protagonists. But I still regret the way his preoccupations and Blomart's are so carefully made to correspond. This leads me to another criticism I would make against this novel: though its construction is close-knit, its substance lacks body. It should spread and ramify; instead it converges on a central point. Even the dialogue I put in my characters' mouths—this is particularly true of Blomart—now embarrasses me with its

strained, costive, breathless tone. Here again we touch on the thorny problem of sincerity in literature. I wanted to speak directly to the reader, and
indeed thought I was doing so; but all the time my voice had been usurped
by a sort of fatuous, didactic vampire. I was dealing with a genuine experience, yet I kept trotting out commonplace platitudes. You are bound to
avoid banality when you catch a moment of existence straight from life,
since it will never be repeated; but the moment a novelist embarks on
speculation he tumbles into cliché forthwith. The originality of any idea
can only be tested in the context of a special branch of learning. If it provides a hitherto unknown key or method which means revising present
concepts, then well and good. But ideas do not germinate in salons or
novels. (Valéry used to think he had ideas, which he noted down with
jealous care. Once he asked Einstein whether he carried a notebook around
with him to jot down his thoughts in. "No," Einstein said. Valéry was
intrigued. "Do you make jottings on your cuffs, then?" he inquired. Einstein
grinned. "Well, you know," he said, *ideas don't happen very often.*" He
estimated he had had two only, in the whole course of his life.) A work
composed *à thèse* not only fails to make any real point but seems invariably
to emphasize the most vapid conclusions.

The moment I began to turn over the themes of *The Blood of Others*
in my mind I foresaw this danger. A note I made at the time reads: "How
intractable this acquisition of social awareness is! How to avoid a moralizing, didactic tone?" In fact, what I refer to as "acquisition of social
awareness" is not a priori either intractable or prone to arouse the moralizing instinct; it was the way in which I approached it that made me slip
into didacticism. I can see how I went wrong when I reread this other
note: "I would like my next novel to illustrate one's relationship with
other people [*autrui*] in all its real complexity. To suppress one's awareness
of the Other's existence is mere childishness. The plot must be far more
closely linked to social problems than in the first novel. It should culminate
in some action with a social dimension—though this is hard to find." *The
Blood of Others* was afterward described as a "novel about the Resistance."
In actual fact it took shape in my mind without any direct impulse from
events; the theme I wanted to tackle was there, but I found it difficult to
excogitate a "social" act which embodied it. It was that October, when I
had actually begun to write the book, that the notion of using guerilla
attacks and reprisals forced itself upon me. This dissociation between the
novel's underlying theme and the episodes in which I gave it shape shows
that *The Blood of Others* was conceived in a wholly different fashion
from *She Came to Stay*. With the latter, the whole concept was there to
begin with, in the shape of various fantasies I had been mulling over
during the past few years. This time I started, again, from a personal
experience; but instead of living it through imaginatively, I formulated it
as an abstraction. I know why.

Till war broke out I had followed my own bent, learning about the
world and constructing a private pattern of happiness. Morality became

identified in my mind with pursuits such as these: it was indeed my Golden Age. Limited though my experience was, I stuck to this attitude body and soul, and never dreamed of discussing it. I got it just enough in perspective to want to make other people conscious of it: this is what I was trying to do in *She Came to Stay*. But from 1939 onward, everything changed. The world became a place of chaos, and my work of construction stopped altogether. My one recourse was the verbal exorcism implicit in abstract moral judgments: I sought desperately for some reason or formula that would justify me in enduring the lot now thrust upon me. I found one or two in which I still have faith; I learned about human solidarity, and personal responsibilities, and the fact that it was possible to accept death in order that life might keep its meaning. But these truths I learned, in a way, against my natural inclinations. I used words to talk myself into accepting them. I expounded them to myself, I turned my powers of persuasion inward and gave myself a regular lesson. It was this lesson I now strove to pass on, ignoring the fact that it might not come as freshly to the reader as it had come to me.

So I embarked upon what I might term the "moral period" of my literary career, which lasted for several years. I no longer took my natural spontaneity for granted; I was drawn to question myself concerning my principles and aims, and, after some hesitation, I even went to the length of composing an essay on the problem.

I was nearly through with *The Blood of Others* by the beginning of 1943. It was at this point that Sartre introduced me to Jean Grenier in the Flore, having recently made his acquaintance himself. Grenier had a scheme for collecting and bringing out in book form various essays typical of contemporary ideological trends. They chatted for a while, and then Grenier turned to me. "What about you, madame," he inquired. "Are *you* an existentialist?" I can still recall my embarrassment at this question. I had read Kierkegaard, and the term "existential philosophy" had been in circulation for some time apropos of Heidegger; but I didn't understand the meaning of the word "existentialist," which Gabriel Marcel had recently coined. Besides, Grenier's question clashed with my modesty and my pride alike. I was not of sufficient importance, objectively considered, to merit any such label; as for my ideas, I was convinced that they reflected the truth rather than some entrenched doctrinal position. Grenier invited me to contribute a piece to the anthology he was editing. To begin with I refused, saying that where philosophy was concerned I knew my own limitations. *Being and Nothingness* had not yet been published, but I had read the manuscript over and over again, and did not see how there was anything I could add to it. But Grenier insisted, saying I could pick any subject I liked.

Sartre encouraged me at this point, telling me to at least try. It was true that I still had something to say about certain of the problems I had tackled in *The Blood of Others*, especially the relationship of individual experience to universal reality, a theme around which I had sketched an idea for a play. I had the notion of a City which demanded from one of its most eminent citizens that he should sacrifice a life—the life, no doubt, of someone he loved dearly. To begin with, the hero refused, but then his concern for the public good made him change his mind, and he consented, only to fall into a state of apathy which made him indifferent to individuals and community alike. Under the threat of mortal peril his fellow citizens vainly besought his help, until someone, probably a woman, managed to revive a flicker of egotistical passion in him. Only then did he regain the desire to save his compatriots. The plot was too abstract, and the play never materialized. But since someone was offering me a chance to deal directly with the problem on my mind, why not take advantage of the fact? So I began to write *Pyrrhus et Cinéas*; I spent three months on it, and it swelled into a small book.

If man is "a creature of distances," why should he transcend himself just so far and no farther? How are the boundaries of his ambitions to be defined? These were the questions I asked myself in an early section. I rejected a merely *ad hoc* morality, and also all those which involved eternity; no human individual can establish a genuine relationship with the infinite, be it labeled God or Humanity. I showed the truth and importance of the idea of "situation" which Sartre brought out in *Being and Nothingness*. I attacked all moral alienation, and refused to admit that "other people" could be used as an alibi. I had likewise realized that in a world at war every project is a matter of choice, and you must—as Blomart did in *The Blood of Others*—consent to violence. The whole of this critical exposé strikes me today as fair enough, though very summary.

In the second section, my problem was to find some positive basis for morality. I restated, in greater detail, the conclusion of the novel I had just completed: liberty, the foundation stone of all human values, is the only end capable of justifying men's undertakings. But I was also drawn toward Sartre's theory, that whatever the circumstances, we have a liberty of action that enables us to surmount them; and if this freedom is a *donnée*, how can we properly regard it as an end? So I distinguished two separate aspects of liberty: Liberty is the very modal essence of existence, which willy-nilly, in one way or another, subsumes to itself all external influences: this internal movement is indivisible, and thus a totality for each individual. On the other hand, actual concrete possibilities vary from one person to the next. Some can attain to only a small part of those opportunities that are available to mankind at large, and all their striving does no more than bring them near the platform from which their luckier rivals are departing. Their transcendency is lost in the general mass of humanity, and takes on the appearance of immanence. With a more favorable situation, the project makes a genuine advance, constructs a new future. An activity is good when you aim to conquer these positions of privilege, both for yourself and for others: to set freedom free. In this way I attempted to reconcile Sartre's ideas with the views I had upheld against him in various lengthy discussions: I was establishing an order of precedence among various "situations." Though, subjectively speaking, salvation was always possible, one should still choose knowledge rather than ignorance, health rather than disease, and prefer prosperity to penury.

I do not disapprove of my anxiety to provide existentialist morals with a material content; the annoying thing was to be enmeshed with individualism still, at the very moment I thought I had at last escaped it. An individual, I thought, only receives a human dimension by recognizing the existence of others. Yet, in my essay, coexistence appears as a sort of accident that each individual should somehow surmount; he should begin by hammering out his "project" in solitary state, and only then ask the mass of mankind to endorse its validity. In truth, society has been all about me from the day of my birth; it is in the bosom of that society, and in my own close relationship with it, that all my personal decisions must be formed. My subjectivism was, inevitably, doubled up with a streak of idealism that deprived my speculations of all, or nearly all, their significance. This first essay only interests me today insofar as it marks a stage in my development.

This dialogue between Pyrrhus and Cinéas is very much like the one I had with myself, and noted down in my private diary, on my twentieth birthday. In both cases a voice asked, "What use is it all?" In 1927 that voice had denounced the vanity of earthly pursuits in the name of the Absolute and Eternity, while in 1943 it invoked Universal History against the finite limitations of individual projects; but it always beckoned me toward a mood of indifference and abstention. Now as before, my response remained the same. Against sluggish reason, and the void, and everything else, I set up the incontrovertible evidence of a *living affirmative*. If it seemed perfectly natural for me to accept the ideas of Kierkegaard and Sartre, and to become an "existentialist," that was because my whole past history had prepared me for it. Ever since I was a child my temperament had inclined me to trust my wishes and desires, and from all the doctrines that had contributed to my intellectual development I selected those which served to strengthen this disposition in me. By the age of nineteen I was already convinced that man, and man alone, is responsible for the direction of his life, and can direct it adequately. Yet I was never to lose sight of that dizzy void, that dense blackness where all his impulses lurk; I will return to this topic later.

Pyrrhus et Cinéas was finished in July and accepted by Gallimard. *She Came to Stay* would be out in a month or two; and I felt that with *The Blood of Others* I had made definite progress. I was satisfied with myself. My second novel could not be published before the Liberation, but I was in no hurry. The important thing was that a day would come when the future was open again. We no longer had any doubts about this, and we even went so far as to predict that there would not be long to wait now. All the happiness I thought I had lost forever now bloomed again; indeed, I felt it had never flourished so abundantly.

Chapter 8

HE ENTRANCE EXAMINATIONS TO SÈVRES WERE held in June, and I found myself free from the end of that month. I wanted to get away again during the summer holidays but this time we picked Central France, an area where provisions were still as plentiful as anywhere. I fixed a rendezvous with Sartre for July 15, and caught a train to Roanne: there was no longer any zonal border. I had reserved my seat, and took up the reservation long before departure time; if I hadn't, I might well have been left standing on the platform. Some passengers traveled on the footboards, others were crammed into the w.c.'s. At stations along the way women burst into tears because they couldn't force their way into a compartment. By an odd coincidence my traveling companions spent a long time discussing *Nausea*, which they compared to Camus's *The Stranger*; after this they had an argument over *The Flies*, which I described in a letter to Sartre: "One man said it was odd the play hadn't proved more successful, and that he'd heard from Alquié that you were annoyed because Valéry didn't care for it(?). He personally found it not without interest." In the same letter I noted that "Roanne seems very poor, as poor as Paris, even though I had real *café au lait* for breakfast. Still, for 25 francs I got a meal consisting of radishes, a huge dish of spinach— as good as any spinach can be—excellent potato croquettes, and two rather moldy apricots. I had plenty of everything because the helpings were being served for two, and my table companion ate nothing. Better here than in Paris. Yet even the best hotels can offer nothing except spinach and beets." I only quote this extract because, when I look through the letters I got at the time, it is very striking how all my correspondents are at great pains to describe their meals; even Olga never fails to do so. Food was a crucial problem.

I spent three weeks cycling on my own. I went back to Limousin, and spent a day at Meyrignac with my cousin Jeanne, surrounded by a swarm of blond children. The house had been enlarged: the woodshed, the coach house, and the laundry had all been converted into living quarters. The wisteria and bignonia that once covered the walls had vanished; there were statues of the Virgin under the trees, and the ornamental park was fenced in with barbed wire. There was little of the past left for me here.

My bicycle was giving me trouble: one of the tires went flat every hundred miles or so. I wrote to Sartre and gave him the address of a small garage proprietor: if he said he'd been recommended to him by some distant relation of Bost's, he would be able, for 250 francs, to obtain a new inner tube. When he alighted on the station platform at Uzerche, he was lugging two tool bags, and had a rubber tire slung over one shoulder. We sat on the terrace of the Hôtel Chavanes, overlooking the Vézère, and he gave me the news from Paris. He told me he had been signed up by Pathé to write scripts for them, and was getting a regular sizable retainer for this service. If things went well, he intended to give up teaching the following year.

This time we didn't hurry things, but traveled in short stages, making leisurely stops at the places we liked. Sometimes it rained, and then we would put on a pair of yellow plastic cycling capes. I can still see Sartre standing under a tree, his rain-soaked head protruding from this tarpaulin-like garment, wiping his bespattered glasses and helpless with laughter. The day we reached Beaulieu it was late in the evening when we arrived, and we went straight in to dinner, leaving our bicycles standing at the curb outside the hotel. Then a storm broke overhead, with such sudden fury that Sartre didn't even have time to rush out and put them under shelter. Already the driving rain had knocked them over, and a torrent of muddy yellowish water had borne off our saddlebags. The manuscript of *Le Sursis* (*The Reprieve*) lay bobbing in the gutter; we fished it out again, but the leaves were waterlogged and mud-stained, and the ink was running badly. It was a long job to dry it all out and reconstitute the text. All the houses were flooded; by noon the following day housewives were still hard at it, bailing, sweeping, and scrubbing off muddy floors.

But for the most part the weather was sunny; we never lacked for energy, and we ate when we felt hungry. Whenever we spotted a farm we would make a detour to see if we could pick up some eggs—very often successfully. Innkeepers thought it quite normal for us to ask them to cook us an omelette over and above the advertised menu. Generally we never had trouble in finding accommodations. At La Roche-Cadillac, however, every room was taken: in the end someone told us to try a certain farm: it was a fair way off, but the owner was a hospitable sort, they said. We wandered around for some time in the darkness, and when we finally got there dinner was nearly over. There were about a dozen people, all sitting around one big table and eating apple tarts: they offered us some, and the farmer, with a conspiratorial wink, told us that his barn had been packed before, but there'd be plenty of room for us to sleep there tonight. These earlier guests had not, we surmised, been gadding about just for the fun of it; and he obviously thought we were more of the same sort.

We had another glimpse of the Tarn gorges, and at a place known as Les Vignes we found a nice little inn. It was run by an old woman who had no other guests apart from us and who stuffed us full of good ham.

We stayed there several days. The old woman spoke nostalgically of the days when there wasn't a road through, and tourists were unknown, and the Tarn was still a lovely unspoiled river. We also revisited several places along the Lot—Espalion, Entraygues, Estaing, and Conques. At the last-named we couldn't find a room; they were expecting some refugees, and the mayor let us sleep on a couple of the paillasses that had been prepared for them in the schoolroom. Once again we walked through the Grésigne Forest; and at Vaour they served us so delicious a *pâté* at lunch that we decided to stay for dinner too. No accommodations. Fair enough: we'd sleep in the stable. We were bitten by bugs all night, but at least our stomachs were well satisfied.

Our trip ended at Toulouse. We had a few drinks with Dominique Desanti, who was staying at her parents' place, and also ran into Lautmann; but Sartre did not know him very well, and we didn't discuss any serious topic. A few months later we heard that he had been executed.

We spent the last part of August and all of September at La Pouèze, in a state of blissful euphoria. The Allies had taken Sicily during July, and at the beginning of September they made landings in Calabria and at Salerno. Mussolini's resignation, followed by what was described as "Badoglio's treachery," blew the German-Italian entente sky-high. Since the Italian armed forces had surrendered unconditionally, the German Army, on Rommel's orders, occupied the entire peninsula. Mussolini, who had been removed to a hide-out at the summit of the Gran Sasso, was neatly hijacked out of it by some German parachutists. This exploit, however, had no political repercussions, and some important German units found themselves irretrievably cut off in Italy. On the Eastern Front, the communiqués informed us, European forces were staging a "flexible withdrawal" in order to "shorten the front line." You needed only one glance at a map to see what a debacle lay behind this announcement. When D-Day came and Anglo-American forces secured a bridgehead on the French coast, it would be impossible for the Wehrmacht to defend three fronts simultaneously.

We listened to the B.B.C., we congratulated ourselves, and we did a lot of hard work. I began my third novel, for which I had already found a title: *Tous les hommes sont mortels (All Men Are Mortal)*. Sartre was going on with *The Reprieve*. He dropped it temporarily when we returned to Paris, in order to write a new play. Like his first theatrical venture, this was undertaken in order to help tyro actresses. Wanda, Olga's sister, wanted to go on the stage too: she was attending Dullin's classes, and in October he had given her a small part in *The Flies*. Furthermore, Olga the dark-haired one, had just married a man called Marc Barbezat; he was managing director of a factory near Lyon that turned out pharmaceutical products. He also published a most elegant periodical called *L'Arbalète,* which he brought out twice yearly, at his own expense, printing it himself on a hand press. He wanted his wife to get a thorough grounding in the acting profession, and therefore suggested to Sartre that he write a play for her and Wanda, something easy to stage, that could be taken on tour all around the country. He would underwrite the cost of the venture. The idea of writing a short play, with a single set and two or three characters only, intrigued Sartre. He at once thought of a situation *in camera,* as it were: a group of people shut up in a cellar during a lengthy bombardment. Then he had the inspired notion of placing his characters in Hell, for all eternity. The actual writing of *Huis Clos (No Exit)* was easy and quick. Originally he entitled it *Les Autres,* and it was thus that it appeared in *L'Arbalète.*

I had sworn I would not spend a second year on the Rue Dauphine; and well before the holidays I applied to the proprietors of the Hôtel de la Louisiane, on the Rue de Seine, where many of the Flore's regulars lived. I moved in during October. My room contained a divan, several book-shelves, a large and massive table, and a poster on the wall representing an English Lifeguardsman. The day I arrived, Sartre upset a bottle of ink over the moquette carpet, with the result that the proprietress instantly removed it; but the parquet flooring suited me as well as any carpet would have. I also had a kitchen of my own. From my window I looked out over a great sea of rooftops. None of my previous retreats had come so close to being the apartment of my dreams, and I felt like staying there for the rest of my life. Sartre had a tiny room at the other end of the corridor: its bareness more than once surprised his visitors. He did not even own any books; any we bought we lent to people, who never returned them. Lise and Bourla occupied a large, circular studio on the floor below. We often ran into Mouloudji and his charming Lola in the passageway: she was extremely popular in the Louisiane, since she washed and ironed shirts for four or five tenants who belonged to the crowd at the Flore. In those days, when you couldn't get soap to lather, doing laundry for nothing was a real act of kindness.

Financially we were less hard-pressed than the previous year. In accordance with the arrangement he had made, Sartre not only kept his *bacca-lauréat* class at the Lycée Condorcet, but was also turning out scripts for Pathé. The first one he offered them, however, *Les Jeux sont faits (The Chips Are Down),* was not received favorably by the company's experts. Dullin asked him to lecture, taking turns with Camille, on the history of the theater. *Being and Nothingness* was published by Gallimard, but only made its way slowly; it sold very few copies, and was very little discussed. For my own part, I was reveling in my release from fixed hours of work, and limited myself to looking in at the Bibliothèque Nationale twice a week. With Bost's assistance I raided old song collections, joke books, monologues, and ballads, and pieced together the resultant material into radio features. These broadcasts were insipid stuff, but I found their preparation considerable fun.

These various changes all contributed to make my life more agreeable; but there were two factors in particular which altered it for the better: the publication of *She Came to Stay,* and a sudden blossoming of friendships.

When I arrived at La Pouèze, *She Came to Stay* had just been published. I had no idea what sort of reception it would get, and Sartre had been too closely involved with my work to enlighten me on the subject. Various friends had spoken well of the book; but they were friends. "I must confess, I'm astounded," Marco told me in his most ceremonious voice. "I read it at one sitting, and found it most amusing; but it's really a railroad station bookstall novel, isn't it?" I was expecting him to be catty, and so this didn't worry me. All the same, I decided to be modest in my expectations. I had labored over this novel for four years, and ventured everything on it; yet now I felt quite detached about its fate. My natural optimism, which required my life to be a continual process of development, allowed me to regard this apprentice work with lighthearted contempt as just a frivolous love story: I dreamed now of vast "committed" novels. There was a good deal of common sense in this stern self-deprecation; it forestalled any disappointment, and spared me the embarrassment that too high an estimate of my own work might have brought about.

Toward the end of August Sartre went up to Paris to take part in a Resistance meeting: the C.N.E. had held its first plenary assembly at the end of May, and certain regroupings were due to take place. I went to meet him at Angers. From my table outside a café opposite the station I saw him hurrying toward me, waving a paper. The first review of *She Came to Stay* had just come out, in *Comoedia,* written by Marcel Arland. No article had ever pleased me so much. Though he had one or two reservations, Arland spoke warmly of my novel, and sounded as though he took it seriously: this was the thing I found most exciting. It is not very often that one unequivocally achieves a long-cherished ambition. Here was a review, written by a real critic, printed in a real paper, to assure me in black and white that I had written a real book—that I had become, overnight, a real writer. I could not contain my joy.

This mood continued unbroken when I returned to Paris: there were quite a number of other notices, mostly complimentary. Many, however, inveighed against the immorality of the milieu I chose to describe; even Arland found it regrettable that my characters should be so obsessed with jumping in and out of bed. It must be remembered that during this period the Vichy Government banned *Tartuffe* and guillotined a woman abortionist; all women were chaste, all girls virginal, all husbands faithful, and all children innocent. Even so, this finicky mock-modesty took me by surprise: there is really so little bedroom stuff in *She Came to Stay!* On the other hand, I was pleasantly astonished by Thierry Maulnier's observations on Françoise and her struggle to achieve happiness. I felt they were justified, but they caught me off my guard. So my book existed in depth; it was an object, and to a certain extent had passed beyond my control. Yet I was pleased, too, to see that it had not betrayed my original purpose. Gabriel Marcel wrote me a most friendly letter, in the course of which he remarked that Xavière seemed to him a perfect embodiment of the Other. An elderly man solicited a meeting with me, via Marco, and proceeded to tell me all about some obscure and murky political drama in which he had been involved: the central motif of this episode, as had been the case in *She Came to Stay,* apparently involved a death-struggle between two individual personalities. I managed to convince myself, therefore, that my chosen themes had not lost any of their sharpness or impact in the process of communication. I got other letters, too: one from Cocteau, and another, I think, from Mauriac. Ramon Fernandez, who normally never set foot in the Flore, made a special trip there to see me. Since he had gone over to the enemy's camp this gesture of his embarrassed me somewhat; but I found it touching too. As a girl I had been very fond of his books, and his defection saddened me. He had acquired a paunch and sported white spats. He told me stories about Proust's sex life which absolutely flabbergasted me.

Marco, who moved in social circles, heard my name being discussed favorably in various drawing rooms, and retailed the gist of such conversations to me in a half-flattering, half-mocking way. "You must feel your friends haven't done you justice!" he told me. He was, I noticed with some satisfaction, distinctly miffed. An unsuccessful novelist, whom Sartre knew slightly, ran into me upstairs in the Flore one day: "A lot of good luck you had there," he said. "You struck a good subject." He nodded. "Yes, a good subject that: a real bit of luck!" I was expecting some contemptuous comment from Adamov. "Well," I said, "have you seen it? A real novel, with a beginning, a middle, and an end. Does that make you see red?" He shook his head, and stared at me dully. "Not all that much," he said. "There's Xavière, at least. Xavière's something."

Because of Xavière, some of the Flore's regulars allowed me, as it were, extenuating circumstances; but the greater majority looked somewhat askance at me. They complained to Olga and Mouloudji that I had spoken slightingly of the Bal Nègre and its "splendid animalism." They found none of their private myths in the novel, and the character of Françoise exasperated them. The men were unanimous in condemning me; the women were rather more divided. Some of them would approach me and ask, "Might we perhaps see each other occasionally?" I fended off these invitations, which seemed to annoy them. A very good-looking young man called Francis Vintenon, whom I had known by sight for some time, showed his approval in a more graceful fashion: he offered me a pack of English cigarettes, which was a very rare gift at the time. After this he would often bring me cigarettes and English novels, though I knew he was absolutely broke.

So through the medium of my book I aroused curiosity, irritation, even sympathy: there were people who actually liked it. Now at last I was fulfilling the promises I had made myself when I was fifteen; now at last I was reaping the reward for my long, uneasy labors. I did not jeopardize my pleasure by asking indiscreet questions, such as what absolute value there might be in my novel, or whether it would stand up to the passage of time: the future would decide that. For a moment it was sufficient that I had crossed the first threshold: *She Came to Stay* existed for other people, and I had entered public life.

Though I had so often attacked the illusory mirage of "the Other," and indeed denounced it once more in *She Came to Stay,* I fell a victim to it when I saw myself in the guise of a different person. One literary columnist, discussing new books from Gallimard, referred to me as "the firm's new woman novelist." The words tinkled gaily around in my head. How I would have envied this serious-faced young woman, now embarking on her literary career, if she had possessed any name other than my own—but she *was* me! I was so inexperienced in these matters that I somehow contrived to identify myself with my image of me, and benefited by everything tending to enhance it. If I had been awarded the Prix Goncourt that year I should have accepted it with wholehearted jubilation. In fact, the possibility did arise; I was told at Gallimard's in March that I stood a strong chance. (The date of the award had been postponed from December to March; The Prix Renaudot was awarded two weeks later.) Sartre told me that the C.N.E. had no objection to my accepting if I refrained from giving press interviews and publishing articles in connection with the prize. The afternoon that the selection committee met I spent working, as usual, upstairs in the Flore; but I found myself impatiently awaiting the phone call that would tell me the result. I had put on a new dress, made at La Pouèze to Madame Lemaire's design; the fabric was ersatz, but it was a beautiful electric blue. I had also discarded my turban in favor of an elaborate, high coiffure, with the hair piled on top of my head. The idea that at any moment I might become the center of vast publicity I found both terrifying and attractive. Yet I wasn't very upset when I heard that the prize had gone to Marius Grout. A few days later I was assured I was a strong candidate for the Prix Renaudot; I was down at La Pouèze when I read in the papers that the winner in this case had been Dr. André Soubiran, and this time I had not the faintest shadow of regret. It was neither pride nor indifference that led me to accept these disappointments with such equanimity; the friendships I had made both bolstered my *amour-propre* and kept me from overindulging it.

There was little enough left by now of our old friendships; time or distance had worn them thin, absence robbed us of some altogether. We saw scarcely anyone outside the "family," and it made a great change in my way of life when the circle of our acquaintances suddenly expanded.

Michel Leiris's two books *L'Afrique fantôme* and *L'Age d'homme,* had impressed us by their fastidious honesty and their brilliant style—the latter an odd blend of lyricism and aloofness—and we felt we would like to meet the author. Sartre was introduced to him at the C.N.E., and, as I have said, he reviewed *The Flies* in *Les Lettres françaises.* In July, while I was away, Sartre went to dinner with Leiris and his wife, and in October they invited me to come with him. Sartre had forgotten the number of their house, and we spent over half an hour wandering up and down the Quai des Grands-Augustins before we found the right door. What with his shaven skull and formal clothes and stiff gestures I found Leiris a somewhat intimidating character, despite the calculatedly cordial smile he switched on; but his wife Zette at once put me at my ease. A young girl still peeped through those blue eyes, while her voice and the way she welcomed us conveyed almost maternal warmth. Their apartment was furnished in bourgeois style and overflowing with books and modern paintings: Picassos, Massons, Miros, and some beautiful works by Juan Gris; the drawing-room chairs were upholstered with tapestry designed after Juan Gris cartoons. The windows looked out on a wide panorama of river and cobblestones. Leiris worked at the Musée de l'Homme, and Zette managed his brother-in-law Kahn-Weiler's art gallery. Kahn-Weiler had launched most of the great cubists, and owned a vast private collection of Picassos. He was now hiding out in this flat, which often served as a refuge for Jews or members of the Resistance. Both Michel and Zette Leiris knew a large number of famous—or notorious—characters, and told us innumerable anecdotes about them. They were on the closest terms with Giacometti, and talked of him a good deal. Leiris also held forth to us about the heyday of surrealism, a venture into which he had thrown himself with passionate enthusiasm. In those days he used to powder his face white and paint landscape scenes on his shaven cranium. He had taken part in the banquet that was given, just after World War I, in honor of Saint-Pol-de-Roux, and held in the upstairs room of the Closerie des Lilas. He had leaned out of the open window and shouted at the top of his voice: "Long live Germany!" Some passers-by had requested him to come down and explain himself. He did, and woke up in the hospital. His particular blend of masochism, extremism, and idealism had led him into heaven knows how many painful and preposterous scrapes, all of which he related with an air of mildly astounded impartiality.

Queneau was one of Leiris's best friends. I cannot remember exactly how our first meeting with him came about, but it took place in the Flore, and we told Queneau how much we had enjoyed *Les Enfants du limon.* His original intention had been to write a serious study of those illuminati who spent their time trying to square the circle or discover the secret of perpetual motion: he discussed them for some time, with great charm. We were astonished to learn that he was a trained mathematician and was currently reading Bourbaki. He also showed remarkable erudition in numerous other fields; he never showed off, indeed, but he minted his knowledge into a stream of anecdotes, comparisons, and descriptive summaries. His conversation put me in a very cheerful mood, since he was amused by everything one said, and even more by the things he said himself. His eyes twinkled behind his glasses, and he would burst into continual fits of laughter. It was not always clear, on thinking back, just what he had been laughing *at*; but his gaiety was infectious, notwithstanding. His wife, with a great air of ingenuousness, fired off embarrassing home truths and non sequiturs; sometimes she was rather disconcerting, but she had her witty moments.

When Sartre met Camus at the dress rehearsal of *The Flies* he found him a most likable personality. It was at the Flore, in Sartre's company, that my own first encounter with Camus took place. The conversation

turned, after some hesitation, toward literary topics, among other things
to Ponge's *Le Parti Pris des choses,* which both Sartre and Camus thought
highly of. But a happy accident soon led to the ice being broken. Camus
was crazy about the theater. Sartre talked of his new play and the conditions
that would govern its production. Then he suggested that Camus should
play the lead and stage it. Camus hesitated at first, but when Sartre pressed
the point he agreed. The first rehearsals took place in my room. Those
present included Wanda, Olga Barbezat, and a boy called Chauffard as the
bellboy. He was an ex-pupil of Sartre's, who was writing, but whose
main ambition, however, was to be an actor. At present he was working
for Dullin. The readiness with which Camus flung himself into this venture
endeared him to us; it also hinted that he had plentiful time at his disposal. He had only recently come to Paris; he was married, but his wife
had stayed behind in North Africa. He was a few years younger than I.
His youth and independence created bonds between us: we were all solitaries, who had developed without the aid of any "school"; we belonged
to no group or clique. Like us, Camus had moved from individualism
to a committed attitude; we knew, though he never mentioned the fact,
that he had important and responsible duties in the Combat movement.
He relished success and fame, and made no secret of the fact; to carry it
off with a blasé air would have been something less than natural. Occasionally he allowed a touch of original Rastignac to peep out, but he
didn't seem to take himself overseriously. He was a simple, cheerful soul.
In a good mood he was not above somewhat facile jokes; there was a waiter
at the Flore called Pascal, whom he insisted on referring to as Descartes.
But he could afford to allow himself such indulgences; his great charm, the
product of nonchalance and enthusiasm in just the right proportions, insured him again any risk of vulgarity. What I liked most about him was
his capacity for detached amusement at people and things even while he was
intensely occupied with his personal activities, pleasures, and friendships.

We used to meet, sometimes in little groups, sometimes all together,
at the Flore or one of the cheaper restaurants nearby, or, very often, at
the Leirises' apartment. Sometimes I would invite the Leirises, the Queneaus,
and Camus to dinner at my place; eight people could fit round my table
without too much difficulty. Bost, who knew a bit about cookery, used to
help me prepare the meal. I was better provisioned than I had been the
year before, thanks chiefly to Zette, who occasionally got hold of some meat
for me. I would offer my guests bowls of green beans and heaped dishes
of beef stew, and I always took care to have plenty of wine. "The quality's
not exactly brilliant," Camus used to say, "but the quantity is just right."
I had never "received" before, and enjoyed the new experience.

These meetings took up a good deal of our time, and we set a value on
them that our common tastes, opinions, and interests could not wholly explain: it was largely due to the bond of comradeship in day-to-day activities
that united us all. We listened to the B.B.C., and passed on the news
bulletins, and discussed them; we shared our joys and anxieties, our
moments of hate and indignation and hope. Even when we talked about

the weather there was a conversational undercurrent going on in which our fears and expectations found utterance; we only had to be in each other's company to know that we were united, and to sense our joint strength. We agreed to remain leagued together in perpetuity against the systems and men and ideas that we condemned. But their defeat was imminent, and our task would be to shape the future that would then unfold before us: perhaps by political action, and in any case on the intellectual plane. We were to provide the postwar era with its ideology. We had a detailed plan ready. Gallimard was proposing to publish a volume in his *Encyclopédie* entirely devoted to philosophy. Our idea was that Camus, Merleau-Ponty, Sartre, and myself should take over the section on ethics and turn it into a kind of joint manifesto. Sartre had decided to found a literary review, and we would all constitute a joint editorial board. We had come through the night, and dawn was breaking; we stood shoulder to shoulder, ready for a new start. That is why, despite my thirty-six years, these new friendships possessed for me the exquisite bloom of a far more youthful relationship.

It was a lucky chance for me that I embarked upon them at the same time as my literary career began: they helped me to clarify my ambitions. I did not aspire to posterity's marbled fame, but I would not be content with a bunch of snowdrops, either; I recognized my true desire by the joy I experienced at its accomplishment. During the first of the dinner parties I gave in my room, Zette Leiris and Jeanine Queneau recalled the discussions they had had that September as they cycled along the country lanes: they argued about the relationship between Françoise and Pierre in *She Came to Stay* and the attitude each of them had to Xavière, and problems of infidelity versus loyalty, jealousy versus trust. They conveyed to me that these discussions had formed a basis for meditation on various personal problems: I remember the excitement that bubbled up inside me as I listened to them. One remark of Camus's also moved me a great deal. I had lent him a typed copy of *The Blood of Others*; one evening when we were in the Leirises' kitchen, and about to sit down to dinner, he drew me aside and said enthusiastically, "It's a *fraternal* book," and I thought: If a fraternity can be created by words, then writing is well worthwhile. What I wanted was to penetrate so deeply into other people's lives that when they heard my voice they would get the impression they were talking to themselves. If my words multiplied through millions of human hearts, it seemed to me that my existence, though reshaped and transfigured, would still, in a manner of speaking, survive.

Now that I had had a book published, it would have been quite in order for me to attend meetings of the C.N.E., but I was put off doing so by a scruple which often subsequently made me hold back in a similar way. I was so completely in harmony with Sartre's views that my presence would simply have duplicated his, to no useful purpose. To go also struck me as both inopportune and ostentatious. It was not other people's malice I feared so much as my own embarrassment: I would have felt, in my inner heart, that I was making a tactless exhibition of myself. This criticism might not have applied if I had been in a position to accompany Sartre to C.N.E. meetings right from the beginning; and I am sure I would have managed to get there if the sessions had held any real attraction for me; but Sartre regarded them as a great bore. I was glad that Camus asked me to let Editions de Minuit have *The Blood of Others*—though in fact they had not started printing it at the time of the Liberation. I would have liked to "do something"; but the notion of merely symbolic participation I found repugnant, and so I remained at home.

Literature was in the doldrums, but there was a lively enough theatrical season. Barrault put on *The Satin Slipper* at the Comédie-Française. We had objected to a good many things in this play when we read it a few years before; but we had admired Claudel for successfully containing heaven and earth in a love affair. Ever since he had written his *"Ode au maréchal"* we had found him utterly sickening; but all the same, we were curious to see his play and find out how Barrault had dealt with it. The show began at six o'clock and lasted for over four hours, yet it held us absolutely breathless. Marie Bell in male attire I found embarrassing: I had imagined Doña Prouhèze as endowed with more boyish charms. But I was captivated by her speaking voice: she encompassed all Africa and the Americas, the desert and the oceans, in her vocal range; she seared one's very heart. Barrault was a frail Rodrigo indeed beside this burning bush. His production was a wonderful medley of styles. The motions of the sea he indicated by means of human gestures, a happily inspired borrowing from Chinese theatrical convention. There were other devices which recalled Barrault's innovations in *Hunger*. Yet more than once the curtain rose on a set that might have been designed by Châtelet. We walked out afterward asking each other what line he would ultimately decide to follow. Shortly afterward a young company put on a play called *Orage,* adapted from Strindberg, in which Jean Vilar showed great promise both as producer and actor. We had no great liking for the works of Giraudoux, and I cannot think why we went to see *Sodome et Gomorrhe*; but during the performance we, like everyone else, noted the passage of an angel whose name was Gérard Philipe.

Clouzot had now made his film *Le Corbeau,* for which Chavance provided the script. Some members of the Resistance accused him of contributing to enemy propaganda: if the film was screened in Germany it would present a repulsive picture of French society. In fact, however, it never crossed the border. Clouzot's friends made the point that the film attacked anonymous letter-sending, while the Occupation authorities were exhorting Frenchmen to denounce their neighbors on the quiet. We ourselves did not feel that *Le Corbeau* carried any moral message; on the other hand, there seemed no reason for it to arouse patriotic indignation. All we noted was that Clouzot had talent.

I went off early in January for a short skiing holiday. Sartre did not come with me, but Bost did. Some friends of ours had rented a house in Morzine. The white roofs of the village and the smell of damp wood in the streets all brought back nostalgic memories. But I had some setbacks, too. The French method of skiing had been altered, and the instructors now categorically forbade us to use the stem turn: everything had to be learned again from scratch. "I'd gladly sacrifice the Prix Renaudot if I could do a proper Christie," I wrote to Sartre. All the same I enjoyed myself considerably, and ate well.

One morning I went down to the sports store where I had my skis waxed, and found it in a state of chaos: it had been ransacked by the Maquis during the night. The owner wouldn't pay them the contributions they demanded; it was all his own fault—so I was informed by his fellow tradesmen, a more patriotic, or prudent, bunch. At all events, the Maquis was the law in Morzine; another incident, which I described in a letter to Sartre, amply confirmed this:

> The hotel [we took our meals there] is in a fine upheaval; an hour ago—at six-thirty this evening—three Maquisards appeared, clutching revolvers, in search of a woman called Odette, an elegant and unlikable vacationer who dines at the table next to ours and, it appears, is working for the Gestapo. They grabbed some half-witted young woman who had been friendly with Odette during the past few days, went up to her room with her, politely examined her papers, and then brought her down into the lobby again, where the proprietor insisted on standing them drinks. Everyone in the hotel appeared to be wholeheartedly on their side. They decided to wait for Odette, but by the time dinner was over she still hadn't showed up. It was an odd meal, with all eyes fixed on that vacant table. It seems she denounced heaven knows how many people, and everybody in the hotel knew it. I had observed that she was the clinging type, but supposed this was simply garden-variety flirtatiousness. In the evenings she used to go out with the ski instructors; apart from this she looked like a young woman of decent family, and she attended Mass regularly. The three Maquisards announced their intention of bumping her off when they found her; and no one, not even her friend during the past week, seemed in the last anxious to put her on her guard . . .
>
> I also saw two Germans in uniform out on the ski run this afternoon, solemnly practicing turns; it was as startling and incongruous as the sight of a Moslem riding a bicycle . . .

In fact someone must have tipped Odette off, because she never set foot in the hotel again. Three days later, when I was waiting for a connection on my return journey to Paris, I spotted her red blazer on the opposite platform; she was chatting away to a group of people, without an apparent care in the world.

The Allied air forces had conquered the skies; attacks in the press against "Anglo-Saxon terrorism" merely confirmed the news bulletins put out by the B.B.C.: Cologne, the Rhineland, Hamburg, and Berlin had all been devastated. On the Eastern Front the Germans were retreating before a new Soviet offensive. In February, Allied forces landed at Nettuno. The armies advancing northward from Salerno to link up with this new bridgehead were halted at Cassino, and a violent battle took place, in the course of which the famous monastery was reduced to rubble. But the Anglo-American advance was resumed, and very soon their troops entered Rome. Our own liberation was due in a matter of months—perhaps even of weeks. The R.A.F. was preparing for D-Day by stepping up its raids on French targets, pounding at factories, ports, and railheads. Nantes was razed to the ground, and the Paris suburbs hard hit. The Resistance helped this all-out drive by blowing up German trucks, while railroad workers deliberately sabotaged locomotives and weakened the roadbed. In the Savoie, Limousin, and Auvergne areas the Maquis grew steadily. From time to time the Germans would launch an attack on them, imprisoning some and shooting others. Paragraphs were always appearing in the papers to the effect that "fifteen refractory elements" or "twenty bandits" or a whole "band of traitors" had been destroyed. Rumors were rife: from northern and central France and the Dordogne reports came that the Germans had shot the entire male population of some village, driven out the women and children, and set fire to the houses. In Paris the Occupation authorities no longer plastered warning notices over the walls; but they did post up the photographs of those "foreign terrorists" whom they condemned to death on February 18, twenty-two of whom were executed on March 4. Despite the crudeness of the reproductions, all these faces thus held up for our hatred were moving, beautiful even; I stood there a long time, under the arches in the Métro, staring at them, and reflecting sadly how soon I would forget them. There were many other heroes and victims whose features we never knew: the incidence of raids and reprisals was now on the increase. It was during this period, I believe, that Lautmann was executed at Toulouse; certainly it was about now that I learned of Cavaillès' death, and heard that Kahn had been deported. I remembered the little girl with her dark pigtails, and the red-tiled house among its quiet, peaceful chestnut trees: it was hard to realize that happiness could be snuffed out in an instant. Yet it was true. About three times a week Sartre went to meetings of the C.N.E. and the C.N.Th., Comité National du Théâtre; if he was late getting back my heart would leap into my mouth. For the first five or ten minutes I kept telling myself it would be all right; but what would I do after two or three hours? We awaited Hitler's downfall with feverish exultation; but until it came, our lives might still be ruined. Cheerfulness and distress dwelt side by side in our hearts, an uneasy partnership.

One morning we arrived at the Flore to find Mouloudji in a frantic state: Olga Barbezat and Lola had been arrested. They were on fairly intimate terms, and though neither of them was involved in political activities, the previous afternoon they had been to tea with some friends who were in the Resistance, and the police had picked up everyone there. Sartre had a word with the man who said he was Laval's secretary—much to his embarrassment. Though Mouloudji and Barbezat tried every approach they knew, they failed to get the two women released, though at least they received the assurance that neither Olga nor Lola would be deported. As things turned out they remained in Fresnes Prison till June.

Nevertheless, we were all sufficiently inured to anxiety for it not to spoil our capacity for enjoyment altogether. Gallimard had just founded a new prize, the Prix de la Pléiade, and we threw a very gay party for Mouloudji on February 26 when it was awarded to him. The election committee consisted of Eluard, Malraux, Paulhan, Camus, Blanchot, Queneau, Arland, Roland Tual, and Sartre, while Lemarchand acted as chairman. The award had to be for an unpublished manuscript; the winner would get 100,000 francs, and Gallimard would publish his book. Sartre voted for *Enrico,* as did Camus; Mouloudji had no serious competition, and carried off the prize without difficulty. It came in very handy for him, too: that winter he was in the last stages of destitution, without even an overcoat to his name. When he went out in the street he turned up the collar of his jacket, which didn't stop his teeth chattering. Some of his fellow writers from North Africa organized a lunch in his honor at the Hoggar Restaurant, and Sartre and I were both invited. The main dish consisted of lamb chops, and I still recall my disappointment on finding that my chop was nothing but a bone with a little fat gristle adhering to it. Mouloudji's good fortune first flabbergasted Boubal, and then shocked him. When *Enrico* was published in January, 1945, he riffled through the pages, snorting, "A hundred thousand francs for writing this sort of shit! A hundred thousand francs for saying you've slept with your mother! I wouldn't mind admitting it myself at that price!" Mouloudji at once embarked on further stories, which appeared in *L'Arbalète.* The critics upbraided him for his *"misérabilisme,"* but nevertheless gave him a good press.

A little later we took part in another literary occasion. Picasso had just written a play, *Le Désir attrapé par la queue (Desire Caught by the Tail),* reminiscent of avant-garde writing in the twenties: a distant and belated imitation of *Les Mamelles de Tirésias.* Leiris proposed the idea of a public reading, and we fell in with his suggestion. Camus undertook to compère the proceedings. He had a big walking stick in one hand, with which he rapped on the floor to indicate a change of scene; he described the setting and introduced the characters; he also rehearsed the actors—though Leiris was responsible for the casting—during several afternoons beforehand. Leiris had the lead, and delivered the long speeches of Big Foot with enthusiastic fervor. Sartre was Round End, Dora Marr, Fat Misery, and the poet Hugnet's wife, Thin Misery. Zanie Campan, an extremely pretty girl who was married to Jean Aubier the publisher and had ambitions to go on the stage, played The Tart, and I was The Cousin.

The reading took place about seven o'clock at night in the Leirises' drawing room. They had set out a few rows of chairs, but so many people turned up that a large proportion of the audience remained standing at the back, or in the anteroom. We stood in a group with our backs to the window, facing the spectators, who paid great attention to our performance

and applauded it with positively religious zeal. For Sartre and Camus and
me the whole thing was a great lark; but in these circles, or so it seemed,
Picasso's least word and gesture were taken seriously. He was present in
person, and everyone congratulated him. I recognized Barrault, and someone pointed out Braque to me: he was very good-looking. Part of the
audience left, and the rest of us then went through to the dining room,
where Zette's ingenuity and some generous contributions had combined
to produce a real prewar atmosphere. An Argentine millionaire and his
wife, who had had their flat decorated by the finest artists in Paris—
Picasso had painted them a door—brought along an enormous chocolate
cake. It was on this occasion, I think, that I first met Lucienne and Armand
Salacrou, Georges Bataille, Georges Limbour, Sylvia Bataille, and Lacan:
comedies, books, a beautiful doll-like screen personality—all these now become real flesh-and-blood people, and I began to exist a little for them,
too. How much bigger and richer the world had become, all in a few
short months! And how wonderful it felt to be alive! I had gone to
considerable trouble to dress up for the occasion: Olga lent me a beautiful
red angora sweater, and Wanda contributed a necklace of big blue pearls:
Picasso delighted me by commenting favorably on this combination. I
smiled at people, and they smiled back at me. I was pleased with myself,
and with them too: my vanity gave itself an enjoyable airing, and the
atmosphere of amiability went straight to my head. All these polite remarks
and effusive greetings and pleasantries and small talk had some special
quality that saved them from being the usual insipid commonplaces; they
left a sharp yet unacknowledged aftertaste. A year before we would never
have dreamed of gathering together like this and having a noisy, frivolous
party that went on for hours. Prematurely, and despite all the threats that
still hung over so many of us, we were celebrating victory.

About eleven o'clock most of the guests took their leave. The Leirises
made the performers and a few close friends stay on: why not keep the
party going till five in the morning? We assented, and found the irremedi-
able nature of our decision rather amusing. The moment midnight had
struck, choice also became necessity: of our own free will, yet willy-nilly, too,
we were shut up in this apartment till dawn, with a forbidden city all
around us. We had lost the habit of sitting up late, but luckily there was
enough wine left to dispel our drowsiness. We didn't dance, for fear of
annoying the tenants on the floor below, but Leiris played some jazz
records, very softly. Mouloudji sang *"Les Petits Pavés"* in a pleasant, still
childish voice; Sartre, in response to popular request, gave us *"Les Papillons
de nuit"* and *"J'ai vendu mon âme au diable"*; Leiris and Camus read
a scene from one of their favorite melodramas; while the others all cheerfully
produced something or other, though I forgot the individual items. From
time to time a wave of sleepiness would come over me, and it was then
that I relished this unusual night most keenly. Outside, except for the
Occupation forces and their protégés, the streets were thoroughfares no
longer but barriers, which instead of linking up the blocks of houses,
isolated them, and revealed them for what they really were: rows of prison-

ers' barracks. Paris had become one vast Stalag. We had defied the inevitable moment of dispersal, and though we might not technically have infringed the curfew order, at least we had frustrated its intentions. To drink and talk together thus in the heart of darkness was so stealthy a pleasure that it seemed illicit to us, and partook of that special delight to be had from forbidden joys alone.

As a result of this evening's entertainment we made several new friendships. A year or two earlier we had met Dora Marr and Picasso at dinner with the Desnos's, and conversation had dragged. We saw Picasso again, both during the rehearsals of his play and on the actual day of the reading. He invited us to lunch at the Restaurant des Catalans (which in those days was not where it is now, but on the opposite side of the Rue des Grand-Augustins); he ate all his meals there, in the company of Dora Marr. He also asked us around to his studio on several occasions. We normally called on him in the morning, with the Leirises. He lived in the Rue des Grands-Augustins; his bedroom was a bare, cell-like chamber, and there was very little more furniture in the huge barn of a studio where he worked—nothing but a stove, its pipes radiating in all directions, and several easels and canvases, some on view, others turned to the wall. From various exhibitions I had learned the way in which he developed a theme from one painting to the next. He would concentrate on one subject at a time—the sanctuary at Notre Dame, a candlestick, a bunch of cherries—and as one followed the sequence of his various interpretations, it was easy enough to grasp his creative quirks and caprices, where he had forged ahead and where he had temporarily halted. In comparison with his past work, these paintings were more remarkable for technical perfection than for novelty; but this type of perfection had its own value, and I enjoyed seeing the canvases *in situ,* at the very moment of their creation. Picasso always welcomed us with sparkling vivacity; but though his conversation was gay and brilliant, one didn't exactly talk *with* him. It was more a case of his holding forth solo, the effect being spoiled only by his overaddiction to somewhat shopworn paradoxes. What fascinated me most were his expressive features—those quick, darting eyes!—and his remarkable talent for mimicry. He came to dinner at my place once, with Dora and the Leirises, and I bestirred myself to produce something really special. A large salad bowl piled high with blueberries and currants elicited tributes all around.

We established a closer, less formal relationship with Armand and Lucienne Salacrou. He had a keen eye and a quick laugh; his wit was mordant, and he possessed a cynical streak which he quite cheerfully turned against himself, making it appear a sort of agreeable frankness. One charming quality about him was that though, like everyone else, he put on a mask in public, he nevertheless confessed with relish to many things that most people keep quiet about: his private terrors and pet vanities, for example.

Two other people we often met at the Leirises' apartment were Georges Bataille and Georges Limbour. Certain parts of the former's book

L'Expérience intérieure I had found irritating, though others had moved me deeply; and I had very much enjoyed Limbour's novel *Les Vanilliers*. It is often asserted that writers should only be known through their books, and that when met in the flesh they prove a disappointment; but I found that few commonplaces could be less true. I was never once disappointed by my first encounter with any author whose works I admired, whatever might come of our meeting later. They all had an idiosyncratic manner, a keen eye for the world about them, a marked warmth—or bitchiness—of character, and a tone and manner which slashed right through the usual conventions and platitudes. Their charm might after a while wear thin or become mechanical, but it was always *there,* and imposed itself upon one from the start.

One attractive feature about this circle we were now entering was that nearly all its members were former surrealists who had broken away from the movement in the relatively distant past. Our age and university training had kept Sartre and me outside this group, though indirectly surrealism had done a great deal for us: we had inherited both its benefits and its setbacks. When Limbour told us about automatic-writing sessions, or Leiris and Queneau recalled Breton, with his ukases and tempers and sentences of excommunication, their anecdotes—so much more vivid and detailed and *true* than any book—allowed us to glimpse our own prehistory. One day, in the upstairs room at the Flore, Sartre asked Queneau what he still kept from his surrealist days. "The feeling I was once young," Queneau said. His reply impressed us, and we felt envious of him.

There was another advantage which I derived from these new acquaintanceships. I knew very few women of my own age, and none who led normal married lives. The problems that confronted people like Stépha, Camille, Louise Perron, Colette Audry, or me were, as I saw them, individual rather than generic. I began to realize how much I had gone wrong before the war, on so many points, by sticking to abstractions. I now knew that it *did* make a very great difference whether one was Jew or Aryan; but it had not yet dawned on me that such a thing as a specifically feminine "condition" existed. Now, suddenly, I met a large number of women over forty who, in differing circumstances and with various degrees of success, had all undergone one identical experience: they had lived as "dependent persons." Because I was a writer, and in a situation very different from theirs—also, I think, because I was a good listener—they told me a great deal; I began to take stock of the difficulties, deceptive advantages, traps, and manifold obstacles that most women encounter on their path. I also felt how much they were both diminished and enriched by this experience. The problem did not concern me directly, and as yet I attributed comparatively little importance to it; but my interest had been aroused.

To meet for drinks or lunch or dinner, sometimes a few of us, sometimes a larger party, was now not enough: we wanted to repeat the special sort of night we had enjoyed after the reading of *Desire Caught by the Tail.*

So in March and April we organized what Leiris referred to as "fiestas." The first of these was held in Georges Bataille's apartment, which looked out over the Cour de Rohan. The musician René Leibovitz and his wife were in hiding there. Fifteen days later, Bost's mother lent us her villa at Taverny. For a septuagenarian and clergyman's widow she was remarkably broad-minded: she locked up her antique furniture and precious knick-knacks, put away some chessmen that normally stood on a table, and went off somewhere else for the night. In June there was another fiesta at Camille's: I shall return to this later. During the course of my life I had often enjoyed myself a great deal; but it was only on these fiesta nights that I learned the true meaning of the word "fete." Geneviève Gennari, in her essay on me, observes that fetes or parties play a prominent part in my books; it is true that I have described several such occasions in *All Men Are Mortal* and *The Mandarins,* and have also discussed the phenomenon in *La Morale de l'ambiguïté* (*The Ethics of Ambiguity*). It was the fiestas— and the night of August 25 which they anticipated—that revealed the value of such interludes to me.

Caillois, in *Le Mythe de la fête,* and Georges Bataille, in *La Part du diable,* have analyzed this problem far more exhaustively; I only suggest here what significance it had for me personally. All the writers who have touched upon it interpret it after their own fashion: the function of the fete in Rousseau, for instance, had been well illuminated by Starobinski in *La Transparence et L'Obstacle.* For me, then, the fete is primarily an impassioned apotheosis of the present in the face of anxiety concerning the future. When the days pass smoothly and happily, there is no stimulus toward a fete. But if hope is rekindled in the very midst of despair, if you regain your hold upon the world and the times—then the magic moment catches fire, and you can plunge into it and be consumed with it: *that* is a "fete." The distant horizon is uncertain still, half threatening, half promising; that is why every fete has a quality of pathos about it. It faces up to this uncertainty, and doesn't dodge the issue. Nocturnal fetes in honor of young love, gigantic fetes on a day of victory: beneath the lively wine-flown raptures there is always a faint taste of death, but for one resplendent moment death is reduced to nothingness. Dangers still threatened us; after the hour of our deliverance there would still be dis-illusions aplenty in store for us, endless sorrows, and months, perhaps years, of uncertainty and chaos. We did not deceive ourselves about this. We merely wanted to snatch a few nuggets of sheer joy from this confusion and intoxicate ourselves with their brightness, in defiance of the disenchant-ments that lay ahead.

By our common efforts we achieved our end. The details mattered little on such occasions; to be together was enough for us. The atmosphere of gaiety, a thin flickering flame in each of us individually, became a verit-able sun on the faces all about us, that gave us light and warmth: friend-ship played no less important a part in it than the Allied successes. These bonds, as I have said, were vigorous and youthful, and circumstances drew them into an even closer symbolic relationship. We were isolated from our fellows by an impassable circle of silence and darkness. No one could pass either into or out of the ring; we might have been living in the Ark. We became a sort of secret fraternity, performing its rites away from the world's common gaze. To tell the truth, we had to invent charms of a sort, for the landings had not yet taken place, Paris was still unliberated, and Hitler remained alive: how was one to celebrate events that had not yet happened? There exist certain magical conductors that abolish both temporal and spatial distances: the emotions. We worked up a vast atmosphere of collective emotionalism that fulfilled all our longings in a trice: in the fever that it kindled victory became tangible reality.

We employed the most well-worn devices to spark off this flame. To begin with, we let rip on the food and drink. Every fete plays havoc with one's normal economy for the sake of a real blowout; and so, at a modest level, it was with us. It required great care and severe self-restraint to amass the provisions and bottles with which we stacked the buffet; then, suddenly, we found ourselves eating and drinking all we could put away. Abundance, so nauseating when cultivated for the mere show of the thing —I am thinking, for instance, of the picnic I went on with Zaza, along the bank of the Adour River—becomes a most stirring affair when it caters to famished stomachs. We stayed our pangs of hunger with shameless zest. Casual love-making played a very small part in these revels. It was, primarily, drink which aided our break with the daily humdrum round: when it came to alcohol, we never held back, and none of us had any objections to getting drunk. Some even regarded it as a duty. Leiris, among others, set about the task enthusiastically and made a most admirable job of it. I can see him now, bumping down the staircase at Taverny on his bottom, a hilarious expression on his face as he bounced from step to step, yet never losing his somewhat formally dignified appearance. Each of us turned himself, more or less deliberately, into some sort of clown for the others' benefit, and there was no shortage of special attractions: we constituted a sort of carnival, with its mountebanks, its confidence-men, its clowns, and its parades. Dora Marr used to mime a bullfighting act; Sartre conducted an orchestra from the bottom of a cupboard; Limbour carved up a ham as though he were a cannibal; Queneau and Bataille fought a duel with bottles instead of swords; Camus and Lemarchand played military marches on saucepan lids, while those who knew how to sing, sang. So did those who didn't. We had pantomimes, comedies, diatribes, parodies, monologues, and confessions: the flow of improvisations never dried up, and they were always greeted with enthusiastic applause. We put on records and danced; some of us, such as Olga, Wanda, and Camus, very well; others less expertly. Filled with the joy of living, I regained my old conviction that life both can and ought to be a real pleasure. This belief would last into the quiet dawn hours; then it would fade (though it never completely died), and the waiting began again.

We went to La Pouèze for Easter. During our absence Paris was bombed almost every night, and the noise was so appalling (Bost wrote) that he had daydreams about being all alone on a desert island; he found it very hard to sit still with his arms folded and wait for the ceiling to cave in on his head. He lived only a hundred yards away from the Gare Montparnasse, and the R.A.F. was systematically battering away at all the train stations. The rail service had been so effectively disorganized that Bost had taken three hours to get to Taverny, instead of the usual twenty minutes. To begin with, two trains had gone through so crammed that he couldn't even hang on outside, let alone get into a compartment. The one he finally caught took a weird, roundabout route, zigzagging through the outer suburbs and stopping every mile or so. When we got back we found the Gare du Nord, the Gare de Lyon, and the Gare de l'Est closed. To get to Lyon you took a train from Juvisy, and if you wanted Bordeaux you left from Denfert-Rochereau. One night there was such a violent explosion I thought the heavens had fallen: the walls of the hotel shook, and I began to tremble myself when Sartre came and dragged me out onto the hotel terrace. The horizon was glowing a fiery red, and the sky was the most fantastic sight: I was so fascinated that I forgot to be afraid. This noisy and chaotic spectacle lasted for over two hours. Next morning we learned that La Chapelle station had been knocked to bits and was surrounded by great mounds of rubble; bombs had fallen just outside the Sacré-Coeur.

Restrictions were intensified, electricity cuts became more numerous, no Métro trains ran after 10 P.M., and the number of performances in theaters and cinemas was reduced. Food became almost unobtainable. Luckily Zette put me onto a source of supply: the gatekeeper of the Saint-Gobain works at Neuilly-sous-Clermont also sold meat, and Bost and I made several profitable trips out there. We took a train as far as Chantilly, with our bicycles stowed aboard, and then had a thirteen-mile ride. We would go and make our purchases at the works, and have a drink in the village inn. Close by there was a vast open square, deconsecrated now, from which the stony rubble that was once Beauvais Cathedral had recently been cleared. Its present function was as a mushroom bed, and we took a few pounds of mushrooms home with us after each visit. We often heard explosions as we rode along, and the crackle of antiaircraft fire. One afternoon—despite the fact that the station and its immediate surroundings had already been pounded flat—the alert sounded as we were cycling through the ruined town of Creil. Despite the heat, I pedaled across the railroad bridge at breakneck speed: the silence and solitude of the place was terrifying. Out in the country the peaceful atmosphere of fields and meadows was still infected with a strange secret poison. Strips of glittering tinfoil lay thickly strewn about the road; I never found out where they came from, but there was a deadly glint about them. However I was in a triumphant mood when I got back home and unwrapped my pieces of fresh beef.

On walls all over Paris the drawing of a snail appeared, done in English and American national colors, crawling up the Italian coast line. A few days later we learned that the Allies were now advancing on Rome at breakneck speed, and the press did not conceal the fact that landings were liable to take place at any moment. The atmosphere in the Flore began to change. Francis Vintenon told me confidentially that he had recently thrown himself into Resistance work "up to his neck." Laval's pseudo secretary disappeared, and so did Zizi Dugommier. The faces of the two staff writers on *Pilori* and *La Gerbe* grew longer and longer: the day that Pucheu's execution was announced in the morning papers they seemed too exhausted to speak aloud, and merely nodded to one another in greeting. Finally one of them got a couple of words out. "That's the end of us," he said. "Yes," the other replied, and they both sat staring into space. The collaborator on *Pilori* was hanged during the Liberation; I don't know what became of his colleague.

Then, suddenly, the sky above our heads turned black: Bourla was arrested. Lise couldn't sleep because of the bombardments, and never managed to get enough to eat; so she went off to La Pouèze, while Bourla went on living in the same room. On just one occasion, however, he spent the night with his father. At five o'clock in the morning the Germans rang the bell, and carted both of them off to Drancy. Monsieur Bourla was living with a blonde Aryan girl at the time, and she was not interfered with. Bourla kissed her before he left, saying he wouldn't die because he didn't want to die. The girl at once got in touch with a German called Felix (who her go-between was I don't know), and Felix promised to save both father and son for a consideration—say three or four million francs. He bribed a prison guard, and Lise, who had returned to Paris in a state of desperate anxiety, was given a message from Bourla, a few words scribbled on little scraps of paper. They had been rather roughly handled, he said, but they were keeping their spirits up; they trusted Felix to see them through. It looked as though their trust was justified. One morning Felix told the blonde girl that all the internees at Drancy had been deported to Germany, but that he had nevertheless managed to arrange for his two protégés to be left behind.

That afternoon I went to Drancy with Lise. It was spring, and all the flowers were out. In a café near the station we were told that a number of sealed trains had left during the night, and the guard towers were deserted. We walked up to the barbed wire, and saw rows of mattresses being aired on window sills. No sign of anyone in the rooms. We had brought our field glasses with us, and made out two distant figures gesturing toward us. Bourla pulled off his beret and waved it excitedly, revealing a close-shaven scalp in the process. Yes, Felix had been as good as his word. Two days later he informed the blonde girl that Bourla and his father had been transferred to a camp for American prisoners of war. He would soon have them out of there, he said. They were getting good food and spending their time sun-bathing, but they did need some clean linen. Lise and the blonde girl packed a case for them. Lise never actually met Felix herself; all she knew about him was what the blonde girl told her. (She was infatuated with Felix, and used to knit him sweaters.) Lise demanded that Felix get a message through to her from Bourla, but he never brought one. She persisted; she asked for a certain ring that she had given Bourla, and which he always carried about with him. No ring appeared, either. She began to get scared, wondering just what this silence meant. She asked for the exact whereabouts of the POW camp. The question appeared to embarrass the blonde girl. Was she Felix's dupe, or his accomplice? Or was she just trying to spare Lise for as long as possible? At any rate, it took days of persistent nagging to extract the German's answer to this question from her: "They were both killed some time ago."

I was shattered, both by Lise's grief and on my own account. There had been plenty of other deaths to sicken me, but this one touched me intimately. Bourla had been a close neighbor of mine, and I had taken him to my heart: besides, he was only nineteen. Sartre did his honest best to convince me that in a sense *every* life is complete at its end, and that death at nineteen is fundamentally no more absurd than death at eighty; but I did not believe him. How many places and people that boy might have seen and loved, which now he would never know! Every morning, simply by opening my eyes, I robbed him of the world. But the most awful thing was that I did not rob a *person*; there was no one to say, "The world has been snatched from me." No one. Nor was this emptiness anywhere given embodiment: there was no grave, no body, not even so much as a bone. It was as though nothing had happened, absolutely nothing. A note of his was found, scribbled on a scrap of paper: "I am not dead. We are only separated." It was a voice from another age. Now there was no one there to say, "We are separated." This nothingness terrified me. Then I returned to earth, but the sun scorched me. Why had things turned out this way? Why had he stayed with his father on that night of all nights? Why had his father been convinced he ran no danger? Why had we believed him? Were not Felix and the blonde girl, with her talk of a three-million ransom, responsible for his death? After all, he might perhaps have survived his deportation. These were useless questions, but they still tormented me. There was one other that I asked myself, in a scared sort of way. He had said, "I won't die because I don't want to die." He had not gone to his death willingly; it had come to him, without his consent. Had he stood for an instant and seen his end, looked death in the face? And who had been the first to go, he or his father? If he was conscious, I felt certain, he must have cried *No!*, aloud or in his heart, a last frantic, terrible spasm that was all for nothing—and remained thus, rooted in eternity. He had cried *No!*, and then there had been—nothing. I found the very thought unbearable; but I had to bear it.

Of all the periods in my life, I find it hardest to recollect just how things looked to me during this particular phase. The four previous years had been a tightrope walked between fear and hope, patience and anger, desolation and moments of returning joy. Now, abruptly, this precarious emotional equilibrium had been destroyed, and I was torn asunder. For a few months I had felt myself reviving, with a new lease on life hung dazzlingly before me. But now Bourla was gone. Never before had I been brought up against the ghastly uncertainty of our mortal state in so irrefutable a way. There are some people—more sensible, perhaps, or less involved—who do not find such contrasts surprising, who can absorb them into that vague twilight (barely modified, now and again, by a few faint glimmers of light, the occasional touch of shadow) which permeates all their days. I, on the other hand, had always striven fiercely to keep darkness and light apart. Night's black terrors I would embrace for brief instants only, moments of convulsive agony and tears; this was the price I must pay to save myself from skies that were too perfect, too clear, their pellucid surface flawless and unbroken. After a few days of unalloyed grief, my desolation over Bourla's loss fell into this pattern. Because of his death and all it signified, my moments of agony and despair reached an intensity I had never hitherto known, which could only be described as hellish. But no sooner had I shaken off this mood than I was caught up by glorious visions of the future and by all the diverse elements that went into the fabric of my daily happiness.

For some months we had been hearing about an unknown poet whom Cocteau had discovered in prison, and whom he maintained to be the greatest writer of his age. At any rate, this was how he had described him in July, 1943, when composing a letter to the presiding magistrate of the police court in the 19th *arrondissement,* before whom the poet, one Jean Genet, was up for sentence, with nine previous convictions against him for theft already. Barbezat intended to publish some of his poems and an extract from a prose work in *L'Arbalète,* and his wife Olga—brunette Olga, that is—occasionally went to see him in prison. It was from her that I had learned of his existence, and discovered one or two facts concerning his life. He had been placed with foster parents, a peasant family, soon after birth. The larger part of his childhood he had spent in reformatories. His career as burglar and pickpocket had taken him all around the world, and he was, on top of all this, a homosexual. He had taken up reading in prison; this had led to his writing poems and, subsequently, a book. Olga Barbezat was ecstatic about his talent, but I was less impressed than I might have been in my youth. The gutter-Bohemian of genius seemed to me a somewhat stereotyped figure; and knowing Cocteau's taste for the offbeat, not to mention his passion for discovering people, I fancied he might be over-boosting his protégé's claims. But when the first section of *Notre-Dame des fleurs* appeared in *L'Arbalète,* we were very much impressed. Genet had obviously been influenced by Proust and Cocteau and Jouhandeau, but he nevertheless possessed a voice of his own, a quite inimitable style of utterance. It was a most uncommon occurrence nowadays for us to read anything that renewed our faith in literature: these pages revealed the power of words to us as though for the first time. Cocteau had read the situation aright: a great writer *had* appeared.

We were told he was now out of prison; and one afternoon in May, when I was at the Flore with Sartre and Camus, he came over to our table. "You Sartre?" he inquired brusquely. With his close-cropped hair and thin, tight lips and suspicious, rather aggressive expression, he struck us as a pretty hard case. He sat down, but stayed only a moment. But he came back on other occasions, and we saw a good deal of each other.

Hard he certainly was; an outcast from the day he was born, he had no reason to respect the society that had rejected him. But his eyes could still smile, and a child's astonishment lingered about his lips. Conversation with him was easy: he was a good listener, and quick to respond. One would never have guessed he was a self-taught person: he had the boldness of judgment, the sweeping prejudices, the un-self-conscious attitude characteristic of those who take a cultured background completely for granted. He also possessed remarkable powers of discernment. His whole demeanor reminded one irresistibly of the Poet with a Mission; he affected to despise the elegant luxury of salon society, and castigated it for its snobbishness. But he did not keep up this pose for long; he was far too passionate and inquiring a person. His range of interests, nevertheless, was strictly circumscribed: he detested anecdotes and had no time for the merely picturesque. One evening we went up to the penthouse terrace of my hotel, and I showed him the view over the neighboring rooftops. "What the hell am I supposed to make of *that*?" he asked me testily, and went on to remark that he was far too busy with his own reactions to waste time on mere external spectacle.

In actual fact he was an excellent observer when he chose; if an object or person or event had some positive meaning for him, he would find the most appropriate and direct language in which to describe it. On the other hand, he was not uncritically receptive. There were certain truths he was after, and he would seek, even in the oddest byways, for any key that might unlock them. He conducted this quest in a spirit of sectarian fervor, yet also brought to it one of the keenest intelligences I have ever known. The paradoxical quality about him during this period was that though he ran to certain set attitudes, which camouflaged his true nature, he remained nevertheless wholly attached to freedom. The whole basis of his fellow feeling for Sartre was this idea of liberty they shared, which nothing could suppress, and their common abhorrence of all that stood in its way: nobility of soul, spiritual values, universal justice, and other such lofty words and principles, together with established institutions or ideals. In conversation, as in his writings, he was deliberately offhand, and asserted that he would never hesitate to rob or betray a friend; yet I never heard him speak ill of anyone, and he would not permit attacks on Cocteau in his presence. We took his personal behavior more seriously than his declarations of aggressiveness, and became very attached to him from the first moment of our acquaintanceship.

About the time we got to know Genet we conceived the idea of throwing another fiesta, to which I would have willingly invited him; but Sartre objected on the grounds that Genet wouldn't care for such an occasion. There was some truth in this. It suited middle-class people, solidly established in the world, to lose themselves for a few hours in a noisy alcoholic haze; Genet, on the other hand, had no taste for such dissipations. He had started off lost, and now preferred to feel solid earth beneath his feet.

Camille had lent us the vast apartment she now shared with Dullin on the Rue de La Tour-d'Auvergne (it was supposed to have once belonged to

Juliette Drouet) and we invited our friends there for the night of June 5. Zina answered the door when we arrived; there were masses of flowers and ribbons and garlands and various delightful knickknacks hung up all over the hall, the dining room, and the vast circular drawing room, which opened onto an old garden. All the same, Zina seemed upset, and there was a distinct smell of wine on her breath. "*She* is in a bad state!" she told us. It seemed that Camille had begun her preparations bright and early, and had worked like a galley slave; but in order to keep her spirits up she had consumed so much red wine that she'd been forced to retire to bed. Zina obviously hadn't left her to drink on her own, but she at least could still stand up. Dullin welcomed us in his usual generous fashion, though this invasion obviously scared him a little. Besides the usual crowd, Armande and Lucienne Salacrou turned up, and also a friend of Bost's named Robert Scipion, who had written a very amusing parody of *Nausea*. Camus brought along Maria Casarès, who was rehearsing *Le Malentendu* at the Théâtre des Mathurins: she wore a Rochas dress with violet and mauve stripes, and had combed her black hair straight back. She laughed frequently and rather stridently, revealing fine white teeth: she was a very attractive woman. Camille and Dullin had invited one or two student guests of their own from the Ecole, as well as an old friend named Morvan Lebesque. These ingredients didn't mix too well, and Camille's absence created a somewhat constrained atmosphere, so that at first the evening was not as lively as it might have been. Dullin recited some of Villon's poems, very well indeed; but even he couldn't warm up that atmosphere. Jeanine Queneau's reaction to this embarrassing situation was to play the *enfant terrible*: at the conclusion of one ballade she barked like a dog. In order to cover up this little jape, Olga, without turning a hair, gave Camille's bitch an admonitory tap. We put on records and started dancing, the drink flowed, and very soon we were milling around in our usual way. Scipion, who was still unused to liquor, lay down on the floor after a few glassfuls and fell fast asleep with his fists clenched. About three in the morning Camille appeared, smothered with scarfs and jewelry, rouge on her eyelids and blue mascara smeared over her cheeks; she flung herself at Zette Leiris's feet and implored forgiveness, after which she danced a rather tottery *paso doble* with Camus. We caught the first Métro train in the morning, and Olga and Bost came with us as far as Montparnasse. In the faint dawn light the Place de Rennes was quite deserted, and there were notices on the station wall announcing the suspension of all train departures till further notice. What was going on? Sartre and I walked down as far as the Rue de Seine, too sleepy to think, but with a queer feeling of anxiety niggling at us. I slept for four or five hours, and when I awoke it was to the sound of a radio announcer's voice blaring long-awaited yet unbelievable words through my window. I jumped out of bed. Anglo-American forces had landed in Normandy. All Camille's fellow tenants were convinced we'd had secret advance information and were celebrating the event the night before.

The days that followed seemed like one long holiday. People were happy and laughing, the sun shone, the streets had never looked gayer. Since women had taken to bicycles there had been a fashion for brightly colored skirts, and this year they had made them by sewing various squares of material together. Elegant people used high-quality silks, but in Saint-Germain-des-Prés most girls made do with cottons. Lise got hold of some very pretty ones, with a red background, which were quite inexpensive. Lola had recently been released from custody, as had Olga Barbezat; she often went up to sun-bathe on the hotel roof-terrace, together with Lise and other residents. I couldn't bear to lie and swelter on that hard cement surface, but I enjoyed sitting there in the evening, high above the roofs, to read or talk. I would drink ersatz "Turin gin" outside the Flore with Sartre and our various friends, or stroll along to the Rhumerie Martiniquaise, where we got equally ersatz rum punch. But we were building our future, and blissfully happy.

On the evening of June 10 *No Exit* came before the critics and the public. When Olga Barbezat was arrested Sartre abandoned the whole idea of putting the play on tour: there were numerous snags about this anyway. Badel, the manager of the Vieux-Colombier, became interested; but at this point Camus, feeling that he was not qualified to direct professional actors or, indeed, to put on a play in a Paris theater, wrote a charming little note to Sartre releasing him from their prior agreement. Badel entrusted the production to Rouleau, and engaged well-known actors such as his wife, Gaby Sylvia, Balachova, and Vitold. Of the original cast only Chauffard kept his old part. The first night was a great success; the line "We have unlimited electricity" brought the house down—something which Sartre had not anticipated. He watched the performance from the wings, but mingled with the spectators afterward. As he was walking across the foyer a stranger came up and asked for a private word with him. He said he had it from an unimpeachable source that the Germans intended to arrest Sartre and have him shot. "When they level their rifles," he hissed, "think of me!" He advised Sartre to go into hiding, but meanwhile arranged to meet him at noon the following day outside the church of Saint-Germain-les-Prés: as the twelfth stroke sounded, all the passers-by would embrace each other, the bells would peal out, and universal peace descend upon the earth. Sartre, much relieved, went home to his own bed and slept soundly, but out of politeness he went along to the Place Saint-Germain-des-Prés at the appointed time. The stranger met him, smiling. "Five minutes to go!" he said, eyeing the clock complacently. Midday struck, first from one clock, then from another. The man waited a second or two, looking rather disconcerted. Then, apologetically, he explained that he must have gotten the day wrong.

No Exit was followed, on the same bill, by a Toulet comedy, such insipid stuff that the audience began to leave during the intermission; Badel decided to reverse the order and put the comedy on as a curtain raiser—but didn't change the programs or posters. One evening, as Sartre was strolling down the Rue du Vieux-Colombier, he met some of the audience pacing to and fro outside the theater. The curtain had gone up fifteen minutes earlier, but now there had been an electricity failure. Sartre spotted Claude Morgan, who shook his hand in a rather embarrassed way, and said, "Frankly, I just don't understand it—after *The Flies,* too! Why on earth did you write *this?*" He thought Sartre was responsible for the Toulet masquerade: he had only watched the beginning of it, and was still somewhat in a daze.

A few days after *No Exit* opened, Jean Vilar, who had been organizing a series of lectures, asked Sartre to give one on the theater. The meeting took place in a hall overlooking the Seine, and was well attended. Barrault and Camus both raised points with Sartre afterward, and so did Cocteau— this was the first time I had seen him at close quarters. When the meeting broke up, a large number of ladies asked Sartre for his autograph: I spotted Marie Le Hardouin, and Marie-Laure de Noailles, who was wearing a delicious little straw sailor hat. Cocteau had not yet seen *No Exit*; he went to it later with Genet and discussed the production with him in most warmly enthusiastic terms. Generosity of this sort is common enough among writers, but I have seldom observed it in playwrights. Genet arranged for Sartre to meet Cocteau one evening at the bar of the Hôtel Saint-Yves, on the Rue Jacob, which was then a popular rendezvous for certain types of persons. Cocteau's work and legendary personality had exercised a great attraction over me when I was young, and I accompanied Sartre to the meeting. Cocteau looked just like the pictures of him, and his torrential flow of conversation made me dizzy. Like Picasso, he dominated the conversation, but in his case words were his chosen medium, and he used them with acrobatic dexterity. Fascinated, I followed the movements of his lips and hands. Once or twice I thought he was going to trip up; then—hoopla!—he recovered himself, the knot was neatly tied, and he would be off again, tracing a new series of complex and hypnotic arabesques in mid-air. He expressed his admiration for *No Exit* in several most gracefully turned compliments, and then began to recall his own early days in the theater, and especially the production of *Orpheus*. It was at once apparent that he was absolutely absorbed in himself, but this narcissistic streak neither constricted his vision nor in any way cut him off from contact with other people: the interest he had shown in Sartre and the way he talked about Genet both offered ample proof of this. When the bar closed we walked down the Rue Bonaparte till we reached the *quais*. We were standing on a bridge, watching the Seine rippling beneath us like black watered silk, when the alert sounded. Pencil-thin searchlight beams swept the sky, and flares exploded. By now we had become used to these noisy apocalyptic displays, but tonight's seemed an especially fine one; and what good luck to find ourselves stranded near this deserted river, alone with Cocteau! When the antiaircraft fire died away, all was silent except for our footsteps—and the sound of his voice. He was saying that the Poet should hold aloof from his age, and remain indifferent to the follies of war and politics. "They just get in our way," he went on, "—the Germans, the Americans, the whole lot of them—just get in our way." We didn't agree with this at all, but we still felt most amiably disposed toward him; and his unwonted presence here, in the darkness that was crisscrossed now with rays of fresh hope, we found strangely appealing.

Every morning the B.B.C. bulletins and newspaper headlines keyed up our expectations still higher. The Allied armies were approaching. Hamburg had been destroyed by phosphorus bombs; waves of "outrages" and sabotage broke out all over the Paris area. On the morning of June 28 Philippe Henriot was killed. Meanwhile the Germans, terrified at the prospect of their imminent defeat, revenged themselves on the civilian population. A letter was circulated from hand to hand containing an account of the tragedy at Oradour-sur-Glane: on June 10 thirteen hundred persons, mostly women and children, had been burned alive, either in their homes or in the church where they had fled for refuge. At Tulle, the S.S. had hanged eighty-five "refractory elements" from the balconies along the main street. In the Midi people had seen children dangling from butcher hooks, which were thrust through their throats. Another member of our circle was arrested. One afternoon we went to Desnos's apartment and Yuki told us that Desnos had been arrested by the Gestapo two days previously. Some friends of his had telephoned him in the small hours to warn him; but instead of bolting instantly, in his pajamas, he had started to get dressed. He hadn't even put his shoes on when the ring at the door came.

Vague fears began to insinuate themselves into our hopes. There had been talk for some time now of the secret weapons Hitler was preparing, and at the end of June the first rockets fell on London. They dropped at random, without any warning of their arrival; at any moment you could imagine that some dearly loved friend had just been killed. This vague, omnipresent insecurity seemed to me the worst possible sort of ordeal, and I dreaded the thought that I might one day be called upon to face it myself.

But for the present we remained in ignorance of this. We went for walks and had drinks together and discussed things. We attended the Concerts de la Pléiade, under the patronage of Gaston Gallimard; we read the volume of critical essays that Blanchot had just published, under the title of *Faux Pas,* and quoted bits of Queneau's *Ziaux* to each other:

> We lizards love the Muses,
> And the Muses love the Arts.

Early in July we went to the opening of Camus's play *Le Malentendu* (*Cross Purpose*). We had read the script some months earlier, and had told him that we much preferred *Caligula*; so we were not surprised to find that, despite a fine performance by Casarès, the play didn't really come across in the theater. In our opinion this was not a serious setback, and our friendly feelings for Camus were not in the least disturbed by it. What *did* infuriate us was the self-evident satisfaction of the critics, who emphasized every weak line by sneering laughter: they knew only too well what side Camus was on. Yet we laughed too, during the intermission, as we watched them strolling up and down the street with such ostentatious un-self-consciousness. They were talking volubly, and Alain Laubreaux was waving his hands about a great deal. "They know," we told each other. Almost certainly this was the last opening they would ever attend as reviewers. Any day now they would be thrown out—from their papers, from France, and from the future. And they knew it. Yet they had not modified their arrogance one jot. When we heard their acid remarks, and saw the falsely triumphant expressions on their faces, our motives for willing their downfall (the bitter pill which they had already swallowed in secret) became only too apparent. Thanks to this odd combination of circumstances, I discovered that hatred can at times be a positively joyous emotion.

I had been working hard all that year. My new novel was begun in September; but I will discuss this elsewhere, since it took a very long time to write. In July I finished a play. It had been begun three months earlier, and the title I gave it was *Les Bouches inutiles* (Useless Mouths).

Ever since I had attended the rehearsals of *The Flies* I had been thinking of writing a play. I had been told that the best thing in *She Came to Stay* was the dialogue. I knew that stage dialogue was something quite different from novel dialogue, but this simply sharpened my desire to try my hand at it. To my mind it ought to be as bare as possible: the speeches in *The Flies* seemed overprolix to me, and I much preferred the dry, pregnant dialogue of *No Exit*.

But first I had to find a subject; I have already mentioned one of the possibilities which I turned over in my mind and then discarded. Over the Easter vacation at La Pouèze I read some of Sismondi's chronicles of Italy: Sartre had got all twelve volumes of him out of the library for me, since I had a notion to make the hero of my novel rule over one of these city-states as a young man. One point which emerged from several of these accounts impressed itself on me especially. During a siege, in order to stave off famine, the actual combatants used to get rid of all "useless mouths" —women, children, old people. I told myself I would use such an incident in my novel (in fact I did so), and then, suddenly, I paused: it occurred to me that I had stumbled on an eminently dramatic theme. I remained quite still for a moment or two, staring at nothing, while a wave of intense excitement surged through me. There was an interval, often quite a long one, between the decision's being taken and its actual execution. What must have been the feelings of the chosen victims during this period—and of the fathers, brothers, lovers, husbands, or sons who had condemned them? The dead, in the normal course of events, remain dumb. But if they still had a mouth, and could speak forth, how could those that survived them endure their despair and their fury? This was what I wanted to show in the first place: the transformation of loved ones into souls awaiting execution, the relationship of flesh-and-blood men to these angry ghosts.

But my original purpose changed somewhat. If my characters were merely to suffer their appointed fate, I reflected, I could hardly extract much in the way of action from their lamentations. It was essential that their fate should still lie in their own hands, so I chose as my main characters the town's most respected magistrate and his wife. I also wanted their dramatic dilemma to have a more basically interesting background than the transition from one tyranny to another, so I shifted the setting to Flanders, where similar incidents had, in fact, taken place. A city that had just overthrown a democratic regime found itself threatened by a despot. Then the question of means versus ends was to arise: has one the right to sacrifice individuals for the general future good? Partly to satisfy the needs of the plot, and partly through what was, at the time, my natural inclination, I slipped into a moralizing role.

I made the same mistake as in *The Blood of Others* (from which I also borrowed numerous leitmotivs): my characters became reduced to mere ethical viewpoints. The leading male character, Jean-Pierre, is another version of Jean Blomart: since he cannot formulate a code of conduct which does justice to all men, he opts for abstention. "How can you measure the weight of a tear against the weight of a drop of blood?" he asks.* Then he comes to see that his withdrawal makes him an accessory to crimes committed without his participation, and, like Blomart, he plunges into action. Clarice, like Hélène—though she also shares some of Xavière's characteristics—passes from obstinate individualism to a more generous position. The principle of evil [le Mal] is personified in her brother, the Fascist Georges, and in the ambitious François Rosbourg: by their underhanded scheming they demonstrate that oppression is not something one *chooses* to take part in: from the moment it creeps into any society it rots it throughout. The means are inseparable from the envisaged end, and if the two come into conflict, it is the end which is perverted. By adopting dictatorial methods to preserve their liberty, the citizens of Vauxelles plunged their own town into a reign of tyranny. Finally, however, they became aware of this, and asserted the kinship of combatants and "useless mouths": all of them then made a sortie against the besiegers, the outcome of which I left in the air. (The heroine's question, "Why should we choose peace?" reflects—as does the end of *The Blood of Others*—the moral implicit in Kierkegaard's *Fear and Trembling*.)

My condemnation of this play is not without certain reservations. In the first half especially, the dialogue has a certain power, and some passages produce a fine effect of dramatic suspense. It was daring of me to try and put an entire town on the stage; but this audacity can be defended on the grounds that at the time we were, quite fortuitously, living at the height of a critical period of history. As for the denouement, it is no worse and no better than any other. My mistake was to pose a political problem in terms of abstract morality. The idealism which permeates *Les Bouches inutiles* I find

* I note that ten years later I put this remark almost word for word into the mouth of Anne Dubreuilh, the heroine of *The Mandarins*. But there is one great difference. Anne's attitude, which is closely bound up with her character as a whole, represents neither "truth" nor "error." It is set in contrast to that of Dubreuilh and Henri Perron, and the novel shows no preference for one view rather than the other. But in Jean-Pierre's case, as in Blomart's, abstention per se forms one stage in a process of moral evolution, and they both finally outgrow it. This leads to a simple, unambiguous, and morally edifying conclusion; whereas in *The Mandarins* no firm decision is made, we are not told who is right and who is wrong, and the condition of ambiguity is preserved.

embarrassing, and I deplore my tendency to didacticism. It is a work in the same vein as *The Blood of Others* and *Pyrrhus et Cinéas,* but the faults they share are less tolerable on the stage than in any other medium.

Sartre, besides belonging to the C.N.E. and C.N.Th., had connections, through Camus, with the Combat movement. About mid-July one member of the network was arrested, and managed to get word out that he had confessed certain names to the authorities. Camus advised us to move, and the Leirises offered us hospitality. It was enchanting to stay with friends in Paris, as though we were up from the country; we spent several days there, in a big, brightly lit room, and Leiris made me read the works of Raymond Roussel. Then we made our way, by train and bicycle, to Neuilly-sous-Clermont, where we took rooms in the village *auberge-épicerie.* It would be easy enough to get back from here when events started moving. We stayed there for about three weeks. We had lunch and dinner and did all our work in the main public bar, with the locals playing cards and billiards all around us. Rows were not uncommon. In the afternoons we would trudge up country lanes where larkspur was in bloom along the hedgerows, and climb hillsides over which ripe corn rippled in the wind. I often used to write out of doors, sitting under a tree. R.A.F. planes came over and strafed German convoys on the road; more than once I heard the sound of machine-gun fire quite close to me. About ten o'clock at night Vi's would go grunting overhead, and we would see a flicker of red flame in the sky. Every time I wondered whether they would drop on London, and if anyone would be killed.

Zette and Michel Leiris came out and spent an afternoon with us, and we also had a visit from Olga and Bost. They told us the news that didn't get into the papers—among other things, the German attack on the Vercors Maquis. Whole villages had been burned to the ground, and hundreds of peasants and Maquisards slaughtered. Among the victims was Jean Prévost. We also found out that Cuzin had been executed in Marseille. The local militia had laid an ambush for the Oraison Maquisards; Cuzin got wind of it and tried to warn his comrades, but fell into the hands of the militiamen, who turned him over to the Germans.

On August 11 the papers and radio announced that the Americans were on the outskirts of Chartres. We hastily packed up and mounted our bicycles. The main road, we were told, was out of the question: German troops were retreating along it, constantly harried by low-level R.A.F. attacks. So we took a side road, which brought us out at Chantilly by way of Beaumont. Despite the blazing sun we pedaled along feverishly, gripped by the sudden fear of finding ourselves cut off from Paris: we had no wish to miss the actual Liberation. A few trains were still running from Chantilly to Paris; we stowed our bicycles in the baggage car and chose a compartment about halfway back. The train traveled a few miles, passed through a small station, and then came to a halt. There was the roar of a plane overhead, and the stutter of machine-gun bullets: I flung myself on the floor, yet felt no emotion of any sort—the incident seemed quite unreal to me. Then the shooting stopped, the plane vanished in the distance, and all the passengers got out and ran for the nearest ditch. We followed them. Ambulance attendants were already on the scene. They rushed into the front compartments, and emerged carrying the wounded—perhaps the dead, too—on improvised stretchers made from the wooden benches they found inside. One woman had lost a leg. Now that it was all over I suddenly felt afraid. People were grumbling: "Why are they shooting up Frenchmen?" They were aiming at the engine," someone explained. "They weren't interested in what it had behind it." The objections died away. We knew how efficiently these British pilots had gone about the task of paralyzing rail communications in the Paris area, and were only too anxious to find an excuse for them. Then the driver blew his whistle, and we were off again. Several passengers refused to board the train again, but Sartre and I carried on, albeit somewhat apprehensively. Throughout the remainder of the trip nobody smiled or uttered a word. In the afternoon heat the brown-paper parcels in the luggage racks began to give off a sweetish smell which I knew only too well. In my mind's eye I once again saw those blood-splashed bodies, and felt I would never be able to eat meat again.

As a safety precaution we did not go back to the Louisiane but checked in at the Hôtel Welcome about ten yards down the street, at the corner of the Rue de Seine and the Boulevard Saint-Germain. There was a storm brewing. We had a drink with Camus outside the Flore. He told us that all the Resistance leaders were in agreement on one point: Paris should liberate itself. What form would this uprising take? How long would it last? No one was sure; but it would certainly cost lives. Already there was an unusual atmosphere about the place. The Métro was closed down altogether, and the only means of transport was by bicycle. The electricity had been cut off, and candles were unobtainable; brown tallow dips provided such light as there was. Food could not be had at all, and we were forced to fall back on our provisions—a few pounds of potatoes and some packets of pasta. Every policeman suddenly vanished from the streets, presumably into hiding. On August 16 the gas was cut off. At dinner time we went around to the Hôtel Chaplain, where Bost had rigged up a sort of stove, fueled with old newspapers: but to cook so much as a handful of noodles on this contraption was a major undertaking. These deprivations were so complete that they gave the final conflict a tangible reality for us. Tomorrow or the next day there would be an explosion. But this feeling of certainty was tempered with nervous forebodings. How would the Germans react to the situation? Shooting had been heard inside the prisons, and from around the Gare de l'Est and the ancient fortifications. They were still arresting and deporting people. There was one possible danger that threatened us all. When they withdrew from Paris, they might blow the whole city sky-high. Well-informed characters were saying that underground mines had been laid right round the area surrounding the Sénat:

which meant that we were liable to be blown up ourselves, either in the Rue de Seine or Montparnasse. But to brood over such an eventuality was pointless, since there was absolutely nothing to be done about it.

On the afternoon of August 18 I saw trucks crammed with troops and packing cases moving along the Boulevard Saint-Michel, making for the North. Everyone stopped to watch them. "They're pulling out!" people whispered. Leclerc's army was almost at the gates of Paris. Perhaps the Germans were going to evacuate the city without a shot being fired; the rumor went around that they had emptied their desks and burned their archives. As I fell asleep that night I thought: Perhaps this time tomorrow it will all be over.

When I woke up I leaned out of my window. The swastika was still flying over the Sénat; housewives were shopping as usual in the Rue de Seine, and a long queue had formed outside the baker's shop. Two cyclists rode past shouting, "The Préfecture's fallen!" At the same moment a German detachment emerged from the Sénat and marched off toward the Boulevard Saint-Germain. Before turning the corner of the street the soldiers let loose a volley of machine-gun fire. Passers-by on the Boulevard scattered, taking cover as best they could in doorways. But every door was shut; one man crumpled and fell in the very act of knocking, fists drumming at the panels, while others collapsed along the sidewalk.

Then the Germans marched off down the Boulevard, while stretcher bearers, who had popped up from heaven knows where, proceeded to carry the wounded away. Various front doors opened again, and one concierge calmly began to scrub the red stain on the step outside, incurring some rude comments in the process. The Boulevard took on its normal appearance once more, even down to the old women gossiping on the benches. I walked away from the window. Sartre went off for a C.N.Th. meeting at the Comédie-Française, and I walked around to the Leirises'. From their window I could see the French flag flying over the Préfecture. The uprising had been launched that morning. The City Hall, the Gare de Lyon, several police stations, and the majority of the city's public buildings were now in the hands of the Parisians. A detachment of the F.F.I., Forces Françaises de l'Intérieur, had jumped out of a truck on the Pont Neuf and fired on a German convoy. Numerous German vehicles had been set on fire. The phone kept ringing all day, and a constant stream of friends kept coming and going, bringing the latest news. Some said that negotiations were going on with the Germans, and a truce would soon be declared. That evening Zette and Michel Leiris and I cycled over to the Hôtel Chaplain, where we found Sartre as well. While we were opening a can of sardines, a street vender came down the Rue Bréa, pushing a cartload of tomatoes, and everybody rushed out to buy some. Some youths rode past on bicycles calling out that the Germans had asked for a cease fire.

There was a storm during the night, and in the morning the swastika flag was still there. Sartre and I went out together: there was a feeling of nervous strain in the air. Leclerc's division was now said to be only three or four miles from Paris; tricolor flags and banners suddenly blossomed from every window. Despite this, housewives shopping in the Carrefour Buci had been shot at. The F.F.I. cordoned off a house on the Rue de Seine and overpowered a band of Japanese snipers on the roof. We spent the day wandering around the *quartier*. About four o'clock loud-speaker trucks drove down the Boulevard, with the official announcement that fighting had ceased: the Germans were being allowed to evacuate Paris, and were surrendering a number of prisoners in return. Despite this, people reported continued firing from Les Gobelins, the Place d'Italie, and other areas. As evening drew on an uneasy crowd began to wander around the Place Saint-Germain-des-Prés. An elderly, harassed-looking woman, who was pushing a bicycle, called out to us: "If there's so much as a shot fired, the Germans are going to bombard Paris—the guns are trained on the city. Pass on the news." She trudged on her way, repeating the message in an exhausted voice. Was she a Fifth Column agent or merely crazy? No one took any notice of her; yet her grim phophecy fitted in well with the day's fluctuating fortunes. A lot could yet happen.

Next day Sartre went back to the Théâtre Française, and I returned to the Leirises' apartment. Michel had joined his Resistance group at the Musée de l'Homme. I found Zette in, together with one of her friends who was cooking for F.F.I. personnel in a canteen on the Rue Saint-André-des-Arts. Fighting had broken out again. The morning scene looked peaceful enough; I could see some anglers sitting beside the Seine, and one or two youths in swimming trunks, sun-bathing. But F.F.I. men were hidden behind the balustrades along the *quais,* Zette told me, and there were more in the neighboring apartment blocks, and yet more in the Place Saint-Michel, on the steps leading down to the Métro station. A German truck passed by under the window, with two flaxen-haired young soldiers in it, sitting bolt upright, Tommy guns at the ready. Twenty yards ahead death lay in wait for them, and one instinctively wanted to shout a warning at them. A burst of fire ripped out, and they fell. F.F.I. men cycled up and down the *quais* asking invisible combatants if they had enough ammunition. Then we saw another column of German trucks and armored cars approaching. Zette's girl friend left and returned. She told us that the insurgents now held Les Halles, the Gare de l'Est, and the Central Telephone Exchange. They had also taken over the printing presses and editorial offices abandoned by the collaborationist newspapermen, and *Combat* and *Libération* were on sale in the streets. She also told us something more alarming. German tanks were said to be on the way, and about to shell the buildings along the *quai*. But Zete was not disturbed by this report, and in any event nothing of the sort happened. Late that afternoon I left the apartment. I had decided to move into the Hôtel Chaplain for the time being, since the Rue de Seine was now decidedly unhealthy: every time a column of armored cars left the Sénat, they gave it a peppering. Despite this, I wanted to go by there first to pick up some of my belongings and a few potatoes. It was a lengthy expedition. There were pools of blood at the corner of the Rue Saint-André-des-Arts, and bullets were flying everywhere. F.F.I. patrols were handling the passers-by like traffic policemen:

"Stop!" they would yell, and then "Go"—at which one scurried across the street.

The following day Sartre had an appointment to meet Camus, who had installed himself in the offices of *Paris-Soir,* on the Rue Réaumur: he was now editing *Combat.* We walked down toward the river soon after midday. Children were playing hopscotch in the back streets, and their elders were lounging about in a carefree way; but when we emerged on the *quai* we froze in our tracks. The roadway and sidewalks were deserted, and bullets were whining through the air. Behind us lay a peaceful summer afternoon, but in front was a no man's land, from which all living creatures had fled. We ran across it at top speed, and those who crossed the bridge bent double, so as to have the protection of the parapet. There wasn't a soul in sight along the *quai* on the Right Bank; but further on, the whole *quartier* was steeped in peace, and the Liberation an accomplished fact. We went to 100 Rue Réaumur, and rang the bell at the back entrance, which was guarded by young men carrying Tommy guns. The whole building was a hive of tremendous chaos and tremendous gaiety, from top to bottom. Camus was exultant. He asked Sartre to write a descriptive report of the Liberation period for him. After this we returned to the Left Bank. Men were busy erecting barricades in the Place Saint-Germain-des-Prés and along the Boulevard. I ran into Francis Vintenon, with a rifle slung over his shoulder and a red handkerchief knotted around his throat: he looked splendid. Liaison officers were cruising up and down the Boulevard Montparnasse on bicycles, exhorting passers-by to go and help with the barricades, and showing them where to assemble. Occasionally a tank or an armored car full of S.S. men would come down the Boulevard Raspail, interspersed with Red Cross ambulances, bearing their cargoes of wounded. Somewhere the guns were thundering. I began to get anxious once more: why were the Allied armies so long? Was there a chance that the Germans still might bombard Paris? What would it be tomorrow?

But next morning the city seemed calm enough. We went to have lunch with Armand and Lucienne Salacrou at their home on the Avenue Foch. Snipers had been firing from the roof of the building opposite, and some bullets had embedded themselves in their drawing-room wall. We had lunch in one of the rooms looking out on the courtyard. After coffee Salacrou and Sartre made their way gingerly into the drawing room in order to switch on the radio. While the B.B.C. was telling us, triumphantly, that the fighting was over and the Liberation of Paris accomplished, we could still hear shots being fired outside.

Sartre went back with Salacrou to the Comédie-Française, which was now occupied by the C.N.Th. He spent the night and all the following day there, while I was trudging hither and thither round Paris: there were always provisions to be hunted for somewhere or other, and I believe I also took the first installment of Sartre's report on the Liberation to Camus. I remember the weird, scorching silence in the streets, broken only by the sound of an occasional stray bullet, or the passage of an armored car: some were still out on patrol. One particularly stubborn sniper covered the whole of the Rue Dufour in his field of fire, and one had to run the gauntlet to cross it between bursts. I had dinner—two potatoes—that evening at the Hôtel Chaplain with Olga, Wanda, Bost, and Lise. Some cyclists going past shouted out that the Leclerc Division had just reached the Place de l'Hôtel-de-Ville. We pushed down to the Carrefour Montparnasse; people were gathering from all quarters. The guns fired, all the bells of Paris began to peal, and every house was lit up. Someone kindled a bonfire in the middle of the road; we all joined hands and danced around it, singing. Suddenly a warning voice shouted: "Tanks coming!" A German tank was, in fact, approaching from the direction of the Rue Denfert-Rochereau. Everyone hurried back home; but we stood for a while in the hotel courtyard, talking to our fellow tenants. "If they're going to blow the place up," one woman remarked, "it'll have to be tonight."

At six o'clock the following morning I ran up the Boulevard Raspail to find the Leclerc Division debouching in columns onto the Avenue d'Orléans, and a huge crowd packed along the sidewalks, cheering them. In the Rue Denfert-Rouchereau there stood a little group of orphans, prinked out with tricolor rosettes and waving little flags. The cripples from the Infirmerie Marie-Thérèse had been lined up outside in their wheel chairs. From time to time a shot would crack out from some roof-top sniper, and someone would collapse and be carried away. But no one took any notice of these little eddies in the crowd: excitement had driven out fear.

All that day Sartre and I walked the flag-draped streets of Paris. I saw women in their best clothes clinging round soldiers' necks; the tricolor shone resplendent from the summit of the Eiffel Tower. What a tumult of emotions surged through my heart! Seldom indeed does one achieve a long-awaited pleasure and find it all one could have hoped for; but such was my good fortune on this occasion. We met various acquaintances of ours who frowned and said our real troubles were only just beginning, we'd get them in every size and shape and color from now on. I was sorry for them; this feverish, buoyant excitement escaped them precisely because it had not been in their nature to desire it. We were no blinder than they; but come what might thereafter, nothing was going to take these moments from me, and nothing has ever done so: they shine out from my past with perennial and untarnished spendor.

Some of our friends, very much against their will, were kept away from these celebrations. While we were visiting with the Leirises they had a phone call from Zanie and Jean Aubier, who said they were telephoning on all fours because fighting was going on all around their house, and it was impossible to get out. Some Germans had dug themselves in behind the Luxembourg Gardens and were proving very hard to dislodge.

De Gaulle marched down the Champs Elysées the following afternoon. Sartre watched the procession from a balcony in the Hôtel de Louvre, while Olga and I and the Leirises went to the Arc de Triomphe. De Gaulle himself was on foot, surrounded by a horde of police officers, soldiers, and F.F.I. men, the latter wearing the most exotic accoutrements and marching arm-in-arm, laughing happily. We mingled with the vast crowd and joined in the cheering. It was not a military parade we acclaimed so much as a magnificent, if chaotic, popular carnival show. Then, suddenly, I heard a familar and half-expected sound: the noise of firing. The crowd around me streamed up a road that ran at right angles to the Champs Elysées, and I went with them, hanging onto Olga's arm. We turned into another street; some shots rang out, and one or two people fell flat on the asphalt. I decided that flight was preferable. All the doors were shut, but some men forced one of them open, and we plunged into the shelter thus provided: it was a sort of basement store, full of cardboard boxes and wrapping paper. We stood there and got our breath back. Gradually things quieted down again, and after a while we returned to the street. As Olga and I walked down toward the Alma we passed some ambulances and stretcher bearers carrying off the wounded. I wondered a little uneasily how the Leirises had fared, and went around to their place: they returned shortly afterward, unscathed. Sartre met us on the Quai des Grand-Augustins. He had been on a balcony with other members of the C.N.Th. When the shooting began; the F.F.I. had taken them for militiamen and started firing in their direction, upon which they had very smartly retreated inside, to the other end of the room. We had dinner with Genet, Leiris and his wife, and an American friend of theirs called Patrice Valberg. He was the first American we had spoken to, and we stared at his uniform with incredulous eyes. He told us of his entry into Dreux, and later Versailles, and how excitedly the inhabitants had welcomed them, and what his own reactions had been. We had just got up from the table when a plane roared overhead, so loud that it might have been circling at rooftop height. Then there was a loud explosion, quite close by. At that moment I really did know what fear was. One German airplane flying over Paris in the fierce frustration of defeat, loaded with bombs and hatred, was far more terrifying than an entire Allied squadron. We were on the fifth floor; I suggested we might go down to ground level. Valberg grinned at my pusillanimity; I don't know how far this went to reassure the others, but they raised no sort of protest. Most of the tenants had gathered in the courtyard. Fresh explosions came, and the windows rattled. Then the night became calm once more. We learned next day that the bombs had not fallen far away. The Halle aux Vins had gone up in flames, and an apartment house on the Rue Monge had been knocked flat.

That was the end of it. Paris was liberated now: the world and the future had been handed back to us, and we flung ourselves upon them. But first I want to try and recapitulate what I had learned during those five years.

At the beginning of the war someone at Gallimard told me, approvingly, a remark that had been made by a certain attractive young woman who was married to one of the firm's authors: "What difference does the war make?" she observed. "It does not change my attitude to a blade of grass." I found myself both fascinated and embarrassed by such serenity: it was true that blades of grass no longer mattered much to me. But my state of perplexity soon vanished. Not only had the war changed my attitude to everything; it had radically transformed the objects of my attention: the skies over Paris (and Breton villages, women's mouths and children's eyes.) After June, 1940, I no longer recognized anything—objects, people, seasons, places, even myself. The age I lived in, which for ten years had revolved on a firm axis, now abruptly shifted out of orbit and dragged me with it. Without even quitting the streets of Paris, I found myself more *dépaysée* now than I would have done after crossing the high seas in the old days. With all the naïveté of a child who believes in the absolute vertical, I thought that there was an absolute truth governing the world. This truth might still be half buried under some matrix that the years would slowly wear away, or which might be shattered suddenly by the impact of the revolution, but *substantially it did exist*. In the peace which had been granted us, justice and reason worked like a yeast. I built my happiness on firm ground and beneath immutable constellations.

What a misapprehension this was! It was not a fragment of eternity I had lived through but a transitory period, the prewar years. The earth turned, and revealed another of its faces to me. Violence and injustice were let loose, with every kind of folly, scandal, and horror. Not even victory would turn back the clock and revive the old order that had been temporarily disrupted: it ushered in a new era, the postwar period. No blade of grass in any meadow, however I looked at it, would ever again be what it had been. The ephemeral was my lot. And down the stream of Time, History bore its vast jumble of incurable ills, its brief moments of glory.

Yet now, at the end of August, 1944, I contemplated the future with some confidence. History was not my enemy since, in the last resort, my hopes had been fulfilled. Indeed, it had just bestowed on me the most poignant joy I had ever experienced. How fond I had been, on my travels, of slipping away and losing myself among trees and rocks; and yet I shook off my own personality even more radically when I plunged into the hurly-burly of daily happenings. All Paris was incarnate in me, and I recognized myself in every face I saw. I was stunned by the sheer intensity of my own presence: through some miraculous communal intimacy it extended my awareness till it encompassed every other living soul. I seemed to have grown wings; henceforth I would soar above the narrow confines of my personal life and float in the empyrean that was all mankind. My happiness would reflect the magnificent adventure of a world creating itself afresh. I was not forgetting its darker side; but that moralistic streak I have mentioned helped me to face it. To act in concert with all men, to struggle, to accept death if need be, that life might keep its meaning— by holding fast to these precepts, I felt, I would master that darkness whence the cry of human lamentation arose.

Or would I? Those suffering voices pierced my barricades and threw them down. It was impossible for me to return to my former optimistic outlook: defeat and shock and horror can neither be made good nor left behind. That at least I knew, and would never forget. Never again would

I slip back into the fantasies of a divided mind, by which for years on end I had contrived, or imagined I had, to bend the universe to serve my will. I remained indifferent to many things that most people take seriously; but my life ceased to be a game, I knew what my roots were, and I no longer pretended that I could escape my own human condition. Instead I endeavored to bear it. Henceforth I took reality at its proper weight and valuation. At times I found it repugnant to accept it. By renouncing my illusions, I had also lost my intransigence and my pride: that is perhaps the greatest change that took place in me, and sometimes I regretted it bitterly. Françoise, in *She Came to Stay,* once asked herself angrily: "Am I going to resign myself to being just a woman?" If I chose to make Françoise a murderer, that was because I found anything preferable to this kind of submission. But now I was ready to submit, since despite all the deaths that lay behind me, despite all my anger and rebelliousness, I had re-established myself in the condition of happiness. Of all the blows I had endured, none had broken me. I had survived; indeed, I was unscathed. What thoughtlessness, what inconsistency!—yet neither less nor worse than other people's; and so in feeling ashamed of myself I also felt shame for them. Yet I bore my unworthiness so lightly that, save at rare and fleeting moments, I was not even conscious of it.

This shock, this defeat that I was up against—now refusing to accept, now acknowledging its presence, at times irritated by my own docility, and on other occasions upholding it—had a specific name: death. Never did my own death, or other people's, obsess me so violently as during those years. Now is the appropriate time to discuss this preoccupation of mine.

From the time I knew I was mortal I found the idea of death terrifying. Even when the world was at peace and my happiness seemed secure, my fifteen-year-old self would often turn giddy at the thought of that utter nonbeing—*my* utter nonbeing—that would descend on its appointed day, for ever and ever. This annihilation filled me with such horror that I could not conceive the possibility of facing it coolly: what people called "courage" I could only regard as blind frivolousness. I would add, however, that neither during this period nor in the years that followed did I show myself exceptionally pusillanimous. When I put on skis or tried to swim I lacked boldness, it is true: I never dared to move really fast on a snowslope, or to get out of my depth in water. Being physically clumsy, I was afraid of breaking a leg, or choking, of being obliged to call other people to my assistance: death did not enter into it. On the other hand, I felt no qualms about scaling precipitous mountains, in espadrilles, or working my way across stretches of screes or firn where one false step might well have cost me my life. The morning I fell from a very considerable height and ended up in the bed of a stream, I simply thought, in an interested way: Well, that's that; these things do happen. I had the same reaction when a fall from my bicycle stunned me; that is, I observed with great detachment this unforeseen but by and large normal event, that is, my death. In both cases I was caught unawares; I don't know how I would have behaved if I had been faced with a really serious danger and my imagination had had time to get to work on it. I have never had the occasion to take the relative measure of my cowardice and my courage. The raids on Paris and Le Havre did not make me lose any sleep; but then the risks I ran were minimal. What *is* certain is that, granted the actual circumstances in which I was variously placed, fear never stopped my taking any particular course. My optimism acted as a check against excessive precautions; besides, I did not even fear the prospect of death, insofar as it was bound to arise in my life at a certain moment. It would be the final point of life for me, true, but still a *part* of life; and on the occasions when I believed myself face to face with it, I surrendered myself calmly to this lively adventure, never giving a thought to the void that yawned for me on the farther side. What I rejected, with all my heart and soul, was the horror of that endless night, which, since it did not exist, would never *be* horrible, but held infinite horror for me, who *did* exist. I could not bear to think of myself as finite and ephemeral, a drop of water in the ocean; at times all my endeavors seemed vanity, happiness became a false lure, and the world wore the mocking, illusory mask of Nothingness.

At least death guaranteed me against an excess of suffering. "Rather than endure *that,*" I used to say, "I will kill myself." When war broke out this resolve hardened: misfortune became a daily possibility, and so did death. For the first time in my life I ceased to rebel against it. Sitting on the Pointe du Raz, in September, 1939, I told myself I had had the life I wanted, and that it could end now—at least it *had existed.* I can also remember myself leaning out of a train window, the wind whipping past my face, and thinking: Yes, perhaps the moment may come to rule a line across the page: so be it, I agree. And because I accepted it in my heart without any feeling of shock, I realized that one *could* defy it: a few years more or less matter little when set against the freedom and peace of mind one achieves the moment one stops running away from death. There were phrases that I had always regarded as hollow and meaningless, the truth of which I now discovered in the most intimate fashion: you must accept death when there is no other means of preserving your life; or, death is not always an absurd and lonely accident, but sometimes creates living bonds with other people, and then it has both meaning and justification. A little later I thought I had had the experience of what death was like, and had discovered that it was, precisely, nothing at all. At some point I ceased to be afraid of it, and even to think about it.

But I did not rest in this condition of indifference. One summer evening, a few days before the first night of *The Flies,* Sartre and I had dinner at Camille's, and were on our way back from Montmartre by foot when the curfew sounded. We checked in at a hotel on the Rue de l'Université. I suppose I was a little drunk, in that room, decorated in red. Death suddenly appeared to me. I wrung my hands, and wept, and banged my head against the wall, as vehemently as I had done at the age of fifteen.

One night in June, 1944, I tried to exorcise death with words. I excerpt some of my notes here, just as they came from my pen:

I was lying in bed, my stomach resting on the mattress, my knees and feet pressed against the ground. The silence of the night turned to a sound of water and rustling leaves, characteristic noises from my childhood. Death closed over me. A little patience yet, and I would drift to the other side of the world, enter that region which never reflects the light. I would be alone, far from the rest of mankind, in that state of pure being that is, perhaps, the diametrical opposite of death, and which I scarcely knew save in my dreams. Vainly I seek it, at times, in the wilderness of mountains and high plateaus; solitude retreats elusively the instant you seek it open-eyed. I was going to escape into some mysterious dimension that would pass judgment on my life and bring me face to face with my essential being; and perhaps at the end of the road I would meet death, that dream of death which I take, every time, for the final truth, letting myself slip in a sort of glad abandon into the abyss of the Void while a voice cries: "This time it is forever, there will be no awakening." And someone is still there, to say, "I am dead"—and in this miraculous instant, dreaming of death as a living being may dream, life attains the ultimate distilled essence of my naked being. Scarcely a week passes without my playing this game, whose counters are anguish and certitude. But tonight my body rejected the surrender of sleep, would not embrace death even in dreams, were it but to deny it, would not sleep; and there was no anguish in my heart, for this refusal carried such violence that death lost its importance, time was abolished, and being asserted itself unaided, irrespective of other beings, or of the future. But this flame demanded fuel. For an instant it burned bright, feeding on memories, and the phrases that formed on my lips sufficed to make glad my heart: life swelled, pressing in on me. But how to live in the dark night of this room, in the heart of a barred and bolted city? I turned the light on, and wrote these words sitting up in bed. I have written the beginning of the book which is my last and greatest recourse against death, the book I have so long desired to write; the labor of all these years may have had no other purpose than to give me the courage—and the excuse—to write it.

*   *   *   *

And perhaps this death, which has terrified me all my life, will be over in a second, without my perceiving it. Illness or accident, it may well be astonishingly *easy*. One act of submission leads to another. I shall be dead to others; I shall not see myself die.

*   *   *   *

I am sure I shall die in my bed. My bed frightens me: it is a ship bearing me away, a giddiness. I am moving out, out from the bank, motionless now, close to someone who talks and smiles, whose features vanish from the surface of the water as I plunge into it; I plunge, and glide, moving out and away to nowhere, on my bed, carried by the stream, by the flowing hours of darkness.

The dreams to which I allude in the preceding paragraphs played a large part in my disputes with death. Heaven knows how many times I was shot through the heart, or sank in quicksands, went numb, fainted, passed into utter oblivion. I welcomed this self-annihilation, and got great relief from it. I was projecting the true nature of my death, just as I had so often tried in vin to project the true nature of war or separation: to explore all around them, to possess and, thanks to this possession, annihilate them. I passed through death as Alice passed through the Looking Glass, and once on the other side, I could possess myself of it. Instead of dissolving into it, I absorbed it into myself; in short, *I survived it.* As I breathed my last I would say, "This time it's forever; this time there'll be no awakening!" But someone still remained to say, "I am dead." This presence subdued death's power: I was dead, yet here was this voice whispering: "I am there." Then I would awake, and the truth would catch me by the throat: when I am dead, that voice will speak no more. It sometimes seemed to me that if I succeeded in being *there* at the exact instant of my death, if I coincided with it, then I would compel it to *be*: this would be one way of preserving it. But no, I thought, death will never lie within my grasp; never will I be able to concentrate all the horror with which it fills me into one final, all-embracing spasm of anguish. There is no help for it, the small squeamish fear will remain, the persistent night thoughts, the banal image of a black ruled line terminating the series of measured spaces that stand for years—and after it nothing but a blank page. I shall never apprehend death; all I will ever know is this illusive foretaste, mingled with the flavor of my living days.

I was afraid of growing old, too: not because my features would change and my powers diminish, but because of the ever stronger taste of death that would poison my every living moment, the black ruled line's slow but inexorable approach. In those days the line was still lost on the far horizon; but inevitably, sooner or later, the time of separation, of not being, would come. When I cycled through the countryside and saw it all drenched in sunlight and fresh life, my heart would contract at the thought of it going on when I was no longer there to behold it. As a child I wanted to catch a little soul on the wing—one that had not yet found a body— and take its place, and say "I" as that soul. But now I imagined, instead, that some person would lend me his conscious mind, that the self which looked out through those eyes would be mine. Emily Brontë had stared at the moon, with its halo of reddish muslin, and thought: One day I shall see it no longer. It was the same moon that all our eyes reflected; why then, in the equation of time and space, were we all isolated elements, irreducible one to the other? Death is common to all of us, yet each individual faces it alone. While life still exists, we can die together; but in dying we pass beyond this world, to a place where the word "together" no longer possesses any meaning. My greatest wish was to die with the one I loved; yet though our bodies might lie side by side, such contact would remain illusory. Between nothing and nothing there can be no bond.

I had a foreshadowing of this illimitable darkness through the deaths of others. Zaza still came to me by night, her face yellowed beneath the pink hood she wore. There was Nizan, too, and, closest to me of all, Bourla. Bourla had gone from us into the silent void of separation; and one day we had learned to give this separation a new name: death. Time had passed, but Bourla was not done with death, he would never be done with it. Often, especially at night, I would say to myself, "Let's bury him, and think of him no more." How convenient a good old traditional funeral is! The dead man vanishes into the grave, and his death goes with him. You drop earth on him, you walk away, and that's the end of it; if you like, you can return from time to time and shed tears over the spot where death is pinned down. You know where to find it. Besides, in the normal course of things people die in their beds, in a house. Their absence is simply the obverse of their former presence. His chair is empty, they say; about now he would have been turning his key in the lock. When I walked through the Paris streets and thought of Bourla, I tried to say, He is not there. But whichever way you looked at it, he would not have been in the precise spot where I was. From where, then, *was* he absent? From nowhere and everywhere: his loss affected the entire world. And yet the world was full; no place is left for the one who lets his place go vacant. This separation is a kind of betrayal then: our very heartbeats momently deny his life and death alike. One day we shall have forgotten him entirely. And one day I, too, will similarly be gone, and forgotten.

Yet even the desire to escape this fatal curse was lacking; if our lives were infinite, they would merge into universal indifference. Though death challenges our existence, it also gives meaning to our lives. It may be the instrument of absolute separation, but it is also the key to all communication. In *The Blood of Others* I had attempted to show death laying siege in vain to the fullness of life. In *Pyrrhus et Cinéas* I wanted to demonstrate that without it there could be neither projects nor values. In *Les Bouches inutiles,* on the other hand, I intended to portray the fearful gulf that yawns between the living and the dead. When I began *All Men Are Mortal,* in 1943, I envisaged it in the first place as a sort of protracted wandering around the central theme of death.

I intend to discuss this novel on a later occasion, since its texture was considerably enriched during the first year after the war. There is only one comment I would like to make here. Before writing *She Came to Stay* I spent years fumbling around for a subject. From the moment I began that book I never stopped writing, except during brief periods when circumstances either kept me wholly occupied or else paralyzed my activities altogether. The transposition of my experience into literary terms no longer posed a major problem for me. The same applies to most writers; my case is in no way exceptional. It therefore seems all the more opportune to examine it in closer detail. Why was it that from this point on I always had "something to say"?

In the first place I knew my job rather better, and had gained extra confidence. When I turned the idea for a book over in my mind, I was quite certain that book would be published: I believed in its existence, and this helped me to make it exist. But there was another and far more basic reason. As I have already remarked, it was only when my experience cracked and showed faulty that I was able to take a step back and discuss it in perspective. After the declaration of war things finally ceased to be a matter of course. Misfortune and misery had erupted into the world, and literature had become as essential to me as the very air I breathed. I am not suggesting that it constitutes a remedy against absolute despair; but I had not been reduced to such extremities, far from it. What I *had* experienced, personally, was the pathetic ambiguity of our human condition, its twin elements of misery and splendor. I had realized my own incapacity both for seeing those elements steadily and whole, and for articulating either of them individually in my own person: I always remained well on this side of life's triumphs and atrocities alike.

Conscious of the gulf that lay between my impressions and the factual truth, I felt the need to write, in order to do justice to a truth with which all my emotional impulses were out of step. I believe many vocations to literature can be explained in similar terms. "Literary honesty" is not what it is commonly taken to be: a writer's business is not to transcribe the thoughts and feelings which constantly pass through his mind so much as to point out those horizons which we never reach and scarcely perceive, but which nevertheless are there. That is why it requires infinite pains if we are to deduce an author's living personality from his work.

As for the author himself, the task upon which he is engaged is never-ending, for each of his books says both too much and too little: though he spend scores of years repeating and modifying his ideas, he will never succeed in capturing on paper—any more than in his heart or his physical self—the multitudinous reality that lies all about him. Frequently the effort he makes to achieve this end sets up a sort of dialectical scaffolding within the work itself; this is clearly apparent in my own case. I was not satisfied with the ending of *She Came to Stay*: murder is not the solution to the difficulties engendered by coexistence. Instead of stepping around them I wanted to face them squarely. In *The Blood of Others* and *Pyrrhus et Cinéas* I attempted to define our true relationship with other people [*autrui*]. I reached the conclusion that, whether we like it or not, we do impinge on other people's destinies, and must face up to the responsibility which this implies. But such a conclusion also produced its opposite corollary: though keenly aware of my responsibilities, I nevertheless felt myself wholly incapable of action. This impotence was one of the main themes I tackled in *All Men Are Mortal*. I also attempted to correct the moral optimism of my two previous works by describing death, not only as a common link between the individual and mankind, but also as the major peril of loneliness and separation. Thus each book thenceforth impelled me toward its successor, for the more I saw of the world, the more I realized that it was brimming over with all I could ever hope to experience, understand, and put into words.